49th International Computer Music Conference (ICMC 2024)

Sound in Motion

Seoul, South Korea
7 - 13 July 2024

Editors:

Hee Seng Kye
Richard Dudas

ISBN: 979-8-3313-1131-5

Printed from e-media with permission by:

Curran Associates, Inc.
57 Morehouse Lane
Red Hook, NY 12571

proceedings.com

Some format issues inherent in the e-media version may also appear in this print version.

Printed with permission by Curran Associates, Inc. (2025)

For permission requests, please contact International Computer Music Association at the address below.

International Computer Music Association
1819 Polk Street #330
San Francisco, CA
94109

Phone: (734) 878-3031

www.computermusic.org

Additional copies of this publication are available from:

Curran Associates, Inc.
57 Morehouse Lane
Red Hook, NY 12571 USA
Phone: 845-758-0400
Fax: 845-758-2633
Email: curran@proceedings.com
Web: www.proceedings.com

International Computer Music Conference 2024 in Seoul

ICMC2024
SEOUL

July 7, 2024 - July 13, 2024

Sound in Motion

Proceedings

ICMC 2024

icmc2024.org

Sound in Motion

Seoul, July 7 – July 13, 2024

Proceedings

Hosted by the Hanyang University Center for Research in
Electroacoustic Music and Audio Technology – CREAMA
한양대학교 전자음악연구소 – CREAMA

Hanyang University, Seoul Campus

Proceedings of the 49th International Computer Music Conference 2024
July 7 — July 13, 2024
Hanyang University, Seoul, S. Korea

Sound in Motion

Hee Seng Kye, Richard Dudas, editors

Published by:
The International Computer Music Association
2040 Polk Street, Suite 330
San Francisco, CA 94019
United States of America

Sponsored by:

Greetings from the ICMA

Dear 2024 ICMC Delegates,

On behalf of the International Computer Music Association (ICMA), I welcome you to the 2024 International Computer Music Conference in the vibrant city of Seoul, South Korea. Founded in 1974, the ICMA sponsors the ICMC each year, hosted by computer musicians like you worldwide. This year, we are privileged to gather in the dynamic metropolis of Seoul, offering a unique blend of sights, sounds, and mountain vistas. This year's conference theme, *Sound in Motion*, resonates with the number of people travelling to Seoul for ICMC 2024.

ICMC is the preeminent conference for practice under the broad umbrella of 'computer music'. We can find research, art, music, and more addressing computer music history, analysis, theory, philosophy, aesthetics, perception, cognition, social and environmental studies, DSP, sound design, spatialization, machine learning, algorithmic composition, software and hardware, MIR, and every topic in between.

The face of ICMC has evolved significantly since its inception in 1974. Originally a predominantly technical conference featuring cutting-edge research and some music, ICMC now reflects a balance of humanities and arts with science and engineering. It has also become the largest international conference for music and installation art, with hundreds of submissions each year. This evolution is a testament to the progressive and dynamic nature of our community, of which you are an integral part.

Accordingly, the ICMA has adjusted its focus. With increased efforts in promoting diversity, equity, and inclusivity through financial and promotional support, ICMA encourages arts practice while maintaining its commitment to research. We require gender and geographical diversity in the formation of the ICMA Board and the keynotes at ICMC. We presented regional ICMA music showcases and are deliberating with regional electronic and computer music organizations to discover how best to serve our communities. We continue to provide travel grants to student members of the ICMA and monetary awards for Best Music, Best Student Music, and Best Paper at ICMC. The Best Paper recipient can expand their paper for inclusion in the Computer Music Journal. Array, once our Association's newsletter, is now a peer-reviewed journal. ICMC and the ICMA demonstrate how, unique to computer music, research and art work hand-in-hand.

We could only do this with our ICMC hosts, especially this year's hosts at Hanyang University. Their contributions are invaluable, and we deeply appreciate their efforts in making this conference a success. With unprecedented speed, the conference committee headed by Taehi Kim and Richard Dudas successfully organized and operated ICMC2024. Their tireless efforts with others, often in awkward time zones, exemplify the best of interdisciplinary, international collaboration that computer music is known for.

We wish you the best in sharing your practice, learning of your colleagues' practices, exploring Seoul and Hanyang University, making new connections and collaborations, and enjoying social events and informal gatherings – all of the moments and events that continue to make ICMC the most important convening of our discipline's minds.

Kerry L Hagan
President, International Computer Music Association
www.computermusic.org

Welcome from the ICMC 2024 Organizers

Welcome to the 49th International Computer Music Conference – Sound in Motion – and welcome to Hanyang University!

We would like to extend a warm welcome to all of this year's ICMC delegates, whether attending the conference in person here in Seoul, or participating remotely. This is the second ICMC to be held in Korea (the first was in 2018 in Daegu), and the first time the conference takes place in its capital city, Seoul, a vibrant city with a rich musical and cultural life. It is also the first time that the ICMC takes place at an academic institution in Korea – the Hanyang University College of Music.

This year marks the 50th anniversary of the International Computer Music Association, which was founded in 1974 in conjunction with the first conference. The to connect individuals and institutions involved in the technical, creative, and performance aspects of computer music on an international level. The ICMC, organized yearly by different host institutions around the world has become the preeminent conference for the field of electronic and computer music.

This year we received over 700 submissions from participants representing 46 countries, and accepted around 380 of the highest quality works in three tracks – music, installation, and paper tracks – based on a double-blind peer-review process.

The theme of this year's conference is Sound in Motion. The sounds we perceive result from the motion of particles in the air, and those in turn result from some kind of physical – or electric – motion, either natural or human-induced. The works of our invited keynote speakers, Atau Tanaka, Laetitia Sonami and Tae Hong Park, tie in with this theme, as they are all active as computer music performers in addition to being composers. We also welcome the Erämaa Trio, who will be assisting with the evening performance linked to Atau Tanaka's keynote address.

Also in motion are the performers of L Contemporary Group, who are performing many of the instrumental works at this year's concerts, and the teams of Remember Stage, and JoeunSorine who are providing the equipment and direction, respectively, for our concert halls.

We thank the teams of the Hanyang University Museum and Hanyang University History Museum for collaborating with us and providing fantastic spaces for the installations presented at this year's conference. We also thank the administrative team and Dean at the Hanyang University College of Music for their unwavering support. We also thank our external sponsors, the Korea Tourism Organization and Seoul Metropolitan Government for their assistance.

Enjoy the conference and enjoy your visit to Seoul!

Richard Dudas, Conference Chair
Taehi Kim, Conference Co-Chair, Music Chair
Hee Seng Kye, Paper Chair
Jae hyun Ahn, Technical Chair

Welcome to the Hanyang University College of Music

I am very pleased to welcome you to the Hanyang University College of Music, whose Composition Department's computer music studio and research center CREAMA is hosting the 2024 International Computer Music Conference.

With more than 60 years of history, the College of Music aims to cultivate musicians and music educators with the highest level of artistic expression, creativity, personality and professional knowledge. The college's five departments – voice, composition, piano, instrumental, and Korean traditional music – encompass both Western and Korean music, and, together with the Graduate School, offer degrees at bachelor's, master's, and doctoral levels. The College of Music is dedicated to producing professional musicians – performers, composers, computer musicians, music scholars, and music educators – via hands-on experience and international exchanges through projects such as this year's ICMC.

Hanyang University's founder Lyun-joon Kim – known by his pen-name Paiknam – was a baritone vocalist, a poet, and composer of more than 1600 art songs, so music not only has a very special place at the heart of our university, but also constitutes an important facet of Hanyang University's history. I am therefore pleased that we are be able to host the first ICMC in Seoul at our flagship Seoul campus in order to welcome the international computer music community to the College of Music at the heart of our campus.

Concerts at this year's ICMC will principally take place at the College of Music's Paiknam Concert Hall and Recital Hall, and paper presentations will be held in our seminar and lecture rooms. We are hosting sound installations in collaboration with the Hanyang University Museum and Hanyang University History Museum, the latter of which is located in the historical first building at Hanyang University (originally the Main Building of the Hanyang College of Engineering, built in 1956).

Last but not least, I would like to thank the conference chairs Taehi Kim and Richard Dudas whose tireless efforts have made this conference possible at our campus.

I wish you all an enjoyable conference and pleasurable visit to Korea's and its capital city, Seoul!

Kyungmee Rhee
Dean, Hanyang University College of Music

Welcome from CREAMA

The Center for Research in Electroacoustic Music and Audio Technology (CREAMA) at the Hanyang University College of Music was founded in its first incarnation as the Electronic Music Research Institute in 1996 by Donung Lee, and was among the first computer music studios set up in academic settings in Korea. It is the home to the postgraduate degree programs in Computer Music Composition, and Audio Technology at the Hanyang University's College of Music.

Its principal aims are:

• to increase the visibility of electro-acoustic music within the sphere of contemporary music,
• to foster education and understanding of contemporary acoustic and electro-acoustic music,
• to promote the use of new technologies and methods in the arts,
• to spearhead technological research in the arts, and
• to nurture collaboration and exchange with similar centers and with other disciplines in the arts.

Throughout the years, CREAMA has had a long-standing informal connection to the ICMC through its people – composers, researchers, performers, both professional and student – who, over the years, have shared their thoughts, ideas, and research with the international computer music community through their musical compositions and conference papers which have been performed and presented at ICMCs around the world over the past few decades. This year's ICMC has been organized by a team largely consisting of faculty, staff, researchers and postgraduate students currently involved in the studio's activities, as well as graduates of our program – both recent and erstwhile – who have been working in the greater music and professional audio fields. We are delighted to be able to host this year's ICMC at Hanyang to welcome you to share your thoughts, ideas, and research with the slice of the computer music world attending this year's conference.

Welcome!

Richard Dudas
Director, 한양대학교 전자음악연구소 CREAMA

ICMC 2024 Music Peer-Review Committee

ICMC 2024 Paper Peer-Review Committee

Miriam Akkermann
Alejandro Albornoz
Rebecca Brown
Rodrigo F. Cádiz
Antonio A. Carvallo
Paulo C. Chagas
Lamberto Coccioli
Cathy Cox
Paul Doornbusch
Arne Eigenfeldt
Aaron Einbond
Tom Erbe
Carl Faia
John ffitch
Omar E. Guzmán Fraire
Lauren Hayes
Revital Hollander
Eric Honour

Kittiphan Janbuala
David Kim-Boyle
Andrew King
Panayiotis Kokoras
Jonathan J. Kulpa
Johnathan F. Lee
Serge Lemouton
Jose I. Lopez
Cory McKay
Andrew McPherson
Romain Michon
Mikako Mizuno
Jeff Morris
Yunze Mu
Chryssie Nanou
Jon Nelson
Max Neupert
Vesa Norilo
Felipe Otondo

Ken Paoli
Juan A. Parra Cancino
Aki Pasoulas
Thiago Rossi Roque
Danilo Rossetti
Robert Rowe
Jøran Rudi
Carla Scaletti
Wenyi Song
Adam Stanović
Ricardo de Oliveira Thomasi
Sever Tipei
Pierre Alexandre Tremblay
Juan Carlos Vasquez
Henrik von Coler
Jiayue Cecilia Wu
Guilherme Zanchetta
Michael Zbyszyński

ICMC 2024 Installation Peer-Review Committee

Teresa M. Connors
Arne Eigenfeldt

Nikolas Gomes Ferranddis
Omar E. Guzmán Fraire
Javier Jaimovich

Yunze Mu
Max Neupert

ICMA Paper Awards

Each year the ICMA recognizes the best paper submitted with the Best Paper Award. The top scoring papers written by ICMA members are given to a panel elected by the ICMA Board, and a winner is decided from among these top submissions. The Best Paper Award for ICMC 2024 is being awarded to two papers:

ICMC 2024 Best Paper Award

Nick Hwang (University of Wisconsin-Whitewater) and
Anthony T Marasco (Michigan State University)

– for –

MoNoDeC: the Mobile Node Controller for audience-involved sound diffusion

~

MoNoDec by Nick Hwang and Anthony T. Marasco is a multichannel, network-based, audio system designed for interactive and immersive audio experiences that leverages audience mobile phones as loudspeakers systems with great potential for interactive audience-based performance and sound diffusion. The ICMA board-appointed panel of judges found this paper to be "a compelling and innovative approach to audience-involved sound diffusion," and, for at least one member of the Committee, "it stands out more [because] the technology is not developed for just one artist or project, but is suitable for broader applications, thus contributing significantly to the field."

– and –

Matthew Barnard (Music, School of The Arts University of Hull),
Adam Martin (Music, School of Arts & Humanities University of Huddersfield), and
Mark Slater (also from Music, School of The Arts University of Hull)

– for –

Nightports at Hull Minster: Transporting a Site-Specific Musical Work Across Physical and Virtual Spaces

~

The Hull Minster is an Anglican minster (i.e., monastery) and England's largest parish church, located in Kingston-upon-Hull in Yorkshire, England. The panel of judges were impressed the "use of ambisonic recording and real-time spatialization to create immersive audio experiences" and, in particular, the impact of "site-specific compositions and the integration of the acoustic properties of historical buildings into musical performances" or making it "available for headphone listening."

Both of these papers show innovation in the future of spatialization and networked musical performance. After discussion, and without the ability to come to consensus of one paper over the other, the ICMA board-appointed panel felt that, on this occasion, a joint award for Best Paper Award was appropriate.

Congratulations to Nick Hwang and Anthony T. Marasco, and to Matthew Barnard, Adam Martin, and Mark Slater – joint recipients of the ICMC 2024 Best Paper Award!

The Best Paper award entails guaranteed publication of an extended version of the paper as an article in Computer Music Journal.

2024 ICMC Best Paper Award Committee:

Cecilia Wu – ICMA At Large Director
Mengjie (Maggie) Qi – ICMA At Large Director
Henrik Von Coler – ICMA At Large Director
Douglas Keislar – Editor, Computer Music Journal
Anthony De Ritis – Research Coordinator, ICMA
Hee Seng Kye – Paper Chair, ICMC 2024
Kerry L Hagan – President, ICMA
Richard Dudas – ICMC 2024 Conference Chair

At the end of the conference, a Best Presentation Award will be *chosen by conference attendees* who submit their votes by ballot. The award announcement will be published in the following year's proceedings. Be on the lookout for the ballot box and cast your vote at this year's conference!!

ICMA Best Music Awards

Each year the ICMA recognizes the best music submissions in both professional and student categories. The top scoring musical works composed are given to a panel elected by the ICMA Board, and winners are decided from among these top submissions.

ICMC 2024 Best Music Submission Award

Nicola Fumo Frattegiani

– for –

Luar

Luar *is a fixed media work, a stereophonic audiovisual composition, by Nicola Fumo Frattegiani of the Accademia di Belle Arti di Macerata.* Luar *is a Portuguese word that means "moon light," with words of Portuguese poet Fernando Pessoa, that describe this "this descent towards never-ending subjectivity".* Luar*'s synchronization of timbre, text, and video is compelling, if not oftentimes disturbing – a masterful setting of the text.*

ICMC 2024 Best Student Music Submission Award

Dariush Derakhshani

– for –

Pulsar Rays

Pulsar Rays *by Dariush Derakhshani, a Ph.D. candidate at the University of California, Santa Barbara, is an acousmatic composition that alludes to the sound navigation of dolphins and bats. It is a mature work with an engaging formal structure, and intriguing use of timbre and space that holds one's interest for its full ten minutes, not so easy to do.*

2024 ICMC Best Music Awards Committee:

Marc Battier – ICMA Asia Regional Director
Paulo C. Chagas – ICMA Americas Regional Director
Steven Leffue –ICMA Americas Regional Director
Anthony De Ritis – ICMA Reseach Coordinator
Juan Parra – ICMA Publications Coordinator
Chryssie Nanou – ICMA Treasurer/Secretary
Richard Dudas – Conference Chair, ICMC Seoul 2024
Kerry Hagan – ICMA President
Taehi Kim – Music Chair, ICMC Seoul 2024

ICMC 2024 Organizing Team

Organizing Committee

Conference Chair:	Richard Dudas (Hanyang University)
Conference Co-Chair:	Taehi Kim (Hanyang University)
Music Chair:	Taehi Kim (Hanyang University)
Late Night Concert Chair:	Yemin Oh (Sangmyung University)
Technical Chair:	Jae hyun Ahn (JoeunSorine)
Installation Chair:	Shinwon Ahn (Hanyang University Museum)
Installation Coordinator:	Nayoung Hwang (Hanyang University Museum)
Installation Manager:	Yoonjae Choi (Indiana Univ. Jacobs School of Music)
Paper Chair:	Hee Seng Kye (Hanyang University)
Web Technology Team :	Taehi Kim (Hanyang University) Sujin Kim (Hanyang University)
Designers :	Daeun Kim (CREAMA, Hanyang University) Yugyeong Lee Hyunjoo Ji (Hanyang University) Minjoo Song (PSL)
Concert Coordinators :	Taehi Kim (Hanyang University) Seunghyun Jang (Creative Village Mippeuda Inc.) Sujin Kim (Hanyang University)
Performance Chairs:	Hyeyeon Jung (L Contemporary Group) Jonghyun An (L Contemporary Group)
Performance Organizer :	Youkyung Kim (L Contemporary Group)
Administrative Manager :	Minjoo Song (PSL)
Stage Directors:	Jieun Jeong (JoeunSorine) Juyeon Park (JoeunSorine)
Staff Manager :	Daeun Kim (CREAMA, Hanyang University)
Staff:	Hyunjoo Ji (Hanyang University) Hyeonmuk Na (Hanyang University) Dohyun Bang (CREAMA, Hanyang University) Piao Yisong (CREAMA, Hanyang University) Yongwoo Lee (CREAMA, Hanyang University)

Interns

Hanyang University
- Hyunjun Bae
- Jaeyoung Chang
- Kyusang Cho
- Haneul Jin
- Jihyun Jung
- Chanhee Kim
- Joonhee Kim
- Minju Kim
- Seungho Kim
- Eunsun Kwon

Kukje Universty of Arts
- Garam Kim

Baekseok Arts University
- Seunghyeon Park

Univ. for Music and Perf. Arts Vienna
- Seoyoon Jang

Sangmyung University
- Doa Kim

Seoul National University
- Minjoon Choi

Sungshin Women's University
- Yubin Kim
- Yumin Lee
- Jisoo Park

Sookmyung Women's University
- Nayeon Kim
- Yihyeon Kim
- Jiwon Lee

Cate School
- Philip Choi

Indiana Univ. Jacobs School of Music
- Minho Kang

San Francisco Art Institiute
- Heejin Jang

Seoul Jazz Academy
- Seohee Kim
- Dong Woo Lim

University of Central Missouri
- Taylor Gardner

Korean National University of the Arts
- Da Hyun Kim

ICMA Board of Directors 2024

OFFICERS

President:	Kerry L Hagan
Vice President for Membership:	Qi Mengjie (Maggie)
Vice President for Conferences:	Rodrigo Cádiz
Vice President for Asia/Oceania:	PerMagnus Lindborg
Vice President for the Americas:	Eric Honour
Vice President for Europe:	Nikos Stavropoulos
Vice President for Preservation:	Tae Hong Park
Treasurer/Secretary:	Chryssie Nanou
Publications Coordinator:	Juan Parra Cancino
Research Coordinator:	Tony De Ritis
Music Coordinator:	Ping JIN
Array *Editor*:	Miriam Akkermann
Social Media Office:	Patrick Hartono

BOARD OF DIRECTORS

At-Large Directors:	Cecilia Wu Qi Mengjie (Maggie) Henrik Von Coler John Thompson
Americas Regional Directors:	Paulo C Chagas Steven Leffue
Asia/Oceania Regional Directors:	Marc Battier Mikako Mizuno
Europe Regional Directors:	Miriam Akkermann Juan Parra Cancino

EX OFFICIO

ICMA Administrative Assistant & Bookkeeper: Sandra Neal

List of Previous Conferences

2023 Shenzhen, China
2022 Limerick, Ireland
2020-2021 Santiago, Chile
2019 New York University, New York, USA
2018 Daegu, South Korea
2017 Shanghai, China
2016 Utrecht, The Netherlands
2015 Denton, Texas, USA
2014 Athens, Greece
2013 Perth, Australia
2012 Ljubljana, Slovenia
2011 Huddersfield, England, UK
2010 New York City, New York, USA
2009 Montreal, Quebec, Canada
2008 Belfast, N. Ireland, UK
2007 Copenhagen, Denmark
2006 New Orleans, Louisiana, USA
2005 Barcelona, Spain
2004 Miami, Florida, USA
2003 Singapore
2002 Gothenburg, Sweden
2001 Havana, Cuba
2000 Berlin, Germany
1999 Beijing, China
1998 Ann Arbor, Michigan, USA
1997 Thessaloniki, Greece
1996 Hong Kong, China
1995 Banff, Alberta, Canada
1994 Aarhus, Denmark
1993 Tokyo, Japan
1992 San Jose, California, USA
1991 Montreal, Quebec, Canada
1990 Glasgow, Scotland, UK
1989 Columbus, Ohio, USA
1988 Cologne, Germany
1987 Champaign/Urbana, Illinois, USA
1986 Den Haag, Netherlands
1985 Burnaby, British Columbia, Canada
1984 Paris, France
1983 Rochester, New York, USA
1982 Venice, Italy
1981 Denton, Texas, USA
1980 New York City, New York, USA
1978 Chicago, Illinois, USA
1977 San Diego, California, USA
1976 Cambridge, Massachusetts, USA
1975 Champaign/Urbana, Illinois, USA
1974 East Lansing, Michigan, USA

Keynote Address 1 - Monday, July 8, 2024

Atau Tanaka

From mainframes to microcontrollers: Composing and performing computer music 1988-2024

Abstract

This keynote address will describe a personal history of computer music systems for composition and performance, spanning over 35 years. We will start with the share system mainframes preceding the personal computer revolution, then look at developments in workstations, early digital signal processing (DSP) hardware and the possibility of real-time performance. The miniaturization and possibility to run sophisticated synthesis algorithms on commodity platforms including mobile telephones has opened up the field of application of computer music beyond the lab into the street. Finally, in the most recent era, the increasing computational power of microcontroller systems lead to a new period, potentially of what I call "post-computer music".

~

Atau Tanaka studied electronic music with Ivan Tcherepnin (brother of modular synthesizer designer Serge) at Harvard University. There he met John Cage during his Norton Lectures. Tanaka went on to carry out his doctoral work with John Chowning and Max Mathews at CCRMA Stanford and there began his work with the BioMuse (ICMC1993).

Atau has carried out research at IRCAM, Apple France, and Sony Computer Science Laboratory (CSL) Paris in areas of music human-computer interaction (HCI), network performance, and human-centred machine learning.

In the '90s he formed Sensorband with Zbigniew Karkowski and Edwin van der Heide and performed in the Japanese noise scene. He has performed at festivals such as Ars Electronica, WOMAD, Sonar, CTM, and exhibited at Eyebeam, the Musikinstrumenten-Museum Berlin and SFMOMA.

His research has been supported by the European Research Council (ERC), UK and French research councils. He was artistic co-director of STEIM Amsterdam and Edgard-Varèse Guest Professor at TU Berlin.

He is professor at Goldsmiths, and works with Bristol Interaction Group and MSH Paris Nord.

Keynote 2 - Tuesday, July 9, 2024

Laetitia Sonami

REPETITION and DESIRE: Echo, Narcissus, AI and I

Abstract

I revisit the myth of Echo and Narcissus and how it perdures in the technologies we design, our perception of reality, and our criteria for what we consider meaningful representation.

While Echo's imprints are easily traced, Narcissus hides its lovely face in many manifestations of AI.

I present examples of synthetic voice as benchmarks of technological innovation and share my explorations of ML for dynamic mapping, and, finally, my discovery of a strange vocal persona.

~

Laetitia Sonami is a pioneering French sound artist and performer known for her innovative use of technology in her work. After studying with Eliane Radigue in Paris, she moved to the United States in the late seventies to pursue her electronic music studies.

Sonami has created several unique instruments for live performance, amongst which the lady's glove and her current Spring Spyre which applies AI to real time audio synthesis.
Sonami's work often explores themes of embodiment and is credited for inspiring the many offshoots from her gestural controllers.

She has exhibited and performed at major international festivals and venues and has mentored many young artists in the field.

Keynote 3 - Friday, July 12, 2024

Tae Hong Park

Music, Computers, and Computer Music: Observations from an Unlikely Journey

Abstract

In this talk, we will explore the evolution of "computer music" over the past three decades through my personal, and somewhat unlikely, journey of discovery that began as a hobby. We will explore the key observations, experiences, and milestones that have shaped my understanding, appreciation, and engagement in the field and its community, while also considering what may lie beyond the horizon.

~

Born in Vienna, Austria, Tae Hong Park is a composer, bassist, and music technologist. Park received his Bachelor of Engineering degree in Electronics from Korea University in 1994 and worked in the area of digital communication systems and digital musical keyboards at the LG Central Research Laboratory in Seoul, Korea, from 1994 to 1998.

He also holds degrees from Dartmouth College (M.A.) and Princeton University (M.F.A. and Ph.D.). His current interests primarily lie in the composition of electro-acoustic and acoustic music, signal processing, computer-aided music analysis, cyber-physical systems, soundscapes, and new media studies.

His works have been performed throughout the world at various venues, conferences, and festivals by groups and performers such as the Ahn Trio, Argento Ensemble, Brentano String Quartet, California E.A.R. Unit, Ensemble Surplus, Wayne Dumaine, Edward Carroll, Entropy, Kaleidoscope, Zoe Martlew, Nash Ensemble of London, New Jersey Symphony Orchestra, and the Tarab Cello Ensemble. Park served as a board member of SEAMUS, Chief Editor of the Journal SEAMUS, and currently serves as an Editorial Consultant for Computer Music Journal.

He has also served three terms as President of ICMA, chaired the 2006, 2018, and 2019 ICMC, and has served as Chair of ICAD 2013, SID 2015, and Noisegate 2016 conferences. He is the author of "Introduction to DSP: Computer Musically Speaking," published in 2010. After teaching at NYU for more than a decade, he is now an Associate Professor and Chair of the newly formed Department of Music at Purdue University.

Table of Contents

Paper Session 1 – Piece and Paper I

Paper Session 2A – Piece and Paper II

Paper Session 2B – Musical Gestures and Analysis

Paper Session 3A – Piece and Paper III

Paper Session 3B – Software and Hardware Systems I

Paper Session 4A – New Instruments for Musical Expression I

Paper Session 4B – Perception and Cognition

Paper Session 5A – Piece and Paper IV

Paper Session 5B – Software and Hardware Systems II

Paper Session 8A – Computer Music History and Culture II

Paper Session 8B – Computer Music History and Culture III

Paper Session 9A – Piece + Paper V

Paper Session 9B – New Instruments for Musical Expression II

This page intentionally left blank.

Time Travels, So Does the Sound: Exploring Memories Stuck in Between

Sophie Jung
University of the Sunshine Coast
sophie.jung@research.usc.edu.au

ABSTRACT

As a PhD research student and Korean who has relocated to Brisbane, Australia, the author has endeavored to examine the role of self-reflective soundscape listening in understanding the traumatized inner self, enhancing self-resilience, and assisting individuals dealing with grief and trauma due to sudden bereavement, as well as expressing ineffable emotions through soundscape music compositions. Drawing from personal experiences and cultural differences, the author's journey serves as a critical lens in exploring these inquiries.

This paper explores the intersection of sound, time, and emotion, utilizing recorded jet engine sounds collected over the years alongside other soundscape recordings from Korea and Brisbane. Providing a compelling illustration of the author's research project, the focus is on the composition 'Entropy', embodying the concept of 'Emotions in Time in Motion'. Through this exploration, the author aims to illuminate the potential of self-reflective soundscape listening in navigating the complexities of emotions and facilitating memorialization through soundscape music compositions.

1. INTRODUCTION

The ritualistic act of recording sounds, specifically capturing the thunderous roar of jet engines during takeoff, has been a deeply personal soundscape recording practice for the author over the years. The jet engine sounds mixture with train sounds, symbolizing both departure and arrival, become a metaphor for the temporal and emotional dimensions inherent in the human experience. In addition, the live recording of Korean traditional music was embedded in the highlight of the composition.

This paper delves into the intricate relationship between sound, time, emotion, memories, and reminiscence, using these recordings as the cornerstone for a soundscape composition. This composition creates an invisible space for listeners to revisit the times spent traveling, bridging the gap between past memories and the present moment of listening.

2. SOUNDSCAPE MUSIC

Soundscape music serves as a powerful channel for intertwining the concepts of time, space, and the listener's self, offering a unique perspective on the intricate dynamics at play. For example, consider the confined space of an airplane, where listeners are enveloped in the cabin's soundscape amidst the thunderous engine sounds from the outside world. As a soundscape listener myself, sitting within the plane fosters a unique connection between the self and the airborne vessel. Simultaneously, the mind, engaged in listening, may wander into distant realms while absorbing the cacophony of sounds from the swiftly traversing aircraft.

Time, a dynamic component in the experience of air travel, is keenly felt. As a soundscape composer, the author consistently ponders the profound relationship between time and space during the creation of musical compositions. The transformative power inherent in the compositional process and the music itself emerges as a force capable of evoking memories and emotions.

The subsequent sections explore the author's fascination with the multifaceted nature of soundscape music, highlighting its ability to evoke a sense of time, space, and self within the intricate tapestry of sonic experiences.

3. MEMORIAL SOUNDSCAPE

The author's soundscape compositions represent her exploration of time spent, spaces experienced, and loved ones who once accompanied her but now exist solely in memory. She asserts that the soundscape genre serves as an effective medium for articulating and creating a new realm for memorializing lost loved ones.

Her research project focuses on 'memorialization through self-reflective soundscape music creation', utilizing contextualized field recordings from sites of trauma or personally meaningful sounds.

Self-reflective soundscape listening is a method the author is personally developing for the research, evoking and stirring up personal memories in an unpredictable and powerful manner. The process involves reminiscing about the past, revisiting places where valuable time was spent with loved ones, all accumulated within memories. Her research argues that self-reflective soundscape listening should be deeply personal, drawing upon field recordings that explore personal trauma, memories, and experiences.

The author's soundscape composition, *Entropy*, based on self-reflective listening and field recordings, elucidates her experiences and the emotions evoked through listening and music creation with a mixture of sonic elements.

The soundscape compositions created by the author through her research will be shared with the public ultimately via a Soundscape Memorial website. The author hopes that her compositions will evoke emotions and inspire sentimental reflections in listeners.

4. SOUND IN MOTION

4.1 Soundscape's Storytelling

The theme, 'Sound in Motion', aligns with the dynamic nature of jet engine sounds as they soar into the skies. Takeoff serves as a poignant metaphor, evoking a spectrum of emotions from nervousness to excitement. In this context, the sound of a plane in motion transforms into a captivating canvas for exploring the emotional nuances of life's journey. Thus, listeners embark on a journey of sonic storytelling.

As jet engine sounds reverberate, they encapsulate not only the physical motion of the plane but also the myriad emotions experienced during air travel. Nervous anticipation, the thrill of exploration, uncertainties, and untold stories intertwine within our imagination as we share the concurrent soundscape, inhabiting the same time and space with fellow travelers. This exploration of emotional nuances through sound serves as a dynamic storytelling mechanism within the soundscape composition.

In the vast expanse of air travel, every human becomes a protagonist in their own story, including the author, who has regularly traversed the skies.

The author was struck with awe witnessing the musicians perform *Samheonyukgak*, a piece listed on the Korean National Intangible Cultural Heritage. The musicians, consisting of six instrumental players — one each for daegeum, haegeum, janggo, buk, and two for piri [1]— impressed with their dedication to preserving a musical tradition spanning over thousands of years without written scores, leaving a lasting impression. The cross-legged sitting postures of the six musicians wearing traditional Korean white cloths, Hanbok, on the wooden floor in a Korean traditional house used for the performance venue, was memorable as well as their unity of progressing the music. Simultaneously, the author felt a sense of sentimentality as the live recording, hurriedly made before catching a train, left behind a lingering regret brought about by time constraints. As the author consciously realized that the time in the moment would never return and faced the sudden risk of losing both time and space, leaving behind only memories, the memorial soundscape recordings and the process of self-reflective listening helped to appreciate the moments in the past, embrace the moments in the present listening experience, and thus create new moments of time and space for the future with the listened memories.

Soundscape, as an artistic medium, harbors a collective narrative yearning to be expressed. Envision the multitude of people within a plane, each possessing a unique perspective. If every individual were to craft their own soundscape composition, the auditory landscape would echo with an anthology of diverse and intertwining stories.

4.2 Sonic Experiences Shared

Sounds traverse through the air. The intentional selection of jet engine sounds acts as a potent focal point, their massive and enveloping nature serving as a metaphorical embrace. This purposeful focus directs attention to the present moment of listening, reminiscent of a contemplation of life and mortality. The compelling energy of sounds actively shapes and merges different times and spaces intrinsic to the soundscape music composition, creating an entirely new spacetime for the listener to inhabit.

The continuous and steady rhythm of jet engine sounds possesses a remarkable quality — not only the capacity to distill the essence of a ten-hour flight into a condensed timeframe but also indicating that the flight is cruising smoothly. Likewise, the train sounds departing the platform intentionally interwoven with the taking of jet engine sounds indicate no dissimilation. Rather, throughout the soundscape listening experience, open questions might arise about a safe landing at the destination or whether the person who recorded the sounds managed to board the train before the door closed. This last part of the composition implicitly suggests that the person in the recording finally returned to reality after a journey to a home country that now sounds slightly foreign to the author. This mixture of emotions intrigues the author, who endeavors to convey the self-reflective process through the soundscape journey.

While the collected recordings span various years, their juxtaposition and interweaving within the composition defy chronological constraints. This temporal ambiguity reflects the essence of memory — a confluence of past experiences brought together in the present moment of composition and listening. While time is in perpetual motion, our reality is in a transient state: we cannot step into the shoes of time-travelers; a fact that brings a sense of melancholy.

5. EMOTIONS IN TIME IN MOTION

This paper, accompanied by a soundscape composition, seeks to capture the intricate relationship between time and sound in motion. The jet sounds, representing both departure and arrival, symbolize the perpetual cycle of life and death, drawing from the author's own experiences navigating the uncertainties of air travel. Listening to the recorded jet sounds brought back vivid memories of deep fear experienced during a smooth plane trip to NYC for field recordings, specifically for a soundscape memorial project for 9/11. This emotional turbulence mirrors the physical motion of the plane, connecting sound and sentiment while reflecting on past experiences. The recorded sounds become a vessel for expressing the fleeting nature of life and the constant interplay between anticipation and fear.

Additionally, while listening to a live recording of Korean traditional music, *Samheonyukgak*, from Hanok Village in Jeonju, South Korea, previously unheard, all the way across the globe in Brisbane, Australia, the author experienced a mix of happiness and sadness. The music evoked fond memories of time spent with loved ones, juxtaposed with the author's longing for those still in Korea. The elegant traditional Korean dance music, while enjoyable, also stirred feelings of turbulence, reflecting the complexity of emotions intertwined with memories lost to time.

Moreover, contemplating overseas travel often leads one to ponder the possibility of revisiting a place in the future or returning home. However, what if the sudden loss of a loved one erases the hope of sharing the future with them? The author's research project is a response to contemplating the impact of sudden bereavement, striving to address intense emotions by paying tribute through the memorial soundscape project. It seeks to provide solace for those grappling with the grief of personal loss, resonating with the unexpected tragedies.

6. ENTROPY

In crafting Entropy, the composer endeavors to encapsu late a narrative journey, tracing the linear trajectory of a trip from Korea to Brisbane within an approximate 18- minute duration, allowing listeners to embark on this au ditory expedition. Commencing with the raw recording of a jet taking off and culminating with the closing of Bris bane's train doors, the composer arranges a tapestry of soundscape recordings, each evoking the essence of trav el. Despite originating from disparate past trips and jour neys, these recordings coalesce to form a cohesive sonic narrative. The integration of Korean traditional music recordings into the journey imbues the soundscape with a dreamlike quality, reminiscent of floating amidst clouds with the backdrop of humming jet engines. Deliberate alterations in timbre and timing enhance the ethereal at mosphere, while the incorporation of raw recordings as compositional elements adds layers of authenticity.

Through repeated engagement with the original Korean traditional music recordings, the composer delves into the accumulated practice time of the musicians, imbuing the piece with a sense of lineage and continuity spanning generations. This intertwining of past, present, and future creates a palpable anticipation, as the composer navigates between temporal realms, infusing each moment with significance.

The composition culminates with the phrase "mind the gap," serving as a poignant reminder of the inevitable passage of time and the transient nature of existence. This intentional inclusion of the Brisbane City Train an nouncement in the piece serves to contextualize the recordings, providing listeners with a sense of place and journey progression. While human voice sounds are typi cally edited out of the composer's soundscape recordings, this deliberate choice adds a layer of familiarity for Bris bane residents, who may recognize the ambient sounds of birds alongside the train, reflecting the city's unique soundscape. Similarly, the use of the phrase "mind the gap" deviates from the composer's usual practice, serving as a deliberate attempt to convey a specific meaning to listeners. While its interpretation may vary, the composer seeks to elucidate its significance within the context, of fering insight into their creative intentions.

Through the manipulation of sounds, the composer seeks to underscore the finite nature of human experi ence, employing the brief sound of train doors closing as a metaphor for life's abrupt endings amidst the relentless march of time.

7. MEMORIES STUCK IN BETWEEN

As the sound travels through time, it brings forth the realization that memories, stuck in between, remain a profound testament to our existence.

A crucial aspect of the composition is the acknowledgment that the author, at different junctures, was physically present on the plane, with distinct memories associated with each recording. However, those moments are irreversibly gone, leaving behind only the recorded sounds interwoven with memories. This mirrors the broader human experience of losing loved ones, where memories endure even as physical presence fades.

In the author's composition notes, the emphasis lies on the essence of our reality, particularly the boundless time that captures every human being with limited time. Through captured sound recordings and the creation of soundscape music compositions, the author strives to evoke moments of appreciation for life—a life whose time inevitably closes its switch at the end, leaving behind unforgettable memories embedded somewhere in the universe that we collectively share.

By bringing the soundscape of memories to the forefront of our current listening experience, the author hopes to further accelerate the appreciation of life moving forward and the relationships we have celebrated thus far.

8. CONCLUSIONS

Memories, inherently personal, are clearly expressed in the creation of memorial soundscape music, as reflected in the presented soundscape composition. Nevertheless, the personal has the potential to transcend individual experiences and become universal.

The soundscape piece, *Entropy*, enriched by the immersive sounds of traveling jet engines, extends an invitation for everyone to reflect on their unique personal stories and memories, embracing the diverse elements of our shared travel experiences.

Acknowledgments

I extend my sincere gratitude to the six musicians who performed *Samheonyukgak* at Hanok Village in Jeonju, South Korea, on 27th October 2023. Their exceptional musical talents and dedication to preserving cultural heritage left an indelible mark on my research and enriched my understanding of the profound traditions within Korean music. Their contribution is sincerely appreciated.

9. REFERENCES

[1] S. Kim, "The Formation and the Distortion of the Term, Samheonyukgak," *Journal of the Society for Korean Historico-Musicology*, vol., no. 65, pp. 35–71, 2020.

AlloThresher: Multimodal Granular Synthesizer

Myungin Lee
Immersive Media Design & Computer Science
University of Maryland College Park
myungin@umd.edu

Jongwoo Yim
Department of Composition
Seoul National University
jongwooyim@snu.ac.kr

ABSTRACT

AlloThresher is a multimodal instrument based on granular synthesis using the gestural interface. Granular synthesis is a sound synthesis method that creates complex tones by combining and mixing the simple micro-sonic elements called grains. Using two smartphones with gyroscopes and accelerometers in both hands, the user can precisely and spontaneously trigger the parameters of the granular synthesis in real-time. The devised gestural interface includes an adaptive filter and reverberation, adding expressiveness. The modulated spectrogram of each grain and post-processing generate the corresponding visuals, morphing and blending dynamically with the instrumentalist's performance. The entire software is programmed in C++, optimizing the real-time multimodality. By removing conventional interfaces like knobs and sliders, this seamless connection between modalities utilizes the profound advantage of the gestural interface. The instrumentalist's physical presence and gesture become part of the space and the performance so that the audience can simultaneously observe and cohesively connect the audio, visual, and interface.

1. INTRODUCTION

Granular synthesis is a sound synthesis method that assembles intricate tones by combining and mixing simple micro-sonic elements called grains [1]. While the method generates unique and dynamic timbres, it requires multiple parameters to control, and this has been one of the challenges of mastering granular synthesis, especially in real-time. This aspect has also been a limitation from the audience's point of view since the audience can barely understand the interface and the instrumentalist's intention while the instrumentalist is controlling the dozens of knobs and sliders. On the other hand, granular synthesis is often considered sound clouds, dynamic agglomerations of sonic particles that move around the sonic landscape over time and frequency domains. While this concept motivated composers to involve cloud-like visual scores or videos for audiovisual representation, such a process required post-processing and was barely applied to live performances.

Within this context, we propose a novel multimodal instrument, AlloThresher, based on granular synthesis using the gestural interface with visual representations of the sonic clouds. AlloThresher utilizes two smartphones. The gestural interface interpreted from the smartphones' sensors enables the player to precisely and spontaneously decide and play the multiple parameters of the granular synthesis in real-time. The audio analysis-based visualization presents a coherent multimodal experience. This instrument design allows simultaneous control of multiple parameters for the performer with coherent graphics and, from the audience's perspective, provides a connection between the performer's gesture and the corresponding audiovisual. The instrument is scaleable from laptop to large-scale distributed facility such as the AlloSphere with 26 stereo projectors and 54.1 channels of audio [2].

2. RELATED WORKS

Since Gabor proposed a scientific model using a grain system to reproduce sound in 1946 [3], composers have frequently utilized granular synthesis to shape large masses of sound with unique timbres. In 1959, Xenakis created granular sounds using hundreds of tiny slices of magnetic tape and analog tone synthesizers [4]. Xenakis's Pithoprakta and its visual score show the probabilistic mass of short and numerous sounds played by acoustic instruments in an audiovisual way [5, 6]. Truax created Riverrun in 1986 using real-time granular synthesis, and its spectral analysis depicts the time-frequency landscape [7]. In 1995, Roads devised Cloud Generator equipped with a graphical interface that can create large clouds of grains [8]. Still, to deliver a coherent audiovisual experience, composers had to record or post-process the additional graphics and combine them as a video [9, 10]. In 2020, EmissionControl2 [11], Roads introduced an open-source standalone interactive real-time granular synthesizer with sound file granulation.

In the multimodal cases, Borderlands [12] by Carlson incorporates the concept of grain clouds and sound quads into the audiovisual interface for Granular synthesis. Droljc's work [13, 14] shows a real-time audiovisual granular synthesizer combined with a particle system. GrainTrain [15] proposed by Çamcı uses a multi-touchscreen to control waveforms in real-time granular synthesis.

Meanwhile, having many different parameters to control using the GUI is one of the challenges of using granular synthesis, especially in real-time.

3. DESIGN OF MULTIMODAL GRANULAR SYNTHESIS

The instrument design is based on the intimate interconnection between the granular synthesis, gestural interface, and graphics. Each component is not simply utilized to map specific parameters in different modalities but communicates back and forth, establishing a crossmodally correspondent experience. Such experience in digital mediation provides the most veridical estimate of events or stimuli by combining the perceptual from different unisensory referring to the identical event while keeping those estimates separately [16]. Therefore we deliberately designed the multimodal experience loop in our system. Figure 1 shows the schematic of AlloThresher instrument.

The software is implemented on a single C++ platform using open-source libraries including *AlloLib*, *OpenGL*, and *RtAudio* [17, 18, 19]. C++ allows direct access to low-level hardware and system resources, optimizing efficiency, performance, and quality, which are crucial for real-time instruments.

The following sections delve into detailed domains of the instrument, including gestural interface, audio, and graphics. These sections comprehensively examine the project from theoretical, technical, and artistic perspectives.

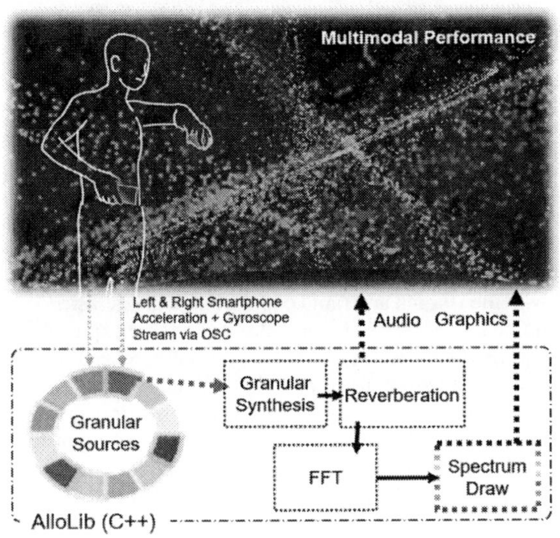

Figure 1. Schematic of AlloThresher instrument

3.1 Audio

The granular synthesizer implemented in C++ comprises the audio. The implemented code can read, truncate, manipulate, filter, short-time Fourier transform (STFT), spatialize, and playback. Therefore, the instrument can access parameters in every domain in real-time. Motivated by Road's design [11], we created a granular synthesis with parameters including grain source, start position, amplitude, duration, playback rate, number of grains, and spatial position. The grain source includes recorded noises, wave sounds, acoustic instruments, voices, Tibetan Monk Om Chanting, and Korean Emile Jong. These sources can be easily replaced, added, or removed.

When such parameters are controlled using conventional types of knobs and sliders for real-time performance, from the instrumentalist's perspective, manipulating these multiple parameters is challenging. Moreover, the audience finds it hard to relate the instrumentalist's decision to the performance since such control is barely observable from their perspective. From this observation, we developed the multimodal granular synthesizer with graphics and a gestural interface.

3.2 Interface

The proposed gestural interface allows spontaneous control for the instrumentalist and enables the audience to connect the relationship between the gesture, audio, and graphics coherently.

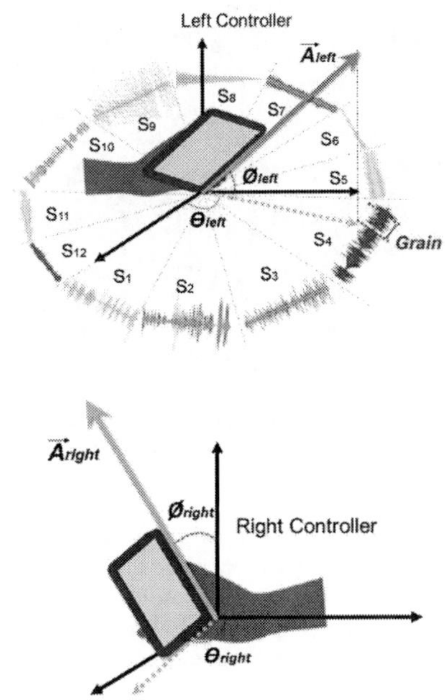

Figure 2. Parameters of the left and right smartphones

The smartphone, on each hand, composes the interface as the controller. The smartphone's brand or model is irrelevant. The gestural data, including gyroscopes and accelerometers, is parsed from the device and sent to AlloThresher's server device via OSC [20]. Figure 2 shows the parameters of the left and right controllers. A_{left} indicates the left controller's vector, and A_{right} is the right controller's vector.

Smartphones have different rules: the left hand decides the source to granulate, and the right hand grinds the grain. The left-hand gyroscope emanates the directional information of the gesture, which determines the sound source (θ_{left}), grain position (θ_{left}), and reverberation (ϕ_{left}). In the case of Figure 2, the fourth sound source (S_4) is selected among the 12 sound sources (S_{1-12}). The grain start position is $(3{*}30-\theta_{left})/30$ between 0 and 1 and $\phi_{left}/90$ amount of reverberation between 0 and 1 is applied.

The right controller behaves more dynamic role to actuate the grains. A_{right}'s absolute acceleration determines the amplitude and duration of the synthesis. This design allows the synthesizer to actuate only if the acceleration exceeds a certain threshold, preventing unintentional continuous actuation.

Vertical direction ϕ_{right} decides the number of grains, and the horizontal direction θ_{right} maps to the playback rate from -1.5 to 1.5. The direction of the right hand stroke provides a dynamic spatial panning effect supporting stereo to any number of channels.

3.3 Graphics

The graphic components are designed to visually represent the granular parameters and corresponding audio. Figure 3 shows the exemplary graphics of AlloThresher.

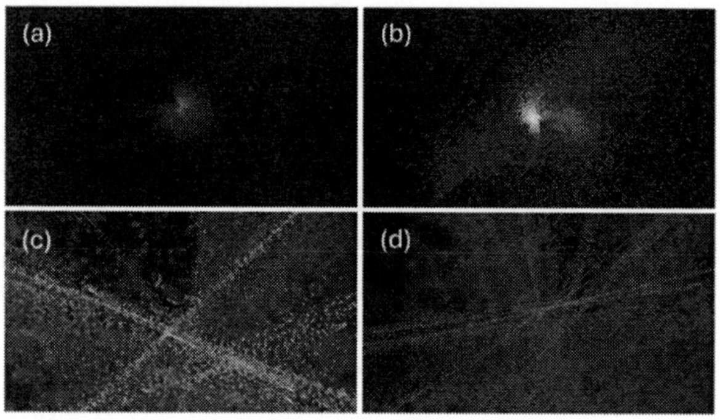

Figure 3. Exemplary graphics of AlloThresher (a) Small actuation with single granular source (b) Moderate actuation with multiple sources, (c) Dynamic actuation, (d) Actuation with high reverberation

We tied the granular synthesis's characteristics to the graphics. For instance, time-frequency observation using the STFT shows agglomerations of particles that assemble dense sound clouds. The proposed software analyzes the STFT in real time, scales logarithmically, and plots it as a dynamic mesh composed of spectral particles according to the playback rate of the granular. When the playback rate is positive, the spectral mesh comes closer, and the mesh diminishes if the rate is negative. The graphic frame feedback effect depicts reverberation by copying and applying the frame buffer. This effect creates a diverging smooth texture, resembling acoustic reverberation in a large space. The color represents the source of the grain.

As a result, inspired by clouds of sound, dynamically morphing and blending spectrograms of the sound actuated by the gesture comprise the visual components. Likewise, the visual elements explain the multiple factors of granular synthesis, assist the audience's understanding, and enhance the multimodal experience.

4. EXPERIENCING ALLOTHRESHER

AlloThresher is designed as a multimodal instrument for real-time performance. The instrumentalist can use one's spatial awareness and motor system to precisely decide the granular synthesizer's factors. Using this property, the instrumentalist can establish counterpoints such as tension versus resolution and prediction versus unpredictability. These counterpoints become the building blocks of the multimodal composition. To demonstrate, we composed various motives and compositions for the performance. Figure 3 shows the multimodal performance of AlloThresher in an immersive environment with 36 speakers and two stereo projectors with a curved screen. The audiovisual demonstration is available online [21].

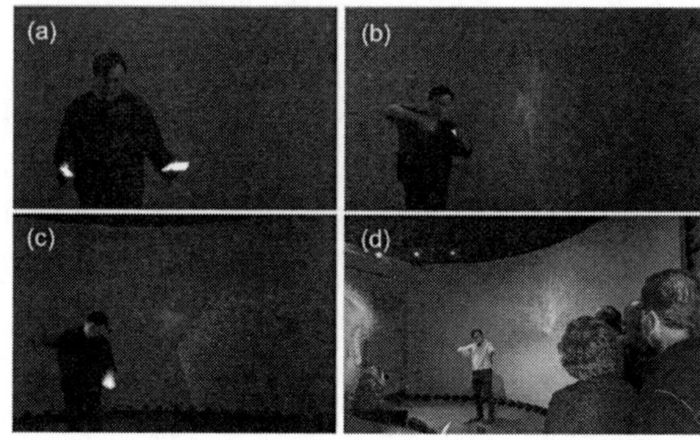

Figure 4. Photographs of AlloThresher's performance with the instrumentalist's gesture and the corresponding graphic behind (a) stable pose, (b) grinding gesture (c) stroke gesture (d) public performance

4.1 Audience's Response

The performances invited a diverse audience of musicians, dancers, engineers, students, and the general public. Most of the audience was impressed with the immersive experiences. For instance, engineers and musicians showed interest in the real-time implementation of granular synthesis and its graphical mapping, and dancers were impressed with the smooth and rapid expression of the gesture to multimodal experience. Even without a specific explanation of the interface, audiences showed fast comprehension of the instrument. Audiences including trained musicians including Curtis Roads and JoAnn Kuchera-Morin shared their experiences through the interview that they often find it hard to understand the interaction of computer music when the player is playing one's instrument behind the laptop controlling indistinguishable knobs.

After the performance, the audience was invited to play the instrument. While most of them began by enjoying the improvisation, they started to understand the mapping of the gestures and tried to make their own motive. Such results showed diverse differences in the cases. This demonstrates how AlloThresher invites new players as an enjoyable tool; at the same time, the player can train and grow virtuosity to master a particular motive, phrase, and piece.

5. DISCUSSION

Avoiding conventional interfaces such as knobs and sliders, we build a seamless connection between the instrument and the profound expressiveness of the gesture. As if observing the vibrant and sophisticated gesture of the conductor is a part of the orchestra experience, in AlloThresher performance, the instrumentalist's presence and gestures become part of the performance and the space. Correspondingly, the audience can naturally observe and relate the audio, visual, interface, and performance more comprehensively. This observation brought echoing dialogue to trained musicians including Curtis Roads and JoAnn

Kuchera-Morin, and developed in to coherent multimodal instrument design research [22] which suggests numerical analysis method by measuring and computing the correlation between multimodal experience from audience's perspective.

Utilizing our program's compatibility without dependency on commercial programs and customizable characteristics, we could share the instrument through Git [23] and adjust the components, including graphic configurations and granular sources. This allows creative opportunities for artists and general users to experience a new instrument with their laptops and smartphones with any scale.

For future work, we are gathering instrument users and targeting to open an open call for the piece. We are developing a method to document the notes of the pieces by visually recording the time-variant information on a 2D score.

6. CONCLUSIONS

This paper introduces a novel multimodal instrument based on a granular synthesizer. Using custom C++ codes with open-source libraries, AlloThresher can be installed in any operating system, providing an optimized and scalable multimodal experience. While audio, interface, and graphics are introduced separately to explain the details, the modality design of the AlloThresher is connected as a loop pursuing a crossmodally correspondent experience. For the instrumentalists, such component provides natural motivation from gesture to audio, gesture to graphics, audio to graphics, and vice versa. The audience understood the instrument easily by relating the audio, visual, and gesture. The audience response was positive and vibrant evoking the discussion on the conventional computer music interfaces. While the progression of digital technology is accelerating the automation of music and graphics, AlloThresher aims to reconnect the physicality and expressiveness of our gestures to the users.

Acknowledgments

This work is supported by the Immersive Media Design Program and the Department of Computer Science at the University of Maryland College Park, the AlloSphere Research Group at the University of California Santa Barbara, and the College of Music at Seoul National University. We thank JoAnn Kuchera-Morin and Curtis Roads for their remarks. We thank Tae Kyeong Rhee for rendering the figures.

7. REFERENCES

[1] C. Roads, *Microsound*. The MIT Press, 2004.

[2] A. Cabrera, J. Kuchera-Morin, and C. Roads, "The Evolution of Spatial Audio in the AlloSphere," *IEEE Computer Music Journal*, vol. 40, no. 4, pp. 47–61, 2016.

[3] C. Roads, "Introduction to granular synthesis," *Computer Music Journal*, vol. 12, no. 2, pp. 11–13, 1988.

[4] A. Di Scipio, "Formalization and Intuition in Analogique A et B," pp. 95–108, 2005.

[5] I. Xenakis, *Formalized music: thought and mathematics in composition*. Pendragon Press, 1992, no. 6.

[6] M. Solomos, "The granular connection (xenakis, vaggione, di scipio...)," 2006.

[7] M. Clarke, P. Manning *et al.*, *Inside Computer Music*. Oxford University Press, USA, 2020.

[8] C. Roads, "From grains to forms," pp. 1–40, 2012.

[9] ——, "The path to Half-life," *POINT LINE CLOUD*, 2004.

[10] A. Munster, "Signaletic immediations: Sensing new media as relational events and ecologies," *Immediation I*, p. 228, 2019.

[11] "EmissionControl2," 2023. [Online]. Available: https://github.com/EmissionControl2/EmissionControl2

[12] C. Carlson and G. Wang, "Borderlands-An Audiovisual Interface for Granular Synthesis." in *NIME*, 2012.

[13] T. Droljc, "Composing with isomorphic audiovisual gestalts," 2018.

[14] "Particle-based Granular Synthesis," 2018. [Online]. Available: https://youtu.be/ajCYefU61e8?feature=shared

[15] A. Çamcı, "GrainTrain: A hand-drawn multi-touch interface for granular synthesis," in *Proceedings of the International Conference on New Interfaces for Musical Expression*, 2018, pp. 156–161.

[16] C. Spence, "Crossmodal correspondences: A tutorial review," *Attention Perception Psychophysics*, 2011.

[17] "AlloLib: A Cross-platform Suite of C++ Components for Building Interactive Multimedia Tools and Applications," 2024. [Online]. Available: https://github.com/AlloSphere-Research-Group/allolib

[18] D. Shreiner, G. Sellers, J. Kessenich, and B. Licea-Kane, *OpenGL Programming Guide: The Official Guide to Learning OpenGL, Version 4.3*, version 4.3 ed. Boston, MA, USA: Addison-Wesley, 2013.

[19] G. P. Scavone and P. R. Cook, "RtMidi, RtAudio, and a synthesis toolkit (STK) update," *Synthesis*, 2004.

[20] M. Wright, A. Freed, and A. Momeni, "2003: OpenSound Control: State of the Art 2003," *A NIME Reader. Current Research in Systematic Musicology*, 2017.

[21] "AlloThresher: Video Demonstration," 2024. [Online]. Available: https://www.myunginlee.com/allothresher

[22] M. Lee, *Coherent Digital Multimodal Instrument Design and the Evaluation of Crossmodal Correspondence*. University of California, Santa Barbara, 2023.

[23] "AlloThresher," 2024. [Online]. Available: https://github.com/MyunginLee/allo_thresher

Mollspeak — Unreal Spatial Synthesis for a Narration

Olivier Pasquet
Goldsmiths, University of London
o.pasquet@gold.ac.uk

ABSTRACT

Mollspeak is a permanent immersive sound installation that explores the lives of eighteenth-century maidservants through an intimate portrayal of home life. The piece examines the cultural significance of domestic spaces and their impact on social dynamics. This article outlines the creative processes behind the piece and discusses the technical solutions used to realize it, including photogrammetry, physical model synthesis engines, and software for simulating surreal room acoustics. The sound piece showcases an innovative approach to immersive storytelling using abstract voice, and is part of a larger research endeavor in music-theatrical directions.

1. INTRODUCTION

Mollspeak is a permanent sound installation at the Museum of the Home in London, premiered on May 18th, 2021, and also aired as a 25-minute radio binaural version on October 12th 2021. The installation combines synthetic sounds, music generation, and acoustic architecture designed for the museum's building, featuring a text by Maria Fusco and voiced by actress Maxine Peake.

The project is part of a long-term artistic research exploring the connections between spatial representations of time and narration, stemming from the authors' backgrounds in theater, architecture, and music composition. Spatialization plays a crucial role in the piece, with all sounds and the composition's timeline generated and positioned in space and time using 3d scans of museum objects and a dedicated synthesis engine called *Dürer*.

The paper discusses how various tools and concepts come together to create a cohesive aesthetic for a series of pieces, showcasing an artistic research path that merges expertise, imagination, failures, and surprises.

2. SCENARIO

Maria Fusco's text reveals the pains, desires, and routines of eighteenth-century maidservants, drawing from extensive archival research and objects in the Museum's collections (fig. 1). *Mollspeak*, is a phrase employers coined to mock their servants' dialectical speech. Maria Fusco's original script mingles research with historic poetic form to give voice to a working class's story – reflecting on duties, desires and place in the world – to create a plainly spoken, yet lyrical portrait.

Exploring homes and home life requires intimacy and familiarity, which affects anthropological and cultural aspects. Subconscious memories shape our definition of home, with physical spaces and objects playing a crucial role. The sonic component of this piece explores the subconscious connections between objects and their spaces, leaving uncertainty about their origins. This ambiguity creates a fertile ground for composition.

Figure 1. *The Management of Servants by a member of the aristocracy*, eighteenth-century.

3. USE OF THE MUSEUM'S COLLECTION

3.1 Photogrammetry of objects of the museum

The piece is based on classified objects from a museum, each representing a social aspect of British society. The resonant characteristics of each object were recorded and 3d scanned using photogrammetry to avoid physical contact with the fragile items (fig. 2). This allowed for the digital creation of physical models that could be transformed into unconventional forms later on.

3.2 Experiments using physical model synthesis engines

The initial concept involved using 3D scan data to generate resonances from quadrangle meshes [1, 2]. Tools like Modalys and Faust were used to apply finite element methods and create resonant models. However, the results only became musically interesting after applying transient design techniques, including compression, valve distortion, emphasizing mid-high frequency transients, and controlling low-frequency decay using specific plugins and tools [3, 4].

We prefers fast rhythms with sharp attacks to clearly understand musical structure. As a result, incorporating long-term resonances wasn't feasible. We realized that a less continuous approach was needed to maintain a pulsating style and thus prevent listener apathy [5].

Figure 2. Photogrammetry scans of horn beakers and a paper doll. Many of the museum objects were scanned. Some of them are not supposed to resonate, to make any sound...

3.3 Alternative symbolic strategies

We explored alternative interactions with 3D scans of museum objects, such as scratching or shaking, using tools like the Sound Design Toolkit (SDT) to create non-linear sounds [6] [1]. However, we opted for a more poetic approach, introducing temporal elements to sonic materials and imbuing objects with symbolic meaning to create metaphors and ostinati. This approach allowed for contrasting elements and meaningful comparisons.

Another strategy involved using actress Maxine Peake's voice in a musical manner, juxtaposing it with the text. The outcome was a blend of meaningful text and dadaistic composed phonemes derived from voice processing. Techniques using the yin fundamental frequency estimator included separating voiced and unvoiced elements of her voice, rhythmically playing them as percussive elements, and combining them to create textual meaning [7]. The text was often deconstructed and not read linearly, but Peake's declarative style added an emotional foundation [8].

The result is a seamless blend of narrative sound objects, musical metaphoric elements, fragmented words, and an intensely delivered text. The delivery is as forceful and insistent as the commands given to servants. Sound examples can be heard here:
`https://www.opasquet.fr/mollspeak/.`

3.4 Other alternative strategy with spatial synthesis

The tool *Dürer*, developed for this piece, is an audio synthesis and virtual acoustics tool for Rhino's Grasshopper, based on image source model room simulation (fig. 3). It pays homage to Albrecht Dürer and Vera Molnár [9]. It consists on representing time by space and displacement in the most straight forward way in order to create descriptive scores with a specific granular esthetics in the near future.

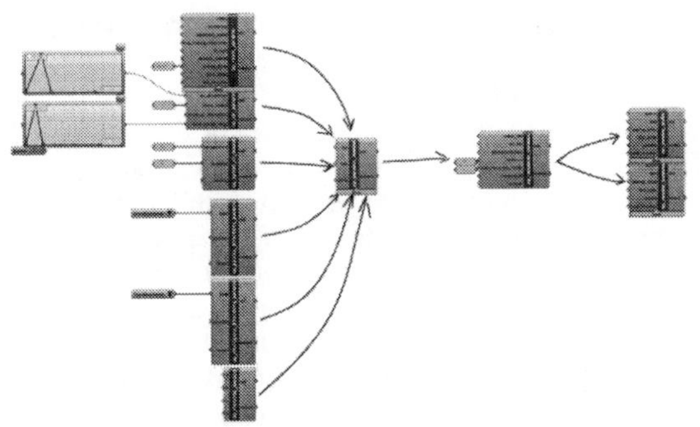

Figure 3. Components for *Dürer*'s renderer in Grasshooper's Rhino plugin. It consists on three parts: physical parameters (materials, directivities, scattering etc), renderer parameters (IR size, instances etc) and export (IR audio format, convoluted file etc).

The first development process began with a hack and the integration of the *Pyroomacoustics* Python library from EPFL, Lausanne, into Rhino [10, 11] [2]. The engine renders multichannel impulse responses either from a beam of microphones (beamforming) or a virtual Eigenmike, allowing manipulation of directivity, delays, and virtual ambisonics (fig. 4). For *Mollspeak*, Rhino imports all the 3D scans of objects within the museum, ensuring that meshes are closed. These meshs may undergo transformation and simplification to enhance rendering speed. Mesh reduction is a nuanced process that varies depending on specific requirements. We have developed a technique for mesh simplification, utilizing a genetic algorithm solver called Galapagos, which preserves reflections acceptably [12].

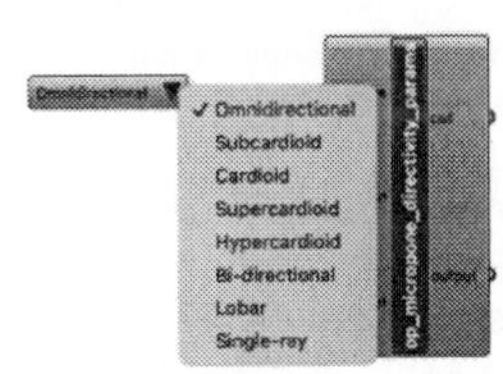

Figure 4. Available directivities for *Dürer*'s virtual microphones. "Single-ray" is not feasible in reality, which is precisely what we are interested in.

Dürer is primarily designed for unrealistic room acoustics. It can generate multichannel impulse responses and apply convolution to a set of sound files. It is also possible to create sound synthesis related to space using physically

[1] https://github.com/SkAT-VG/SDT

[2] https://github.com/SkAT-VG/SDT

unrealistic characteristics. A torus with specific face angles can produce intriguing click rhythms and oscillations, and the visual outcome closely correlates with the sound (fig. 7).
For example, one can play with:
- unattainable parameters such as room temperature, speed of sound, air absorption...
- amplifying materials positioned with precision to create oscillations (absortion >1.)
- RIR denoising by only synthesising a limited amount rays or bounces.
- an impractical number of virtual speakers or microphones.

The most interesting aspect, in conjunction with the piece's sharp aesthetics, is to capture the sequence and power of rays bouncing off mesh faces. Each object from the museum thus receives a unique characteristic derived from the topology of its surfaces. We voxelize the space, quantify distances and ray angles to get perceivable rthymical coherency (fig. 5). We also empirically adapt the number of rays, their initial directivity and intensity as if we were reconstructing acoustic directional characteristics of sources. In our specfic case, it has been found that it only makes sense to use a train of dirac impulses as sources to avoid any question about phases. Shortening the length of ray paths and setting mesh faces to be fully reflective creates a clear texture.

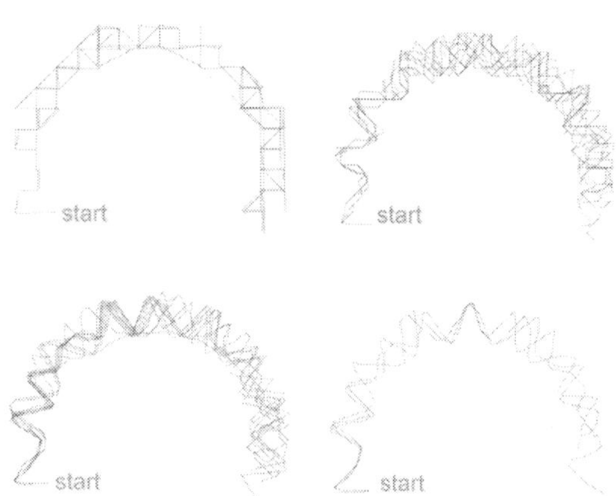

Figure 5. Four semi-torus used as meshes. The two top ones use a voxelized space. The two at the bottom have quantized ray angles and distances. They all use a small number of rays for the demonstration.

This concept remains easily comprehensible, both aurally and visually, when using a limited number of rays. However, employing a large number of rays enables a sense of continuity in the resulting RIR, effectively yielding rhythmic synthesis. The mesh's form and its topological coherence create temporal consistency and discontinuities from sample to sample, akin to resonance. For example, squeezing the object has a pronounced impact on the outcome (fig. 6).

Computational power, combined with geometric tools in Rhino and the described computational granular propagation, enables rapid construction and deconstruction of objects, transitioning seamlessly from continuous to discontinuous forms (fig. 7). We have explored various optimisation techniques for forms finding in order to generate specific rythms and clusters within the RIR. This unfortunately have not been further for *Mollspeak*.

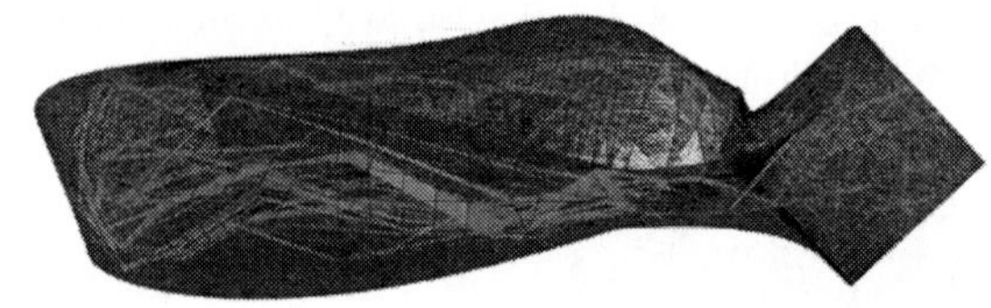

Figure 6. Distorted torus. By constraining and discretizing ray angles, parallelism and convergence emerge, yielding a construct showcasing intricate ray interactions and interferences.

Figure 7. Two "expensive donuts": the one on top is flat and will give complex early reflections, faces of the bottom one are set for a specific rhythm.

3.5 Radio version of the piece and download *Dürer*

It is possible to listen to the linear 25-minute radio stereo and binaural version of the piece online. *Dürer* requires the architecture design software Rhino 3d [3] .
`https://www.opasquet.fr/mollspeak/`
`https://github.com/opasquetdotfr/Duerer`

4. FUTURE DEVELOPMENTS

Several developments have been done after *Mollspeak* and more is to come:
Our recent works, *The Nudge* and *The Impossible Trilemma*, both premiered at CLab in Taipei, feature "uncontrolled" transformers of Bark text-to-speech model [4] . These pieces blend abstract narration with uncanny vocal effects, pushing the boundaries of music and meaning. They draw a

[3] https://www.rhino3d.com
[4] https://github.com/suno-ai/bark

direct inspiration from previous vocal works composed by Georges Aperghis [13].

Meanwhile, our ongoing project *Dürer*, initially used as a visual score generator for the collection of large-scale paper prints *Toi-1842b*, has evolved using an experimental multi-thread version of *Dürer* with Pytorch, a Python library initially used for machine learning [14] [5]. We also have the intension to use that spatial technique to explore latent spaces.

5. CONCLUSION

Mollspeak was a major step in stylistic research on our pieces using text and music. The deployment of diverse techniques, including those tailored specifically for that piece, allowed for experimentation and ultimately essential advances for ongoing long-term progress.

Dürer was built in the realm of generative forms and spatial-temporal representation. It serves as a personal artistic notation and generative tool for composition utilizing spatial computation [15]. We have described, with *Mollspeak*, a simple framework and individual workflow for a series of specific concepts that can ultimately be materialized into sound pieces, prints, or fabricated in 3D.

Acknowledgments

We would like to thank Maria Fusco, Sinead McCarthy, Christina Karpodini, Jan Schacher, Toro-Pérez Germán, Atau Tanaka, the Museum of the Home in London, and the entire team of ICST at ZHdK without whom *Mollspeak* would have never been realized.

6. REFERENCES

[1] R. Michon, "Faust-STK: A set of linear and nonlinear physical models for the Faust programming language," 2011. [Online]. Available: https://api.semanticscholar.org/CorpusID:4844055

[2] A. Stegaru, "Modalys Reference Manual Finite Element Objects," 2003.

[3] P. A. Tremblay, G. Roma, and O. Green, "Enabling Programmatic Data Mining as Musicking: The Fluid Corpus Manipulation Toolkit," *Computer Music Journal, vol. 45, no. 2, pp. 9–23*, 2021.

[4] G. Roma, O. Green, and P. A. Tremblay, "Stationary/transient audio separation using convolutional autoencoders," 2018. [Online]. Available: https://api.semanticscholar.org/CorpusID:186844125

[5] B. Riley, *L'Esprit de l'Oeil*, 2008.

[6] S. Baldan, S. D. Monache, and D. Rocchesso, "The Sound Design Toolkit," *SoftwareX*, vol. 6, pp. 255–260, 2017. [Online]. Available: https://api.semanticscholar.org/CorpusID:55869488

[7] A. de Cheveigné and H. Kawahara, "YIN, a fundamental frequency estimator for speech and music." *The Journal of the Acoustical Society of America*, vol. 111 4, pp. 1917–30, 2002. [Online]. Available: https://api.semanticscholar.org/CorpusID:1607434

[8] H.-T. Lehmann, "Postdramatic Theatre," 2021. [Online]. Available: https://api.semanticscholar.org/CorpusID:235209773

[9] V. Molnar, "Léonard de Vinci s'il eut eu un ordinateur..." 1981.

[10] D. Rutten, "Evolutionary Principles Applied to Problem Solving - Grasshopper," 2010.

[11] R. Scheibler, E. Bezzam, and I. Dokmanić, "Pyroomacoustics: A Python Package for Audio Room Simulation and Array Processing Algorithms," *2018 IEEE International Conference on Acoustics, Speech and Signal Processing (ICASSP)*, pp. 351–355, 2017. [Online]. Available: https://api.semanticscholar.org/CorpusID:11855208

[12] D. Rutten, "Galapagos: On the Logic and Limitations of Generic Solvers," *Architectural Design*, vol. 83, pp. 132–135, 2013. [Online]. Available: https://api.semanticscholar.org/CorpusID:62481370

[13] M. Woo, "L'interprétation musicale des phonèmes, des gestes et des images dans Machinations de Georges Aperghis," 2011.

[14] B. Rozemberczki, P. Scherer, Y. He, G. Panagopoulos, M. S. Astefanoaei, O. Kiss, F. Béres, N. Collignon, and R. Sarkar, "PyTorch Geometric Temporal: Spatiotemporal Signal Processing with Neural Machine Learning Models," *Proceedings of the 30th ACM International Conference on Information & Knowledge Management*, 2021. [Online]. Available: https://api.semanticscholar.org/CorpusID:233289399

[15] A. Spicher, O. Michel, and J.-L. Giavitto, "Spatial Computing as Intensional Data Parallelism," *2010 Fourth IEEE International Conference on Self-Adaptive and Self-Organizing Systems Workshop*, pp. 196–205, 2010. [Online]. Available: https://api.semanticscholar.org/CorpusID:9328536

[5] https://pytorch.org

Liquidation: Bridging Acoustic Piano and Electronic Soundscapes through Real-Time Performance System

Sujin Kim
CREAMA, Hanyang University
Sjin967@hanyang.ac.kr

Daeun Kim
CREAMA, Hanyang University
tothestar21@hanyang.ac.kr

ABSTRACT

The Liquidation system is a real-time performance system for solo piano, implemented in Max, that focuses on enhancing piano performances with live electronics. Utilizing sound modulation techniques such as 32-channel ring modulation, multi-delay, and daisy chain reverb, and inspired by Arnold Schoenberg's composition concept of 'Liquidation,' the system algorithmically manipulates the piano's audio signals, blurring the lines between traditional piano sounds and electronic sounds. Additionally, by using algorithms to simply modify the values of cues, the system has been designed to allow easy control without the need for deep knowledge of electronic music. This paper highlights the technical and creative potential of merging traditional musical instruments with contemporary electronic sound manipulation by collaborating live electro-acoustic piece Glacial Echoes.

1. INTRODUCTION

Most of today's creative music works involve digital tools to some extent. Among lots of these programs, Max is regarded as one of the most effective tools for live electronics, offering a customizable environment and intuitive visual-based programming. However, synthesizing sound within Max requires a deeper understanding compared to DAW programs like Logic and Ableton. Hence, beginners might find it challenging to engage in live electronics with Max.

The *Liquidation* system, designed for solo piano, simplifies the creation of specific sounds, aiming to apply 'liquidation' - one of Arnold Schoenberg's composition techniques - electronically. By adjusting values for each audio effect through 'cues', the algorithms assigned to each audio effect automatically calculate the values, allowing users to design varied sounds without extensive signal processing and sound programming knowledge. This system aims to blend acoustic and electronic timbres seamlessly, through a distinct signal processing algorithm and simple adjustments.

2. BACKGROUND

Efforts to combine acoustic instruments with electronic music to design diverse sounds and control them effectively have been varied to date.

It's a multidisciplinary field that combines elements of music theory, digital signal processing, and composition. Especially in digital signal processing (DSP), there are various techniques for sound synthesis, so the variety of which sounds to use as the main material and which technique to choose from them is very diverse. Therefore, it is important to choose the right sound materials and techniques by focusing on the musical goals pursued. In this paper, we intend to design a tool that applies compositional techniques electronically to enhance the sound spectrum of acoustic instruments and to control them efficiently. Thus, we will mention a few representative studies related to this topic.

One notable example is Karlheinz Stockhausen's *Mantra* [1]. In this piece, the ring modulators are key in sculpting the piano's sound textures. In *Mantra*, the first pianist's modulator is tuned to each section's fundamental notes, minimizing effects for aligned notes while intensifying dissonance. The second pianist's modulator uses an inverted pitch sequence to deepen harmonic complexity. While both *Mantra* and the *Liquidation* system use ring modulation on piano material, the focus in *Mantra* is on changing pitches, whereas the *Liquidation* system aims to 'dilute' the characteristics of the acoustic itself through diverse audio effects, marking a distinct difference between the two approaches.

Another attempt to combine piano with electronic sound is Cort Lippe's research [2]. This research was conducted at IRCAM, and it features the ability for performers to adjust various aspects of DSP and control algorithms in real-time. The primary audio effects are analysis/resynthesis and convolution, particularly highlighting the real-time interaction between the piano and computer. Although both use Max for DSP, the *Liquidation* system highlights the importance of making electronic music accessible to performers without extensive DSP knowledge by simplifying control over complex processes. Lippe's setup, while also user-friendly within a performance context, requires a deeper understanding of the underlying technologies for its full utilization.

There is also research that has developed a 'hybrid piano' as an augmented instrument [3] done by Lauren Hayes. In this study, she utilized haptic technology to allow performers to adjust DSP and control algorithms in real-time. While both her research and the *Liquidation* system focus on real-time electronic sound control, she utilizes haptic feedback mechanisms to give performers physical sensations corresponding to their digital interactions, aiming to replicate the traditional feel of acoustic instruments. The *Liquidation* system, however, uses audio effects processed in Max to algorithmically alter the sound of the piano, creating a hybrid sound environment without the need for tactile feedback.

3. AUDIO EFFECT SYSTEM

Liquidation is one of Schoenberg's composition techniques. In his book [4], Liquidation refers to the process of progressively removing distinct features from musical phrases or themes in order to transform them into a simpler structure. We sought to electronically reconstruct this composition technique through The *Liquidation* System. In this system, acoustic piano sounds are transformed into blurred electronic sounds, and the features of original acoustic instrument sounds disappear. The piano was chosen as the acoustic instrument to be transformed because it was thought to be suitable for expressing the liquidation technique, in that the reverberation can be controlled through the pedal. In addition, it seemed that the sound range, which is wider than that of other instruments, and the wide dynamics can enrich the musical effect of liquidation.

In this system, the effects—ring modulation, delay, and reverb—can be individually toggled on or off according to user preference, allowing for selective utilization of the desired effects as shown in Figure 2. It provides a comprehensive framework for applying electronic sound modulation techniques by using a cue system that operates with an algorithm.

Figure 2. The *Liquidation* System

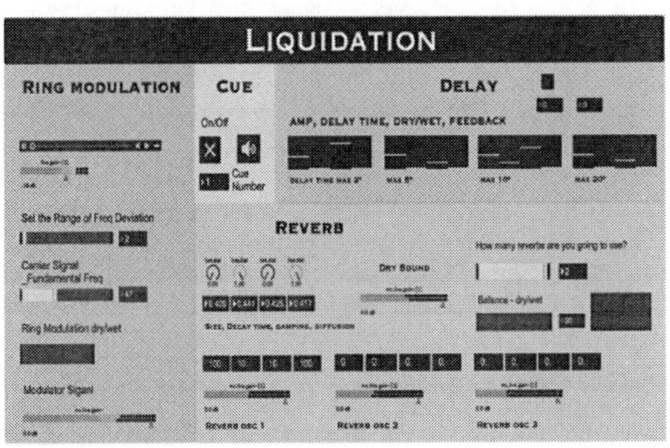

3.1 32-Channels Ring Modulation

In the *Liquidation* system, ring modulation is implemented through the use of the `mc.cycle~` object, which extends the processed carrier signal across 32 channels. These carrier signals, derived from the piano's input signal, are replicated across 32 sound channels, each with a unique frequency. The fundamental frequency of the 32-channel carrier signal is determined by the `sigmund~` object [5], which tracks the frequency of the input signal. Users can control the degree of deviation within a range of 0 to 127 of the fundamental frequency, generating a variety of sounds through the combination and difference with the modulator signal.

This process transforms the original sound of the piano into a new acoustic landscape characterized by complex and metallic textures. The variation in sound is determined by the degree of deviation and modulation depth, with the modulation depth increasing as the volume of the input signal increases, utilizing an envelope follower.

3.2 Multi-Delay

The implementation of delay serves to create echoes that form a complex interplay with the original signal. To achieve a nuanced sound texture characterized by multiple overlapping delayed sounds, the *Liquidation* system utilizes the `mc.poly~` object. This approach diverges from conventional delay effects by incorporating a total of four delay oscillators within the `mc.poly~` object. Each oscillator is individually managed through the `multislider~` object, allowing for precise control over four distinct parameters: amplitude, delay time, dry/wet balance, and feedback. Among these parameters, delay time is variable, with maximum settings of 3, 5, 10, and 20 seconds, respectively, while the settings for the remaining parameters of oscillators are kept uniform. Through four delay oscillators each set with their own values, it is possible to design more complex and three-dimensional delay sounds.

To address the potential issue of clipping noises that can occur with changes in delay time, a careful routing strategy is used. In this strategy, sound is alternately sent through two `tapout~` objects from a single `tapin~` object. This technique ensures that the development of delayed sounds aligns with the ongoing musical performance, creating a more organic and engaging auditory experience.

3.3 Daisy Chain Reverb

In the *Liquidation* system, three `yafr2` objects, which are used to generate reverb, are connected in sequence like a daisy chain to effectively create a spatialization as shown in Figure 3. Sound passing through the first `yafr2` object subsequently moves through the second and third `yafr2` objects. As the sound traverses multiple reverb systems, it becomes increasingly 'blurrier'. By connecting several reverbs in sequence, akin to a daisy chain, the aim was to create multiple layers of spatialization.

These three `yafr2` objects are capable of being individually configured by accepting parameter values through messages in real-time. Given that the `yafr2` objects are designed to process mono signals exclusively, multi-channel audio signals are initially mixed down to mono. Subsequently, the processed reverb signal is reconstituted into a two-channel format, achieved through the utilization of the `mc.pack~` object. The `slider` object is deployed for fine-tuning the balance between the direct and delay-affected sounds. This setup provides the flexibility to adjust the quantity of reverbs applied concurrently, further enabling the selection of how many of the three reverbs to use, enhancing the depth and immersion of the sound experience.

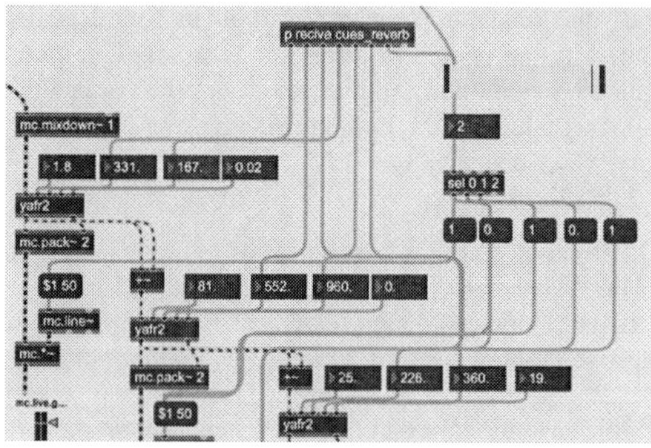

Figure 3. The reverb system connected in sequence

4. THE PERFORMANCE SYSTEM FOR PIANO SOLO

4.1 Cue

In music, a cue is a sign given by a conductor to signal specific instructions to each musician during a performance. Similarly, the *Liquidation* system has a role for cues. Through cues, the corresponding values are transmitted and calculated through algorithms to be applied to each effect. Thus, cues allow for the effective simultaneous control of various effectors. The *Liquidation* system is designed to allow easy control by simply adjusting values, without requiring deep knowledge of electronic music, through algorithmic calculations. The *Liquidation* system transmits a total of ten types of values, as follows in Table 1.

Audio Effects	Values				
Ring Modulation	dis_ envfol				
Delay	del_ amp	del_ on/off	del_ bal	del_ time	
Reverb	rev_ num	rev_ bal	rev_ decay	rev_ damping	rev_ on/off

Table 1. Types of values for audio effects

This approach allows the values for each of the three audio effects to continually change, rather than being fixed. It was deemed more effective to provide guidelines as variables rather than setting static values. This method enables the creation of a musically richer texture.

4.1.1 32-Channel Ring Modulation

For the ring modulation effect, the operational parameters of the envelope follower are defined by a list value named 'dis_envfol,' which includes two numerical values. These values determine the operational state—either enabled or disabled—of the ring modulation effect and the applied modulation depth. This setup facilitates precise adjustment of the effect, ensuring the modulation depth aligns with the piano's sound to naturally transform it into a more metallic tone.

4.1.2 Multi-Delay

In the intermediate transformation algorithm for delay, 'del_amp,' 'del_on/off,' 'del_bal,' and 'del_time' refer to amplitude, the on/off state of the delay effect, the balance between wet and dry sound, and delay time in a delay effect, respectively. The amplitude values are randomized using the `metro`, `uzi`, and `random` objects to ensure that each value changes unpredictably. The same algorithm is applied to adjust the balance between the dry and wet signals. For the delay time, among the four delay oscillators, only the value from 'delay oscillator 1' is initially received, after which approximate values are calculated randomly using the `uzi` and `random` objects like other values. The on/off feature for delay was designed without a separate algorithm, allowing users to arbitrarily decide how many of the four delays to use.

4.1.3 Daisy Chain Reverb

Reverb requires the most values, including 'rev_num', 'rev_bal,' 'rev_decay,' 'rev_damping,' and 'rev_on/off'. These are designed to specify the number of reverb effectors used, the balance between wet and dry sound, the decay time, the degree of damping, and whether to use the reverb effect, respectively. A similar algorithm to that used for calculating values for delay effect was employed. Likewise, the `metro`, `random`, and `uzi` objects were utilized to generate random values within a specific range. The values for the reverb's decay and damping are computed through this algorithm, whereas the number of reverb effects to use and the balance of dry/wet are determined directly by the values coming from the cues, without a separate algorithm. By automatically changing the reverb values to random ones within a predefined range every three seconds, it aims to effectively use three reverbs. The continuous change in reverb decay and damping values allows for the experience of multiple layers of spatiality.

4.2 Musical Application

To practically verify the musical functionality of the *Liquidation* system, Daeun Kim's piano piece and Sujin Kim's sound design collaborated to create *Glacial Echoes*, a live electroacoustic piece for piano. This composition metaphorically depicts the process of glaciers breaking apart, where the characteristic acoustic sounds of a piano solo are electronically fragmented through the *Liquidation* system.

4.2.1 Glacial Echoes

The piece for piano and live electronic music, *Glacial Echoes* is composed of five scales derived from 'A, F#, F, D, A#', as illustrated in Figure 4. Each of the five scales signifies massive ice blocks. Through the piano and electronic music, the five glaciers, distinct and solidly merged, are delicately depicted as they gradually splinter and scatter with the flow of time, becoming increasingly faint from their clustered form.

Figure 4. five scales of *Glacial Echoes*

In this piece, the transformation of the glaciers is divided into three parts. Firstly, the initial section features firm keystrokes on the piano and long phrases of five scales symbolizing the sturdy nature of the glaciers. However, in the second part, the clusters of the five scales start to break apart into irregular patterns as electronic music begins to interpose itself into this structure. The use of delay effects gradually reveals the acoustic process of disintegration as the glacier decomposes and fragments. In the final part, as the disintegration progresses, the once-clustered piano scales increasingly disperse and dim. Electronic part uses delay and ring modulation to weave together different chords, forming clusters of sounds or applying reverb, with the effect that over time the original form of the scale becomes increasingly indistinguishable, eventually disintegrating completely.

4.2.2 The Role of Cues in Glacial Echoes

The *Liquidation* system effectively employs cues to control a variety of effects, facilitating a gradual fusion of the piano with electronic soundscapes. Cues were deliberately positioned at specific points within a sequence. The settings for cues and the values of each parameter are as follows in Figure 5. This approach highlights the nuanced integration of traditional and electronic musical elements, offering a detailed exploration of their synergistic potential in sound production.

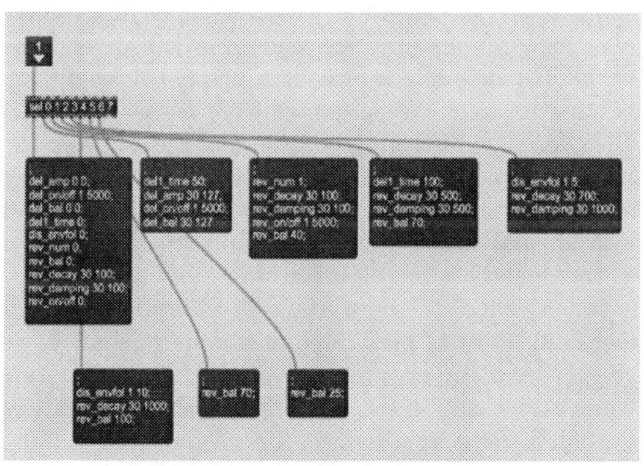

Figure 5. Values for the Cues

In *Glacial Echoes*, a total of seven cues were utilized. In Cue 1, the algorithm begins with values solely for reverb, initiating a gradual reverb effect on the piano sound source to enhance spatiality. In Cue 2, the piano sound is delayed for algorithmically determined durations within a preset range. At this point, the delay balance (del_bal) value is randomly generated within a range from a minimum of 2 to a maximum of 10, aiming for a very subtle delay sound. In Cue 3, to express the delay sound more formally, the range of the 'del_bal' value is increased between 30 and 80. Cue 5 seeks to gradually apply ring modulation by increasing the distortion balance (dis_bal) value through a line object. Cue 5 corresponds to a highlight in the piece; thus, in addition to the delay and reverb effects that began in the previous cues, ring modulation is also added to bring about the most significant change to the piano acoustics. After the highlight of the piece, Cue 6 turns off the delay and ring modulation effects, leaving only the reverb effect to pursue a momentary musical pause. In Cue 7, effects such as delay and ring modulation are gradually reapplied, ultimately leading to the piano fading away, leaving only the electronic effect as a resonance to conclude the piece.

5. CONCLUSIONS

The design of the *Liquidation* system was developed for piano solo and live electronics, focusing on exploring its musical applications. In this system, Schoenberg's compositional technique of liquidation was applied in a digital sound context, transforming the acoustic sound of the piano into a blurred electroacoustic sound. The audio synthesizing technique of the *Liquidation* system is divided into three main parts: 32-channel ring modulation, multi-delay, and daisy chain reverb.

To explore the musical diversity of this system, *Glacial Echoes-* live electro-acoustic piece serves- as a compelling exploration of the possibilities of various types of sounds using the *Liquidation* system. In this piece, a total of seven cues were utilized, in keeping with the concept of liquidation. The *Liquidation* system, with its adaptive cues and sound manipulation capabilities, proves to be an effective tool in realizing this artistic vision, demonstrating how to apply acoustic compositional techniques to electronic sound aiming for artistic purposes. This study can also be seen as a case presentation on the vast creative potential of efficiently processing DSP through algorithms.

6. REFERENCES

[1] "Stockhausen- Mantra," https://stockhausenspace.blogspot.com/2014/06/opus-32-mantra.html, accessed May. 5, 2024.

[2] C. Lippe, "Music for piano and computer: A Description," *Information Processing Society of Japan SIG Notes*, vol. 97, no. 122, pp. 33-38, 1997.

[3] L. Hayes, "Haptic Augmentation of the Hybrid Piano," *Contemporary Music Review*, vol. 32, no. 5, pp. 499–509, 2013.

[4] A. Schoenberg, *Fundamentals of Musical Compo sition*. Faber & Faber, 1967.

[5] "sigmund~," https://music.arts.uci.edu/dobrian/Max-cookbook/keywords/sigmund, accessed Feb. 11, 2024.

Zen of Aggression: Composing the Transformational Hybrid

Berk Yagli
University of the Arts London
Orcid-id: https://orcid.org/0009-0006-0775-7059, byagli9@gmail.com

ABSTRACT

Increasingly, academics are taking into consideration hybridized compositions due to the proliferation of current music-making. As a direct result, a wide variety of written works have emerged to explore and clarify various forms of hybridity while also analyzing the cultural and social connotations of the works (that are linked to or described by this term). Even though there is a lot of current scholarly engagement on the subject, there are no formalised or systematic methods for the creation of hybrid works. In this paper, we examine some of the diverse definitions of hybridization that have been proposed in the literature to date. As the paper progresses, a hybrid composition (which is created by drawing inspiration from one of these definitions- as put forth by Levinson is explored. The paper investigates how the practice could expand upon the definition (Transformational hybrid) of hybridization, and key findings are explained and supported with specific examples. While the main focus of the paper is on the broad-scale of hybridity, the accompanying composition 'Zen of Aggression' delves into compositional ideas through the hybridization of two distinct genres: heavy metal and electroacoustic.

1. INTRODUCTION

In recent years, there have been a substantial number of newly composed musical works that blend two or more genres or musical traditions. Examples include works such as Polyphia's *ABC* [21], Igorrr's *Very Noise* [15], Drumcorps's *The Importance of Stealth* [13], The Algorithm's *floating point* [24], Orestis Karamanlis' *bitvox* [16], Ake Parmerud's *Growl* [19], among many others. Although there are many terms through which one may refer to these works, they are most often descried as hybrid.

Arguably, music has always been hybridised to one degree or another. For example, *The Firebird* [22] and *The Rite of Spring* by Stravinsky [23], *Turkish March* by Mozart (Mozart 1783, republished 2021) [17], *Köçekçe* by Ulvi Cemal Erkin [14], are among many other examples from the classical canon. Along similar lines, one may also note that music has always been influenced by cultural exchanges, and this results in the sharing of practice and ideas that has much in common with the blending of two or more genres or traditions. There is something quite specific and unique about the contemporary blending of music, however, that goes beyond these historic examples.

Understandably, given this development within contemporary music-making, scholars are increasingly turning their attention to works that are hybridised. We now have a substantial body of written work that explores and explains various types of hybridity, while considering the cultural and social meanings behind works that are described using this term. Despite this breadth of literature on the broad topic of hybridisation in music, however, there are no formalised or systematic methods for the creation of hybrid works. Forming the creation process of a method with the influence of some of the current concepts regarding hybridity is the central focus of this article, with findings presented in two forms. Firstly, findings are presented in a theoretical (written) format in which methods for hybrid composition are articulated and discussed. Secondly, finds are presented in the form of a practical composition, *Zen of Aggression*, which exemplifies a start for a working method for hybridisation. Theoretical and practical aspects are, of course, inherently fused; ideas explored in theoretical terms inform compositional planning and decision-making, and the practice of composition provides valuable insights into the production and re-thinking of novel methods.

Although the central focus of the article is on the broad notion of hybridity (or, more specifically, methods for hybridity), the compositional explorations in the accompanying composition involves the hybridisation of two specific genres: electroacoustic music and heavy metal. The rationale for this is explained at length below. Briefly, however, these genres have certain conspicuous differences, with electroacoustic music prioritising experimentation with recorded or synthetic sound to generate novel materials and musical forms, while metal prioritises instrumental thinking, drawing upon tonality and rhythm as core materials and building-blocks of musical form. As a consequence, these two genres present various challenges in terms of their integration, and this proves valuable in terms of exploring diversity and distinctiveness, while also enabling the listener to hear the various ways in which these genres have been combined within the accompanying portfolio. We start by exploring existing definitions of hybridity.

2. DEFINITIONS AND TYPES OF HYBRIDITY

Attempts to define and explain the term *hybridity* are extremely varied. In this section, we survey some of the main contributors, providing insights into how this term has been distinctively defined and explained.

2.1 Emmerson

The composer Simon Emmerson uses the terms poly-stylism, Oedipus hybrid, and eclecticism to talk about hybridisation of music in 'Where next? New music, new musicology'. Emmerson argues that hybridisation becomes stronger by the order of these terms [5]; poly-stylism engages in hybridity on the surface (by bringing material from some other source level to create 'cultural tension' in a single work), while eclecticism requires the composer to make decisions from his/her palette of experiences as a composer in different genres (multi-styles exchanging and blending on a more equal level as material). Hybrids may be asymmetric in their weighting towards one of other genre, perhaps involving strong forces of attraction or repulsion – what is rejected may be as important as what is accepted, and this suggests the possibility of an Oedipus hybrid – a form of a hybrid which owes to two sources but strongly embrace one while rejecting the other [5] .

Although Emmerson's terminology is not framed as a method, per se, it can certainly be used as such. For example, Rob Bentall talks about the specific methods that he uses in some of his hybrid works [2]. He mentions that these methods are designed to produce works associated with Emmerson's notion of polystylism, focusing specifically upon the following musical elements: Harmony; Melody; Rhythm; Spectral Dislocation; Reconstructive Sampling; Durational Expansion.

Bentall argues that Smalley's notion of spectromorphology (1997) lays out electroacoustic music's main parameters as gesture, texture, and timbre, adding rhythm/harmony/or melody and working mainly with these notation/instrumental music-based qualities arguably starts to make the music hybrid. This kind of argument, however, needs more debate since current electroacoustic music canon include many pieces that include rhythm, harmony, and melody to a greater or lesser extent, including, for example, Trevor Wishart's Globalalia [25], Ake Parmerud's La vie Mécanique [20], and Robert Normendau's Murmures [18].

2.2 Perks

Guitarist, composer and musicologist Richard Perks, like Emmerson, provides a list of terms that enable one to unpick hybrid works. Unlike Emmerson, however, his focus is upon cultural hybridity (in the context of improvisation), and is therefore distinct from, but entirely relevant to, the current discussion [10]. Perks makes the following distinction between types of hybridity:

· Exclusion: Reflecting one music-culture only, leaving no room for the others; non-hybrid.

· Partial Exclusion: Two music-cultures have combined successfully (in some perceptible form), but the third is not present.

· Homogenization: All three music-cultures are present, though each in a notably diluted form: a bland unification.

· Coexistence: All three music-cultures are discernible; whilst capably functioning side-by-side, each music-culture resembles/maintains its native form for the most part; individual music-cultural traits remain distinctly identifiable.

· Assimilation: All three music-cultures have sufficiently combined; some multi-directional enrichment has occurred, however, one (or two) music-culture(s) appears dominant; individual music cultural traits remain identifiable.

· Synthesis: All three music-cultures have effectively combined through mutual exchange; the borrowing and adaptation of various musical properties and/or performative conventions has resulted in the emergence of a highly distinctive, collective, musical voice; individual music-cultural traits are only partially identifiable, if at all.

Perks' terms are not merely interesting because they further expand our vocabulary for discussing hybridity. They also transfer the discussion from one focused upon genres and elements to one focused upon musical cultures. His intention is not directly stated; he may wish to side-step the otherwise complicated issues associated with genre identification. He may also wish to signal a broadening of the discussion by placing cultures at the heart of hybridity.

2.3 Shpinitskaya

In a similar way to Perks, musicologist Julia Shpinitskaya in Masters dissertation 'A Theory of Multicultural Texts: The Music of Erik Bergman As a Phenomenon of Multicultural Europe' focuses upon cultural construction of hybridity, albeit using the term cultural mixtures, rather than hybrids. Shpinitskaya sets out three forces that defines connections within a mixture [27]:

1. Confrontation: Negation of the integration
2. Neutrality: Some degree in between confrontation and association
3. Association: Integration of the cultural elements

Then, she offers three main models of cultural mixtures:

1. Mosaic: a simple confrontation of entire cultural blocks without a real concordance or coordination between them, produced like a horizontal montage (they may interact but do not mix) [27]
2. Superimposition/application: the vertical coexistence of several cultural layers without interpenetration ("In a way, the elements are touching each other but do not diffuse through the inward space of each other" [27]
3. Assimilation: Adoption of another source with the subsequent transformation of both sources ("In assimilation there is no room for a quotation or imitation. This is not a matter of stylization or modelling" [27]

After describing the three main models of cultural mixtures, Shpinitskaya connects them with Yuri Lotman's five stages of cultural dialogue [27]

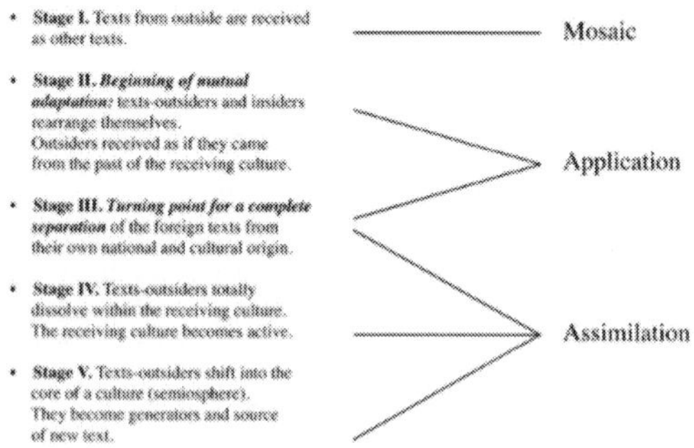

Figure 1: Five stages of cultural dialogue mixture [27]

Shpinitskaya (2016, pp. 86) also considered other categorizations of mixtures, according to the layer of culture they belong to, or the type of art that they are: horizontal mixtures combine "texts of the same temporal layer, but of different geographical locations"; vertical mixtures combine "different historical points having the same geographical location"; differentiated or heterogeneous mixtures combine "texts of different classes or habitats in the arts and society"; and combined mixtures "submit to the conditions of two or three of these combinations simultaneously" [27].

2.4 Filho

Composer Paulo Rios Filho (2010) provides one of the clearest cases in which specific compositional methods for hybridisation have been articulated. According to Filho there are four main strategies that composers may employ, each of which is linked to a set of procedures; strategies are described as compositional decisions of medium-long proportions (macro-decisions), while procedures are micro-decisions that are consequently subordinate to those strategies. The four strategies, and their associated procedures, may be summarised as follows:

1. Borrowing: The extraction of materials from its original context and placing it into an alternative environment (High degree of representation-because borrowing deals with surface materials and not inner structures).

Three different procedures are associated with this strategy:

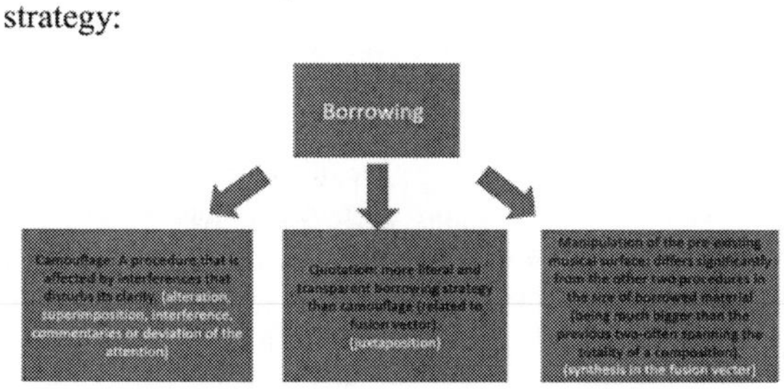

Figure 2: Three Sub-categories of Borrowing - Filho

2. Reflection of materials, structures, and principles: The modelling of materials and principles from alternative musical practices. It is a form of replication rather than appropriation (or borrowing) of specific materials. Once again, there are three procedures associated with this strategy:

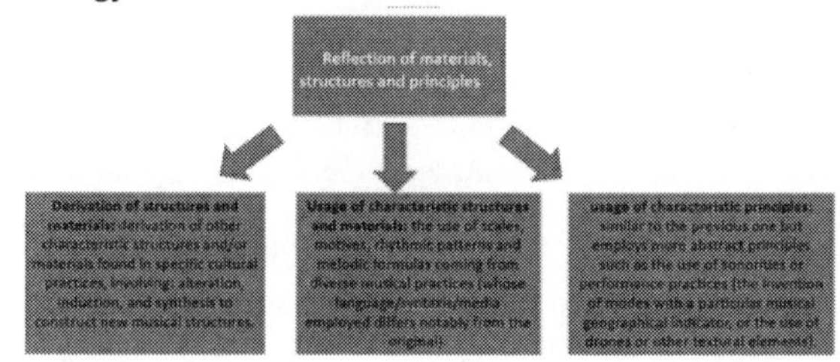

Figure 3: Three Sub-categories of Reflection of materials, structures and principles-Filho

3. Translation of philosophical conceptions and attitudes: The representation of non-musical concepts in musical ways.

It is associated with three sub-categories:

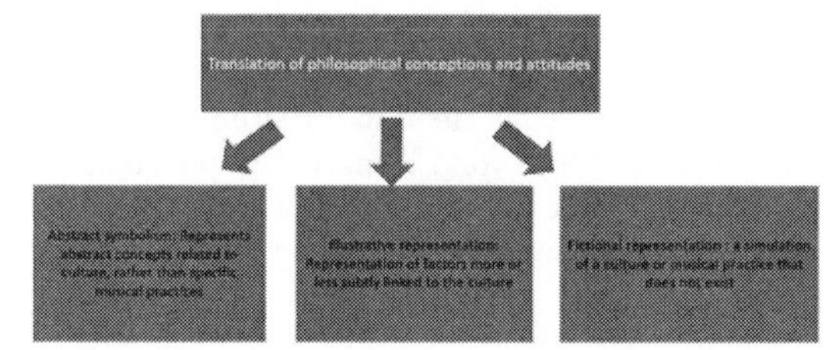

Figure 4: Three Sub-categories of Translation of philosophical conceptions and attitudes.

4. Syncretism: The adoption of sonic and/or stylistic parameters of a musical-cultural practice by means of another (high degree of direct representation-since in most cases it deals with surface materials).

This strategy contains five different sub-categories:

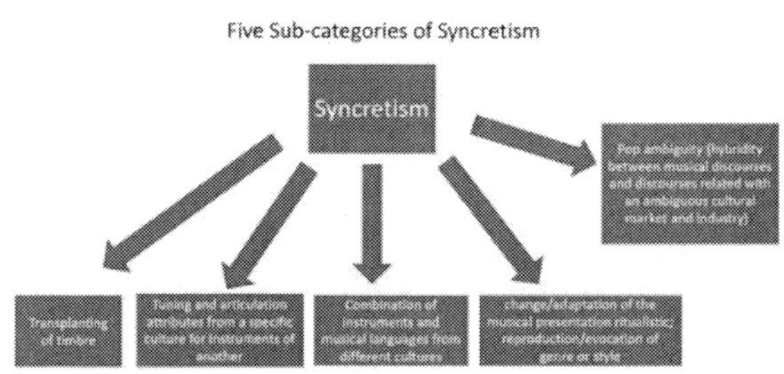

Figure 5: Five Sub-categories of Syncretism.

It is also important to mention that Filho also offers very similar ideas about musical hybrids to others; Filho mentions higher and lower orders of hybridity, using terms such as juxtaposition, superimposition, interpenetration, and synthesis. He suggests that there is a degree of 'fusion' between the elements becomes stronger once we go through the various orders, which he describes as fusion vectors - internal processes that affects entire compositions [28].

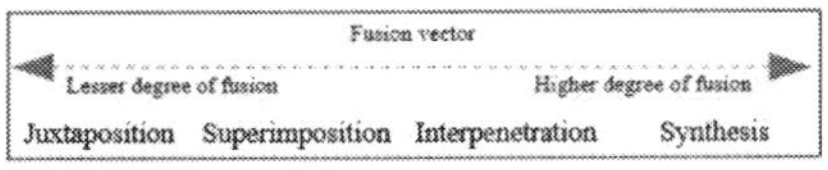

Figure 6. Fusion vector [28]

3. QUESTIONS AND METHODS

As we have seen, definitions of hybridity vary in terms of their core terminology. Even so, they all tend to focus upon the ways in which musical elements or genres are combined in existing works. It is important to note that hybridity, as it has been described above, is articulated as a suite of distinctive combinations of elements or genres: works are not hybrid in one distinct way. Rather, there are different types of hybridisations, which authors have described using diverse terminology. Despite this, methods for achieving hybridity, however, are conspicuously absent; in the examples cited above, only Filho frames their terms in the form of a method, but these are not accompanied by any sense of how one might achieve or produce a hybrid work. Rather, the terms appear to function only a form of inspiration or stimulus for a composer looking to create hybrid works. In this respect, they are no different from the descriptive terminology provided by others, except that they are instructional; encouraging a composer to work with a specific hybrid type in mind. There are, to date, no systematic methods for the creation of hybrid works that a) demonstrate a holistic and/or systematic approach to the composition of hybrid works and, b) provide clear examples of works that have been composed relative to such a method.

In what follows, we introduce part of a new working method for the hybridisation of works, and consider this method in relation to the creation of a specific work. In doing so, we focus on the hybridisation of two specific musical genres – electroacoustic music and heavy metal. These have been chosen because the compositional methods employed in these respective genres offer a point of contrast. We shall briefly consider this point.

Electroacoustic music mostly utilizes method of GRM's bottom-up approach. This approach is exactly the opposite of top-down approach which most of the popular music genres employ. While in the top-down approach composers tend to come up with the musical form way before the composition finishes (and even in most cases before anything is written; common in pop repertoire), in the bottom-up approach the musical form emerges from experimentation with sound materials and through micro-decisions that happen in the composition process. In other words, a form emerges from the composer's decisions rather than the decisions are being made to fit the pre-selected musical form. In electroacoustic music, due to the nature of its unique musical materials (which includes arguably all of the available sounds; recorded, synthesized, musical, non-musical) and due to its unique building blocks of composition (gesture, texture), a top-down approach is not feasible.

In contrast to electroacoustic music, metal music has a top-down approach. This can take many forms: A composer can decide on a musical form before composing the materials, a composer can come up with certain related but not connected riffs and puts them in a sequence to get a specific form in mind or to logically find the perfect fit (and the form emerges as a result). It could take type of improvisation and the new materials would then be composed in accordance with the initial section. Moreover, it could also start just from drum grooves and written drum parts and riffs. Metal musicians and composers put their focus on instrumental thinking and create novel forms by exploring new approaches to instrumental techniques. In this genre, more often than not, novel approaches to songwriting have a direct relationship with the development of using the instruments in different forms. The instrumental aspect of metal music also has a significant impact on the way the composers compose (in regards to the top-down approach). Unlike pop, country, or blues musicians/composers who use their instruments, metal composers focus on creating riffs and blocky-sectional materials (different from relying exclusively on chord progressions).

As can be seen from the significant differences between the approaches of composing the two different musical traditions (metal and electroacoustic music), building hybridity between them offers unique challenges. The compositional study of the article 'Zen of Aggression' [26] was composed in order to come up with an initial method for combining these two traditions while using Perks' Transformational Hybrid as influence.

4. ZEN OF AGGRESSION: COMPOSING A TRANSFORMATIONAL HYBRID

The remainder of this article focuses on the piece Zen of Aggression [26] to discuss the fruitful and problematic methods when approaching to compose a Transformational hybrid between electroacoustic music and metal. During the composition of the piece, these terms were borrowed from Levinson's descriptive terminology (about different types of hybrids) [29] to be used as an inspiration for creating the piece. As a result, it is hoped that we will turn description (by Levinson) into a method, and demonstrate/debate the results.

4.1 Transformational Hybrid

To start the discussion, it is beneficial to introduce the term Transformational Hybrid (specifically in the context of the piece 'Zen of Aggression' [26]. According to Levinson, the Transformational Hybrid is a type of hybrid in which A is transformed in a B-ish direction (unlike synthesis in which a resultant hybrid is more or less like a halfway point between A and B) [29]. Levinson points out that the main differentiator between synthesis and transformational hybrid is the type of art of the hybridised elements and how similar and different they are (in terms of material, temporal status, and other characteristics). The more different they are is more likely to result in alteration of the materials (Transformational Hybrid) instead of fusion (Synthesis Hybrid) [29].

It is also interesting to find many similarities when comparing Emmerson's Oedipus Hybrid [5] with Levinson's Transformational Hybrid [29]. In Zen of Aggression, these ideas of Synthesis and Transformational Hybrid act as a starting point for experimentation (to build different points of blending the two genres: electroacoustic and metal together). Since the description provided by Levinson falls abstract and not specific for building the materials in a composition setting, the composer (when composing Zen of Aggression) set specific rules (in addition to Levinson's description) for each terminology (to start composing the compositional statements). The starting point follows as:

Synthesis: A type of hybridity in which the resulting musical statement gets away from the juxtaposition of the materials and focuses on finding common ground between the hybridised genres (while not altering the inner structures).

The initial strategies for Synthesis ('Zen of Aggression'):

1- Building compositional statements through focusing on recontextualisation of materials (instead of focusing on strategies related to juxtaposition of musical structures and materials)
2- Building electroacoustic and metal-derived materials to alter/shift their structure/context

Transformational Hybrid: A type of hybridity that is achieved through a composition process which relies heavily on one genre while rejecting the other (with the focus on shifting/altering the compositional structures).

The initial strategies for composing ('Zen of Aggression'):

1- Composing electroacoustic and metal-derived materials (usage of certain cliché materials/musical ideas to alter/shift their structure/context
2- Focusing on certain characteristic/qualities of metal and electroacoustic music (which do not strictly define the genre for building hybridity (such as the dynamics, timbral quality, and strategies for building musical form)

Even though the initial strategies was helpful in the initiation of the composition process, it is important to understand the significant differences (when considering to use of them as an influence for composition) both these descriptions imply. Firstly, building a compositional statement in which two genres are distinguishable from each other (juxtaposition) requires separate thinking (in terms of genre conventions) and mostly can done more naturally through composing two different compositional statements (in different genres). The process then would follow as finding ways to 'appropriate' them together. The two different compositional statements would focus more extensively on over-used genre clichés or in a usual format in terms of instrumentation/timbre/the way the materials function and are being treated (to be highly referential).

On the other hand, composing a Transformational Hybrid might work better by composing a compositional statement that focuses on shifting the functions of materials (that are originally attributed to a certain genre). In this way of composing, masking/abstracting the attributes of a certain genre(s) (which would create high-referentiality) would be the main aim rather than creating high referential parts. The composer could still work on highly referential cliché genre parts to form hybridity, however, the main difference in attitude (when compared to Juxtaposition) would be to shift the function of the materials to transform the convention (an example of this strategy can be found around 3'11" to 3'28"). This distinction became relatively helpful in turning the influence of Levinson's descriptive approach into a method for composing the piece.

In summary, we can say that the Transformational Hybrid approach was achieved by:

- The compositional statements built through conventional genre structures and materials (such as the conventional usage context of metal vocals) to find ways for shifting the context/recontextualising the function to transform the material (give new function/meanings)
- Using one genre's material in the context of another (such as composing a metal statement and using the whole statement without breaking it into different sections-stems in the same function (context) of gestural functioning of electroacoustic materials
- Starting with one genre's material (mostly metal) and transforming it through the usage of other genre's techniques (mostly electroacoustic music)
- Using one genre's functional vocabulary strategically (in this piece's context-electroacoustic music's triggers) to shift/alter the context of the hybridity and help the fluidity (of the hybridity).
- Using one-genre-dominated non-hybrid sections (mainly electroacoustic to have more sparse sections (less energy) and preparing for the next section of hybridity).

When we look at the different sections composed using the Transformational Hybrid approach, we can say that even though the initial strategy is quite similar for each section (building the section through recontextualisation of genre materials to transform/alter them), each section provided significantly different approaches/strategies to follow depending on the purpose of the section.

For instance, the section between 2'53" to 3'11" was strategically composed to resemble a metal section while not being explicitly metal (to break away from the traditional acousmatic/electroacoustic approach as well as to get away from the Polystylism/juxtaposition approach). To achieve this an open-chord metal section was recorded through traditional means (specifically for this piece and section) and extended (both in timbre and harmony through utilizing electroacoustic techniques and approach) via using/processing different sound materials on top of the recorded open-chord-mainly with textural purposes (and in doing so also reshaping the original metal ensemble sound). Moreover, the hierarchy/usual function of metal elements was aimed to be conserved but redesigned by using different voices (mainly shaped with electroacoustic music techniques) functioning in the same way as a lead-singer in metal music while the rhythm section (drums and bass) were replaced with break-beat/glitch music influenced processed drums (but still functioning in a similar way to the traditional metal music context).

The structure and power dynamics suddenly shift during the section of 3'12" to 3'28". In this section's new dynamic the vocals no longer function in the context of metal music but work closer to electroacoustic music (as a texture and gesture) while traditional gestural materials of electroacoustic music emerge in the context of metal music (in which the gestural materials strictly follow beat and use repetition instead of following spectromorphology).

The context re-shifts again in the section of 3'28" to 3'46" with the vocals functioning in the context of metal (lead-vocal) while around the end of the section another vocals emerges (with more spectromorphological function).

On the other hand, for the section between 5'49" to 6'07", the recontextualisation and transformation occur differently (and perhaps in a more balanced way). In this section, there is a clear sense of tonality and rhythm with references to metal (even though they are not explicit) such as the use of kick-drum-like gesture to indicate the beat as well as more traditional use of gestural material (in spectromorphological context).

In the section of 7'12" to 7'37" it is also possible to find traces of the recontextualisation strategies and ideas explored in sections 5'49" to 6'07" and 2'53" to 3'46". This section continues on the idea of recontextualising the function of metal and electroacoustic music materials. This section stand mainly pitch and rhythm-based with no explicit relationship to metal. It uses non-metal vocal materials (processed and shaped through electroacoustic techniques) within the context of lead-vocal usage in metal. The rhythm and tonality is achieved through similar strategies that got utilized around 5'49" to 6'07".

The section of 8'09" to 8'37" acts as a reminder of the section 00'00" to 2'54" (in which nearly the whole section uses ascending as a tool for building hybridity as well as to form the structure for the whole compositional statement) as the section has a considerable use of ascending as a tool for forming the structure of the statement (but less so in forming hybridity). Unlike the section from 00'00" to 2'54" however, this section builds hybridity mainly by relying on the metal cliché of question and answer (instead of relying on ascension as a tool for building the hybridity). When building the metal cliché section, a metal dominated section was composed as a base (with a traditional metal ensemble) but was masked through the usage of electroacoustic techniques . On top of the metal-dominated base section different electroacoustic dominated (spectromorphology-based-to an extent) gestural and textural materials were added. Unlike traditional electroacoustic parts, however, this section's electroacoustic materials mainly followed while still having a certain amount of freedom to follow spectromorphology.

The section of 8'37" to 9'56" acts as a reminder of the introduction section (right before 1'26") and acts as the outro section of the piece. It is once again mainly electroacoustic dominated (like the very beginning of the piece) with spectromorphological thinking and similarly functioning musical materials (to the introduction section). This section is helpful in the context of hybridity (when thinking about the form of the piece) for glueing different sections together.

The section of 00'00" to 1'26" acts as an introduction to the piece. It is mainly electroacoustic music dominated and within the spectromorphology-based thinking.

The section of 1'26" to 2'53" is mainly using ascending (in pitch and intensity) as a tool for building the compositional statement. The constant ascension in intensity is used as a way with the aim to hybridise both of the genres in a more abstract way.

The section of 00'00" to 3'47" uses mainly spectromorphological thinking and elements (gesture, texture). The section utilizes the idea of triggers (which helps to suddenly change the context/flow of the section) that is heavily driven by acousmatic music vocabulary. The main sonic elements were composed to fit with the aesthetics of aggression (the usage of heavy compression, granulation, glitch, and low dynamic range). There is also usage of explicit metal elements-mainly in the complete song format. However, it should be noted that the usage of these materials is recontextualised in the sense that they are being used mainly gestural-and sometimes gestural elements (mainly to be switched on and off through the usage of triggers) rather than in the usual function of metal song format.

The section of 3'47" to 5'37" is mainly electroacoustic (spectromorphology-based) and acting as a bridge. Even though this section is one of the non-hybrid section of the piece it can be argued that it helps tremendously for the hybridity of the other sections as well as the overall piece. The main aim of the section of 6'07" to 6'43" is to act as a bridge and to prepare the listener for the main climax which starts at 7'12". The section from 6'43" to 7'12" is the last section acting as a bridge and can also be considered as the climax section for the trigger ideas (which was mainly explored at the beginning of the piece) explored in the piece (the compositional idea resembling the TV Switch-which turns things on and off).

The ideas explored around the section of 5'49" to 6'07" get extended and explored more deeply in the section of 7'12" to 7'37" as it is the beginning of the climax of the piece.

It is possible to create a graph summarising the main strategies and function of each section in the piece to see the structure/context of the piece more clearly (which would in turn hopefully help us to approach the piece critically within the context of transformational hybridity).

Figure 7, 8, 9 and 10 illustrate the structure of Zen of Aggression in terms of its hybridity strategies. The piece has three main different strategies (utilized in different ways throughout different sections of the piece):

1-Usage of ascension in pitch and intensity for building hybridity

2-Shifting/changing the context/function of the genres (traditional usage of metal vocals shifting purpose/function)

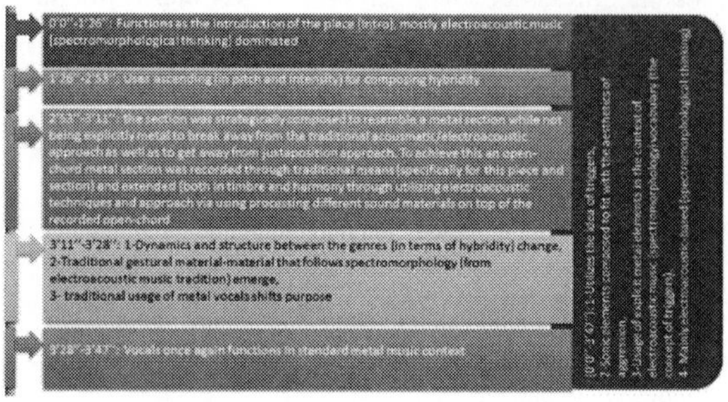

Figure 7. Structure of Zen of Aggression in terms of its hybridity strategies

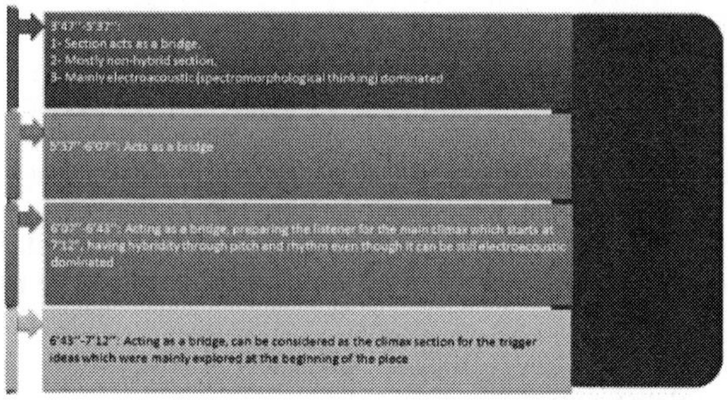

Figure 8. Structure of Zen of Aggression in terms of its hybridity strategies

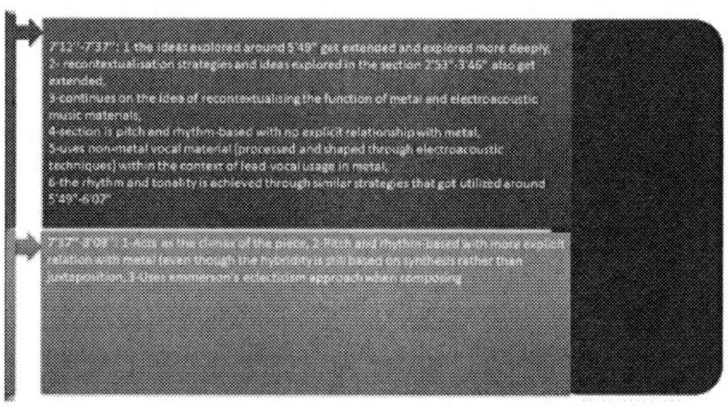

Figure 9. Structure of Zen of Aggression in terms of its hybridity strategies

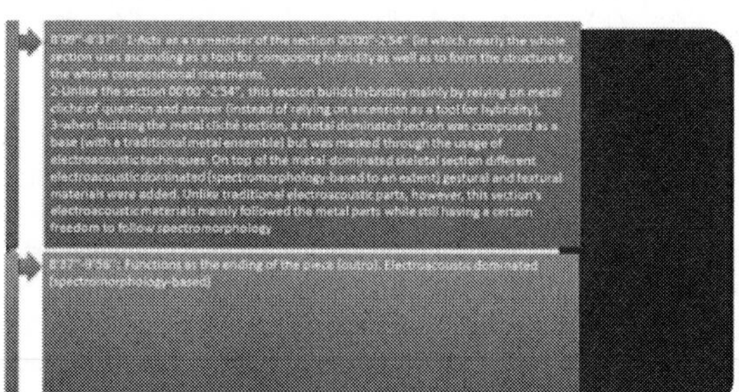

Figure 10. Structure of Zen of Aggression in terms of its hybridity strategies

3-Usage of electroacoustic (spectromorphology-based) sections to balance the high-energy-material sections (when considering the whole structure of the piece) as well as to prepare the next section's hybridity

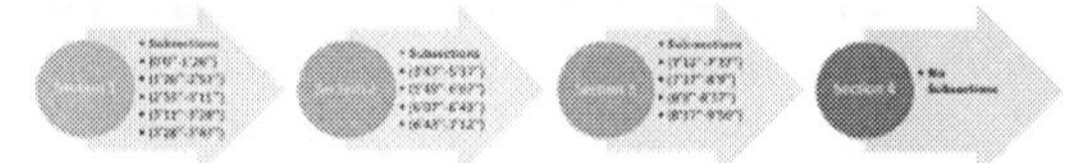

Figure 11. Sections and sub-sections of Zen of Aggression

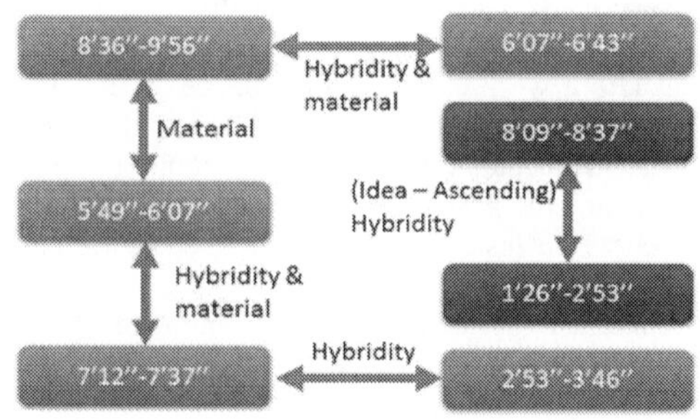

Figure 12. Structural relationship in Zen of Aggression

Figure 11 illustrates all the sections and sub-sections happening in Zen of Aggression. The main sections (four in total) are divided in relation to their macro function while the sub-sections (thirteen in total) are divided about their micro functions.

Figure 12 illustrates the structural relationship in Zen of Aggression. These structural relationships indicate to us that some of the significant sections throughout the piece are related to each other either through their hybridity approach or material.

Overall, Zen of Aggression uses the concept of Transformational Hybrid from the descriptive terminology of Levinson (Levinson, 1983) as an influence to initiate experiments to find out how a practice might be evolved upon the hybridization definition.

The piece uses three main strategies for composing transformational hybridity (please see above for details). It is possible to say that the strategies related to recontextualising/shifting the function of the materials are the most successful for generating fruitful outcomes while the strategies of using spectromorphology-based (electroacoustic dominated) sections with the concept of recontextualisation were arguably less successful. This is mainly because having one dominating genre as a skeletal structure (in which the recontextualisation happens on top of it) creates problems (such as clashing with the concepts of juxtaposition instead of synthesis) when one aims to approach hybridity through the lens of transformation.

5. CONCLUSIONS

This article focuses on various ways hybridisation has been defined and conceptualised within the existing literature. As a study,one of those definitions (proposed Levinson) have been used as inspiration to compose a hybrid work to find out how practice might build upon these two hybridisation definitions. The exploration of compositional ideas in the accompanying composition ('Zen of

Aggression') involves two specific genres: electroacoustic and metal (even though the central focus of the article is on the hybridity as a broadscale-which could be applied to various genres). The article gathers its findings through compositional exploration and forming discussions between what has been done, its implications, and what worked and not worked. The findings included certain approaches that have been done through getting influenced by Juxtaposition, Synthesis, and Transformational Hybrid and display certain strategies to recontextualise the function of electroacoustic and metal materials. As future work, a study that incorporates and explores specifically the ideas of recontextualisation of different genre materials and investigation of composing and decomposing as a tool to generate recontextualisations and hybrid would be useful as the explorations done through composing 'Zen of Aggression' come to a conclusion that this way of recontextualisation offers the most promising and unique outcomes.

5.1 Acknowledgments

I would love to thank Adam Stanovic for his invaluable and continuous support throughout the process of this research. This paper would not be possible without his help. I would also like to thank Russ Bestley for his support on the genre parts of my research.

6. REFERENCES

[1] M. Allen, "Against 'hybridity'in genre studies: blending as an alternative approach to generic experimentation." Trespassing Journal, 2, pp. 3-21, 2013.

[2] R. Bentall, "Methodologies for Genre Hybridisation," Organised Sound, vol. 21, no. 2, pp. 117–126, 2016. doi:10.1017/S1355771816000042

[3] D. Chandler, "An introduction to genre theory." 1997.

[4] D. Duff, "Modern Genre Theory." Longman, 2000.

[5] S. Emmerson, "'Where next? New music, new musicology.'" EMS : Electroacoustic Music Studies Network, 2007.

[6] S. Emmerson, L. Landy, "The analysis of electroacoustic music: the differing needs of its genres and categories." In Proceedings of the electroacoustic music studies network conference meaning and meaningfulness in electroacoustic music, 2012.

[7] S. Friar, "Hybrid Music in Theory and Practice." Ph.D. Princeton University, 2017.

[8] R. B. Gill, "The uses of genre and the classification of speculative fiction." Mosaic: a journal for the interdisciplinary study of literature, pp. 71-85, 2013.

[9] C. R. Miller, "Genre as Social Action (1984), Revisited 30 Years Later (2014)." Letras & Letras, Pp. 56-72, 2014. doi:10.14393/LL63-v31n3a2015-5

[10] R. Perks, "Strung Together: Realizing Music-cultural Hybridity within a Limited Time Frame." Music & Practice, 9, 2021.

[11] D. Smalley, "Spectromorphology: Explaining sound-shapes." Organised Sound, 2(2), 107-126, 1997. doi:10.1017/S1355771897009059

[12] T. Wishart, "On Sonic Art (S. Emmerson, Ed.) (1st ed.)." Routledge, 1996. https://doi.org/10.4324/9781315077895

7. DISCOGRAPHY

[13] Drumcorps, "The Importance of Stealth." Recorded by Morning Under Leaves, 2021.

[14] U. C. Erkin, "Köçekçe." Recorded by B. F. Orkestrası, London, 2014.

[15] Igorrr, "Very Noise." Recorded by Metal Blade Records, 2020.

[16] O. Karamanlis, "BitVox: For Beatboxer & Live Electronics." Recorded by G. Gargalas, Athens, Greece, 2019.

[17] A. W. Mozart, "Turkish March." Recorded by B. Apostolov, 2021.

[18] R. Normendau, "Murmures." Recorded by empreintes DIGITALes, 2012.

[19] A. Parmerud, "Growl." Recorded by empreintes DIGITALes. 2015.

[20] A. Parmerud, "La vie mécanique." Recorded by Ymx media, 2004.

[21] Polyphia, "ABC (feat. Sophia Black)." Recorded by Rise Records, 2022.

[22] I. Stravinsky, "Stravinsky: The Firebird (Ballet Suite)." Recorded by O. d. Bastille, 2009.

[23] I. Stravinsky, "The Rite of Spring." Recorded by R. L. Orchestra, 2017.

[24] The Algorithm, "floating point:" Recorded by FiXT, 2016.

[25] T. Wishart, "Globalalia." Recorded by Orpheus The Pantomime, 2008.

[26] B. Yagli, "Zen of Aggression." Recorded by B. Yagli, 2022.

[27] J. Shpinitskaya, "A Theory of Multicultural Texts : The Music of Erik Bergman As a Phenomenon of Multicultural Europe." 21: The Semiotic Society of Finland, 2016.

[28] P. R. Filho, "Cultural Hybridization as a Methodological Horizon for Contemporary Music Creation." Master Thesis, 2010.

[29] J. Levinson, "Hybrid Art Forms." Journal of Aesthetic Education, 1984. doi: 10.2307/3332623

Go To Music - Move 37

Sébastien Thon
LIS Laboratory, Aix-Marseille University, France
sebastien.thon@univ-amu.fr

ABSTRACT

Black and white like musical notes or the keys of a piano, arranged on a board where they form meaningful patterns, the Go game stones resemble notes that two musicians would take turns writing on a same musical score.

To explore this idea, we developed GOTO MUSIC, a Python program that generates music from records of Go games, by establishing a correspondence between a stone that is placed and a pentatonic scale of notes widely used in Korean traditional music. We used it to write a piece of music in 5 parts from the moves played in 2016 during the famous 5-game Go match between the Korean champion Lee Sedol and the artificial intelligence program AlphaGo.

Thus, our algorithm finds sound in motion, as it generates music and also animation from moves on a board.

1. INTRODUCTION

Generative music refers to music that is automatically composed by algorithms. The concept, which dates back to the avant-garde experiments of the 20th century, has seen significant advancements with the advent of AI and machine learning technologies. The origins of generative music can be traced to the early experiments in computer-assisted music composition by Hiller and Isaacson, exploring the potential of algorithms to generate musical structures, laying foundational concepts for future explorations in generative music [1]. Composers like John Cage [2] and Iannis Xenakis [3] also explored aleatory and stochastic processes in their music.

Recent years have seen AI and machine learning emerge as powerful tools for creating music. Algorithms such as Markov chains, genetic algorithms, and neural networks are now commonly used to generate complex musical compositions [4].

The application of AI in music has transformed the field, with deep learning models like recurrent neural networks (RNNs) and generative adversarial networks (GANs) being used to create music that can often be indistinguishable from that composed by humans [5].

Multiple experiments of sonification [6] have also been made to generate music from various data sources, such as stock market movements, weather data, literature, or even biological signals.

In this paper, we propose a new translational model for algorithmic generation of music, by writing music from the moves played during a Go game.

Go is a strategy board game for two players invented in China more than 2,500 years ago. One player uses white stones and the other black. The players take turns placing their stones on the vacant intersections on a board covered by a 19×19 grid of lines (Beginners often play on smaller 9×9 and 13×13 boards). The aim is to capture more territory than the opponent by fencing empty space off.

We can find many analogies between the game of Go and music. First, the round black and white stones bring to mind musical notes, but also the keys of a piano. The lines on the Go board recall the lines of a musical staff, in 2D instead of 1D. At the start of a game, the Go board is empty and is gradually filled with stones, like notes on a score that is being written. The score is blank at the start, a simple white page with empty staffs. The stones on a Go board during a game present a very graphic appearance which becomes more complex with each move, revealing meaningful graphical patterns.

Thus, we may be tempted to analyze these patterns to find a hidden meaning, to try to decipher information encoded on the board like music in a score. Every Go game is a story, and music is a powerful way for storytelling. So, we propose our music generation approach as one musical way to tell the story of a Go match.

2. GO TO MUSIC

2.1 From stones to notes

Could it be possible to get music from the record of a game of go, to get sound from moves? To explore this idea, we wrote GOTO MUSIC, a program in Python that automatically creates music from records of Go games.

Such records, called *gibo* in Korean or *kifu* in Japanese, take the form of a diagram representing the grid of the board (19 lines by 19 columns for the standard size) and all the stones played with their numbers (Figure 2).

Previously written exclusively on paper, kifu are now available in the form of computer files. The most used file format is the *Smart Game Format* (SGF), a mark up text format used for storing records of board games, particularly Go. Most Internet Go servers and Go software from 1990 support this format.

For a given SGF file of a game, our program analyzes the moves played one after the other. For each stone placed on the board, a value is computed from the stone and the eventual 8 stones surrounding it at that moment. This value is then used to determine a musical note.

At first, we started by counting a semitone for a black stone and a tone for a white stone, and adding them up to directly get the note, but the result was too dissonant. Instead, we count 1 for black and 2 for white, and the sum is used as an index to get a note in a pentatonic scale of notes widely used in Korean traditional music (Table 1).

Index	Note	Index	Note
1	G3	10	Eb5
2	A3	11	G5
3	Bb3	12	A5
4	D4	13	Bb5
5	Eb4	14	D6
6	G4	15	Eb6
7	A4	16	G6
8	Bb4	17	A6
9	D5	18	Bb6

Table 1. Correspondence between index and a note in a pentatonic scale.

We process like this for each stone placed by a player, to get a note for each move (Figure 1).

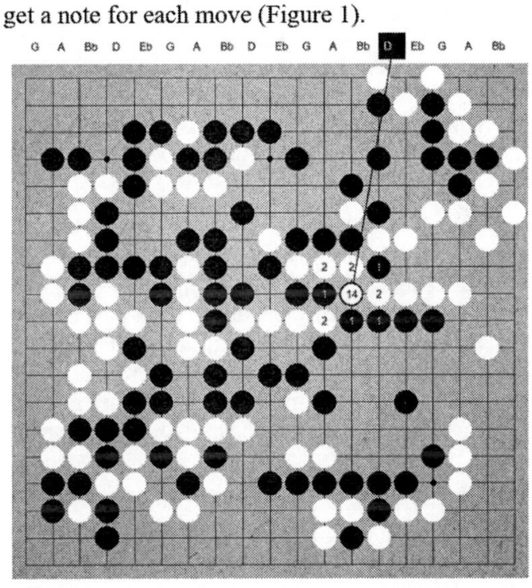

Figure 1. The white stone placed by Lee Sedol at move #168 during the second game gives the value 14 (black: 1+1+1+1 + white: 2+2+2+2+2). This value is used as an index in a pentatonic scale and gives the note D6.

With this algorithm, if a stone is isolated, the corresponding note is low. If the stone is surrounded by several others, the note will be higher, reflecting a great activity in this local area for the conquest of the board. The music gradually rises in pitch as the game progresses, while the board fills up with stones.

2.2 Music tracks

The algorithm stores the computed notes in two MIDI scores, one for each player. Each score finally contains as many notes as moves were played during the game by the corresponding player.

We could have respected the times between each move as the same amount of time between each note, but the duration of a game of Go can be very long, sometimes several hours, with a move sometimes taking more than ten minutes. We have instead opted for regular time intervals between each note, as if a person reading the record of the game would read it at a different pace from that of the game itself.

A piece of music is then written with a DAW on a computer, built around these two MIDI tracks. Each MIDI track is played by a different virtual instrument (VSTI) to give an identity to each player.

2.3 Video

In addition to music, our program also produces animation. For each move, a square image is generated, reproducing the Go board and the location of the stones at this moment. The stone which has just been placed appears with a number, calculated as described previously in section 2.1. The stone is connected to the corresponding note in a pentatonic scale, which appears at the top of the image (Figure 1).

3. MUSIC GENERATED BY MAN AND AI

3.1 Lee Sedol vs AlphaGo

Between March 9 and 15, 2016, a 5-game Go match was held in Seoul between Lee Sedol, a South Korean professional player considered the best in the world at the time, and AlphaGo, a Go program based on Artificial Intelligence developed by Google DeepMind. This match saw the first victory of a program against a professional of the highest level, AlphaGo winning the first three games as well as the fifth, Lee Sedol only managing to win the fourth (Table 2).

Game	Black	White	Winner	Moves
1	LS	AG	AG	186
2	AG	LS	AG	211
3	LS	AG	AG	176
4	AG	LS	LS	180
5	LS	AG	AG	280

Table 2. Results of the 5 games between Lee Sedol (LS) and AlphaGo (AG) in March 2016.

With our GOTO MUSIC program, we created a piece of music in 5 parts from the 1033 moves played during the 5 games between Lee Sedol and AlphaGo. The SGF files of the records are available online [7].

3.2 The instruments

The MIDI scores generated by our program for the two players are played on a computer. We use a virtual instrument reproducing the *gayageum* (traditional Korean zither) when Lee Sedol plays, to evoke his Korean nationality and the millennial past of the game of Go. We use a simple electronic pluck sound when it is AlphaGo's turn.

The two instruments are placed in stereo space, like two opponents on either side of a Go board. The electronic sounds for AlphaGo are on the left, the gayageum for Lee Sedol on the right, as they were placed during the official competition.

3.3 The 5 parts of the music

3.3.1 Part 1

The first game took place March 9, 2016 and lasted 3h27. Lee Sedol resigned after 186 moves (Figure 2).

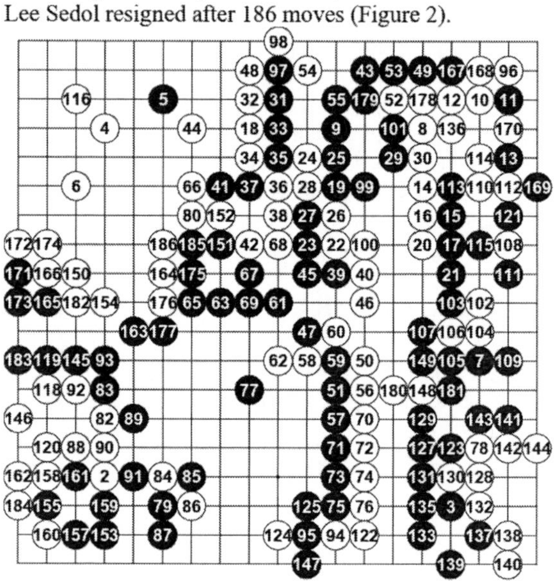

Figure 2. *Kifu* of the 186 moves of the first game between Lee Sedol and AlphaGo (Lee Sedol is black)

The indices of the notes computed by our algorithm for this first part are shown in table 3. These numbers are then used in a pentatonic scale to determine the note to play as seen in table 2.

1	2	1	2	1	2	1	2	1	3	4	7	2	2	3	5	4	2	1	6
4	2	3	4	5	6	7	9	5	7	3	5	8	5	10	10	6	9	4	5
4	4	1	3	5	5	1	5	3	2	3	6	5	3	5	5	4	4	9	10
3	5	1	5	4	3	7	10	6	6	4	6	4	6	4	6	3	2	1	5
1	3	4	3	4	6	4	7	4	10	8	6	4	5	4	5	8	7	6	9
8	3	4	6	4	9	5	2	4	4	5	5	10	9	7	4	6	6	5	6
8	7	3	3	8	5	4	6	5	9	6	7	2	6	8	13	6	5	3	5
3	7	9	5	8	6	6	6	7	2	8	11	1	4	1	6	5	9	8	6
13	7	4	3	3	5	6	10	5	8	4	5	5	9	6	7	5	14	8	9
4	12	8	9	9	8														

Table 3. Notes indices for the 186 moves of the first game alternatively played by black then white (read from left to right, top to bottom).

In the corresponding first part of our music piece, the gayageum starts first, since Lee Sedol had black for the first game (Black always starts first in Go). The two instruments then respond to each other, alternately playing a note corresponding to the stone placed by one of the two players. Then, drums appear at the first third of this music part, corresponding to the moment when AlphaGo's statistics began to show its dominance in the first game. In traditional Korean music, like *sanjo*, the gayageum is accompanied by the *janggu*, an hourglass-shaped drum. In our music, these percussions are like heartbeats to reinforce the dramatic tension of the game which will culminate in the first defeat of the human champion against the machine after 186 moves.

3.3.2 Part 2

The second game took place March 10, 2016 and lasted 4 hours. Lee Sedol resigned after 211 moves.

During this game, move #37 played by AlphaGo stunned the Go world. Many players believed that it had been placed in the wrong place. A human player would never have dared to play it, it was too difficult to estimate the consequences.

At the press conference which followed this second game, Lee declared: "*I thought that AlphaGo was based on probability calculations and that it was just a simple machine. But when I saw this move, I changed my mind. Certainly, AlphaGo is creative. This move was really creative and beautiful.*"

In the second part of the music, to reflect this extraordinary move, a very pronounced bend ornament (called *nonghyeon* in Korean) is applied to the note played by the gayageum for move 38, Lee Sedol's response, to represent the turmoil in his mind at this revolutionary moment.

3.3.3 Part 3

The third game took place March 12, 2016 and lasted 3h51. Lee Sedol resigned after 176 moves.

Percussions accompany the entire third part of the music to emphasize the tension of all the spectators and Lee Sedol himself. If he does not win this third game, he will have no chance of defeating AlphaGo during the tournament. Unfortunately, this game was won by AlphaGo.

3.3.4 Part 4

The fourth game took place March 13, 2016 and lasted 3h59. It was the only one won by Lee Sedol, after 180 moves.

The fourth part of the music forms a calm break in the piece, without percussion. It is underlined by a layer constructed from a human voice to evoke this temporary victory of man over the machine. This part evokes the calm of this last human resistance before the final domination of the AI in the fifth and last part.

3.3.5 Part 5

The fifth and last game of the tournament took place March 15, 2016 and lasted 4 hours. Lee Sedol resigned after 280 moves.

The fifth part of the music gradually degrades into glitchy electronic sounds, as well as the video which becomes more and more glitched, to mark the historic victory of the machine over man in the game of Go.
The final music and animation can be found here:
https://vimeo.com/912987229

4. ANALYSIS OF THE RESULTS

Our method allows us to produce polyphonic music, with the overlapping of two independent melodic lines corresponding to the moves of the two players.

The notes have equal durations and are placed alternately between the two lines, giving a regular rhythmic pattern. This pattern contributes to a clear rhythmic texture and rhythmic interaction between the two melodic lines, translating the alternating sequence of moves between the players.

The lowest notes correspond to isolated stones, mainly played at the start of the game when the board is still empty. Higher notes are heard when a placed stone has many neighbors, reflecting competition for dominance of the board. Higher and higher notes are heard as the game goes on, because the board fills with stones with each move played. Certainly, stones are removed from the board when they are captured, but it is still increasingly rare that a stone placed has not at least a neighbor.

Music generated with our algorithm generally has the same starting sequence for approximately the first 5 to 8 notes, if the players play Go in the classical style. Indeed, to have the best chances of conquering territories on the board, traditional wisdom says the priority is to play corner enclosures, then to extend to the middle of the sides, and finally to the center because it is easier to secure territory in the corners than on the sides or in the center. This starting phase is called *fuseki* in Japanese. Thus, players play approximately the first 8 moves by placing their stones in isolated places at the corners and sides, which results in the two lowest musical notes in our range (G3 for black, A3 for white). This fuseki phase ends when it is no longer possible to place a stone without triggering an immediate combat, because the free spaces are no longer sufficient for this stone not to be in danger. Consequently, a stone is placed next to another one, and a higher note is computed by our algorithm. It is interesting to see how the sonification of the game with our algorithm allows us to hear when the fuseki phase ends. Thus, this phase serves as an introduction to the music generated by our algorithm, before the game really begins with the first attack.

Unlike the sonification of some real-world data which are extracts without beginning or end of a continuous flow (ocean wave heights, weather data, stock prices, etc.), with values which may appear stochastic, a game of Go has a beginning and an end and tells a story, which is very close to the flow of music.

Instead of only stone neighborhood, higher level Go concepts could be considered in our algorithm to better tell the story of a Go game through music: connection and separation, life and death, thickness and lightness, attack and defense, *sente* and *gote*, *ko* fighting, *joseki* use, etc. This opens many avenues of research for future work.

5. CONCLUSIONS

We presented an algorithm capable of interpreting a game of Go like a music score, by playing on the many similarities between stones on a Go board and notes on a musical staff.

Our software produces both music and animation. We used our program on a series of 5 very famous games played in 2016 between the Korean champion Lee Sedol and the artificial intelligence AlphaGo, which experienced for the first time the domination of the machine over man in Go at such a level. We produced a musical piece in 5 parts from these games. The two players are like two musicians who write alternately on the same score. Their parts are played with different instruments, a gayageum for Lee Sedol, to recall his Korean nationality and the millennial past of the game of Go, and very electronic sounds for his artificial challenger.

Since a few years, there is more and more use of AI to generate music. In this paper we take a roundabout way, using the joint action of man and AI to generate music, but indirectly, by computing the notes from games of Go between man and machine.

Our program therefore finds sound in motion, in the moves played on the board, but also in the shock wave caused by this victory of AI over man in a field that was then thought to be beyond its reach.

Acknowledgments

We would like to dedicate our music piece to Lee Sedol. Despite the excessive media exposure of this tournament against the AI where he had to pose as champion of humanity, he showed a lot of courage and tenacity. This tournament was one of the symbols of the dominant advent of AI in all fields.

6. REFERENCES

[1] L.A. Hiller and L.M. Isaacson, "Experimental Music: Composition with an Electronic Computer", 1959.

[2] J. Cage, "Silence: Lectures and Writings", Wesleyan University Press, 1961

[3] I. Xenakis, "Formalized Music: Thought and Mathematics in Composition", 1971.

[4] E.R. Miranda and J.A. Biles "Evolutionary Computer Music", Springer, 2007.

[5] J.-P. Briot, G. Hadjeres and F.-D. Pachet, "Deep Learning Techniques for Music Generation, Computational Synthesis and Creative Systems", Springer, 2019.

[6] Kramer, G, Auditory display: Sonification, audification, and auditory interfaces. Proceedings of the First International Conference on Auditory Display (ICAD), 1992.

[7] Records of Go games between Lee Sedol and AlphaGo, 2016 https://www.alphago-games.com/#leesedol

Frasi ipermetriche
Hypermetrics in a Computer-Assisted Algorithmic Composition Environment

Ken Paoli, DMA
College of DuPage
Glen Ellyn, IL USA
paolik@cod.edu

ABSTRACT

Frasi ipermetriche is a work for three virtual instruments that employs an algorithmic patch that generates arrays with shared rhythmic material to create a rhythmic output with motivic cohesiveness. The program takes a "top down" approach to set a timed duration in which the same rhythmic values will be generated in a group of arrays to form a type of "hypermetric phrase." New rhythmic and melodic components for the hypermetric phrase are generated with every change of the "real world" clock. The patch allows the user to pre-determine several aspects of the composition and allows for parameter changes during the generation of material. This paper provides a brief description of hypermeter, the generative processes involved in the patch and the realization steps leading from compositional data to finished work.

1. HYPERMETER

Hypermeasure and hypermeter are terms credited to Edward T. Cone, an American theorist and composer, who first used them in his book *Musical Form and Musical Performance* (1968) [1]. Cone believed that while the usual definition of the phrase involved the alternation of strong and weak beats at both the measure level and also at the beat level, inside the measure, it fell short of "a more organic rhythmic principle that supports the melodic and harmonic shape of the phrase and justifies it acceptance as a formal unit." The term hypermeasure appears in the second essay and the term hypermeter appears in the third essay and, when it is used, it has a negative connotation describing the "tyranny of the four-measure phrase" as it relates to the music of Chopin [1].

From this rather negative beginning hypermetrical analysis has been embraced by Schenkerian theorists who apply his hierarchical approach to the metrical aspect of compositional analysis [2]. Not all theorists involved in the study of hypermeter are Schenkerian; other theorists' studies are concerned with distinguishing hypermeter from what Lerdahl and Jackendoff refer to as "grouping" [3]. Regardless of the specific concerns of the varying approaches, hypermetric studies tend to be hierarchical in nature.

Traditional phrase structure and hypermeter may unfold "in unison" but the focus of hypermeter is an examination of metrics apart from phrase structure. Rothstein points to the conflicts that may arise between hypermeter and phrase structure as a "basic compositional resource" [2]. While much modern music has eschewed the language-based notion of organization in phrases, hypermeasures may serve as a compositional resource for algorithmic organization of rhythm. In discussing the organization of Romantic music Cone states that "one can find long stretches in which phrases combined into phrases that are themselves metrically conceived" [1]. This is what he refers to as hypermeasures. Cone goes on to state that hypermeasures "are likely to occur where several measures in succession exhibit similarity of motivic, harmonic and rhythmic construction" [1]. Lerdahl and Jackendoff distinguish two types of rhythmic structure: grouping and metric, which they maintain should be kept separate. The interaction of these rhythmic elements creates interest and variety in music [4]. Applying grouping to music of the post-Common Practice period can allow for hypermetric analysis if the definition of elements that create a sense of meter can be expanded.

Young has argued that the concept of meter should include "gesture, timbre, and the initiation points of phrases" to broaden the definition of meter [4]. Another notion is to allow for uneven metrical spacing of "strong beats" creating irregular hypermetric structures. Young maintains that "as we move into repertoires not driven by functional harmony, we can modify the definition of phrase to be a directed motion in time from one entity to another, whether those entities are tonal, timbral, textural, or otherwise. Additionally, we can consider pitch-directed motion, even in music that does not use functional harmonic progression as its vocabulary" [4]. While promoting an expanded notion of the "hypermetric phrase" which allows for irregularity, Young admits that in contemporary music metrics may be "obscured at the surface level" [4]. For the author, this points to the importance of rhythmic patterning in non-metrical works. The notion of initiating a time span and generating shared rhythmic and perhaps, melodic material that endures for the duration of the time span became the departure point for the patch which is the basis of this paper.

2. THE HYPERMETRIC PATCH

The Hypermetric Patch was programmed in *Music Wonk*, a Wintel program by the late John Dunn, that uses visual-based programming, but confines itself to MIDI manipulation. It has extensive data manipulation capabilities and for composers whose work begins with MIDI data, *Music Wonk* provides an excellent set of generative tools. Since the death of its creator in 2018, *Music Wonk* has been available as shareware (http://www.geneticmusic.com/).

The impetus of the Hypermetric Patch was to create a routine that would generate rhythmic motives and employ these motives for a specific time span to create rhythmic cohesiveness between musical voices. While algorithmically generating material, it was important that the user interface would allow for changes of patch parameters during data generation. While this particular use of the patch was to produce material for a chamber piece, with the addition of a MIDI control surface and some minor output additions, this patch could just as easily be "outfitted" for live performance.

The discussion on the generation of rhythmic material which is the main feature of the patch and will be presented first. That will be followed by a consideration of several additional sub-patches or macros that were added for the benefit of enhancing the musicality of the patch.

2.1 The Master Clock

A top-down approach to organizing rhythmic patterns required designing a patch using a real-time clock measuring time in milliseconds. This clock defines the time span of the hypermetric phrase and, during this time span, rhythmic patterns are generated and held by various patch components. The Master Clock section is organized as follows.

The patch uses a **Duration Clock** (**MS Clock**) that is timed in milliseconds to set the time span for the hypermetric phrase. The duration range is from 2000 to 20,000 ms (2" to 20") and the time range may be:

- manually set (with a beginning default time of 4").
- automated (using a random number generator).
- an array with values from 1" to 4" (executed in either ascending or descending order), which can lengthen or shorten phrase components.

The **Duration Slider** displays the current phrase length in seconds. The **Duration Limit Slider** displays the user determined maximum phrase duration. The strobe output of the **Duration Clock** toggles a **Hold** switch. The **Hold** function is an attribute of all clock modules and in this case, a single **Sync Clock** (**AS Clock**) is employed as a timing strobe for several sub-patch components. When the **AS Clock** is "held", the output of any module connected to it is stopped. This arrests the **Write** input to the rhythmic arrays, which then "hold" the current array values until the next **Duration Clock** cycle. The result is a set of six rhythmic values that remain in use for the length of the **Duration Clock** cycle. When the **Duration Clock** refreshes, the arrays refill with values that are again, held for the current duration. This creates the "hypermetric" aspect of the algorithm. The data flow of this portion of the program is displayed in Figure 1.

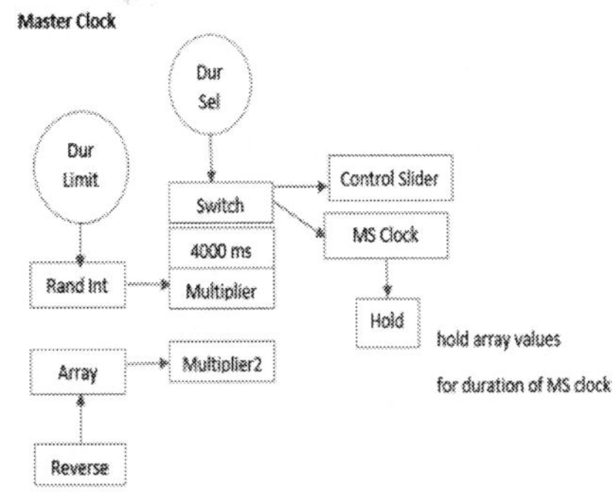

Figure 1. Master Clock Flow Chart

2.2 Rhythmic Value Arrays

The rhythmic values in MIDI span the numeric range from 2 to 192 (a 32nd note triplet to a double whole note). For the purpose of this patch the values were limited from 2 to 96 (a 32nd note triplet to a whole note). To represent both duple and triple values, two arrays were populated:

- **Value Array 1** has 47 rhythmic values divisible by 2.
- **Value Array 2** has 30 rhythmic values divisible by 3.
- A third array, **Value Array 3** has 10 "fast" values in a range from 3 to 12 (a 32nd note to an 8th note).

The high and low range of the value arrays are adjustable from the **Control Panel** allowing the user to set the minimum and maximum array range.

The **Value Arrays** outputs are controlled by the user with a **Value Array Knob** that allows the selection of the array to be random or selects a specific Array (duple, triple or "fast"). The selected output is passed to the Write Value of the **Main Array**. See Figure 2.

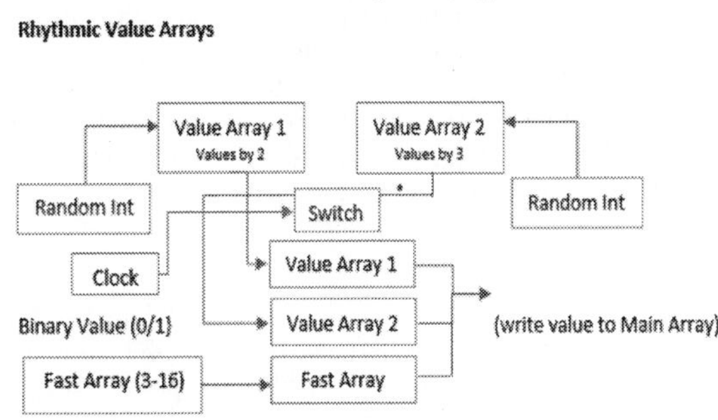

Figure 2. Rhythmic Value Arrays

2.3 Main and Secondary Arrays

The selected output of the **Value Arrays** is sent to the **Main Array**. As stated earlier, this array contains six (rhythmic) values (this number could easily be adjusted to accommodate additional array values). The output of the Main Array is sent to an **Array Slider** which provides a graphic display of the current values in the array. The **Main Array** values are outputted to two additional arrays which share the same write clock with the **Main Array**. The **Secondary Arrays** also accommodate six values.

Two clock modules are needed: a **Stepper Module** which allows the values "held" in the array to be played while the **Addresser Module** continues to output read values from the array. The read/write capability of the **Main Array** allows, a single Addresser module to supply different ordering of the rhythmic material to the two additional arrays. The result is the same rhythmic values are shared between the three arrays; however, each array has a different ordering of those rhythmic values. This allows for motivic integrity of the generated rhythmic patterns in the hypermetric phrase. See Figure 3.

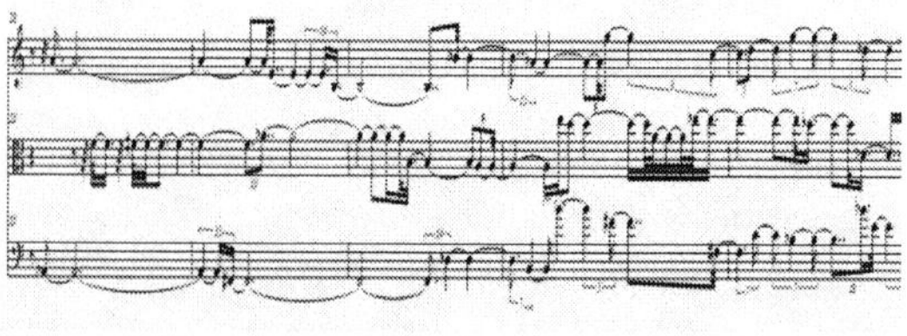

Figure 3. Unquantized Rhythm Array output

3. SUB-PATCHES

The clock and array information presented above comprise the methodology concerning the generative aspects of the patch. The sub-patches that follow are meant to enhance the musicality of the patch.

3.1 Tempo

Tempo can be set manually or automated with a range from M.M. 30 to 200. Selections are as follows:

- The manual setting defaults to 60 and maybe adjusted by the user on the Control Panel.
- If automated, a **Random Integer Module** generates a tempo value between 30 and 200.

A conversion module changes the tempo to milliseconds which is output to the System Clock. This clock controls the global timing of the patch.

Exported tempo data was "mapped" to the MIDI range and recorded. Original values were restored "by hand" and entered into the DAW tempo map.

3.2 Quantization Sub Patch

The ability to quantize note values is an included option that allow the user to choose to quantize the outputted rhythmic values or not. If the resultant output is meant to be scored in traditional notation, quantizing is recommended as it reduces the amount of editing necessary to produce a legible score.

3.3 Unirhythm Sub-patch

In the course of data testing and evaluating the output of the program, it was deemed desirable that, besides the three independent rhythmic outputs from the **Main and Secondary Arrays,** one array could supply the same rhythmic values to all three **MIDI Voice Modules**. This sub-patch is called **Unirhythm,** although the effect it produces is musically best described as homorhythm.

Unirhythm is accomplished by selecting one of the three rhythmic arrays using a manual **Unirhythm Control** that is available for each voice. A series of switches reduces the output to a single option; that note duration information is output to all **MIDI Voice Modules**. Figure 4 displays the homorhythmic output of the sub-patch.

Figure 4. Unquantized Unirhythm Output

3.4 Augmentation/Diminution Sub Patch

The augmentation and diminution of rhythmic values was deemed desirable to allow for greater rhythmic contrasts of the three voices. The inputted values are multiplied or divided that either doubles, or halves the rhythmic values. These values are controlled by an **Aug/Dim Knob** that allows the user to select either rhythmic manipulation on the Control Panel. A second control is the **Rhy/+- Knob** that allows the user to select whether to engage this rhythmic manipulation or not.

The interaction of the Unirhythm and Aug./Dim. Sub-patches create additional compositional choices. All three voices can play homorhythmically; two voices can share the same values while the third plays values from any array (which may be rhythmically augmented or diminished).

3.5 Pitch Class Sub Patch

Many varying methods for generating pitch information could be utilized, but the programmatic goal was rhythmic patterning under a hypermetric "umbrella." It was decided to use serial techniques to generate melodic material in this iteration of the program. A previous version used sieves to generate melodic material.

The same Prime Row is used for the source material and the user can choose the row version for each voice. The **Pitch Row Display** provides user input of the row and gives a visual display of the Prime Row.

Transposition of the row may be applied manually or automated. If the automated option is chosen, the **Duration Clock** will change transposition in time with the hypermetric phrase change.

3.6 Octave Sub-Patch

The Octave Sub-Patch allows the used to set the octave and the lowest pitch for each voice of the patch. This allows the patch to be tailored for various instruments.

The octave displacement uses the clock signal from the **PC Macro** to trigger a Random Integer which adds 3 to 6 octaves to the pitch. This output is sent to the transposition input of the **MIDI Voice Module**.

3.7 Velocity Sub Patch

Changes in "note on" Velocity messages create the variety of attack nuance that yields a more musical output. In this iteration of the patch velocity zones are used.

The note velocity range is divided into three overlapping velocity "zones." This allows for velocities yielding three different levels of note dynamics. A separate **AS Clock** determines the duration of the current velocity layer yielding velocity changes that are independent of the hypermetric clock.

3.8 Textural Variation Sub Patch

Having three voices continually outputting data that produces music with no textural variation whatsoever is of limited aural appeal. A textural variation sub-patch was developed that allows for any voice to be a soloed and three possibilities for duets. Of course, complete silence was ruled out as the changes of output from this sub patch are controlled by the **Duration Clock** which could result in long silences. Having all voices playing is the default texture if this sub patch is not engaged.

3.9 MIDI Output

The MIDI output of the **MIDI Voice Module** is the equivalent of a software playback device and is of less importance to the patch since it receives data and passes it through a virtual MIDI interface to a DAW program for compositional manipulation.

4 REALIZATION

4.1 Preliminary Considerations

While the generation of the material is accomplished in the Hypermeter Patch, the recording of the MIDI data occurs in a DAW. The MIDI tracks are "orchestrated" by virtual instruments and recorded tempo information is visible on a Tempo Track that controls the master clock of the DAW.

It should be noted that this patch is not intended to be a "black box" program. The generated material is often surprisingly good, at times it yields patterns too "trivial" to pursue. The generated material has to be evaluated and sculpted into a musical "shape" by the composer.

4.2 Recording

Before recording, the following aspects of the patch should be set:

- The Prime Form is entered into the Control Panel.
- The Row Forms for the three voices are selected.
- The Row transpositions are selected.
- Duration and Tempo are set.
- The range of rhythmic values are chosen.
- The Unirhythm section may be engaged, or not.
- Variable texture can be preset to insure all of the instruments play together, or, if engaged, the voices will enter alone or in "duets."
- The range and low notes for the three voices should be set to the range of the proposed instruments.

Once the settings are completed, recording can begin.

Several runs of material were recorded. Initial runs maintained a single row transposition to produce stable pitch sections. Later runs allowed for row transposition changing with the hypermetric phrase for sections with a less centric character. Unirythm yielded homorhythm for all three voices and when combined with texture variations created interesting contrapuntal material.

Conceived as a sting trio, appropriate samples were chosen for the orchestration and typical instrument placement in a stereo field was used. Articulations for the strings were applied using expression maps.

The ordering of the generated material is not linear; sections were ordered to suit the exigencies of the composer. Defining a phrase as "directed motion from one entity to another… whether the musical nature is tonal, textural, or otherwise," the author has freely assembled this piece [4].

4.3 Digital Conversion, Mixing and Mastering

Once the MIDI version of the work is completed, the output is converted to monophonic wave files and processed with equalization. The resultant tracks were routed to a stereo effect bus for the addition of reverb. The three tracks were then exported as a stereo wave file. This mixdown was mastered using a linear parametric equalizer to insure smooth equalization curves and a phase correction processor to remove phase loss from the file. Compression was not employed to preserve the subtleties of the acoustic instruments.

5 CONCLUSIONS

Computer-assisted algorithmic composition encompasses a variety of techniques to generate data in the process of creating compositions. The preference of the author is to develop programs based on theoretical notions and attempt to apply them in a compositional setting. Most programs go through several layers of refinement before they yield satisfactory results, much like traditional compositional approaches. The computer composer invests time to investigate and evaluate, at every step, the results of the algorithmic processes. While the generation of material for evaluation is quick and convenient, programs of this type do not make composition an easier endeavor. However, having an algorithmic composition "assistant" makes composition and data manipulation almost irresistible.

6. REFERENCES

[1] Cone, Edward T. *Musical Form and Musical Performance*. New York: W.W. Norton, 1968.

[2] Rothstein, William N. "Rhythm and the Theory of Structural Levels." New Haven: Yale University ProQuest Dissertation Publishing, 1981.

[3] Yust, Jason. *Organized Time: Rhythm, Tonality and Form*. New York: Oxford University Press, 2018.

[4] Young, Samuel M. *Hypermeter and Phrae Structure in Selected Works by Stravinsky, Crumb and Adams*. 2018. University of California Los Angeles, Doctoral Dissertation.

Promotion and Development of Music Programming Language in Music Universities in Southwest China - An Example from Sichuan Conservatory of Music

Wanjun YANG
Sichuan Conservatory of Music, CHINA
yangwanjun@163.com

Jinhao HAN
Sichuan Conservatory of Music, CHINA
1016941374@qq.com

ABSTRACT

Using music programming for electronic music composition has been a significant method in electronic music research and creation for over half a century. However, teaching students to develop their strengths in coding and composition remains a challenge for educators. This paper discusses the experiences and achievements in electronic music education and composition using music programming technology by Chinese researchers. Focusing on the Sichuan Conservatory of Music, explore how to integrate new technologies with the essence of Chinese culture in electronic music composition and composer training. We aim to find new forms and examine the impact of the intermingling and collision of different cultures on advancing music art and technology.

1. A HISTORY OF MUSIC PROGRAMMING TECHNOLOGY RESEARCH IN SOUTHWEST CHINA

As an inland province in southwest China, Sichuan was comparatively isolated in terms of information dissemination. However, after China opened its doors in the late 1970s, new ideas and technologies began to flourish, and music scholars in Sichuan started to actively learn and explore. The Sichuan Conservatory of Music (SCCM), the only professional music conservatory in western China, saw the beginning of electronic music composition and sound synthesis language studies during this period.

In the 21st century, the Electronic Music Department (EMD) at SCCM has actively pursued ties and academic exchanges with international electronic music institutions. It has established partnerships with GRAME (France), CCRMA (USA), and ZKM (Germany). Esteemed figures such as Professor John Chowning from Stanford University and Professor Jeffrey Stolet from the University of Oregon have visited to conduct academic lectures, workshops, and concerts, providing substantial support for the study and research of electronic music at SCCM.

2. TEACHING MUSIC PROGRAMMING TECHNIQUES IN THE EARLY DAYS OF SCCM

In search of theories and technologies to better serve Chinese electronic music, a group of composers and researchers with backgrounds in both computer engineering and music composition have convened at SCCM. Their goal is to conduct research on electronic music composition tailored to Chinese culture, formally incorporate music programming technology into their teaching programs, offer courses based on music programming technology, and create an electronic music community rooted in Chinese culture. These initiatives provide students with more options for creating electronic music, offer researchers new directions for investigation, and expand the genres and possibilities for producing electronic music compositions.

3. TEACHING AND RESEARCH IN SOUND DESIGN AND COMPOSITION

3.1 Course offerings

Since the early 1980s, Chinese scholars have explored electronic music, initially focusing on synthesizers with limited supporting literature. Over the decades, academic electronic music gained traction, though many relied on commercial sound processors. In 2003, the introduction of Max/MSP revealed new possibilities in sound design through graphical programming and bringing new creative methods to students. In 2010, Professor Jon Christopher Nelson visited the SCCM and introduced Csound, which highlighted the importance of unique sound design and suggested we develop a new course to foster design thinking. The course, initiated in 2010 and using Csound as its main tool, which has received global support to incorporate sound design into the curriculum and to encourage innovative approaches to sound processing. By 2011, electronic music became an independent research area and received financial support from college executives to encourage publications on music coding and the development of a Chinese electronic music curriculum. SCCM students were deeply involved in Csound and Max/MSP, contributing to Chinese-language academic databases and advancing the field.

3.2 Compilation and publication of books

In order to improve the accessibility of sound design literature to Chinese students and to address the language barrier, I have translated a large number of English materials into Chinese, organized and published them. These include China's first Csound tutorial, 'Manual to Csound Music Programming,' which was published in 2015 with funds raised by me and is now widely used in educational institutions across China. After updating the Csound course, I guided students in exploring object-oriented programming in electronic music with tools like SuperCollider and Sonic Pi. Over the past decade, the acceptance of sound design principles and music coding has grown significantly among professional music institutions in China, influencing new generations of composers.

4. PROBLEMS AND SOLUTIONS IN THE IMPLEMENTATION OF MUSIC PROGRAMMING TECHNOLOGY IN CHINESE MUSIC UNIVERSITIES

4.1 Current status of electronic music research in universities

Since the initiation of the Csound series of courses in 2010, there has been an ongoing discussion about the relevance of teaching music programming, particularly computer theory, to students of electronic music. Many new undergraduates, trained primarily in instrument performance and art theory, struggle with the mathematical and logical demands of electronic music, impeding their research. At SCCM, students' concerns about the purpose of electronic music training and job prospects were also a challenge. In addition, economic disparities affect students' access to quality electronic music resources, especially those from low-income areas. Addressing these challenges requires adapting students' understanding of electronic music.

4.2 Addressing the inner confusion and creative needs of learners

Maintaining student engagement and securing long-term institutional support in music education is challenging when the focus is solely on technical skills. Young composers and researchers value their student careers and need to see the acquisition of practical applications of what they have learned.

Teaching music programming in isolation can easily lead students to believe that programming is reproducing the functionality in their DAWs, Thus making them think they can get better sound design by using the DAW directly. Considering that, we decided to put DAWs in the classroom together with programming, Allow students to experience the difference between programming and DAWs in actual composition.

Once the students have developed an interest in learning music programming, we start addressing the short-term employment of the students. Our response is to integrate the music curriculum with Chinese music culture in our teaching and research, to meet the learning and creative needs of our students, and to gain support from the society and enterprises. By combining theoretical and practical learning of Csound and Sonic Pi, we've encouraged their adoption in composition and research, enhancing educational outcomes and fostering collaboration. This course has been successful for over a decade.

4.3 Promotion of music programming techniques among students

The study of electronic music requires not only a willingness to explore new things but also an effective research system. Unfortunately, most current electronic music production platforms are quite expensive, making them unaffordable for many students from modest backgrounds. At the Sichuan Conservatory of Music, many students come from mountainous or remote prefectures and cannot afford the high costs associated with research, leading them to resort to using pirated software for their studies. This issue became particularly pronounced with the introduction of Max/MSP, Kyma, and GRM tools. To reduce students' dependence on commercial electronic music production platforms, open-source and free electronic music production tools or platform languages have been introduced into the curriculum. This initiative addresses their practical difficulties and encourages more students to actively engage in electronic music research and creation. In recent years, an increasing number of students have participated in research, leading to significant breakthroughs and progress. Many government- and academy-funded projects have been approved, resulting in new findings in electronic music and the publication of many papers. This has provided localized research materials for subsequent students.

4.4 Strategies and approaches for different students

For general learners, we provide paradigms and templates to facilitate learning and applying the language. For instance, we offer specific functional modules and composition templates, enabling them to quickly engage in application without losing patience and enthusiasm due to the extended period required for basic learning.

For students with a strong foundation in composition, we guide them to integrate coding techniques with the creation of works featuring local cultural elements, such as traditional Chinese instruments like the Zheng, Sheng, and Dizi. By employing audio synthesis and digital audio processing techniques, we assist students in tape music and acousmatic design, encouraging them to learn and design sound processing programs in a coded manner. Through real-time audio processing techniques, students can incorporate their patch-playing skills into the design of electro-acoustic music or interactive electronic music.

For students with some design skills, we instruct them to use widget-related technologies to design interactive electronic music using graphical objects. They are taught to use MIDI, OSC, and DMX protocols to interact with additional hardware devices or software, designing new media works that integrate audio and visuals.

These methods enable students to view creation as a motivation for learning, satisfying their need to produce their own work during the learning process and guiding them to engage more deeply with Csound learning.

4.5 Intensive training in sound design for process-oriented programming

Learning music programming languages takes longer than learning musical instruments, posing challenges for mastery through regular classes. To aid deeper learning, I offer weekly composition tutorials for enthusiastic students, providing a platform for sharing and improving sound design techniques. Additionally, we provided a dedicated academic space for these students, facilitating collaboration and the storage of research materials.

Learning music programming also requires strong computer skills, which most Chinese students majoring in music lack, necessitating guided research. In the advanced Csound course, we collaborate with students to modify code, research efficient algorithms, and improve their understanding of programming methods by creating a strong connection between students and instructors.

For a process-oriented music programming language, the focus is on the rational design of signal flow for sound signal processing. This involves modifying, recombining, modulating, and resynthesizing the sound signal piece by piece, relying on robust sound algorithms for operation. As our research evolved and listener demand increased, we gradually shifted towards modulating and analyzing recorded samples with sound algorithms. This transformation allowed us to use real-world sounds as compositional material, and even as control signals to guide the music's progress and development, facilitating interaction between the real world and the work. Guided by the concept of interaction, our research has advanced to the real-time analysis and processing of instrument sounds. We use real-time sound signal analysis techniques to convert instrument signals into data streams that can drive synthesizers and oscillators, allowing real instruments to control virtual ones and create a blend of real and virtual sounds.

4.6 Intensive training in object-oriented programming for music composition

For students who have acquired a good understanding of process-oriented programming in sound design and have progressed to the actual music composition stage of programming practice, they often encounter unpredictable problems. These challenges include sound components differing from what was imagined, algorithms that are difficult to control, and the pursuit of sounds that exceed the limits of existing algorithms. In response, I teach object-oriented programming languages such as SuperCollider or Sonic Pi, which use SuperCollider as a core, in addition to process-oriented programming languages for students interested in using music programming languages to create a wider variety of music. Unlike process-oriented programming, which requires the invocation of sound algorithms, object-oriented programming allows for the customization of methods and composition algorithms. This offers more flexibility to develop functions or invoke methods for specific needs and is suitable for those pursuing unique sounds.

The freedom of object-oriented programming is not limited to customization alone but also extends to the modularity of musical composition. In music composition, it is important to manage repetition and variation without necessitating the composer to rewrite the code and call methods for each iteration. Object-oriented programming enables custom encapsulation of methods and algorithms, making sound design modular, easy to organize and coordinate, and simple to call repeatedly. This reduces the workload and complexity for the composer. Studying and researching object-oriented programming allows students to move beyond reliance on established sound processing methods and towards designing their own sound processing methods and composing pieces with an independent identity.

5. METHODS AND PRACTICES OF PROMOTING CODED MUSIC

5.1 Establish standardised assessment criteria

The assessment system for coded music is more quantifiable than that for traditional music. Assessing the integrity, feasibility, and innovation of the algorithm at a linguistic level enables students to better utilize language in their compositions.

The methods taught in classroom lectures need to be validated through practical work. As a requirement for course completion, all students, in addition to their regular assignments, are required to compose works using Csound and present them in a concert hall at the end of the course. This serves as a means to assess students' learning and also applies some pressure on them to work harder with Csound. It encourages them to think about how to use the techniques they have learned for composition, thereby integrating learning with creation.

5.2 Leading students to form research groups

After starting the Csound course in 2010, I not only devoted myself to conducting creative research but also founded a Csound research group. The initial team consisted of myself and several students who were enthusiastic about Csound. We focused on new ways of creating and designing interactions, striving to uncover new possibilities for traditional Chinese instruments. As research progressed, the scope of the Csound research group's work expanded annually. The works created by group members have become typical examples of Csound research and serve as excellent demonstrations.

5.3 Conducting professional academic activities

Young composers are increasingly using coding techniques to compose electronic music, and regular classroom performances no longer suffice, so we present the latest works in an annual event called "The Night of Coding", which has expanded to twice a year in recent years. It was inspired by Miller Puckett's "The Night of Linux". The event provides a comprehensive platform for presenting and discussing coding work, offering venue, equipment, funding and media support for live and online presentations. Additionally, it includes interactive salons for composers to share their experiences and promote coding skills. To further inspire and educate, we frequently invite international electronic musicians to Sichuan Conservatory of Music for lectures and live performances. Over the past decade, notable figures like Professor Takayuki Rai and Professor John Chowning have significantly contributed by teaching composition techniques and advanced audio technologies, enriching students' learning and encouraging the development of personalized compositional methods through ongoing in-person and online engagements.

5.4 Composition based on traditional Chinese culture

In addition to studying programming and composition techniques, we have also explored how to better integrate technology with composition and how Csound-related compositions can distinguish themselves among the numerous outstanding electronic music languages, software, and hardware available. The sounds of traditional Chinese instruments are inherently unique and culturally specific, making the unique attributes and cultural traditions of traditional Chinese music a constant source of inspiration for young Chinese composers. After numerous attempts and discussions, we believe that combining Chinese musical culture with research focused on its characteristics is a crucial starting point for Csound research and composition in China. Selecting suitable Chinese cultural symbols to align with the characteristics of Csound compositions, identifying instruments and timbres, and using Csound to synthesize unique Chinese scales and tunings are all strategies we employ in our compositions. Building on the ideas mentioned, we composed works with traditional cultural elements and characteristics. Works such as "CHINA", "911", "Cycle Etude", "Fragment of Iliad", "Spring Breeze Sweeps beyond Yumen Pass" and "DTMF" have been selected by prestigious events like ICSC, ICMC, NYCEMF, and Musicacoustica. These compositions not only convey the creative ideas and individuality of young Chinese composers but also showcase Csound's Chinese research in various forms on the global music stage.

5.5 Promoting teaching with research projects

In China, research projects play a crucial role in the assessment of academic research. For Csound to establish its presence in Chinese academic research, it must align with the requirements for research project submissions and completions. Over the past decade, the Csound research group has submitted eight projects related to coding composition, application, and plug-in development. These projects have not only provided the necessary financial support for research and application but also enhanced presentation opportunities. As a result, there has been a significant increase in the motivation of group members to research and create with Csound. Furthermore, it has broadened the awareness and acceptance of Csound and computer music programming among researchers in related disciplines and educational research authorities. This development has paved the way for a broader platform and laid a stronger foundation for future researchers and creators.

5.6 Establishing a database of Chinese language subjects

In Chinese music education, while learning foreign languages such as English, French, and Italian is important, it typically focuses only on learning musical terminology and does not encompass comprehensive language studies. Consequently, when students encounter English-based music programming, they find it challenging to engage in research. To address this issue, I have compiled and summarized my research findings with my students during our study of music programming. Additionally, I have authored several textbooks in Chinese, adopting a mindset that makes the material accessible to students with basic English skills. Throughout years of teaching and research, several students have chosen music programming as the topic for their dissertations and have published numerous research papers in Chinese. These contributions provide valuable research samples for other students and enrich Chinese academic databases.

6. CONCLUSION

Based on the discussion above, we believe that the inherent excellence of a technology and language forms the foundation for its existence and application. However, in practice, teaching and promotion also require strategic approaches to study, compose, and present them, ensuring they are adopted and their outstanding features are aptly showcased to the world. This approach aims to ignite the desire in other learners and researchers to learn, study, apply, and compose about them. There's a Chinese proverb, ' fragrant wine fears no dark alley (quality goods need no advertising),' which underscores the idea that quality inherently draws interest. In the education and promotion of music programming languages, it is crucial not only to explore the potential of the language but also to integrate and promote cultural aspects. This ensures that the music programming language can take root in specific cultural soil and flourish.

It is our hope that the experiences and methods outlined in this paper will inspire other educators and researchers, providing guidance in the teaching, application, and dissemination of music programming languages.

7. REFERENCES

[1] Lazzarini, V. et al.: Csound: A Sound and Music Computing System. Springer (2016)

[2] Miller Puckette.: The Theory and Technique of Electronic Music. World Scientific Publishing Co. Pte. Ltd. (2007).

[3] Lee Tong Soon: ROUTLEDGE HANDBOOK OF ASIAN MUSIC: CULTURAL INTERSECTIONS. Routledge. (2021)

[4] Thom Holmes.: Electronic and Experimental Music Technology, Music, and Culture FIFTH EDITION. Routledge. (2017)

[5] Will Kuhn and Ethan Hein.: Electronic Music School, A CONTEMPORARY APPROACH TO TEACHING MUSICAL CREATIVITY. Oxford University Press. (2021)

Microphone-based Data Augmentation for Automatic Recognition of Instrumental Playing Techniques

Nicolas Brochec
Tokyo University of the Arts
nicolas.brochec@pm.me

Tsubasa Tanaka
Tokyo University of the Arts
tanaka.tsubasa@ms.geidai.ac.jp

Will Howie
Japan Society for the Promotion
of Science International Research Fellow,
Tokyo University of the Arts
wghowie@gmail.com

ABSTRACT

Within existing research on the automatic classification of musical instrument playing techniques, few available datasets include enough playing techniques to cover the full range of a given musical instrument's expressive ability. However, creating a new large dataset requires recording many samples for many performance techniques, which is costly and time-consuming. Therefore, in this study, we attempt to augment data by increasing the number of recording microphones without increasing the recording duration and verify the effectiveness of this data augmentation method. As a result of recording flute playing techniques using multiple microphones, the accuracy and macro F1-Score of a convolutional neural network-based classifier improved when using a combination of the five most close-to-source microphones. The classifier's performance further improved when data were combined with a data augmentation method based on pitch shifting.

1. INTRODUCTION

Throughout the history of contemporary art music, composers have diversified Instrumental Playing Techniques (IPTs) to foster musical innovation. In contemporary mixed music, real-time digital audio effects are often applied to the live performance of acoustic instruments. The performer, a foot pedal, or a computer operator usually triggers these effects. However, automated triggering could reduce the burden on the operator and expand creative possibilities. This burden originated the development of score follower systems such as Antescofo [1]. Antescofo tracks the performer's temporal position on the score and automatically switches effects, reducing the burden on the operator. However, using Antescofo requires the score input information for each piece of music which adds an extra burden. Moreover, Antescofo's machine listening is based on pitch and rhythm detection, which does not allow for the recognition of IPTs. This research aims to develop a system that automatically recognizes IPT and switches audio effects according to it, thereby reducing the burden on the operator and the cost of music score input.

Several existing studies demonstrate that the development of automatic recognition of IPT systems suffers from a lack of large common sound banks [2, 3], with proposed systems often relying on commercial sound banks. Commercial sound banks are primarily recorded for industrial music production that does not require advanced contemporary instrumental techniques. These banks typically only include one sample per pitch per instrumental playing technique, severely limiting the available audio samples to train a classification algorithm.

One way to improve classification accuracy is to increase the number of audio samples by using data augmentation methods. Existing research [3, 4, 5, 6] proposes generating new audio samples by applying various digital audio transformations to the original data such as pitch shifting. However, these experiments have shown that the accuracy is still too low to put automatic recognition of IPT into practice.

Another possible data augmentation method is to record audio samples at different distances from the sound source. It would augment the number of samples without increasing the recording duration. In this study, we propose a novel method of data augmentation using multiple microphone positions, and evaluate its efficacy for automatic recognition of IPTs.

2. PROPOSED METHOD

To evaluate the efficacy of the microphone-based data augmentation method, we first simultaneously captured audio samples of flute playing techniques from different source-to-microphone distances. We then made several datasets, trained a neural network-based classifier, specifically Convolutional Neural Network (CNN), and tested it on a dataset originating from a different sound bank. Finally, we assessed the performance of the classifier with different metrics. We selected the flute as our instrument of focus because the first author of this study is familiar with this instrument. Furthermore, this study continues our previous study on the automatic recognition of flute IPTs [4].

2.1 Microphone Set

Diverse flute playing techniques were captured with seven microphones placed at different distances from the source, as described in Table 1. The microphones **A**, **B**, **C**, **D** were oriented toward the source, focusing on direct sound capture. Microphones **E** were oriented toward the ceiling to capture the room's natural reverberation. The "main

Microphone	Distance	Height	Nbr of Mics	Letter
DPA 4099	33 cm	/	1	**A**
DPA 4011	80 cm	/	1	**B**
DPA 4011	100 cm	/	1	**C**
DPA 4006	140 cm	179 cm	2	**D**
DPA 4006	458 cm	277 cm	2	**E**

Table 1. Microphones used to record the sound bank.

aeolian	flatterzunge	key click	multiphonics
ordinario	pizzicato	play and sing	staccato
tongue ram	trill	whistle tone	

Table 2. Flute playing techniques in 11 categories.

stereo" pair **D** microphones were 38 cm apart, while the microphones within the "ambient" pair **E** were 300 cm apart. Microphone positions **A**, **B**, **D**, and **E** are typical of contemporary studio and live recording/amplification microphone techniques. We placed microphone **C** at a distance of 1m from the source to the microphone because this distance is typically used for acoustic and electroacoustic measurements. The DPA 4099 is frequently used for live acoustic instrument amplification, while DPA 4011 and 4006 microphones were chosen for their flat frequency response, allowing for more accurate acoustic information capture. The height of **A**, **B**, and **C** is equal to the distance from the floor to the flute head hole.

2.2 Selection of Flute Playing Techniques

The flute can produce a chromatic scale from medium (C3≈261 Hz) to treble pitch (C6≈2093 Hz). The sound of the flute is produced by the friction of the air on the mouthpiece, while different changes in the velocity and characteristics of the blown air allow for playing diverse techniques [7, 8, 9]. In our previous study [4] we selected 19 different flute IPTs from the FullSOL library [10], and we showed that some IPTs are unsuitable for our investigation. Indeed, classifiers get confused when classifying the *harmonics*, *discolored fingering*, and *aeolian and ordinario* techniques because the *ordinario* technique is very close to them. We also concluded that similar techniques should be grouped together to reduce the number of classes and increase the number of samples per class. For instance, a minor second trill and a major second trill fall under the *trill* category. Playing a whistle tone with or without glissando is essentially performing a *whistle tone*. Playing and singing at the same pitch or not is performing a *play-and-sing* technique. As a result, we use in this study 11 flute IPTs (see Table 2).

All seven microphones simultaneously captured each flute playing technique played pitch by pitch chromatically within their respective register at *mezzoforte*. Some techniques have a small range of pitches (*aeolian*) or produce a short duration sound (*key click*, *staccato*, *pizzicato*, *tongue ram*). This can cause an imbalance in the training datasets because of the difference in sample duration for each class. We therefore recorded each short-duration playing technique twice more to increase available data. Our sound bank includes 2.85GB of audio files recorded at 96 kHz / 24-bit resolution [11].

2.3 Datasets

We designed two experiments to investigate which microphone combinations produce the best results for automatic recognition of flute playing techniques. For this purpose, we created multiple training datasets based on different microphone combinations and tested them on a separate test dataset (heterogeneous datasets).

2.3.1 Training Datasets

We first made a dataset for each monophonic recording (**A**, **B** and **C**), and for each stereo recording (**D** and **E**). We then combined these monophonic and stereophonic recordings to make new training datasets. First, we combined **A** and **B**, **B** and **C**, and **C** and **A**. Then, we combined **A**, **B** and **C**. After, we combined **A**, **B**, **C** and **D**, and **A**, **B**, **C**, and **E**. A final dataset was also created using all the datasets (**ABCDE**). We created a total of 12 different datasets. For stereo recordings **D** and **E** we use both channels as two different monophonic signals.

2.3.2 Test Dataset

For a comprehensive evaluation of the classifier, we tested it on a separate test dataset. The test dataset is made from the FullSOL sound bank [10], and includes flute playing techniques similar to those found within our datasets. To match the flute playing techniques from FullSOL with those from our training datasets, we deleted any unused techniques, and combined similar techniques into the same categories, as we did for our own datasets.

2.3.3 Validation Dataset

Our experiments used a validation dataset to measure the accuracy at each step of the training. This dataset is made from 20% of the test dataset. The selection of samples is stratified, which means that the proportion of samples in each class is proportional to the original test dataset.

2.4 Audio File Pre-processing

To prepare our data, we followed an existing methodology [4]. We downsampled the audio file sample rate to 24 kHz, as 12 kHz (the Nyquist frequency) is sufficient to cover most flute harmonics. We removed any silence within the audio file, as it is irrelevant. We edited the audio file into 15-frame-long sequences (≈ 320ms). We analyzed the sequences with a Log-Mel-Spectrogram (LMS) analysis. We computed the LMS on 128 bins, and the FFT window is fixed at 2048 samples with a hop size of 512 samples (≈ 21.3ms). The minimum frequency is set to 150 Hz because bass frequencies are irrelevant for the flute. Each sound file was edited into a maximum number of data samples according to the number of frames used. When the length of a given chunk was less than 15 frames, we padded the audio sample with zeros. We then normalized the data.

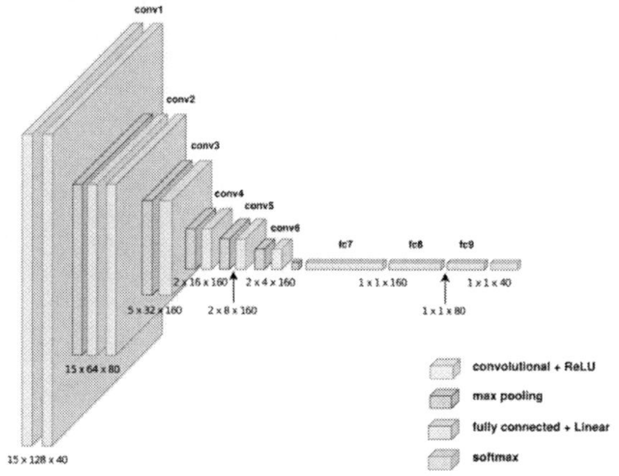

Figure 1. Schematic representation of the proposed architecture.

2.5 Methods of Classification

2.5.1 Classifier Architecture

To perform our experiments, we chose to implement a deep Convolutional Neural Network (CNN) architecture, which has been shown in several previous studies to have high efficiency for instrument-related audio classification tasks [3, 5, 6, 12, 13, 14, 15, 16]. In the domain of automatic recognition of IPT, existing research proposes design strategies to create CNN architectures [3]. We propose augmenting the capacity of these CNN architectures by adding several layers and by selecting the hyper-parameters that favored a rise in accuracy. A schematic representation of our architecture can be seen in Figure 1. We found that a kernel size of *2x3* works better for conv1, conv2, and conv3 modules than square-like sizes. Conv4, conv5, and conv6 use a *2x2* kernel size. We use batch normalization [17] and dropout layers [18] after each convolutional layer to speed up the training process and reduce overfitting. After the sixth convolutional layer, we connect three fully connected layers (fc7, fc8, and fc9) with a linear activation function.

2.5.2 Training

The neural network weights are initialized using Xavier Normal Initialization [19]. Training minimizes cross-entropy loss through mini-batch gradient descent with ADAM optimization. The learning rate begins at $lr = 0.001$, decaying exponentially, with validation accuracy monitored on the last 10 epochs. Training lasts for a maximum of 100 epochs on an A100 GPU machine, halting if validation accuracy has not improved in the last 20 epochs.

3. EXPERIMENTS

We performed two experiments to test whether microphone-based data augmentation can be effective. We first trained our classifier on the original data with different combinations of microphones. Then, in a second experiment, we augmented the number data by applying pitch shifting to the original audio data.

3.1 Transformation-based Data Augmentation

For audio classification tasks, digital audio transformations are often applied to the original data to augment the number of samples within the training datasets [20]. In the case of IPT classification, audio transformations are commonly utilized to represent the real-world environment(s) of musical performances [3, 4, 5, 6]. The aim of adding transformed audio data samples to our original data is to verify whether combining microphone-based data augmentation with transformation-based data augmentation would increase the accuracy. We only chose pitch shifting for that purpose because it increases accuracy [20]. The tuning of each of our audio samples is randomly modified in a range of 200 Hz around the tuning frequency (440 Hz).

3.2 Metrics

We evaluated our classifier by conducting two types of measurements. Firstly, we measured the accuracy of the model state achieving the highest accuracy on the validation dataset. Due to variations in sample durations per class, our datasets are unbalanced. To address this, we opted for the macro F1-Score, providing a more representative measure of classifier performance considering no difference between highly and poorly populated classes [21]. We repeated the training and testing five times per dataset and calculated the average accuracy and macro F1-Score on the five tests.

We computed confusion matrices to understand how well our classifier identified the playing techniques. For each of the five tests, a confusion matrix is generated. The final confusion matrix is the average of five individual matrices from the tests. We provided the average confusion matrices for the best-performing models based on average accuracy scores.

4. RESULTS

We performed two experiments, with and without the addition of pitch-shifted audio samples.

4.1 Accuracy and Macro F1 Score

Dataset	Original		Pitch-shifted	
	Accuracy	Macro F1	Accuracy	Macro F1
A	84.83	66.38	84.78	69.12
B	86.00	65.28	85.42	64.02
C	80.96	60.06	84.16	65.62
D	81.40	59.98	85.45	63.79
E	71.74	51.74	82.53	54.99
AB	86.19	68.05	89.18	73.18
BC	86.66	66.92	88.71	71.55
CA	85.78	69.19	87.07	71.03
ABC	**87.86**	**70.76**	89.72	72.82
ABCD	84.47	68.95	**91.32**	**75.56**
ABCE	85.40	68.89	90.35	72.36
ABCDE	84.91	67.98	90.84	74.05

Table 3. Comparison of accuracy and F1-Score results with and without adding pitch-shifted audio samples. Results averaged on five tests (%).

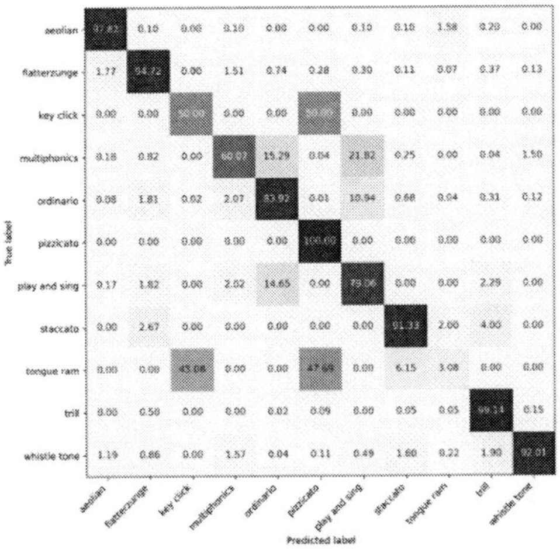

Figure 2. Original audio samples. **ABC** microphones. Confusion matrix averaged on five tests (%).

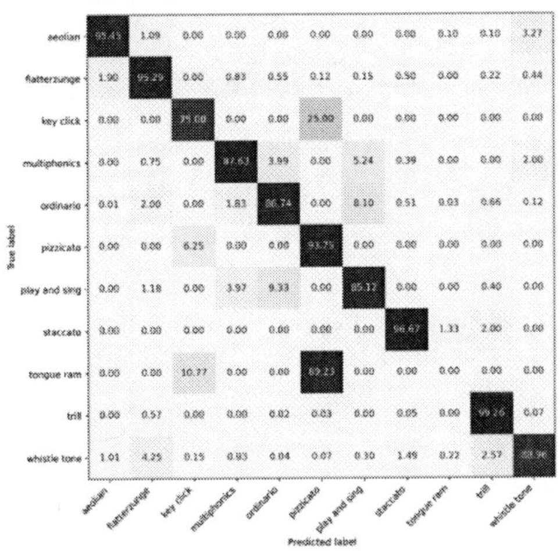

Figure 3. Pitch-shifted audio samples added to original audio samples. **ABCD** microphones. Confusion matrix averaged on five tests (%).

With original audio samples, we measured the highest accuracy and macro F1-Score of 87.86% and 70.76% with the combination of **ABC** microphones. When adding the pitch-shifted audio samples, we measured accuracy and macro F1-Score of 91.32% and 75.56% with the combination of **ABCD** microphones.

4.2 Confusion Matrices

The confusion matrix Figure 2 shows that the majority of playing techniques are well-identified when the classifier is trained with original audio samples. However, the *key click* and the *tongue ram* techniques are misidentified. The confusion matrix Figure 3 shows that the majority of playing techniques are better identified when the classifier is trained with the addition of pitch shifted audio samples.

5. DISCUSSION

We found that the combination of **ABC** microphones gave the best accuracy (87.86%) and macro F1-Score (70.76%) when using original audio data samples. The ambient sound microphones **E**, placed farthest from the source and oriented towards the ceiling, yielded the lowest accuracy and macro F1-Score. This indicates that for the classifier, the acoustic information of the room's natural reverberation is less important than the direct signal. Adding more microphones increased the accuracy by 1.86% and the macro F1-Score by 5.48% compared to the best-performing single microphone **B**. However, using more than three microphones caused drops in accuracy and F1-Score.

Adding pitch-shifted audio samples to the original samples improved accuracy and F1-Score. The best scores were achieved with microphone combination **ABCD**, with an accuracy of 91.39% and macro F1-Score of 75.37%. The lowest accuracy and macro F1-Score were measured with the microphones **E**. Adding microphones improved accuracy by 5.9% and macro F1-Score by 11.54% compared to microphone **B**. Using more than five microphones decreased accuracy and F1-Score.

For a single microphone, the microphone **B** yielded the highest score in both experiments. When included in other datasets, it also yielded high accuracy scores. We think this is likely because the microphone used to record the FullSOL sound bank was placed at a similar distance.

Using more than three microphones in both experiments improved the classifier's generalization ability. However, using more than five microphones degraded performance. We think using more than seven microphones would not enhance the classifier's performance.

The confusion matrices show that *key click* and *tongue ram* techniques are poorly identified when using original audio samples. Using pitch-shifted audio samples improved the accuracy of *key click*, but *tongue ram* remains misidentified. We think leveraging self-supervised learning for general-purpose audio representation systems such as BYOL-A [22, 23] is an approach to consider. The model learns meaningful representations from massive unlabeled audio data using self-supervised learning during pre-training. The variety of internal representations would improve the model's robustness when fine-tuned for a specific task. Further research is required to assess BYOL-A's efficiency in automatically recognizing IPT.

6. CONCLUSION

In this study, we proposed a microphone-based data augmentation method for automatically recognizing instrumental playing techniques (IPTs). We created datasets of audio samples recorded at different distances from the sound source. Training a classifier with these datasets improved its performance, especially with close-to-source microphones and the addition of pitch-shifted audio samples. This method achieved state-of-the-art results with an accuracy score of 91.37% and a macro F1 Score of 75.56% on heterogeneous datasets. Although our study focused on flute IPTs, our method can be applied to other musical instruments as well.

The proposed classifier has shown high performance in most flute playing techniques included in the two experiments. However, the accuracy of short-duration IPTs is low, and adding pitch-shifted audio samples to the original audio samples did not enhance the accuracy. We will address this particular concern in a future study.

Acknowledgments

We want to thank Kanami Koga, the flutist whom we recorded the sound bank. This research is related to ERC Reach Project (GA #883313).

7. REFERENCES

[1] A. Cont, "ANTESCOFO: Anticipatory Synchronization and Control of Interactive Parameters in Computer Music." in *International Computer Music Conference (ICMC)*, 2008, pp. 33–40.

[2] V. Lostanlen, J. Andén, and M. Lagrange, "Extended playing techniques: the next milestone in musical instrument recognition," in *Proceedings of the 5th international conference on digital libraries for musicology*, 2018, pp. 1–10.

[3] J.-F. Ducher and P. Esling, "Folded CQT RCNN for real-time recognition of instrument playing techniques," in *International Society for Music Information Retrieval*, 2019.

[4] N. Brochec and T. Tanaka, "Toward Real-Time Recognition of Instrumental Playing Techniques for Mixed Music: A Preliminary Analysis," in *International Computer Music Conference (ICMC 2023)*, 2023.

[5] J.-F. Ducher and P. Esling, "Apprentissage profond pour la reconnaissance en temps réel des modes de jeu instrumentaux," in *Journées d'Informatique Musicale*, 2019.

[6] A. Martelloni, A. P. McPherson, and M. Barthet, "Real-time Percussive Technique Recognition and Embedding Learning for the Acoustic Guitar," *arXiv preprint arXiv:2307.07426*, 2023.

[7] N. H. Fletcher and T. D. Rossing, *The physics of musical instruments*. Springer Science & Business Media, 2012.

[8] P.-Y. Artaud and G. Geay, *Flûtes au présent: traité des techniques contemporaines sur les flûtes traversières à l'usage des compositeurs et des flutistes*. Editions Jobert & Editions musicales transatlantiques, 1980.

[9] C. Levine and C. Mitropoulos-Bott, *The Techniques of Flute Playing I/Die Spieltechnik der Flöte I*. Bärenreiter-Verlag, 2019.

[10] C. E. Cella, D. Ghisi, V. Lostanlen, F. Lévy, J. Fineberg, and Y. Maresz, "OrchideaSOL: a dataset of extended instrumental techniques for computer-aided orchestration," *arXiv preprint arXiv:2007.00763*, 2020.

[11] N. Brochec and W. Howie, "GFDatabase: A Database of Flute Playing Techniques," Apr. 2024. [Online]. Available: https://doi.org/10.5281/zenodo.10932398

[12] V. Lostanlen and C.-E. Cella, "Deep convolutional networks on the pitch spiral for musical instrument recognition," *arXiv preprint arXiv:1605.06644*, 2016.

[13] Y. Han, J. Kim, and K. Lee, "Deep convolutional neural networks for predominant instrument recognition in polyphonic music," *IEEE/ACM Transactions on Audio, Speech, and Language Processing*, vol. 25, no. 1, pp. 208–221, 2016.

[14] T. Park and T. Lee, "Musical instrument sound classification with deep convolutional neural network using feature fusion approach," *arXiv preprint arXiv:1512.07370*, 2015.

[15] P. Li, J. Qian, and T. Wang, "Automatic instrument recognition in polyphonic music using convolutional neural networks," *arXiv preprint arXiv:1511.05520*, 2015.

[16] M. Blaszke and B. Kostek, "Musical instrument identification using deep learning approach," *Sensors*, vol. 22, no. 8, p. 3033, 2022.

[17] S. Ioffe and C. Szegedy, "Batch normalization: Accelerating deep network training by reducing internal covariate shift," in *International conference on machine learning*. pmlr, 2015, pp. 448–456.

[18] N. Srivastava, G. Hinton, A. Krizhevsky, I. Sutskever, and R. Salakhutdinov, "Dropout: a simple way to prevent neural networks from overfitting," *The journal of machine learning research*, vol. 15, no. 1, pp. 1929–1958, 2014.

[19] X. Glorot and Y. Bengio, "Understanding the difficulty of training deep feedforward neural networks," in *Proceedings of the thirteenth international conference on artificial intelligence and statistics*. JMLR Workshop and Conference Proceedings, 2010, pp. 249–256.

[20] S. Wei, S. Zou, F. Liao *et al.*, "A comparison on data augmentation methods based on deep learning for audio classification," in *Journal of physics: Conference series*, vol. 1453, no. 1. IOP Publishing, 2020, p. 012085.

[21] M. Grandini, E. Bagli, and G. Visani, "Metrics for multi-class classification: an overview," *arXiv preprint arXiv:2008.05756*, 2020.

[22] D. Niizumi, D. Takeuchi, Y. Ohishi, N. Harada, and K. Kashino, "Byol for audio: Self-supervised learning for general-purpose audio representation," in *2021 International Joint Conference on Neural Networks (IJCNN)*. IEEE, 2021, pp. 1–8.

[23] ——, "BYOL for audio: Exploring pre-trained general-purpose audio representations," *IEEE/ACM Transactions on Audio, Speech, and Language Processing*, vol. 31, pp. 137–151, 2022.

This page intentionally left blank.

A Switching Beat-Following Algorithm for Interactive Conducting Systems

Zengguang Wu
Deakin University
s224053735@deakin.edu.au

William Raffe
Deakin University
william.raffe@deakin.edu.au

Michael Hobbs
Deakin University
m.hobbs@deakin.edu.au

ABSTRACT

An interactive conducting system takes the role of an orchestra, and provides the user with a conducting experience. The beat-tracking and music-playing components of conducting systems have been well developed, but the beat-following algorithm still has room for improvement. Through a survey of past and present beat-following algorithms, we found a necessity for the algorithm to be able to handle different musical situations and user preferences. To address this issue, we developed a mobile conducting app with a novel beat-following algorithm, which can switch between different behaviours to accommodate those differences. To show its capability, we put it into action, and performed some excerpts from the orchestral repertoire.

1. INTRODUCTION: Interactive Conducting Systems

Conducting an orchestra had been a privilege reserved for professional conductors, until we got interactive conducting systems. A conducting system takes the role of an orchestra, and provides the user with a conducting experience.

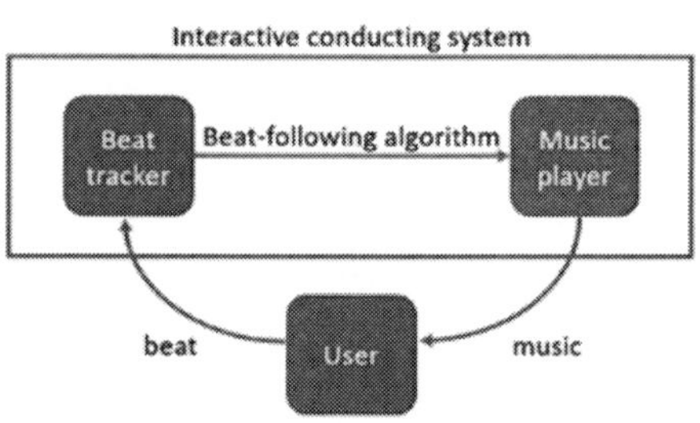

Figure 1. The structure of an interactive conducting system

A typical conducting system has three major components (Figure 1): a beat tracker that takes the user's gestures, a music player that plays the music, and a series of mappings from features of the gestures to elements of the music. Of these mappings, the one involving time is of great importance. It determines how the music follows the user's beats, and has been referred to as the beat-following algorithm [1].

Conducting systems have been seen in the forms of mobile apps [2, 3], computer programs [4, 5] and multimedia installations [6, 7], and have been thoroughly researched by scholars [8]. Arguably, the beat-tracking and music-playing components, thanks to their respective connections to the mature areas of pattern recognition and audio processing, have been well developed; but, the beat-following algorithm, a seemingly simple part, has not drawn enough attention, and still has room for improvement.

2. BACKGROUND: Beat-Following Algorithms

What makes a good beat-following algorithm? On the one hand, it should be stable, and play music smoothly; on the other hand, it should be flexible, and provide a good response to the user. Between these two aspects, there is an apparent dilemma, forcing the algorithm to focus on one aspect or the other.

2.1 Algorithms

There is a **responsive algorithm** used by some mobile conducting apps [2]. At the start of a piece, the user gives two beats. The music starts playing at the user's second beat, and at the tempo indicated by the time between the two beats. After the start, the music still follows the user closely. (Figure 2)

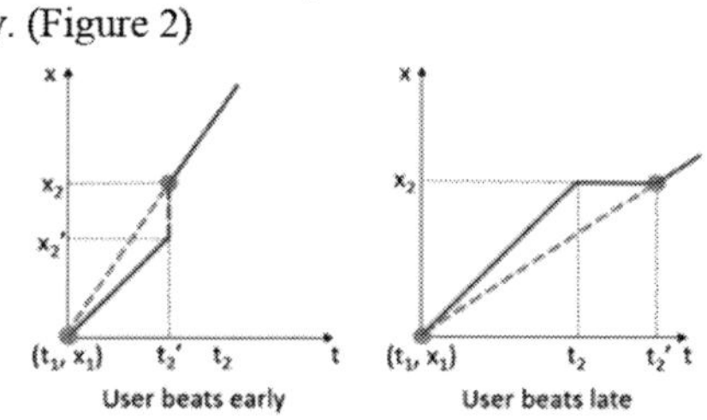

Figure 2. The responsive algorithm

In these position-time graphs, the horizontal t-axis is the real time, and the vertical x-axis is the position in the MIDI file. On the graph, each orange dot is a beat from the user, and the blue line is the system's position in the music file. The tempo of the music is the slope of this blue line, with a steep slope indicating a fast tempo. As shown, when the user beats early, the music chases the user by skipping to the corresponding beat; when the user beats late, the music waits for the user by staying at a position just before the beat. In both cases, a new tempo is calculated from the time between the last two beats from the user. This algorithm provides a good response to the user, but at the price of the continuity of the music.

In contrast, there is also a **smooth algorithm** [3] that maintains the continuity of the music. Here, once the music starts, it plays by itself without waiting for or chasing the user. Every time the system receives a beat from the user, it sets the tempo of the music to the average rate of the user's last several beats. This algorithm keeps the music smooth, but may lose contact with the user. For example, suppose the user wants to speed up, and starts beating quicker. Because of the averaging, after several beats, each beat from the user will be much earlier than the corresponding beat in the music, and this correspondence will be broken. The music will no longer respond to the user's individual beats, and the conducting experience will be compromised.

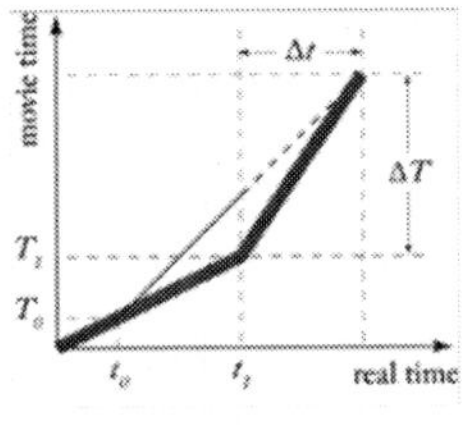

Figure 3. A mixed algorithm [1]

Lee et al.'s [1] beat-following algorithm (Figure 3) can be seen as a mix of the above two core ones. When the user beats early, the system chases the user as in the responsive algorithm, but in a slightly different way. Instead of skipping to the current beat and catching up with the user instantly, it changes to a tempo faster than the user's new tempo, catches up with them at the next beat, and then plays on at the user's new tempo. This algorithm provides a balance between stability and flexibility, but does not solve the dilemma in between.

The Live Tempo feature of Avid Sibelius [4] has a similar algorithm with an extra "sensitivity" slider, which allows the user to adjust the weighting between smoothness and responsiveness. However, this slider sits in a dialog; during the performance, this setting cannot be changed, and remains the same for all beats in the piece.

2.2 Discussion

Dannenberg and Bookstein [5] provided a total of 13 "hints" for a proper interactive conducting system. (Table 1) Many of these hints deal with the beat-following algorithm, and some will be reflected later in our own implementation. For example, they found it necessary for there to be some information in addition to the music itself to help the user control the system, and suggested a "conductor's part" (Hint 1). For another example, they "found a conflict between the necessity for fine control of tempo in the slow, expressive passages, and the necessity in very rhythmically stable passages for the computer to be less sensitive". They suggested disabling conducting in some sections (Hint 2) and implementing some other functions for the user to change the tempo (Hint 4).

Not only can different passages have different characters, but even within a single passage, different beats can also have different natures. Because of musical phrasing, some beats are to be played exactly on time, while some other beats allow a certain degree of variation.

To help the algorithm follow the user better in different musical situations, Baba et al. [6] made use of expressive templates. A template contains tempo information extracted from existing recordings of a piece, and is a "standard" interpretation of the piece. In their system, the tempo of the music depends not only on the user's beats, but also on the tempo variation in the template. Their conducting system was successful, but when an expert conductor performed an excerpt from Tchaikovsky's Sixth Symphony, his tempo intention was significantly different from the template, and it did not work very well.

Whereas the previous issue was with a user with too much musical proficiency, Lee et al. [7] faced the opposite problem. When developing a conducting system for young children, they noticed the unreliability of their gestures. To address this, they adjusted their approach, and associated the tempo directly with the speed of the user's gesture. This approach worked well for the children, but not surprisingly, professional conductors were not satisfied.

To summarise, music passages and beats can have different characters and natures, and users can have different proficiency levels and preferences. In order for an interactive conducting system to embrace all pieces and users, its beat-following algorithm needs to accommodate all these differences. The algorithms mentioned above each have their own advantages, but none of them can do a decent job on their own.

#	Hint	Flexible/Stable
1	The score must contain a carefully constructed conductor's part (do not assume a conducted beat on every quarter note).	Flexible
2	Conducting should be disabled in some sections.	Stable
4	Provide tempo increment and decrement functions.	Flexible
5	Provide a sequence mode that plays the score without conducting input.	Flexible
6	Anticipate the conductor by compiling tempo changes.	Flexible
7	Implement a command that sets the tempo to a predefined value.	Flexible
8	Maintain compatibility with standard formats.	Stable
9	Tempo averaging is important.	Stable
10	Limit the sensitivity of the system to conducted tempo change.	Stable
11	Limit how far the performance can lead the conductor.	Stable
12	Various recovery strategies can avoid unnatural performances.	Stable
13	Facilities to support rehearsal are critical.	Flexible

Table 1. Dannenberg and Bookstein's "hints" for interactive conducting systems

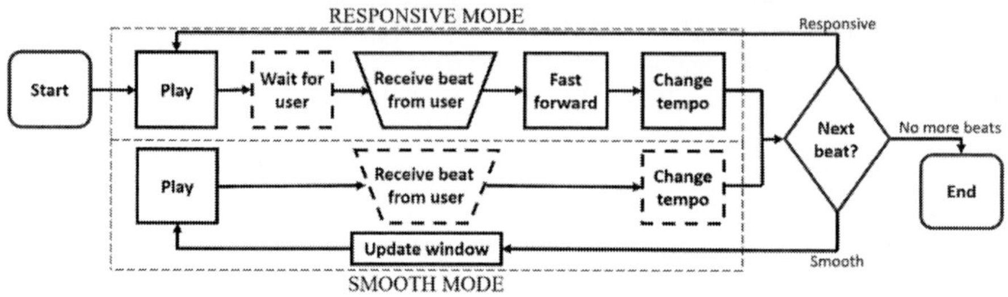

Figure 4. The switching beat-following algorithm

3. IMPLEMENTATION: A Switching Beat-Following Algorithm

Our implementation is an iOS conducting app equipped with a switching beat-following algorithm. The app gets the user's beats with the iPhone's built-in gyroscope, and plays MIDI files with the system's own MIDI player. The main innovation is the beat-following algorithm, which can switch between different behaviours to accommodate different musical situations and user preferences.

3.1 The Switching

In the sense of Dannenberg and Bookstein's "conductor's part", together with each MIDI file, there is a text file specifying the settings for each beat. According to the setting, the algorithm can switch between two modes: a responsive mode and a smooth mode. (Figure 4) The responsive mode behaves in the same manner as the responsive algorithm mentioned earlier. It follows the user closely, and can chase or wait for the user when necessary. The user's beats are compulsory, and the music will only play on if the user gives beats. The smooth mode is like the aforementioned smooth algorithm, but with significant differences.

3.2 The Smooth Mode

Like the smooth algorithm, the smooth mode maintains the continuity of the music, and there is no chasing or waiting. The user's beats are optional, and the music will play on whether the user beats or not. But, unlike the smooth algorithm, here each beat from the user corresponds to a beat in the music. For each beat in the music, there is a time window of ±0.25 beats for the user to give the corresponding beat, meaning they can be early or late by at most a quarter beat. When a beat is received outside the windows, it can be ambiguous. For example, if a beat falls halfway between beats 1 and 2, the system would not be able to tell whether it is beat 1 late by half a beat or beat 2 early by half a beat. Therefore, beats received outside the windows are ignored by the system, and have no impact on the music.

Also different from the smooth algorithm, the new tempo is based on whether, and to what extent, the user's beat is earlier or later than the corresponding beat in the music.

Figure 5. The conducting scene

Suppose the previous beat of the music was at time t_0, the current beat is expected at time t, and the user's beat is received at time t'. First, we calculate the user's intended duration change c as the ratio between the new beat duration $t'-t_0$ and the old beat duration $t-t_0$:

$$c = \frac{t'-t_0}{t-t_0} \quad (1)$$

Then, we modify c by the following formula:

$$c' = \frac{c+m}{1+m} \quad (2)$$

m is a modifier that indicates the system's resistance to tempo change. A positive m would shrink the change and stabilise the tempo; the larger the m, the stronger the effect; an m between 0 and -1 would magnify the change, and is reserved for some special cases. Finally, we multiply the old tempo v by the reciprocal of the duration change, which is the tempo change, $1/c'$, and get the new tempo v':

$$v' = \frac{v}{c'} \quad (3)$$

As an integral part of the switching beat-following algorithm, this smooth mode is slightly different from some of the hints, but works to the same effects. Tempo control (Hint 4) requires nothing more than beats from the user, and can be limited (Hint 10) by setting m large, or disabled (Hint 2) by setting m even larger.

3.3 The User Interface

Although each MIDI file comes with a text file containing the default settings, these settings can be adjusted via the user interface, which serves as a rehearsing facility (Hint 13). The user interface of the app contains a few setting scenes and a conducting scene, which is designed to initiate conducting and then not be looked at while the user moves their phone through traditional conducting gestures. In the conducting scene (Figure 5), the user can navigate through the beats and adjust the settings before conducting the piece, choosing between smooth and responsive modes. During the conducting, if they find a certain setting not to their taste, they can pause the music, change the setting, and pick up from a point of their choice. In a separate scene, they can also change the settings on a global scale by setting all beats to a certain mode or restoring them to default.

4. THE ALGORITHM IN ACTION

The novel beat-following algorithm is yet to be formally tested. To show its capability, we put it into action, and performed some musical excerpts that have been motivating the algorithm to some degree. As mentioned above, in a passage of music, different beats can have different natures. A good example is the famous opening of Beethoven's Fifth Symphony (Figure 6).

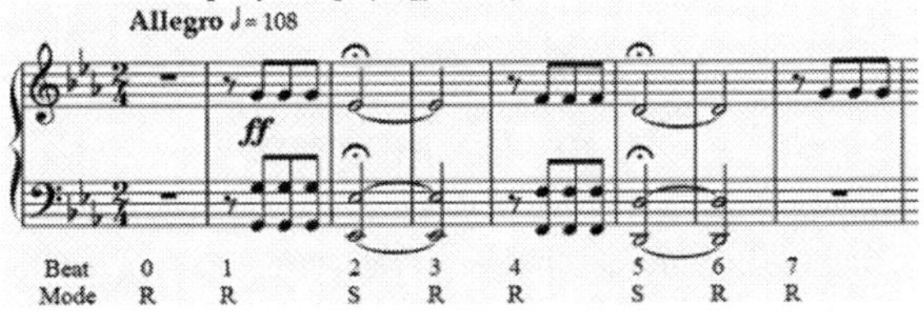

Figure 6. Beethoven: Symphony No. 5 (excerpt) [9]

As in real-world conducting, at the start of a piece, the conductor gives two beats (0-1); the orchestra starts playing at the conductor's second beat, and at the tempo indicated by the time between these beats. The system is supposed to follow these beats closely, and is therefore set to the responsive mode. On beat 2 sits the fourth note of the "fate" motif. Playing it early or beat would upset the rhythm, so a beat or late beat from the user is likely an imperfection rather than an intention. So, at this beat, to prevent the system from chasing or waiting for the user, and keep the music flowing, we set the system to the smooth mode. The situation after a fermata is the same as the start, so beats 3-4 & 6-7 are similar to beats 0-1, and also set to the responsive mode. The situation at beat 5 is exactly the same as at beat 2, and therefore also set to the smooth mode.

Whereas the previous example showcases the system's capability to accommodate beats of different natures, passages of different characters can also be handled well with the proper settings. Figure 7 is an excerpt from the fourth movement of Brahms's First Symphony. The first four bars, populated with a fast three-note phrase derived from the main theme of the movement, is a typical "rhythmically stable passage" in the words of Dannenberg and Bookstein, and requires the smooth mode. At beat 9, the music takes a dramatic turn, and recalls a chorale theme from the movement's introduction. This passage, consisting of a series of long chords, invites the conductor to do whatever they want with the tempo, and calls for the responsive mode.

Also in the finale of Brahms 1, and not far from the above excerpt, there is a long accelerando, where we can see our smooth mode in action with the music's tempo being "dragged" by the user's beats. Putting them together, we performed the last 2 minutes of Brahms' First Symphony with our app: https://www.youtube.com/@wab108

5. FINAL REMARKS

In this paper, we took a look at the beat-following algorithms of past and present interactive conducting systems; we implemented a novel algorithm that can switch between different behaviours to accommodate different musical situations and user preferences; we put the algorithm into action, and performed some excerpts from the orchestral repertoire.

We have been aware of some limitations of the current system. When the user waves the phone, they cannot see the screen display. To fix this, we are currently developing a desktop conducting app with the smartphone as a controller. Also, it might not be comfortable for a conductor to hold a smartphone, so we have been considering some alternatives, such as smartwatches.

With this paper, we want to draw some attention to the beat-following algorithms, a relatively overlooked component of interactive conducting systems. We believe with better beat-following algorithms, conducting systems can do a great job for both educational and entertaining purposes. We hope with better conducting systems, more people will be able to make their own interpretation of classic orchestral works, and such experiences will enhance their appreciation of both orchestral music, as well as conducting as an integral element of orchestral performance.

6. REFERENCES

[1] E. Lee, T. Karrer, and J. Borchers, Toward a framework for interactive systems to conduct digital audio and video streams. Computer Music Journal, 30(1), 21-36, 2006.

[2] Hello Design, Bravo Gustavo, mobile app, 2009.

[3] Micro App Brewery, Air Conductor, mobile app, 2019.

[4] Avid Technology, Sibelius, computer program: the Live Tempo feature, 2024.

[5] R. Dannenberg, and K. Bookstein, Practical aspects of a midi conducting program. ICMC 1991.

[6] T. Baba, M. Hashida, and H. Katayose, "VirtualPhilharmony": A Conducting System with Heuristics of Conducting an Orchestra. NIME 2010.

[7] E. Lee, T. M. Nakra, and J. Borchers, You're the conductor: a realistic interactive conducting system for children. NIME 2004.

[8] K. Lee, M. J. Junokas, and G. E. Garnett, A Review of Interactive Conducting Systems: 1970-2015. ICMC 2016.

[9] L. Beethoven, Symphony No. 5 in C minor, op. 67, 1808.

[10] J. Brahms, Symphony No. 1 in C minor, op. 68, 1876.

Figure 7. Brahms: Symphony No. 1 (excerpt) [10]

GB-ABBX : A Framework for Enhancing Beatbox Performance Using Gesture Sensing

Kento Otani
Kwansei Gakuin University
gwm00491@kwansei.ac.jp

Mitsuyo Hashida
The University of Fukuchiyama
hashida-mitsuyo@fukuchiyama.ac.jp

Haruhiro Katayose
Kwansei Gakuin University
katayose@kwansei.ac.jp

ABSTRACT

Human beatbox is a musical performance technique that uses the human vocal organs to generate percussive sounds, beats, rhythms, melodies, and various other sounds. Recently, advanced techniques and unique styles employing sound effects have been developed, and competitions have also been organized. We have been working on extending beatbox performances by applying IT technology. This study specifically demonstrates the technical configuration for extending beatbox performances using gesture sensing and presents a musical work created for this technology.

1. INTRODUCTION

Human beatbox is a musical technique that transforms the human vocal tract into a variety of percussion instruments, and it has evolved significantly since its inception in the 1970s. Originating to complement the early hip-hop music, human beatbox has established its status as an independent performance art that transcends cultural and geographical barriers. Today, professional beatboxers exist worldwide, and global competitions that attract large audiences are held annually.

A notable competition in human beatbox is Grand Beatbox Battle (GBB), which features several categories. In Producer Showcase category, performers are allowed to use not only hardware such as loopers, effectors, and MIDI controllers, but also software such as DAWs, and are allowed to use the performer's voice as a sound trigger. This format corresponds to what is referred to as live electronics in the context of computer music. Live electronics, a music form that has grown since the 1960s, has seen various experiments and technological advancements [1] [2], yet the intersection with beatbox performance has been limited.

Therefore, this study proposes the GB-ABBX (Gesture-Based Augmented Beatbox) system, which enables musical control in live electronics using beatbox through pose gestures, and aims to create new points of intersection between beatbox performance and live electronics by producing musical works using this system.

2. HUMAN BEATBOX

Human beatbox [3] [4] is a form of music that involves using the human speech organs, such as the mouth, tongue, throat, and lips, to mimic various sounds. It is used both as a part of creating musical rhythms and as a standalone performance technique, as shown in Figure 1 [5] [6] [7] [8]. This technique enhances the diversity of music and enables new musical expressions.

(a) Solo Beatbox **(b)** Solo Battle **(c)** Tagteam **(d)** Loopstation

Figure 1: Scenes of beatbox performance

The origins of human beatbox can be traced back to the 1970s American hip-hop scene, particularly in New York. Originally, the term "beatbox" referred to a device designed to automatically play rhythm patterns. However, these devices were expensive, and DJs and MCs who could not afford them began using their oral cavities to create music rhythms. Thus, human beatbox emerged as a new method for creating music rhythms and as an improvisational performance in situations where instruments were not available. It developed as part of hip-hop culture and spread worldwide.

Human beatbox has evolved significantly from its origins. While early human beatbox focused primarily on mimicking simple rhythms and beats, over time, it has become capable of imitating more complex rhythms and timbres. Furthermore, advancements in technology have further evolved human beatbox performances, allowing for the use of electronic devices such as loopers and effect pedals, as well as software like DAWs, to enable more diverse and rich musical expressions. Looper, as the name suggests, are electronic devices that can record and loop playback of sounds input through microphones or instruments, and some models can apply effects processing to the input or track sounds. In particular, the loopstation series manufactured by BOSS, especially the "RC-505" (Figure 2 [9]), is commonly used in beatbox performances and competitions. These advancements have made human beatbox a platform for exploring new realms of music, expanding its possibilities. Competitions have also evolved from initially only having solo categories with a microphone to now including various categories such as tag team divisions for pairs, crew divisions for groups of four to five people, and loopstation categories utilizing loopstation.

Figure 2: RC-505mkII (New version of RC-505). The five round buttons at the bottom of the device serve as tracks, and by pressing these buttons, audio can be recorded and looped for playback. The A, B, C, and D buttons at the upper left/right of the device can be pressed to use input/track sound effects.

3. GB-ABBX: OVERVIEW

In live electronic music, performers use gestures to transform and develop musical performances in real-time. Here, the term "gesture" includes not only so-called motion gestures but also acoustic features, or acoustic gestures, and various methods have been considered [10] [11].

As mentioned in Chapter 2, the range of musical expressions has expanded through the combination of beatbox with various musical instruments and software. However, there are still some drawbacks at the stage of sound production and during live performances. For example, when controlling sound with equipment, one limitation is that the parameters of built-in effects can only be adjusted by physically touching the equipment. This means that the number of controllers needed increases with the number of required sound controls, leading to complexity in mapping and an increased rate of performance failures due to operational errors. Additionally, the number of controllers, such as buttons and pedals, is limited by the equipment, thus limiting the methods and number of parameter controls. Therefore, it is considered that beatbox performances require further support through IT technology. This study aims to solve these problems and further enhance musical expression by integrating the use of both acoustic and motion gestures, utilizing triggers from diverse gestures and mapping, and integrating sound and video processing in current beatbox performances.

Furthermore, from the perspective of competition rules in beatbox, it's clear that entirely new IT technology supports that do not exceed the scope of the rules are possible. For example, rule number 5 of the GBB's Producer Showcase Wildcard (video qualification) [12] states "All sounds must be sourced or triggered by the mouth." However, there is no rule mentioning that a microphone must be used to generate sound, so theoretically, generating sound through image processing of the mouth captured by a camera would not be considered a violation under the current rules. Thus, pursuing IT technology supports that are not regulated by the current rules could enable innovative beatbox performances in current competitions.

GB-ABBX is a system that allows for the control of sounds generated by beatbox through pose gestures captured by a camera. This enables parameter manipulation without directly touching musical equipment, allowing for more flexible and diverse sound control. This study aims to enable various sound controls for beatbox through the movements of different parts of the hands and face. The system diagram is shown in Figure 3.

Currently, there are three main modes of sound control in GB-ABBX, which can be switched during the performance through key operations. The first mode is "Volume Synth", where the synthesizer is triggered when the mouth opens beyond a certain point, and the volume of the synthesizer can be controlled by the Y-coordinate (vertical position) of the left wrist. The second mode is "Formant Synth", which uses multiple parameters related to the mouth to determine its shape and simultaneously applies four band-pass filters to the synthesizer, altering the formant to match the vowel corresponding to the mouth shape. Notably, the trigger for the synthesizer in this control is done through input from the microphone. The third mode is "Drum Machine', where performing specific hand gestures triggers the corresponding drum sounds, which are then quantized to match the tempo and beat of the song. This allows for the correct placement of drums in the song using only hand gestures.

4. IMPLEMENTATION

For the implementation of GB-ABBX, Mediapipe and Max were used. Mediapipe [13] is an open-source machine learning library developed by Google, used in this study to extract gesture information from video data obtained via a webcam. Additionally, Max, developed by Cycling '74, is a graphical integrated development environment for music and multimedia. In this study, it is used to receive gesture information output by Mediapipe and to perform corresponding controls as musical parameters.

In GB-ABBX, it is possible to perform various types of controls by changing the recognized pose gestures and the parameters assigned to them. Currently, three main types of gesture recognition by Mediapipe are used. The first is "Handpose", which measures the coordinates of each landmark on the user's left and right hands in the camera's video. The second is "Hand Gesture Recognition", which detects hand gestures of the user's left and right hands. The detectable gesture labels include "Closed_Fist", "Open_Palm", "Pointing_Up," "Thumb_Down", "Thumb_Up", "Victory", and "ILoveYou". The third is "Face Landmarker," which measures the coordinates of facial parts such as the lips and eyes, to calculate numerically the degree of mouth opening vertically and horizontally, and the movement of the eyes, among others. The correspondence between these three sound control modes and the gesture recognition technologies introduced in Chapter 3 is as follows: "Volume Synth" uses "Handpose" and "Face Landmarker", "Formant Synth"

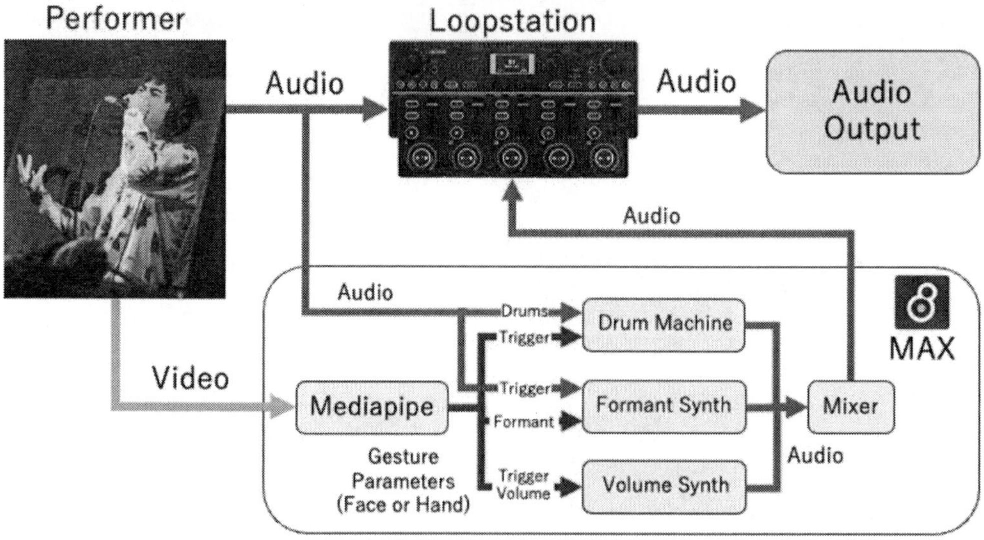

Figure 3: System diagram of GB-ABBX. The blue arrows represent audio, the green arrows represent video, and the red arrows represent hand/face gesture information extracted by Mediapipe.

uses “Face Landmarker”, and “Drum Machine” uses “Hand Gesture Recognition”.

5. EXAMPLE OF BEATBOX MUSIC CREATED FOR GB-ABBX “ IT ’ S THE LIGHT ”

A musical work titled “It's The Light” was created for GB-ABBX. In “It's The Light”, the word “Light” is imagined as hope residing in people's hearts. While weaving the words “It's The Light” repeatedly, the music plays a bright yet ephemeral tune, embodying the wish not to forget the light within the heart and to find a new light in a heart where the light has faded. Moreover, this musical work exclusively utilizes vocals produced through live electronics with beatbox, thereby adhering to the rules of the GBB's Producer category mentioned earlier.

The devices used and their signal flow for the creation of this work are shown in Figure 4.

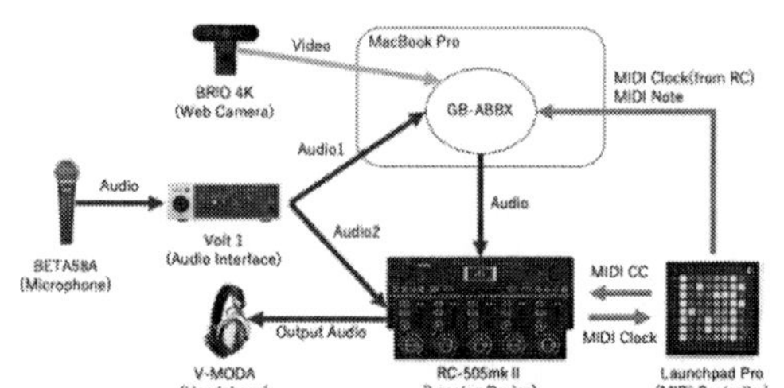

Figure 4: Devices used in “It's The Light” and their signal flow. The blue arrows represent audio, the green arrows represent video, and the orange arrows represent MIDI information.

First, sounds such as beatbox and vocals are input through the "BETA58A" microphone and output to the "Volt 1" audio interface. From there, sounds requiring GB-ABBX processing are output to the GB-ABBX Max patch on the “MacBook Pro” for corresponding audio processing and then output to the looping device “RC-505mkII”, while sounds not requiring GB-ABBX processing are directly output to the “RC-505mkII”. In this work, all sounds except for vocals are output through GB-ABBX. The “RC-505mkII” plays a crucial role in increasing the number of sounds by recording the input sounds onto tracks and adding variation to the song by applying built-in sound effects to the input and track sounds. The MIDI controller “Launchpad Pro MK3” is used for MIDI CC parameter control within the “RC-505mkII” and for playing the oscillator built into the GB-ABBX Max patch with a MIDI Note sequencer. It also serves the role of synchronizing the tempo of the “RC-505mkII” with the Max patch via MIDI Clock for “Drum Machine”. The webcam “BRIO 4K” is used to send the performer's camera information to Mediapipe, which is loaded in the Max patch.

In the application of GB-ABBX within this work, “Volume Synth” is first used for two types of sub-melodies added within the drop, with the second melody expressing an effect similar to slow gear by gradually raising the left hand from bottom to top. Next, “Formant Synth” is used for the chord synthesizer played at the beginning of the song, changing the formant of the synthesizer in the same way by changing the shape of the mouth in the order of “a”, “o”, and “u”. Lastly, “Drums Trigger” is used for various sounds including the drum parts and pluck sounds of the song, with the left hand's “Thumb_Up” triggering the kick, “Pointing_Up” triggering the hi-hat, the right hand's “Open_Palm” triggering the snare, and “Pointing_Up” triggering the shaker. Additionally, the pluck sound is realized by applying a very short delay effect to the kick sound.

The screen capture of the Max patch when playing “It's The Light” is shown in Figure 5.

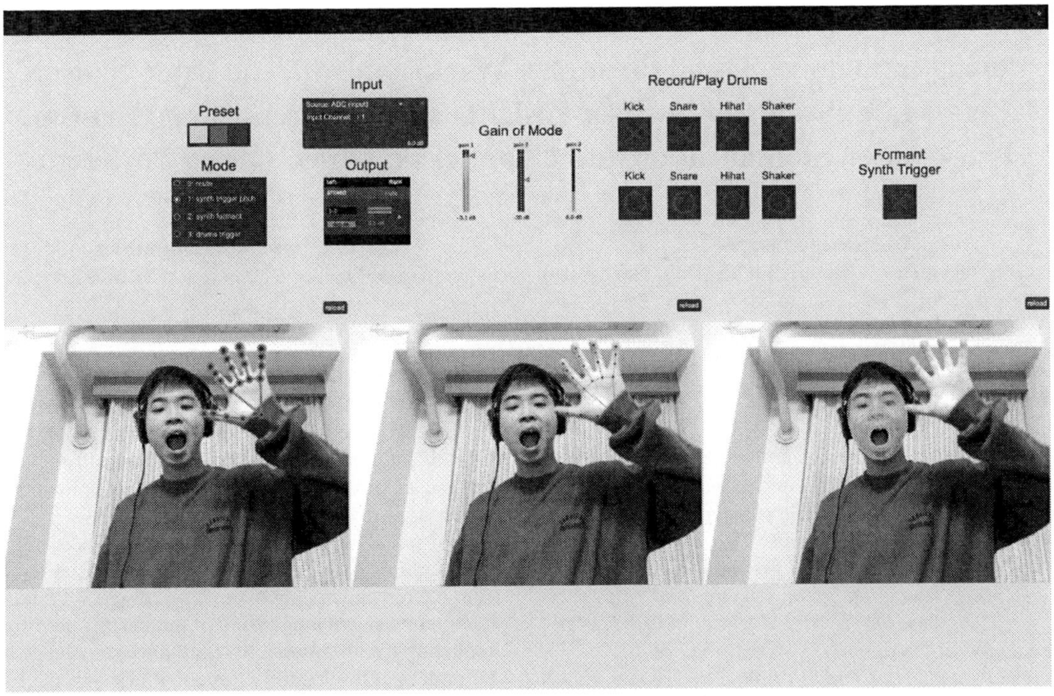

Figure 5: Screen capture of the Max patch during performance. 3 camera images show, from left to right: "Handpose", "Hand Gesture Recognition", and "Face Landmaker" measurement previews.

6. CONCLUDING REMARKS

In this study, we proposed the GB-ABBX system, which enables musical control through pose gestures, and used this system to produce musical works with live electronics via beatbox.

As future work, we consider implementing mechanisms for coordinating with machine learning software such as Wekinator for musical control and for creating visual expressions corresponding to pose gestures.

7. REFERENCES

[1] P. Cook, "Principles for Designing Computer Music Controllers," in *Proceedings of the CHI'01 Workshop on New Interfaces for Musical Expression (NIME-01)*, Seattle, USA, 2001.

[2] D. Morrill and P. R. Cook, "Hardware, Software, and Compositional Tools for a Real Time Improvised Solo Trumpet Work," in *Proceedings of the International Computer Music Conference, (ICMC)*, Aug. 1989.

[3] A. Kuch and I. Tedjasukmana, *Beatbox Complete. English Edition: Sounds, Patterns, Styles*. HELBLING Publishing, 2014.

[4] H. Yates. Shooting From the Lip: A Brief History of Beatboxing. Roland Corporation. [Online]. Available: https://articles.boss.info/shooting-from-the-lip-a-brief-history-of-beatboxing/

[5] LurningCurve. Helium — HUMAN BEATBOX. HUMAN BEATBOX. [Online]. Available: https://www.humanbeatbox.com/beatboxers/helium/

[6] Dutch Beatbox Battle - Official Website. DUTCH BEATBOX BATTLE. [Online]. Available: http://www.dutchbeatboxbattle.nl

[7] JPN CUP ALL STAR BEATBOX BATTLE. M-Plus. [Online]. Available: https://www.jpncup-beatbox.com

[8] A. Rosenschein. BOSS x SBX: Creating " Walk " with Saro. Roland Corporation. [Online]. Available: https://articles.boss.info/boss-x-sbx-creating-walk-with-saro/

[9] BOSS - Loop Station. Roland Corporation. [Online]. Available: https://www.boss.info/jp/categories/loop_station/

[10] F. Visi, R. Schramm, and E. Miranda, "Use of Body Motion to Enhance Traditional Musical Instruments: A Multimodal Embodied Approach to Gesture Mapping , Composition and Performance," in *Proceedings of the International Conference on New Interfaces for Musical Expression(NIME)*, Jul. 2014.

[11] alex nowitz. gesture-controlled live electronics. [Online]. Available: https://nowitz.de/gesture-controlled-live-electronics

[12] Kilaa. GBB 2024 Wildcard Competition Rules and Application. Swissbeatbox. [Online]. Available: https://swissbeatbox.com/newsfeed/gbb-2024-wildcard-competition-rules-and-application/

[13] C. Lugaresi *et al.*, "MediaPipe: A Framework for Building Perception Pipelines," Jun. 2019.

Exploring Immersive Sound through a Workshop with the Open Source Tool Live 4 Life: Summary of User Insights and Preferences on Event vs. Track-based Spatialization and Channel vs. Object-based Paradigms

Christophe Lengelé
Université du Québec à Montréal (CIRMMT, Hexagram)
christophe.lengele@yahoo.fr

Philippe-Aubert Gauthier
Université du Québec à Montréal (CIRMMT, Hexagram)
gauthier.philippe-aubert@uqam.ca

ABSTRACT

Live 4 Life, an open-source spatial performance tool developed in SuperCollider, features an 8-track interactive sequencer with pre-defined spatial trajectories, algorithms and a multichannel effects system. This tool emphasizes discrete finite event-based spatialization, blending channel- and object-based paradigms, for synchronized control of time (tempo, rhythm, duration) and space, in order to articulate temporal distribution of spatialized events.

This paper summarizes findings from a survey integrated within a workshop, evaluating the tool's practical use. It investigates participants' preferences in spatialization systems (event vs. track) and paradigms (channel vs. object), alongside their perceptual preferences for specific spatial models. The outcomes indicate that event- and channel-based spatialization should be more prominently considered, especially in rhythmic contexts. This finding confronts the industry's prevailing trend and standardization towards track- and object-based approaches, suggesting a potential shift in spatial sound practices.

1. INTRODUCTION

Initiated in 2011, *Live 4 Life* is an interactive spatial performance tool crafted to enhance the creation and real-time control of masses of spatialized sound objects in diverse loudspeaker configurations, such as stereo, quadraphonic, octophonic, or dome setups. This tool embracing the philosophy of playing the place and the music at the same time, is not just about spatialization; it's a comprehensive sound creation system to play with sequences of parameters (divided in three main categories: rhythm, sound and space), integrating spatialization at the heart of each sound synthesis and loudspeaker. This tool's holistic approach was presented at the ICMC conference [1], providing an overview and categorization of various spatial composition techniques (abstract/concrete). The compositional architecture of the tool, as detailed in the 2021 ICMC proceedings [2], demonstrates the integration of patterns and value series from different modules to define spatialized sound events. Additionally, an article in Organised Sound highlights *Live 4 Life*'s improvisational capabilities through interfaces like the GUI, the keyboard, and MIDI/OSC controllers, integrating insights and examples from actual performances to demonstrate its practical application in live settings [3].

This spatial research, which questions ways of associating rhythmic and spatial parameters, is based on the concept of free and open works, advocating for both improvisational form and the sharing of the open-source codebase, reflecting a commitment to communal knowledge and collaboration. Developed in SuperCollider [4], the tool's innovative design architecture includes a layer- and event-based spatialization. This design allows sequences of spatialized sound particles or choruses (copies or echoes of the same event with micro-delays or spectral/spatial variations) to meet a multichannel effect system, creating an immersive environment for sound exploration.

Distributed as an open-source project on Github [1] in 2022, *Live 4 Life* is a long-term dream against capitalism and loneliness. It embodies a vision that tries to break free from commercial limitations, fostering a truly open and free community within the spatial sound performance domain. Expanding on this concept, the next logical steps involve developing and conducting workshops. These workshops are designed not only to disseminate and teach the usage of the tool but also to study user preferences and interactions, thus refining *Live 4 Life*'s capabilities in response to real-world user feedback and needs. The detailed results of this user survey are integrated within the online user manual [2].

2. DEVELOPING A WORKSHOP: SPATIAL SOUND CREATION AND IMPROVISATION WITH *LIVE 4 LIFE*

2.1 Workshop overview

In 2023, seven training workshops focused on immersive sound creation with this open-source project were organized. These sessions were held in various locations in Montréal – five at the Centre for Interdisciplinary Research in Media Music and Technology (CIRMMT), two at Hexagram-UQÀM – as well as one in Paris during the International Symposium on Electronic Arts (ISEA). The recruitment for the workshops was organized via an online form, with the link disseminated through the websites and mailing lists of the institutions hosting the events, as well

[1] https://github.com/Xon77/Live4Life
[2] https://github.com/Xon77/Live4Life/wiki

as through various social media platforms. In total, these workshops attracted over 20 participants. At the conclusion of each workshop, participants were invited to voluntarily complete a survey. This survey, which was ethically approved by CIEREH-UQÀM, included questions about their spatial preferences in terms of creation and perception.

2.2 Workshop structure, formats and adaptation

In the announcement, the workshop was described as follows: "Participants will learn how to create and improvise with spatialized sound on multiple speakers using the open source tool *Live 4 Life*, which the author has been developing in SuperCollider since 2011. After a short introduction to the tool on its goals and possibilities, you will learn 1. how to install and configure the tool, 2. how to interact with the GUI and controllers, 3. how to define your own personal spatial configuration, 4. the code structure in detail, and finally 5. how to send the generated pattern data to another program like Processing via OSC to generate visuals." The following prerequisites were mentioned: "An interest in spatialization and a basic knowledge of SuperCollider are recommended, but not required, to modify the source code of the tool. All code is available on Github, including the installation and configuration process. Before registering for this workshop, please carefully read the sections on usage, supported platforms, and licensing to see if you will be able to use this tool on your computer." The mail of the workshop organizer was also given to answer any questions about the workshop or the installation of the tool.

The three initial workshops, which were held in the main conference room at CIRMMT, lasted three hours. However, given the lengthy installation and setup process of the spatial tool, this duration was deemed insufficient for thoroughly discussing the spatialization concepts underpinning the tool and demonstrating its practical interaction. Subsequently, a full-day was organized for subsequent workshops. Conducted in either English or French, the workshops featured different spatial configurations, adapting to the available space and loudspeakers – featuring a 32-loudspeaker dome at Hexagram-UQÀM, and quadraphony in other workshops. The survey or certain parts of it, particularly those concerning perception, were sometimes omitted for various reasons, including participant fatigue and unsuitable spatial setups for answering perception-related questions.

3. PARTICIPANTS' PREFERENCES IN SPATIAL COMPOSITION

After this workshop explaining different spatial systems (continuous input-based / finite event-based spatializations and object-based / channel-based paradigms), the survey included a critical question regarding participants' preferences in spatial composition and performance systems.

3.1 Continuous (track) input-based vs. finite event-based spatialization systems

Here, we propose a distinction between continuous (track) input-based spatialization vs finite event-based spatialization. Contrary to most tools with input-based spatialization from a fixed number of tracks, the tool is based on layer- and event-based spatialization, which allows to control the temporality (rhythm, density, duration and amplitude) of spatialized sound events. By continuous input-based spatialization, we mean that the user selects the position or trajectory of each continuous input (like in most spatialization plugins such as *Ircam Spat*[3]). According to the tool creator's experience, it tends to slowly create track after track more simple and clear spatialization. By finite event-based spatialization, we mean that the user selects (among a pre-defined library) the position and trajectory for several layers of events with different times of beginning and durations (like in some creation systems allowing to control both time and space of events, such as *Live 4 Life* or *Sound Particles* [5]). From the tool creator's experience, it tends to quickly create in a generative way more complex and confusing spatialization.

Fourteen workshop participants were asked to rate their preference on a scale from 1 (indicating a preference for continuous input-based spatialization) to 9 (favoring finite event-based spatialization), with an intermediate option of 5 representing a balance of both systems. The average score was 5.57, with a variance of 2.57, indicating a moderate consensus leaning towards a hybrid or balanced preference between the two spatialization approaches.

Based on written comments, several participants favored continuous input-based spatialization, citing its adequacy in a variety of musical practices and situations. One participant, who identifies as a composer of "cinema for the ears," expressed a need for spatialization that responds to continuous input flows, emphasizing the method's suitability for creating immersive soundscapes.

On the other end of the spectrum, finite event-based spatialization was praised for its ability to create complex spatialized textures and finer control over performance and space adaptation. One user described it as offering "an additional dimension, the possibility of emergence, the unexpected, a feeling of freedom."

Interestingly, a significant number of respondents rated their preference at the midpoint, indicating a desire for the flexibility to combine both spatialization methods. These participants highlighted the contextual nature of composition and performance, suggesting that having both options available is important. They pointed out that each strategy might serve different creative strategies — composition on one hand and improvisation on the other — and therefore, a hybrid approach could be advantageous.

For this reason, the intention is to enhance the tool with the capability for continuous mono input/track spatialization. This feature could be implemented by controlling the sound source's position along a trajectory through a singular, continuous control mechanism—a percentage-based index, similar to the approach utilized by Sound Trajectory [6]. This approach could be extended by introducing two or more control values: the first for selecting a specific trajectory from a pre-defined set, and the second for pinpointing the exact location on that trajectory, which could also be played back in loop with a specific speed.

[3] https://www.flux.audio/project/spat-revolution

3.2 Channel-based vs. object-based spatialization paradigms

In the pursuit of enhancing spatial sound composition tools, it is important to understand user preferences when it comes to choosing between channel-based and object-based spatialization paradigms. Here, we define these concepts in the following manner.

Object-based spatialization involves sending sound or effect to a virtual 3D position, facilitating reproduction across different spatial setups. From the author's experience with the tool, the spatial algorithm tends to make forgive the presence of loudspeakers and be more CPU-intensive, potentially limiting the number of spatialized events in real time. Conversely, channel-based spatialization, which involves sending a sound or effect to a physical speaker position, is not easily replicated in different spatial configurations. Based on the tool creator's experience, the simple treatment of sending directly a sound to a specific channel tends to reinforce the presence of loudspeakers and is more CPU-efficient. This efficiency can facilitate a higher volume of spatialized events in real time, offering potentially a practical advantage in live performance settings.

The survey conducted among *Live 4 Life* tool users delved into this subject, asking participants to express their preference on a scale from 1 (channel-based) to 9 (object-based), with 5 representing an equilibrium between both paradigms. The collected data from 14 participants yielded an average preference score of 5.07, with a variance of 5.46, suggesting a diverse range of opinions and no strong consensus towards either paradigm.

Proponents of the channel-based approach highlighted its concrete, physical, and intuitive nature. They valued the precision it offers, considering it to be more anchored in the physicality of hardware and the materiality of loudspeakers. Comments such as "The channel-based approach can be more precise," and "Loudspeaker as a material object is important," emphasize the perceived tangibility and exactitude of this approach.

Conversely, some participants favored the object-based paradigm for its flexibility, particularly in allowing for varied configurations and adaptability to different performance setups. One user mentioned, "I want to be flexible about playing again the piece/composition on different setups," highlighting the adaptability of object-based spatialization in various performance environments.

A noteworthy portion of the feedback indicated a preference for the integration of both paradigms, reflecting a desire for versatility in spatial sound tools. Participants recognized the distinct advantages of each approach, with comments like "Both paradigms have their benefits and drawbacks," and "It depends on whether you plan to change the existing setup often," suggesting a pragmatic view that the choice of paradigm should be tailored to the specific needs of the project and the flexibility required by the composer.

Despite the tendency towards object-based paradigm for reasons of simplicity, standardization and reproduction in every space regardless of speaker setup, mixing channel- and object-based paradigms to be used on every sound event allows to take advantage of the strengths of channel approach. It can also have much more impact (and at least more CPU-efficient) than sending it at the exact same coordinates of the loudspeaker through e.g. Vector Base Amplitude Panning (VBAP) algorithm [7]. This desire to mix these two paradigms, and to move away from standardization towards the object-oriented model, is also a way of questioning the norm, as Feda Wardak, creator of plastic architectural installations in public space, says: "I thwart the norm, I provoke it, because I think the norm inhibits things. At a certain point, over-norming sanitizes things, it industrializes, it standardizes. And I think common sense should take precedence over the norm." [8]

4. PARTICIPANTS' SPATIAL PERCEPTION PREFERENCES BETWEEN TWO ROTATING MODELS: FIXED POSITIONS IN SEQUENTIAL ROTATION VS. CIRCULAR TRAJECTORIES

The survey conducted among users of the *Live 4 Life* tool included a focused inquiry into their perceptual preferences between two spatial sound models: fixed positions with rotation towards the adjacent loudspeaker at each new events' onset (a sound event is directly sent to a loudspeaker and next events are sent to the nearest speaker, forming a sequence of fixed positions in circle or spiral for 2D or 3D setups) vs. continuous random circular trajectories throughout each event (utilizing either equal-power panning for 2D setup or VBAP algorithm for 3D setup with varying ascending or descending trajectories). This comparison was made across four distinct spatial sequences: one with texture elements, two that mixed texture and percussive elements, and one rhythmic sequence in loop. It should be noted that the first three generative sequences are based on exactly the same parameter patterns. Only the sound folder changes, following the patterns of the sound files module within the respective folder.

Ten participants answered the survey results for each example, which showed a range of scores from 1 (favoring fixed positions with rotation) to 9 (favoring circular trajectories). The responses, gathered from seven participants using a quadraphonic setup and three participants in a 32-loudspeaker dome environment, revealed nuanced preferences that varied according to the complexity and nature of the sequences. The average scores across the four examples varied, reflecting the subjective nature of spatial sound perception and its contextual dependency.

In the quadraphonic setup, participants generally found circular trajectories to be more enveloping and dynamic, providing a more filled space and apparent movement. For instance, in the generative sequences mixing texture and percussive elements, circular trajectories were said to have "more movement," thus capturing the attention more effectively than fixed positions with per-event rotation. However, for the rhythmic sequence in loop, preferences leaned towards fixed positions, which were considered to better articulate the rhythm and structure of the musical piece.

In contrast, participants experiencing the 32-loudspeaker dome emphasized different aspects, although fixed positions with per-event adjacent speaker rotation were also praised for offering a clearer understanding of rhythm, in the same way as the quadraphony. It is somewhat surprising to find that spatialization, corresponding to rotating fixed speaker positions, is perceived as more diffuse or vague but more enveloping and with a better sense of space than circular spatializations. This contrasts with comments on quadraphony, especially regarding the enveloping aspect, sense of space, movement, and spatial imaging of the circle. This is likely due to the combined change in spatial configuration and algorithm for circular trajectories, hence their importance in perception vs. trajectories. The number of loudspeakers and spatial algorithm may influence the perceived clarity and effectiveness of the spatial model. The fact that there are more speakers gives a stronger sensation of enveloping movement in a spiral for static positions rotating. Also, the use of the VBAP algorithm for ascending or descending circular trajectories reduces this impression of movement and circular sensation.

The tempo of sequences plays as well a significant role in spatial sensation and the differentiation between the two spatial models. Participants observed that denser sequences often appeared more blurred. A preference for slower examples was noted, with dense sequences offering nonetheless an intriguing auditory contrast. Slow spatializations with trajectories were preferred for their enhanced sound quality. Slow movement sequences allowed for a better appreciation of sound characteristics and spatial localization, echoing the slow spatial approach Stockhausen mentioned in *Oktophonie* [9]. Conversely, rapid sequences were so dense that distinguishing between the two spatializations became challenging.

The nuanced findings from this survey underscore the complexity of spatial sound perception, highlighting how different factors such as spatial configuration, algorithm, and tempo influence user preferences. These initial insights point towards the need for further investigation with a broader participant base, to deepen our understanding of these phenomena. It also suggests a flexible tool that can navigate between these spatial paradigms and systems (continuous input-based vs. finite event-based and channel-based vs. object-based) would be beneficial.

5. CONCLUSIONS

The article summarizes findings from first workshops using the tool *Live 4 Life*, exploring user preferences in spatial sound composition. Participants' feedback on preferences in spatialization systems (event vs. track and channel vs. object), and perceptual preferences for specific spatial models were discussed. The survey highlighted a preference for event- and channel-based spatialization in rhythmic contexts, challenging the industry's focus on track- and object-based approaches. For a comprehensive understanding and validation of these results, further surveys involving a larger participant pool are suggested. This would not only refine the findings but also potentially reveal new insights into user preferences and tool optimization. The study underscores the importance of continuous development and user feedback in enhancing spatial sound tools, advocating for an approach that is both open-source and user-centric for future research and development.

Attempts to initiate collaborations, particularly in the audiovisual sphere, encounter obstacles due to a prevalent inclination towards commercial software like Ableton and Max MSP within the community. This inclination challenges the tool author's firm commitment to developing exclusively on open-source platforms and collaborating solely with individuals who utilize non-commercial software. Despite the positive reception of the tool and its workshops, its adoption faces hurdles due to the complexity inherent in the SuperCollider platform and the tool's comprehensive design, aligning with a maximalist vision.

Proposals include extending workshops to provide ample time for thorough engagement with the tool and exploring unconventional venues for workshops to reach a broader spectrum of communities, thereby enhancing the tool's accessibility and appeal. Recent enhancements have introduced a visual component in Processing, that represents sound parameter patterns for an immersive experience. Furthermore, developments are steering towards establishing participatory performance installations, enabling attendees to interact directly with *Live 4 Life* and step into the role of a performer.

Acknowledgments

This postdoctoral research, which received the ethics certificate (2023-5339) by CIEREH-UQÀM, was made possible thanks to research grants from FRQSC (Fonds de Recherche du Québec - Société et Culture / B5 - 318691) and the support from CIRMMT and Hexagram-UQÀM.

6. REFERENCES

[1] C. Lengelé, "Live 4 Life - A spatial performance tool focused on rhythm and parameter loops," in *Proceedings of the International Computer Music Conference*, Daegu, South Korea, 2018, pp. 213–218.

[2] ——, "The story and the insides of a spatial performance tool: Live 4 Life," in *Proceedings of International Computer Music Conference*, Santiago, Chili, 2021, pp. 133–139.

[3] ——, "Live 4 Life: A spatial performance tool to play the ephemeral and improvise with space and playback speeds," *Organised Sound*, vol. 26, no. 1, pp. 89–99, 2021.

[4] J. M. Cartney, "Rethinking the computer music language: SuperCollider," *Computer Music Journal*, vol. 26, no. 4, pp. 61–68, 2002.

[5] N. Fonseca, "Immersive Sound Design Using Particle Systems," in *Audio Engineering Society Convention 138*, May 2015.

[6] M. Mercier, "Sound Trajectory en pratique live," in *Proceedings of Journées d'Informatique Musicale*, Paris, France, 2023.

[7] V. Pulkki, "Virtual sound source positioning using Vector Base Amplitude Panning," *Journal of the Audio Engineering Society*, vol. 45, no. 6, pp. 456–466, 1997.

[8] Arte.tv, "Feda WARDAK - ADAGP / Atelier A," https://www.youtube.com/watch?v=dfAqGN_ddKY, accessed February 1, 2024.

[9] K. Stockhausen, *Score Oktophonie: Elektronische Musik vom Dienstag aus Licht.* Kürten, Germany: Stockhausen-Verlag, 1994.

Foresta di Corpi Elettrici
Reflections between Field Recording and Spatialization Techniques

Valentina Ciniglio
Sound artist, PhD researcher at the Faculty of Music, University of Cambridge
valentina.ciniglio.e@gmail.com

ABSTRACT

What can be learnt from the field about spatialization possibilities and its consequences for acousmatic music? As a composer who heavily bases her work on field recording, and as a researcher, I asked this question myself many times.

This paper is a reflection about the salient technical and aesthetic aspects underpinning the piece "Foresta di corpi elettrici", and its theoretical background.

It analyses some aspects of the research I have been doing about the relationship between sound, space and bodies through in-ear binaural microphones, and how these considerations affected the way the space was conceived in the piece, and how sound objects were put in motion.

I draw on decolonializing practices, sound studies, electroacoustic and acousmatic literature to bring up topics that can be valuable not only on a theoretical level, but also on a technical and aesthetic level, when composing.

1. INTRODUCTION

The sonic material for this acousmatic composition consists of field recordings carried out with different techniques (binaural, contact mics, geophone, re-amping), encoded to be diffused on a 4-channel system.

I draw on Denis Smalley's [1] spectromorphology, which provides listening tools such as the different grades of surrogacy of the gesture and the texture, useful to analyze a sound and work on it. Indeed, the sound objects are considered according their belonging to the natural or instrumental world (source-bounded), as more remote levels of surrogation where the sound can hardly, or impossibly, be linked to any known sound source.

I also considered his reflections on spatiomorphology [2]; the idea that sound, whether source-bounding or not, is trans-sensorial implies that it transmits also visual, tactile sensations related to the experience of that sound, including the spatial hints in which it takes place. Sound is thus considered a space-bearer. The transmodal perceptual process entails a body in motion, surpassing any distinction between perceptual and thought awareness, a point that has been of pivotal importance for my research about the sound-space of the dhikr, and later considerations about the space-form of the composition.

I rely on the reflections of eco-acoustic music, inspired by David Monacchi's [3] experience with natural eco-systems, and the eco-acoustic studies of Almo Farina [4]. According to the eco-acoustic paradigm, sounds are localised in frequency beams, or niches, and electroacoustic composition techniques derive from its internal features and are meant not to alter its structure. While Monacchi's work concentrates on natural sonic eco-systems, endangered by deforestation and climatic change, my practice has so far engaged with almost completely anthropic sonic events, whose environment is endangered by savage real estate development and urban planning strategies.

For this reason, the recordings carried out during my fieldwork will be part of a future sonic archive documenting the heritage of the dhikr and its community.

In Foresta di Corpi Elettrici, the sound is conceived as being an organic entity; the samples of the dhikr that I used have been selected to reflect the different positionalities in the hadra, giving different suggestions of movement and space. At the micro-level, each sound is born, grows and goes through different internal metamorphosisthroughout the composition, to eventually die. At the macro-level, I tried to make the sounds interact together as different organs of a creature, due to their different levels of surrogacy. They influence each other, co-existing and interfering with each other in time, creating an ambivalence that has no solution.

2. RECORDING THE SONIC-SPACE OF THE DHIKR

The field recordings mainly employed for this piece are the result of my field work in Egypt, since 2019, for a PhD project about the relation between sound, bodies and space, and the use of binaural technology as a tool for a decolonializing practice of the ear.

The decolonial thinking, as defined by Rachele Borghi (5) with the term decolonialise[1], means for me the con-

[1] "Decolonializzare ha il vantaggio di poter rimandare ad una dimensione micro, quella di te, del tuo corpo, del tuo spazio, del tuo contesto. Permette di indicare non solo la volontà di uscire dal colonialismo ma anche l'azione costante di cercare, sperimentare, portare avanti pratiche, esercizi per uscire dalla colonialità e raggiungere la decolonialità (*ibidem*, p.38)". (Delocolonialising has the advantage to refer to the micro dimension, your dimension, your body, your space, your context. It allows to point at the will to get out of colonialism but also the constant action of seeking, experi-

stant awareness of the ethnographer, of her epistemological advantage and of the power relationships between her and the local community in the process of producing knowledge in the academic context, as well as the semantic and symbolic places where she cannot access. Her practice passes through the use of her body as the starting point to reflect on her own positionality and privilege, by putting herself in the game of explicating where one comes from, and where one is located in the dominant Western system, in the form of militant performances.

In the literature, the dhikr is described as a Sufi ritual which expresses the remembrance of God. The ritual expresses the feeling of love towards God, and plunges its roots in the Sufi current of Islam. It consists of religious chants, performed by a *munshid* (singer), usually during the ḥaḍra, group meetings that can take place within the Sufi confraternities, *leyla* (concerts) or during the *mawlid*s, religious festivals celebrated in honor of saints.

The performance of the dhikr is mainly based on musical improvisation according to a fixed structure that begins with a slow intro, without percussion; the nay or kawala – reed flutes – and the oud improvise according to one of the Arabic modal scales, and the voice follows. The verses are usually interpolations of verses taken from poems, or the munshid's own compositions, usually concerning themes such as spiritual love, separation, grief, devotion to the saints. The rhythm comes in gradually, slow and with a contained dynamic. It is the mushid's voice that acts as a guide, giving the signal at the end of a verse to the rest of the band, to move to a faster rhythm and a more consistent dynamic. A fundamental sound element during dhikr is the type of strong and sonorous breathing that the participants perform together following the rhythm of the percussion, while moving.

The fieldwork itself draws an already existing tradition of documenting the dhikr, started since the 80's with tape recorders, and then with video cameras and phones, which has led to the habit to consume this type of music in other contexts, either in private, in shops, cars, or gatherings.

During the fieldwork, I have been using different recording configurations: only in-ear binaural microphones; in-ear binaural microphones and direct line from the mixer; in-ear binaural microphones, direct line from the mixer, and omnidirectional microphones or binaural microphones ("ears"). Therefore, every set gives a different sonic image of the dhikr.

The choice of the set depended on the location of the dhikr (see Figure 1 for example), for example either it was easy to move around or place fixed microphones with stands, on the sides of the dhikr, in the back of the crowd dancing, or behind the musicians. The position of the microphones was affected by the location of the loudspeakers: when too close, they masked the other sound sources that did not pass through the mixer/are not amplified, given the high sound pressure level of the amplification system. Another factor influencing the recording technique was whether there was enough space on the sides of the dhikr: for example, when in a narrow street, or courtyard, or on the contrary when the outside space is wider and busy with passers-by.

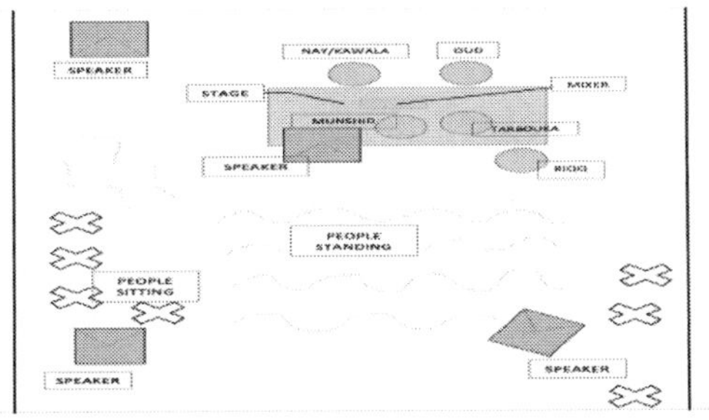

Figure 1. Overhead map of one possible spatial organization of the ḥaḍra.

Therefore, it can be a difficult task to find a good spot to record all the elements of dhikr, as the riqq – a wooden frame drum with cymbals - and the sagat – little brass finger cymbals – are not amplified through the mixer, and the breath and the voices of the crowd, which are the core of the dhikr. Indeed, they function as an engine that spurs the munshid to go on for hours, in turn guiding and inspiring the musicians. Staying very close to the percussions will catch also the high sound pressure of the tarbouka, resulting in a crackled sound which adds to the already distorted sound coming from the loudspeakers, thus masking the crowd. Also, being too far in the back, it might be either too close to the loudspeakers in the back, or too far from the speakers in the front; moreover, the voices from the crowd as well the two percussions might be too far from the microphone.

The loudspeakers are often positioned in the back of the stage or on the other side behind the crowd, though oriented towards the outer space of the dhikr. This is so to reach the people that cannot fit the space right in front of the singer, and therefore stands or sits along the tiny alleys, or outside the building or the shrine. The position of the loudspeakers in the space is then a clue of an acousmatic dimension of the dhikr, which is not only a way to surround the people in the proximity of the band, but also a way to extend the reach of sound beyond the direct source.

3. RESONANCE AND SONIC INBETWEENNES

The dhikr starts late at night; it begins with the voice and the kawala or nay answering to it, with the oud playing a bordone underneath. People is still, sitting or standing; There is a solemn mood spreading throughout the people. The munshid gives a sign for the percussions to come in. The people get up, and start breathing loud, moving slowly from left to right, and back. Sometimes people start by

menting, carrying forward practices, exercises to exit the coloniality and reach the decoloniality. Translation mine).

standing in two rows facing each other, swinging back and forth, before changing to the main configuration where people stand in rows in front of the munshid.

The words of the munshid lead at the same time the musicians and affect the crowd, which shouts, answers back, already individually charged by their own personal background and stories, propagating an energy through the crowd in the form of collective excitement. Bodies shake, the breathing increases in volume, eventually transferring also the energy back to the munshid and the musicians, creating a resonating sound-space.

There is grieving, pain, ecstatic sensations, embodied through the lyrics of the munshid, which however do not come in a vacuum but are sustained in a stream of sound which is at first soft and sad or inspired, like at the beginning when the kawala phrasing behind the munshid; secondly, at the end of the mushid's verse, the musicians build up to a faster rhythm where the kawala's sound turns into a thick drone, due to the "octaver" pedals – pitch shifting effects – employed by the kawala/nay players. In these moments, the breathing is less audible as the music is very loud, coming distorted and full of feedbacks through the loudspeakers all around. The munshid spurs the crowd by dancing from the top of a chair or the stage, sometimes wielding a stick or any other objects in his hands. In these moments, the movements of the people are wider, wilder, and the spiritual energy is very intense. The sound all around is wrapped around the bodies, and its internal spectral characteristics changes with the movements of the bodies around, which work as a dynamic filter.

What allows for the dhikr to work is what I would call the *in-betweenness* of the sound. This in-betweenness is at the same time physical (as an acoustic phenomenon) and cultural.

Sound, as a physic phenomenon affecting our bodies, is charged with spiritual and haunting power by the same bodies resonating together with the sound objects. The in-betweenness is the space between me and the other (something to nothing), me and God, it is the affective expression of the tension between the subjects' desire of transcending their selves while invoking the saint's and the Prophet's baraka and love on them, and the impossibility of transcending one's condition. It is therefore the space of this impossibility, half way from the self and the other.

The in-betweenness is sonic to the extent that it is arising from the mutual constitution of sound objects and listening entities: sound objects as physical phenomena engage with both psychological and bodily affections through vibration, carrying within them already the energy resulting from the affective processes the musicians and the munshid are going through when they look at the people, and engage with them, with the general gaw (the atmosphere).

At the same time, the sound objects become charged with an affective haunting power: they become something more, something other than just sound. Something that cannot be fully explained or caught by language, or writing. The music is loud, with heavy saturation and high reverbation; the position of the speakers, usually one behind the musicians and one on the back of the attendants on the other side, leads to heavy feedbacks from the microphone of the munshid, creating a specific sonic frame within the dhikr takes place.

Following McCallum's reading of Derrida (2007) [7], I understand in-betweenness as a frame within which there is the possibility for the otherness to be temporarily experienced. Thus, the haunting power arises from the collectivity, from its movement, its screams, its responses to the music. It is a mutual practice; it is culture produced and lived through the relational dimension of the sound space of the dhikr. The collectivity is hit by the frenzies of the percussions, the heavy phrasing of the nay or the violin, the drone of the oud; the music carries and is carried by the words of the munshid, words like hints: the "door", to "get drunk", the "boat", the "knife", the "water", the "iron", the "electricity", the "love"; references sometimes not completely understandable (and even when not explicit, still sensible), if not put in the spatial and temporal context of the dhikr.

I explored different ways people listen to the dhikr, and what they think about the relation between their listening and the sounding object/entities, considering the medium of the recordings as the structure through which the knowledge about the dhikr unfolds between the observant and the participants. At the same time, I matured also a way of staying and developing my own relation with the sound space of the dhikr, the way it was affecting me and engaging with my memories, my feelings: sometimes I would myself record with the in-ear binaural microphones, or I would just attend the dhikr, interacting with people, moving around or entering the center of ḥaḍra. One of the chapters of the project is indeed dedicated to the sound objects of the dhikr, which is the result of my personal experience and the listening-sessions I had afterwards.

Doing field-work through the in-ear binaural microphones does not mean to have a perfectly accurate fidelity in reconstructing a 3d sound image. The HRTF variates from one person to the other, meaning that we acknowledge in advance the uniqueness of the medium, and consequently the limits of ethnography itself. I did not consider using a HRTF correction coefficient in post-production; I tried to develop a methodology which is indeed an attempt to highlight the limits of the ethnographer as a way to renounce to every attempt to "give justice" to the Other, with the aim to reflect on and accept the impossibilities to solve the dilemma of how to make the "native's claim" equal to that of the ethnographer, codifying new ways for objective knowledge, focusing rather on developing practices to stay in this impossibility.

The recording sessions took place during the performance of the dhikr, like tents opened to the public, or public spaces such as small alleys, courtyards, and people are free to join and leave at their own will. They are carried out by me and other participants by wearing a pair of

Soundman binaural microphones directly into the ears, connected to a Tascam MKIII. The resulting recordings served to a re-listening session, to which a discussion followed about the experience, the sounds which are present and the way they are perceived, the memory of the feelings.

4. MOTION: FROM THE FIELD TO THE COMPOTISION

Reflecting about positionality and how it affects my listening experience opens up different options, when working on the compositional level.

I treated the sounds as if they were organisms of the same ecosystem, whose spectrum can give indication of their location in the virtual space of the composition, their interdependency, and also their fallibility by simulating audio masking effects, as it happens in the sound-space of the dhikr. I nailed the spectrum of each sound object to fit in a specific niche of frequencies. In time, the sound develops migrating to other frequencies, or expanding or shrinking to lower or higher frequencies.

The first acoustic window is dedicated to the birth of the sounds that will evolve throughout the whole composition, like the sound of the kawala, or the intermittent impulses, that will return in the end, though morphed and with increasing short intervals, the sound of an iron surface being scratched, and the electric short gestures in the low register.

The evolution follows the structure of the dhikr: the intro is slow, marked by the recalling of sound of the kawala; then the more sustained part comes in with the start of the movement of the bodies, indicated by the movement of the boat; finally, the increased path which leads to the end, characterized by the overlapping of all the sound objects, sobbing, interfered with sounds of electricity, representing the tiredness and the euphoria of the faster movement, in a drunken state of mind.

The sound objects are inspired by some of the symbols and words sung by the munshid in the dhikr, like to "get drunk", the "boat", the "knife", the "water", the "iron", the "electricity", the "love". The result is a composition which is anecdotal, but at the same time re-interprets, recreates the idea of that sonic-space: at 3'35" for example, we can hear the sound of a boat starting the engine and leave, or the gestures and glitches of electricity at 4'53", the water starting at 3'31"; other sounds referred instead to a symbol by assuming a similar behavior, more than directly recalling it, as for the behavior of the voices in the last acoustic window, which are increasingly frenzied to give the sense of drunkenness, hyperventilation, or the drone starting at 3'36" which is a granulated sample of a kawala playing a drone, stretched and pitched down, whose spectrum gradually loses its higher frequencies to fade away.

Also, the acousmatic dimension created by the disposition of the speakers at the mawlid inspired my approach to spatialization in different ways. The sound object is spread to mimic the soundspace of the dhikr from different vantage points, through filtering and reverb, in order to change the depth and perspective from which they are perceived.

We can hear the first voice of the munshid at 3'34" spatially closer to our ears, even if the sound is treated in a way that results small, like coming from far, as if we were standing in front of him, but listening to him through a small device. The second voice starting at 5'12", interrupted and overlapped with the heavy breathing, is located just in front of as, as if we were hearing it from the loudspeakers from the first row of the ḥaḍra, while the breathing is just next to us. The third voice, in the closing, represents instead the sound object perceived as if we were gradually leaving the ḥaḍra behind.

The voice, naturally echoed, distorted and reverberated, is then played with in a way that its spatial behavior is a referral to the reflections of the sound on the walls of the small alley (like in the case of the first voice), or in widenings like cemeteries (the third one).

Also, the voice has been treated to the extent that it is audible its mediated nature through a technological medium: cracklings, disturbances from tape recorders, buzzes from loudspeakers, which are treated as sound objects of their own that would come in, towards the last acoustic window, and interact with the vocal elements.

Finally, I worked with impulsive sounds like audio interferences and audio cassette recorder to punctuate the space. The reference to the audio cassette recorder is a personal tribute to the long tradition of recording the dhikr, while the audio interferences are inspired by the amplified audio in the context of the dhikr where technical problems in the disposition of the loudspeakers or the low quality of the equipment result into feedback, sudden cuts in the sound, and heavy saturation.

5. CONCLUDING THOUGHTS

Foresta di Corpi Elettrici is a piece for 4-channel system; however, the piece can also be spatialized on a wider array of speakers, positioned in a circle of 4 speakers, and 4 additional speakers turned towards the external space of the circle, in a configuration which is meant for the audience to move around an acousmonium which has no real center or front. In this way, around the center there is another acoustic space interested by the reflections of the sound on the surfaces of the room.

The practice of field recording I have carried out for the last two years has had an impact on my relationship as a composer with the spatial dimension of sound.

At the compositional level, I started thinking about structuring different listening perspectives of the same acoustic ambient, intersecting different listening points. The changing relation in time between us and the location of the sound objects gives space to different spatial "planes", reproduced at the same time. The different planes would coexist together by being stretched over diver frequential clusters, by filtering, altering the pitch and time stretching.

The distance from the sound source plays an important role in creating a multidimensional sound space, which nevertheless is modified also by the acoustic characteristics of the space where the piece is played.

Indeed, I started also reflecting on how the different early and late reflections, the size of the space, the number of loudspeakers available, the number of people present in the physical space would become an integrating part of the compositional process, being an extension of the virtual space of the piece. In this way, differently from space-conservative approaches, we become aware of the medium through which we experience sound, and we can swing our positionality from considering the intrinsic aspect of a work to how the spectrum can be morphed by the material, size and distance of the surrounding surfaces and become charged with new timbrical colorations, different behaviors and eventually, different effect on the listeners. I believe this breaking of illusion of the immersivity can open up interesting directions to play with the behavior of sound; its interplay with the materiality of the ambience around us, its phenomenology on the aesthetic level can always return different outcomes and perspectives about the very sound objects, in constant feedback.

Acknowledgments

I would like to thank the University of Cambridge, the Faculty of Music, and my supervisor prof. Peter McMurray for giving me the chance to dedicate myself to my research interests.

I want to thank Abdo Zein alDin, for supporting and trusting me and this project.

I thank all the people I met at the mawlids, for welcoming me, for their inspiring presence and experiences whose bits were shared with me. I will make sure that this knowledge is never alienated from the community it belongs to.

Finally, I want to thank my maestro Elio Martusciello for his inspiring thoughts, and his support.

6. REFERENCES

[1] D. Smalley, "Space-form and the acousmatic image," *Organised Sound*, vol. 12, no. 1, pp. 35–58, 2007. doi:10.1017/S1355771807001665

[2] D. Smalley, "Spectromorphology: explaining sound-shapes," *Organised Sound*, vol. 2, no. 2, pp. 107–126, 1997. doi:10.1017/S1355771897009059

[3] D. Monacchi, *L'Arca dei Suoni Originari.* Mondadori, 2019.

[4] A. Farina, *Soundscape Ecology: Principles, Patterns, Methods and Applications.* Springer Science+Business Media Dordrecht, 2014.

[5] Borghi, Rachele, *Decolonialità e Privilegio: Pratiche femministe e critica al sistema-mondo.* Meltemi, 2022.

[6] A. M. O. Gautier, *Aurality: Listening and Knowledge in Nineteenth-Century Colombia.* Durham, NC: Duke University Press, 2014.

[7] P. McCallum, "Questions of Haunting: Jacques Derrida's 'Specters of Marx' and Raymond Williams's 'Modern Tragedy'". *Mosaic: An Interdisciplinary Critical Journal*, June 2007, Vol. 40, No. 2, pp. 231-244, 2014.

This page intentionally left blank.

A City the Goes Away: Constructing a Contemporary Patrimonial Memory through Electroacoustic Composition in the Case of *El Filo Errante*

José Ignacio López Ramírez Gastón
jlopezramirezgaston@gmail.com

ABSTRACT

The present paper discusses the use of electroacoustic music to construct artistic representations of traditional cultural soundscapes fading away amid contemporary and social urban developments and technological progress. Through an analysis of my composition El Filo Errante 2.1 (2021), I examine the use of creative compositional technology-based tools for the generation of an intangible cultural heritage in construction in which the historical sound elements of the city of Lima-Peru, those that accompany my early years and are slowly fading away, acquire new life through artistic modern representations and reformulations. This musical piece argues for the use of local soundscapes as organic and contextual material to be rediscovered and reformulated into new representative sound products, and against an exclusively archivist view that sees to resolve a possible loss of cultural memory, positioning the sounds of a city as rigid atemporal objects to be preserved. As sound elements and musical pieces exist only when being perceived by the human being, the sound of the past is only relevant when experienced in a particular context, in this case: the contemporary context of computer music and the Lima of the 21st century.

1. INTRODUCTION

Upon returning to Peru in 2011 after nearly two decades abroad, I embarked on a journey to contribute to the development of cultural and academic spaces dedicated to sound experimentation and technology-based musical arts within the nation. In the particular case of Peru, sound arts and musical education are intimately linked with local identity politics and the nationalistic paradigms that have accompanied our short republican history. Making music in Peru or attempting to make *Peruvian music* requires an understanding of a complex set of believes and ideological narratives.

This work is not directly related to the way in which local discourses determine musical practices, but the present discussing regarding the construction of alternative contemporary representations of traditional sound sources from the city of Lima sets itself in contrast with a common traditional national point view in the country that has historically been suspicious, and even uncomfortable, with the introduction of musical practices considered foreign, like is the case of electronic and computer music.

During my time at UCSD working on my doctoral dissertation, I focused on the challenges and intricacies involved in bringing academic electronic music into Peru's education system. A revised version of my research was published in 2022 by the Universidad Nacional de Música (formerly Conservatorio Nacional de Música) [4]. Additionally, I have addressed some of these obstacles in detail, including the strategies taken to surpassed them, in a previous ICMC paper [3], and I intend to keep documenting the country's advancements as they unfold.

The musical composition presented here is politically influenced by a countercultural stance that seeks to reshape, among other aspects, the prevailing local perceptions of heritage, identity, nationhood, Peruvian identity, and memory, along with their connection to sound-related artistic practices and musical education. In this context, El Filo Errante 2.1 functions not only as an illustration of contemporary Peruvian computer music but also as a social declaration advocating for an alternative, comprehensive, and inclusive approach to constructing a national sonic landscape through the use of digital sound arts.

2. CONCEPTUAL AND HISTORICAL BACKGROUND

2.1 Soundscaping the city

Bartalucci and Luzzi mention that a soundscape is defined as an "acoustic environment as perceived or experienced and/or understood by people, in a specific context" [1]. The document they refer to, ISO 12931, generated in 2014 by the ISO (the International Organization for Standardization) goes into more detail, clarifying a differentiation between the physical phenomenon of sound (acoustic environment) and soundscape, understanding the latter as a perceptual construct defined by human perception, experience or understanding of the sound by a human or a group of people within a particular context.

Musicians are quite familiar with the term, normally in connection with Murray Schafer's World Soundscape Project. While Schafer seemed initially to be particularly interested in the development of an ecology of sound and the preservation of sound environments, his later work with the project has been directly linked with the development of compositional techniques and musical sound arts that relate to what *we can listen to* in an artistic way.

The influence of the initial world of soundscape culture that Murray formulated in musical arts, has given our contemporary world a long range of musical activities and aesthetics, many times related to electronic music and other technology-based sound arts. Going further, authors like Zhiyong Deng, considered that "soundscape composition has its own musical features, musical functions, musical types and connections to other music genres" and that "soundscape composition can be regarded as a distinct, and therefore new, genre category." [7][1] The term has also been used in a more generic way in reference to musical *ambients*, textures and other musical elements, or by popular electronic musicians to define the locality of their work, even if the work does not include local acoustic environments or representative recordings with identity or native value.

In the case of the composition analyzed here, there is an emphasis in a combination of a perceptive contextual and historical sound source, and an artistic compositional technique that reconfigures (or deconstructs) the sounds to keep them from a direct representation of and existing sound environment. In other words, the initial material gets dramatically detached from its representative nature to represent a new sound world, one that seems alien to its own origins.

2.2 Peruvian musical patrimony

From a global perspective, understanding music *in general* as intangible cultural heritage might seem not to require a further discussion. A contemporary concept of cultural heritage includes both the memories from the past and the visions for the future. It would also regard technological advancements and innovations not only as mechanisms for the preservation of something previously existing, but as sources for the construction of contextual musical materials that represent news models for awareness of place, time, and identity.

For the most part of contemporary history, governmental models for Peruvian cultural have stressed the need to stay away from the influence of the west. As I have mentioned before: "it is within a plural and ambiguous set of nationalists, nativist, socialist, anti-foreign and indigenist ideologies, analyzed in this work, that we can identify a constant: the suspicion towards, and ultimately, the rejection of technologically based musical traditions as an element in the construction of a history of Peruvian music." [5]. Moving away from a traditional set of characteristics that tend to stereotype the notion of Peruvian culture or attempt to maintain a romantic notion of what is native and therefore *ours*, the composition here presented represent an alternative sense of peruvianness as the expression of cultural soundscapes presented by the city of Lima that are not particularly related to the nationalistic notions promoted by the Peruvian government and intrinsic to the Peruvian population by the unifying rhetoric of the national institutions.

3. EL FILO ERRANTE 2.1

El Filo Errante 2.1 (2021) is an electroacoustic representation of the culture of the *afilador de cuchillos* (knife sharpener), an important part of the traditional soundscape of the Peruvian capital, Lima. The knife sharpener represents and old cultural practice of door-to-door hawking that is normally accompanied by the sound of a pan flute call, as a distinctive custom melodic phrase, the announces his presence in the neighborhood. In this piece I unified three elements: (1) a nostalgic rendition and reconfiguration of the concept of "una Lima que se va¨ (José Gálvez, 1965) adding the theme of the transformation of the soundscape of the capital, (2) the change of paradigm on a Peruvian informal economy that favors commercially massified products over street services, and (3) the role of music aesthetics, practices and instrumentation in the aural representation of cultural contexts.

3.1 *Una Lima que se va*

Vieja ciudad, calma ilusión, bella verdad,
mi inspiración, la Lima antigua que se va.
Chabuca Granda, 1948

In 1921, the emerging modernist poet José Gálvez released his renowned book "Una Lima que se va" [2]. In this piece, Gálvez depicted a romanticized portrayal of Lima. The title has since been employed to evoke a sense of nostalgia for Lima's vanishing past. The book encapsulates a discourse that cherishes the conventional settings of a prosperous and progressive modern city that thrived before the War of the Pacific (1879-1883) and the subsequent alterations resulting from the conflict. Chabuca Granda, arguably the most renowned Peruvian singer of the 20th century, revisits the concept of this traditional city that is slipping away in her song Lima de Veras (1948).

The composition El Filo Errrante 2.1, refers to the soundscapes of a Lima that is abandoning us, and the sounds of my childhood that are abandoning me. It endeavors to reconcile the sounds that marked my early years in the Miraflores district of Lima with the sounds that define my present life as a computer music composer. The composition uses two sound sources and electronic

[1] This has been discussed previously from a different perspective by Truax [6]

processing in Pure Data. The sound sources been used are (1) a piano, and (2) recordings of a knife sharpener taken at my apartment's door.

3.2 Peruvian informal economy

If the recording of the knife sharpener's *performance* at my doorstep primarily represents the sound of my childhood, it also encapsulates one of the most fundamental aspects of the Peruvian economy: informality (see figure 1). In that sense, the composition not only evokes the past but also sheds light on a shadow economy prevalent in the city (and the country). Both the piano and the sound of the knife sharpening represent the contradictions of a city in constant flux and transformation, grappling with issues of technology, modernity, and its identity as the capital of a country that has yet to undergo the industrial revolution. Lima exists as a hybrid entity, straddling the line between a bustling metropolis and a quaint town, a dichotomy reflected in its soundscape.

Figure 1. An old knife sharpener in downtown Lima.

3.3 Electronic Music as cultural representation

The use of electronic music and a programming language like Pure Data, also reflects on the ambiguous nature of a country in a constant conflict between a past to be rescued and a future to be embraced. Is for that reason that together with the sounds of the knife being sharpen I integrate the traditional sound of a piano, to be deconstructed through the process in order for it to loss its original identity while style being identifiable.

In that sense, the aesthetic of electroacoustic music plays an ambivalent role. While electroacoustic music could be perceived as a sound of the past in a global context, within the Peruvian environment and academic musical education, it continues to resonate as the sound of the future and innovation. The ambivalence lies in the contrast between the established history of electroacoustic music globally and its relatively recent introduction and exploration within the Peruvian musical landscape. As a genre that often pushes the boundaries of traditional musical practices, electroacoustic music represents an avant-garde and forward-thinking approach to sound creation in the local academic context, opening up new possibilities and horizons for musical expression in the country. It stands as a testament to the dynamic interplay between tradition and modernity, serving as a bridge that connects the rich musical heritage of Peru with contemporary global trends in music composition and technology yet to be implemented.

4. STRUCTURE AND PATCHING

El Filo Errante 2.1 represents a variation of a composition originally crafted in 2020. This piece found its place in the inaugural compilation of Peruvian electroacoustic composers from the new generation, released by the Laboratorio de Música Electroacústica y Arte Sonoro of the Universidad Nacional de Música in Lima, a lab that I inaugurated in 2017. El Filo Errante serves as the opening track on this record, a collaborative effort that features contributions from both me and my students specializing in electroacoustic music at the university. The 2.1 version of the composition was subsequently developed in 2021, reflecting an ongoing evolution of the sonic exploration initiated in its earlier iteration.

It is noteworthy to highlight the challenges faced in fostering a comprehensive dialogue on the role and practice of electroacoustic compositions within the university setting. Notably, there is a lack of awareness and knowledge concerning computer music programming at the institution, except for the content covered in the courses Taller de Electroacústica I and II, which I personally conducted until 2024. This situation underscores the need for future attention and efforts to address and enhance the understanding and integration of electroacoustic music within the academic framework.

El Filo Errante 2.1 in constructed in Pure Data, as it is the main programming language I have used to teach computer music at the Universidad Nacional de Música between 2017 and 2024. In order the bring the students closer to practices uncommon in the traditional academic environment of Peruvian music training, the patch itself has been used to generate a graphic representation or symbolic *notation* (see Figure 2). In my observation, traditionally trained Peruvian composers have exhibited limited interaction with other art forms in recent decades. Recognizing this gap, I have found it crucial not only to convey my artistic interests through my compositions but also to utilize them as a means of broadening the awareness of students who, for the most part, may be unfamiliar with the history of contemporary art in the 20th century.

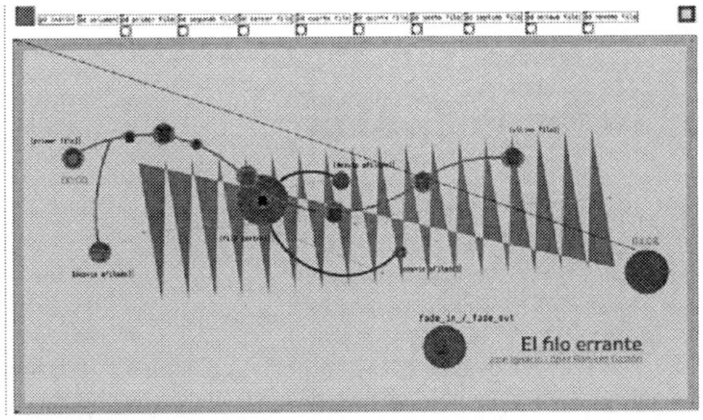

Figure 2. El Filo Errante 2.1. Main patch in Pure Data.

The piano is visually symbolized by the color red and circular elements, embodying its *harmonious* and melodic qualities, while the sounds of the knife are depicted by the color black and sharp triangular elements, reflecting its percussive, harsh, and cutting nature.

The composition is intricately divided into 9 distinct *filos* (edges or borders), each capable of independent play and processing. This modular design not only enhances the interactive nature of the piece but also aligns with my previous compositional work, which is grounded in the exploration and application of modular models [x]. This intentional division allows for a dynamic and flexible performance, where each section can be manipulated and experienced autonomously. This flexibility allows for different execution formats and there is a version of the piece for three computers to be performed by the Ensamble de Laptops de la Universidad Nacional de Música – ELUNM (see figure 3). This configuration underscores the versatility of the composition, allowing for diverse interpretations and collaborative engagements.

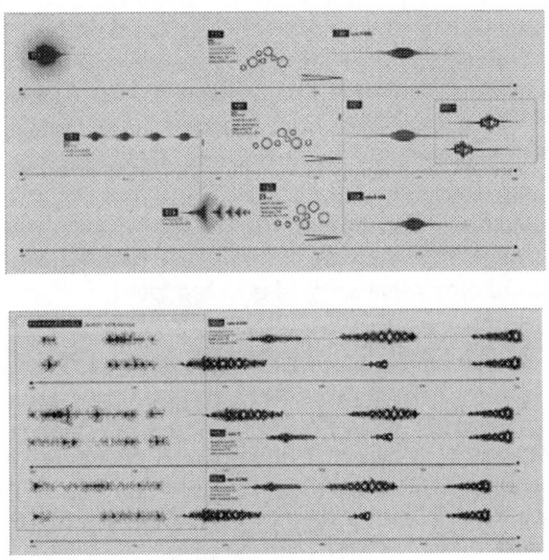

Figure 3. Two different sections of a version for three computers.

El Filo Errante 2.1 can be heard and downloaded from: https://archive.org/details/filoerrante-2-1

5. CONCLUSIONS

In the realm of electroacoustic composition, we are granted the remarkable capability to forge alternative soundscapes that transcend the conventional boundaries of representing a mere sound environment. This creative medium empowers us to explore uncharted auditory territories, allowing for the conception and realization of sonic landscapes that extend beyond the constraints of natural or familiar settings. This holds true not just as a recognition of the subjective and perceptual aspects inherent in sonic events but also in its capacity to enhance the essence of our sonic cultural and historical heritage by reshaping how we engage with intangible cultural patrimony. Our perception of the past is inevitably filtered through the lens of the present. Therefore, crafting new sonorities rooted in our contemporary context, personal experiences, and historical involvement contributes to the enrichment and reinterpretation of our understanding of history. It signifies a dynamic and evolving relationship with our cultural legacy, allowing for a more nuanced and resonant connection between the past and the present.

Acknowledgments

To the city of Lima and the complex nature of our history, for pressing me to search for alternative ways to communicate and transform our heritage

6. REFERENCES

[1] C. Bartalucci and S. Luzzi, "The soundscape in cultural heritage," *IOP Conference Series: Materials Science and Engineering*, 2020, 949.

[2] J. Gálvez, *Una Lima que se va (crónicas evocativas),* Euforion, 1921.

[3] J. I. López Ramírez Gastón, "Reconfiguring Instrumental Performance in Perú: Ensamble de Laptops de la Universidad Nacional de Música – ELUNM," *Proceedings of the 2021 International Computer Music Conference*, Santiago, 2021, pp. 351-355.

[4] J. I. López Ramírez Gastón, "Composición Musical Modular. [re]configuraciones peruanas a viejos paradigmas (2071-2021)," *Quispe Art & Research Journal*, 2021.

[5] J. I. López Ramírez Gastón, *Este futuro es otro futuro: El papel del discurso social en el (sub) desarrollo de la música electrónica académica en el Perú.* Universidad Nacional de Música, 2022.

[6] B, Truax, "Soundscape composition as global music: electroacoustic music as soundscape," *Organised Sound,* 13(2), 2008, 103-109.

[7] Z Deng, J Kang, and D Wang, "Soundscape composition as a new music genre," Proceedings of ICMEM, Sheffield, 2015, pp. 23-25.

Catástrofes (2023): Creative Processes in Synthesis, Audiovisual and Sound Spatialization

Danilo Rossetti
Universidade Federal de Mato Grosso/
Universidade Estadual de Campinas
d.a.a.rossetti@gmail.com

ABSTRACT

Catástrofes[1] *(2023) is an audiovisual electroacoustic work combining different types of sound synthesis and ambisonics spatialization. The piece is malleable regarding the spatialization possibilities, considering ambisonics orders, 2D or 3D sound fields, and multichannel diffusion. It is conceived as a sound continuum in which the textures and sound masses are gradually achieved from the addition of up to 26 voices employing different synthesis techniques. Three main sound masses are juxtaposed and formed by different superpositions of partials. Their transitions are gradually performed through timbre interpolation. From this structure, psychoacoustic phenomena such as roughness and beats emerge as saliences and ruptures in listening. We propose an analysis of the sound morphology of the piece employing a methodology based on audio descriptors. This composition was conceived in a multidisciplinary research combining artistic and technological methodologies. It is a part of our recent research involving electroacoustic composition, synthesis, timbre, spatialization in ambisonics, and video.*

1. INTRODUCTION

Catástrofes (2023)[2] is an audiovisual electroacoustic work entirely programmed in a Max patch using different types of sound synthesis (e.g. additive, ring modulation, frequency modulation, and granular). The additive synthesis can have up to 26 oscillators, each one considered as a sound source in the sonic space of diffusion.

The synthesis is combined with an ambisonics spatialization system using objects of ICST Ambisonics [1] and Spat [2] libraries. It means that the piece has a malleability regarding its spatialization possibilities, depending on different features such as 1) ambisonics encoding and decoding order, 2) 2D or 3D sound fields, 3) quantity of loudspeakers available in the sound-field array, and 4) binaural decoding for headphone listening, simulating spatial properties. The ICMC 2024 version has 8-channel and 2D decoding of the 3rd order of ambisonics.

The term "*catástrofes*" refers to the "*catastrophe*" concept by René Thom (in French) [3], *i.e.*, a methodology that permits organizing the experience data in dynamic systems resulting in continuous and discontinuous morphologies. The catastrophes are the critique points of those systems where ruptures occur, such as continuity breaks resulting in qualitative leaps (in perception), that organize the morphologies in different manners.

This composition is part of the context of our research, in which we recently presented a paper at ICMC 2019 [4]. This research involves electroacoustic composition in its different forms of expression, synthesis, timbre, spatialization in high-order ambisonics, and video. In that article [4] we described a system that combined granular synthesis and spatialization in high-order ambisonics and analyzed the results of this combination. On the other hand, this present work aims to describe and analyze mainly sound synthesis based on the generation of harmonic and inharmonic partials (additive, ring modulation, FM) and how these different partials are spatialized in a high-order ambisonics system.

Our compositional hypothesis is that space has a considerable influence on the way we listen to music. Different spatial configurations of diffusion can influence the way we listen to the same musical work. By allocating the sound sources at different points in a 2D (x, y) or 3D (x, y, z) space of the partials generated by the synthesis, we may create new ways of listening to the sound textures produced, as a type of spatialized timbre.

The question we are asking, in the case of *Catástrofes*, is what it would be like to listen to this timbre produced in the composition and realized in the electroacoustic diffusion in one or more sound diffusion spaces, in different configurations of loudspeakers or in a binaural reduction. We will try to briefly discuss these issues through the analysis of the work focused on the sound morphology that we will develop later.

2. SOUND SYNTHESIS AND PSYCHOACOUSTIC PHENOMENA

The musical part of *Catástrofes* is conceived as a sound continuum in which the textures and sound masses are achieved from the synthesis techniques utilized. The synthesis voices of different frequencies are gradually added forming complex textures and sound masses. This implementation generates the perception of psychoacoustic phenomena such as roughness [5] and beats [6] that are considered the saliences and ruptures in listening (or catastrophes).

The duration of the piece is Ca. 11'19'', and three main sound masses (parts) formed by different frequencies' superpositions are juxtaposed. The transitions between those masses are gradually performed, using a method of

[2] The binaural version of *Catástrofes* is available at: https://youtu.be/ggMbu-cVM4A?si=h8vN97u1_PQ34Zri

timbre interpolation [7]. In Table 1 we present the partials used in the structuration of the piece.

Part	Partials (Hz.)
1	94,6; 101,49; 109,18; 137,6; 140,94; 148; 168,21; 181,88; 203,74; 241,65; 271,23; 273,97; 361,71; 446,27; 900; 1316,81; 2210.
2	30,03; 48,96; 54,21; 60,47; 73,56; 107,17; 113,41; 130,25; 150,37; 162,8; 190,55; 203,78; 211,56; 222,35; 230,83; 249,87; 263,93; 515,09; 559,2; 652,66; 782,59; 831,34; 947,28; 1565,19; 1813,56; 1878,36.
3	56,76; 60,48; 63,46; 117,47; 122,3; 141,8; 148,15; 161,02; 198,2; 249,38; 297,19; 310,14; 322,88; 426,66; 458,79; 510,59; 659,97; 682,82; 1284, 28; 1364,90; 1403,88; 1577,51.

Table 1. Frequencies of partials employed in the three main sound masses of *Catástrofes*.

3. AMBISONICS SPATIALIZATION

The spatialization in 3rd order of ambisonics was implemented with ICST Ambisonics and Spat 5 libraries and programmed using 26 sound sources.

We observe in Figure 1 the encoding and decoding of the 26 sound sources in 3rd order, as well as the utilization of light compression and a simulation of 8 virtual speakers in case of phone monitoring, as an option for the main output in 8 channels (dac~ 1-8). This configuration was programmed for the diffusion of the work according to the instructions of ICMC 2024 for an 8-channel system.

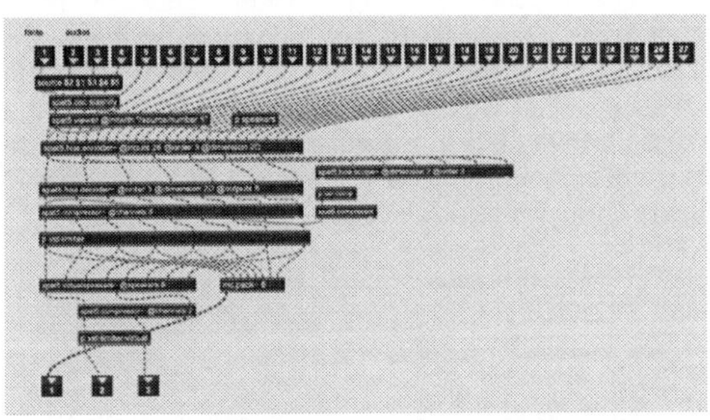

Figure 1. Max subpatch for the 3rd order ambisonics spatialization.

We created a type of notation for the spatialization of the piece in Max/MSP. For this notation in total, 67 entrances are found, 66 considering the 3 parts of the piece (17 for the 1st part, 26 for the 2nd part, and 22 for the 3rd part), and the last one considering the four voices that remain frozen until the end of the piece.

In Figure 2, we show the subpatch containing the information on the trajectories of the second part of *Catástrofes*, containing 26 entries.

The main idea was to create textural imagery that converge with the timbre created, which was derived from the superposition of sound layers. This visual image is always in movement and gradual transformation. In Figure 3, we present the Jitter subpatch in Max/MSP for the video.

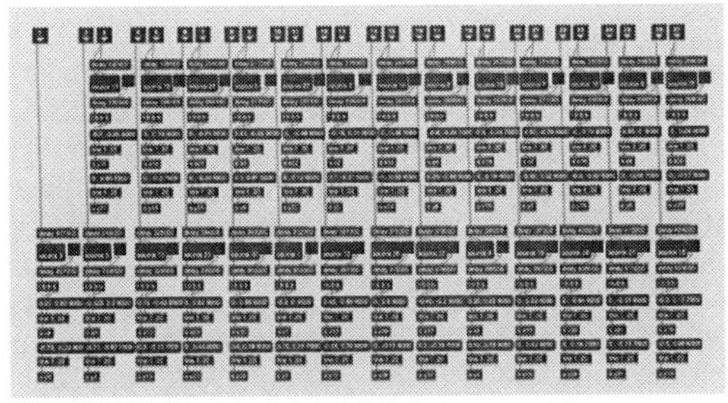

Figure 2. Spatial information of the second part of *Catástrofes*, containing 26 entries.

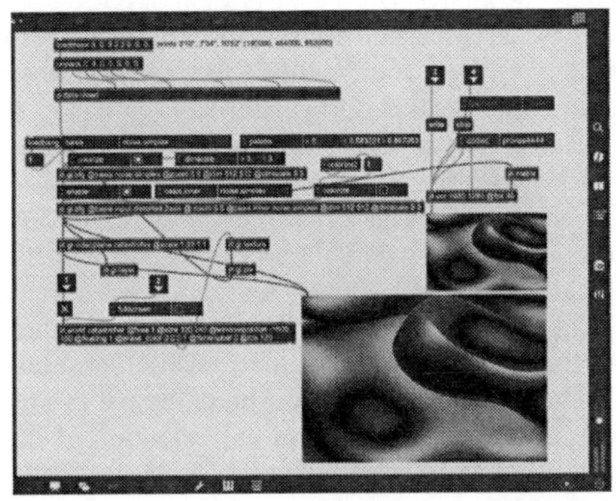

Figure 3. Max subpatch for the visuals, programmed in Jitter.

The texture and color variations in the images are obtained by gradual and continuous changes in the scale, offset, and palette parameters of the jit.bfg object. Figure 4 shows a frame from the video produced during the performance of the piece employing the programming of Figure 3.

Figure 4. Frame of the video of *Catástrofes*.

4. ANALYSIS

Here, we propose an analysis of the sound part of *Catástrofes* based on a methodology that employs audio descriptors to address the sound morphology, texture, and timbre of musical works [8].

For the case of his piece, we base our analysis on the utilization of bark coefficients, spectral flatness, spectral centroid, and spectral flux audio descriptors. We will not present a definition of those descriptors in this article. It can be found in other works [9, 10, 11].

On the other hand, the choice of these descriptors is justified by the fact that they provide information on different features of the perceived timbre (spectral, intensity, and psychoacoustic information), forming a model with complementary information on the timbre. Spectral flatness and spectral centroid are descriptors that present different characteristics of the analyzed sound spectrum, which can be complementary. Spectral flux is an intensity descriptor, focused on the energy variation of the spectrum. Bark coefficients are a psychoacoustic descriptor that measures the frequency regions (bark) that concentrate the sound energy perceived.

We will focus the analysis on the interpretation of the perception of timbre based on listening and the data obtained by the analysis of the descriptors. Figure 5 presents the graphical representation of the 8-channel waveform of *Catástrophes*, bark coefficients, spectral flatness, spectral centroid, and spectral flux descriptors (from top to bottom). This graphical representation was made in the *Sonic Visualiser* software.

By listening, we refer to the idea of an active listening, as described by Pascale Criton [12]. This active listening exhibits operational features, searching for articulations and transversal connections, identifying structures and layers that relate and interconnect each other, and creating individual listening relationships. We believe that this attitude in listening is relevant in a situation of listening to music through a large number of loudspeakers (multichannel system array).

As we proposed in the introduction of this article, *Catástrophes* is structurally divided into three parts, where three different main textures are defined by different harmonic and density configurations: Part A: From 0' to 3'10''; Part B: From 3'10'' to 7'30''; Part C: From 7'30'' to 11'19''. These three parts are disposed of in time with the configuration below. In Figure 5, the division of the parts is marked with a red line.

Bark coefficients are a psychoacoustic measure based on the inner ear properties of the critical bandwidth model of the basilar membrane. This model divides the range of the frequency into 24 nonlinear bands between 0 and 15.500 Hz (bark 1 has a size of 100 Hz, while bark 23 has a size of 3.500 Hz.) [8, 10].

In the graphic representation of the bark coefficients in Figure 5, it can be seen that part A of *Catástrofes* has a subtle presence of sound density in the bark bands. Part B begins with a similar configuration, with a concentration of energy in the bark from 1 to 7 showing an accumulation of energy. From 7' onwards there is a concentration of energy in the bark above 20. Part C shows a greater general concentration of energy and a greater density of timbre, mainly in the bass (bark 1 to 7) and treble (bark 20-24) regions, but also with some concentration in the middle region.

Spectral flatness determines if the spectra have more noise-like (values close to 1) or tone-like characteristics [8, 9, 11]. In the spectral flatness curve in Figure 5 (in orange), we can see that part A has the lowest values (between 0 and 0.3), part B has medium values (close to 0.3) and part C has values close to 0.4. From 11' onwards, the values are between 0.5 and 0.6. Therefore, we find a gradual increase in the amount of noise in the timbre throughout the piece.

Spectral centroid is the barycenter of the spectral content concerning each window of analysis. The higher is the frequency values of the spectral components, the higher is the value of the spectral centroid [8, 9. 11]. Observing the spectral centroid curve in Figure 5, in part A, after a start near 1,900 Hz and a decay in the curve, there is an increase in the initial values from 300 to 1,400 Hz.

Part B begins close to this value, with a subsequent decrease to 600 Hz and a further increase to around 2,000 Hz. and reaches 2,500 Hz close to 10'. From 11' onwards, the spectral centroid values are close to 4,000 Hz.

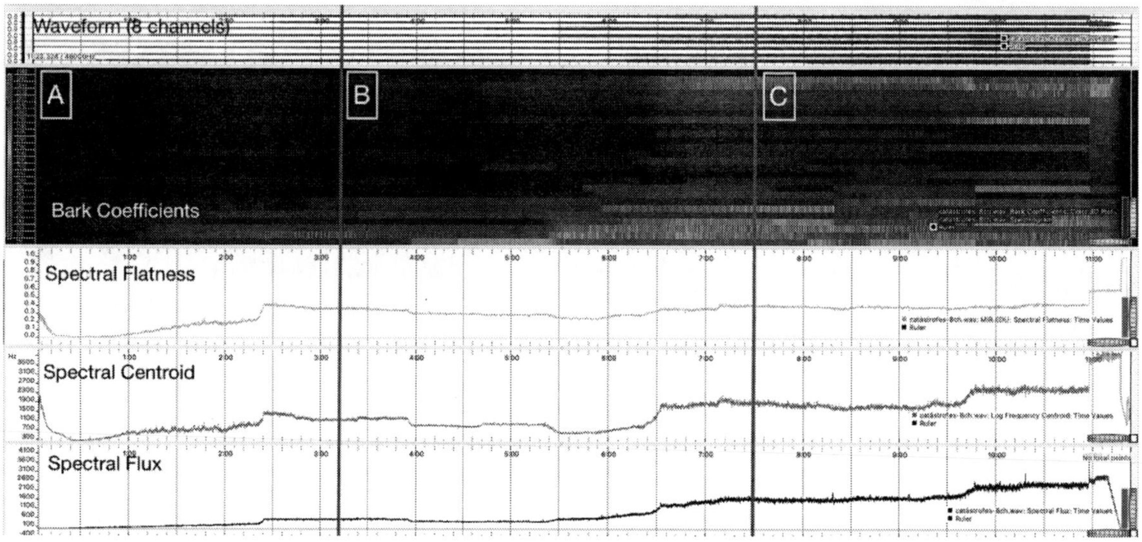

Figure 5. Graphical representations of Bark Coefficients, Spectral Flatness, Spectral Centroid, and Spectral Flux descriptors applied to the 8-channel audio of *Catástrofes* in *Sonic Visualiser* software.

Spectral flux is a measure of the level of change in the power of the spectrum. The lower the changes in the power spectrum, the lower the level of the spectral flux values [8, 9, 11]. In the spectral flux curve in Figure 5, we observe a gradual growth in its values. It means that in *Catástrofes*, the variation of the power spectrum increases gradually in the piece with part C presenting a higher level of variation concerning part A.

5. DISCUSSION AND CONCLUSIONS

Based on the data provided by the descriptors and an active listening of *Catástrofes*, we perceive a densification of the timbre throughout the piece, with a great concentration of energy in the low and high frequencies. The middle region of the frequencies is less explored, gaining importance towards the end of part B.

It can also be seen that the variation in the curves and graphical representations of the descriptors used often does not correspond exactly to the segmentation of the piece into 3 parts. In this sense, we could think of another formal segmentation if that were our aim. This gap between the variation in the values of the descriptors and the formal segmentation determined in the creative process is due to the gradual transformation of the 26 voices into other frequencies when a new part begins. Thus, the spectral configuration of the next part is defined just before the end of the previous part.

Due to the significant densification of the sound spectrum from the end of part B, spatialization in ambisonics in possible 2D and 3D configurations plays a preponderant role in listening to the piece. By defining spatial positions or movements of frequencies (partials), we reduce the potential for roughness or dissonance between them. It is thus possible to explore the psychoacoustic phenomena of roughness and beats from another perspective.

Finally, this composition was conceived in a multidisciplinary approach, combining artistic and technological methodologies for sound and video creative processes. The relationship between perception and action was strongly employed during the creative process through an active listening.

This piece is related to the field of compositional research, in which the creative process is a means of experimenting, testing, verifying hypotheses, and constructing apparatuses and technical objects [13]. Moreover, it deals with sonological emergent psychoacoustic phenomena [14], and subjective experience. The visual part of *Catástrofes* seeks to converge with the sound part through the gradual and continuous transformations that occur in the imagery textures. This combination of multichannel electroacoustic music and video will lead us to future research into levels of presence and immersion in these types of creations, and ways to analyze them.

Acknowledgments

We thank the Muscom Research Group (UFMT-CNPq) "Composition, Analysis, and Performance with computational methodologies".

6. REFERENCES

[1] J. Schacher, "Seven Years of ICST Ambisonics Tools for Max/MSP – A Brief Report", In Proc. The Ambisonics Symposium, Paris, 2010, pp. 1-4.

[2] T. Carpentier, M. Noisternig, O. Warusfel, "Twenty Years of Ircam Spat: Looking Back, Looking Forward", in Proc. International Computer Music Conference (ICMC 2010), Denton, 2010, pp. 270-277.

[3] R. Thom, Parábolas e catástrofes: Entrevista sobre matemática, ciência e filosofia conduzida por Giulio Giorello e Simona Morini. Dom Quixote, 1985.

[4] D. Rossetti, J. Manzolli. "Creating Timbre in Space: Granular Synthesis and Ambisonics Spatialization Study and Composition", In. Proc. of International Computer Music Conference, New York, 2019, pp. 1-4.

[5] P. Vassilakis, "Perceptual and physical properties of amplitude fluctuation and their musical significance", Ph.D. Dissertation, University of California, 2001.

[6] H. Fastl and E. Zwicker, Psychoacoustics: Facts and Models. Springer, Berlin, 2007.

[7] G. Grisey, Écrits ou l'invention de la musique spectrale. Éditions MF, 2008.

[8] D. Rossetti, M. Antunes, J. Manzolli. "Musical Analysis of Sound Feature Emergences Using Acoustic and Psychoacoustic Descriptors, in Música Hodie (22), 2022, pp. 1-36.

[9] G. Peeters. "A Large Set of Audio Features for Sound Description (Similarity and Classification) in the CUIDADO Project", Report, *Ircam*, 2004.

[10] H. Fastl, E. Zwicker. Psychoacoustics: facts and models. Springer, 2006.

[11] D. Rossetti, W. Teixeira, J. Manzolli. "Emergent Timbre and Extended Techniques in Live-Electronics Music: An Analysis of *Desdobramentos do Contínuo* performed by Audio Descriptors. *Música Hodie,* vol. 18, no 1, pp. 16-30, 2018.

[12] P. Criton, "Mutation et processualité dans la pensée musicale d'Horacio Vaggione", in M. Solomos (Org.), Espaces composables: Essais sur la musique et sur la pensée musicale d'Horacio Vaggione. L'Harmattan, 2007.

[13] A. Sèdes. "Méthodologie de la recherche: Séminaire de Composition et Recherche", Université Paris 8, 2014.

[14] C. Anderson and A. Di Scipio, "Dynamic Networks of Sonic Interactions: An Interview with Agostino Di Scipio", in Computer Music Journal, 2005, pp. 11-28.

Emergent Patterns: Music Generation through Markovian Feedback

Felipe Tovar-Henao
University of Cincinnati College-Conservatory of Music
tovarhfe@ucmail.uc.edu

ABSTRACT

This paper presents a feedback-based implementation of Markov decision processes for symbolic music generation, aimed at addressing a well-known trade-off between novelty and coherence in regular nth-order Markov chains — novelty used here to denote the degree to which the output sequences deviate from the input sequences, and coherence defined as the long-term presence and persistence of patterns in the output sequence. The simplicity of Markov models, relative to state-of-the-art deep-learning architectures, serves as a framework for exploring potentially transferable and scalable solutions to the perennial problem of preserving complex, long-term musical dependencies in generative music.

1. INTRODUCTION

Recent breakthroughs in artificial intelligence have caused a dramatic shift in generative music research, favoring the use of deep learning architectures, such as transformer models [1], over more traditional, rule-based approaches, including cellular automata, constraint satisfaction problems, and Markov chains [2]. Notable examples of state-of-the art (SOTA) generative music models include [3], [4], [5], capable of directly generating raw audio data given a text prompt. Despite these nontrivial improvements, one of the remaining problems in generative music is that of preserving complex, long-term musical dependencies in the output [6], [7]. In other words, maintaining pattern relationships over long spans of time.

To explore this issue, this paper considers a deliberately simpler case, namely Markov decision processes, as a framework for exploring potentially transferable solutions to more complex cases, such as deep learning architectures. In particular, it introduces a web-based feedback-based implementation of Markov models for symbolic music generation in which long-term dependencies emerge in the generated output, without durational constraints.[1]

1.1 Markov models

Markov models and variants thereof have traditionally been used as an analysis/resynthesis approach to symbolic music generation [8], [9], [10]. This consists of generating *nth*-order probabilistic models of pre-existing musical data, usually in MIDI format, from which new musical sequences can be generated through Markovian predictions. These models are formalized as finite-state transition probability matrices, describing the probability of every state transitioning into all other possible states (see Figure 1).

FUTURE (output)

PRESENT (input)	*state 1*	*state 2*	...	*state* n
state 1	0.1	0.2	...	0.7
state 2	0.6	0.3	...	0.1
...	...	...	...	...
state n	0.3	0.2	...	0.5

(Transition probabilities)

Figure 1. A transition probability matrix, where each row represents the normalized probabilities of the present state transitioning into all other possible future states.

In the context of symbolic music generation, a Markov state often stands for a musical event, such that new musical sequences can be stochastically generated by repeatedly predicting the next state or musical event, using the n most recent predictions as input. However, *nth*-order Markov models suffer from a well-known tradeoff with respect to their order — namely that lower-order Markov models generate sequences with long-term dependency problems (i.e., pattern-lacking), while higher-order Markov models result in sequences too similar to the input data. This can be understood as a *novelty-coherence* tradeoff— *novelty* used here to denote the degree to which the output sequences deviate from the input sequences (i.e., dissimilarity), and *coherence* defined as the long-term presence and persistence of patterns in the output sequence.

In light of this limitation, a feedback-based implementation of a Markov model is presented here, which affords the generation of polyphonic music sequences with high

[1] The source code and examples are available on https://github.com/felipetovarhenao/markov-feedback/.

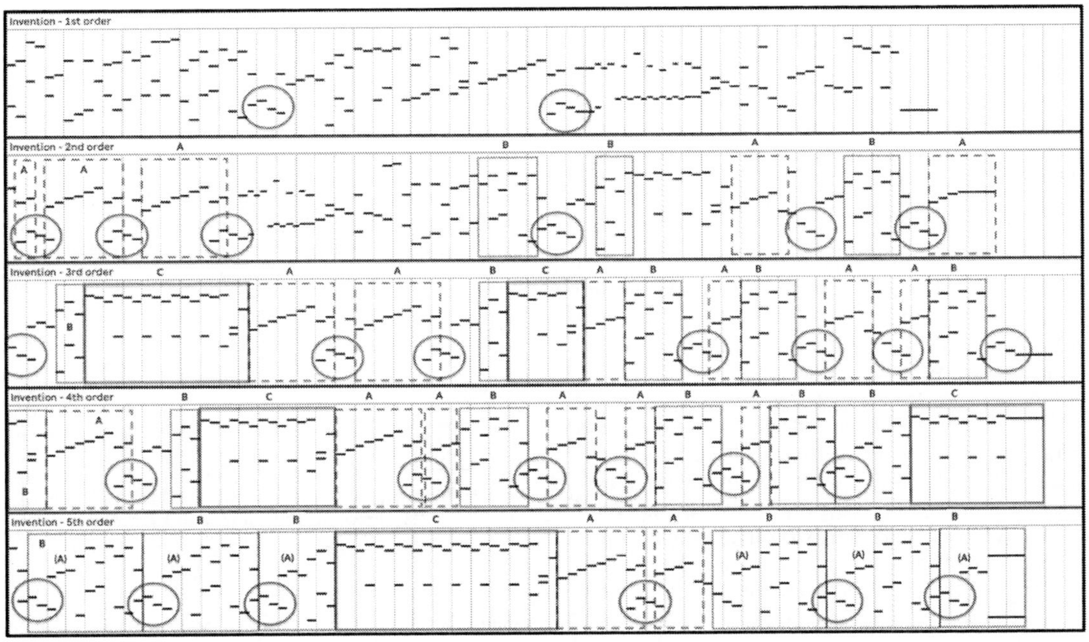

Figure 2. Piano roll visualization of a 5-stage order-boosting feedback, using J.S. Bach's *Invention No. 4 in D minor* (BWV 775) as input data. Sequential segments that repeat at least once within each sequence are highlighted and differentiated by label and enclosing shape.

levels of both novelty and coherence, as defined previously, relative to regular *nth*-order Markov models.

1.2 Background

The implementation presented here is motivated by two common approaches in machine learning: *reinforcement learning* and *diffusion models*, both of which are based on Markov processes.

1.2.1 Reinforcement learning

This paradigm, popular for being used to train computer agents how to play games, consists of cumulatively rewarding an agent for taking actions that lead to a desired outcome, thus increasing the probability that the system will make optimal, or nearly optimal decisions in future opportunities. While establishing a desired outcome in the context of music generation is a highly subjective, and thus limiting approach, reinforcement techniques can still be a useful mechanism to increase the probability of repeated transitions between Markovian states, which in turn increases the chances of pattern emergence in a musical sequence.

1.2.2 Diffusion models

Diffusion probabilistic models are a type of deep-learning architecture that is commonly used for image generation tasks [11]. During the training process, these models gradually apply Gaussian noise to the input data over multiple timesteps, and then learn how to remove the noise iteratively. Since the state of the data at any given timestep is only dependent on the previous state, the data noising and denoising stages can be described or modeled as Markov processes.

This idea of generating data by way of iteratively removing or sculpting noise, comparable to subtractive audio synthesis techniques, motivates the approach taken in this implementation.

1.3 Method

The web-based implementation presented here makes use of two relatively simple but core mechanisms, here referred to as *order-boosting feedback* and *prediction reinforcement*. These are inspired by *diffusion models* and *reinforcement learning*, respectively.

1.3.1 Order-boosting feedback

This consists of first building a low-order transition probability matrix, typically of 1st-order, based on the original input sequence, and then generating a new sequence from it. This new sequence can then be used as input or training data to repeat the same process but increasing the Markov order by 1 with each iteration. The lower the order of the initial Markov model, the noisier or more pattern-lacking the first generated sequence is — i.e., more *novel*. A possible interpretation of what this feedback process does is the promotion of *pattern emergence*, whereby repetitions of increasingly larger segments start to the emerge from the "musical noise" generated by the initial lower-order Markov model. This process is shown in Figure 2, using J.S. Bach's *Invention No. 4 in D minor* (BWV 775) as the initial input sequence. All intermediate generated sequences, each around 150-notes long, are also included.

In the first iteration, the generated sequence is noisy, with a short pattern that only repeats once, highlighted with an oval-shaped enclosing. With each subsequent iteration, more and larger pattern repetitions begin to emerge, until the final sequence contains mostly repeated patterns. It's also worth noting how these patterns seem to gradually converge into meso-formal sections whereby, in the fifth iteration, segments A and B appear to blend into a single section, while segment C stands on its own, thus resulting in a ternary structure. Crucially, the final sequence contains novel patterns relative to Bach's *Invention No. 4* and it's able to maintain long-term dependencies.

1.3.2 Prediction reinforcement

Prediction reinforcement is used to continuously update the transition probability matrix as the sequence is being generated. It consists of indiscriminately rewarding every new Markovian prediction, by increasing the transition probability between the current state and the predicted state. The transition probability of the predicted state is thus multiplied by a *reinforcement factor*, and then normalized along with all transition probabilities for the current state such their sum is equal to 1. The matrix is updated with every new prediction, so as to incentivize repetitions between transitions throughout the output sequence. However, since this may result in undesirably high repetitions, a *maximum reinforcement threshold* can be set, which ensures that reinforced transition probabilities are clamped when such threshold is exceeded. This reinforcement step can be expressed mathematically as:

$$f(M,i,j) = \min\left(kM_{ij}, \frac{h\left(\left(\sum_{n}^{N} M_{in}\right) - M_{ij}\right)}{1-h}\right) \quad (1)$$

where M is the transition probability matrix, i and j are, respectively, the row and column indices of the prediction's transition probability, N is the number of matrix columns, k is the reinforcement factor, and h the maximum reinforcement threshold, in the [0, 1) interval.

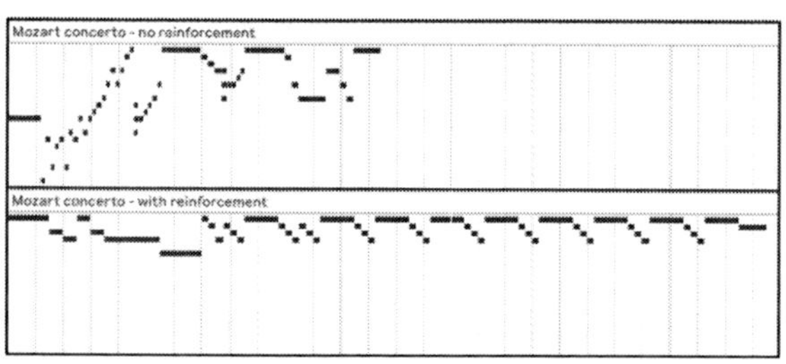

Figure 3. Two sequences generated by a 1st-order Markov model, based on the clarinet part of Mozart's *Clarinet Concerto in A KV. 622* (Adagio). The first with no reinforcement, and the second with a *reinforcement factor* of 2 and no *maximum reinforcement threshold.*

An extreme case of this reinforcement mechanism's impact on the output can be visualized in Figure 3, where two sequences, both generated by a 1st-order Markov model, are compared: the first with no reinforcement, and the second with a reinforcement factor of 2 and no maximum reinforcement threshold. The result is a lack of repetition in the first sequence, and the second sequence quickly locking into a loop. While this degree of repetition is generally undesirable, using more moderate values for the reinforcement factor and maximum reinforcement threshold can prove useful in promoting pattern emergence when combined with order-boosting feedback.

1.4 Implementation

A visual representation of the implementation, including the preprocessing stage and the two previously described mechanisms, is shown in Figure 4. The reader is encouraged to experiment with the web-based implementation[1].

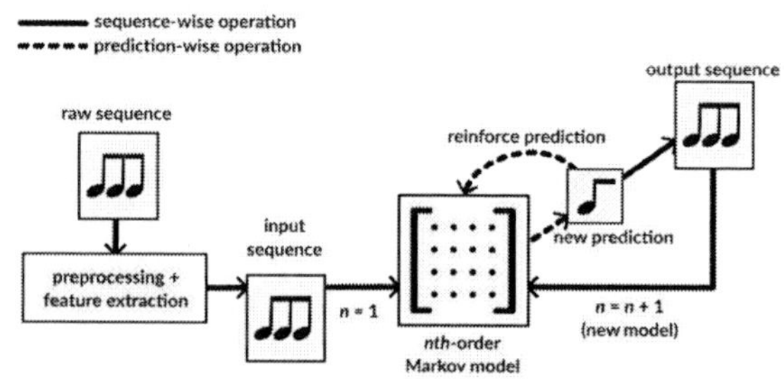

Figure 4. Visual representation of Markovian feedback generation.

1.5 Sequence generation

18 different musical sequences were generated using the current implementation. Details related to the training and generated MIDI files, as well as the input parameters used, are included as part of the paper's supplementary files.

1.5.1 Training data

The data used as input to generate the examples consisted of five, well-known piano works from the Western Classical repertoire, in MIDI format. The motivation behind this choice was to facilitate the perceptual comparison between the generated sequences and music that the reader would likely be familiar with.

1.5.2 Preprocessing

The preprocessing stage consisted of performing the following operations on the input MIDI files:

a) *Sorted array representation:* For each MIDI file, all note events were sorted by the following 3 features, in order of priority: (1) start time, (2) pitch, and (3) instrument MIDI number. Each MIDI file would then be represented as an array of note events and, where multiple files were used to generate a sequence, these were concatenated into a single input sequence.
b) *Key signature normalization*: All MIDI files were transposed so as to start on either C major or A minor, depending on the mode of the initial key. In cases where the MIDI file didn't have a specified key signature, key estimation was performed.
c) *Inter-onset interval (IOI) quantization*: This consisted of approximating the ticks-per-quarter-note (TPQN) value of IOIs to the nearest value from a list of allowed durations — in this case, multiples of 16th-, 24th-, 20th-note subdivisions. This allowed the model to better

[1] https://felipetovarhenao.github.io/markov-feedback/

generalize rhythmic information present in the input data.

1.5.3 Feature extraction

Each Markov state encoded the following 4 note event features:

d) *Pitch*: the MIDI pitch value, in the range of 0-127.
e) *Forward note-wise IOI*[1]: temporal distance between the current and the next note. A zero value would indicate that the next note is synchronous with the current note — i.e., both belonging to the same chord.
f) *Backwards chord-wise IOI:* temporal distance between the current note, and the previous chord.
g) *Forward chord-wise IOI*: temporal distance between the current note, and the next chord.

The last two features were particularly useful in capturing contextual information that would otherwise be missed by only focusing on note-level features.

2. CONCLUSIONS AND FUTURE WORK

This paper introduced and described a feedback-based implementation of a Markov process, capable of generating polyphonic music sequences with high levels of novelty and coherence, relative to regular *nth*-order Markov models. The simplicity of Markov models relative to SOTA deep-learning architectures serves as a "toy model" or framework for exploring potentially transferable solutions to the problem of maintaining long-term dependencies in generative music.

Some possible avenues for improvement and experimentation include the use of other traditional reinforcement learning techniques, such as *noise injection* or *epsilon-greedy Q-learning*, which might further increase the novelty of the generated sequences by promoting exploration during generation. Another option to be tested is implementing this approach with Hidden-Markov Models to generate sequences with more complex musical features.

More broadly, while deep learning architectures dominate current research, it's worth considering the foundational and educational role that Markov models have played in the field of symbolic music generation, and how improving upon simpler and historically traditional algorithms might offer new insights that are applicable to the current state of the art.

3. REFERENCES

[1] P. Dhariwal, H. Jun, C. Payne, J. W. Kim, A. Radford, and I. Sutskever, "Jukebox: A Generative Model for Music." arXiv, Apr. 30, 2020. doi: 10.48550/arXiv.2005.00341.

[2] Ö. Sandred, *The Musical Fundamentals of Computer Assisted Composition*, 2nd ed. Audiospective Media, 2022.

[3] A. Agostinelli *et al.*, "MusicLM: Generating Music From Text." arXiv, Jan. 26, 2023. doi: 10.48550/arXiv.2301.11325.

[4] J. Copet *et al.*, "Simple and Controllable Music Generation." arXiv, Jan. 29, 2024. doi: 10.48550/arXiv.2306.05284.

[5] S. Forsgren and H. Martiros, "Riffusion - Stable diffusion for real-time music generation," 2022, [Online]. Available: https://riffusion.com/about

[6] P. Bodily and D. Ventura, "Steerable Music Generation which Satisfies Long-Range Dependency Constraints," *Transactions of the International Society for Music Information Retrieval*, vol. 5, no. 1, pp. 71–86, Mar. 2022, doi: 10.5334/tismir.97.

[7] C.-Z. A. Huang *et al.*, "Music Transformer: Generating Music with Long-Term Structure," presented at the International Conference on Learning Representations, Sep. 2018.

[8] L. Hiller and L. M. (Leonard M. Isaacson, *Experimental music; composition with an electronic computer*. New York, McGraw-Hill, 1959. Accessed: Apr. 01, 2023. [Online]. Available: http://archive.org/details/experimentalmusi00hill

[9] A. Sigit Ramanto and N. Ulfa Maulidevi, "Markov Chain Based Procedural Music Generator with User Chosen Mood Compatibility," 2017, doi: 10.20668/adada.21.1_19.

[10] A. Yanchenko, "Classical Music Composition Using Hidden Markov Models," 2017.

[11] J. Sohl-Dickstein, E. A. Weiss, N. Maheswaranathan, and S. Ganguli, "Deep Unsupervised Learning using Nonequilibrium Thermodynamics." arXiv, Nov. 18, 2015. doi: 10.48550/arXiv.1503.03585.

[1] All inter-onset interval values were quantized and expressed in MIDI ticks-per-quarter-note units.

rr: the Development of a New Max Package Facilitating Gradual or Randomized Parameter Changes Across Note Sequences

Jonathan Pitkin
Royal College of Music
jp@jpitkin.co.uk

ABSTRACT

rr is a new Max package designed to facilitate the creation of successions of similar sounds which change either gradually or randomly within specified limits. It consists of three abstractions which output MIDI Note and Control Change messages which may be routed to plugins, recording modules, Max for Live devices or MSP objects within the Max environment, or to external applications. As well as describing the capabilities of the abstractions, this paper traces the package's evolution and sets it in the context of other toolkits, and other approaches to algorithmic composition.

1. INTRODUCTION

The rr package is a collection of Max[1] abstractions designed to generate sequences of MIDI Note and Control Change (CC) messages which enact either gradual transitions between defined start and end states or pseudo-random variations of one or more of their parameters or characteristics. It is suited to the creation of successions of inter-related sounds which are timed either unpredictably or according to precise non-metrical patterns which do not fit easily or meaningfully within the standard grid-based temporal framework associated with established software environments such as Digital Audio Workstations (DAW's).

The rr package evolved out of programming designed to meet specific needs identified by the author in the course of composing a piece for live electronics entitled *Study: Boots...* . It therefore embodies a particular approach to randomization and the algorithmic generation of musical events. As well as outlining this, this paper will discuss aspects of the process of adaptation involved in preparing the package for distribution through the Max Package Manager[2]. In this way the entire project will be presented as a case study in how a composer's vision for a single musical work can act initially as a catalyst for the development of a set of tools which might also appeal to a range of other users, and then ultimately as a showcase for the kind of musical outcomes these tools can be used to achieve.

2. BACKGROUND

The author's composition *Study: Boots...* is essentially an exercise in making a lot out of a little. It takes as its basic material the bass drum and hi-hat sounds that are fundamental to Electronic Dance Music[3], and subjects them to extensive transformations and recombinations. These needed to be structured in two different ways:

First, there would be gradual transitions (or 'ramps') between two different versions of a sound over the course of a series of repetitions (usually accelerating or decelerating). For example, as a ramp decelerated, its constituent sounds might also gradually decrease in pitch, move in space, and so on. Second, there would be continuous sequences of similar sounds which varied at random between given limits in respect of several different parameters, either independently or in proportion with one another. For example, a series of bass drum sounds might be made to change randomly in duration, with changes in pitch and decay length 'locked' in step with this, while reverb level and spatial placement both varied independently. Randomization was also to be used in extended, continuous series of the kinds of ramps described above, to define the parameters of the start and end state of each one (again within specified limits). In both cases it was considered advantageous that these musical passages would be created afresh in each performance, rather than being pre-programmed and then selected for inclusion in a fixed, definitive version of the piece.

Conventional DAW's are not well suited to the flexible approach to musical timing that all of this would entail, especially if the composer wishes to make quick adjustments when auditioning his material. As is often pointed out, DAW platforms mostly handle musical time in a way which lends itself to a conventional framework of regularly-spaced beats and their equal subdivisions [1, 2, 3]. And while certain plugins might allow a degree of randomization of parameters from note to note, this can only take place separately from any randomization in the timing of the notes themselves.

Even in its basic form, Max allows the user to treat matters of timing in a much more flexible way; however, the

1 www.cycling74.com/products/max

2 https://docs.cycling74.com/max8/vignettes/package_manager

3 The title refers to a popular 'script' for producing a basic beat-box version of an EDM beat: boots and cats and boots and cats and...

higher-level objects it makes available for navigating these possibilities still tend to favour metrical thinking over any other kind of organizational principle: Glennon and Didkovsky note (albeit in 2010) that Max's object set for temporal structure generation and manipulation is "quite limited", and that objects such as seq and timeline have "many of the limitations that typical sequencer software does" [2] (p.131).

Despite this, Max was used to design the modules needed for *Boots*... , with the intention of making these available to other Max users, in a more versatile and easy-to-use form, at a later stage. rr is the result of that subsequent process of adaptation.

3. AESTHETIC MOTIVATIONS

The use of randomization in *Boots*... was motivated by essentially the same conviction that Laurie Spiegel expresses in a 2018 essay [4]: "The representation of many individual sonic events as a general description of process can be a faster and more efficient method of musical fabric generation than having to specify every aspect of each individual note"(p.107).[4] What is more, in *Boots*... the lower-level decisions the computer makes – about exactly where, within the specified ranges, the parameters of each note or ramp should fall – simply do not matter all that much. The Polish composer Witold Lutosławski – persuasively described by both Krupowicz [5] and Wiggins and Forth [6] as an "algorithmic composer" despite making no use of computer technology in his own works – expressed a comparable awareness of the relative lack of importance of those musical variables of which he allowed himself to relinquish control:

> "...the primary intention is always a certain specific sound vision whose most essential features survive intact in spite of the differences between each performance... However, it must be the kind of vision that will not basically be altered by the eventuality of certain notes, or even groups of notes, not always being played in the same order..." [7] (p.57)

There is one further feature of computerized randomization from which *Boots*... benefits: the escape it offers from the fixity associated with traditional 'tape' music and its successors. The uniqueness of each algorithmically-generated performance, even if it only in terms of fine detail, might be seen to provide something approximating the unpredictability of live performance by human musicians.[5]

4. CONTEXT

Many of the opinions referenced above regarding the limitations of DAW's and Max are expressed in the context of introductions to tools which seek to overcome them in various ways [1, 2, 3; see also 9, 10]. Some of these are versatile Max packages with points in common with rr.

In Glennon and Didkovsky's TimeStruct package [2] "A composer makes high-level compositional decisions...by specifying certain general properties about the form of a desired time structure while leaving details about its contents to chance" (p.131). The idea of a nested or hierarchical structure of Timestruct-generated events (see p.132) has a parallel in rr's algorithmically-generated sequences of ramps which themselves consist of sequences of algorithmically-generated notes or sounds. Essl's Real Time Composition Library[6] (RTC-Lib [9]), meanwhile, includes a number of objects for generating random pitches, rhythms and other values using a range of methods and probability weightings[7], as well as introducing the idea of 'rhythm scales', a close analogue for rr's 'ramps'. Finally, Agostini, Daubresse and Ghisi's cage package [10], makes similar capabilities available to the user through its cage.noterandom, cage.notewalk and cage.weightbuilder objects, while accelerations and decelerations can be created and extensively edited using the cage.timewarp object, though this requires an 'unwarped' sequence of regularly-spaced durations to be created first.

Both RTC-Lib and cage (by design) are relatively low-level, modular libraries, and as such they balance flexibility against the need for the user to integrate and build around the objects they contain before tangible musical results might be achieved. So whilst one could certainly use them to build patchers which offered similar possibilities to the rr objects, the latter can be put to use (in an admittedly narrower range of musical applications) more quickly.

5. DESCRIPTION

5.1 Overview

The rr package consists of three objects[8] – rr.rampr, rr.randomrampr and rr.randomizer – which output MIDI Note and CC messages. These are designed to generate (respectively):

- accelerating or decelerating sequences (ramps) of notes, alongside optional CC messages to bring about concurrent gradual transitions from one parameter state to another
- continuous successions of such sequences, randomly varying the initial and final values of each parameter, within specified limits

---

4 Glennon and Didkovsky make a similar point: "specifying certain general properties about the form of a desired time structure while leaving details about its contents to chance" allows composers "to work with the event timing and general temporal structure of their material from a higher level" [2] (p.131).

5 Hagan's discussion of these issues is particularly nuanced. [8]

6 Coincidentally this project was also originally conceived to meet the needs of a specific composition: Essl's Lexicon-Sonate of 1992-2010.

7 Amongst these there does not, however, seem to be an equivalent of rr.randomizr's 'min leap' setting, described in section 5.4.

8 Although all three are actually abstractions created entirely in Max, they are designed to function in the same way as objects, and are therefore referred to as such hereafter.

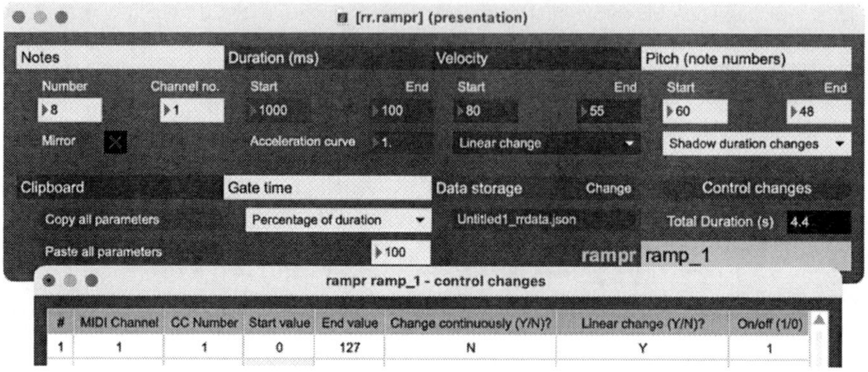

Figure 1. rr.rampr main UI window and CC programming window (detail).

- continuous streams of notes, with designated parameters varying randomly (either in proportion with one another or independently) within specified limits.

The output of each object may be passed directly to MIDI-literate instruments within the Max environment (such as VST plugins or Max for Live devices), routed to other applications, or reformatted as required to control effects plugins and MSP objects. Output may be recorded and edited either within Max (for example using the mtr object) or elsewhere.

The settings of each rr object may be adjusted by double-clicking on them to open a UI window; they may also be changed programmatically by sending messages. This makes it possible, for example, to use hardware controllers or line/bline objects to bring about gradual changes in the characteristics of continuous textures created by rr.randomrampr or rr.randomizr.

5.2 rr.rampr

The rr.rampr object (UI shown in Figure 1) is programmed by specifying the number of notes in the ramp, the starting and ending durations, and the acceleration curve factor. A gate time setting (expressible either as a percentage of duration or a constant adjustment up or down) allows the user to determine the degree of overlap or separation between each note. Start and end values for pitch, velocity and any CC parameters may also be specified; these may change either in linear fashion or with the same curve factor as the durations. Each CC transition may take place either continuously (generating a stream of messages encompassing every value between the start and end points) or as discrete messages sent out with each note onset; they may also be temporarily muted. Any parameter may be kept constant throughout the ramp by setting it to the same start and end value. Finally, a 'mirror' toggle determines whether the ramp immediately retraces its steps, in reverse, upon reaching its destination.

5.3 rr.randomrampr

The rr.randomrampr object (see Figure 3) allows the user to set a range of possible values for the starting and ending durations, pitches, velocities and CC parameters, as well as for the acceleration curve and gate time of each ramp in the sequence. Minimum and maximum durations may also be set for the gaps between ramps. The shape of pitch and velocity transitions may be set to 'all linear', all curved ('shadowing duration') or a randomized mixture of the two; similarly, mirroring can be always on, always off or mixed at random. A 'reversing' toggle introduces the possibility of start and end values being exchanged.

The start and end values for pitch, velocity and any CC parameter may be set to vary independently or 'locked' to vary in proportion with the randomization of the starting and ending durations. As before, identical min and max

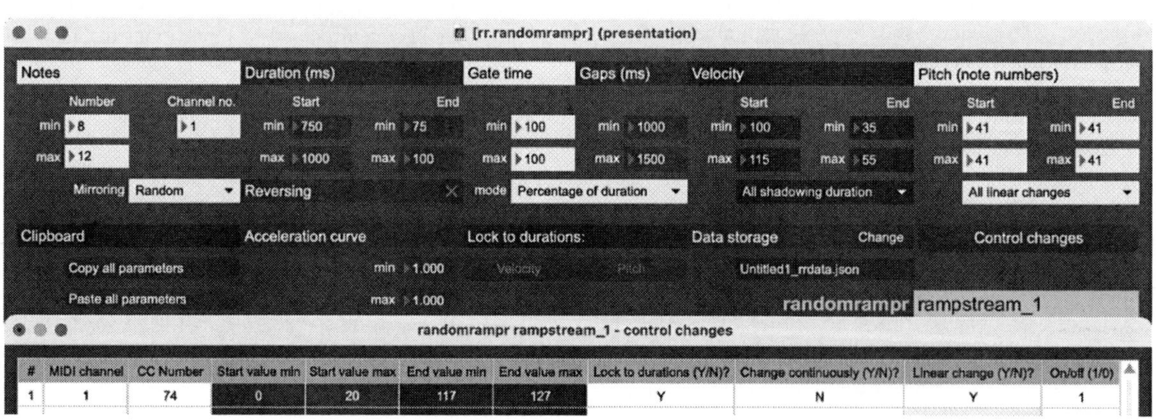

Figure 2. rr.randomrampr main UI window and CC programming window (detail).

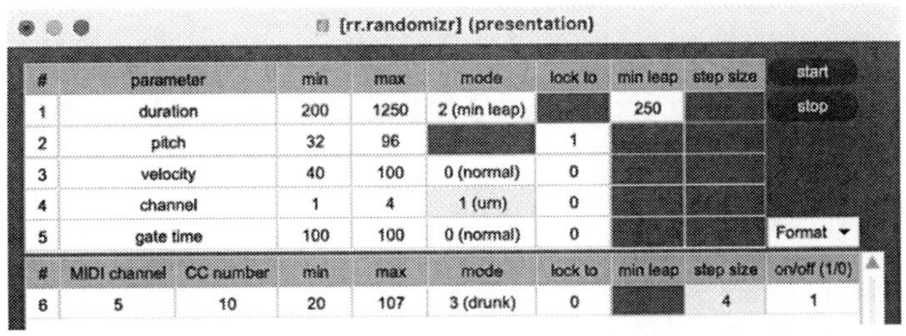

Figure 3. rr.randomizr UI window (detail).

values for both the start and end ranges may be used to maintain constant parameter values.

5.4 rr.randomizr

The rr.randomizr object (see Figure 3) is programmed by specifying minimum and maximum possible values for the duration, pitch, velocity, channel, gate time and optional CC parameters of each note, and the mode to be used to generate a random value in each case. Three of these correspond to familiar Max objects: normal (uses random), urn (uses urn, but resets and continues once the urn is empty), and drunk (uses drunk); a fourth, 'min leap', allows the user to set a minimum difference between consecutive values.

As in rr.randomrampr, each parameter may be varied independently or locked to follow the variation of any other, in direct or inverse proportion. Once again, parameters may be fixed by giving them the same min and max values.

6. EVALUATION AND FUTURE WORK

The rr package has passed through various stages of informal evaluation. The process of disentangling the programming of the three objects from its original context involved drawing a careful distinction between those capabilities which were intrinsically linked to their immediate artistic purpose and those which were easier to imagine being of value in other musical settings. In fact, some controls were added to rr which had not been needed in *Boots…* .

Several example patchers and tutorial videos were prepared with the intention of encompassing a wide range of musical and programmatic contexts (some quite different from those for which the package had originally been designed). The process of creating this material served as a kind of stress testing, not just of the stability of the programming itself, but also of the package's versatility. It was also guided by suggestions and feedback from an internal testing team at Cycling 74: one such idea which may be revisited in a future update was for a graphic display within the UI to show the effect of changes to the acceleration curve values in rr.rampr and rr.randomrampr.

In the meantime, the package is being introduced to Composition students at the Royal College of Music, London, who are beginning to integrate the objects into their own patching and to feed back their reactions and suggestions for expansion. The reactions of Max users who download rr from the Package Manager are also keenly anticipated.

7. REFERENCES

[1] D. Trueman, "The Cyclotron: A tool for playing with time", *Proceedings of the International Computer Music Conference*, Belfast, UK, 2008, pp.69-72.

[2] A. Glennon and N. Didkovsky, "The TimeStruct toolkit: Imposing temporal structure in Max", *Proceedings of the International Computer Music Conference*, New York, USA, 2010, pp.131-134.

[3] P. Vandemast-Bell and J. Ferguson, "Perspectives on Musical Time and Human-Machine Agency in the Development of Performance Systems for Live Electronic Music", *Innovation in Music: Performance, Production, Technology, and Business*, R. Hepworth-Sawyer, J. Hodgson, J. Paterson, and R. Toulson, Eds., New York, USA: Routledge, 2019, pp. 87-99.

[4] L. Spiegel, "Thoughts on Composing with Algorithms", *The Oxford Handbook of Algorithmic Music*, R. T. Dean and A. McLean, Eds., New York: Oxford University Press, 2018, pp.105-112.

[5] S. Krupowicz, "Witold Lutosławski: An algorithmic music composer?", *Proceedings of the International Computer Music Conference*, Denton, Texas, USA, 2015, pp.46-49.

[6] G. A. Wiggins and J. Forth, "Computational Creativity and Live Algorithms", *The Oxford Handbook of Algorithmic Music*, R. T. Dean and A. McLean, Eds., New York: Oxford University Press, 2018, pp.267-292.

[7] W. Lutosławski, "About the element of chance in music", *Lutosławski on Music*, Z. Skowron, Ed., Lanham, Maryland, USA: Scarecrow Press, 2007

[8] K. L. Hagan, "The intersection of "live" and "real-time" ", *Organised Sound*, vol. 21, no. 2, pp.138-146, 2016.

[9] K. Essl, "Real Time Composition Library", 1992-2022. https://www.essl.at/works/rtc.html (accessed 29th Jan 2024).

[10] A. Agostini, E. Daubresse, and D. Ghisi, "*cage*: a high-level library for real-time computer-aided composition", *Proceedings of the International Computer Music Conference*, Athens, Greece, 2014, pp.308-313.

The Aliased Complex Oscillator as a Paradigm for Analog Physical Modeling Sound Synthesis

Clemens Wegener
The Center for Haptic
Audio Interaction Research
clemens@chair.audio

Max Neupert
The Center for Haptic
Audio Interaction Research
max@chair.audio

ABSTRACT

This paper describes a versatile stereo resonator which can rotate the signals in a matrix by any angle around the center. Its signal path is fully analog, and the delay lines are implemented with bucket brigade delays. The design draws inspiration from a digital algorithm (which itself was inspired by an analog concept) and re-implements and extends it as an analog circuit. The resulting resonator creates vivid physical modeling sound synthesis with an analog waveguide in the popular Eurorack format.

1. INTRODUCTION

Much of the knowledge for analog circuit design lies buried in skewed and over-compressed scans of magazines from the 1970's [1] [2] or with some luck in plain hypertext web pages petrifying on *archive.org*. The heyday of analog signal processing has passed, and since then, digital audio computation has become the dominant paradigm, as it proved more powerful and flexible. The availability of online resources on the field reflect this, and at the same time manufacturers have retired a substantial part of their analog component portfolios.

Gerzon describes a stereo reverberator in his 1971 article (pictured in Fig. 1), where he lays out the theory for such, but laments that actually building one would be too costly or outright impossible with the parts available: **Tape delays** are "much longer than the required 30 ms and produce flutter-echo" [2], while "At the present stage of development, small signal degradations introduced in each stage of the line render the **bucket brigade delay** (BBD) line unsuitable for delaying high quality audio more than a few milliseconds". Gerzon has hopes that **digital delays** will solve this issue, but complains that they "are only available in precise multiples of 5 mS [sic]. It is very important for the delays to be incommensurable [1] for the stereo spread to be obtained. Hopefully, manufacturers will soon remedy this deficiency..." [1]

40 years later, Puckette unearths Gerzon's article and implements the reverberator in Pure Data [3]. He is not using it for room acoustics, but as a resonator for physical audio.

[1] The delay times shall be of different, high prime numbers, so that they never fold on-top of each other.

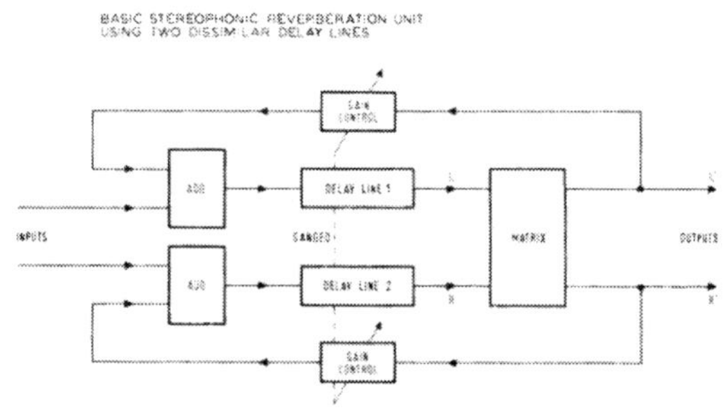

Figure 1: Gerzon's diagram of the hypothetical stereo reverberation (originally figure 3) in [1].

This topic is very much within our research focus in acoustic excitation and intimate control. Such algorithms, which are changing the timbre of the sound through reverberation with their non-linearity and in-harmonic spectral energy, are particularly interesting to us and have led to several publications. [4] [5] [6]

Our attention was attracted to the question if the device which Gerzon described theoretically in 1971 can be built with today's knowledge of analog circuitry. Even more of interest is the question of what kind of timbral qualities and character such analog design would come with. Today the modular Eurorack synthesizer format has arguably revived some of the interest in the analog and its unique sound aesthetic.

2. POWER PRESERVATION AND PHYSICAL REPRESENTATION

The stereo signal in a matrix is a powerful and simple way to simulate reflections. When a rotation matrix is used the total energy in the two channels is preserved at all times as is shown in [2] and applied in [7]. It can be understood and visualized as a rotation of a stereo signal mapped to a x, y plane. This configuration is equivalent to two waveguides [8] with a non-physical scattering junction where the mathematical operation of a rotation (relative to the point of origin) or reflection is calculated.

It can also be understood as an extension of the Karplus-Strong algorithm [9], simulating two strings instead of one, while signals can be mirrored or rotated into each other—or can recombine into one longer string.

Some parametrizations have physical meanings allowing the comparison to a real world model while others have not—or those physical meanings are not obvious and intuitive. The signal processing was originally designed for use in (room) reverb effects [1], where its physical representation is imagined as two adjacent rooms interconnected with an open door. Our implementation can produce quite convincing reverbs when delay lines are set long/slow. However, our proposed use is for creating physically inspired instruments.

3. WHY ANALOG PROCESSING MATTERS

Analog synthesizers come with their own imperfections and instabilities which are very difficult to model in the digital and result in a special sound aesthetic and is subsumed as "character". Analog processes, and in particular the saturation of capacitors in analog delay lines, have a musical character through its nonlinear behavior. The 1st harmonic emerges which is akin to overblowing a flute. An analog signal path is beneficial for musical applications with its absence of any latency or jitter in processing. When comparing the output of the analog resonator with the digital simulations of it, we notice that the spectral color of resonances depend on the system's state and their variance is greater in the analog version. This makes the resonances sound very lively and captivating. Gerzon's dismissal of BBDs (as quoted in section 1) is not applicable to our implementation because of three reasons: 1. The musical qualities of signal saturation in capacitors described above, 2. The quality and signal to noise ratio of the BBD units have greatly improved after 1971, and 3. Since we are using the delay as a reverberator and not a room reverb we only need a few milliseconds and in such short delays the signal degradation is not significant.

4. TRANSLATION INTO ANALOG

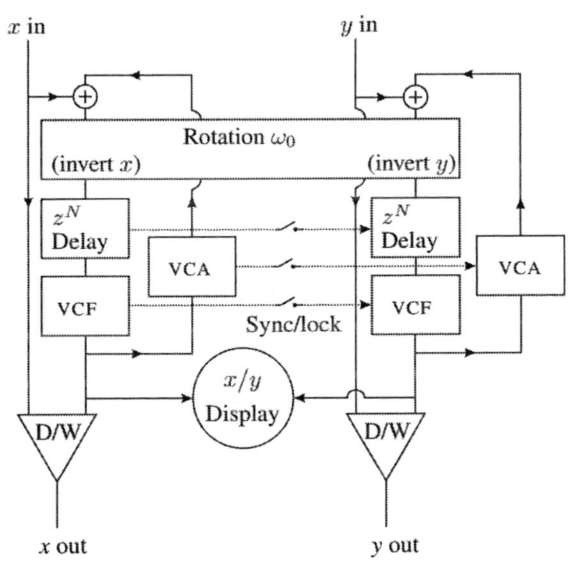

Figure 2: Signal flow block diagram.

The stereo signal in our waveguide is represented by a point in a two-dimensional space. Mathematically this point can be rotated (relative to the point of origin)[2] with the help of a matrix. Practically this is a multiplication with sine and cosine. This rotation is done in four analog multipliers, while the coefficients $sin(), cos()$ to the multipliers are produced digitally from a lookup table.

$$Rot(\omega_0) = \begin{bmatrix} \cos\omega_0 & -\sin\omega_0 \\ \sin\omega_0 & \cos\omega_0 \end{bmatrix} \quad (1)$$

Inversion of the signal happens here as manipulation of the coefficients. When the y signal is inverted the matrix operation is equivalent to a reflection around an axis going through 0 with an angle $\omega_0/2$.

$$Ref(\omega_0) = \begin{bmatrix} \cos 2\omega_0 & \sin 2\omega_0 \\ \sin 2\omega_0 & -\cos 2\omega_0 \end{bmatrix} \quad (2)$$

Timing (e.g. speed/pitch) of the delay is driven by a high precision oscillator. The content of the delay lines is stored as electric charges in BBDs. BBDs are integrated circuits with a serial array of capacitors which are available in different sizes, some with a tap out at half the size. A clock signal causes the capacity in each cell to move on to the next cell. Note that the delay of the BBD chips is fixed to 512 samples in our case. So instead of modulating the amount of samples in the delay line, the sample time (respectively sampling frequency) itself is modulated. These chips were originally produced by Panasonic. They still find their application today, mostly in analog flanger and delay stompboxes for guitarists. Their current manufacturer not only reproduces the Panasonic chip, but also the original datasheet, in which only the new brand name was inserted into the facsimile.

Figure 3: User interface and prototype faceplate of the waveguide module

Following the signal path (shown in Fig. 2) out of the delay: a subsequent filter and decay (feedback amount) which can be driven by a control voltage (CV) input, are all realized in analog circuits, including the gain stage and dry/wet mixer. If no input is provided at the second channel, it is equal to the first channel. Delay times, VCF and

[2] Where the origin is the zero point of both signals.

VCA can be locked together, so that the knobs for x will control y as well.

5. DELAYED MODULATED COMPLEX EXPONENTIAL DECAYING SIGNAL

Here we want to describe the time and frequency behavior of the resonator. In the special case that the two delay times are equal and none of the channels is inverted we can regard the system as an aliased complex oscillator. The two delay lines can be represented by a single complex valued delay line and a phasor $e^{j\omega_0}$ is applied to rotate the complex signal each time it has traversed the VCF and VCA stages.

Since time in BBD chips is sampled at discrete points, we can formalize the signal to be discrete and use the Discrete Time Fourier Transform (DTFT) to analyze its frequency response. For simplicity we also assume that the clock frequency to the BBD chips is fixed, such that the sampling frequency and delay time does not change.

Now, we can formalize the different operations that are applied to the input signal $x[n]$ as follows:

$$s_{out}[n] \quad = \quad e^{j\omega_0 \lfloor n/M \rfloor} \alpha^{\lfloor n/M \rfloor} \overline{s_{in}}[n \ mod \ M] \qquad (3)$$

Where

$$\begin{array}{lll} \overline{s_{in}}[n] & \ldots & \text{complex input signal} \\ & & \text{with finite support } M \\ s_{out}[n] & \ldots & \text{complex output signal} \\ \alpha & \ldots & \text{feedback factor} \\ \omega_0 & \ldots & \text{rotation angle} \\ \lfloor\ \rfloor & \ldots & \text{integer division} \\ M & \ldots & \text{delay time in samples} \end{array} \qquad (4)$$

So after delay M, which in our case is fixed to 512 samples, the rotation about angle ω_0 and the feedback (or gain) factor α is applied. The input signal is fed into x_{in} and y_{in} and the output is propagated to x_{out} and y_{out}, which are real and imaginary inputs and outputs of s_{in} and s_{out}, respectively.

We can now apply the DTFT as follows:

$$\begin{aligned} & S_{out}(e^{j\omega}) \\ & = \sum_{n=-\infty}^{\infty} s_{out}[n] e^{-j\omega n} \\ & = \sum_{p=0}^{\infty} \sum_{n=0}^{M-1} \alpha^p e^{j\omega_0 p} \, \overline{s_{in}}[n] \, e^{-j\omega(pM+n)} \\ & = \sum_{p=0}^{\infty} \alpha^p e^{jp\omega_0} e^{-jp\omega M} \sum_{n=0}^{\infty} \overline{s_{in}}[n] \, e^{-j\omega n} \\ & = \sum_{p=0}^{\infty} \alpha^p e^{jp(\omega_0 - \omega M)} \overline{S_{in}}(e^{jw}) \\ & = \frac{1}{1 - \alpha e^{j(\omega_0 - \omega M)}} \overline{S_{in}}(e^{jw}) \end{aligned} \qquad (5)$$

where $p = \lfloor n/M \rfloor$.

The frequency spectrum has peaks at

$$\omega_p = \frac{\pm\omega_0 + 2\pi k}{M}, k = \ldots, -1, 0, 1, 2, \ldots \qquad (6)$$

where negative frequencies $-\omega_0$ alias back into the spectrum because the delay effectively subsamples the produced modulation frequencies.

Fig. 4 shows the magnitude spectra of one of the outputs for the delay clock at 1024 kHz which results in a delay time of $1ms$. The spectra are shown for different rotation angles ω_0. Note that rotations will generally result in inharmonic spectra, expect for a rotation angle of 0 and π.

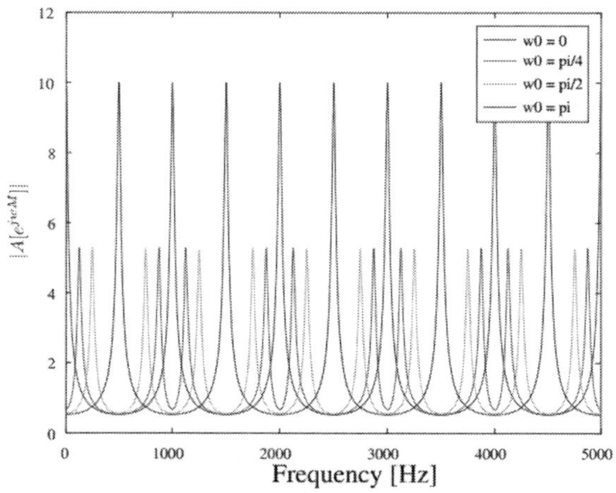

Figure 4: Spectral distribution for the delay clock at 1024kHz, resulting in a delay time of 1ms.

6. VISUAL REPRESENTATION

A display is an important element for this waveguide synthesizer. It displays a stereo analyzer, imaging the two channels of output signal as axis x, y in a plane. As such it visualizes the complex oscillating signal in the resonator. Sinusoidal signals with a rotation create torus knots or Spirograph forms, while other inputs result in patterns resembling orbits, Lissajous curves or petal-shapes. It is possible to generate circles, triangular or rectangular outlines depending on the rotational angle and delay speeds. These forms resemble Chladni figures on a resonating plane. Saturating feedback lets these forms disintegrate and become more chaotic, while more "pure" sounds generate clearer corresponding forms. The wide range of forms and movements is mesmerizing to watch and allows for a synaesthetic experience of the instrument. The visual representation of the signal also assists the experienced user to remember and recreate parameter settings for specific sounds.

7. SUPPLEMENTARY MATERIAL

Audio recordings of the analog waveguide module can be found at zenodo.org/records/11181487. A video with a short demo and an explanation can be found on YouTube youtu.be/nZmAcIOcRoQ.

8. CONCLUSIONS

We've taken the original concept from Gerzon, extended it with the algorithmic versatility added by Miller and fused it into a hardware synthesizer with an analog signal path.

We added eighteen knobs for all parameters, control voltage inputs, three switches for imposing the first channel's parameters to the second, two switches to invert the signals at the reflection node, and a display for visualization. Our resonator is complex, yet stunningly simple considering that the same sound would need hundreds of oscillators if recreated as a filter bank. Depending on the settings the two delay lines can be reflections of each other or joined to a longer delay, with a wide array of possible sounds exceeding the traditional or extended [10] Karplus-Strong techniques and even comb-filter feedback delays [11].

The analog waveguide module is a unique, versatile yet extremely playful synthesizer which creates highly characteristic stereo sounds alongside a fascinating visual representation.

Acknowledgments

We'd like to thank Miller Puckette for digging up the interesting concept by Gerzon in his paper and answering our questions in conversations and email exchanges. In addition we'd like to acknowledge Bauhaus-Universität Weimar for their institutional support, Jörg Brinkmann for his performance, and Superbooth Berlin for presenting and documenting the Analog Waveguide in their "Gesprächskonzert" format.

9. REFERENCES

[1] M. Gerzon, "Synthetic Stereo Reverberation Part One," *Studio Sound*, pp. 632–635, Dec. 1971. [Online]. Available: https://www.worldradiohistory.com/Archive-All-Audio/Archive-Studio-Sound/70s/Studio-Sound-1971-12.pdf

[2] ——, "Synthetic Stereo Reverberation Part Two," *Studio Sound*, pp. 24–28, Jan. 1972. [Online]. Available: https://www.worldradiohistory.com/Archive-All-Audio/Archive-Studio-Sound/70s/Studio-Sound-1972-01.pdf

[3] M. Puckette, "Infuriating Nonlinear Reverberator," in *Proceedings of the 2011 International Computer Music Conference*. Huddersfield: International Computer Music Association, 2011, p. 4.

[4] C. Wegener and M. Neupert, "Excited Sounds Augmented by Gestural Control," in *Proceedings of the 2019 International Computer Music Conference*. New York, N.Y: New York University, Jul. 2019, p. 5.

[5] M. Neupert and C. Wegener, "Interacting with digital resonators by acoustic excitation," in *Proceedings of the 16th Sound & Music Computing Conference*. Malaga: Universidad de Málaga, May 2019, pp. 80–81. [Online]. Available: http://smc2019.uma.es/articles/D1/D1_01_SMC2019_paper.pdf

[6] P. Schmalfuß, M. Neupert, and B. Kessler, "Efficient Snare Drum Model for Acoustic Interfaces with Piezoelectric Sensors," in *Proceedings of the 23rd International Conference on Digital Audio Effects (DAFx-20)*, Vienna, 2020, p. 4.

[7] M. Puckette, "Music 206: Feedback and Distortion," 2015. [Online]. Available: http://msp.ucsd.edu/syllabi/206.15w/index.htm

[8] J. O. Smith III, "Physical Modeling using Digital Waveguides," *Computer Music Journal*, vol. 16, no. 4, pp. 74–91, 1992. [Online]. Available: https://ccrma.stanford.edu/~jos/pmudw/pmudw.pdf

[9] K. Karplus and A. Strong, "Digital Synthesis of Plucked-String and Drum Timbres," *Computer Music Journal*, vol. 7, no. 2, p. 43, 1983. [Online]. Available: https://www.jstor.org/stable/3680062?origin=crossref

[10] D. A. Jaffe and J. O. Smith, "Extensions of the Karplus-Strong Plucked-String Algorithm," *Computer Music Journal*, vol. 7, no. 2, pp. 56–69, 1983, publisher: The MIT Press. [Online]. Available: https://www.jstor.org/stable/3680063

[11] J.-H. Ahn and R. Dudas, "Musical Applications of Nested Comb Filters for Inharmonic Resonator Effects," in *Proceedings of the 2013 International Computer Music Conference*, vol. 2013. Perth: International Computer Music Association, 2013, pp. 226–231.

Reality Check - a framework for preserving real-time electronic music realizations

Miller Puckette
IRCAM; UCSD
msp@ucsd.edu

ABSTRACT

A framework is proposed for protecting an ongoing music production using a continuous integration (CI) paradigm. An enabling technology named Reality Check *is described, which has been applied so far to two existing and one in-progress electronic music production. The benefits are at least two-fold: the pieces that are included in the CI system can be monitored for their continued viability; and also, the various software components used in their realization can use the pieces as unit tests to ensure their own continued back-compatibility.*

1. INTRODUCTION

Live electronic music has a durability problem. Any realization more than a few years old is likely to require maintenance to adjust for changes in hardware or software. Pieces of live electronic music often fall into disuse for lack of the resources necessary to keep them current. Together with fixed-medium music, pieces of live electronic music can become unavailable because of deterioration of physical media, unavailability of equipment that can read the media, and/or difficulty of deciphering proprietary file formats and disk filesystems. In addition to these problems, live electronic music faces unique challenges.

Even if we suppose that we can access the primary digital materials used in a live realization, it can easily happen that essential software components used in a live electronic realization simply disappear or become unusable because of an operating system update or a lost copy protection key. Moreover, a dependency of this sort might not be evident at the time a piece is first realized - it might be hidden in a system library, plug-in, or configuration file stored somewhere else than the digital archive that supposedly constitutes the realization.

The purpose of this paper is twofold: first, to introduce a new software framework called Reality Check that aims to help keep both an electronic realization and its supporting software available over time; and second, to argue for a cultural change among practitioners of live electronic music that can help slow the processes by which the live music repertory degrades over time.

A further affordance of this work lies in its contribution to DAFNE+, a project supported by the European Commission to apply blockchain technology toward the development and versioning of collaborative artistic projects. One major problem facing this project is that items on (or pointed to from) a blockchain are fixed digital documents that could easily fall into the same time traps as any other such document. In particular, if a live electronic realization is built up over a long collaborative process among several stakeholders, the problem of ensuring the continued usefulness of the data itself is multiplied. For example, an NFT describing a realization of a piece of electronic music is worthless if the realization doesn't work. If blockchain technologies are ever to become relevant to the real art world their contents will have to offer more than GIF animations.

It will certainly not be possible for any one effort, such as this one, to permanently solve the problem of realization rot. In many situations it will simply not be possible to use the tools or ideas described here. But even to somewhat mitigate the problems we now face will be well worth the effort.

In the sections that follow we first give a brief description of recent related work; then give a functional description of Reality Check and its use both in existing and one ongoing musical production. Finally we discuss the cultural and practical issues that arise in adopting Reality Check (or another such framework) in the development and production of live electronic music realizations.

2. A STATE OF AFFAIRS

Works in the electronic music repertory are constantly falling into disrepair[1]. Both hardware and software slide perpetually into the oubliette as new, more exciting hardware and software appear. New techniques and tools energize composers as they pursue new and unexplored musical possibilities. But pieces of "new" electronic music, once no longer so fresh, are forgotten even as they are replaced by ever newer ones. There is clearly a problem here.

The worst pain is felt by those who turn to specialized hardware to overcome the limitations of standardized hardware. Until about 1990, for example, general-purpose processors could not approach the speeds necessary to generate anything beyond the most simple electronic sounds in real time. Composers, both in institutions and as individuals, turned to off-the-shelf synthesizers and sound processors. At IRCAM for example, there was even the idea that composers who wrote for "personal systems" such as computer-controlled MIDI synthesizers would find their work much more easily portable outside the walls of the lab and, perhaps, longer-lasting as a result. The reality has been the opposite. Pieces from the late 1980s by Michael Jarrell and André Dalbavie[2] were not only never performed without IRCAM's direct involvement but quickly became obsolete, even despite their occasional revivals after much hard work on the part of later generations of computer music producers.

One might think that we are now free of such problems, since the audio signal processing required in real-time electronic music performance is normally well within the capacity of a modern CPU and can thus be realized portably. But no such luck: the new vogue for applying machine learning in real time means that some of the work is often offloaded onto "graphics processors" using specialized packages and programming languages that will certainly go the same way as the Yamaha TX816s of the 1980s. New papers along the lines of Akkerman's will continue to appear.

The last couple of decades has seen the appearance of a few constructive responses to the overall problem, such as GAMELAN[3], ASTREE[4], and Integra[5]. None of these appear to be still available online. It appears that they have fallen into one or both of the following two traps. First, there has been a tendency to provide supporting software for the development of the piece itself (as opposed to its preservation). Integra, for example, provided an entire infrastructure including sequencing and specific types of audio effects. There is a tacit assumption that these tools would expand over time to meet the needs of an ever wider range of musical tasks, but instead, the existing structure was not one into which a great number of composers wanted to fit their work, and so there were not very many pieces produced within it.

This leads to the second problem, which is that of maintenance of the infrastructure itself. To muster the will to maintain a system such as Integra requires a critical mass of composers or other workers who are invested in the project. Such a mass seems not to have gathered, perhaps as a result of the first issue cited above.

As an alternative to building a framework for realizing new works, we propose that live electronic music realizations, both new and old, be placed into a CI framework in order to toughen them against the ravages of time. This has the advantage of not imposing a particular structure upon any given realization, other than its ability to be virtualized in order to run automated tests on it. In principle at least, not only can the structure of a piece (whether through-written, improvised, generative, or other) be freely determined by its creator, but also the software used can be chosen by the artist.

There nonetheless remains an important obstacle: any tools used in the live performance must be regenerable in some way, either by virtualizing a binary image or, much preferably, by compiling from open source. A complete realization of a piece should contain not only all documents specific to it but also the wherewithal to regenerate all the software that needs to run in real time. This includes not only the environment (Max, Pure Data, Supercollider, Csound, or whatever) but also any dependencies such as plug-ins or "externs".

This is not a trivial demand. A composer under the time pressure imposed by a looming concert date will understandably want to grab a favorite old tube compressor emulator that might be ready to hand. Such plug-ins are often encrypted and copy-protected, and there is little hope that any given one will be runnable once the boutique software house it came from inevitably withers away. Not just for CI-readiness but also in general, a composer or realizer must always choose between expediency and long-term viability.

In the following section we introduce Reality Check, one such possible CI system. It is implemented in Pure Data (Pd) and has been available in preliminary form on the web since 2020. The occasion for introducing it to a wider audience today is a new, large-scale music production that is using Reality Check as its CI system, in the hopes of guaranteeing its long-term viability.

3. REALITY CHECK

Reality Check is implemented as a Pd patch that can test other Pd patches (presumed to be realizations of musical pieces) to verify that they generate the correct output given a standardized input. The standardized input consists of a soundfile, and a text file containing all MIDI, network packet, and GUI (mouse and keyboard) events. To prepare the test, we generate a standardized output soundfile by running the piece with the standardized input.

At any later time we may then present the standardized input to the realization patch to verify that it still produces the same output, to within a predetermined tolerance (by default, one ten-millionth of maximum amplitude). If the test passes, this verifies not only that the realization patch is correct, but also that the real-time environment is still capable of playing the piece correctly.

A simplified block diagram is shown schematically in figure 1. The right-hand side of the figure shows the setup for a live performance of the piece. In the performance, microphones and other sensors (MIDI controllers and mouse or keyboard events) are sent in real time to a Pd patch which generates audio output to be played in the concert hall. During a performance of the piece (or perhaps a rehearsal or even a studio mock-up), all these inputs, and optionally the audio output, are recorded.

To set up the CI system, the realization patch is then run, virtually, in the interior of Reality Check, supplying it with the recorded inputs and in turn recording its audio outputs. The realization patch runs in a sub-process using the `pd~` object. If desired, extra output points may be inserted in the realization patch to allow finer-grained testing. This process results in an output soundfile, typically containing several audio channels.

At any subsequent time the realization patch can then be tested as shown at left in the figure. The recorded audio and control inputs are again played by the Reality Check patch into the realization patch, but this time the output is compared, sample by sample, with the earlier recorded output. If the two agree, the piece has been shown to be running correctly. If not, something has gone wrong and maintenance is needed.

Problems can come from at least three different sources: the underlying hardware and operating system, the application software, and the composer. Upgrades to the hardware and operating system should be made at a time when the older, working system is still available and running

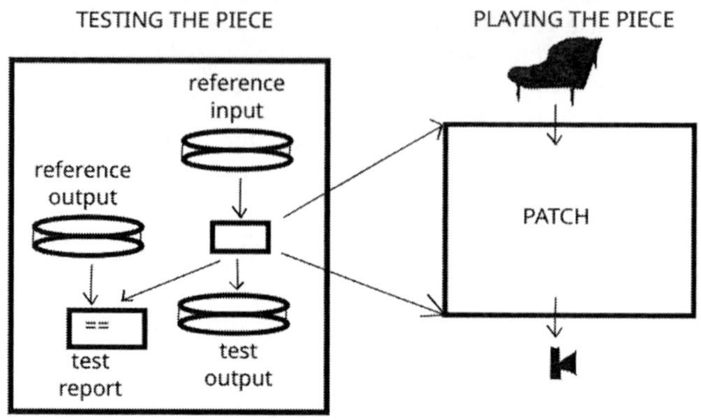

Figure 1. *Reality Check block diagram.*

on a different computer. If the CI test succeeds on the older system but fails on the new one, this must be corrected in the application software. In the simplest case the software simply doesn't run on the new system and needs recompiling—for which we will need the sources to all the software at play. Most of the software components will doubtless be maintained separately, but the maintainer must be prepared for some software components eventually to be orphaned. The upkeep of all orphaned components then becomes part of the task of maintaining the realization.

Second, the application software may have become available in a new version that isn't strictly compatible with the one used in the realization. The temptation here would be to keep up the older software version, but this is dangerous, since the maintainer may end up in the position of maintaining an orphaned version of the software. The more forward-looking solution would be to use the existence of the CI test itself to apply gentle persuasion to the upstream software developers to maintain compatibility. As we will see below, this can be a practical approach in the case of widely used open-source software.

Finally, the composer might want to bring changes to bear on the piece itself. There are at least two classes of alterations that might be desired. First, the piece might be customized for a new concert hall or a new performer. A new concert hall might require reworking the spatialization of the patch's audio output. In the example currently under development, we are anticipating this by using the IRCAM spatializer software ("SPAT") as a separate process, considered as part of the specific performance production and not of the realization of the piece itself.

For another example, a performer might play along with one or more pre-recorded samples or tracks of the same instrument, and it might be desirable that the recordings be replaced by those of each new performer. This and similar adaptations can be made without bringing them back into the CI system.

On the other hand, often a composer decides to revise timings or levels or other parameters that are baked into the realization itself, either during rehearsals for a new performance or in a post-mortem studio session. In this case it is appropriate to re-introduce the changes into the CI system. And while for the later delight of musicologists we will want to keep both the new and old versions, we can probably leave off maintaining the older version in the CI system in favor of the newer one.

4. TEST CASE

A production is underway for an opera, to premiere in 2025, that will certainly put this whole framework under an excellent stress test. The software components being used are Pure Data, Antescofo[6, 7], the `vstplugin~` Pd external object[8], and the Synful VST3 plugin[9]. Two of these systems are open-source and the other two, Antescofo and Synful, are in the process of being released in open source as well. As suggested above, the output of the realization patch is not spatialized but is instead realized as 32 audio tracks that are passed on to IRCAM's spatialization software. For purposes of testing the 32 tracks are optionally mixed down by a reference spatializer inside the Pd patch that is only adapted for a specific 6-channel speaker arrangement. There are currently only four audio inputs but as the production unfolds this will grow to about twenty. A twenty-channel DAW project will serve as a mock-up of the inputs before the actual production, and a bounce of the 20 outputs of the DAW will serve as the initial reference input for Reality Check.

Conceptually, the realization of the piece consists of a Pd patch that is already stable, plus a growing Antescofo script that constitutes the electronic "score". Since the Antescofo script is still under continuous development, it was deemed desirable to also make a test script that exercises all the elements of the patch systematically. CI tests have been built that separately verify the patch using the test script, and also verify the script for the piece itself. This last test is updated as the piece takes shape.

Along with the ongoing production, we are starting a CI regime in which the piece, along with three other pre-existing ones, are run automatically at regular intervals, thus flagging any problems that crop up. This CI system will have to be periodically updated in the future as hardware, operating systems, and software components evolve.

This regime has already borne fruit by catching, on two occasions, regressions in Pd that were since corrected, as well as calling attention to variations in floating-point rounding that do not appear make an audible difference (in our examples so far at least) but which now needs to be studied in more detail.

5. ET TU, MAX?

There is much more music written in Max than in Pure Data, and the question comes up: can we do the same thing with Max (and indeed, with other environments such as SuperCollider) as with Pd? Recently the Max developers have introduced a `max~` object that can embed one virtual instance of Max within another, in much the same way as Max can be embedded inside a VST plug-in. The Max scheduler can optionally be configured to run control and DSP operations in a deterministic execution order. So there is a reasonable chance that the technique described here can be adapted to Max as well as Pd. We will be investigating this possibility in the future.

6. OBSERVATIONS AND CONCLUSIONS

A CI system such as this one can only work if some person or institution will take on the task of maintaining it. In our particular case, the host institution has a team of several permanent computer music designers who understand from years of bitter experience why this will be a good thing to do. Furthermore, we hope that once the procedures described here become widely used inside our own house that other centers that maintain repertories of live electronic music will adopt this or a similar methodology. If adoption is widespread enough, software developers will be able to take advantage of separately maintained CI repertories as a very useful collection of unit tests that their own software can benefit from to maintain backward compatibility.

For Reality Check or any other CI system to work in this way requires that the software components used be able to run in a virtual environment (such as inside `pd~`) and also be deterministically able to guarantee exact reproducibility of audio output from one run to another, given identical inputs. This is apparently the case for the components used in our main test case, as shown by the fact that the CI system currently passes the realization. Precisely which real-time computer music environments offer this possibility is not known.

This requirement of determinism does not forbid the use of stochastic processes in a realization, provided they rely on pseudo-random number generators, as are almost universally used in computer music software. It would nonetheless be forbidden, for instance, to use the current date or room temperature as a random seed; such a seed would have to be fixed. Certain other non-deterministic operations are also forbidden, such as measuring CPU time or querying the current OS version.

There is also the issue of truncation errors that arise from rounding in floating-point computations. In the pieces being tested so far these give variations in the audio output that are very small in magnitude and fall beneath the declared error threshold in the CI system. But running an unstable process such as a Lorenz attractor would give rise to wide divergences in output for different rounding schemes. This is currently a problem for the developers of Pd, Antescofo, and Synful to attend to.

We have nonetheless shown that a CI system can be devised that helps in the maintenance of live electronic music realizations. The system not only flags problems, but its very existence is an invitation to composers to develop their music in CI-controllable form, using deterministic and reproducible software components. It is already also useful as a tool for software maintainers to catch and correct any incompatibilities that might crop up in progressive versions of their programs.

Acknowledgments

This work is supported by IRCAM and by the DAFNE+ project under Horizon Europe Grant Agreement number 101061548.

7. REFERENCES

[1] S. Lemouton, "The electroacoustic repertoire: Is there a librarian?" *array*, pp. 7–14, 2020.

[2] M. Akkerman, "'This hardware is now obsolete.' Marc-André Dalbavie's Diadèmes." in *Proceedings of the International Computer Music Conference.* Ann Arbor: International Computer Music Association, 2017.

[3] A. Vincent, A. Bonardi, and J. Barthélemy, "Pourrons-nous préserver la musique avec dispositif électronique?" in *Sciences humaines et patrimoine numérique*, 2010, pp. 1–1.

[4] A. Bonardi, "Rejouer une œuvre avec l'électronique temps réel: enjeux informatiques et musicologiques," 2015.

[5] J. Rudi and J. Bullock, "The Integra project," in *Proceedings of the 2011 Electroacoustic Music Society Conference*, 2011.

[6] A. Cont, "ANTESCOFO: Anticipatory Synchronization and Control of Interactive Parameters in Computer Music." in *International Computer Music Conference (ICMC)*, 2008, pp. 33–40.

[7] J.-L. Giavitto, J.-M. Echeveste, A. Cont, and P. Cuvillier, "Time, Timelines and Temporal Scopes in the Antescofo DSL v1. 0," in *International Computer Music Conference (ICMC)*, 2017.

[8] C. Ressi, "[vstplugin~]–A Pd external for hosting VST plugins," *Revista Vórtex*, vol. 9, no. 2, pp. 20–20, 2021.

[9] E. Lindemann, "Music synthesis with reconstructive phrase modeling," *IEEE Signal Processing Magazine*, vol. 24, no. 2, pp. 80–91, 2007.

Music-Centric Description of Performance with Data-Driven Musical Instruments

Jeffrey Stolet
University of Oregon
School of Music and Dance
stolet@uoregon.edu

ABSTRACT

Much published literature about musical performance with contemporary digital musical instruments is narrowly focused on performance interfaces and their technical features. This short essay proceeds from the perspective that (1) the entire musical instrument, as opposed to just the interface, should be a point of concentration; that (2) musical knowledge, rather than technology-centric knowledge, needs to be emphasized in descriptions and analyses about musical performance with data-driven instruments; and that (3) the human component of musical performance with digital instruments are essential and should be made more central to these discussions. Departing from these three propositions the text serves as a non-comprehensive introduction to some aspects of musical performance with data-driven instruments.

1. CONTEXT

Musical performance is about *doing*. Musical performance deals with shaping, projecting, controlling, dramatizing, achieving, operating, and manipulating, in the service of beauty, passion, and musical expression. Excellence in any area of endeavor rarely 'just happens.' Instead, such brilliance is the product of the connection of knowledge, discipline, and work ethic guided by values related to the specific arena of activity. We admire great doers inside and outside of music. In musical performance we might think of a great performer who pushes against physical human limits and overcomes the barriers created by technological invention. Musical virtuosity inspires us to attain elevated versions of ourselves. Many great doers outside of music also provide similar types of inspiration.

If one has followed topics associated with digitally-related performance interfaces, you may have noted that considerable emphasis has been granted to technical discussions that focus on such things as inductor-capacitor circuits, electromagnetic resonance, resonant inductive coupling, capacitive sensors, LDRs, IRs, or laser alignment triangulation.[1] But in formulating music of the present and future, deemphasizing hundreds of years of knowledge about how music is played is a particularly bad idea. As a counterbalance to this technological emphasis I will specifically approach this topic from a musical, rather than from a technological frame of reference.

So instead of dwelling on technology-centered depictions of musical interfaces, we are better off if we consider the entire musical instrument rather than emphasizing the interface, and we are better off if we describe how the instrument serves musical objectives. These objectives include how to achieve basic tasks such as starting musical events, stopping musical events, and exerting ongoing control over musical events as they occur.

Traditional Western notation confirms the importance of starting and stopping musical events as does the need to perform musical events in a coordinated and synchronized way, especially during ensemble performances. Additionally, these musical events are not static and require ongoing control as they occur. It is also important to note that musicians create music by using spatial metaphors or their conceptualization of literal space. We can observe this spatial orientation in Western musical scores where vertical positions of note heads signify events in "pitch space," and where a note's horizontal placement in space indicates its position in time. We can also observe the musician's spatial conceptualization when we describe where the physical position of a note on an instrument "is." For example, on a piano we say low notes are to the left and high notes are to the right; and on string instruments the location of the left hand on the fingerboard is described in terms of higher and lower positions.

2. DEEP ENTANGLEMENTS

Working towards the creation of new real-time electroacoustic compositions for data-driven instruments often involves three distinctive activities that intermingle in exciting and often complicated ways. Despite these messy sets of entwinements and the hybridities they promote, the three roles of composer, performer, and instrument builder can be easily observed and comprehended.

First, there is the work that the composer does. Composers make up stuff, mostly stuff that is music and sound

[1] See Miranda, Eduardo R. and Marcelo M. Wanderley. *New Digital Musical Instruments: Control and Interaction beyond the Keyboard.* Middleton, WI: A-R Editions, 2006.

related. Compositional work involves such things as determining the sonic events that will occur within the timeframe of the composition and making judgements about how specific such determinations need to be. As a point of clarity, let me say that I recognize that composers may sometimes determine that the precise events will be indeterminate and the precise outcome of such indeterminacy will only be known at its point of realization during the timeframe of the composition. In the Western art music tradition, the compositional determination of events typically occurs prior to the sounding of the work. As many readers will know, indeterminacy is not randomness and the indeterminate musical substance will almost always be narrowed to a range of desired outcomes. For instance, the specific sounds or notes that are to occur within a composition will not be selected from all possible sounds or notes, but rather from a narrower array of desired outcomes like the sounds from the collection of ten audio recordings of babies crying, or from the equal-tempered notes between MIDI note numbers 60 and 72.

Second, there is work that the performer does. Beyond actualizing compositions through the general directives provided by composers, performers provide beautiful universes of vital musical substance and detail to compositions. This substance and detail that can change a musical experience from the mundane to the sublime. A performer's contribution to nuance at the micro-level is especially critical because there exists no reasonable manner for a composer to specify all the musical detail required to produce an effective musical experience prior to the sounding of a composition. Shaping the tonal and pitch inflections, the musical dynamics, the duration or spatial location of each sound or note has often been seen as better delegated to the performer who can make assessments about how such sonic parameters may need to be adjusted during the course of a composition's performance.

Performance certainly matters because the way something, virtually anything, is expressed, deeply influences how it will be felt and understood. I believe that the qualities of intangibleness and invisibleness in music actually grant the musical performer extreme influence in the domain of micro-musical nuances. In real-time electro-acoustic music, such performative shaping ranges from the micro to the macro and involves things like actualizing the exact temporal placement of composed sonic events, specifying musical balance and dynamics of content, recording audio or control input, or actualizing loop points. Additionally, this performative work may extend to include important musical matters like cultivating a general expressive tone for an entire composition.[2] It is obvious as well that performers must provide the judgement that shapes these musical decisions that have been left to their discretion.

These general areas of composition and performance do not exist in such neat silos. For instance, in jazz many musical events are often determined during the timeframe of the composition by an individual who is also the performer. Because some of the work jazz performers do is compositional yet occurs within the timeframe of the composition, such clear conceptual models are not concise. The boundaries between those things of the compositional domain and those of the performative domain are especially fuzzy. Consider also, for a moment, that for the most part compositional stuff is executed primarily prior to the sounding of a piece, whereas performance stuff is executed within the timeframe of the work. The messiness of such borders becomes evident when one notes that much of what is executed by the performer within the timeframe of the composition is determined prior to the performance in practice and rehearsal sessions. Further, there are instances when a composer "outsources" compositional decisions to the performer which become finalized during the sounding of the composition. Additionally, if an algorithm is making compositional determinations, it might be very unclear who is responsible for different aspects of the sonic outcome – the composer who created the algorithm or the performer who provided the input to the algorithm.

Third, there is the work that the instrument builder executes. In the context of this discussion, instrumental building involves the conceptualization, design and fabrications of the complete mechanism that will be operated by the performer and which will be heard.[3] In all likelihood this work would involve the assemblage of a performance interface that produces data and a software layer that maps and routes this data to sound-producing algorithms capable of responding to this data. With the inclusion of this third activity, the entwinement of composition, performance, and instrument building becomes even more intense with elements such as sound design reasonably belonging to both the compositional and instrument building arenas. And, of course, a certain interface design impacts performance technique (and vice versa). Compositional needs, too, impact performance and instrumental requirements, and so on. The ways one works in these three areas is probably in parallel, not serially, like balancing on a tightrope strung between two buildings where the distribution of physical weight needs to be coordinated. This entanglement creates collaborations among the various roles that exist within a single practitioner where applying the leverage of imagination in these three realms produces beauty and meaning.

3. DATA-DRIVEN INSTRUMENTS

Whereas traditional instruments are driven by energy exerted into their physical systems, new instruments – data-driven instruments – replace energy's function with data streams. These instruments are played through the "operation" of performance interfaces that produce data which is routed to sound-producing algorithms that respond to the data with sonic output. A data-driven instrument is typically not a single thing, but rather a con-

[2] A fascinating example of a performer shaping the tone of previously created compositions is the recordings of Glenn Gould. While Gould was best known for his interpretation of J.S. Bach, his performances of Mozart and Chopin are especially notable in this regard.

[3] I will exclude the amplification and final transduction of signals by amplifier/speaker mechanisms in my descriptions of electronic music instruments. It is not that I am categorically against such an approach, but in my particular discussions, such an inclusion only muddles the primary points I wish to convey.

figuration formed by three interconnected conceptual elements:

1. a section where data is created or acquired through human operation of some interface device,

2. a software layer (or layers) where each generated value input to it is mapped to an output value, or where each value input to it is analyzed, and, on the basis of that analysis, new replacement data is created, and then routed as control data to

3. a sound synthesis section capable of receiving and responding to this modified data by producing sonic outcomes in realtime.[4]

Rather than depressing keys on a piano or plucking strings of a violin to perform music, music is played using performative actions that create data streams which actuate musical events and expressively control musical parameters. A *performative action* is a specific physical motion that directly causes a musical event or events to occur. The specific physical action that depresses a piano key, taps the head of a bongo drum, or plucks a string are all straightforward examples of performative actions.

Just as the amount of energy exerted into acoustic instruments affects musical parameters like volume and timbre, numerical values affect musical parameters contained in sound-producing algorithms. *This means that a performer's task is to create data that will produce aesthetically interesting or pleasing results when the data is used to control musical parameters.* Whether aesthetically interesting or pleasing results are produced is determined by human judgement, the best of which is informed by a broad range of knowledge about musical and cultural history, and theoretical and actual practice as they connect to human life experience, and is further enhanced by an understanding about how humans physically move and how they play musical instruments.

4. PERFORMANCE INTERFACES

While there exists a spectacular diversity of interfaces that can be used for musical performance—some newly invented and fabricated, others appropriated, or appropriated and hacked—the essential structure of these devices is a simple one that contains two broad categories of interfacial elements: buttons and faders.

The humble button is found in many contexts—on our houses, so that visitors can announce their arrival, and on automobiles to start their engines, to name just two examples. In the music systems that I'm describing, the primary characteristic of the button is that of an interfacial element that produces a single value or a packet of values at a specific timepoint when it is depressed. Buttons are useful in specifying when we want to start or stop musical events. While buttons are great for starting and stopping stuff, they don't offer much in the way of ongoing control. In this way, a doorbell is a rather unsophisticated musical instrument in that once its tone is triggered, the button offers no manner to shape musical parameters such as pitch, musical dynamics, or timbre over time.

In the context of data-driven instruments, the conception of a fader is that of an interfacial element that idiomatically produces a continuum of values. In contrast to the button, which outputs a data packet when it is pressed, the fader, when it is moved, outputs what is best characterized as a "data stream" whose numbers unfold over time and whose values are defined by the fader knob's position. Faders are good for providing ongoing control, a fundamental component of musical expressivity. Faders also occur in multi-dimensional forms, most commonly as two-dimensional faders, that simultaneously articulate two values across the X and Y spatial dimensions (understood as occurring across a flat surface), and three-dimensional faders that simultaneously articulate three values across the X, Y, and Z dimensions (conceptualized as occurring within a spatial cube). A Wacom tablet and the Gametrak game controller are examples of performance interfaces possessing two and three spatial dimensions, respectively.

5. INSTRUMENTAL MUTABILITY

Data mapping and sound-producing algorithms employed by data-driven instruments may change during the course of a musical performance. These changes to the instrumental structure can be understood under the concept called *mutability*. A unique feature of data-driven instruments is the extent to which they can change how they operate and sound over the course of a performance. These changes often occur in the software mapping and sound-producing components of the instruments. The reason that instrumental mutability is generally located within software, rather than within hardware, relates to how difficult, inelegant, and time-consuming rearranging the physical world is as compared to the intangible, instantaneously responsive software domain.

Accordingly, the most direct manner to generate such mutability is by changing the data mapping or sound-producing algorithms. In the best cases, the changes in the instrument are developed like the musical material of the composition and, in fact, become part of the composition. In such instances, the composition and the instrument are no longer separate entities, but fused into one.

6. OBSERVABILITY

The notion of observability relates to how well an audience can see what a performer is doing to actuate musical outcomes. This is especially critical with respect to data-driven instrumental performance because of the vast number of ways a data-driven instrument may be played. If one is creating a work whose performance is expected

[4] A similar version of the data-driven instrumental model is offered in Miranda and Wanderley's aforementioned New Digital Musical Instruments and in other places. This three-part structure is not a new idea, but a very old one that can be traced back to early acoustic keyboard instruments like the piano. In this model, the complete pianistic instrument is comprised of (1) the keyboard "operated" by a performer (performance interface), (2) the mechanical assembly that translates downward force into the keyboard into upward motion of the hammers into the strings (data mapping layer), and (3) the strings of the piano (sound-producing algorithm).

to be viewed by an audience, then how to make the performative operation of an interface observable, can be one of the most important considerations when conceptualizing and structuring a musical work.

There are many reasons why seeing a musical performance is valuable. Let me provide just one simple example. When an audience observes what they believe to be a preparatory performative motion, this visual domain input permits listeners to better anticipate future musical events, thus expanding and enhancing the temporal dimension. Such motions might be hand or arm movements or an inhalation that precedes a chord, sound, or phrase. Thus, a musical moment can be both anticipated, and then also experienced in a musical present, giving it both a temporal future and present. If one were to experience the same music without the visual domain, the sonic event might be experienced only as a temporal present.

7. PROBLEM WITH THE CONCEPT OF TRACKING WITHIN MUSICAL PERFORMANCE

The notion of tracking in the context of playing a musical instrument is detrimental because it misdirects attention from what is actually occurring and negatively impacts the understanding of playing a musical instrument. The concept of tracking in playing instruments (1) implicitly transfers the power and responsibility of musical expression from the human to an invented device, (2) erodes the culture of human expertise, transferring it to a technology, (3) and places the technology, which has no capacity to bring an emotional state, a personal history, or an ability to commune with an audience, at the performative center of music instead of the human.

Instrumentalists from all over the world play music in many different musical styles. I would venture to say that all of them would be surprised to find out their instrument has been tracking them. In musical performance, whether the instrument is a traditional acoustic or a newer data-driven instrument, it is unequivocal that the human is operating the instrument and the instrument does not track the performer. I would go even further to say that the concept of tracking, in situations of musical performance, attempts to outsource musicality from humans to technology. Such outsourcing reduces the incentive to think about what needs to be musically and physically accomplished, thus deforming musicality.

Performers throughout history have worked to control the finest details of musical timbre, pitch, and rhythm as well as many other musical nuances. We teach lessons in musical performance and we offer degrees in musical performance all under the premise that there is knowledge to be passed and skills to be developed. These efforts would seem ridiculous if the technology could, or was doing, the work. The circumstances are no different with data-driven instruments: performers operate interfaces that produce data that is routed to sound-producing mechanisms.

The fallacy of correlating gestural motion with data outcomes is simply a case of misinterpreting association with causation. The reasoning that is said to exist is quite simple: data that is produced at the same time as physical motion reflects and is caused by the physical motion. This is incorrect. The device does not report about physical movement – the device knows little about actual physical movement. Instead, the performative interface is reporting about its current state which is reflected in the data that it outputs.

As a performer, I intentionally push buttons and move faders to produce the data I choose that is destined to initiate sound and control sound-producing algorithms. On the other hand, when my cat walks on the piano in the middle of the night, the resulting pitches, are indeed, a kind of objective reporting or tracking of where my cat is standing or sitting or jumping, rather than a musical performance. Why is this? Because my cat has no knowledge about how the instrument works. My cat has no knowledge of the mappings involved—what key is associated with what sound. In contrast, a great musician, like the Chinese pianist Lang Lang, knows that when he plays the note called middle C, that a certain pitch will occur, meaning that he can act with intention. My cat, on the other hand, not possessing this knowledge, has no chance to initiate her musical or performative intent. In addition, Lang Lang possesses sophisticated notions of past, present, and future as they relate to music. Clearly my cat has no conception of time (walking on the piano at 3:00 a.m.), let alone an understanding that facilitates the shaping of present music to be associated with past and future music. Whereas tracking is an objective reporting of events that is not intention-driven and has no sense of past and future, playing a musical instrument is intention and knowledge driven, emotionally rich, and temporally sophisticated. *This temporal sophistication permits musicians to shape the powerful forces of memory and anticipation.* Human operators forge the musical destinies connecting musical presents with pasts and futures; trackers objectively measure and report a status in the present. And, of course, an interface's requirement for direct human intervention is the same reason your piano doesn't play by itself. This should not surprise anyone, because, after all, an interface serves as a border or point where a human and device meet and communicate. If no human exists in this human/device pairing, then an interface has no function. Human operation is essential. Humans operate, humans perform. And this work is performed in the service of beauty, passion, and musical expression.

8. REFERENCES

Magnusson, Thor. "Designing Constraints: Composing and Performing with Digital Musical Systems." *Computer Music Journal* 34, no. 4 (2010): 62–73.

Miranda, Eduardo R. and Marcelo M. Wanderley. New *Digital Musical Instruments: Control and Interaction beyond the Keyboard.* Middleton, WI: A-R Editions, 2006.

Stolet, Jeffrey. *Do: Notes about Action in the Creation of Musical Performance with Data-Driven Instruments.* Morrisville: Lulu Press, 2021.

dlld: a Tangible sound object at hand

Sergey Kasich
UC San Diego
skasich@ucsd.edu

ABSTRACT

We present some key concepts behind the prototyping of a simple, expressive electronic music instrument, which embodies a natural step in the merging worlds of electronic and acoustic musicking. It has a rather random name, "dlld," and is a monophonic "sound object" with the possibility of flexible timbral morphology. A performer can take it in one hand and place it anywhere in physical space. It can be operated haptically like a tangible physical body (an affordance typical of acoustic instruments). This development serves as an example of the practical application of the idea of morphological evolution of musical interfaces (MEMI). The instrument is crafted through a series of stages, evolving in form while retaining its name and the main node of its "DNA" (described as the interactive kinematic concept). Because the stages in this approach are understood non-hierarchically, the instrument becomes potentially affordable for production at different financial levels. We provide three prototypes for the instrument.

1. INTRODUCTION

Electronic music instruments can be identified through a separation of systems of control and sound generation [1, 2, 3]: see Figure 1. This historically has led to the use of various types of performative interactions with the instruments. For a number of reasons though the mass market of music technologies is dominated by the instruments, which have very homogeneous interaction doctrines. Keyboards, buttons, knobs and sliders - that is the alphabet of sound control in the majority of marketed devices. At the same time, we can find products, which challenge this mass-culture reality, trying to introduce concepts, which existed long enough in the domain of academic NIME (New Instruments for Musical Expression) research. Examples here are some gestural controllers (Leap Motion, MiMu gloves, etc.), as well as multi-axes interfaces (ROLI Seaboard, Haken Continuum). Very few of them address another important front of separation between electronic and non-electronic music instruments - the output system.

1.1 Output system

In the case of electronic devices - the output is usually standardized to line level and is designed for the external amplifier, which in-turn usually connects to some sort of standardized speaker. Though it is sometimes underestimated in computer music theories (as shown in Figure 1), we could argue that the output is important in many aspects. Besides it influences the sound, it also results in a mechanical resonator, which is exactly the spot, where the worlds of electronic and acoustic sound generation naturally meet: see Figure 2. The creative approach to the output is a prospective path for developments in the field of music technology, which has been explored by artists and engineers, and waits for more [4, 5, 6].

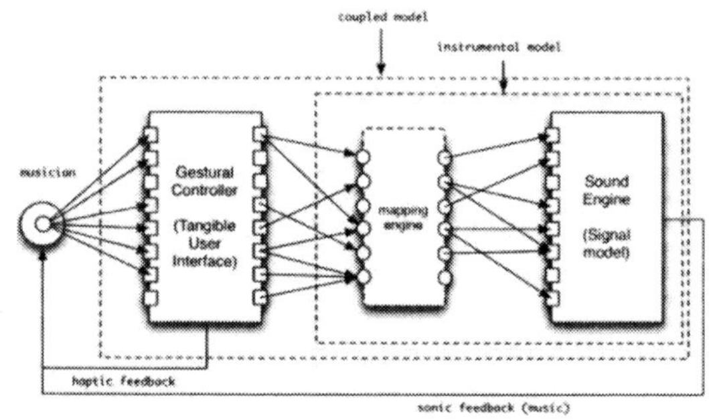

Figure 1. A typical explanatory model of an electronic musical instrument (taken from [1] p.36).

1.2 Haptic elements

Another perspective topic in music interfaces research, as well as in HID in general, is haptics. Specifically haptic display, haptic feedback and etc [4, 7]. We can take our schematic from Figure 2, and use it to mark haptic elements in both electronic and acoustic instruments: see Figure 3. We can argue that because all three (control, generator and output) systems within the acoustic instrument are merged - the acoustic instrument is usually all haptic. This also means, that when playing an acoustic instrument - a performer can influence the sound generation process by directly introducing their body into the physical process of sound generation. It is obvious in case of idiophones, membranophones and most of chordophones (using Hornbostel-Sachs classification), but maybe less so in case of aerophones, especially when interaction is mediated by machinery like in case of pipe organ. This is until one tries to pull their hand into the pipe of the organ during a performance. In situation of acoustic sound generation our body as a mechanical system can always be introduced into the mechanical system of the instrument as it's part, and receive sensible (haptic) feedback in real-time in a form of vibration, pressure, temperature and/or humidity change. This is possible in case of electronically

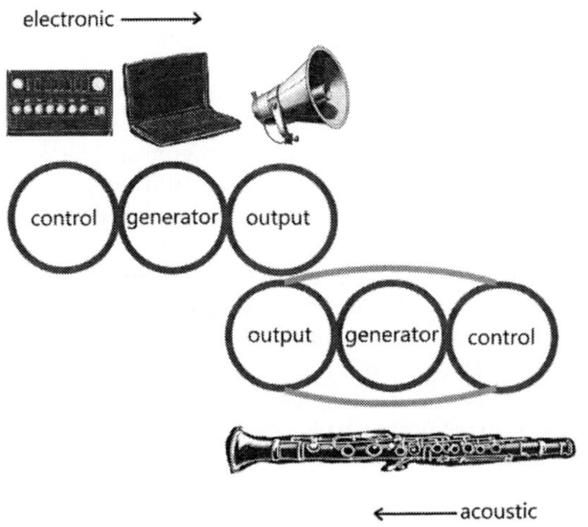

Figure 2. Outputs meet. Electronic and mechanical (acoustic) music instruments consist of similar systems (blue). Though in an acoustic instrument all of them are interconnected and merged (green). This picture tries to illustrate the meeting point of both worlds in the fact that the sound as a mechanical phenomena to appear requires a resonator - which is the same thing in electronic and in acoustic instruments. The morphological similarity between a speaker cone and a bell of a clarinet is also an evolutionary illustration to this fact.

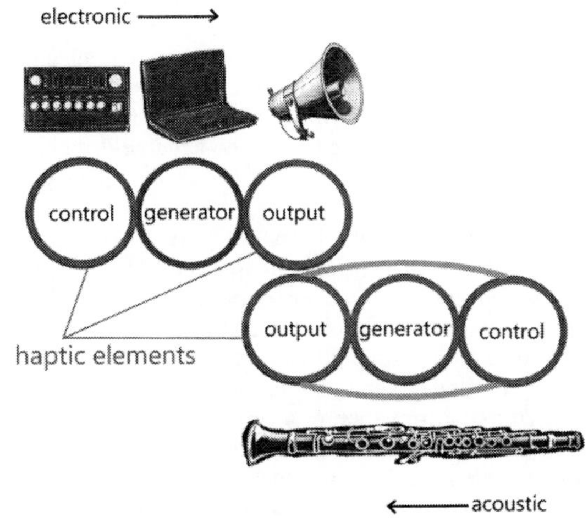

Figure 3. Haptic elements (magenta) in both instruments schematics. Output is haptic in both worlds.

mediated instruments, if and when we consider our body as an electric system. Examples here may include capacitive and/or resistive control for the electronic instruments, with direct contact between body and electronic scheme, especially with sensible levels of electrical current. This approach is central for Circuit Bending movement, various music hacking techniques, it also lies in the core of one of the earliest electric instruments - the Theremin, and is explored in modern developments like FingerRing (FrR) and similar [8, 9, 10]. It is important to state that it is different from digital registration of resistive and capacitive sensors for subsequent mapping, because in case of direct contact 'mapping' happens without digital conversion.

1.3 One-hand-held operation

Electronically mediated interaction can be freed from the limitations, which are natural for mechanical (acoustical) music instruments. Such as the size of a resonator, which determines the size and shape of the instrument and as a result determines the way of interaction. But besides that fact we still can observe certain historically inherited inertia in electronic (including digital) instrument design. This may not be obvious from the beginning, but the fact that most of the interfaces require use of hands and in majority - both hands - most probably is the consequence of this inertia. Simply speaking, nothing prevents a designer of an electronic music instrument from putting all necessary systems (control, generator, output) into the most minimised interaction context - one hand. In fact this has been done in the world of consumer electronics with smartphones. An interactive sound generating mobile app - is an example of hand-held instrument, which this paper is about. And the concept, outlined in next parts can be implemented in such a form as illustrated in Figure 4. This would be an adaptation of general purpose device, which we decide to leave for future explorations. In this paper we concentrate more on other implementations of the one-hand-held instrument.

Figure 4. Illustration of how a smartphone with an attached speaker can embody the discussed concept.

1.4 A tangible sound object (at hand)

In this project we address two problems posed above: the output and interaction (haptics and one-hand operation). We propose a very simple design, which conceptually represents a one-hand operated "sound object" - an electronic music instrument, which constructively merged with it's output system, and from particular angle can be described technically as an advanced mobile speaker.

We use the term 'sound object' in this paper not in the sense, in which it is traditionally defined in electronic music and related disciplines, initiated by Pierre Schaeffer [11]. There it is understood as an abstraction of a sound material - a necessary step to develop a methodology for electronic (acousmatic) composition. We take this abstraction and put it back into a physical reality by attaching a sound to the tangible object, held in hand. In our case a 'sound object' - is a physical object, which can radiate any type of sound. It i possible to speculate, that if Schaeffer's abstraction of sound material into non-tangible sound objects was natural for subsequent work in electronic music composition, - the abstraction to the one-hand-held tangible sound objects is natural for the work with electronic music performance. Other imaginative perspective to this argument would be referring to this type of device as a sort of "sound rock", similar to the one-hand-held rock tools used for other types of creative activities by our ancestors: see Figure 5.

Finally, the "at hand", but not "in hand" - is also important. This way we stress, that portability and mobility of our conceptualized device is essential. In [2] Spitzer shows how the socio-economic and cultural changes were connected to the design of musical instruments. How stationary big instruments like harps and pianos can be attributed to the formation of a certain economic classes in society. With modern property crisis effecting every generation, born after 70s - we can argue, that it makes a lot of sense to design portable and mobile tools. Especially if we would like to add to the musical expression possibilities of a large social categories of people.

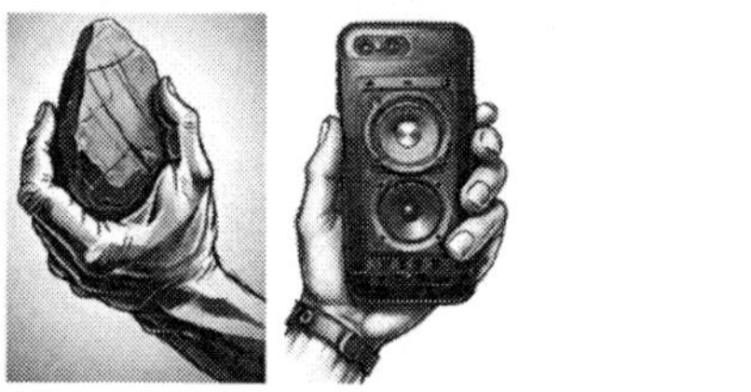

Figure 5. One-hand-held instruments were here with us long time ago

2. MORPHOLOGICAL EVOLUTION OF MUSICAL INTERFACE

We approach the development from the perspective of Morphological Evolution of Musical Interface (MEMI) - showing a recapitulated design practice. Thus the instrument can exist in three evolutionary stages: mechanically - acoustical, electronically-acoustical, digitally-acoustical [10].

Despite our instrument itself was inspired by an electroacoustic speaker, - its mechanically-acoustical embodiment does not involve electrical mediation.

Due to space limitations, we will not go into the details of the MEMI methodology in this text. They can be found in [10]. For our project, we can stress three important points.

First. Instruments can be prototyped through different evolutionary stages. These stages can be derived from research or theories.

Second. There is a non-physical part of the instrument that stays consistent through the evolutionary stages—its metaphorical DNA. This connects every implementation of the instrument with the name of its class (e.g., piano).

Third. A significant part of that DNA is the "interactive kinematic concept" (i.k.c.), which is identified as the learned performative kinematics specific to the instrument.

2.1 Precondition: speaker as a sound object

As mentioned earlier, speakers represent a standard method for sound signal output in electronic music. While the evolution of speaker technology is beyond our current scope, we believe exploring new designs for "output" electro - mechanics is both possible and intriguing. For this project, we must work with existing speaker models available in the market.

In many cases, speakers are concealed behind covers, remaining untouched. But despite this, they have been extensively tested in sound arts and experimental music practices, revealing aspects not commonly utilized in traditional music performance – the physicality and objectivity of the device itself [5, 6]

Instances of creative musical use of the speaker body can be observed in John Bowers's "Victorian Synthesizer", celebrated in the synth-makers community [8], and Maywa Denki's "Otamatone" - a popular Japanese toy-instrument. These instruments, along with similar ones, serve as precursors to the design exploration in our project.

3. DESIGN CASE: DLLD

The dlld (referred to as "dillidee" with each letter doubled) is an expressive electro-acoustic instrument designed to be held and played with a single hand.

Genetic Blueprint (or DNA): This instrument is intended for solo performance, allowing accompaniment for vocal performances. It is capable of producing tones with either diatonic or chromatic scales. Depending on the generator system - large variability of sounds can be produced.

i.k.c.: The design emphasizes one-handed operation, facilitating maximum expressivity through a limited number of controls, mostly operated by fingers. Optionally, the second hand may be employed to manipulate acoustic properties of sound propagation. Notably, natural vibrato is achieved acoustically through hand shaking rather than digital sensing.

Ontogenetic Development Phases: Drawing inspiration from the Magnusson's concept of Epistemes [1], the ontogenetic development of the dlld proceeds through distinct stages:

Acoustic Stage: Assembled utilizing repurposed existing objects, as depicted in Figure 6.

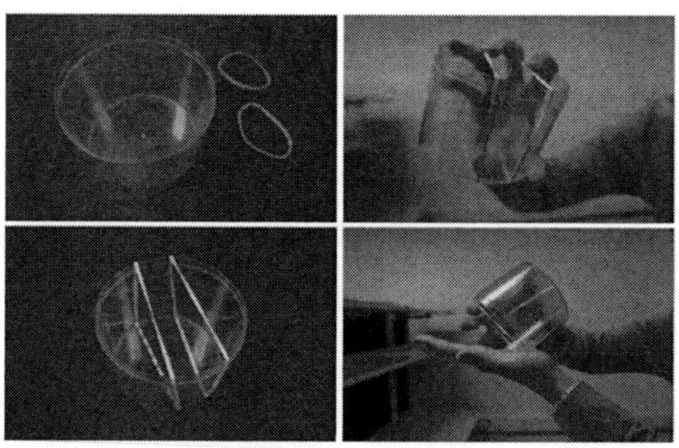

Figure 6. The acoustic dlld uses a resonator and two rubber strings. It is possible to play it with just one hand. Its sound resembles that of some folk African instruments.

Electronic Stage: Involves the integration of pre-assembled components of both electric and acoustic nature, as illustrated in Figure 7.

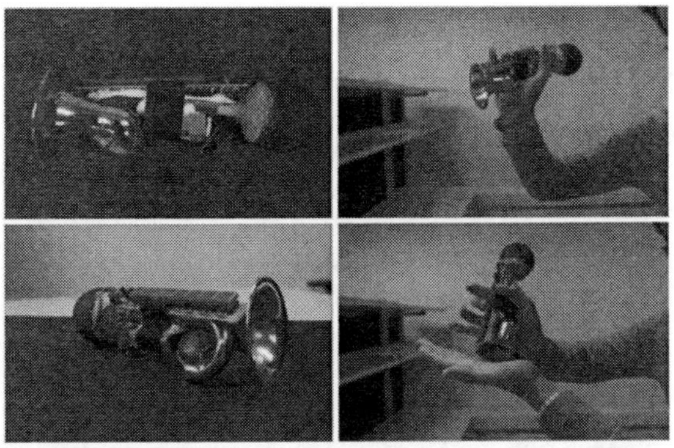

Figure 7. The electronic dlld is assembled using a pre-made board with a 555-oscillator and 8 buttons. A bicycle klaxon is used as an acoustic amplifier and a waveguide, thanks to which the natural acoustic vibrato becomes very expressive. It sounds like a very simple harmonica.

Digital Stage: This phase entails the utilization of a DSP board and DAC programming in conjunction with a specifically designed corpus, as depicted in Figure 8. The current prototype uses 2.5W mono D-class amplifier with an Arduino board as a simple DSP. The control system uses 16 Kailh mechanical key-switches, as well as natural mechanically-acoustical interaction between body and a speaker.

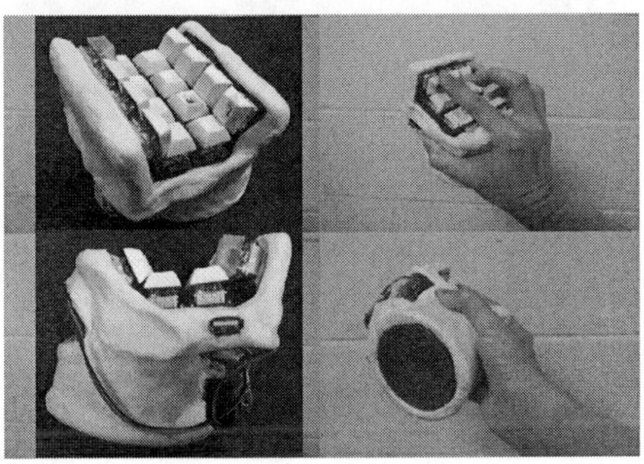

Figure 8. The digital dlld uses an Arduino board as a generator of a simple pulse tone. It has 16 keys assembled in a way that they are reachable by three fingers. This dlld is diatonic in C-major and currently has the range of two octaves plus one tone. It is hard to describe its sound in words, but readers can imagine all the funny effects one can achieve with a well-isolated speaker fed with an 8-bit pulse.

4. CONCLUSIONS

We have developed three prototypes of a one-hand-held music performance instrument, which embodies the idea of a tangible sound object and can be used for all sorts of sound activities. We approached the design of it from the perspective of MEMI methodology, which was outlined in the first part of the paper. This development shows possible solution to two problems in current electronic music instruments: consideration and creative use of the output system and natural interaction between technical system and a human body. As the MEMI methodology is new, we may argue that the instruments designed with it's use, may create new class of music instruments. But this can be a topic for future methodological research. At the same time, the future exploration of the proposed dlld designs may include the above mentioned adaptation of smartphones, utilisation of more powerful DSP boards and tools for digital fabrication, like 3D printings and CNC.

5. REFERENCES

[1] T. Magnusson, *Sonic writing: technologies of material, symbolic, and signal inscriptions*. Bloomsbury Publishing USA, 2019.

[2] M. Spitzer, *The Musical Human: A History of Life on Earth–A BBC Radio 4'Book of the Week'*. Bloomsbury Publishing, 2021.

[3] J. Schacher, "Capture and express, question and understand: Gloves in gestural electronic music performance," *Wearable Technologies*, vol. 3, p. e5, 2022.

[4] A. R. Jensenius, *Sound actions: conceptualizing musical instruments*. MIT Press, 2022.

[5] S. A. Cluett, *Loud speaker: Towards a component theory of media sound*. Princeton University, 2013.

[6] ——, "The loudspeaker in art practice: a preliminary taxonomy," *Sound Art: Sound as a Medium of Art*, pp. 476–490, 2019.

[7] L. Jones, *Haptics*. MIT press, 2018.

[8] N. Collins, *Handmade electronic music: the art of hardware hacking*. Routledge, 2009.

[9] D. Pangburn, "This DIY Electronic Soundsystem Turns Your Body into an instrument," *VICE*, November 2016. [Online]. Available: https://www.vice.com/en/article/9anxgv/diy-body-instrument-electronic-soundsystem

[10] S. Kasich, "Morphological evolution of musical interface: design case studies," May 2023. [Online]. Available: http://nime.org/proceedings/2023/nime2023_78.pdf

[11] P. Schaeffer, "Traité des objets musicaux," in *Lexikon Schriften über Musik*. Springer, 2022, pp. 735–744.

Long-Term, Store-Front Robotics: Interactive Music for Robotic Arm, Caxixi and Frame Drums

Richard Savery
Macquarie University
richard.savery@mq.edu.au

Fouad Sukkar
University of Technology Sydney
Australian Cobotics Centre
fouad.sukkar@uts.edu.au

ABSTRACT

This paper presents an innovative exploration into the integration of interactive robotic musicianship within a commercial retail environment, specifically through a three-week-long in-store installation featuring a UR3 robotic arm, custom-built frame drums, and an adaptive music generation system. Situated in a prominent storefront in one of the world's largest cities, this project aimed to enhance the shopping experience by creating dynamic, engaging musical interactions that respond to the store's ambient soundscape. Key contributions include the novel application of industrial robotics in artistic expression, the deployment of interactive music to enrich retail ambiance, and the demonstration of continuous robotic operation in a public setting over an extended period. Challenges such as system reliability, variation in musical output, safety in interactive contexts, and brand alignment were addressed to ensure the installation's success. The project not only showcased the technical feasibility and artistic potential of robotic musicianship in retail spaces but also offered insights into the practical implications of such integration, including system reliability, the dynamics of human-robot interaction, and the impact on store operations. This exploration opens new avenues for enhancing consumer retail experiences through the intersection of technology, music, and interactive art, suggesting a future where robotic musicianship contributes meaningfully to public and commercial spaces.

1. INTRODUCTION

The integration of interactive music systems and robotic musicianship into commercial retail environment is a largely under-explored area [1]. More commonly, such systems have been confined to laboratory settings or specific art installations and performances, where the controlled conditions differ vastly from the unpredictability and diversity of the real world [2]. Robotic musicians however have extensive potential in the real-world to engage with a range of audiences.

This project centers around a three-week-long interactive in-store installation featuring a UR3 industrial cobot (collaborative robot) arm, custom-built frame drums, and an adaptive music generation system. The store front was in the city center of one the largest world cities at ANON. The installation was designed to interact with the ambient soundscape of the store, creating a dynamic and engaging musical experience for patrons. This paper demonstrates the technical feasibility of such an integration and also explores the artistic and commercial implications of embedding interactive robotic musicianship within a retail environment.

Figure 1: Photo of store-front display

This project's core contributions include the development of a robotic arm integrated with actuated frame drums to forge a distinctive musical instrument, deploying interactive music to elevate the commercial store's ambiance, and showcasing the robotic system's resilience through its uninterrupted operation for a three-week span. Crucially, the project navigated the retail environment's unique challenges by prioritizing system reliability to avoid any disruptions or negative impacts on the customer experience.

We also delve into the critical outcomes and reflections arising from the deployment of our interactive music system in a commercial context. Central to our discourse are the pivotal themes of system reliability, the nuanced dy-

Figure 2: In-shop view of the installation

namics of human-robot interaction within the retail sphere, and the implications of robotic agency as perceived by store staff and patrons. We finally explore the strategic design choices that underpinned the system's integration into the retail environment, ensuring its alignment with the store's brand identity while enhancing the customer experience.

2. RELATED WORK

2.1 Robots, Music and Retail

Recent studies have increasingly recognized the transformative potential of robots in retail environments, primarily focusing on their ability to enhance customer engagement and sales [3]. These include applications to enhance physical shopping experience, such as recommendations on purchases [4]. It is unclear however, the extent to which robots can impact the shopping experience, with studies not pointing to clear findings about best practices to engage customers [5]. Some studies have used robots specifically for entertainment, such as SoftBank's Pepper Robot, to quiz customers about the store inventory [6].

Music plays a pivotal role in shaping the retail atmosphere, with many businesses curating licensed playlists to influence consumer behavior and enhance the shopping experience [7]. Music has been shown to improve product evaluations and behavioural results in retail when effectively used, both through music choice and volume levels [8]. Like music, the strategic design of store-front displays is crucial in attracting customers and establishing a store's brand identity [9] and is extensively researched [10].

2.2 Robotic Musicianship

Robotic Musicianship encompasses a multifaceted area of research that integrates musical mechatronics - concerning the mechanical systems that produce sound - and machine musicianship, which involves the development of algorithms and cognitive models for music perception, composition, performance, and theory [11]. Drumming and percussion playing robots are likely the most widely addressed area of robotic musicianship. Projects have include egg-shaped rattles and drums controlled by direct actuation mechanisms [12]. Many systems have been built that use solenoid motors for various percussion[13]. Recent approaches have focused on techniques such as using Brushless Direct Current (BLDC) motors for high speed and dynamic range [14]. Other projects have focused on adding extra degrees of freedom, allowing for variation in where the drum is hit [15] or adding a flexible joint to the system to improve drum roll performance [16].

There have also been multiple projects extending findings from robotic musicianship into other fields. These include using approaches from robotic musicianship for real-time music generation to interact with individuals to complete basic tasks [17, 18]. Other applications include in education for children with autism [19] and custom devices for interaction [20]. This body of work, spanning from the development of percussion-playing robots to the application of these technologies in educational and therapeutic contexts, showcases the versatility and potential impact of robotic musicianship beyond traditional performance settings.

3. FRAME DRUMS

For this system, we chose to focus on the frame drums, selected for their versatility and adaptability to diverse musical styles, which aligns with the objective of creating an interactive music system that resonates with a broad audience. Their wide range of sizes and tunings, coupled with a potential uniform hitting mechanism, enabled the integration of these instruments into the robotic setup without

Figure 3: Close-up view of the drum actuation mechanism

necessitating significant alterations for each drum size.

The physical design of the frame drum actuation system incorporates motors equipped with dual beaters, enabling hits on both the rim and the interior surface of the drum (see Figure 3). This design choice expands the tonal possibilities while also clearing displaying movement to the audience, through longer than required beater arms. Cabling for the actuation mechanism is routed through the beater holder, to maintain a clean appearance. The drums are positioned at a slant, primarily for aesthetic reasons, to draw attention to the central robotic arm and create a visually engaging setup that complements the store's ambiance.

The actuation mechanism is powered by six Dynamixel XC430 W240 T motors, controlled through a U2D2 motor controller. This setup facilitates precise control over the drum strikes, with each motor's range of motion preconfigured and stored within the motor's firmware. The entire system is managed via a Linux-based control platform, utilizing Python for motor control and system integration. This approach allows for real-time adjustments and synchronization with the central robotic arm, ensuring a cohesive performance.

The control software is designed to interface directly with the U2D2 motor controller, enabling dynamic control of the drum actuation system. Python serves as the backbone for the software architecture, providing a flexible and powerful tool for programming the musical sequences and integrating the frame drums with the broader system. This software layer is critical for achieving the desired musical output and ensuring that the frame drums contribute effectively to the interactive music experience.

The integration of frame drums into the robotic music system was designed around best practices for robotic musicianship, focusing on displaying movement to humans, even if at the cost of mechanical efficiency. This design choice reflects the overarching goal of the project: to create an engaging and immersive musical experience that leverages the unique capabilities of robotic systems while respecting the aesthetic and acoustic properties of traditional instruments.

(a) UR3 robot arm with mounted caxixi.

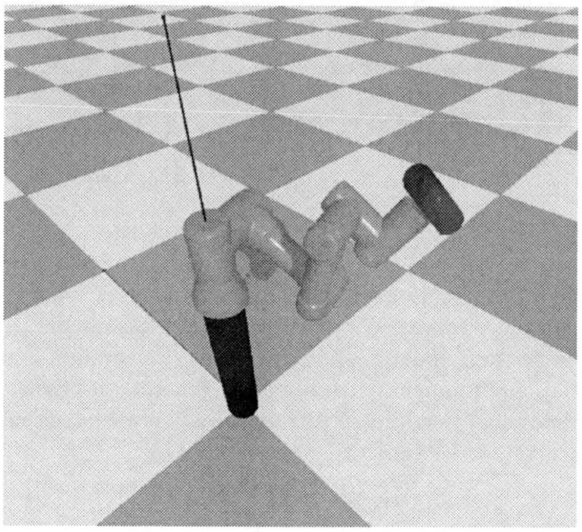

(b) UR3 robot arm with mounted caxixi.

Figure 4: Robot arm simulation and hardware setup.

Figure 5: Motion capture system for recording human percussionist.

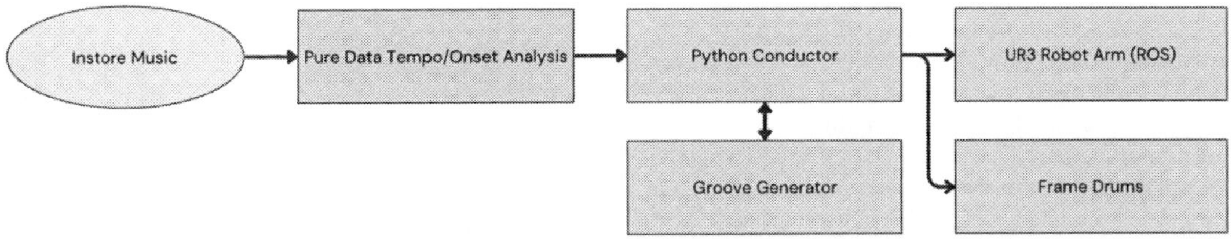

Figure 6: Flowchart of system

4. ROBOTIC ARM PERCUSSIONIST

For imitating a percussionist playing the caxixi, we utilised an off-the-shelf UR3 robot arm which is designed to be safe to operate around humans due to its auto-shutoff capability which utilises internal force sensing to detect unexpected external forces, such as colliding with an object. The UR3 is a highly capable robot with six degrees of freedom (DOF) which means that it can reproduce any arbitrary motion, within its workspace and motor limits, that a human can perform. Robotic arms have recently been used in multiple musical works, such as guitar performance and to convey dancing [21].

The caxixi was attached to the end effector of the robot using a 3D-printed mount, shown in Fig. 4a. To execute motions on the arm we utilised Robotic Operating System (ROS) [22] which has ready-to-use robot specific drivers. To simulate the robot and environment we used Pybullet [23] with OpenAI Gym and IKFast plugin [24], shown in Fig. 4b. This was used for ensuring the commanded trajectories were executable and also for avoiding environment collisions.

To program the playing of the caxixi we utilised a recording of a human percussionist using a VICON motion capture system. We track the trajectories of the both the percussionist's back palm and the caxixi relative to their shoulder. The marker setup is shown in Fig. 5. The VICON captures 3D position and orientation, which we refer to as a pose, at 300 Hz.

To reproduce this trajectory on the robot arm we utilise Gaussian process (GP) regression, a non-parametric probabilistic interpolation method [25]. First a GP is fitted to the trajectory and then using GP regression a smoothed out trajectory of poses at any arbitrary time sequence can be generated. The amount of smoothing can be controlled by adjusting the length-scale parameter of the GP kernel which is useful for ensuring the trajectory is executable on the robot arm which has physical joint velocity limits. More details can be found in [26].

We then took three snippets from this recording with different rhythmic signatures and then translated this motion to the robot arm. For mapping this trajectory to the robot arm we calculate the inverse kinematics solutions for each pose. Since a 6-DOF robot arm can produce multiple solutions for the same pose, for example elbow-up or elbow-down, we bias these solutions to be visually close to the natural configuration of the percussionist's arm. The robot arm also has an option of moving to a random pose to emulate a lively feel. For ensuring executability, we experimentally chose a GP kernel length-scale which ensured the arm did not violate its joint limits or cause an unintended safety stop.

5. MUSIC ANALYSIS AND GENERATION

For the music analysis and generation component of the installation, Pure Data (Pd) was selected for its ability to run on linux. The decision to utilize Pure Data (over pure Python) was also motivated by its capacity to provide a straightforward interface for store staff, ensuring that the system could be managed and troubleshooted with minimal technical expertise. This aspect was crucial for maintaining the system's operational integrity throughout its deployment in a commercial setting.

The Pure Data patch designed for this project was intentionally kept simple, focusing on stability and ease of use. The primary goal of the patch was to analyze the in-store music in real time and output two key pieces of information: the beats per minute (BPM) and the density of the music. This simplicity in design was essential for ensuring that the system could remain functional over extended periods without requiring complex interventions and avoiding (or at least lowering) the chance of crashing.

The analysis process begins with a volume threshold mechanism. If the in-store music's volume falls below this threshold, the system remains inactive, ensuring that the installation does not generate output in the absence of sufficient audio input. For detecting musical onsets, the patch employs the Bonk object, a widely used tool within Pure Data for onset detection. The number of detected onsets over time is then used to calculate the density of the music, providing a measure of its rhythmic complexity.

To determine the BPM of the in-store music, the patch utilizes the Beat object from the ELSE library by Alexandre Torres Porres. The patch monitors the stability of the detected BPM, and in cases of significant variation that suggests instability, it temporarily ceases to generate musical output. This safeguard ensures that the installation's responses are musically coherent and aligned with the ambient music.

After analyzing and detecting the BPM and density, a Python script creates drum rhythms. The generative systems uses a stochastic model that operates on the incoming level of density, combined with a random value for syncopation. Utilizing these parameters, the system allocates drum strikes across a two-bar grid, determining positions for drum hits. Elevated levels of syncopation facilitate an increased frequency of placements off the beat, whereas density levels dictate the quantity of notes generated. Subsequently, each note is given a probability of being played during each cycle. This secondary layer of probability ensures a continuous variability in the rhythm.

The design of the Pure Data patch was designed for flexibility to accommodate the diverse range of music played in the store, which included genres as varied as classical, jazz, pop, rock, and soundscapes. By focusing on the fundamental aspects of music analysis—tempo and density—the system was equipped to adapt to this wide array of musical styles. This adaptability was key to achieving the project's objective of enhancing the retail environment with an interactive musical experience that could dynamically respond to the store's soundtrack, regardless of its genre.

6. SYSTEM INTEGRATION

The integration of the interactive music system is orchestrated through a central Linux laptop, which serves as the center for all operations. This centralized approach ensures cohesive control and synchronization over the system components. Audio input is analyzed by a Pure Data patch, which creates the density and BPM that are then streamed to a Python script. The script interprets the BPM and density data to generate a rhythmic grid for the frame drums, using a rule-based system to create varying patterns. This rhythmic grid, structured as a 2-bar pattern repeats until there is a significant change in music density or when it has played for 32 bars, and dictates the activation signals for each frame drum hit and the robotic arm movement (See figure 6). The robot arm is sent either an instruction to play one of the three caxixi rhythms, or to move to a random pose in-time with the beat. The random pose ensures that the robot is relatively active, while not constantly playing the caxixi and distracting from the retail experience.

One of the critical challenges in system integration is ensuring the synchronization of musical output with the detected beats. This requires considering any digital latency and accounting for the physical time required to actuate the frame drums and robotic arm. To manage this, the system implements a delay strategy for playtime, by the distance between each beats minus 120 ms, accounting for the movement time and system latency. This formula ensures that the actuation of the drums and robotic arm is precisely timed to match the rhythm of the music being analyzed.

To enhance the system's usability, especially for staff, auto-run scripts are configured on the desktop of the central Linux laptop. These scripts enable easy system startup and restart, ensuring that the interactive music installation can be maintained with minimal effort and technical knowledge.

7. LIVE PERFORMANCE

In conjunction with the installation, a special three hour live performance was organized towards the project's culmination (Fig. 7). The primary objective of this event was to explore the acoustic dynamics of the space further and to highlight the installation's presence and capabilities. This initiative served not only as a demonstration of the system's versatility but also as an opportunity to engage the audience directly with the interactive elements of the robotic musicianship in a more pronounced and focused setting. We invited musicians to improvise on violin, alto saxophone and djembe.

Figure 7: Human-robot live band performance

From a technical standpoint, modifications to the setup for the live performance were minimal. The key change involved the integration of a Rode Bluetooth clip-on microphone, which was employed to capture the audio from live musicians. This adjustment facilitated a direct and seamless connection between the musicians' performances and the installation, allowing the system to process and respond to live musical input in real time. The live performance was an exploratory venture into the soundscapes that could be generated within the given space, involving all combinations of the three instruments. This exploration was aimed at showcasing the dynamic interaction between human musicians and the robotic installation, drawing attention to the robot's role as an autonomous performer.

8. DISCUSSION

This section reflects on the key outcomes and insights derived from the deployment of the interactive music system in a commercial storefront, emphasizing the significance of reliability, the perception of robotic agency, the dynamics of store operations, and the strategic design choices that influenced the system's integration and reception.

8.1 Reliability is Key

The operation of the interactive music system underscored the importance of reliability in public installations. Continuous operation without technical failures not only ensures the system's viability as a permanent fixture in a commercial environment but also builds trust and acceptance among the staff and patrons. We heard from staff that past installations in the space have been left not running after requiring constant intervention. Throughout the three weeks the frame drum continued to work, with the arm stopping only three times, likely due to a safety stop as a customer touched the arm.

8.2 Perceived Robotic Agency and Human-Robot Interaction (HRI)

During the course of this project, a significant observation was made regarding the staff's interaction with the robotic elements within the retail environment. The staff's practice of anthropomorphizing the robotic system—evidenced by them assigning names to the robot and engaging with it on a daily basis—highlights a deep-seated human tendency to attribute human-like characteristics and agency to non-human entities. This behavior is not only indicative of the staff's acceptance and integration of the robot into their social space but also underscores the crucial role of anthropomorphism in fostering meaningful interactions between humans and robots, a phenomenon well-documented in the broader field of HRI [27].

We believe the inclination of the staff to engage in anthropomorphic behavior towards the robot was significantly influenced by the robot's interactive capabilities and its designated role within the retail environment. We noted on visiting that staff would note when the music stopped and discuss with Gary what the next song would be. Such interactions suggest that the perceived intelligence of the robot, along with its relational attributes—manifested through its capacity to musically engage and dynamically respond to the store's ambient soundscape—were instrumental in building a rapport and a sense of connection between the robotic system and human users. The anthropomorphic interactions not only facilitated a smoother integration of the robot into the daily routines of the store but also leveraged the unique capabilities of robotic musicianship to enrich the retail space, transforming it into an interactive and socially engaging environment.

8.3 Approaches to Musical Generation

The diversity of music that could potentially play in the store environment, ranging from classical to pop, jazz to electronic soundscapes, presented a significant challenge for designing a system that can appropriately respond to and interact with such a varied musical landscape. We initially considered curating custom playlists, however reconsidered in due to the importance of maintaining the existing store ambiance and branding. Altering the musical environment could inadvertently affect the overall store experience, potentially alienating customers who have specific expectations based on the store's established identity. Given these considerations, the approach to musical generation was focused on enhancing the interaction between the robotic system and the ambient soundscape of the store, and creating interesting movement and interaction.

8.4 Evalutation in a Retail Setting

Evaluating the impact of interactive music systems and robotic musicianship is challenging in any situation. The store we partnered with has a no-camera or recording policy for customer privacy, and directly asking customers was not an option. The effectiveness of such installations can instead be inferred from technical reliability, qualitative feedback from staff and customers, and the potential for future projects within the same venue. These indirect metrics serve as acted as our primary indicators of the system's acceptance and performance, offering insight into its integration within the retail atmosphere and its influence on the customer experience.

In future installations, store Key Performance Indicators (KPIs) could play a role in assessing the system's success, focusing on metrics such as the increase in customers' desire to stay longer within the store and the extent of word-of-mouth sharing [28]. An enhanced store atmosphere, attributed to the novel integration of robotic musicianship, is hypothesized to positively affect these KPIs. The assumption is that by creating a more engaging and interactive shopping environment, customers are more likely to enjoy their experience and share it with others, thereby amplifying the store's appeal and drawing in a wider audience. Despite the inherent difficulties in measuring the system's direct impact on specific customer behaviors, the positive feedback and technical performance offer substantial evidence of its value and effectiveness in enhancing the retail experience.

8.5 Long-Term Effect and Novelty

The concept of the novelty effect, as discussed by Reimann et al. (2023) in their study on a wine recommendation robot deployed in a supermarket, offers a pertinent lens through which to examine the interactive music system and robotic musicianship installed in the retail setting of our project [29]. In their research, Reimann observed that the novelty of the robot attracted individuals with no initial intention of buying wine, indicating that the robot's presence significantly influenced customer behavior and engagement patterns within the store. This divergence between expected and actual user interaction, coupled with the variance between behavioral data and survey responses, underscores the complexity of evaluating social robots in real-world settings and the impact of novelty on user engagement.

Drawing parallels to our work, the deployment of a robotic music system in a commercial environment likely elicited a similar novelty effect among patrons. The installation's uniqueness not only drew in the attention of shoppers but also potentially altered their in-store behavior, encouraging longer stays and increased interaction with the system. This phenomenon aligns with Reimann et al.'s findings, where the novelty of the robot became a focal point for customer interaction, irrespective of the initial intent to engage with the product being promoted.

Moreover, the observation by Reimann et al. that groups interacted more with the robot than individuals resonates with our experience, suggesting that the presence of innovative technology facilitates social interaction among store visitors. This behavior highlights the social dimension of technological novelty in retail spaces, where the introduction of interactive systems can transform shopping from a solitary activity into a collective experience.

A significant insight from Reimann et al.'s work is the importance of identifying and understanding the indicators of the novelty effect in field studies. By proposing a set of indicators and thresholds to recognize this effect, their research emphasizes the need to differentiate between short-term engagement driven by novelty and long-term interest based on genuine utility or enjoyment. Applying this perspective to our project, it becomes crucial to evaluate whether the interactive music system meets real user needs and continues to engage customers beyond its initial novelty.

8.6 Dynamics of Store Operations and Feedback

The support and involvement of the store staff were pivotal, highlighting the importance of designing systems that can be easily operated and managed by non-technical personnel. Feedback from the staff suggests a positive reception towards the technology, although it also emphasizes the need for systems that are robust and require minimal intervention to maintain their operation. This feedback is invaluable for future iterations, suggesting that while the novelty and engagement offered by such systems are well-received, their long-term success hinges on their ability to operate unobtrusively and reliably.

8.7 Always On

The decision to keep the system operational without requiring daily activation or deactivation by the staff presents an interesting case study in the deployment of interactive systems in public spaces. This approach minimized operational overhead for the staff and allowed for a continuous experience for patrons. However, it also raises questions about the long-term durability of the technology and the potential need for periodic maintenance or downtime to ensure continued optimal performance.

8.8 Less Is More

The strategic decision to design the system with high thresholds for beat consistency and tempo, prioritizing accuracy and relevance of musical output over frequency of interaction, reflects a nuanced understanding of the retail environment. In such settings, the potential distraction or annoyance of out-of-sync or overly frequent musical interjections outweighs the desire for constant engagement. This design philosophy underscores the importance of context in the deployment of interactive systems in retail, where the goal is to enhance rather than disrupt the ambient environment.

9. CONCLUSION

This project successfully demonstrated the feasibility and potential of integrating interactive robotic musicianship into a commercial retail environment. By deploying a UR3 arm alongside custom-built frame drums within a storefront, we showcased a novel application of automation in artistic expression but also enriched the ambient retail experience for customers. By focusing on enhancing the interaction between the system and the store's ambient music, rather than attempting to alter the store's musical landscape, we have demonstrated a novel approach to enriching the customer experience without compromising the store's brand identity.

Our exploration into the realms of anthropomorphism, human-robot interaction, and musical adaptability underscores the nuanced relationship between technology, music, and retail spaces. The spontaneous anthropomorphization of the robotic elements by store staff, attributing agency and character to the system, highlights the potential of such installations to become integrated, engaging parts of social and commercial settings. This project has also addressed the technical challenge of designing a system capable of responding to a diverse array of musical genres, emphasizing interaction and adaptability as central to the success of the installation. The system's ability to operate continuously for three weeks without significant interruptions highlights its reliability and suitability for long-term installations in public spaces.

Moving forward, this project serves as a foundation for future research and development in the intersection of music, robotics, and retail. It invites further exploration into how these systems can be optimized to meet diverse user needs, adapt to changing environments, and contribute to the creation of innovative retail experiences. By continuing to focus on the seamless integration of technology with human-centric design principles, we can unlock new possibilities for enhancing public spaces with interactive, engaging, and meaningful installations.

10. ACKNOWLEDGEMENTS

This research is partially supported by the Industrial Transformation Training Centre (ITTC) for Collaborative Robotics in Advanced Manufacturing (also known as the Australian Cobotics Centre) funded by ARC (Project ID: IC200100001)

11. REFERENCES

[1] E. Frid, "Musical Robots: Overview and Methods for Evaluation," *Sound and Robotics*, pp. 243–284, 2023.

[2] J. Sullivan and M. Wanderley, "Stability, Reliability, Compatibility: Reviewing 40 Years of NIME Design," Ph.D. dissertation, McGill University/Université McGill, 2018.

[3] L. De Gauquier, M. Brengman, and K. Willems, "The rise of service robots in retailing: literature review on success factors and pitfalls," *Retail Futures: The Good, the Bad and the Ugly of the Digital Transformation*, pp. 15–35, 2020.

[4] R. Graef, M. Klier, A. Obermeier, and J. F. Zolitschka, "What to buy, pepper?–Bridging the physical and the digital world with recommendations from humanoid robots," *Journal of Decision Systems*, vol. 32, no. 2, pp. 439–465, 2023.

[5] D. Golchinfar, D. D. Vaziri, G. Stevens, and D. Schreiber, "Let's Go to the Mall: Investigating the Role of User Experience in Customers' Intention to Use Social Robots in a Shopping Mall," in *Designing Interactive Systems Conference*, 2022, pp. 377–386.

[6] L. De Gauquier, M. Brengman, K. Willems, H.-L. Cao, and B. Vanderborght, "In or out? A field observational study on the placement of entertaining robots in retailing," *International Journal of Retail & Distribution Management*, vol. 49, no. 7, pp. 846–874, 2021.

[7] A. Michel, C. Baumann, and L. Gayer, "Thank you for the music–or not? The effects of in-store music in service settings," *Journal of retailing and consumer services*, vol. 36, pp. 21–32, 2017.

[8] M.-A. Trompeta, K. Karantinou, C. Koritos, and T. H. Bijmolt, "A meta-analysis of the effects of music in tourism and hospitality settings," *Journal of Business Research*, vol. 138, pp. 130–145, 2022.

[9] B. Cornelius, M. Natter, and C. Faure, "How storefront displays influence retail store image," *Journal of Retailing and Consumer Services*, vol. 17, no. 2, pp. 143–151, 2010.

[10] C. d. C. Webber, J. O. Sausen, K. Basso, and C. G. Laimer, "Remodelling the retail store for better sales performance," *International Journal of Retail & Distribution Management*, vol. 46, no. 11/12, pp. 1041–1055, 2018.

[11] R. Savery, L. Zahray, and G. Weinberg, "Shimon sings-robotic musicianship finds its voice," *Handbook of Artificial Intelligence for Music: Foundations, Advanced Approaches, and Developments for Creativity*, pp. 823–847, 2021.

[12] E. Singer, J. Feddersen, C. Redmon, and B. Bowen, "LEMUR's musicsinger2004lemural robots," in *Proceedings of the 2004 conference on New interfaces for musical expression*, 2004, pp. 181–184.

[13] A. Kapur, E. Trimpin, A. Singer, G. Suleman, and G. Tzanetakis, "A comparison of solenoid-based strategies for robotic drumming," in *ICMC*, 2007.

[14] N. Yang, R. Savery, R. Sankaranarayanan, L. Zahray, and G. Weinberg, "Mechatronics-driven musical expressivity for robotic percussionists," *arXiv preprint arXiv:2007.14850*, 2020.

[15] J. Murphy, D. A. Carnegie, and A. Kapur, "Little drummer bot: Building, testing, and interfacing with a new expressive mechatronic drum system," in *Proceedings of the International Computer Music Conference. ICMC*, 2014.

[16] S. M. Karbasi, A. R. Jensenius, R. I. Godøy, and J. Tørresen, "A Robotic Drummer with a Flexible Joint: the Effect of Passive Impedance on Drumming," 2022.

[17] R. Savery, L. Zahray, and G. Weinberg, "Emotional musical prosody for the enhancement of trust: Audio design for robotic arm communication," *Paladyn, Journal of Behavioral Robotics*, vol. 12, no. 1, pp. 454–467, 2021.

[18] ——, "Before, Between, and After: Enriching Robot Communication Surrounding Collaborative Creative Activities," *Frontiers in Robotics and AI*, vol. 8, p. 116, 2021.

[19] A. Taheri, A. Meghdari, M. Alemi, and H. Pouretemad, "Teaching music to children with autism: a social robotics challenge," *Scientia Iranica*, vol. 26, no. Special Issue on: Socio-Cognitive Engineering, pp. 40–58, 2019.

[20] A. Savery, "Enhancing Violin Performance through Real-Time Interaction: Design and Evaluation of a Wireless Audio-Visual Interface," *Chroma: Journal of the Australasian Computer Music Association*, vol. 39, no. 2, 2023.

[21] A. Rogel, R. Savery, N. Yang, and G. Weinberg, "RoboGroove: Creating Fluid Motion for Dancing Robotic Arms," in *Proceedings of the 8th ICMC*, 2022, pp. 1–9.

[22] Stanford Artificial Intelligence Laboratory et al., "Robotic Operating System." [Online]. Available: https://www.ros.org

[23] E. Coumans and Y. Bai, "PyBullet, a Python module for physics simulation for games, robotics and machine learning," http://pybullet.org, 2016–2021.

[24] Cambel, "Cambel/ur_ikfast: Python Ikfast Library for universal robots," https://github.com/cambel/ur_ikfast, 2024.

[25] C. E. Rasmussen and C. K. I. Williams, *Gaussian Processes for Machine Learning*. The MIT Press, 2006.

[26] F. Sukkar, R. Savery, N. Haque, C. L. Gentil, R. Guenot-Falque, and T. V. Calleja, "A Robotic System For Imitating Human Percussionists," in *Proc. of Australian Conference on Robotics and Automation*, 2023.

[27] M. Blut, C. Wang, N. V. Wünderlich, and C. Brock, "Understanding anthropomorphism in service provision: a meta-analysis of physical robots, chatbots, and other AI," *Journal of the Academy of Marketing Science*, vol. 49, pp. 632–658, 2021.

[28] M. G. Elmashhara and A. M. Soares, "Linking atmospherics to shopping outcomes: The role of the desire to stay," *Journal of Retailing and Consumer Services*, vol. 64, p. 102744, 2022.

[29] M. Reimann, J. van de Graaf, N. van Gulik, S. van de Sanden, T. Verhagen, and K. Hindriks, "Social Robots in the Wild and the Novelty Effect," in *International Conference on Social Robotics*. Springer, 2023, pp. 38–48.

Musical Agents, Agency, & AI: Towards a Phenomenological Understanding

Ted Moore
Johns Hopkins University, Peabody Institute
tmoore97@jh.edu

ABSTRACT

Creating AI musical agents is an interest to many electronic music artists and researchers. This paper suggests a phenomenological understanding of "musical agency" determined by four criteria: in order to perceive a technological system as a collaborative agent it must (1) be perceived as separate from the user, (2) be surprising to the user, (3) be intended as a collaborative agent, and (4) mirror the user's own musical intentions. Each criterion is explored through practitioners' writings, with modular synthesizers as an example of using complexity to fulfill these criteria. The aim is to pursue a broad identification of "AI" in music technology towards any systems that fill the criteria, thereby avoiding definitions that use specific categories of algorithms or implementations.

1. INTRODUCTION

Using AI to create musical agents is a current topic of interest to many electronic music artists and researchers. "Musical agency," a "musical agent," or an "AI improviser" is often defined subjectively using criteria along the lines of "you know it when you see it." This paper examines the mechanisms by which technical or musical objects are perceived as musical agents, why practitioners pursue musical agency, and what it reflects about the human user.

This paper suggests a phenomenological understanding of agency in music-technology systems that provides a framework of subjective criteria that can flesh out the "you know it when you see it" approach. I suggest that in order to perceive a technological system as a collaborative agent it must (1) be perceived as separate from the user, (2) be surprising to the user, (3) be intended as a collaborative agent, and (4) mirror the user's own musical intentions. This phenomenological approach suggests that "artificial intelligence" (at least in music technology systems) should be a broad, inclusive grouping based on perceptions rather than technological implementations.

2. CONTINGENCY & SURPRISE: WHY WE WANT TECHNOLOGICAL COLLABORATORS

Collaboration with music technologies has been part of creative practices from the discipline's beginning. As seen in the accounts below, the goals of these collaborations are often to solicit *surprising* sonic forms from technological processes in the hope of exploring new sonic ideas. Once surprised, a user can then choose to pursue, extend, or discard the results from the technology.

2.1 Analog Contingency

For electronic musicians, the desirable moments of surprise while using technology have often been rooted in the imprecision of analog systems. Harry Collins and Trevor Pinch describe the concepts of control and contingency playing out between the desires of synthesizer engineers and musicians saying, "The history of the synthesizer can be seen as a battle ground between the engineers' desire for control and repeatability and the artists' desire for contingency...The engineer wants the machine to be reliable...The artists...want an *instrument* not a *machine*–something that will play something unique, something which, although subject to control...can surprise them." (emphasis mine) [1] Collins and Pinch further describe this relationship, writing of early analog synthesizers, that, "Musicians would talk about getting an incredible sound at night in the studio only to return to the instrument the next morning to find they couldn't reproduce it. This imprecision was a source of constant delight for some musicians." [1]

2.2 Improvisational Contingency

In their ethnography of group-improvisation from a human-computer interaction (HCI) perspective, Kang, Jackson, and Sengers found that many performers described the "tension" from improvisational uncertainty "as a source of both fragility and potential failure, but also energy and creativity." [2] They go on to describe the pursuit of this contingency using "coder" terminology, saying, "musicians and artists may seek to exploit or create uncertainty as a mechanism of discovery and expression, making breakdown in effect a *'feature'* rather than a *'bug'*." (emphasis mine) [2]

Similarly, when describing her improvisational practice, New Renaissance Artist The Honourable Elizabeth A. Baker explains, "I always have one piece of gear that will probably blow up or I make a new configuration at the beginning of a show that will probably go wrong and I specifically do this so that when it goes wrong...I have to think on my feet...I find the joy of de-escalating the bomb." [3]

2.3 Time-Varying Contingency Towards Musical Expression

In discussion of his computer program *Voyager*, George Lewis equates unpredictability-as-agency on multiple time scales, saying, "If the computer is not treated as a musical instrument, but as an independent improvisor, the difference is partly grounded in the form of program responses that are not necessarily predictable on the basis of outside input... *Voyager*'s response to input has several modes, from complete communion to utter indifference...while tendencies over a long period of time exhibit consistency, moment-to-moment choices can shift unpredictably. It is a fact, however, that the system is designed to avoid the kind of uniformity where the same kind of input routinely leads to the same result." [4] Lewis has explicitly programmed into *Voyager* an added layer of agency: the ability to autonomously change the degree of its contingency throughout a performance.

2.4 Contingency in Machine Learning Systems

The desire for unpredictability, or systems "difficult to control" [1], that these artists exhibit can also be seen in contemporary artists working with artificial intelligence. Rebecca Fiebrink argues that machine learning transforms 'bugs' into creative opportunities, stating "One of the great things about using machine learning as opposed to coding, as I mentioned it's faster, but also the kinds of mistakes it makes are different. If you make a mistake while you're writing code, often you're going to get a compiler error or...silence, or...a filter blowing up. With machine learning the way that a lot of these systems are configured, if it gives you something unexpected...it's going to do something and that's often just more creatively useful than having nothing happen and that can lead you to experiment further." [5] Fiebrinks's description makes a strong argument for why a creator interested in employing contingent technologies as a collaborator would want to use machine learning: the exercise of trial and error is primed for creative surprise and potential instead of discouragement.

Laetitia Sonami–a sound artist, performer, and researcher based in Oakland, CA–says of her work with machine learning, "...in a way, you don't want the instrument to perform like a well-trained circus, you kind of want it to be a little wild, and you want to adapt to it somehow, like riding a bull...I think the machine learning allowed more of this". [5] Furthermore, in an interesting turn on the control vs. contingency paradigm of Collins and Pinch [1], Laetitia Sonami describes using machine learning to *control* the *degree* of *contingency* in her instrument, stating, "The unpredictability...depends on how 'wide' the machine learning is. If I feed the system training examples whose sounds encompass wide changes...the trained models will move through all these points in unpredictable ways as the springs settle to a resting place...I can thus easily scale the instrument between predictable and unpredictable results by changing how I train....This 'predictability index' is very easily modified and unique to ML." [6] Even with this control over contingency, Sonami still chooses to inject the imprecision of analog mechanisms into her instrument, adding, "I was looking for more complex inputs and opted for a partially chaotic system which would 'fight' the intention of ML and not learn (!)." [6]

2.5 Balancing Control and Contingency

These accounts reveal how others have identified technology as perceived, described, and designed to be agential. These writers also acknowledge the fluidity of these distinctions and the precarity of the relation between them. Collins and Pinch hedge against their contingency-vs.-control dichotomy saying, "Life is compromise and artists sometimes long for control just as scientists dream of the serendipitous discovery." [1] Lewis' *Voyager* performs this interplay and balance by varying the degree of it's "communion" and "indifference" towards its interlocutor [4]. Sonami balances the degree on contingency in her performance instrument by adjusting what she calls machine learning's "predictability index." [6]

3. PERCEIVING AGENCY

3.1 Collaborative Agency Requires Separation

In order to perceive a technology as agential, it must first be perceived as having musical actions separate from a user, designer, or performer. This perception essentially amounts to creating the moment of "surprise" described by many practitioners above.

3.1.1 Solo vs. Duet

In 1991, Robert Rowe offered a few classification systems for interactive music technologies, including the "instrument" and "player" paradigms. [7] He describes "instruments" as being "concerned with constructing an extended musical instrument: performance gestures from a human player are analyzed by the computer and guide an elaborated output exceeding normal instrument response. Imagining such a system being played by a single performer, the musical result would be thought of as a solo," which is contrasted with, "Systems following a player paradigm try to construct an artificial player, a musical presence with a personality and behavior of its own, though it may vary in the degree to which it follows the lead of a human partner. A player paradigm system played by a single human would produce an output more like a duet." [7]

3.1.2 Intention Bonding

Another way of considering how systems are be perceived as agents is by analyzing the *sonic* relationship between the human and technology in real-time performance. Sam Pluta presents a two-dimensional continuum in which to position relationships between human sound inputs and computer music outputs. A computer's response with no delay and no distortion relates closely to the human's intention, while increased temporal offset or timbral distortion indicates greater perceived agency.

Pluta's continuum recalls the agency of Lewis' *Voyager* into which was programmed agency to behave at different positions on Pluta's continuum at different moments during a performance.

3.1.3 First- and Third- Person Descriptions

In his chapter on musical intentionality, Marc Leman offers a useful distinction for phenomenologically determining if one is identifying music as agential saying, "third-person descriptions are about repeatable measurements of phenomena", while "first-person descriptions in musicology draw upon interpretations of intentions attributed to music...moving sonic forms receive the status of actions to which intentionality can be attributed". [8]

Leman's third person descriptions ("repeatable measurements of phenomena") are useful for identifying non-agential technologies. [8] A system's measurable repeatability based on similar human inputs (e.g., every time the human does x, the technology does y) will be perceived as a non-agential, "solo" relationship. The repetition of this relationship further establishes and maintains it as non-agential, preserving the perception of shared intention even as musical content transforms over time. This perception of non-agential technology is precisely what Lewis was aiming to avoid with *Voyager*, stating, "It is a fact...that the system is designed to avoid the kind of uniformity where the same kind of input routinely leads to the same result." [4]

Using a first person description requires a listener to first *perceive* a moving sonic form as an "action": only then can intentionality be attributed. The attribution of intentionality depends on the performance context. According to Rowe's paradigms, if the intentionality is perceived as separate from the human's, creating a collaborative "duet," the technological collaborator would be agential. If the intentions behind the moving sonic forms are perceived to originate from and extend the human performer's intentions, the technology would not be seen as agential, only assisting the performer. [7]

First-person descriptions suggest perceptions of collaborative, agential technologies, while third person descriptions suggest predictable extensions of a user's intentions.

3.2 Collaborative Agency Requires Surprise

Modular synthesizer performer Richard Devine describes using modular synthesizer systems as, "Things would happen unexpectedly...It was like a living organism that sort of does its own thing. These circuits would come to life...it's almost like it has its own personality." [9] By using these first-person descriptions, [8] Devine is expressing his perception of agency in his modular system.

This moment of "surprise" is also described by Deniz Peters in his study using motion tracking with dancers. [10] When the dancers would experience "motion tracking glitches", "a foreign agency would seem to gain presence." [10] Peters says, "the instrument [(the motion tracking software)] may...turn into [an] agency, particularly if its response is less predictable than that of a static object." [10]

3.3 Collaborative Agency Depends on Intention

Devine's description makes the moment of "surprise" a *goal* (i.e., desirable and/or planned) rather than a *glitch* (i.e., undesirable and/or unplanned). In order to experience a moment of surprise from a system (as a goal *or* glitch), one must have an established facility with it, such that one's interactions can create predictable outcomes. When one's interactions then produce an unpredictable outcome, one can be surprised. Peters describes this necessary facility saying, "the instrumental action becomes transparent, disappearing as a resistance to our sonic intentions. The instrument seems to become part of one's body. This transparency is a facet of the technical mastery attributed to virtuosity" [10]. Peters' description of the technology as being "part of one's body" echoes Rowe's perception of a "solo" performance [7] as it extends and elaborates the dancers' intentions, and therefore only when it "glitches" does it take on a sense of agency. The dancers' perceptions of agency reflect Leman's first-person descriptions, [8] a consequential distance from the origin on Pluta's continuum, [11] as well as Rowe's perception of a duet. [7] Perceiving a surprising result as a glitch implies that the technology's *intention* is non-agential, while perceiving a surprising result as a desired outcome implies the *intention* to be an agential collaborator.

3.4 Collaborative Agency Requires Mirroring

In addition to an agent being *surprising*, *separate*, and *intended*, the last step in the perception of a collaborative agent is described by Leman, saying, "Attribution of intentionality is likely to occur on the basis of mirroring, that is on the basis of a simulation of the perceived action in the subject's own action. Actions of others are understood as intended actions because the subject can simulate them and understand them as its own intended actions." [8] He clarifies that, "This intentionality can be attributed to subjects as well as to objects (or, rather, events)." [8] Regarding AI music systems, including modular synthesizers, in order to perceive the system as an agential collaborator it must be perceived as a separate, but *similar*, actor. The actions (i.e., sounds) it makes when it surprises the user must be recognizable as sounds that the user could make and might desire to make using such a system.

4. THE USE OF COMPLEXITY

While Peters' dancers experience surprise via unplanned "glitch", Devine is able to achieve his *goal* of surprise in spite of his virtuosity. I say "in spite of" because one may suppose that a "virtuosic" user performing virtuosic execution would be in control at all times (and therefore not-surprisable). How does Devine, a virtuosic user of these systems, achieve his "goal" of surprising himself? How can one create a transition from control to contingency?

Agency can emerge when a system becomes too complex for the user to keep track of all the interconnections and relations necessary to precisely predict the outputs of the system, *yet mirroring still occurs*. Furthermore, for many users, creating this agency is a goal of using the system, as one can then employ that agent as a collaborative partner in the creation of music. The value of this collaboration is heightened by the mirroring property of the agent: that the user and agent share a sense of musical intentionality.

When beginning to create a modular synthesizer patch, Devine says that he "just kind of start[s] from nothing and then patch[es] up and see[s] what happens" [12]. Early in this process Devine would be able to provide Leman's third person descriptions of the sound being produced, using objective, measurable descriptions such as, "the square wave oscillator is being filtered by the low pass filter, the cutoff frequency of which is being modulated by a triangle wave LFO." These descriptions point towards the system currently being non-agential, not offering surprise, only extending the user's intentions.

As one works with a patch, the complexity tends to grow to the point where it becomes difficult to keep track of all the interconnections contributing to the resulting sound.

At this stage, it becomes challenging to provide a third-person, objective description of the system. Instead, one starts using first-person descriptions that, as Leman says, "draw upon interpretations of intentions attributed to music." [8] Devine achieves his *goal* by pursuing complexity to the point where he is surprised by the sonic results, indicated by the use of first-person descriptions such as, "a living organism that sort of does it's own thing." [9] He also emphasizes the value he finds in collaborations with mirroring agents, stating, "It may give you something that you were looking for...it may give you something...that's even cooler than what you were trying to come up with." [12]

5. WHAT DO WE MEAN WHEN WE SAY AGENCY?: TOWARDS A PHENOMENOLOGICAL DEFINITION

At the 2020 inSonic conference, panelists discussed what is meant by "artificial intelligence", particularly in the context of creative music making. Rather than outlining technological categorizations, the panelists' responses about identifying AI all focus on the perception of intention or agency in collaborative technology. Lewis described that, while performing with *Voyager* "people have to feel that they can get the machine's attention, that they can dialog with it, that it, quote, 'understands' them somehow, and if that's AI, I'm prepared to go with that as one potential method of thinking about AI" [13] Palle Dahlstadt adds, "if there's a certain kind of complexity–and that threshold is really quite low–it can be perceived as an agent that actually plays with you." [13] He goes on to explain how low this threshold can be, stating that, "even such relatively simple systems that contain complex internal states and latency and feedback, they start to behave...like playing with another musician because it's so complex." [13]

For these practitioners who have been working with AI in musical creativity for decades, the identification of what is an "intelligent" system is not determined by a category of algorithm or even a high degree of complexity, but rather by a perception or attribution of agency in a technological system. The panel also reveals that a common strategy for inducing this perception is the use of complexity, that of which may involve a machine learning algorithm. This view is nicely summarized by Lewis at the end of his article about *Voyager* titled *Too Many Notes*, saying, "Rather than asking if computers can be creative and intelligent...*Voyager* asks us where our own creativity and intelligence might lie–not 'How do we create intelligence?' but 'How do we find it?'" [4] Lewis' suggestion places the onus for identifying artificial intelligence, not in the contents of the machine, but in the perception of the user.

6. CONCLUSION

In order for a technological system to be perceived a collaborative agent it must (1) be perceived as separate from the user, (2) be surprising to the user, (3) be intended as a collaborative agent, and (4) mirror the user's own musical intentions. For these criteria to arise a system must be sufficiently complex for a user to become unable to predict the system's outcomes (although, as Dahlstadt's observed, the required threshold of complexity is "really quite low"). [13] I propose that the identification of "Artificial Intelligence" in collaborative music technology systems should be a broad grouping based on phenomenological perceptions of agency. The inclusivity this definition offers connects the lineage of collaboration with contingent technologies from early synthesizers (and before) up through the current interest in AI systems. A phenomenological understanding avoids the apotheosis of ever newer technologies, instead rooting one's attention to the experience of artistic practice and the spirit of experimental creativity.

7. REFERENCES

[1] H. Collins and T. Pinch, "On Chance and Contingency," *Public*, no. 33, 2006.

[2] L. Kang, S. J. Jackson, and P. Sengers, "Intermodulation: Improvisation and Collaborative Art Practice for HCI," in *Proceedings of the 2018 CHI Conference on Human Factors in Computing Systems*, 2018, pp. 1–13.

[3] T. H. E. A. Baker, "Talking Free Music with Elizabeth A. Baker," YouTube, 10 2020. [Online]. Available: https://www.youtube.com/watch?v=5WjmVLd7XEM

[4] G. E. Lewis, "Too Many Notes: Computers, Complexity and Culture in Voyager," *Leonardo Music Journal*, vol. 10, no. 2000, pp. 33–39, 2000.

[5] CeReNeM, "Rebecca Fiebrink: Machine Learning as Creative Design Tool," YouTube, 08 2019, centre for Research in New Music. [Online]. Available: https://www.youtube.com/watch?v=Qo6n8MuEgdQ

[6] R. Fiebrink and L. Sonami, "Reflections on Eight Years of Instrument Creation with Machine Learning," *NIME 2020 Proceedings*, 2020.

[7] R. Rowe, *Interactive Music Systems: Machine Listening and Composing*. MIT Press, 1993.

[8] M. Leman, *Embodied music cognition and mediation technology*. MIT press, 2008.

[9] I. D. of Wires, "Richard Devine: IDOW Extended Interview #8 (Analog Voodoo Effect)," YouTube, 02 2013. [Online]. Available: https://www.youtube.com/watch?v=Z7naEUAYDfg

[10] D. Peters, "Haptic illusions and imagined agency: Felt resistances in sonic experience," *Contemporary Music Review*, vol. 32, no. 2-3, pp. 151–164, 2013.

[11] S. Pluta, "Laptop Improvisation in Multi-Dimensional Space," Ph.D. dissertation, Columbia University, 5 2012.

[12] SweetwaterSound, "Richard Devine Interview - The Sweetwater Minute, Vol. 256," YouTube, 09 2014. [Online]. Available: https://www.youtube.com/watch?v=K_5mb_utKdM

[13] Z. Karlsruhe, "inSonic 2020: Syntheses - Day 2," YouTube, 12 2020. [Online]. Available: https://www.youtube.com/watch?v=sooNxK6oQ4c

Visualization of Melodic Gravity in Pops – Computational Model of Hierarchical Implication Realization by Complementary Use of IRM and GTTM –

Hiroki Sawamura
Kwansei Gakuin University
gjn06497@kwansei.ac.jp

Mitsuyo Hashida
The University of Fukuchiyama
hashida-mitsuyo@fukuchiyama.ac.jp

Haruhiro Katayose
Kwansei Gakuin University
katayose@kwansei.ac.jp

ABSTRACT

We discuss melodic gravity, which is considered to be one of the music cognitive structures related to musical emotion for active music appreciation, and propose a method for analyzing expectations along melodic trends toward a computational model for analyzing melodic gravity. We propose a method for analyzing expectations along melodic trends toward a computational model for analyzing Melodic Gravity. In doing so, we propose a method to analyze and describe the hierarchical implicit realization of a piece of music by using the time span tree of GTTM, and discuss its applicability.

1. INTRODUCTION

Music is an art form experienced over time, perceived by our ears as sound, which is essentially the subtle variations in air pressure. Musical notation serves as a means to visually document and convey musical information. The oldest known notations trace back to ancient Greece before the common era. This notation system has evolved into a robust mechanism for capturing ephemeral musical expressions, playing a pivotal role as a language for both composition and conceptualization. Subsequently, the appreciation and education of music have been shaped by a framework reliant on sounds, musical scores, and verbal interpretations. This framework has persisted beyond the widespread adoption of personal computers. The advent of MIDI technology enabled the linkage of acoustic signals with visual cues through piano rolls, music, and synchronized playbars, yet this integration has not become predominant in music education.

The landscape began to shift post-2010. The inception of YouTube in 2006 marked the rise of YouTubers who professionalized video content creation. Beyond 2010, tutorial videos by YouTubers emerged as a key genre, expanding their role from mere entertainment to valuable educational resources. In the realm of music, such videos are enhanced with synchronized graphics and captions, enabling users to concurrently process auditory and visual information on a unified timeline. An exemplary advancement in this domain is the interactive music appreciation platform Songle[1].

Songle, an innovative music player embedded within video sharing platforms, leverages acoustic signal analysis to enrich the user experience. It displays musical elements like melodies and chords, along with structural components such as verses and choruses, complemented by navigation buttons for easy access to these segments. While Songle's introduction marks a progressive step in music appreciation and education, its focus predominantly lies on perceptual aspects rather than on a comprehensive musical cognition.

Our goal is to develop an interactive music appreciation interface that not only resonates emotionally but also presents cognitive information akin to that found in music explanatory videos.

In the following sections, Chapter 2 will delve into the management of emotionally resonant content, Chapter 3 will overview the foundational aspects of handling melodic gravity, Chapter 4 will explore the hierarchical approach to managing IRM, deemed promising for encapsulating melodic gravity, and Chapter 5 will elaborate on the design and execution of a system aimed at analyzing and visualizing musical cognitive structures.

2. HANDLING INFORMATION THAT APPEALS TO EMOTIONS

2.1 An Overview of Songle

Songle is a music player that is integrated into video sharing platforms, augmented by the application of acoustic signal analysis technology. Figure 1 depicts the interface of Songle.

Within Songle, not only are melodies, chords, beats, and measures extracted from the acoustic signals, but information on sections such as verses and choruses, derived from the analysis of repetitive structures, is also displayed. A distinctive feature of Songle is its synchronization with the video, enabling users to comprehend the musical structure in conjunction with the auditory output. Additionally, the platform provides buttons that facilitate navigation to these musical sections. The incorporation of an interface in the presentation of musical information suggests a potential paradigm shift in the modalities of music appreciation and education. Conversely, music explanatory videos have their own unique allure and lucidity, aspects that ought to be taken into account in the development of forthcoming active music interfaces. The subsequent section will delve into the allure of music explanatory videos.

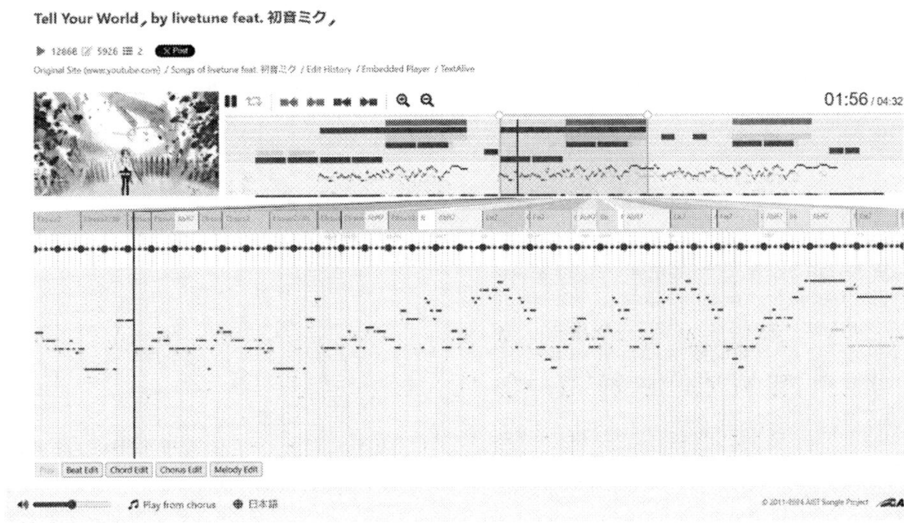

Figure 1. Interface of Songle The interface of Songle, as presented by Goto et al., showcases the automatically estimated results for repeated and Chorus sections of a song, which are accessible by clicking. It also displays the estimated results for chords, beats, measures, and melody pitches, alongside user-corrected values. Edited values would appear in gray. The left side of the figure indicates past times, while the right side points to future times, with the black vertical line marking the current time. The prominently displayed analysis section at the bottom corresponds to the dimmed sections at the top, and its length can be adjusted by dragging either edge. Furthermore, magnifying glass icons with plus and minus signs enable zooming in and out of the section displayed. Chords are represented by colors that match their root notes, accompanied by chord symbols. Activating the chord editing mode triggers the playback of synthesized chord tones to facilitate chord identification. Beats are marked by red circles, with the initial beat of each measure denoted by a larger circle. Melody pitches are illustrated with red lines. Engaging the melody editing mode brings up a piano roll behind the melody to help editing, with beep sounds mirroring the frequencies of the melody pitches.

2.2 The Allure of Music Explanatory Videos

Among the recent popular music explanatory channels is "Dr. Capital's Music Channel [1] ". Focusing predominantly on pop music, this channel elucidates the captivating elements of songs in an accessible manner, frequently referencing related examples. Comparable approaches are employed in television programming, such as in "The Essence of Music (Fuji TV, 1993)" and "Kameda Music School (NHK, 2013–)".

While music theory can often be perceived as intricate, these platforms leverage well-known songs to underscore emotionally evocative aspects like "the intensity of emotion" or "the depth of sorrow", elucidating engaging terminologies and their underpinnings in music theory. This methodology enables even those generally indifferent to music to gain an intuitive grasp of its underlying principles. "Dr. Capital's Music Channel" has addressed concepts such as melodic gravity, serving as an exemplar of this approach.

3. MELODIC GRAVITY

Melodic gravity is the phenomenon where the progression of notes within a melody exhibits a tendency to be "drawn" toward specific pitches or chords. Although the terminology has not been universally standardized, the underlying concept has been acknowledged for centuries and has increasingly been referenced in both scholarly and digital media discussions since the early 2000s.

[1] https://www.youtube.com/c/DrCapital

In the realm of music theory, melodic gravity is associated with notions such as "resolution" and "cadence" and is frequently employed within the framework of musical analysis. Nonetheless, its formalization as a computational methodology for the analysis of actual music pieces remains somewhat elusive.

In the sections that follow, we explore established definitions of melodic gravity within music theory and address the complexities encountered when considering melodic gravity from a temporal standpoint.

3.1 Melodic Gravity within Music Theory

melodic gravity assumes a pivotal role in the study of harmony and counterpoint. For instance, the perfect cadence, typified by the progression from the V (dominant) chord to the I (tonic) chord, serves as a quintessential manifestation of harmonic "gravity," imparting a pronounced sense of resolution. Notable musical elements associated with this concept include:

Resolution to the Tonic The directional movement of a melody toward the tonic note, which serves as the foundational pitch in the key or scale of a piece of music.

Employment of Leading Tones The penultimate note of a scale, known as the leading tone, exhibits a propensity to resolve naturally to the tonic.

Chord and Non-chord Tones The resolution of melodic notes to chord tones, which are the constituent pitches of a chord.

3.2 Temporal Aspects of Melodic Gravity

The considerations outlined above predominantly adopt a static viewpoint. However, incorporating a dynamic or temporal perspective, particularly in relation to emotional responses, is crucial. According to Gestalt theory, it is reasonable to expect that a sequence maintaining a consistent directional tendency would perpetuate unchanged, with repeated occurrences intensifying the emotional connection to the sequence. Moreover, a melodic line that navigates a series of deviations before culminating in a pronounced instance of melodic gravity is likely to exhibit enhanced gravitational pull. Similarly, the recognition and subsequent repetition of a motif can also invoke a sense of melodic gravity as the listener anticipates and traces the recurring theme.

These examples underscore the necessity of interpreting melodic gravity as a function of time. L.B. Meyer broached this topic, incorporating a narrative dimension into the discourse [2]. Subsequently, E. Narmour introduced the Implication Realization Model (IRM) as a cognitive framework for music theory, addressing the questions posed by Meyer[3]. The IRM endeavors to elucidate the cognitive structures underpinning melody by conceptualizing melodies as sequences of note triplets (i.e., Tri-Grams) and analyzing their sequential relationships. While IRM stands as a promising theoretical model for capturing melodic gravity, it faces challenges, including its non-intuitive nature and the absence of a detailed methodology for examining the hierarchical organization of musical compositions.

In the following discussion, we propose strategies for applying IRM at various hierarchical levels within musical analysis.

4. HIERARCHICAL HANDLING OF THE IMPLICATION-REALIZATION MODEL

This section delves into strategies for addressing the challenges associated with the Implication-Realization Model (IRM) highlighted in the preceding section. To mitigate the issue of IRM's concepts being non-intuitive, we introduce a computational model that remains true to the foundational texts, alongside methods for the intuitive visualization of computational outcomes. Moreover, we propose a novel approach for the analysis of melodies' hierarchical structures through the application of Time-span Reduction from the Generative Theory of Tonal Music (GTTM).

This section concentrates on the concept of *melodic archetypes* within IRM. We will:

1. Provide an overview of melodic archetypes.
2. Discuss methods for their intuitive visualization.
3. Describe techniques for hierarchical handling.
4. Outline computational methods for their derivation.

4.1 Overview of Melodic Archetypes

IRM fundamentally segments melodies into trigrams to facilitate the analysis of implications and realizations. A key element in this framework is the concept of *melodic archetypes*. According to IRM, a small initial interval suggests a similar following interval in the same direction.

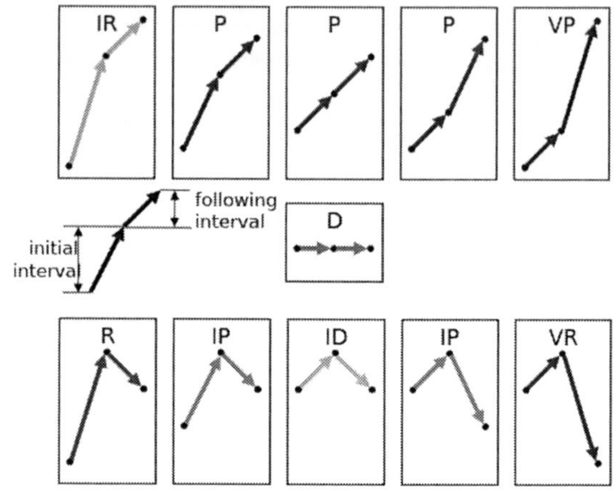

Figure 2. Intervals and Registral Directions of Melodic Archetypes This figure arranges melodic archetypes by interval differences: ascending movements are placed at the top, descending at the bottom, and lateral in the middle. Arrows between pitch dots show interval changes, with left arrows for initial intervals and right arrows for subsequent ones. Arrow lengths indicate interval sizes, and directions represent registral movements: up, lateral, down. Although only upward-starting archetypes are shown, downward-starting ones use mirrored symbols. Colors are chosen based on symbol components: blue for P, green for D, red for R, with reduced saturation for I and brightness for V, aligning colors with Narmour's symbolic meanings.

This expected continuation is represented by the symbol P (*process*) and, when three consecutive notes has equal pitch, by D (*duplication*). Conversely, a large initial interval suggests a contrasting following interval in the opposite direction, which is represented by R (*reversal*) upon its realization.

An important concept to understand here is *registral direction*, which indicates whether two notes are moving upwards, maintaining the same pitch, or moving downwards. IRM assesses the realization of an implication by examining both the registral direction and the interval. If the realization aligns only with the registral direction, the symbol is prefixed with V (*registral*), forming VP or VR. If it aligns only with the interval, the symbol is prefixed with I (*intervallic*), resulting in IP, ID, or IR.

Moreover, the analysis momentarily disregards the magnitude of the initial interval, focusing instead on the similarity and direction between the preceding and following intervals for symbol assignment. This method classifies the implications as either *prospective* or *retrospective*, with the former represented by the direct symbols and the latter by enclosing the symbols in parentheses. For example, a significant disparity between the preceding and following intervals that move in the same direction leads to the assignment of IR for a large initial interval and (IR) for a small one. Notably, both prospective and retrospective variants exist for all symbols, enabling the assignment of a melodic archetype to any pitch sequence trigram, though the uniqueness of this assignment is subject to ongoing investigation.

4.2 Intuitive Visualization of Melodic Archetypes

The concept of melodic archetypes in IRM, while rich in analytical potential, presents challenges in terms of intuitive understanding. Melodic archetypes such as IP, VP, ID, IR, and VR, which are prefixed with an interval or registral direction, derive from the foundational archetypes P, D, and R. Consequently, symbols such as P and IP or R and VR are treated as adjacent concepts within the IRM framework, as depicted in their symbolic representations.

Figure 2 plots the outlines of melodies corresponding to these melodic archetypes. The color scheme in the figure assigns similar hues to melodic archetypes considered adjacent within the IRM framework. Specifically, symbols containing P, D, or R are distinguished by unique hues, with those containing I depicted with reduced saturation and those with V depicted with reduced brightness. The arrows in the figure illustrate the pitch differences between two events, where the start and end points represent pitch events, the vertical span indicates the interval, and the arrow direction (upwards, rightwards, downwards) signifies the registral direction. Following the principle of Narmour's *parametric scale*, symbols towards the figure's left indicate smaller following intervals relative to preceding ones, with the right side indicating larger ones. It's important to note that the left and right ends of the figure do not connect.

Upon examining this figure, it becomes apparent that the allocation of symbols to melodic archetypes by Narmour might not be entirely intuitive. While archetypes related to P and D appear relatively adjacent, concepts related to R, such as VR, are positioned distinctly. Moreover, while V-related archetypes can be aligned vertically, the arrangement of I-related and unprefixed archetypes poses interpretative challenges. Furthermore, the configurations of significantly different symbols, such as IP and VR or IP and R, exhibit similarities. This observation underscores the complexity of intuitively grasping the melodic archetype concepts within IRM.

Plotting such configurations, as illustrated in Figure 3, suggests that adjusting brightness and saturation based on the interval differences between subsequent and preceding tones, and significantly altering the hue based on the progression direction, may facilitate a more intuitive assignment of colors to similar entities and distinct colors to differing ones. However, this discussion pertains to the arrow shapes plotted on paper rather than the actual sounds targeted by IRM. While the utility of visual representations for verifying the alignment of theoretical concept similarities and differences with intuition is discussed, the appropriateness of color assignments for the sounds represented by each melodic archetype remains uncertain. Future endeavors will involve integrating a melody analysis module based on IRM into the music analyzer currently under development, as discussed in the forthcoming section. This integration aims to explore representations of IRM symbols that provide intuitive explanations for actual musical compositions, thereby addressing the challenge of IRM's complex concepts hindering their applicability.

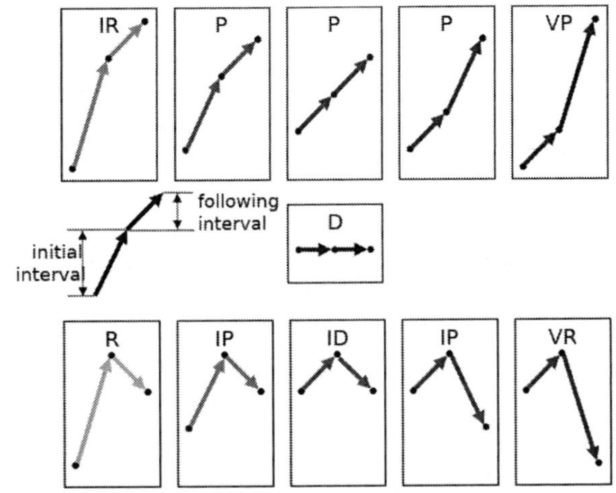

Figure 3. **Proposed Interpretation of Archetypal Melodies** In this figure, we have altered the color scheme for the arrows, previously established in Figure 2, to represent the directionality of pitch movements within the melodic archetypes. Arrows that denote ascending pitch sequences are now depicted in various shades of blue, contrasting with those that signify descending sequences, which are rendered in red hues. When the initial and subsequent intervals are of equal size, we employ primary colors. Further, the intensity of the color is adjusted to reflect the relative sizes of the intervals: arrows representing larger subsequent intervals than their initial counterparts are depicted with diminished brightness, whereas those with smaller subsequent intervals see a reduction in saturation. Additionally, black was assigned to the D archetype, characterized by neither ascending nor descending movements, with both the initial and following intervals having a magnitude of zero, signifying a lack of pitch change.

4.3 Extraction of Hierarchical Structure and Selection of Representative Tones

As outlined in Section 3, expectations with a melody's tendencies can emerge not only between adjacent melodies but also across the higher levels of a melody's hierarchical structure. The Time-span Reduction technique from GTTM is employed to elucidate this hierarchical structure. GTTM consists of four sub-theories: Grouping Structure, Metrical Structure, Time-span Reduction, and Prolongational Reduction, with Time-span Reduction analyzed through the lenses of Grouping Structure and Metrical Structure. In this context, the segments considered as groups in Time-span Reduction correspond to those defined in the Grouping Structure. Furthermore, events not designated as the head within a time-span are regarded as refinements of the head, implying that events identified as the head can be viewed as representatives of their respective group structures. Consequently, it is plausible that Time-span Reduction can unveil the hierarchical structure of melodies and facilitate the selection of representative tones for each hierarchical level.

4.4 Derivation of Archetypal Melodies

The subsequent discussion focuses on the analytical approach prescribed by IRM. Specifically, the concepts articulated in Narmour's publications are formalized herein.

Initially, pitch sequences are segmented into 3-grams. For instance, the 3-gram at a given time t is represented as (p_{t-2}, p_{t-1}, p_t), with p denoting the note number. Subse-

up/up: mR/AA	lateral/up: mL/AB	down/up: mL/AB
up/lateral: mL/AB	lateral/lateral: mN/AA	down/lateral: mL/AB
up/down: mL/AB	lateral/down: mL/AB	down/down: mR/AA

Table 1. Changes of Registral Direction

quently, the registral direction and interval for each 3-gram are ascertained, followed by the determination of changes in these parameters on their respective parametric scales. The final step involves assigning a *melodic archetype* to each 3-gram.

4.4.1 *Registral Direction and Interval*

The method begins with the determination of the registral direction and interval. The difference in pitch $(\Delta p)_t = p_t - p_{t-1}$ from one time point $t-1$ to the next t allows for the definition of the registral direction v_t as follows:

$$v_t = \operatorname{sgn}((\Delta p)_t) = \operatorname{sgn}(p_t - p_{t-1})$$

Here, v_t assumes values of $1, 0, -1$ corresponding to up, lateral, and down movements, respectively. The interval is defined by:

$$|(\Delta p)_t| = |p_t - p_{t-1}|$$

In this scenario, the initial interval i_{t-1}, referred to as such, is derived as:

$$i_{t-1} = |(\Delta p)_{t-1}| = |p_{t-1} - p_{t-2}|$$

The differential in intervals, denoted as $(\Delta i)_t$, is then derived as:

$$(\Delta i)_t = (\Delta p)_t - (\Delta p)_{t-1} = |p_t - p_{t-1}| - |p_{t-1} - p_{t-2}|$$

4.4.2 *Parametric Scale Changes*

This section determines the *direction* and magnitude of changes on the parametric scales for both registral direction and intervals. Terms used in this method are first summarized, followed by the methodology. The term "changes" on the parametric scale simply refers to "changes," and likewise, "direction of change" and "magnitude of change" are used. The *parametric scale* is derived from the tables provided by Narmour [3, 4]. The scales for registral direction (*V-scale*) and intervals (*I-scale*) are discussed there. The table positions more *closural* elements on the left and more *non-closural* elements on the right. Thus, the direction of change,

- *mL* (*motion left*), indicates a change towards more *closural,*
- *mN* (*motion nil*) indicates a change with no effect on *closure,*
- *mR* (*motion right*) indicates a change towards more *non-closural.*

The magnitude of change includes *AA* for *similar* and *AB* for *different*. The magnitude of the preceding interval includes aa for similar and ab for different, with a threshold th added [2]. The magnitude and direction of each change are then determined. Initially, changes in registral direction are determined using Table 1. For *up* $v_t = 1$, *lateral* $v_t = 0$, and *down* $v_t = -1$ registral directions, the pair of consecutive registral directions (v_{t-1}, v_t) is used to assign the direction and magnitude of change in registral direction according to Table 1. For example, for a pair of consecutive registral directions (*lateral, up*), the change in registral direction corresponds to the static/ascending entry in the table, yielding mL/AB. Thus, it can be expressed as:

$$(V_{\text{dir}}, V_{\text{dir}}) = (\text{mL}, \text{AB}) \quad \text{where } (v_{t-1}, v_t) = (\textit{lateral}, \textit{up})$$

The same logic applies to other cases.

Next, a threshold C is defined to determine the magnitude of change in intervals as follows:

$$I_{\text{mgn}} = \begin{cases} \text{AA} & \text{where } |\Delta i_t| \leq C \\ \text{AB} & \text{where } |\Delta i_t| > C \end{cases}$$

The threshold C is determined based on the magnitude of change in registral direction:

$$C = \begin{cases} \text{M3} & \text{where } V_{\text{dir}} = \text{AA} \\ \text{m3} & \text{where } V_{\text{dir}} = \text{AB} \end{cases}$$

Where M3 represents a major third interval (4 semitones) and m3 represents a minor third interval (3 semitones). Furthermore, the magnitude of the preceding interval is determined as follows:

$$\text{mgn}(i_{t-1}) = \begin{cases} \text{aa} & \text{where } i_{t-1} < \text{P4} \\ \text{th} & \text{where P4} \leq i_{t-1} < \text{P5} \\ \text{ab} & \text{where P5} \leq i_{t-1} \end{cases}$$

Where P4 represents a perfect fourth interval (5 semitones), P5 represents a perfect fifth interval (7 semitones). The direction of change in intervals is then determined by the following equation:

$$I_{\text{dir}} = \begin{cases} \text{mL} & \text{where} \Delta i_t < 0 \\ \text{mN} & \text{where} \Delta i_t = 0 \\ \text{mR} & \text{where} \Delta i_t > 0 \end{cases}$$

4.4.3 *Assignment of Melodic Archetypes*

Melodic archetypes are derived from changes in registral direction and intervals, as shown in Figure 4. To develop an algorithm from the table, implications such as reverse, duplicate, and process for the 3-gram (p_1, p_2, p_3) are determined first, followed by identifying whether the implication was realized by the interval alone, the registral direction alone, or both. Note that while terms like "implication" and "realization" evokes the sense of implications and realizations, the derivation is strictly based on a table-driven algorithm, meaning the algorithm does not necessarily contain the causes or mechanisms of implications.

Determination Implications for Melodic Archetypes: Implications for melodic archetypes in a 3-gram are determined.

1. Firstly, melodic archetypes R, IR, VR, implying reversal, are determined only when the direction of change in either the interval or the registral direction is mL, and the magnitude of change in the interval is AB.

[2] The original texts [3, 4] use $a + a$ and $a + b$ but to avoid confusion with the addition symbol, alternative notations aa and ab are used

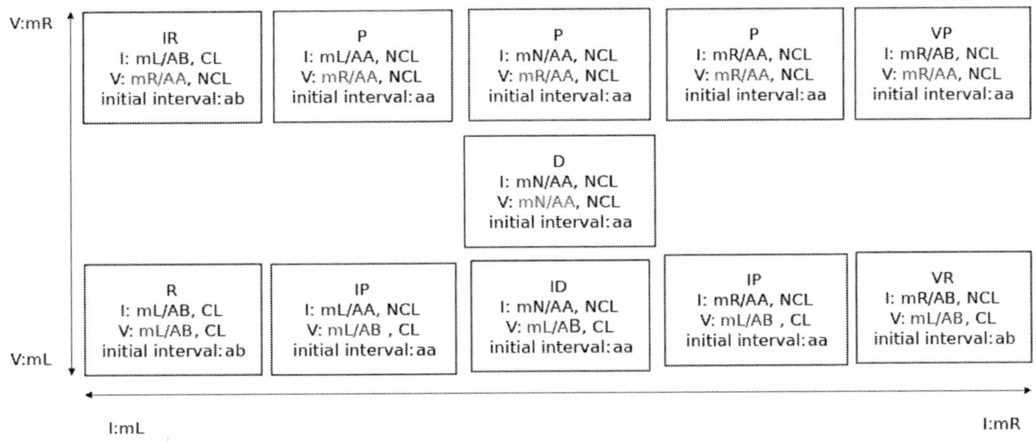

Figure 4. Relation Between Pitch Differences and Melodic Archetypes This figure is organized in accordance with Figure 2, substituting arrows for the properties attributed to each melodic archetype as delineated in IRM [3, 4]. The notations mL, mN, and mR signify motion towards the left (motion left), absence of motion (motion nil), and motion towards the right (motion right), respectively, on the parametric scale established by Narmour. Horizontally, this diagram signifies the intervallic parametric scale, with mL allocated to the left, mN to the center, and mR to the right. In the vertical arrangement, the diagram signifies the registral parametric scale, situating mL at the lower end and mR at the upper end. The labels AA and AB delineate the similarity in intervals and registral directions, where AA implies similarity and AB denotes divergence. Observing this diagram, the horizontal alignment of melodic archetypes according to the differences in intervals aligns with the intervallic parametric scale, allowing for AA and AB to be interpreted as the extent of movement on said scale. The terms CL/NCL denote closural and non-closural states, respectively. The diagram clearly categorizes only the mL/AB condition as closural. Furthermore, the magnitude of the initial interval, critical for identifying prospective archetypes as outlined in 4.1 –that is, the resemblance between the initial two pitches in the triplet– is indicated by either aa or ab. Melodic archetypes that possess an initial interval not depicted in the figure (if aa is displayed, then ab; if ab is shown, then aa) are classified as retrospective. Although the aforementioned descriptions provide a qualitative overview of properties through symbols, as expounded in 4.4, it is possible to quantitatively calculate each property to ascertain its specific value.

2. Next, melodic archetypes D, ID, implying duplication, are determined only when the direction of change in the interval is mN, and the direction of change in the registral direction is not mR.
3. Finally, melodic archetypes P, IP, VP, implying process, are determined for all other cases.

Determination Realizations for Melodic Archetypes: Realizations for melodic archetypes in a 3-gram are then determined. Initially,

- if the implication for the melodic archetype is reversal, the change resulting in realization is mL/AB;
- if the implication is duplication, the change resulting in realization is mN/AA;
- if the implication is process, the change resulting in realization is mR/AA.

Based on this, whether the implication was realized by the interval alone, the registral direction alone, or both is determined. For example, if the implication is reversal and the change in the interval is mL/AB, but the change in the registral direction is not mL/AB, then it is determined that only the interval realized the implication, identifying the melodic archetype as IR. Additionally, if the implication is reversal, the archetype is considered prospective if the magnitude of the preceding interval is ab; for all other implications, the archetype is considered prospective if the magnitude of the preceding interval is aa. If the magnitude of the preceding interval is neither, then the archetype is considered retrospective. However, if the magnitude of the preceding interval is th, whether it is prospective or retrospective is undetermined.

Simplification of Conditions for Determining Realizations: Regarding the Determination Realizations for Melodic Archetypes, if the implication for the melodic archetype is reversal, as per (1), only the direction of change in the interval and the registral direction (limited to mL or mR) needs to be examined; if the implication is duplication, as per (2), only the direction of change in the registral direction needs to be examined; if the implication is process, as per (3), only the magnitude of change in the interval and the registral direction (AA or AB) needs to be examined. From the above discussion, Algorithm 1 is derived.

This revised section elucidates the hierarchical approach to IRM, emphasizing melodic archetypes' conceptualization, visualization, and computational analysis. The proposed modifications aim to enhance the clarity, coherence, and academic rigor of your technical report.

5. SYSTEM IMPLEMENTATION

As discussed in Chapter 1, the aim of this research is to analyze information that corresponds to musical cognition in pop music and to develop an interactive music appreciation interface that is capable of visualization and providing emotionally resonant explanations. The implementation of analyses for chord functions and resolutions of nonharmonic tones has made considerable progress, which is described in this chapter. The visualization of melodic gravity is discussed in Chapter 6.

Algorithm 1 Algorithm for Assigning Melodic Archetypes Based on Interval and Registral Direction Changes

Input: $(V_{\text{mgn}}, V_{\text{dir}}, I_{\text{mgn}}, I_{\text{dir}})$
Output: (is_prospective, archetype)
if $I_{\text{mgn}} = \text{AB} \wedge (I_{\text{dir}} = \text{mL} \vee V_{\text{dir}} = \text{mL})$ **then** ▷ Reversal
  if $\text{mgn}(i_{t-1}) = \text{ab}$ **then** is_prospective = true
  else is_prospective = false
  if $I_{\text{dir}} = \text{mR}$ **then** archetype = VR
  else if $V_{\text{dir}} = \text{mR}$ **then** archetype = IR
  else archetype = R
else if $I_{\text{dir}} = \text{mN} \wedge V_{\text{dir}} \neq \text{mR}$ **then** ▷ Duplication
  if $\text{mgn}(i_{t-1}) = \text{aa}$ **then** is_prospective = true
  else is_prospective = false
  if $V_{\text{dir}} \neq \text{mN}$ **then** archetype = ID
  else archetype = D
else ▷ Process
  if $\text{mgn}(i_{t-1}) = \text{aa}$ **then** is_prospective = true
  else is_prospective = false
  if $I_{\text{mgn}} = \text{AB}$ **then** archetype = VP
  else if $V_{\text{mgn}} = \text{AB}$ **then** archetype = IP
  else archetype = P
end if
if $\text{mgn}(i_{t-1}) = \text{th}$ **then** is_prospective = undefined
return (is_prospective, archetype)

The system is designed as a web-based application that is accessible instantly without any need for installation. This design allows end-users to access music analysis features directly through their browsers without requiring additional software installations.

The architecture of the system is illustrated in Figure 5. This system accepts the acoustic signal of a song as input and implements a process to visually present the results obtained through analysis algorithms based on music theory on the client side. Figure 5 depicts the data flow and processing steps within the system, from the reception of the acoustic signal to the presentation of the final analysis results to the client. Acoustic signal files of the input songs are forwarded to both the chord estimation module and the melody estimation module. The estimated results from each module are then sent to their respective analysis modules for chords and melodies. Finally, the outcomes from the analysis modules are transmitted to the client and displayed in the browser. Data exchange between components of the system uses the JSON format, which is easily interpretable across different programming languages and readable by humans, thereby enhancing the system's extensibility and maintainability.

5.1 Estimation Modules

The implementation of various estimation modules is as follows: The chord estimation module calculates the chroma vectors of the song using NNLS-Chroma [5] and converts these vectors into chord symbols with AutoChord [6] to estimate the harmonic structure of the song. The chord estimation module utilizes NNLS-Chroma to extract chroma features from the song and employs AutoChord to map these features to chord symbols. NNLS-Chroma was selected for its high accuracy, and AutoChord was chosen for its precision in predicting chord progressions. Furthermore, the melody estimation module leverages advanced source separation technology with Demucs [7] to precisely isolate the vocal track from the song. The isolated vocal track is then subjected to f0 estimation with CREPE [8], followed by quantizing the obtained pitches to semitones, thereby determining the pitch, onset time, and duration of each melody note.

5.2 Analysis Modules

The implementation of various analysis modules is as follows: The chord analysis module calculates the tonal distances between chords using Tonal Pitch Space [9] and determines the key of each chord through the method proposed by Sakamoto et al. [10]. By computing the intervals between the tonic of the key and the root notes of the chords, the functions of the chords are determined. The melody analysis module examines the intervals of the melody notes in relation to the root notes of the chords and the estimated melody, analyzing the melodic gravity where the melody tends to resolve to harmonic tones, and the melodic gravity where the melody progresses semitonally towards the major third and tonic notes. Analyses using GTTM and IRM are contemplated to explore "expectations with the tendency of the melody." The formalization presented in Section 4.4 is applied for IRM analysis. Additionally, the possibility of employing deepGTTM-IV [11], capable of accurately determining time-span trees, is under consideration for GTTM analysis.

5.3 Presentation of Analysis Results

The analysis results are conveyed from the server side to the client side and visualized to provide users with information in an intuitive and effective manner. This process employs a combination of textual information and colors to represent analysis results, aiding in the comprehension of melodies and chord structures. The use of the piano roll format enables the visualization of information along the pitch and time axes, offering an intuitive layout that is widely recognized in score videos and digital music production. The display includes a music player, ensuring that the analysis results corresponding to the playback time are shown at the relevant positions on the piano roll as the analyzed song plays. Chord tones are distinguished by color-coding based on the pitch of their root notes. Different colors are assigned to each pitch class by dividing the color wheel into 12 equal parts, allowing chord tones to be color-coded based on the root note for easier visual identification. Displaying chord symbols below the piano roll and nearby Roman numerals indicating chord functions enhances understanding. To represent MelodicGravity, arrows extend from rectangles denoting melody pitches to the next anticipated notes, visually depicting melodic expectations.

6. DISCUSSION

Visualizing musical cognitive structures, including melodic gravity, remains a significant challenge and may necessitate a considerable amount of time to address effectively.

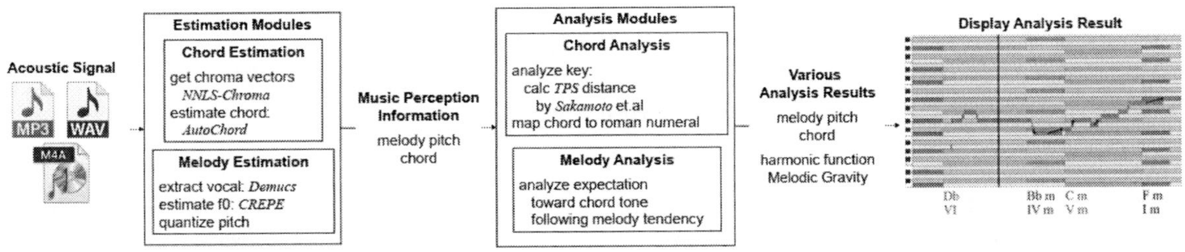

Figure 5. System Architecture Diagram This figure illustrates the modular structure of the system and the sequence of data processing steps. Initially, the system processes an acoustic signal, then estimation modules are applied to determine the melody pitches and chords. Following this, analysis modules are engaged to examine the harmonic functions and melodic gravity. The final stage involves presenting the analysis findings. Detailed operations within each module are further delineated in a list format.

We consider the notions of "implication" and "realization" within the Implication-Realization Model (IRM) as promising approaches to enhance the analysis of melodic gravity. However, as noted in Section 4.2, the theory underlying IRM is intricate, and the interpretation of its symbolism is not inherently intuitive. Consequently, our approach involves initiating the development of methods that can effectively visualize the concepts of IRM. Building upon this foundation, we aim to progress towards visualizing the expectations with the tendencies of melodies.

Acknowledgments

This research was supported in part by Grant-in-Aid for Scientific Research 22K00233.

7. REFERENCES

[1] M. Goto, K. Yoshii, H. Fujihara, M. Mauch, and T. Nakano, "Songle: A Web Service for Active Music Listening Improved by User Contributions." in *International Society for Music Information Retrieval (ISMIR).* Citeseer, 2011, pp. 311–316.

[2] L. B. Meyer, *Emotion and Meaning in Music.* The University of Chicago Press, 1961.

[3] E. Narmour, *The Analysis and Cognition of Basic Melodic Structures: The Implication Realization Model.* the University of Chicago Press, 1990.

[4] ——, *The Analysis and Cognition of Melodic Complexity: The Implication Realization Model.* the University of Chicago Press, 1992.

[5] M. Mauch and S. Dixon, "Approximate Note Transcription for the Improved Identification of Difficult Chords." in *International Society for Music Information Retrieval (ISMIR)*, 2010, pp. 135–140.

[6] C. J. Bayron, "Autochord: Automatic Chord Recognition Library and Chord Visualization App."

[7] A. Défossez, N. Usunier, L. Bottou, and F. Bach, "Demucs: Deep extractor for music sources with extra unlabeled data remixed," *arXiv preprint arXiv:1909.01174*, 2019.

[8] J. W. Kim, J. Salamon, P. Li, and J. P. Bello, "Crepe: A convolutional representation for pitch estimation," in *2018 IEEE International Conference on Acoustics, Speech and Signal Processing (ICASSP).* IEEE, 2018, pp. 161–165.

[9] F. Lerdahl, *Tonal pitch space.* Oxford University Press, USA, 2001.

[10] S. Sakamoto, S. Arn, M. Matsubara, and S. Tojo, "Harmonic analysis based on tonal pitch space," in *2016 eighth international conference on knowledge and systems engineering (kse).* IEEE, 2016, pp. 230–233.

[11] M. Hamanaka, K. Hirata, and S. Tojo, "deepGTTM-IV: Deep Learning Based Time-span Tree Analyzer of GTTM," *Proceedings of the 16th international symposium on computer music multidisciplinary research,* 2023.

Examining the Effect of Phrase Structure Introduction on Performance Timing Prediction

Koki Domoto
Kwansei Gakuin University
hbi43991@kwansei.ac.jp

Mituyo Hashida
The University of Fukuchiyama
hashida-mitsuyo@fukuchiyama.ac.jp

Haruhiro Katayose
Kwansei Gakuin University
katayose@kwansei.ac.jp

ABSTRACT

This paper examines the effects of integrating phrase structure into conventional deep learning-based prediction models with the aim of enhancing the accuracy of performance timing predictions in automatic accompaniment technology. Traditional models struggle to predict timing that fully captures the performer's intentions. Thus, this study seeks to improve the precision of predicting the timing of the next beat in human performances of known pieces of music by incorporating new input information and refining the learning model based on existing methods. Specifically, we explore the effectiveness of including phrase structure as input information alongside score and performance data, as well as the method of its representation. We also redesign the model by employing a learning approach that excels in processing time-series data. Our experiments demonstrate a 35% reduction in prediction error compared to models where timing is predicted using a moving average. It was also seen that the prediction accuracy improved the most when appropriate phrase structure information was incorporated.The obtained results suggest that the introduction of phrase structure information is effective in improving the accuracy of timing prediction.

1. INTRODUCTION

Research focused on human performance, including studies in the fields of aesthetics and psychology, has a storied history. The earliest research can be traced back to Seashore's studies in the 1920s, which identified the "misalignment" between a performance and its corresponding score [1]. Initially, studies primarily adopted an aesthetic perspective, but the advent of PCs and MIDI in the mid-1980s marked the beginning of research based on data measurement. For instance, Shaffer and Todd explored tempo fluctuations at phrase boundaries in music performances by various composers [2]. Concurrently, Palmer investigated the occurrence of overlapping notes in legato expressions during piano performances [3].

Around the same time, research expanded into generating computer-based, human-like performances, or performance rendering. In 2002, a contest for performance rendering was held [4], marking the modeling of performance expressions as a significant field of study in music information processing. Recently, deep learning and generative AI technologies have emerged as new applications for modeling performance expressions. For instance, the Dear Glenn project developed a system capable of generating performances in any piece of music that mimics the expressive style of the famous pianist Glenn Gould [5]. This method applies modeling of performance expressions by linking features of Gould's performances with score information and learning from this data.

Modeling performance expressions is essential not only for generating computer-based performances but also as a core technology for automatic accompaniment. This technology necessitates real-time coordination with a human soloist's performance, based on a score provided beforehand. Just as an accompanist in a human ensemble interprets the performance expressions of the soloist, including the soloist's intentions, automatic accompaniment technology predicts the timing of the soloist's performance based on these interpretations to achieve synchronization. Thus, modeling performance expressions, especially in terms of timing prediction, is crucial in crafting accompaniment with a natural sound.

In the early stages of timing prediction, approaches based on performance experience were mainstream [6]. However, in recent years, methods employing deep learning have been proposed. Maezawa has adopted a method for timing prediction that relies on information from previous performances and scores, enabling predictions for pieces that have not yet been performed [7]. This approach, however, does not consider the performer's interpretation of the score. By focusing on this aspect, an improvement in prediction accuracy is anticipated.

This study aims to enhance the accuracy of timing prediction by addressing the previously mentioned limitation. Specifically, our objective is to improve prediction accuracy by incorporating "phrase structure" into the timing prediction model, acknowledging its significant influence on performers' interpretation and expression of a piece. It is also confirmed that the effect is most improved when phrase structure information written for the performance in question is included, and the appropriate data for improving accuracy is examined by comparing phrase structures written in different ways.

The structure of this paper is organized as follows: Section 2 introduces related work in the field. Section 3 explains our proposed approach. Section 4 elaborates on the experiments conducted to validate the effectiveness of our approach. Section 5 compares prediction results with actual cases and discusses issues encountered throughout the study. Finally, Section 6 concludes the study with a summary of our findings and contributions.

2. RELATED WORK

This section reviews related work on two distinct approaches to timing prediction in automatic accompaniment technology: one leveraging rehearsal data and the other employing deep learning techniques, setting the focus of this study.

A seminal work in the realm of coordinated performance within automatic accompaniment technology is the study conducted by Vercoe [6]. This research proposed a method for statistically analyzing individual performance tendencies by conducting multiple rehearsals prior to the actual performance. This analysis is then used to tailor the accompaniment. Specifically, the method involves calculating the mean value and standard deviation of the soloist's timing for each note from data gathered during rehearsals. These statistics inform the planning and design of the accompaniment performance. Moreover, accounting for these statistical variations during live performance allows for adjustments to subtle changes in the soloist's expressive timing. However, a notable drawback of this method is the requirement for multiple rehearsals, which can be cumbersome for performers.

Maezawa's research represents a significant advancement in timing prediction for automatic accompaniment technology without the necessity for rehearsal [7]. This study models the timing of the next beat as an autoregressive process, employing a deep neural network (DNN) to generate linear prediction coefficients. The model inputs include information from previous performances and the musical score, predicated on the hypothesis that performers rely on both the score's contextual cues and past performance data to ascertain the timing of subsequent notes. By incorporating these elements as score features and performance features, the model was able to predict timing up to eight beats ahead, which is equivalent to the duration of a whole note. The architecture of the DNN comprises two fully-connected layers, augmented by Batch Normalization and Leaky ReLU activation functions. Evaluation experiments demonstrated that this method reduced prediction error by 18% compared to traditional approaches, which model performance timing as a moving average. Notably, Maezawa's method [7] can be applied to pieces being performed for the first time, marking a pivotal development in the field by broadening the predictive capabilities. Nonetheless, this method does not account for the performer's interpretation of the score, suggesting that incorporating this aspect could further refine prediction accuracy.

3. APPROACH

The Maezawa [7] model is an exceptional framework capable of predicting the outcomes of unperformed musical pieces. However, this model falls short in capturing the performers' intentions and facial expressions. In this study, we aim to enhance the prediction accuracy of timing by incorporating phrase structure as new input information to align with the performer's interpretation of the score and by refining the learning model, as illustrated in Figure 1.

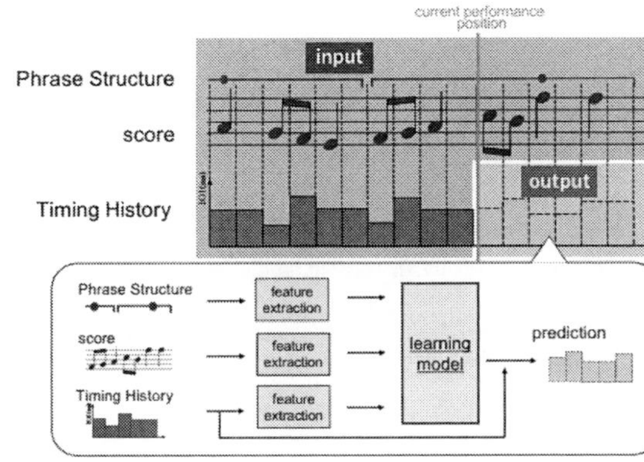

Figure 1. Our approach. (Reference: Maezawa [7])

The setup of this issue mirrors that of Maezawa's study [7]. This study also does not delve into the interplay between soloists and accompanists in an ensemble but instead focuses solely on an individual performer assumed to be in a live performance setting, concentrating on the prediction of performance timing. An eighth note is defined as a single beat, with predictions generated for each beat.

The following subsections elaborate on the details of the model and its enhancements.

3.1 Input information

In Maezawa's research [7], it was posited that leveraging both "timing history information" from the performer's past performances and "score information" from the current piece being played could enhance prediction accuracy. This approach was based on the assumption that the timing of an upcoming beat is influenced by both the performer's previous execution and the structural elements of the score. However, this method presents limitations when considering the diversity of performers' intentions and interpretations of the same musical piece. The variability in performance intentions and interpretations indicates that relying solely on historical timing and score information may not fully capture the "performance plan," which encompasses future expressions and tempo changes.

In this study, we delve into the utilization of "phrase structure information" as a novel input to address the aforementioned limitations. Phrase structure, a concept deeply rooted in the hierarchical organization of performances, offers a symbolic representation of the performer's intended expression, as illustrated in Figure 2. This hierarchical grouping aligns with the principles outlined in "A Generative Theory of Tonal Music" (GTTM) [8], which seeks to understand music's structural organization through cognitive processes. A phrase, in the context of music, is defined as a coherent sequence of melodies through which a performer conveys the flow and emotion of the piece. Building upon this foundation, we also integrate the concept of the "apex" from Hoshina's theory [9], a notable framework in the interpretation of phrase expression. The apex, identified as the most impactful note within a phrase, is considered a critical element of the phrase structure in our study. Incorporating the apex alongside phrase is anticipated to

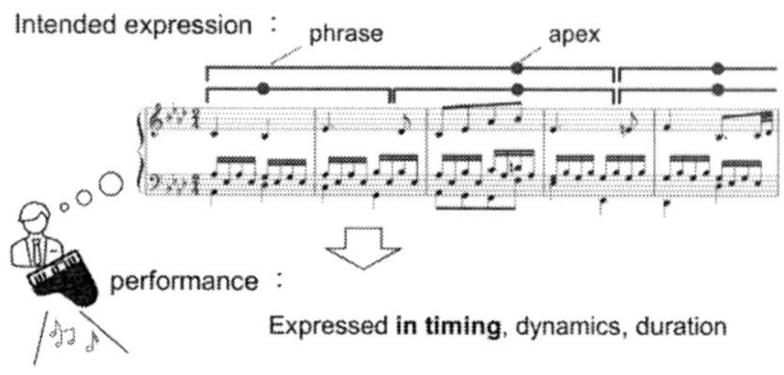

Figure 2. Phrase Structure and Performance Relationships.

significantly enhance the accuracy of future performance timing predictions.

The utility of incorporating phrase structure into performance prediction models has been substantiated through various studies focused on performance rendering. Notably, Itou's research highlighted that employing phrase structures for generating performances can lead to the creation of expressive, human-like renditions of high quality [10]. This evidence underlines the potential of phrase structure not only in enhancing the expressiveness of performances but also in improving the modeling of performance expressions. Given the demonstrated impact of phrase structures on the quality and expressiveness of performance generation, it stands to reason that their inclusion as input information could similarly enhance timing prediction accuracy.

In the experiments outlined in Section 4, we aim to validate the effectiveness of incorporating phrase structure information as an additional input, alongside timing history information and score information, which Maezawa's study [7] previously demonstrated to be beneficial.

3.2 Learning model

In the domain of timing prediction, capturing the subtle nuances of rhythm and timing changes in real-time performances is essential. Consequently, this study employs deep learning for the predictive model .

Maezawa's study [7] utilized a Deep Neural Network (DNN) with a simplistic network structure. In contrast, our research employs a Recurrent Neural Network (RNN), which is adept at processing time-series data, and Long Short-Term Memory (LSTM) networks, renowned for their capability to model dependencies over long-term data. We aim to compare and explore the effects of these models.

To compare and explore those approaches, we have redesigned a timing prediction model based on existing learning models. Our objective is to predict existing patterns and trends in performance using past information (including timing history, score, and phrase structure from past performances) and to anticipate rhythmic and timing variations in future performances using future information (including score and phrase structure for future performances). We adopt a model that inputs each set of past and future information into distinct layers, drawing inspiration from the DeepBach [11] model. Specifically, our network structure inputs past and future information into separate layers; their outputs are then combined and passed

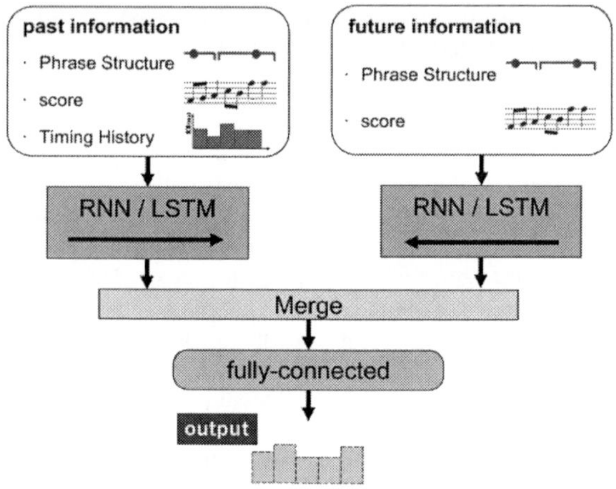

Figure 3. RNN/LSTM model.

through a fully-connected layer, as illustrated in Figure 3. This approach facilitates the learning of both instantaneous changes and the overall development of the performance simultaneously, which is expected to enhance the accuracy of timing predictions.

In the experiments described in Section 4, we compare the DNN model, which features a simple network structure consisting of two fully-connected layers, batch normalization, and leaky ReLU, with the redesigned RNN model and the LSTM model. We then explore which learning model is more effective at improving accuracy.

3.3 Model input/output layer design

This subsection provides a detailed explanation of the design of the input and output layers in the model. First, we describe the three input layers: score information, timing history information, and phrase structure information.

In the first input layer, concerning score information, we employ pitch, the position of each beat within a bar, and the time signature of the piece to capture the fundamental structure of the music. The pitch is digitized using the piano roll format, which allows for the simple and effective digital representation of the score's structure by marking pitches with 0s and 1s along a timeline. The beat position and time signature are encoded using one-hot encoding.

In the second input layer, regarding timing history information, various elements such as the dynamics and tempo of each beat are generally considered. This study utilizes the history of the Inter-Onset Interval (IOI), following the approach used in Maezawa's study [7]. In the DNN model, the history of IOI is standardized to a mean of 0 and variance of 1, as was done in Maezawa [7]'s model.

In the third input layer, regarding phrase structure information, we utilize the information about the starting point and apex of the phrase, which are its main components, to capture the significant features of the phrase structure. These representations are compared using three different methods, as illustrated in Figure 4. The first method is the "one-hot vector representation," a straightforward approach that employs one-hot encoding to represent the starting point and apex positions. The second method is

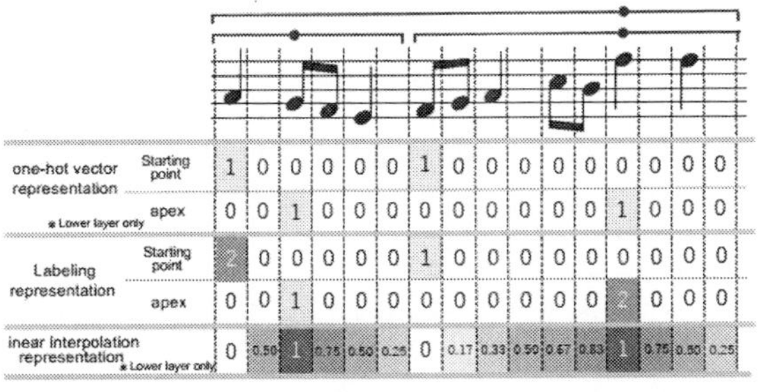

Figure 4. Phrase Structure Representation Methods in Model Input Layer Design.

the "labeling representation," involves labeling points at the starting point and apex in the first layer (lower phrase) as 1, points in the second layer (upper phrase) as 2, and positions without points as 0. In music performance theory, there are findings that suggest a hierarchical structure is expressed by slowing down the tempo at the end of a phrase [12]. Thus, the model is expected to learn more about the differences in tempo fluctuation between the first and second layers compared to the one-hot vector representation. The third method is the "linear interpolation representation," which employs linear interpolation between the starting point and the apex, setting the starting point to 0 and the apex to 1.

To address the limitations of other representation methods and to represent the increase or decrease in a phrase, this method is employed, where the starting and ending points of a phrase are set to 0, and the phrase is represented as increasing from the starting point to the apex, and decreasing from the apex to the endpoint. In the experiments in Section 4, we compare these three methods and explore their effectiveness in improving the accuracy of timing predictions.

In the output layer, we employ a method that calculates the ratio of the IOI one beat before the current position to several IOIs after the current position as the output. This approach aims to learn the subtle increases and decreases in the performance sequence and timing. It predicts the ratio of the IOI for eight consecutive beats, from one to eight beats after the current position, and generates output values for each beat. Consequently, the timing is determined by multiplying the output value by the IOI from one beat ago. Capturing subtle changes in the tempo of a performance is crucial in this study. We believe that this approach will predict changes in the tempo and rhythm of a performance more effectively than merely predicting each IOI individually.

4. EXPERIMENT

This section describes experiments conducted to confirm the effects of incorporating phrase structures and to compare their representations and learning models.

In the experiments, the RNN and LSTM models are configured with two layers, each containing 200 hidden units. The fully-connected layer utilizes 400 units, combining outputs from the preceding layers as its input. Training is conducted using a batch size of 256 and a learning rate of 0.0001, with optimization performed by ADAM [13]. The window size, along with the DNN input beat size, is set at 32 beats, encompassing 16 beats both before and after the current position. All models employ Mean Squared Error (MSE) as the loss function to enhance prediction accuracy. The experiments' evaluation metric is the errors between the predicted timings for four future intervals—up to one beat ahead (eighth note), two beats ahead (quarter note), four beats ahead (half note), and eight beats ahead (whole note)—and their actual timings.

4.1 Dataset

For the training and evaluation of the model in this study, the CrestMuse PEDB version 2 [14] dataset is utilized. This dataset serves as a database for performance expressions of piano pieces in classical music, primarily up until the early 20th century, featuring compositions by J. S. Bach, F. Chopin, and others. It comprises data from a total of 443 performances (67 types) by 12 performers. Each performance data set includes a score file (MusicXML), recording data (WAV/MIDI), score alignment information that outlines the correspondence between score and performance information, and phrase structure data (PDF) authored by the performers themselves.

In this study, approximately 200 performance data from five performers are selected from the dataset and divided in a 6:4 ratio, ensuring that the same piece is not duplicated within the training and evaluation sets. The timing history information is generated based on the score alignment information. Since the PEDB data represents polyphonic musical performances, a beat may contain multiple notes, leading to variations among them in actual performances. In such cases, the average articulation time for each beat is defined as the articulation time for that beat, and the difference from the articulation time of the subsequent beat is calculated to determine the IOI. The score information is generated by converting a MusicXML format score file into a piano-roll format matrix. Phrase structure information is generated by manually extracting the start points and apexes of phrases. Although the phrase structure data in the PEDB is authored by the performers, no standard for description has been established. Therefore, phrase structure data described by the performer and phrase structure data reconstructed by the author are compared in experiments to determine which data is more effective for improving accuracy.

4.2 Experiments 1 and 2: Effectiveness of phrase structure

Initially, two experiments are conducted to verify the effectiveness of utilizing phrase structure information as input for timing prediction.

The first experiment aims to confirm the effect of enhancing accuracy by inputting phrase structure information and to investigate the most appropriate data for accuracy improvement by comparing phrase structure data described using different methods.

The comparison of phrase structure data is necessitated by several issues with the data described by performers. A notable issue is the inconsistency in the rules for describing phrase structures and the granularity of the phrases. In pursuit of improving timing prediction accuracy with phrase structure information that adheres to a uniform standard and consistent interpretation, the first author [1] reconstructs the phrase structure data from sound data, following Fujisaka's rules [15]. By comparing the phrase structure data described by the performers with the phrase structure data reconstructed by the author, we aim to verify which data contributes more effectively to improving the accuracy of timing prediction. The reconstructed data is typically articulated in a two-layer structure. Additionally, regarding the phrase structure data described by the performers, the lack of clear criteria for their descriptions complicates the use of information from multiple layers, leading to a focus on extracting phrases from a single layer. To this end, the author judiciously assesses and rectifies any ambiguities and decides on the layers to be utilized.

The second experiment aims to verify that the improvement in prediction accuracy is greatest when the appropriate phrase structure information is incorporated.

4.2.1 Details of experiment - Experiment 1

To confirm the impact of phrase structure information input on accuracy improvement, the following comparison methods are utilized:

1. MA model: Utilizes the moving average of the timing history information for prediction.
2. AR model: Predicts timing by training an autoregressive process for each beat to be predicted, based on timing history information.
3. No-phrase model: Predicts timing by inputting score information and timing history information into the input layer of the DNN model.
4. Phrase (performer-descriptive) model: Predicts timing by inputting, in addition to music score information and timing history information, phrase structure information described by the performer into the input layer of the DNN model.
5. Phrase (author-descriptive layer 1) model: Predicts timing by inputting, in addition to music score information and timing history information, phrase structure information of the first layer reconstructed by the author into the input layer of the DNN model.
6. Phrase (author-descriptive layer 2) model: Predicts timing by inputting, in addition to music score information and timing history information, phrase structure information of the second layer reconstructed by the author into the input layer of the DNN model.
7. Phrase (author-description layer 1, 2) model: Predicts timing by inputting, in addition to music score information and timing history information, phrase structure information of both the first and second layers reconstructed by the author into the input layer of the DNN model.

The representation method for the input layer of phrase structure information utilizes a one-hot vector representation. As evaluation metrics, the Mean Absolute Error (MAE) and the MSE are calculated.

[1] The author has a history of receiving top honors at piano competitions.

Table 1. Experiment 1: Prediction error (MAE in ms) for each model. 'A' refers to Author, 'P' to Performer, and 'L' to Layer number.

	MA	AR	No-phrase
eighth note	67	54	49
quarter note	122	102	91
half note	223	198	174
whole note	411	381	339

	Phrase (P, L1)	Phrase (A, L1)	Phrase (A, L2)	Phrase (A, L1&2)
eighth note	**47**	**47**	**47**	48
quarter note	89	**85**	89	88
half note	168	**159**	168	162
whole note	319	**297**	315	299

Table 2. Experiment 1: Prediction error (MSE in ms^2) for each model. 'A' refers to Author, 'P' to Performer, and 'L' to Layer number.

	MA	AR	No-phrase
eighth note	13049	9693	5090
quarter note	41784	31738	17247
half note	136535	112698	63498
whole note	443883	386108	232130

	Phrase (P, L1)	Phrase (A, L1)	Phrase (A, L2)	Phrase (A, L1&2)
eighth note	4852	4882	**4539**	4788
quarter note	17305	**16506**	16561	16119
half note	59577	**56399**	58556	56408
whole note	208487	**187037**	204287	187931

4.2.2 Results - Experiment 1

Table 1 shows MAE and Table 2 shows MSE results for each model.

The DNN-based no-phrase model displayed significantly smaller prediction errors compared to the traditional MA and AR models. However, models incorporating phrase information exhibited even smaller errors than the no-phrase model, notably for predictions extending over longer periods, such as 4 beats ahead (half notes) and 8 beats ahead (whole notes), thereby significantly enhancing prediction accuracy. Moreover, a comparison between phrase and no-phrase models revealed differences in both MSE and MAE metrics, with the discrepancies being particularly marked in MSE. This indicates that the introduction of phrase structure information contributes to a reduction in significant prediction errors, including those that would result in outliers. Thus, the utility of incorporating phrase structure information for timing prediction was demonstrated.

Upon comparing the phrase structure data described by performers with that reconstructed by the author, all types of the author-reconstructed phrase information showed improved precision over those described by performers. Furthermore, the first layer of the author-described phrase structure information yielded higher accuracy than the second layer, which contains more generalized information. This suggests that the first layer's phrase structure information, capturing more nuanced performance intentions, contributed to the improvement in prediction accuracy.

4.2.3 Details of experiment - Experiment 2

To verify that the impact of inputting phrase structure information is maximized with the inclusion of appropriate

Table 3. Experiment 2: Prediction error for each input data (ms).

	Appropriate phrase data	Inappropriate phrase data	No Phrase
eighth note	**51**	54	54
quarter note	**95**	99	100
half note	**176**	188	191
whole note	**338**	351	364

phrase structure information, the following data are utilized for comparison:

1. Appropriate phrase data: Uses phrase structure information specifically described for that performance as input information.
2. Inappropriate phrase data: Uses phrase structure information described for a different performer's rendition of the same piece as input information.
3. No Phrase: Does not input any phrase structure information into the input layer.

In conducting this experiment, it is necessary to utilize only pieces performed by multiple performers. Therefore, 167 performances (35 types) from PEDB are employed. The model used is a DNN model, similar to Experiment 1. For the phrase structure data, the author-described data, which demonstrated high accuracy in Experiment 1, is used. The representation method for phrase structure information in the input layer is a one-hot vector representation. As an evaluation metric, the MAE is calculated.

4.2.4 Results - Experiment 2

Table 3 shows MAE results for each input information.

Predictions with inappropriate phrase structure information show smaller errors than those without any phrase structure input but are less accurate than those with appropriate phrase structure information. This indicates the smallest errors occur with appropriate phrase structure information. Therefore, incorporating phrase structure information is most effective when it's appropriate. The lesser errors with inappropriate phrase structure information, compared to no input, suggest even incorrect information may share similarities with the correct structure.

Experiments 1 and 2 demonstrated the effectiveness of incorporating phrase structure information as input and highlighted the importance of accurately describing and applying this information to enhance timing prediction accuracy.

4.3 Experiment 3: Verification of phrase structure representation methods

Next, experiments are conducted to explore the optimal representation method for phrase structure information in the input layer, aimed at enhancing prediction accuracy.

4.3.1 Details of experiment

Five representation methods are compared: (1) one-hot vector representation (layer 1), (2) one-hot vector representation (layers 1 and 2), (3) labeling representation, (4) linear interpolation representation (layer 1), and (5) linear interpolation representation (layers 1 and 2).

The model used is a DNN model, consistent with Experiments 1 and 2, utilizing the phrase structure data described by the author, which demonstrated high accuracy in Experiment 1. As an evaluation metric, the MAE is calculated.

Table 4. Experiment 3: Prediction error in phrase structure representation methods (ms).

	one-hot (layer 1)	one-hot (layer 1,2)	labeling (layer 1,2)	lin interp (layer 1)	lin interp (layer 1,2)
eighth note	**46**	48	47	47	47
quarter note	**85**	88	89	89	89
half note	**159**	162	168	169	168
whole note	**297**	299	320	316	321

4.3.2 Results

Table4 shows MAE results for each representation method.

The one-hot vector representation (first layer) led to an improvement in precision compared to other representation methods. This result is attributed to the simplification of the representation method, which significantly contributes to improved prediction accuracy. In actual performances, tempo changes dramatically just before or after phrase boundaries or apexes. It is believed that the model incorporating the one-hot vector representation for its input was able to learn and adapt to these nuances, leading to enhanced accuracy. However, the linear interpolation representation, which assumed a linear approximation of phrase structure peaking at the apexes, was less accurate because the actual phrase structure is more complex than a linear model can capture. Therefore, a simpler one-hot vector representation was found to be more effective for representing phrase structure information in the input layer.

4.4 Experiment 4: Verification of learning models

Finally, experiments are conducted to evaluate the learning model used for timing prediction.

4.4.1 Details of experiment

Three learning models are compared: (1) DNN model, (2) RNN model, and (3) LSTM model.

The phrase structure data utilized is the one described by the author, which demonstrated high accuracy in Experiment 1. The representation of phrase structure in the input layer is the one-hot vector representation, which showed high accuracy in Experiment 3. As an evaluation metric, the MAE is calculated.

4.4.2 Results

Table5 shows MAE results for each learning model.

RNN and LSTM models exhibited smaller errors compared to DNN models. This is attributed to the capability of RNN and LSTM to effectively handle time series information, which is thought to have contributed to the improvement in accuracy.

When comparing RNN and LSTM models, the RNN model demonstrated higher prediction accuracy for short-term predictions, such as one beat ahead (eighth notes) and two beats ahead (quarter notes), than the LSTM model. However, the LSTM model showed significantly better prediction accuracy for longer durations, particularly for predictions eight beats ahead (whole notes). This confirms the effectiveness of LSTM's long-term forecasting

Table 5. Experiment 4: Prediction error in the learning models (ms).

	DNN	RNN	LSTM
eighth note	46	**43**	44
quarter note	85	**80**	83
half note	159	**153**	**153**
whole note	297	291	**285**

capabilities. In the context of timing prediction for automatic accompaniment technology, enhancing accuracy for long-term timing, where deviations are more perceptible, is deemed more crucial than further improving short-term timing accuracy, which is less likely to be detected by humans. Therefore, using an LSTM model, which offers improved accuracy in long-term timing prediction, is considered effective for the learning model applied to timing prediction.

5. DISCUSSION

Following the validation of this approach, a detailed analysis is conducted by comparing the prediction results based on real cases with the model used in Experiment 1, and then discussing the considerations throughout this study.

In this setup, considering real-time performance, the timing is predicted up to 8 beats ahead for each beat and compared with the actual timing of the performance. This analysis uses performances of two pieces not included in the training: "Schumann, Robert: Kinderszenen Traumerai F-Dur Op.15-7" and "F. Chopin: Waltz No.3 in A minor, Op.34-2".

Figures 5 and 6 illustrate the timing predictions for the first and second models, respectively. For both pieces, the model incorporating phrase structure information input aligns more closely with the actual performance than the other models, demonstrating its effectiveness. Specifically, the MAE for the first piece is 412 ms for the model with phrase structure information, 619 ms for the model without phrase structure information, and 803 ms for the MA model. For the second piece, it is 274 ms for the model with phrase structure information, 360 ms for the model without phrase structure information, and 450 ms for the MA model, indicating the smallest errors. However, even within the model incorporating phrase structure information, there were instances where errors reached up to approximately 800 ms, suggesting a need for further accuracy improvements in future work.

5.1 Effectiveness of phrase structure

This study demonstrated that the introduction of phrase structure information effectively improves the accuracy of timing prediction. This suggests that the model can capture the performer's intentions and nuances.

Although the effect of introducing phrase structure information met expectations, there is room for improvement in several areas. The method of representing phrase structure in the input layer through linear interpolation of tempo increases or decreases did not enhance prediction accuracy. This may be attributed to the complexity of phrase structure, which cannot be fully captured by a simple linear model. To address this, exploring more sophisticated

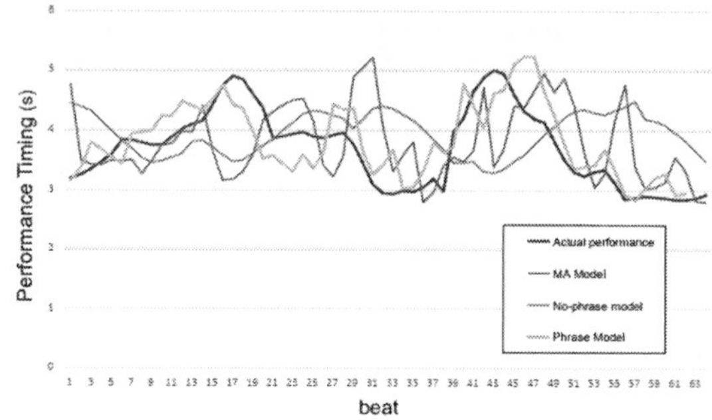

Figure 5. Prediction in "Schumann, Robert: Kinderszenen Traumerai F-Dur Op.15-7".

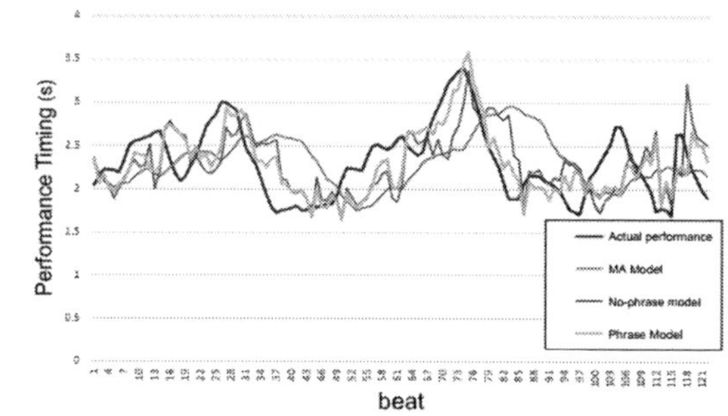

Figure 6. Prediction in"Chopin, Frederic: Valse No.3 a-moll Op.34-2".

mathematical expressions, such as polynomial interpolation in two, three, or more dimensions, is necessary.

In the comparison of phrase structure data, the author-described phrase structure yielded better results than the performer-described phrase structure. This could be because artistic performers are not accustomed to providing logical descriptions of phrase structure, while the author's consistent approach to describing phrase structure, rooted in an engineering background, contributed to improved prediction accuracy. Therefore, further investigation into the criteria for describing phrase structure in timing prediction could lead to enhanced model accuracy. Additionally, manual input of phrase structure information may pose a burden for performers in live settings. To overcome this challenge, developing a model that automatically estimates phrase structure from score and performance data is deemed necessary.

Looking forward, focusing on optimizing the representation of phrase structure information and developing models for automatic estimation is expected to enhance the accuracy and practicality of prediction models. Moreover, exploring ways to utilize phrase structure information more effectively is anticipated to improve the overall performance of the model.

5.2 Model comparison and new model

This study demonstrates that RNN and LSTM models are more effective than DNN models for improving the accuracy of performance timing prediction. This suggests that the capability of RNNs and LSTMs to handle time series data enables them to effectively model the temporal connections within performance data.

Looking ahead, to achieve further improvements in accuracy, it becomes necessary to adopt new models beyond RNNs and LSTMs. The Transformer model, which has been at the forefront of recent research trends, is one such candidate. The Transformer employs an attention mechanism with parallel processing capabilities and the ability to comprehend positional information. Therefore, based on the successes achieved with RNNs and LSTMs, there is anticipation that introducing the Transformer model could lead to enhancements in prediction accuracy.

5.3 Prediction of each note and application to other performance features

The performance timing prediction in this study was based on the assumption that each note within a chord is played simultaneously. However, in real performances, performers may add expression by subtly shifting the timing of each note within a chord, indicating a limitation of this study in fully capturing the expressive nuances of actual performances.

In the future, it will be necessary to extend the model's scope to include timing prediction for individual notes. This approach is anticipated to enable more detailed timing predictions for each note within a chord and a more faithful prediction of performance expression. It is also expected to be applicable to predicting other performance characteristics, such as velocity and duration. Thus, it is anticipated that it will be possible to predict the overall performance expression, including the subtle nuances of the performance.

6. CONCLUSION

In this study, we investigated the effect of incorporating phrase structure into timing prediction and also redesigned the learning model. It was demonstrated that using phrase structure information as input is effective and that the proper description and application of phrase structure are crucial for improving timing prediction accuracy. Moreover, it was found that relatively simple methods for representing phrase structure information in the input layer, such as the one-hot vector representation, are effective. Furthermore, it was shown that the ability to effectively handle time series information is important for learning models, with LSTM proving particularly useful for long-term forecasting. These approaches led to a 35% reduction in the error of timing prediction up to eight beats ahead compared to the traditional method of modeling IOI as a moving average.

Looking forward, the future direction includes an approach to timing prediction for each note to enhance the accuracy of performance representation, along with its application to predicting other performance characteristics such as velocity and duration.

Acknowledgments

A part of this work was supported by JSPS KAKENHI Grant Number 19K21622.

7. REFERENCES

[1] Seashore, Carl E. and Metfessel, Milton, Deviation from the Regular as an Art Principle, Proc. the National Academy of Sciences, Vol.11, No.9, p. 538-542, 1925.

[2] Shaffer, L. H., Todd, N. P., The interpretive component in musical performance, In A. Gabrielsson, (Ed.), Action and perception in rhythm and music, p. 139-152, 1987.

[3] Palmer, C., Mapping musical thought to musical performance, Journal of Experimental Psychology : Human Perception and Performance, 15, p. 331-346, 1989.

[4] Hashida, M., Hirata, K. and Katayose, H., Rencon Workshop 2011 (SMC-Rencon): Performance rendering contest for computer systems, Proc. SMC, Padova, 2011.

[5] Maezawa, A., Yamamoto, K., and Fujishima, T., Rendering Music Performance With Interpretation Variations Using Conditional Variational RNN, Proc. ISMIR, p.855-861, 2019.

[6] Barry Vercoe, THE SYNTHEIC PERFORMER IN THE CONTEXT OF LIVE PERFORMANCE, Proc.ICMC, p.199-200, 1984.

[7] Akira Maezawa, Deep Linear Autoregressive Model for Interpretable Prediction of Expressive Tempo, Proc. SMC, pp.364-371, 2019.

[8] Lerdahl, F. and Jackendoff, R., A Generative Theory of Tonal Music, MIT Press, 1985.

[9] Y. Hoshina, An Approach to Live Musical Expression: Performance Interpretation Methods Based on Energy Thinking. ONGAKU NO TOMO SHA, 1998.

[10] Itou, N., Fukayama, S., Saito, D., Sagayama, S., Generation of Tempo Curve for Performance Rendering of Piano Music with Automatic Phrase Analysis, Proc. Intl. Workshop on Machine Learning and Music, 2012.

[11] G. Hadjeres, F. Pachet, and F. Nielsen, Deepbach: A steerable model for bach chorales generation, Proc. ICML, 2017.

[12] N. P. Todd, A model of expressive timing in tonal music,Music Perception, vol. 3, no. 1, pp. 33-58, 1985.

[13] D. Kingma and J. Ba, Adam: A Method for Stochastic Optimization, Proc. ICLR, p.1-15, 2015.

[14] Hashida, M., Nakamura, E.,and Katayose, H, Hashida, M., Nakamura, E. and Katayose, H., Crest-MusePEDB 2nd edition: Music performance database with phrase information, Proc. SMC, 2018.

[15] A. Fujisaka, M. Hashida, and H. Katayose, How is the performer's intention conveyed to the listener? :Analysis of the effect of visual information on phrase expression, The Special Interest Group Technical Reports of IPSJ, Tech. Rep. 7, 2021.

On the Prowl: A Report of the Approaches to Electroacoustic Improvisation of the Laptop Trio *Totaleee*

Giuseppe Pisano
Norwegian Academy of Music, Oslo
Giuseppe.pisano@nmh.no

Paolo Montella
Napoli Totale Elettronica, Napoli
mail@paolomontella.it

Andrea Laudante
Napoli Totale Elettronica, Napoli
andrealaudante@gmail.com

ABSTRACT

Native to Naples, Southern Italy, Totaleee carries within itself the heritage and experience of different periods and aesthetic directions in free improvisation and electronic music. This awareness is condensed in a few distinctive approaches to their practices, listening and playing styles, but more importantly, it has also informed their methodology for designing devices that favor dynamism and speed, as well as intuitive interfaces, over operational complexity. The ability to respond to a wide range of scenarios and change behavior is crucial to the approach of totaleee, who describe their playing style as being 'on the prowl', managing tension to make the perfect move at the right time. Of course, this has to be made possible by using instruments that offer this possibility, because unlike acoustic instruments, the relationship between gesture and sound on laptops is often not very straightforward. This article describes the trio's design strategies for achieving responsiveness, along with the desired musical results.

1. INTRODUCTION

The electroacoustic improvisation and acousmatic composition trio totaleee is made up of Andrea Laudante, Paolo Montella and Giuseppe Pisano. Although the three artists have independently developed very different tools for live improvisation, they share an ideological orientation that makes interaction and responsiveness its main foundations, placing mutual listening and the will to contribute to the construction of a unified sound at the center of their practice.

2. DEFINING IMPROVISATION

In music, the term improvisation generally refers to the practice of exploring melodies, chord progressions, and rhythms within predefined structures established by specific genres, traditions, cultures, and styles. Baroque music, Flamenco, Indian Ragas and Jazz, they all have their ways to approach improvisation with different rules and codes.

In line with the development of 20th century music, the languages of improvisation have gradually emancipated themselves from idiomatic conventions. The practice we refer to as a trio is what Derek Bailey refers to as "non-idiomatic improvisation" [1], a way of practicing improvisation that aims to deny all references to any existing musical language and thus to renounce categories such as tonality, harmony and rhythm. This means essentially the reinvention of music from scratch, breaking free from pre-established structures and without necessarily adhering to predetermined styles.

The Improvisational process can be intended properly as "being in relation", allowing the exploration of the interactions between material forces and cognitive modalities. In improvisation sessions, sound reveals elements of its origin, describes the path it travels, and establishes relationships with its surroundings. In the practice of the trio, there is no such thing as an isolated sound, and sounds always exist as relational events. The participants to each improvisation session learn about each other and the environment through a language that is codified together during performance, establishing and constantly rewriting rules and structures. Each improvisation configures a language with its own grammar, syntax, and structural functions that exists only for the time of the session. To do all this, sharp senses, high attention, and timing are crucial, and musicians are on the prowl like predators, performing silence as an active practice, ready to pounce at the right opportunity [6]. Totaleee identified reactive response—thus emphasizing active listening—as a key element of radical improvisation. The trio believes that developing the ability to respond quickly to listening can instigate clear sonic behaviors, thereby facilitating the construction of an improvisational discourse.

3. THE ITALIAN CONTEXT

Despite the intention of breaking free of all musical conventions and the active effort to do so, "non-idiomatic improvisation" can probably never be completely be able to avoid all references, and the music that emerges from its practice will always be influenced to some extent by the musical background of the participants and the historical context in which it happens, the series of encounters, developments, directions that define a local "scene" and that sometimes are the result of chance or luck. Totaleee's approach to improvisation is no exception, and falls in the tradition of Italian electroacoustic improvisation, a rather unique subgenre of free music that emerged from very specific conditions that set it apart from other European contexts, and therefore requires a brief digression.

In fact, while in the circuits of conservatories and early Italian research centers, such as the Studio di fonologia musicale RAI in Milan, experiments were taking place that would result in important works of acousmatic music, pieces for instruments and tape, and compositions with live electronics, the birth of a real free improvisation scene using electronics should be sought in the presence in Rome of figures such as Franco Evangelisti and Alvin Curran and the experiences of their respective groups, "Gruppo di Improvvisazione Nuova Consonanza" [2] and "Musica Elettronica Viva - MEV" [3]. In particular, MEV's action ranged widely between free jazz, performing arts, and contemporary art, intersecting with the experiences of Living Theater in the Italian capital and paving the way for a practice that focused much more on the interactive qualities of improvisational work than on technological development of electronic music [4].

The results of this contingency have left a tangible legacy in Rome, particularly in free improvisation formations characterized by the extensive use of electronics, such as IATO Orchestra and Ossatura. A figure of fundamental importance who has undoubtedly elevated the laptop to a central instrument in improvisational practices is Elio Martusciello. Martusciello is also considered to be the main instigator behind the creation of OEOAS, the Officina Arti Soniche Electroacoustic Orchestra of Naples, which originated in the electronic music class at the Naples Conservatory, but now includes musicians from all over Italy with a wide variety of backgrounds.

To date, there are several Italian institutions dedicated to electroacoustic improvisation; in addition to the aforementioned Conservatory in Naples, Francesco Giomi's work between the Conservatory in Bologna and the Tempo Reale research center in Florence deserves special mention [5].

The members of trio totaleee share their education at the Conservatory of Naples and have participated in various collective improvisation experiences that have taken place in the city over the past decade. In addition to the aforementioned OEOAS, there have been experiments such as the concert series Geografie del Suono at the Ex Asilo Filangieri and the various Neapolitan editions of the improvised music festival Multiversale, as well as close contacts with the radical improvisation collective Crossroads Improring and the noise-anarchist milieu of the city.

4. RESPONSIVENESS ABOVE ALL

The need to respond to such a wide variety of situations involving the interplay of acoustic and electronic instruments, as well as the need to react quickly to specific inputs during sessions of conducted impromptu composition for large ensembles with OEOAS, meant that a special focus has been placed on responsiveness. In most conventional instruments, the distance between action and sound production is mediated by simple interfaces. Plucking a string, pressing a key, beating a drum provide an immediate connection between thought, action, and sonic result. Electronic instruments, especially laptops, do not always have this feature [7]. Many interfaces for electronic music and controllers for computers are designed imagining the laptop performer as a soloist, in total control of the performance and its timing.

However, when playing with others, the time between thought, action, and result must be minimized and it is difficult to find a good balance between operational simplicity and sonic complexity. Designing a software electronic instrument that meets the needs of an improviser has been at the core of the individual practice of the members of the trio since the very beginning. The trio relies on a few simple dogmas that simplify the thought-gesture-sound pathway. One of these is certainly to encourage as much tactile control of the device as possible. This means designing interfaces that allow the emancipation of the gaze from the device screen, avoiding, for example, the use of tablets and other types of touchscreen peripherals. Another, however, is the abandonment of control layers, which means keeping all device controls at hand by avoiding the use of control pages, favoring a limited number of controls, and favoring the use of macros. This leads to another important dogma, which is that there is no need to control everything, that certain controls are more effective than others in a system of immediacy, and that sometimes the speed of interaction and the ability to make drastic changes in operation in an improvisational context are more important than a meticulous sound-sculpting. This last point leads us back to a final dogma, perhaps the most important, which is that group improvisation requires enormous attention to ensemble listening and the realization that one's contribution to the unified sound is often made through silence.

5. THE TRIO'S PERFORMANCE PRACTICE

5.1. Meditative Listening and Interdependence, a Look Into Andrea Laudante's Device

The practice and study of Eastern spiritual traditions, particularly the path of Patanjali's yoga and Vipassana meditation [8], have had a profound influence on Laudante's approach to improvisation. Through Vipassana practice, one can personally experience the impermanence and cyclical nature of events, but above all, the emptiness of the self and the interdependence of elements [9]. Engaging in meditative listening has led him to increasingly focus on the cyclical/random nature of sound events and how each sound influences the surrounding environment and vice versa.

As an improviser, Laudante is interested in the possibility of reacting/interacting with his surroundings by acting as a mirror, reflecting his perceptions, and returning part of the original sound source. The machine acts as a filter between him and the external world, condensing infinite possibilities for exploring time and space into a single instrument, juxtaposing sounds from different spaces and times with the reality of the present moment. Laudante's device consists of four different sections: a generative part based on FM synthesis, a bank of samples - memories of sounds and significant moments, a microphone, and an internal feedback system, acting like a digital no-input device (fig. n. 1).

The choice of using a feedback chain in his digital device was necessary to introduce a dynamic source that allowed for a wide range of musical expression. This internal loop happening inside the computer is in fact highly sensitive to changes and can be modulated both internally, through traditional signal processing techniques such as amplification and equalization on separated channels (fig. n. 2), and externally, using the microphone and picking up sounds of the other musicians, blurring the boundary between the "inside" and the "outside".

5.2. Space-Landscape-Field, Paolo Montella Remixing Reality

Paolo Montella's recent artistic endeavors predominantly focus on incorporating field recordings into radical improvisation. Over the years, he has immersed himself in studying the complexities of field recording and the practical application of derived materials. From his perspective, the act of field recording - viewed as a completed operation - requires manipulating the recorded material to unveil its structural connections, language, and syntax, thereby unlocking its intrinsic musical potential [10]. Montella firmly believes that within field recording, there's a distinct orientation towards subjectively representing the world, aimed directly at its artistic transformation [11]. In this context, the operator actively shapes the sonic landscape they inhabit, directing their musical attention intentionally [12]. In his practice, Montella seeks elements filtered through his poetic and artistic sensibilities, capable of revealing at least one aspect of the profound complexity of recorded fields, ultimately offering a subjective representation. While recording, he broadens his microphone's listening horizon as much as possible; during composition and performance, he focuses on isolated details, reintroducing them - with the force of manipulation - into other contexts, often generated through interaction with fellow musicians, aiming to underscore their revelatory power.

The computer device Montella employs during concerts hosts a patch created on Max MSP, precisely tailored to his aesthetic needs. He has chosen a control surface that allows him - through two jog wheels (fig. n. 3) - to directly engage with the sound, emulating the control of a tape recorder. The heart of his device is a granular synthesis algorithm he designed based on Gabor synthesis [13]. Infact, Montella is fascinated by how historically, sound production through this technique is linked to field recording practices, as in the seminal experience of Barry Truax [14].

Sample reading occurs synchronously and overlaid on the playback of the main clip. Through a dedicated algorithm, he can control the degree of deviation from the period which, together with pitch definition, can determine a definitively asynchronous reading (fig n. 4). This type of sound generation and manipulation, besides determining a wide range of possible behaviors, allows him to reproduce sound according to the movement of his hands. The reading index, for both the source and the samples, is directly controlled by the jog wheels. This enables him to isolate small field fragments and cyclically reproduce them in irregular loops. Furthermore, thanks to a series of functions, he can convolve two audio signals through a distortion unit he conceived and designed (fig n.). Consequently, the field materials he uses blend and influence each other, yielding - often unexpected - results with which he constantly interacts. Paolo Montella's practice is characterized by great execution speed and the overlapping of spatial, dramatic, and narrative planes. Through attentive listening, Montella can react responsively to the sonic landscapes created by Laudante and Pisano, further enriching his artistic dialogue.

5.3. Infinite Variation and Morphing, the Textural Approach of Giuseppe Pisano

The device designed by Giuseppe Pisano draws inspiration from Japanese minimalism and the juxtaposition of simple lines in constant dynamic relation. In the design of this instrument Pisano started again from the controlling interface, a Novation Launch Control XL (fig. n. 5), adopting a modular approach in which every column of 3 knobs, one fader, two button would control a single module of the patch.

The instrument was designed in Max/MSP, with the collaboration of Bálint Lazckó and Timo Hoogland, and contains eight complex samplers featuring banks of sounds of different nature that are characterized by different musical behavior. Each has a more or less specific function and therefore slightly different controls. Some samplers have distortions, some others have pitch/rate variations, some others allow for the samples to be played in reverse, some others include advanced spatialization possibilities.

The core of the patch is the [polybuffer~] object that, together with the object [dict] allows to operate polyphonically with banks of samples (fig. n. 6). Once a bank is selected a sample is picked randomly from the bank and played back. At the end of the playback the buffer object reads another random sample from the same bank and plays the new one. Constantly choosing a new one, multiple buffers playing together can create thick bundles of similar sounds with great amount of internal variation and resulting in univocal spectromorphologies of good inherent complexity.

Using [mc.] objects and the external library Spat5 [15] for the spatialization control make the instrument adaptable to any sort of loudspeaker setup by changing the value of just a few number-boxes, which proves especially useful to make full use of non-conventional loudspeaker setups. In the interaction with totaleee this instrument gives Pisano the possibility to establish the context in which the action of the two other musicians will take place as well as operate leaps forward and take the scene with sudden gestures and prominent granular noises.

6. THE PERFORMANCE AT 20ALPHA IN HONG KONG

On October 10th, 2023, the trio held a concert at 20Alpha, a multifunctional space situated on Hong Kong Island that has been dedicated to promoting experimental arts, particularly from the local underground scene, since 2018. The performance, available on YouTube [16] and soon to be released in a record, lasted around 25 minutes and was divided into two sets: the first lasting approximately 19 minutes and the second 6 minutes and 40 seconds. As an illustration of the improvisation practice of totaleee, an brief outline of the second set will be presented.

The set starts with intelligible vocal material played by Montella, characterized by a low level of surrogation that is used to define a communication space - this immediately shaped the syntax of the initial part of their improvisation. The two other musicians are called to respond to this behavior, and they do so using sounds, with a distinct diachronic component, spread across a wide frequency spectrum, framing the vocal counterpoint, which is gradually processed with distortions to add a glitchy patina which creates a timbral bond with the materials surrounding it. The bell-like sounds that characterize the canopy of the sound field, gradually morph their behavior, passing from a textural unfolding to a transient rich hitting-sound that recalls the attack of the vocal material. Through a synthesis process, these voices gradually merged into indistinguishable sound grains. The grains built up towards a strong crescendo, that represented a natural musical rendezvous for the musicians. The three of them interacted with that common vector using different materials in a collective accumulation that was both temporal (adding more speed) and spectral, gradually occupying new, unused, portions of the frequency spectrum. The build-up resolved in a synchronic cut, leaving residues of wet voice in the foreground.

The sonic vestiges left after the cut were necessary to establish a timbral continuum with the previous phase, and to suggest new behaviors for the trio. Soon after the cut, in facts, the trio transitioned into a new phase characterized by faster energetic vectors that dynamically opened and closed different electroacoustic windows. These windows appeared as precise episodes with a distinct beginning and end, and sudden changes in speed, materials used, and vectoriality. Each sudden subtraction of sonic elements caused a behavioural change of the impro. The process of skipping between electroacoustic windows can be intended as a macro-gesture that contains all the windows as micro elements. After some completely unrelated windows, new ones were opened presenting some elements in common with the previous ones. Gradually each new electroacoustic window would be a different version of the previous one: a dense upward gestural vector, with evanescent bands of granular noise and overdriven feedback trajectories.

The intensification of low frequencies and their subsequent modulation suggested a potential conclusion on which the musicians implicitly agreed on.

7. CONCLUSIONS

In conclusion, totaleee draws its strength from the intersection of different solutions to the problem of designing functional interfaces and workflows for laptop improvisation, showing that specific ideological concepts can be applied in different ways to one's own practice and playstyle. A deep knowledge of the cultural background and a deep involvement in the local scenes provide ulterior possibilities to test new solutions, to cross boundaries and to leave one's musical comfort zone, which is the soul and spirit of the language of improvisation.

Acknowledgments

We would like to express our deepest appreciation to Elio Martusciello, who has been a mentor and inspiration throughout the years, for his artistic work and his involvement with OEOAS and in the education at the Conservatory of Naples.

We would like to extend our deepest gratitude to Music Norway, Fond for Utøvende Kunstnere (FFUK) and the Italian Cultural Institute in Hong Kong for funding the trips that allowed Totaleee to be officially born.

A token of appreciation also goes to NOTAM, Oslo, for having the trio as artists in residence, albeit for projects not directly related to improvisation and to l'Asilo in Naples for hosting our concerts, workshops, and activities from the beginning and for making it possible to develop a culture of improvised electroacoustic music in town.

Thanks also to Giuseppe Torre and the University of Limerick for inviting us to present our workshop for electroacoustic improvisation "on the prowl" and therefore helping us sharpen our teaching techniques.

Paolo Montella would like to thank Giuseppe Di Taranto for contributing, through his aesthetic and philosophical sensibility, to nourishing the speculative phase of his research on field recording.

Giuseppe Pisano would also like to thank Bálint Laczkó and Timo Hoogland for their help in programming his instrument.

Author contributions

These authors contributed equally: Giuseppe Pisano, Paolo Montella, and Andrea Laudante.

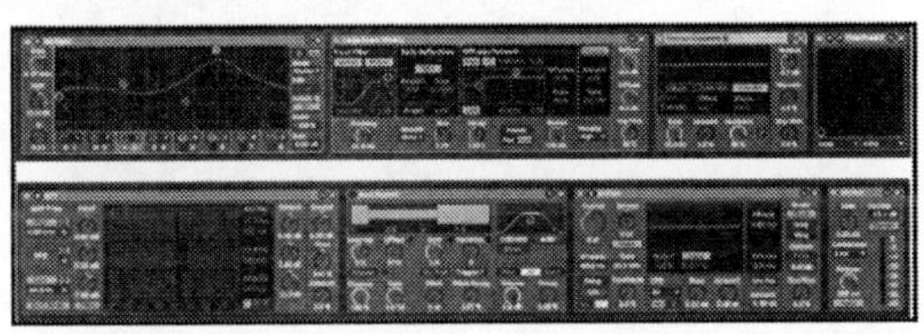

Figure 1. An example of a chain of processes on one of the channels dedicated to the feedback signal

Figure 2. The controller's faders act as a mixer, managing the volumes of individual channels, while the knobs

handle EQ/shifter/chorus, with multiple parameters assigned to each knob. The pads/keys are for synthesis and sound bank.

Figure 3. Reloop Ready is a DJ controller equipped with two jog wheels, boasting compactness and versatility. It's noteworthy for its inclusion of HD pitch faders and the capability for complete customization via SysEx.

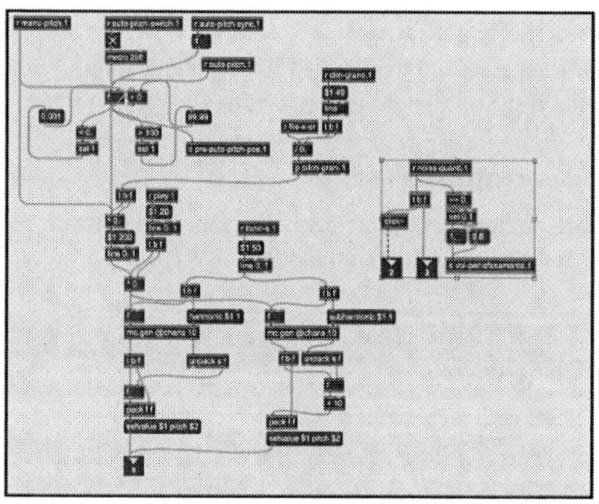

Figure 4. These two components of the patch enable control over both pitch and deviation from the playback period of the source clip.

Figure 5. Novation XL Control: having 8 columns with controls made it logical to organize the instrument as 8 modules with the faders as independent volume controls and the knobs as three macro controls for different signal processing operations.

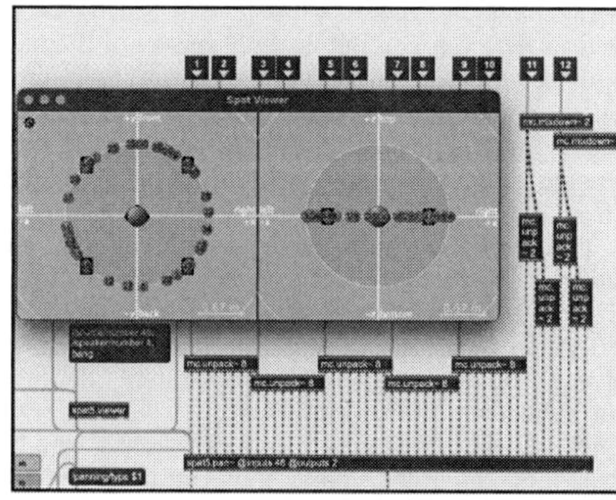

Figure 6. A snapshot of how the spatialization unit is organized, with the potential channels of each polybuffer used as a source in an immersive environment. Sources are distributed over a circle, in 2D and rendered on a stereo field, which can easily be adjusted to become any n-speaker setup.

8. REFERENCES

1. D. Bailey, *Improvisation: its nature and practice in music* Da Capo Press, 1992.
2. V. Mattioli, "Roma 60. Viaggio alle radici dell'underground italiano. Parte seconda", *Blow Up*, n. 188, January 2014, Tuttle Edizioni.
3. A. Cresti, *Solchi Sperimentali Italia. 50 anni di italiche musiche altre*. CRAC Edizioni, 2015.
4. A. Curran, "On spontaneous music." *Contemporary Music Review* 25.5-6. pp. 483-490, 2006.
5. F. Giomi, *Musica imprevedibile. Storia, metodi e training per l'improvvisazione collettiva*. Arcana, 2022.
6. T. Hodgkinson, "Siberian shamanism and improvised music." *Contemporary Music Review* 14.1-2. pp. 59-66, 1992
7. A. Di Scipio, "Sound is the interface: from interactive to ecosystemic signal processing." *Organised Sound* 8.3. pp. 269-277, 2003.
8. S. U Ba Khin, and S.N Goenka, *The clock of Vipassana has struck*, Vipassana Research Publications, 1999
9. T.K.V. Desikachar, *The heart of Yoga*, Inner Traditions Bear and Company, 1999
10. G. Di Taranto, and P. Montella, "Field recording come rappresentazione del mondo – Il processo artistico

nelle registrazioni sul campo", *d.a.t. [divulgazione audiotestuale]*, no. 12, pp. 45-65, 2023.

11.G. Di Taranto, and P. Montella, "Fonografia dell'intenzione. Strumenti analitici per un'arte del field recording", *d.a.t. [divulgazione audiotestuale]*, no. 13, pp. 53-74, 2023 .

12. Ibidem.

13.C. Roads, *The Computer Music Tutorial*, The MIT press, 1996.

14.B. Truax, "Discovering inner complexity: Time-shifting and transposition with a real-time granulation technique", *Computer Music Journal*, 18.2, pp. 38–48, 1998.

15.IRCAM, "Spat 5". Last access 22 February 2024, `https://forum.ircam.fr/topics/detail/45-Spat5/`

16. Totaleee live@ 20α - Hong Kong [set-2], `https://youtu.be/a1vtit6zrAo`

Integrating Higher Order Ambisonics and Cognitive Assemblages in Immersive Sound Composition

Paulo C. Chagas
University of California, Riverside
paulo.chagas@ucr.edu

Konstantin Fontaine
Audio Communication Group, TU Berlin
k.fontaine@tu-berlin.de

ABSTRACT

Immersive sound production has undergone a transformative shift with the introduction of Higher Order Ambisonics (HOA) and advancements in audiovisual practices. This paper explores the foundational principles of "Pune Metamorphosis", an immersive Ambisonics composition crafted in the electronic studio at Technische Universität Berlin (2022-23). The piece unveils a multilayered structure, utilizing original Ambisonics recordings transformed through granular sound synthesis. Our focus lies in non-conscious cognitive sound assemblages, exploring the intricate interplay between human and nonhuman cognizers. This narrative examines cognitive nuances, emphasizing technical agency, human interactions, and the transformative power within dynamic relationships. "Pune Metamorphosis" serves as a case study, showcasing the fusion of HOA and granular sound synthesis to illustrate the synergy between technological advancements and artistic creativity. Our discussion aims to deepen the understanding of how immersive audio composition might engage with and reflect upon cognitive assemblages, influencing the production and perception of sound in a three-dimensional auditory space.

1. INTRODUCTION

1.1 Space and Music: Relational Understanding

Music, sound, and space are deeply interconnected, influencing not only how we perceive sound but also how we experience the space around us. As Born [1] distinguishes, there are three broad ways of conceptualizing space in music, each offering a distinct approach to musical spatiality:

1. **Pitch Space Formalism**: A dominant formalist approach focuses on the internal operations of musical sound, often analyzed through visual and graphic representations in terms of pitch space. This perspective, prominent in score-based music, considers space as an abstract, intra-musical property.
2. **Spatialisation Practices**: Since the 1950s, spatialisation techniques have emerged, particularly in electronic and electroacoustic music. These practices utilize multichannel recording and loudspeaker projection to manipulate and project sound in physical and perceptual space, creating virtual spaces and dynamic sonic movements.
3. **Relational Understanding of Space**: This approach emphasizes the multiplicity of human experiences of music and sound in physical or virtual spaces, considering the social and temporal aspects of these experiences. It highlights the interplay of subjective and collective experiences, the influence of physical locations, and the dynamic evolution of sonic events over time.

In our exploration of *Pune Metamorphosis*, we draw upon this relational understanding to investigate the complex interactions between music, sound, and space, aiming to create immersive and multidimensional auditory experiences.

1.2 Ambisonics Sound Field Reproduction

Ambisonics depicts a sound scene codification format containing information about the directional properties of an acoustic field, namely the propagation of sound pressure and velocity within it. Due to the consideration of evenly distributed spatial segments, it allows representing a full-sphere sound field in a single capture or focal point, and consequently allows for methods to construct, manipulate and playback sound scenes in a flexible manner. The use of adequate microphone arrays furthermore enables the capture and reconstruction of intricate three-dimensional acoustic spaces, as it is the case throughout this work. Depending on the Ambisonics order N, these signal sets then comprise $(N+1)^2$ channels for periphonic systems, of which the first channel contains the omnidirectional sound pressure at the origin of the sound field, while the remaining channels provide directional information.

According to Barrett's insights into the compositional strategies of spatial sound in such formats, the phenomenological blur of a real and synthetic spatial image depicts a critical aspect in terms of artistic options. She thus emphasizes the manipulation of spatial attributes not solely to recreate real-world acoustics but to extend beyond them, allowing composers to experiment with the illusion of space, allusion, and the transformational qualities of sound within virtual environments. This capacity to sculpt immersive, dynamic soundscapes that engage the listener's perception of space and sound source origins significantly enriches compositional paradigms of artists working within the Ambisonics framework [2].

1.3 Spatial Granular Synthesis

In the realm of computer music, intersections of sound synthesis and spatialization have emerged as a key area for expanding the boundaries of sonic creativity in various ways [3–5]. Amongst it, the spatial implementation of granular synthesis depicts a powerful field of techniques for the creation of rich acoustical spaces. Granulation can hereby serve as a method for the diffusion of timbre in space [6], the emulation of aggregate swarm behaviors [7] or as a foundation for particle systems [8].

Due to the large number of resulting sonic objects, these synthesis methods have proven notably favourable for a subsequent spatial distribution, which requires advanced mapping strategies to maneuver their spatial trajectories in a coherent manner. Here the utilization of agent-based systems demonstrates a considered solution to apply complex group behaviours onto the sonic material by the means of few controllable parameters, since they offer a dynamic self-organization and allow for a simulation of various natural phenomena, which can adopt authentically vivid characteristics [9, 10].

Such approaches demonstrate the phenomenological potentials of constituting naturally sounding environments solely based on granulated materials. However, attempts to further enhance their naturalization and thus immersive effects, by correlating them with real, captured sound scenes within dynamic networks, remain relatively limited. Building upon automated models as of Xenakis [11] and Roads [12], Truax has early presented compositional potentials of real-time granulation by leveraging DSP capabilities with appropriate control variables. His proposed system thus exemplary enables manipulations of frequency, grain duration and spacing between grains, either individually or in a synchronized manner, with a fixed sound buffer or by the means of a memory delay line. His implementations within *Riverrun* (1986), showcase a dynamic system of steadily changing synthesis parameters, resulting in a constant state of flux, which he compares to dynamically balanced environmental sounds [13].

1.4 Cognitive Assemblages

In her exploration of cognitive assemblages, Hayles [14] examines the intricate relationships between human and nonhuman cognizers, emphasizing their influence in harnessing material forces. She defines cognitive assemblages as interactions that shape information flow within a system, involving choices and modifications that contribute to cognition.

Inspired by Latour [15], Hayles associates power with the effect produced by mediators, highlighting their role in transforming configurations into durable structures. This perspective aligns with her view of cognizers as transformative actors within technologically advanced societies.

Introducing Deleuze and Guattari's concept of *assemblage* [16], Hayles emphasizes its connotations of connection, transformation, and becoming. She prefers *assemblages* over *networks* for their dynamic, three-dimensional nature, facilitating rich interactions and mutability in cognitive systems.

Cognitive assemblages, viewed as arrangements of systems and actors, perform vital functions by adapting to new situations and evolving through experience. This perspective underscores their transformative nature, operating at various levels and mutating as conditions change.

Highlighting their impact, Hayles points to the Internet as an exemplar of a cognitive assemblage, showcasing its ability to adapt and evolve. These reflections invite reconsideration of cognition within dynamic, interconnected systems, shedding light on the transformative potential within cognitive assemblages.

2. PUNE METAMORPHOSIS: SONIC EXPLORATIONS AND COGNITIVE ASSEMBLAGES

The compositional concept of *Pune Metamorphosis* integrates Ambisonics audio recordings captured during the interdisciplinary research project *Sound Imaginations*, aligning them with Hayle's idea of cognitive assemblages. Initiated in 2016 and concluding in 2019, this project combined scholarship on sound studies with artistic research on immersive sound and audiovisual composition. The recordings spanned diverse locations, including São Paulo, California, Moscow, Mannheim, and Pune [17].

Guided by the concept of listening cultures [18], the project aimed to unravel the relationships between sound, image, space, and culture. The conceptual framework draws heavily from the philosophical insights of Jean-Luc Nancy [19]. Listening, as per Nancy, becomes an intervention in the acoustic environment, shaping our sense of self while preserving our connection to others.

The sonic present is a continuous flux of vibrations, and listening involves navigating an omnipresent network of feedback loops—what Nancy terms *re-soundings*. In a post-human society dominated by technical sounds and electronic interfaces, our sensory perceptions are increasingly influenced by cognitive assemblages, shaping the complex relationship between presence and absence.

Figure 1: Jean Miro (Barcelona 1893 – 1963 Palma de Mallorca) – "Métamorphose" 1936 (1933?), pencil and watercolor, collage.

The Ambisonic recordings made in Pune capture the rich soundscapes of this vibrant Indian metropolis, including urban environments, traffic noise, and the atmospheres of the Ramdara Shiva Temple and Bhuleshwar Shiva Temple. The recordings explore diverse listening approaches related to habits, devices, animals, architectures, and temporal structures, reflecting the local motion in individual and social listening contexts.

For the implementation of the project, an interdisciplinary research was conducted in the electronic studio of the Audio Communication Group at Technische Universität Berlin. This project aimed to explore non-conscious cognitive sound assemblages through spatial granular synthesis, drawing inspiration from surrealist practices like automatic writing and drawing. The exploration of a sound field reactive granulation alongside its clustered spatialization creates a complex ecology reminiscent of the vivid and familiar commotion within Pune's soundscape. By adopting a mindset similar to surrealist automatic practices, the goal was to relinquish conscious control over the creative process, allowing the unconscious mind to influence artistic output.

Joan Miró's artwork *Métamorphose* (Figure 1) adds another layer of inspiration to the Ambisonics composition. Miró's use of automatic drawing techniques, combining drawing, aquarelle, and collage, resonates with the project's intention to explore assemblages operating as automatic systems in granular sound synthesis.

This coherence of cultural, philosophical, and artistic influences within *Pune Metamorphosis* embodies a multifaceted sonic exploration, revealing not only the diverse sounds of Pune but also the intricate relationships between human and nonhuman cognizers in the creation of immersive audiovisual compositions.

3. COMPOSITION

3.1 Dual-Layer Framework

To achieve the intended complex interplay of auditory and cognitive events, *Pune Metamorphosis* is constituted as a dual-structured compositional process that converges the two sonic layers to form a cohesive unit. The foundational layer was constructed from 17 takes of the initial Ambisonics sound field recordings captured in Pune. Since the simple playback of this assemblage on a sufficient constellation of loudspeakers already provides an immersive experience, the concurrent rendering of its abstraction depicts a rich method to achieve the intended cognitive results, when the boundaries between the two layers are blurred by correlating them. To achieve this, the second layer was derived during a real-time processing of the primary Ambisonics soundscapes to nest sound synthesis methods into their playback by the means of a tailored granular synthesis, leveraging the SuperCollider audio programming environment.

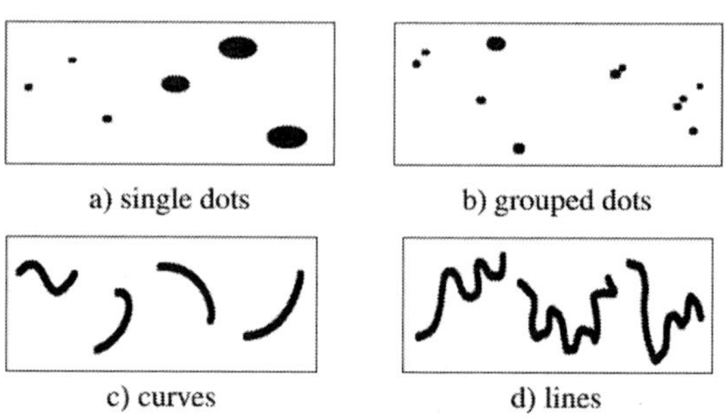

Figure 2: Types of individual elements

Having the above-mentioned characteristics of the Ambisonics signal constellation in mind, the granulation was implemented upon usage of a circular buffer that was fed with the omnidirectional channel of the Ambisonics signal, to maintain a strong cognitive interplay between granulation and decoded sound scene. The technical implementation within SuperCollider benefits from its flexible multichannel processing capabilities, which facilitate individualizing large numbers of grains. Within its environment, an empty audio buffer of arbitrary size is thus aligned with a Phasor signal that dynamically provides the writing position within this buffer. Routing the omnidirectional signal as source input to write onto this buffer provides the reusable signal structure for a subsequent granulation. Buffer length and read pointer delays then determine the degree of cognitive convergence, whereby a constrained latitude of the latter must be assured to avoid the granulation of discontinuous signals.

In consideration of the granular synthesis and its spatialization patterns, a variety of element types were defined, inspired by the analysis of Miró's painting *Métamorphose*. The elements were categorized into two distinct groups, namely single events and grouped swarms. In context of granulation, the latter was interpreted as several parallel streams of grains, whereas single grains represented single events. The behavioral patterns of the two groups were prior defined as partially presented in figure 2 and 3. Individual elements are thus represented by dots, grouped dots, simple curves, lines, or figures, whereas the constellation of swarms is conducted as swarms of dots, swarms of curves, swarms of lines or swarms of figures.

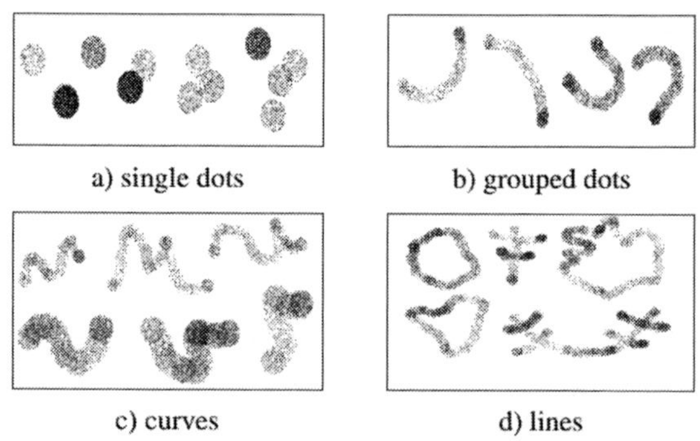

Figure 3: Types of swarms

3.2 Graphic Score Granulation and Spatialization

As presented in Truax, the processes of transformation involve careful, systematic modulation of granular synthesis parameters such as grain size, pitch, dynamics, and space, mirroring Miró's artistic vocabulary in an auditory form. A graphic score was notated for the production process, which is depicted in figure 4. It serves as a visual guide, illustrating the real-time transformations, mapping from visual to spatial sound.

To conduct such modulations within the programming environment an array-based approach was realized, as it provides flexibility in assigning deviating parameter values to granular synthesizers located in distinct array cells, resulting in grouped collections of grain streams. The above-described behavioral characteristics are the ones maneuvering the compositional guideline for synthesis and spatialization parameters, to align sonic and spatial motion. Throughout playback of the assembled soundscape, grain parameters are varied within determined ranges in accordance with the visual score, while the dynamically adapting circular buffer ensures further correlation.

The resulting array of grain streams is routed to a subsequently implemented array of the same size, hosting the Ambisonics encoders and thus forming a grouped collection of encoded sound objects in space. The assignment of swarming algorithms onto the positional data of the individual grain entities then allows an agent-based control of clustered grain swarms, opening out into an authentic motion of the aggregate swarm.

Aligning the grain modulations to spatial parameters then assures an additional close interconnection of musical and spatial events, whereby the swarm's point of orientation depicts a suitable parameter as well as arguments describing the relation and dynamics amongst individual sound objects.

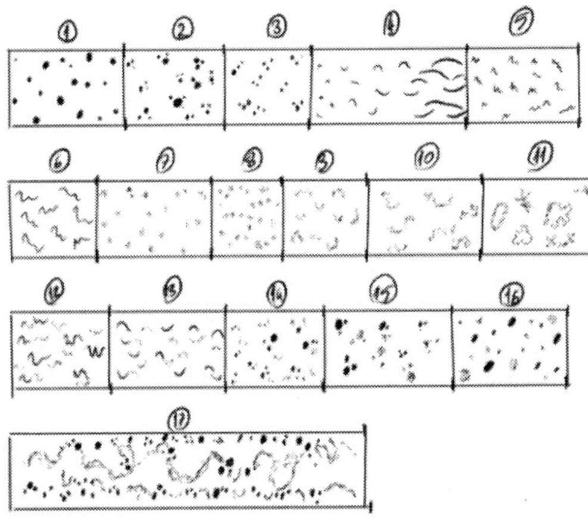

Figure 4: Graphic Score

4. CONCLUSIONS

This research systematically integrates Higher Order Ambisonics with Cognitive Assemblages and granular synthesis to create immersive sound compositions. By coupling the inherent characteristics of the Ambisonics format with dynamically adaptive processes within granular synthesis and aligning the spatial trajectories of a clustered swarm, the crafted soundscapes achieve significant depth and naturalization. This approach highlights nuanced sound spatialization and synthesis, underscoring the role of interdisciplinary collaboration and reflects Hayles' perspective on cognitive assemblages, while influencing both the creation and perception of soundscapes.

The concept of cognitive assemblages, in conjunction with the relational understanding of space, was applied to emphasize the multiplicity of human experiences and the interplay between human and machine experiences. The project's foundation in Pune, India's cultural tapestry, underscores the city's sonic heritage and its potential for inspiring innovative sound art. Pune's diverse soundscapes provide a canvas for exploring the interplay between technology and tradition, highlighting human interaction and cultural heritage.

In conclusion, *Pune Metamorphosis* showcases the technical capabilities of HOA, Cognitive Assemblages, and granular synthesis, while emphasizing interdisciplinary collaboration and cultural context in the evolution of sound art. Future development could involve applying artificial intelligence methods to enhance the complex interactions between humans and machines, expanding the realms of immersive and multidimensional auditory experiences.

Acknowledgments

The recordings of ambisonic sound in Pune, as part of the *Sound Imaginations* research project, were made possible by the support of the Center for Ideas and Society at the University of California, Riverside. The composition and production of *Pune Metamorphosis* received funding from the Fulbright Scholarship Program, was commissioned by the TU Studio, and garnered support from the Stiftung Humboldt Forum and the Staatliche Museen zu Berlin. Special thanks are extended to Henrik von Coler and Eren Utku for their invaluable contributions to the project.

5. REFERENCES

[1] G. Born, *Music, Sound and Space: Transformations of Public and Private Experience*. Cambridge University Press, 2013.

[2] N. Barrett, "Spatio-musical composition strategies," *Organised sound*, vol. 7, no. 3, pp. 313–323, 2002.

[3] D. Topper, M. Burtner, and S. Serafin, "Spatio-operational spectral (sos) synthesis," in *ICMC*, 2003.

[4] R. McGee, "Spatial modulation synthesis," in *ICMC*. Citeseer, 2015.

[5] S. James, "Spectromorphology and Spatiomorphology of Sound Shapes: audio-rate AEP and DBAP panning of spectra," 2015.

[6] D. Rossetti and J. Manzolli, "Creating Timbre in Space: Granular Synthesis and Am-bisonics Spatialization Study and Composition," 2019.

[7] S. Wilson, "Spatial swarm granulation," in *ICMC*, 2008.

[8] D. Kim-Boyle, "Spectral spatialization-an overview," in *ICMC*, 2008.

[9] J. C. Schacher, D. Bisig, and P. Kocher, "The map and the flock: Emergence in mapping with swarm algorithms," *Computer Music Journal*, vol. 38, no. 3, pp. 49–63, 2014.

[10] D. Kim-Boyle, "Spectral and granular spatialization with boids," in *ICMC*, 2008.

[11] I. Xenakis, "Formalized Music. Bloomington, Indi-ana," 1971.

[12] C. Roads, "Automated granular synthesis of sound," *Computer Music J.*, vol. 2, no. 2, pp. 61–62, 1978.

[13] B. Truax, "Real-time granular synthesis with a digital signal processor," *Computer Music Journal*, vol. 12, no. 2, pp. 14–26, 1988.

[14] K. Hayles, *Unthought: The Power of the Cognitive Nonconscious*. University of Chicago Press, 2017.

[15] B. Latour, *Reassembling the Social: An Introduction to Actor Network Theoryy*. Oxford University Press, 2007.

[16] G. Deleuze and F. Guattari., *A Thousand Plateaus: Capitalism and Schizophrenia*. Bloomsbury Publishing, 1988.

[17] P. C. Chagas, "Sound Imaginations: Listening Cultures and Audiovisual Immersion," *ARRAY2023 – Flux. Computer Music in the Anthropocene*, pp. 59–76, 2023.

[18] H. Schultze, "Hörkulturen der Gegenwart. Eine Anthropologie in acht Hörweisen," *Positionen*, vol. 105, pp. 15–18, 2015.

[19] J. L. Nancy, *À l'écoute*. Galilée, 2002.

"J.B. REMEMBERS J.B.": A SYSTEM FOR DYNAMIC IMPROVISATION ACCOMPANIMENT

Jeff Albert
Georgia Institute of Technology
jeff.albert@music.gatech.edu

ABSTRACT

This paper explores the intersection of technical mechanisms and artistic expression in interactive computer music, focusing on the creation of a piece/system that enables a dependable performance sensation for improvising musicians. The piece/system, "J.B. Remembers J.B.," dynamically generates accompaniment that reacts to the performer's improvisation while maintaining a consistent sonic aesthetic.

1. INTRODUCTION

"Does it still sound good if I do not know how it works?" This is a question I often ask myself when working on interactive computer music. It is too easy to succumb to the temptation to rely on the technical mechanism to be the interesting part while depriving the actual sounds of the attention they deserve. This piece started with an interesting technical idea that did not sound as good as I had hoped.

2. GOALS OF THE SYSTEM

Musical systems or settings are commonly developed with a particular sound or set of sounds in mind. A sonic aesthetic if you will. Many improvisers create music in a similar way, with a sonic aesthetic in mind, but another common goal of improvising musicians is the feeling one gets when playing the music. This could be called a performance sensation. How do I feel when I play this music? The system underlying the piece "J.B. Remembers J.B." aims to allow for a consistent performance sensation that includes the feeling of freely improvising while still creating a consistent sonic aesthetic. This is done by dynamically creating an accompaniment that listens to the improvisation and reacts to the performer, yet also creates unexpected musical events with which the improviser can interact. The goal is a feeling of free improvisation for the player with a dynamic accompaniment that nudges toward a consistent aesthetic experience that can be lacking in completely free improvisations.

3. THE RANDOMNESS PROBLEM

Improvisers like interaction, and unexpected or surprising interaction is highly valued. It can be tempting to equate unexpected with random, and it is easy to create seemingly random procedures with computers, so many computer based musical improvisation agents use some form of random or weighted random decision making. George Lewis's 2007 article includes the words "Intending Chance" in the title. [1] The problem is that randomness is only musically interesting some of the time, and the rest of the time it is less compelling.

3.1 Identifying Phrases

My previous work in interactive computer systems has focused on capturing and storing data on pitch and rhythm, then manipulating those data to create musical events in dialogic interaction with the human improviser. [2] That work suffered from "The Randomness Problem." One of the initial goals of this work was to be more aware of musical phrase structures as a mode of organization. While there is work on musical phrase segmentation [3] trying to apply these techniques in real-time can be a challenge.

3.2 Enter the first J.B.

In October of 2023, I heard John Bischoff give a presentation that included his explanation of his piece "Bitplicity." [4] In this piece he improvises phrases on his pulse wave oscillator instrument while marking each phrase beginning and end by pressing a key on a MIDI controller. The computer program then resynthesizes these phrases and he plays in duo with these resynthesized phrases. This concept sparked the idea that would develop into this piece.

4. J.B. REMEMBERS J.B.

Technologically this piece is programmed in Max for Live and hosted in Ableton Live. There are multiple "phrase memory" modules, each having slight variations from the others. Each of these modules keeps track of the pitches played by the performer and the elapsed time between events (or notes). The original module required the performer to use a MIDI foot-controller to mark the start and end of each phrase. This idea was taken directly from Bischoff, although technically implemented in a different way. After some initial play testing, I realized that the requirement to physically mark the phrase ends by tapping a controller could significantly interrupt the musical flow of the improvisation; it required the performer's focus to be in two places. In response to this, I developed other phrase modules that can operate independently of controller input from the performer. Each of the phrase modules extract pitch and duration information from the real time audio input from the improviser, and outputs monophonic MIDI note data that can be routed to any softsynth sound in Ableton Live. These modules have somewhat arbitrary phrase lengths which differ on each module, and the data is manipulated in differing ways with regards to order and direction of reading of the pitch and rhythm data.

One module plays back notes in order from a collection that is 20 notes long. The other module records a 15 note long collection and plays back from it in a palindromic order. The improviser has foot pedal controls that can separately control when each module is playing as well as when each module is listening. This allows the computer to play from a continuously updating pool of notes, recording the performer's note information in real time, or for the performer to "freeze" the set of notes in the pool at any given point. This also allows the performer to let a module continue listening and gathering data, but not playback.

While I initially thought that the way the pitch data were manipulated would be the factor that would determine musical success, in my early prototypes I quickly realized that choices of software instrument sounds and rhythmic placement were more important. The sound world became more important than the specific order of pitches. The sets of pitches used matter greatly but the sounds used to play them are equally as important. It also soon became apparent that where the notes started within the grid of the rhythmic accompaniment was vital to the overall effect. The durations of the notes in the pitched aspects of the dynamic accompaniment are taken from what the system hears from the improviser, but the starting times in relation to the groove grid have been quantized to align with the drum groove parts.

4.1 J.B. No. 2, but Soul Brother Number 1

An important aspect of the consistent sonic aesthetic that I wished to create in this piece is rhythm. Groove based music has played an important role in my musical life and informed my creative activity in defining ways, so I wanted groove to be present in this piece. As I riffed on title ideas and thought about how I wanted to incorporate musical groove, I thought of James Brown. [1] His initials fit perfectly with the title idea of "J.B. Remembers" which referred to John Bischoff and the musical process of remembering phrases, and his music provided perfect inspiration for the rhythmic aspects of this piece, which use some of the features in Ableton Live to lend a certain lifelike unpredictability to the dynamic accompaniment.

This unpredictability comes from the chance operations in Ableton Live, which allows for each note in a drum pattern to have a particular chance of occurrence. At 85% the pattern sounds complete, but the individual notes vary. At 15% the notes are all in time, but the pattern is not obvious. The piece uses four different clips of the drum pattern with chances of occurrence of 13, 25, 50, and 85 percent. The Follow Action feature is weighted to cause the clips to generally move from sparse towards dense over the course of the piece, with the possibility (probability) of some slippage from dense back to toward sparse at times. An Ableton groove setting is applied to additionally vary the dynamic and time placement of the drum parts.

4.2 How it Started, How It's Going

Very few creative projects have a finished form that perfectly aligns with their initial intentions, and this piece is no exception. What started as an exploration of techniques to manually mark phrase lengths in an improvised piece with computer quickly became an exploration of the systematic aesthetic choices that made improvising within the system (and hearing the resulting music) enjoyable. The next steps in this research will involve trying to automate phrase detection in real time in a way that can be aesthetically successful, technically feasible, and not distracting to the performer.

5. CONCLUSIONS

Technologically mediated creativity is always a back-and-forth between technological considerations and aesthetic concerns. An advance in tools and techniques gives new artistic ideas which make us imagine new tools, which then give new creative ideas, in a never-ending techno-creative feedback loop. I originally though this piece was about developing a new technical tool to mark musical phrases while improvising, but it ended up being more of an aesthetic exploration. An exploration that has better prepared me for my next technical experiments.

Acknowledgments

I would like to thank John Bischoff for the idea, James Brown for the music, Katie Young for inviting me to play on that concert, and Alexandria Smith.

6. REFERENCES

[1] G. Lewis, "Mobilitas Animi: Improvising Technologies, Intending Chance," *Parallax*, vol. 13, pp. 108–122, 2007, 4.

[2] J. V. Albert, "Interactive Musical Partner: A System for Human/Computer Duo Improvisations," Dissertation, Louisiana State University, Baton Rouge, LA, 2013.

[3] O. L. Martín Hartmann and P. Toiviainen, "Interaction features for prediction of perceptual segmentation: Effects of musicianship and experimental task," *Journal of New Music Research*, vol. 46, no. 2, pp. 156–174, 2017. [Online]. Available: https://doi.org/10.1080/09298215.2016.1230137

[4] J. Bischoff, "Bitplicity," 2021. [Online]. Available: https://artifactrecordings.bandcamp.com/album/bitplicity-art-3012-2021

[1] "Soul Brother Number 1" is the name of a 1988 James Brown compilation album, and one of his many nicknames, which also included "The Godfather of Soul," and "The Hardest Working Man in Show Business."

Was It Really Just the Dress? Change in Sound through Motion: a Comparison of Subjective Auditory Perception and Measurable Acoustic Phenomena in Swinging Loudspeakers and Moving Body

Peter Faerber
ZHdK/ICST
peter.faerber@zhdk.ch

Annkathrin Poepel
ZHdK/ICST
annkathrin.poepel@zhdk.ch

Angela Stoecklin
the fusion projects
an.stoecklin@bluewin.ch

ABSTRACT

This research investigates the impact of the movement and stillness of a dancer and loudspeakers on pendulums within a sound field. The pendulums with loudspeakers on their lower end are integral components of the kinetic sound sculpture Sounding Influencer. Two pendulums are being used, emitting sine tones with varying pitches. A dancer manually sets the pendulums in motion. Changes in amplitude become noticeable when the pendulum is still and the dancer is moving. When the pendulum is set in motion and the dancer remains still, both amplitude and frequency shifts become evident. When both are in motion, the acoustic effects produced by the pendulum tend to mask those evoked by the dancer's movements. The auditory changes are particularly noticeable when the sound field comprises one or two standing waves.

1. INTRODUCTION

With the introduction of the possibility of sound recording in 1876 by Thomas A. Edison, the reproduction of sound became detached from the sound source [1]. In acousmatics, we perceive sound without seeing what caused it, complicating the reception of music. In Musique concrète, Pierre Schaeffer created *objets sonores*, sounds where the attack is cut off, a crucial element in determining the origin of a sound [2]. In electronic music, sounds are generated without an acoustic-instrumental origin and can only be reproduced through speakers. To enhance the audibility of musical structures over time, these sounds are spatially separated: either through speakers distributed in the space, representing individual sound sources, or through an array of speakers enabling virtual positioning and movement using psychoacoustic effects (stereophony). Stockhausen introduced the fifth parameter, sound place (topik), for this purpose in serial music [3].

Arrays with a certain even number of locally fixed loudspeakers have become the standard in sound engineering. They facilitate immersion in an immersive sound world through techniques like quadraphony [4], holophony, or wave field synthesis. Unlike traditional sound reproduction, speakers don't have to remain in a fixed position but can be set in motion. The movement of speakers not only creates sound movements in space but also induces acoustic effects associated with the motion of a sound source. The Doppler effect (frequency shift) is the most well-known effect [5], accompanied by changes in amplitude, alterations in the sound spectrum, and shifts in sound emission direction [6].

The use of moving speakers began in the mid-20th century to create the Doppler effect and fluid sound movements. Examples include the rotation table used in the realization of *Kontakte* (1959) by Karlheinz Stockhausen [7] or Hermann Scherchen's *Rotierender Nullstrahler* (rotating speaker sphere) (1959) [8]. Since devices became available to simulate these effects, speakers are moved not only for simulation but because the work wouldn't be possible without the speaker's movement, integral to the piece and irreplaceable by simulation. A remarkable example is Gordon Monahan's *Speakers Swinging* (1982) [9]. Speakers are rolled, thrown, made to swim or fly. The pendulum motion of a speaker was first used in the realization of *Poème électronique* (1957) by Edgard Varèse for the 1958 World Expo in Brussels to create acoustic motion effects [10]. Peter Bosch and Simone Simons developed the kinetic sound installation *Electric Swaying Orchestra* (2011) with six swinging speakers for indoor use [11]. Ray Lee designed the massive sound installation *Ring Out* (2017) with eight pendulums for outdoor performances [12]. In contrast to Bosch and Simons' kinetic sound installation, the pendulums are being moved manually. In the participatory sound art installation *Four Swinging Speakers* (2020) by Jesse Austin-Stewart, it is the audience who repeatedly sets the four speakers in motion [13].

Since 2020 we have been working with swinging speakers in various formats, including sound installations and performances. In 2021 a dancer joined the research. From 2022 on our research question has been: What is the influence of motion on sound? Since then, we systematically examine the mutual influence/interaction of sound, motion, body, and space, both quantitatively through analyses of video and audio recordings and qualitatively through subjective auditory impressions and overall perception during the live experience.

2. RESEARCH OVERVIEW

The setup is a frame with two pendulums hanging in it, each two meters in length, with a speaker attached at each end. The frame's height is constructed to position the speakers at the dancer's hip level (see Figure 1). Sinusoidal tones are being used as sound material. This simple waveform enables the detection of minute changes in frequency, amplitude, and spatial propagation.

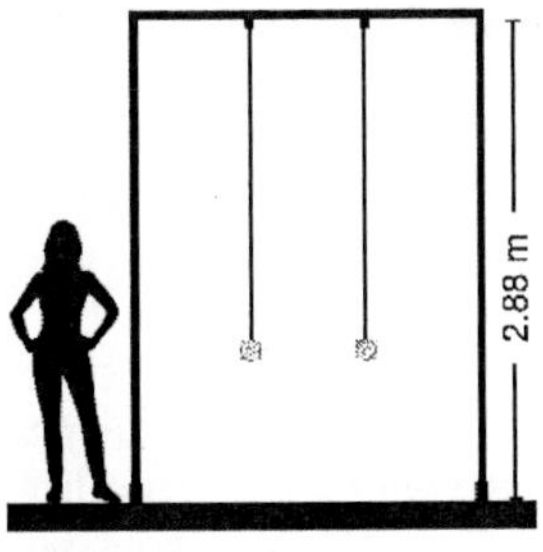

Figure 1. Frame with 2 pendulums with loudspeakers.

2.1 Acoustic effect with swinging speaker

2.1.1 Recording setup for analysis

The recording was made at our Laboratory with a Neumann KM184 microphone. The Laboratory measures 7.58 m x 7.59 m x 5.77 m (width x length x height).

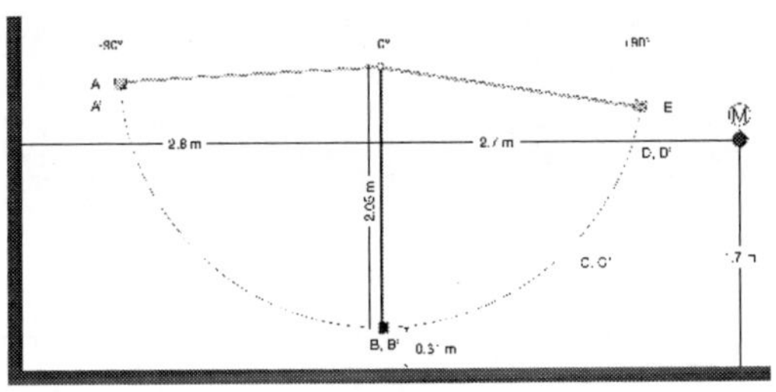

Figure 2. Recording set up. Microphone (M) at audience position. Release position at -90° degrees (A), Point of return (E).

2.1.2 Doppler effect

The pendulum is horizontal at position (A, see Figure 2) at -90°. It is released, falls freely and swings to the reversal point (E) and back again. It accelerates to the maximum speed of 6.2 m/s, which it reaches at 0° (B) and slows down to point (E) at -90°.

In Figure 3, alongside the amplitude, a sonogram of the first period (A-E-A') is depicted. One oscillation period takes about 2.9 seconds. The basic frequency is 370.0 Hz, with a frequency shift of +/- 6.7 Hz.

As the speaker attached to the pendulum approaches and moves away from the microphone, the frequency changes according to the Doppler effect law. During the recording, not only one frequency change occurs, as expected, but also a second shift in the opposite direction (lower trajectory). These are early reflections from the back wall, nearly as strong as the direct sound.

2.1.3 Amplitude modulation

The amplitude depends on the distance between the speaker and the microphone. The volume curve is superimposed with smaller and larger amplitude fluctuations. These arise from the overlay of the direct sound with the early reflections. They constantly change as the speaker's emission position in relation to the floor and walls changes permanently due to the pendulum's movement. The fluctuations are particularly strong when the pendulum swings around its resting point (B and B' accordingly) because the distance to the floor changes rapidly there.

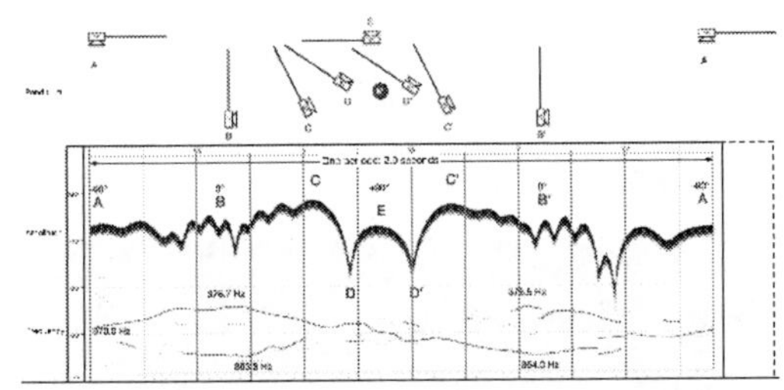

Figure 3. Amplitude and sonogram (1st period). Above: Position of the pendulum, (M): Microphone.
Below: upper part: Amplitude. Lower part: Frequency. X-axis: Time, Y-axis: Amplitude (dB) and frequency (350 – 390 Hz).

2.2 Specifying frequencies

We carried out a room acoustic measurement for the space, where the experiments took place and detected the frequencies resonating the most in there. We only investigated frequencies in the range between 200 and 700 Hz. The most prominent frequency was 383 Hz.

2.3 Movement and stillness

Throughout the research process, various options are systematically being explored.

a. Static sound source (pendulum at rest), static body (dancer still).

b. Static sound source (pendulum at rest), moving body (dancer in motion).

c. Moving sound source (swinging pendulum), static body (dancer still).

d. Moving sound source (swinging pendulum), moving body (dancer in motion).

Each combination is repeated several times for comparison reasons and perceived by three individuals (dancer, composer, and technician) who describe their subjective auditory impressions. Additionally, audio and video recordings of all combinations are being made and further quantitatively analyzed. Sonograms are generated to delve into the acoustic characteristics.

3. RESULTS

3.1 Movement and stillness

a. Static sound source (pendulum at rest), static body (dancer still):

A static sound source and a still body do not result in a change in sound.

b. Static sound source (pendulum at rest), moving body (dancer in motion):

Changes induced by the dancer's movements are subtle but clearly audible (see Figure 4). The dancer's movements around still pendulums lead to significant amplitude changes. Observers experience sound alterations due to the dancer's movements. Frequency shifts caused by the Doppler effect from the moving body are visible in the sonogram but are below the threshold of perception. The fluctuation in amplitude is clearly audible (see Figure 4). Subjective perception varies depending on the listening position in the space, for example, in a position within the direct or diffuse sound field.

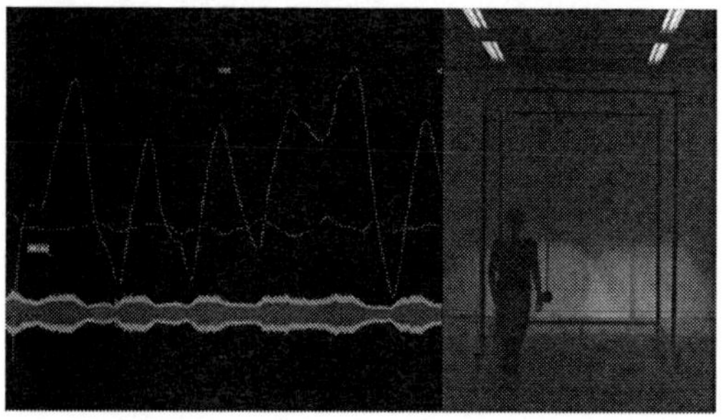

Figure 4. Dancer moves in front of the pendulum.

The intermittent blocking of the speaker is well evident in the amplitude profile. This effect is pronounced, as the direct sound does not reach the listener during the blocking of the speaker.

c. Moving sound source (swinging pendulum), static body (dancer still):

The acoustic changes induced by the swinging of the speaker are notably pronounced (see Figure 5).
Left of the centerline: Manual displacement of the pendulum causes a minimal frequency shift, imperceptible to the listener. The amplitude change is more substantial and distinctly audible, stemming from sound reflections that cause cancellations and elevations.
Right of the centerline: Strong amplitude variations caused by the freely swinging pendulum are evident here. In the frequency profile, the Doppler effect induces a strong pitch shift.

d. Moving sound source (swinging pendulum), moving body (dancer in motion):

As the speakers oscillate back and forth, the subtle changes in sound caused by the dancer's body movements are masked by the Doppler effect of the oscillating speaker.

3.2 Body surface

The dancer wears different clothing during the research, long pants in one session and a knee-length skirt in an other. There is a difference in the impact on the sound field

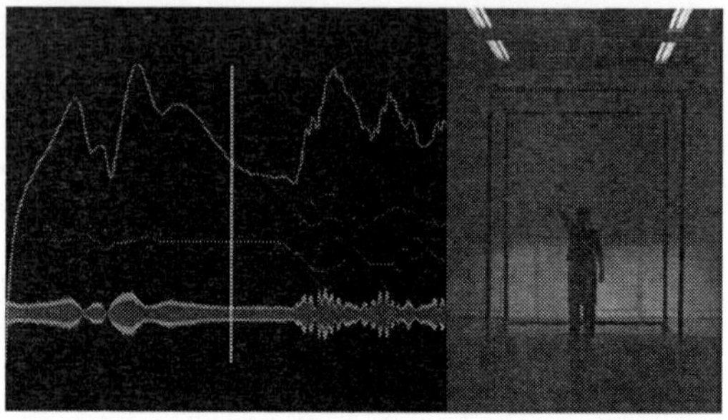

Figure 5. Acoustic effects of pendulum movement Top Line: Amplitude profile (averaged over one second). Middle Lines: Frequency profile. Bottom: Waveform representation. Fundamental pitch: 383 Hz. Deviations ± 4.8 Hz.

when the dancer wears pants or a skirt. The skirt provides a slightly larger and more closed reflective surface, resulting in stronger sound reflection, noticeable in a minimal higher amplitude deviation. This difference can be heard in option b, assuming a listening position in the room where the acoustic effects of the movement are generally well audible (see Figure 6). Reflections and phase changes during the dancer's movements influence the auditory process.

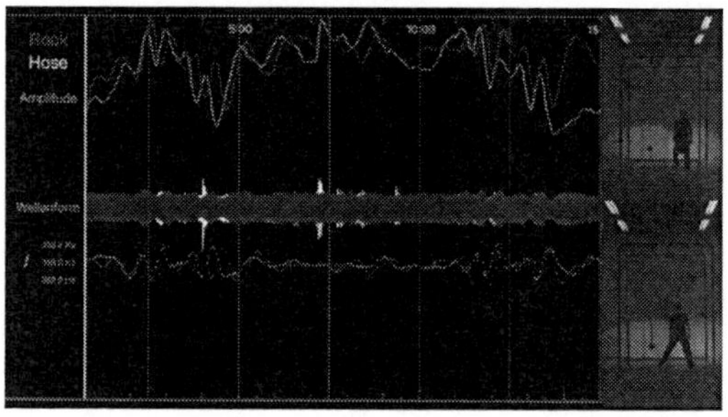

Figure 6. Difference between skirt and pants Top: Amplitude profile (averaged over 1 second). Middle: Waveform representations. Bottom: Frequency profile. Red: Analysis with skirt, White: Analysis with pants. The fundamental pitch is 383 Hz. Deviations are ± 0.2 Hz.

The dancer acts as an instrumental player of the pendulums. Her movements influence the sound, while the sonic alterations influence her movement decisions. In the dancer's subjective experience, the body becomes attuned to the subtle changes in the sine tones.

4. CONCLUSIONS

It has been demonstrated that a moving body, alongside a still sound source, induces changes in both amplitude and frequency response, acting as an acoustic reflector. The size of the body's surface determines its reflective behavior, meaning that the sort of clothing has an impact on this behavior. This change was subjectively perceptible and could also represented graphically through audio analysis. The systematic investigation allows for a deeper understanding of the complex interactions between motion, room acoustics, and perceived sound alterations.

From the dancer's perspective, the relevant initial question was in regards to the impact of the pendulum installation and the emitted sounds on the body, movement, and movement quality. In the first experiments it became evident that the body resonates with the pulse of the pendulums. In guiding the movement to hold, lead, release, and catch the pendulums, the body becomes like a part of the mechanism, without being mechanical.

The guiding of the arms functions in line with the pendulum, and the steps tune into the pulse of the swinging. Alongside this pulse, the dancer applies pauses, oscillations in the same direction or in opposite directions in relation to the pendulums and at times adapts to the oscillation durations of the pendulums. This understanding extends both rhythmically and spatially, approaching a synesthesia of space and time. The sinusoidal tone played through the speakers not only changes due to the pendulum movement but additionally through the body's movement. The body acts as a sound reflector, turning the mover into a collaborator or antagonist of the pendulums, simultaneously playing with the sounds and their transformation. Movement decisions are made based on rhythmic, spatial, and sonic components, creating an interaction between body movement, pendulum movement, and sound.

5. OUTLOOK

Building upon the findings outlined in this paper, we have developed a performance which took place in a different space than the initial investigations. We observed that the auditory experiences vary depending on the recipient's position and the spatial conditions, although this aspect was not systematically examined up to now. However it will be investigated in a subsequent research phase. Therefore we aim to incorporate room acoustics into our explorations and conduct investigations in various locations. This will provide a more comprehensive understanding of how spatial factors impact the interplay between movement, sound, and perception.

6. REFERENCES

[1] T. A. Edison, "The Perfected Phonograph," *The North American Review*, vol. 146, no. 379, pp. 641–650, 1888.

[2] P. Schaeffer, *Traité des objets musicaux. Essai interdisciplines*. Paris: Editions Du Seuil, 1966.

[3] K. Stockhausen, "Musik im Raum (1958)," in *Texte zur elektronischen und instrumentalen Musik. Aufsätze 1952-1962 zur Theorie des Komponierens*, D. Schnebel and K. Stockhausen, Eds. DuMond, 1963, vol. 5, pp. 152–175.

[4] M. A. Gerzon and P. Fellgett, "from quadro to surround sound," *elektor*, vol. 5, no. may, pp. 19–25, May 1977.

[5] C. Doppler, *Über das farbige Licht der Dopplersterne und einiger anderer Gestirne des Himmels*. Prag: Borrosch & André, 1842.

[6] M. Oechslin, M. Neukom, and G. Bennett, "The Doppler effect - an evolutionary critical cue for the perception of the direction of moving sound sources," in *2008 International Conference on Audio, Language and Image Processing*. Shanghai, China: IEEE, Jul. 2008, pp. 676–679. [Online]. Available: http://ieeexplore.ieee.org/document/4590253/

[7] P. Färber, "Der rotierende Lautsprecher - Effektgerät und Klangobjekt," Masterarbeit, Musikwissenschaftliches Institut der Universität Bern, Bern, 2015.

[8] ——, "Scherchens rotierende Nullstrahler (1959): »Idealer« Lautsprecher oder nur Effektgerät?" in *Studies in the Arts - Neue Perspektiven auf Forschung über, in und durch Kunst und Design*, T. Gartmann and M. Schäuble, Eds. Bielefeld: transcript Verlag, 2021, pp. 113–136.

[9] G. Monahan, "Speaker Swinging. An Interview by Robert Johnson, August 7, 1987," in *Sound by Artists*, D. Lander and M. Lexier, Eds. Toronto, Banff: Art Metropol and Walter Philips Gallery, 1990, pp. 141–145.

[10] K. Tazelaar, *On the threshold of beauty. Philips and the origins of electronic music in the Netherlands, 1925-1965*. Rotterdam: V2_Publishing, 2020.

[11] P. Bosch and S. Simons, "our music machines," *Organised Sound*, vol. 10, no. 2, pp. 103–110, Aug. 2005. [Online]. Available: https://www.cambridge.org/core/product/identifier/S1355771805000749/type/journal_article

[12] R. Lee, "Ring Out," 2017. [Online]. Available: https://www.invisible-forces.com

[13] Austin-Stewart, "Four Swinging Speakers (2020)," 2020. [Online]. Available: https://www.jesseaustinstewart.com/four-swinging-speakers

MIDI.CITI: Designing an Experience-oriented Musical Cityscape

Kunwoo Kim
CCRMA, Stanford University
kunwoo@ccrma.stanford.edu

Ge Wang
CCRMA, Stanford University
ge@ccrma.stanford.edu

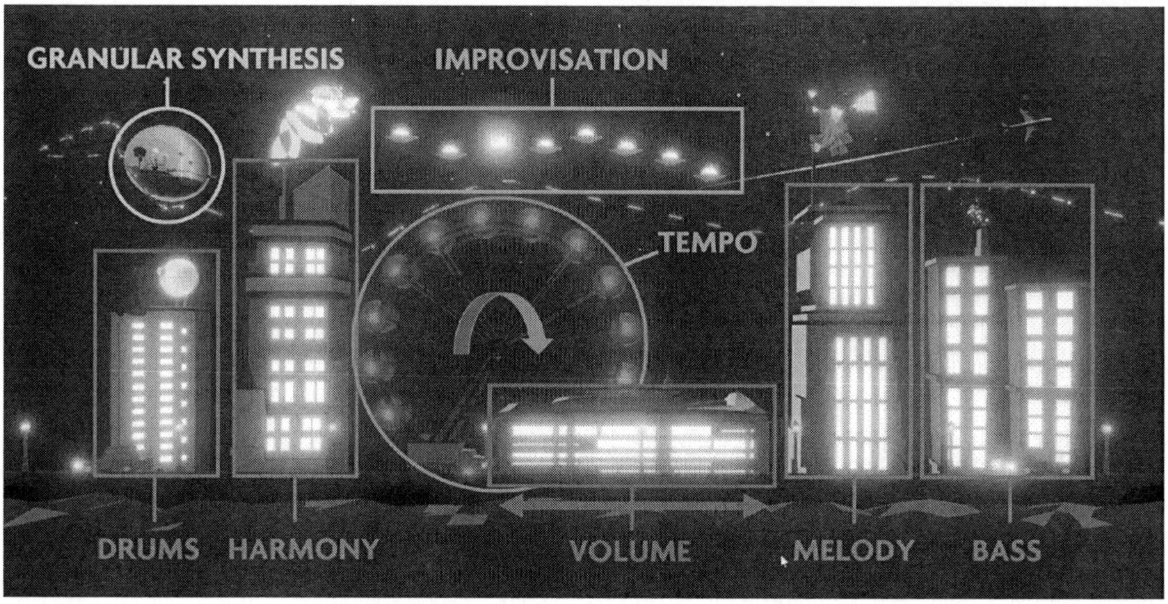

Figure 1: Audiovisual mapping of MIDI.CITI.

ABSTRACT

MIDI.CITI is an interactive audiovisual musical sandbox that offers room for playfulness, expression, and experiential narrative. It contains a real-time algorithmically generated drum machine mapped onto a metaphorical cityscape environment. This paper unpacks the design of MIDI.CITI through the lenses of interaction, play, and designing tools "inside-out", i.e., designing outward from an intended aesthetic experience. We describe its design process as well as its interactions and audio algorithms. Lastly, we put forth a few underlying design principles, including prioritizing the experience, adopting an audio-first approach for tightly-coupled audiovisual correspondence, taking advantage of real-time generative audio, and finding a balance between high-level and direct control. Through these discussions, we aim to provide "things to think with" for creating experience-oriented interactive audiovisual software.

1. INTRODUCTION

MIDI.CITI is an interactive musical sandbox, designed for users to have a playful and expressive experience as they experiment with musical ideas and visual metaphors embedded within a cityscape interface. Despite its name, the software does not use MIDI; it was chosen simply because it rhymes with "city". Instead, MIDI.CITI uses ChucK [1] for generative audio, and is interconnected with graphical and interactive elements using Chunity [2].

Algorithmic processes in MIDI.CITI produce semi-automated musical events that are tightly coupled with the visuals. Chunity's strongly-timed mechanisms allow real-time audio synthesis in tandem with graphics, while precisely governing the audiovisual timing between the two. The synergy of the generative audio, precisely coupled graphics, and interactive elements curates a unique combined experience. MIDI.CITI represents an adaptable design paradigm that can be used for other desktop or VR environments [3].

MIDI.CITI adopts the lenses and design principles of Artful Design [4], aiming to build tools that attend to aesthetic considerations. This translates to critical questions in the design of MIDI.CITI: how might we effectively connect sound, visuals, and interactions to create an expressive audiovisual experience? How can we make use of these underlying mechanics and dynamics to foster playfulness?

In this paper, we unpack the design of MIDI.CITI and its constituent components and a few relevant principles for designing experience-oriented audiovisual tools.

Demo video: https://kunwookim.com/midi.citi

2. MIDI.CITI

The urban elements of MIDI.CITI represent instruments and audio parameters such as tempo and volume. The overall music unfolds as a set of algorithmically-generated audio sequences, programmed in ChucK. The algorithm introduces pseudo-randomization of rhythms and pitches, ensuring sustained engagement across iterations. In tandem with the development of musical layers, the city becomes more visually vibrant, with the addition of lights, cars, planes, trains, and even rabbits on the Moon and UFOs. The rhythm, harmony, and meter are readily modifiable in the ChucK script, facilitating further customization and experimentation.

2.1 The Four high-rise buildings

Users can control the rhythmic complexity of the four different instruments—drums, harmony, melody, and bass—by raising or lowering the amount of window lights in corresponding high-rise buildings (orange in Figure 1). For instance, to intensify drum beats while minimizing melody lines, users can increase the window lights on the drum building, while decreasing lights on the melody building. Moreover, the overall musical sum of the generated loops (e.g., 8 measures, each comprising 12 subdivided beats) maintains uniqueness across iterations through a pseudo-randomized algorithm.

The adjustment of rhythmic complexity is facilitated by the density parameter. First, each instrument is assigned a "trigger array," where each element denotes one of three states: 0 ("do not play"), 1 ("maybe play"), and 2 ("always play"), corresponding to the beat subdivision. Second, the density parameter ranges from 0.0 to 1.0, with unlit windows representing 0.0 and all lit windows indicating 1.0. When the trigger array element is set to 1 ("maybe play"), the density parameter effectively serves as the probability of note generation. Thus, while 0s and 2s establish a fundamental rhythmic structure for an instrument, 1s introduce interesting rhythmic nuances to the sequence.

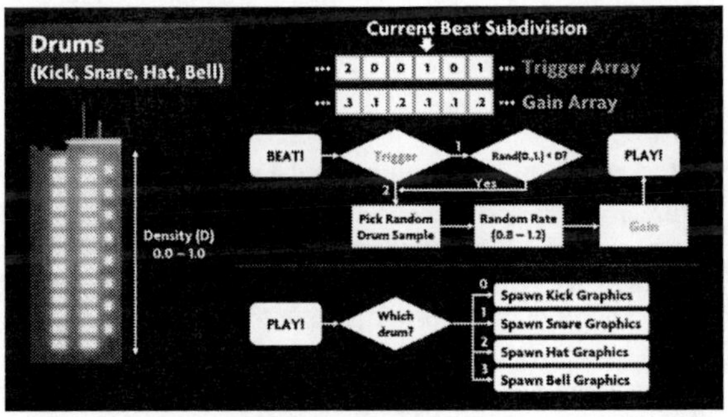

Figure 2. The algorithmic flow of note generation for drums.

The drums consist of kick, snare, hat, and bell, each with a preassigned trigger array (Figure 2). Gain arrays dictate the respective playback volume for each beat subdivision, differentiating between strong and weak beats. Upon receiving a playback signal, the algorithm initiates additional randomization procedures such as randomized sample and playback rate (0.8 to 1.2).

The harmony consists of four `Rhodey` unit generators from ChucK, which establish a four-part chord structure. At the beginning of each measure, it selects one of three trigger array patterns for the measure to maintain rhythmic diversity. With each playback, it generates a chord in either open or closed position, further introducing variability in the accompaniment.

The melody is synthesized using the `ModalBar` unit generator. At the start of each measure, it selects one of five trigger array patterns. Unlike other instruments, the melody exhibits more random rhythmic patterns as its trigger array elements only consist of 0s ("do not play") and 1s ("maybe play"), with no 2s ("always play"). During each playback, the algorithm selects a pitch from a pentatonic scale spanning across three octaves, adapting to the current harmonic context.

The bass is produced using the `Rhodey` unit generator, employing three different trigger array patterns per measure. Unlike the melody, the bass introduces the least amount of randomness in order to uphold the basic structure of the music. Specifically, the first beat of each measure is always played, while its pitch is always the root of the current harmonic context. For subsequent subdivided beats, the pitch is chosen from scale degrees of 1, 3, or 5.

2.2 The Ferris wheel and the low-rise building

Users can rotate the Ferris wheel using their mouse: clockwise to make it go faster and counter-clockwise to make it go slower. This speed of rotation corresponds to the tempo of the whole musical system by changing the beats per minute (bpm) parameter within the main ChucK script that sends global events to each generative instrument process. The tempo can be subtly influenced by rotating the mouse cursor to reinforce or dampen the rotation of the Ferris wheel. In addition, the users can adjust the amount of window lights of the low-rise building, thereby adjusting the overall volume of the music.

2.3 The Moon

Upon flying to the Moon, it is revealed that two rabbits occupy the Moon's dark side, inspired by the East Asian folklore of Moon rabbits. As they pound their mortars and pestles to the underlying rhythm, a granular synthesis train (i.e. grain tram or "tram-ular" synthesis) departs from the Moon back to the city, a musical and symbolic link between the fantastical and the mundane ebb and flow of urban life. The two air balloons on the Moon each control granular synthesis position and volume of the atmospheric soundscape, consisting of four voices of different pitches (Figure 3). The sample used for granular synthesis is a cross-faded interpolation between orchestral and choral sounds, offering a continuous timbre spectrum.

2.4 The UFOs

Lastly, UFOs can be called to appear over the skyline—not to harm anyone, but to play music together! They are the only non-algorithmic, directly playable instruments in MIDI.CITI. Using a computer keyboard, the user can directly improvise different melodies over the algorithmically generated musicscape.

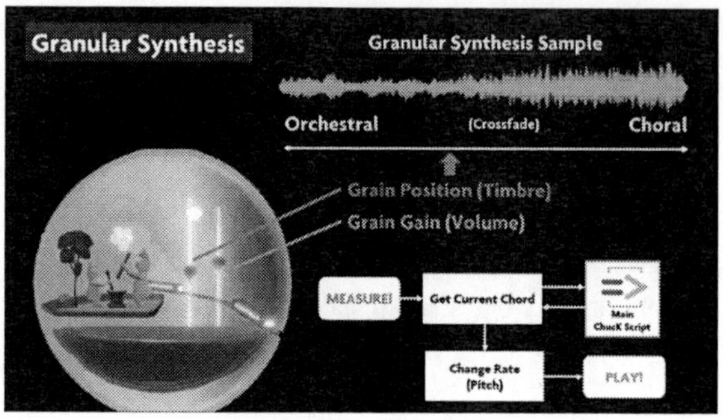

Figure 3. The algorithmic flow of the Moon.

3. DESIGN LENSES

3.1 Interaction

MIDI.CITI's interaction design seeks a balance between automatic generation and direct human control. Principle 5.5 from artful design states, "Have your machine learning—and the human in the loop" [4]. MIDI.CITI uses algorithmically generative audio for its beats, chords, and melodies, but offers a number of simple, yet expressive, metaphorical "knobs" to the user. For example, increasing the density parameter of the building associated with melody introduces additional variations in pitch, rhythm, and dynamics. Similarly, rotating the Ferris Wheel accelerates its rotation speed in tandem with the musical tempo. Together, these simple interactions present many possible recombinations, where the user can create a narrative using the resulting sonic textures. MIDI.CITI adheres to Cook's principle of "instant music, subtlety later" [5], where each interactive urban element allows for instant change in one musical parameter, yet combinations of elements allow for subtle control over the holistic musical outcome.

3.2 Play

Callois states that play is a free, voluntary, uncertain, and unproductive activity, a source of joy and amusement [6]. MIDI.CITI embodies the *paidia* aspect of play, described as "more free-form, expressive, improvisational, recombination of behaviors and meanings" [4]. MIDI.CITI offers iterations of different narratives based on user choice. For example, the densities of different instruments can be maxed out with a fast tempo to achieve exuberance or they can be minimized with a slower tempo to create space for serenity. The users of MIDI.CITI experience open-form aesthetics built on the dynamics of interaction and underlying mechanics of audio algorithms that drive the corresponding graphical output [7].

3.3 Experience

The third lens stems from the idea of designing tools "inside-out" from an intended experience. Artful design's Principle 1.15 states, "Design not only from needs – but from the values behind them", while Principle 2.2 states, "Design inside-out" [4]. MIDI.CITI affords the function of an audiovisual generative drum machine, but was simultaneously designed to prioritize human values such as evoked emotion, playfulness, and expression. As a result, MIDI.CITI aims to follow artful design's principle 1.16, "Design is the radical synthesis of means and ends into a third type of a thing—both useful and beautiful." [4], bringing together complex drum machine algorithms, audiovisual correspondence, and instant yet subtle interactions to ultimately serve an experiential goal.

MIDI.CITI encapsulates its audiovisual interactions within the overarching metaphor of a cityscape, thereby giving form to the experience. It was designed with the conviction that experience-oriented design, with metaphorically aligned audiovisual interactions, have the power to evoke profound reflections and desire for deeper explorations. As one user reflected, it is "a very musical and expressive audiovisual experience that makes me think about the world we live in and how we interact with it." Another user remarked, "I am always left wanting to explore this space more deeply, to go to MIDI.CITI myself and take part in the musical lives of its inhabitants."

4. DESIGN PRINCIPLES

4.1 Don't forget the Experience

Prioritizing experience as the "North Star" of the design is central to value-based design approaches like artful design. This often translates to revisiting a number of questions throughout the design process. What is the end experience? How do we want a person to *feel* within and as a consequence of the experience? How does the system build toward that outcome? How do we invite user participation for play and creative expression?

The metaphor of a musical city provides the framing for MIDI.CITI, where users engage in an experience that is musically creative, playful, whimsical, and expressive, yet uncomplicated and calm. This set of experiential "North Stars" guides the design choices on not only sonic, graphical, and interactive elements, but also the overall balance, narrative, flow, and presentation. It leads to specific design questions that ultimately become the substance of the experience: What if the buildings represented the four instruments in the drum machine? What if the parameters were controlled by window lights? What if a Ferris wheel controlled the tempo? What if we could fly to the Moon? All the while, the "North Star" serves as a set of experiential goals to evaluate each design choice.

4.2 Achieve precise audiovisual correspondence.

A precise correspondence between the audio and the visual promotes functional understanding of the system and enhances the overall aesthetic experience. In MIDI.CITI, every sound the user hears is visualized in the scene with precise audiovisual synchronization (and we can think of the reverse as being true: each visual event is sonified). Whether they are particle effects coming from the rooftops or the animations of rabbits on the Moon, we take the advantage of strongly-timed audio provided by ChucK and use it to precisely drive both audio and graphics. In particular, MIDI.CITI's ChucK code generates audio while sending relevant parameter values and graphical triggers to Unity, enabling a visual element to occur in the nearest frame after a sound has been played. In this way, the audio retains its continuous generation while precisely synchronized with the graphics. The key takeaway here is to synchronize both sound and graphics *from audio*. Indeed, it would have been insufficient here to drive such precise audiovisual synchronization from graphics. A typical video frame rate of 30 fps to 60 fps may not be accurate enough to control a continuous stream of generative audio and its varying nature may result in asynchrony, jitter, or other undesirable artifacts.

4.3 Take advantage of synthesized audio

Synthesized audio has many advantages over pre-recorded audio in interactive software. Various low-level control of audio synthesis parameters including filters and effects, as well as high-level musical parameters such as tempo, dynamics, texture, and rhythmic complexity can be manipulated expressively.

In MIDI.CITI, by introducing pseudo-randomization, the looped sequences of music is rarely repeated in the same manner, yet it can preserve an aesthetic consistency by asserting a prescribed parametric boundary. Also, granular synthesis is used to enrich the overall sonic atmosphere, allowing the user to *resynthesize* a sound stream that interpolates between orchestral and choral timbres.

4.4 Combine high-level and direct control

An important consideration in generative music is finding an appropriate balance between algorithmic processes and meaningful human input. This supports artful design's Principle 7.11A, "That which can be automated should be.", and 7.11B, "That which cannot be *meaningfully* automated should not be". For example, the user has high-level influence over rhythmic variations, musical density, and timbre, but this does not preclude the design from also having direct low-level musical input, such as pitch and note onset.

In MIDI.CITI, the UFOs are mapped in a diatonic scale of the music's overall key and allow for one-to-one action-to-sound interactions. Combined with the semi-automated music environment, this direct-input element enables additional possibilities for play, improvisation, and expression.

4.5 Surprise! Break the established expectation

As users spend time with the design, the mechanics and dynamics of the system get understood and expectations begin to form. An effective way of making the design more interesting is to break such expectations by introducing a novel element that "no one asked for". This can result in a reframing and broadening of the aesthetic experience. For example, in MIDI.CITI, the Moon, initially a visual ornament, serves an unexpected function, wherein the user can fly toward it and interact with Moon rabbits creating grains of sound. Each additional unexpected event builds new layers of mechanics and dynamics, leading to novel ways to aesthetically experience MIDI.CITI.

Breaking the established expectation within the system can be considered a form of *defamiliarization*—a technique that presents a familiar object or situation in an unfamiliar manner to protract the perceptive process and invite fresh context [8]. Such break in expectation sustains the experience, calls attention to its own aesthetics, and invites users to see and hear familiar elements anew.

5. CONCLUSION

As for future work, mechanics for customizing and even programming the musical inner-workings of MIDI.CITI are considered. Currently, the ChucK back-end contains information on probabilities of beats and pseudo-randomized algorithms of pitches. If the user has access to editing these components within the software, it would create another layer for creativity and expression. Moreover, a "free-edit" mode of a city would be an interesting implementation, where the user places different kinds of buildings (or even their own 3D models) and maps them to different audio parameters to customize their own version of a musical city.

In conclusion, we dissected MIDI.CITI as an experience-oriented musical cityscape, unpacking its design through lenses of interaction, play, and experience. We outlined the audio algorithms and pseudo-randomization techniques that aim to create a sustained space for creative engagement. We proposed design principles for using a generative audio-driven system, interconnecting graphics, interactions, and music with the aim of creating a sense of narrative and experiential flow. Overall, if we had a "call to action" in writing this paper, it would be to promote designing more aesthetics-driven audiovisual experiences, as tools for human creativity and expression.

6. REFERENCES

[1] G. Wang, P. R. Cook, and S. Salazar, "Chuck: A strongly timed computer music language," *Computer Music Journal*, vol. 39, no. 4, pp. 10–29, 2015.

[2] J. Atherton and G. Wang, "Chunity: Integrated Audiovisual Programming in Unity," in *NIME*, Conference Proceedings, pp. 102–107.

[3] K. Kim and G. Wang, "VVRMA: VR Field Trip to a Computer Music Center," in *New Interfaces for Musical Expression*, 2024.

[4] G. Wang, *Artful Design: Technology in Search of the Sublime, A MusiComic Manifesto.* Stanford University Press, 2018.

[5] P. Cook, "2001: Principles for designing computer music controllers," *A NIME Reader: Fifteen years of new interfaces for musical expression*, pp. 1–13, 2017.

[6] R. Caillois, *Man, play, and games.* University of Illinois press, 2001.

[7] R. Hunicke, M. LeBlanc, and R. Zubek, "MDA: A formal approach to game design and game research," in *Proceedings of the AAAI Workshop on Challenges in Game AI*, vol. 4. San Jose, CA, Conference Proceedings, p. 1722.

[8] L. Crawford, "Viktor Shklovskij: Diffrance in Defamiliarization," *Comparative Literature*, pp. 209–219, 1984.

Reprogrammable Effects Pedals on the Daisy Seed Platform

Alois Cerbu
UC Berkeley, Dept. of Mathematics
cerbu@berkeley.edu

Carmine Cella
UC Berkeley, Dept. of Music
carmine.cella@berkeley.edu

ABSTRACT

Many creative audio effects are available only as plugins to digital audio work stations, or as boutique hardware devices. We describe the implementation of three realtime digital effects algorithms – a strobe tuner, spectral processor (with denoising & phase vocoder frequency estimation), and realtime granular synthesizer – designed to run on an inexpensive open-source hardware platform powered by the ElectroSmith Daisy Seed microcontroller. The platform has the form factor of a guitar stompbox; we discuss the merits of portable, reprogrammable hardware audio processing solutions for live performance, and future directions for this project.

Figure 1. The three effects discussed, running on the Daisy Seed pedal hardware: from left to right, granular processor, spectral processor, and strobe tuner.

1. INTRODUCTION

Since the 1970s, digital audio processing has become a significant part of music production & performance [1]. Digital audio environments provide canvases on which to superimpose, rearrange, and effect recorded sounds. These effects may be subtle – mixing, compression, equalization, reverberation – or significant alterations – distortion, delay, pitch-shifting, to name a few [2]. Digital audio effects are used both "offline" (in non-realtime settings like composition & production) and "online," for live performance.

Many consumer-grade computers & soundcards cannot guarantee "realtime" processing (sub-10 ms latency) without audio dropouts [3, Chapter 4]. A high-performance laptop with an external audio interface can attain round-trip latencies around 3 ms (assuming input and output buffer sizes of 64 samples at 48 kHz), assuming no latency is introduced by the audio interface or its communication protocol with the host. By comparison, an embedded digital effects unit can, in theory, handle much smaller audio buffers and thus deliver lower latencies. Projects such as Bela [4], Pisound [5], and Norns [6] (and its open-source cousin Shield) implement realtime Linux kernels for single board computers. These hardware solutions offer the flexibility of a DAW with the portability and immediacy of a live instrument. These products require various amounts of assembly and configuration, with Norns requiring the least (it also being the only one that ships with a dedicated enclosure).

This paper describes the implementation of three DSP effects on top of an inexpensive open-source hardware platform, which has the latency profile and form factor of a dedicated effects stompbox with the reconfigurability of a DAW (we measured the roundtrip latency at under two milliseconds). The motivation of the project was to provide open-source versions of processing methods typically found only in higher-end boutique pedals: an accurate strobe tuner, spectral processor, and granular synthesizer. The total materials cost per unit, $140, is comparable to the cost of a standalone strobe tuner pedal, and much less than comparable hardware for granular synthesis.

2. THE DAISY ECOSYSTEM & PEDAL HARDWARE CAPABILITIES

The Daisy Seed is a microcontroller for audio applications [7]. It is powered by an STM32H7 chip (clocked at 480 MHz), with integrated high-quality audio codec and onboard persistent storage. The manufacturer, ElectroSmith, provides an open-source library for interfacing with and configuring the hardware, and which ships with a template makefile that invokes the GNU Arm embedded toolchain [8]. Setting up the buildsystem is amply documented in the Daisy wiki.

Firmware is written in C++, compiled on a computer & sent over USB to the Seed's 128 KB flash memory; the Seed has about an additional megabyte of high-speed onboard RAM, 64 MB of SDRAM, and 8 MB of persistent QSPI storage. . ElectroSmith and its community have also developed tools to port DSP code written in Max gen~, Faust, and PureData to the Seed.

Our code runs on Keith Shepherd's open-source guitar pedal hardware for the Seed [9], which provides a rotary encoder, six potentiometers, two momentary footswitches, a 128×64 OLED, stereo audio i/o, and eighth-inch TRS MIDI i/o, and fits in a 125B-sized aluminum enclosure.

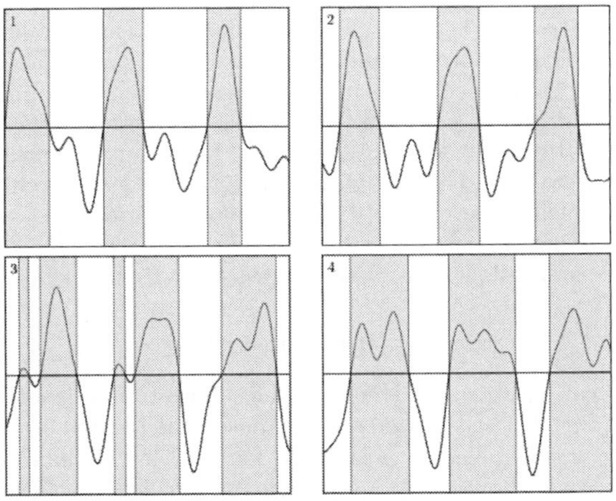

Figure 2. Four frames of the strobe tuner (numbered chronologically), displaying the waveform and barcode pattern. The input signal is an inharmonic sum of sinusoids with frequencies $0.96 \cdot 3f$, $1.85 \cdot 3f$ and $3.11 \cdot 3f$, and with amplitudes 1, 0.5, and 0.25. The overall shape of the barcode phases to the right since the fundamental is slightly flat of a harmonic of f, even though one of the high partials is sharp.

3. THE ALGORITHMS

Keith Shepherd's hardware repository [9] includes firmware for certain idiomatic guitar DSP effects, such as reverb, distortion, chorus & tremolo. The algorithms we chose to implement, described in this section, are meant to demonstrate the platform's capabilities on time- and frequency-domain tasks. All three projects require the firmware to store & manipulate reasonably large buffers of audio; the strobe tuner and granular synth also make extensive use of the screen.

All code and supplemental photo & video documentation can be found in the linked GitHub repository: [10]. The algorithms are implemented in C++; the spectral processor and granular synthesizer are adaptations of algorithms written by the first author for desktop use [11].

3.1 Strobe Tuner

The first algorithm we describe is a simple but accurate strobe tuner. The principle is as follows: we are given an input digital waveform ($n \mapsto x(n)$) and a reference frequency to compare our signal to, f. We set up a phasor ($n \mapsto p(n)$) whose value moves linearly through the interval $[0, 1]$ at frequency f. Given $w = 128$, the width of the screen in pixels, whenever n is such that $w \cdot p(n)$ crosses an integer, we modify a vertical line of pixels at horizontal coordinate $\lfloor w \cdot p(n) \rfloor$, turning the pixels on if $x(n) > 0$ and off otherwise.

If x is harmonic with frequency $f + \delta$, this will produce a barcode-like pattern (capturing the zero-crossings of the signal x) which phases in one direction or the other depending on the sign of δ. If, as in the case of plucked strings, the signal is not harmonic, the barcode represents the phasing of partials relative to fundamental; the fundamental can still be tuned to the reference pitch by eye, as demonstrated in Figure 2, or the user may choose to tune a higher partial to the reference frequency instead.

The source code can be found in `main.cpp`, inside the `tuner` directory of our repository. The heart of the method is line 215: each audio frame, we draw a short vertical line whose horizontal position is a phasor with some fixed reference frequency. For simplicity of implementation, our algorithm displays six simultaneous barcodes with reference frequencies tuned to the open strings of a guitar (relative to $A\,440$); in another mode, the reference pitch can be selected from the chromatic scale using the encoder. In future work, tuning will be possible relative to frequencies other than $A\,440$. We also plan to add pitch-tracking so that the tuner can operate in "chromatic mode," comparing the input signal to the nearest note in a chosen reference scale – this will enable the user to tune to scales other than 12 EDO.

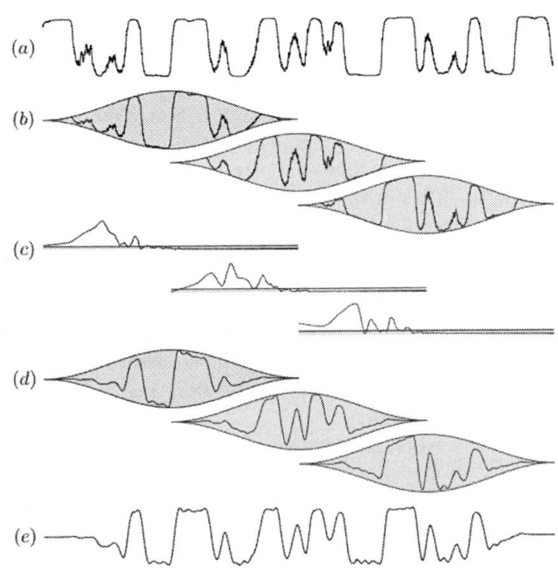

Figure 3. Stages of spectral processing. The input signal (a) is split into overlapping time-domain windows (b), which are then Fourier-transformed (c). In the denoising example we implement, all frequency content with amplitude below the thresholds (represented by shaded rectangles in (c)) is removed. The resulting spectra are inverse-Fourier-transformed, yielding the time-domain signals in (d), which are recombined to yield the output signal (e). Notice the removal of the noise from the original signal, but the global similarity in the shapes of the two waveforms.

3.2 Spectral Processing

The second algorithm is a spectral processor [12]; we define a `Fourier` class which handles windowing and the scheduling of forward- and reverse-FFT methods: an instance of the class is initialized with a callback defining the manipulation to take place in the frequency domain; audio fed to the instance is written to a number of circular buffers (one for each overlapping analysis window). When an input buffer fills up, the class invokes a forward FFT, then the user-defined callback, and then the inverse FFT, writing and windowing the resulting values into a number of overlapping resynthesis buffers, which are summed and returned to the Daisy's audio callback.

In our tests, we succeeded in running FFTs on the Daisy hardware of sizes up to $N = 4096$ with four overlaps or up to $N = 2048$ with eight overlaps. We implement two callbacks: one that denoises the signal by independently mixing the low- and high-amplitude bins, and a second which accurately measures the frequencies present in a signal using the phase vocoder algorithm [12] with bin-to-bin smoothing. A graphical representation of the denoising callback is outlined in Figure 3.

The denoiser separates the harmonic from the wideband elements of a sound; when in the configuration that zeros all frequencies with low amplitude, it smooths out transients. The sounds produced are especially interesting when the input is nearly (but not exactly) harmonic, as when processing, for example, a distorted dyad or triad. The distortion adds harmonics of the pitches present, as well as of common undertones. The spectral processor removes the wideband elements, often leaving behind crisp & distinct high pitches & chirps.

In future work, we plan to implement an accurate polyphonic pitch-tracking algorithm so that the pedal can be used as an online audio-to-MIDI device. We also plan to implement the resynthesis portion of the phase vocoder, for cross-synthesis and frequency-domain pitch shifting [12].

3.3 Granular Synthesizer

The third algorithm we implement is a granular synthesizer. In the taxonomy of Roads' book [13, Chapter 5], our algorithm is "granulation in real time": audio is written into a fifteen-second circular buffer, from which grains are read. We implement a `Granulator` class which writes incoming audio into a circular buffer and handles grain requests. In the same source file we also define a `Granary` object, which is an independently addressable grain generating metronome. The example project uses four granaries, each with its own parameters for the size, density, transposition, direction of playback and predelay of grains, as well randomization control of these parameters. For example, the density parameter determines how frequently the metronome asks for grains, while the spray parameter randomizes the regularity at which these grains are triggered (while maintaining the requested density, on average). The Seed can handle about forty voices of grain polyphony without audio dropouts.

The parameters of the granulation are stored to the Daisy Seed's persistent memory; for difference choices of parameters, the granular synth can be configured as a transposition effect, chorus, reverse delay, or can turn input sounds into textures. These configurations are demonstrated in the video attached to the software repository.

In future work, we plan to include an option to use the effect statically, without constantly overwriting the source audio, to implement "freeze" capabilities, and to make the granulation sensitive to acoustic features of the input signal (like pitch & rhythm).

4. FUTURE WORK

Besides the algorithms we've presented, the Seed guitar pedal could be used for a number of practical musical settings. In future work we plan to implement firmware that performs live beat tracking & pitch detection for coordination of other audio equipment. The spectral processor described in this article is still quite preliminary and there is plenty of room for more interesting frequency-domain processing.

The Seed has enough computational power to evaluate moderately-sized neural networks: a community project for Daisy Seed has emulated a number of guitar amplifiers & distortion pedals [14]. In further work we also plan to port machine learning algorithms, trained on a computer, to the Seed. For example, the pedal could run an algorithm which would perform auditory feature extraction and neural audio synthesis; with much optimization, perhaps even a scaled-down version of IRCAM's RAVE project [15].

5. CONCLUSIONS

We have detailed the implementation of three real-time digital effects algorithms – a strobe tuner, spectral processor, and granular synthesizer – for the ElectroSmith Daisy Seed. The aim of this work is to publish open-source software versions of audio effects that usually are available only either as software plugins for DAWs, or inside specialized or boutique effects hardware. We hope also to generate interest in the further development of effects and synthesizers for the Daisy Seed guitar pedal platform.

6. REFERENCES

[1] J. Watkinson, *The Art of Digital Audio.* Focal Press, 2001. [Online]. Available: https://books.google.com/books?id=eVpITJfPxMEC

[2] U. Zölzer, *DAFX: Digital Audio Effects*, 2nd ed. Wiley Publishing, 2011.

[3] Y. Wang, "Low latency audio processing," Ph.D. dissertation, Queen Mary University of London, 2018.

[4] A. McPherson, "An environment for submillisecond-latency audio and sensor processing on BeagleBone Black," in *Audio Engineering Convention 138*, 2015. [Online]. Available: http://www.eecs.qmul.ac.uk/~andrewm/mcpherson_aes2015.pdf

[5] Blockas. Pisound – Raspberry Pi Sound Card & MIDI Interface. [Online]. Available: http://blokas.io/pisound

[6] Monome. Norns. [Online]. Available: http://monome.org/docs/norns

[7] ElectroSmith. Daisy Seed. [Online]. Available: http://electro-smith.com/products/daisy-seed

[8] ——. libDaisy: Hardware Library for the Daisy Audio Platform. GitHub. [Online]. Available: http://github.com/electro-smith/libDaisy

[9] K. Shepherd. (2023) DaisySeedProjects. GitHub. [Online]. Available: http://github.com/bkshepherd/DaisySeedProjects

[10] A. Cerbu. (2024) GitHub. [Online]. Available: https://github.com/amcerbu/StrobeSpectralGranular

[11] ——. (2021) GitHub. [Online]. Available: https://github.com/amcerbu/huygens

[12] J. O. Smith, *Spectral Audio Signal Processing*, 2011. [Online]. Available: http://ccrma.stanford.edu/~jos/sasp

[13] C. Roads, *Microsound.* MIT Press, 2004.

[14] K. Bloemer. (2023) NeuralSeed. GitHub. [Online]. Available: http://github.com/GuitarML/NeuralSeed

[15] A. Caillon and P. Esling, "Rave: A variational autoencoder for fast and high-quality neural audio synthesis," 2021. [Online]. Available: http://arxiv.org/abs/2111.05011

MoNoDeC: the Mobile Node Controller for audience-involved sound diffusion

Nick Hwang
University of Wisconsin-Whitewater
hwangn@uww.edu

Anthony T. Marasco
Michigan State University
tmarasco125@gmail.com

ABSTRACT

We present MoNoDeC, a multichannel audio system designed for immersive audio experiences by leveraging audience mobile phones and Internet of Things (IoT)-driven speakers. This network-based system uses audience mobile devices and speakers as point-source audio and dynamic audience participation through their mobile displays, allowing users to interact with and influence performances. MoNoDeC enables designers to craft interactive audio environments where audience members can modify musical elements, contribute to a collective canvas, or change instrument timbres. This paper highlights MoNoDeC's ability to foster engaging, immersive, and interactive musical experiences beyond traditional loudspeaker systems, showcasing its potential for interactive audience-based performances and sound diffusion.

1. INTRODUCTION

MoNoDeC, short for "Mobile Node Controller," is a multichannel audio system that utilizes audience mobile phones and IoT-driven speakers as point sources in immersive audio experiences. MoNoDeC is a network-based system currently with two client use cases: audience mobile phones and Raspberry Pi-driven audio devices, allowing for interactive audience-based performances, mobile and connected audio sound diffusion system [1]. Audience phones allow for dynamic interfaces for participatory elements during performance.

Audience participants use their mobile phones to register their location within a customizable audience space (rows, cloud, or free-form), turning their devices into point sources during performances or installations. Designers can choose for mobile users to move about during a performance or experience.

A performance controller manages the state, audio output, and interface data delivery to participants during the performance stage. The controller selects performance parameters and shapes the sound from the mobile devices through mapped touch gestures. Audience members interact with the mobile interface, affecting the experience by modifying musical aspects, contributing to a collective canvas, or altering instrument timbres.

MoNoDeC engages the audience in immersive and interactive experiences and performances unattainable with traditional loudspeaker setups. This paper explores the design, functionality, and capabilities of MoNoDeC as a sound diffusion system and shows examples of the dynamic interfaces it can present to mobile users during performance.

2. PRIOR SYSTEMS & HISTORICAL CONTEXT

Techniques for assembling speaker arrays from audience-provided or readymade devices have been present since the mid-20th century. As radios became more ubiquitous and portable, composers experimented within the limits of this technology to write works around these media players turned instruments. Composers writing new works for radios explored differing approaches to culling sound from the airwaves [2]. Through the advent of the Web Audio API and mobile devices, the evolving social expectation that audience members will be equipped with a device capable of receiving audio and/or control data over the internet has allowed composers to push the boundaries of complexity and collaboration experienced in works for distributed musical networks.

The past decade has seen the rise of frameworks aimed at streamlining the creation of musical networks for installations and live performances. Leveraging the built-in sensors and audio processing systems in mobile phones and single board computers [3], these frameworks allow artists to use mobile devices as both gestural controllers for shaping musical content in performance and portable speakers integrated into the concert hall. Prior research shows a collection of client-server systems similar to MoNoDeC, some developed for conducting specific studies centered on audience participation [4] and others designed to aid in creating new distributed music works. The Soundworks framework [5, 6] allows creators to develop networked musical works featuring bidirectional audio and data transmission between client devices. Both SoundSling [7] and Nü Soundworks [8] combine audience member web browser interfaces with a controller made in the Max programming environment to explore audio diffusion in 1-to-n and n-to-n layouts respectively. Focusing on collaborative improvisation with networked mobile devices, the AuRal framework [9] and the Daisyphone software [10] use a shared music composition workspace and relative geolocation to turn data transmission and local audio generation into communal music-making experiences.

MoNoDeC differs from preexisting systems in a handful of ways. The current version of MoNoDeC's user-facing software elements is web-based allowing its user interfaces to provide dynamic visual feedback for the mobile user that many existing systems do not. MoNoDeC aims to help newcomers develop and deploy projects quickly by including starting templates, preset speaker node layouts, and the ability to save frequently used settings. Additionally, the option to add customizable IoT speaker nodes into a setup is simplified by providing firmware that works to connect embedded computers to the MoNoDeC server.

3. MONODEC

The main purpose of MoNoDeC is to use audience members' mobile phones as point-source sound diffusion speakers. MoNoDeC is also capable of using custom-made IoT devices that we call autonomous hubs as point sources and standalone digital instruments as well. Additionally, MoNoDeC is capable of presenting dynamic interfaces to audiences members which may include providing performance affecting options or digital instruments localized on their own device. MoNoDeC can be used independently as an immersive audio system with sound diffusion or in conjunction with existing paradigms such as loudspeaker orchestras or ambisonic arrays.

MoNoDeC is built with existing communication software created by the authors (Collab-Hub) [1] that uses a web-based server-client framework allowing for two-way communication between web-pages, apps, and IoT Devices. MoNoDeC's interfaces for the controller and audience members are served through web pages or apps, and the autonomous hubs connect directly to the server. Dynamic interfaces for controller and audience provide active participation options during performance. The autonomous hubs are intended to be stationary. Collab-Hub enables the communication pathways of MoNoDeC. For ease of connectivity and setup, currently MoNoDeC relies on the Wide Area Network (WiFi internet) to communicate with the server and audience members' phones, although alternative setups could use a localized version of the MoNoDeC / Collab-Hub server to reduce possible latency.

3.1 Visual Rendering

The controller and audience mobile phone interfaces are rendered with HTML, CSS, and JavaScript. HTML5 Canvas objects render the interactable layouts and instrument control elements with P5.js. [2]. The state of MoNoDeC's data and phases are stored on the remote server.

3.2 Phases

MoNoDeC has three phases which are managed by the controller: layout and design, registration, and performance:

3.2.1 Layout and Design Phase

Layout and Design Phase allows the controller to make decisions on the layout of the available audience spaces. These audience spaces represent predetermined seating for the performance, where during the Registration Phase audience members select their seats. Visual landmarks like the Controllers table / mixing booth, stage, or easily noticeable physical object in the performance help orient the audience to the graphical layout. These graphical landmarks can be added during this Layout and Design Phase. The controller may select from premade or saved layouts. This phase can occur anytime before a performance; the layouts are saved on the server and can be recalled.

3.2.2 Registration Phase

Registration phase occurs prior to performance and once the audience is seated. During this phase audience members' interfaces display the phase name and the interactable interface displays the selectable seat options on their mobile device. Audience members are instructed to select their seat. Upon selection, their seat graphic will change colors and new text will instruct audience members to await the next phase.

The controller's interface displays the entire layout with seats with colors indicating unregistered (blue) and registered colors (red). During this phase the controller is unable to change the layout, but is able to return to Layout and Design Phase. If the controller returns to the previous phase, all audience member's selections reset. The controller is able to advance to the Performance Phase once audience members have finished selecting their seats.

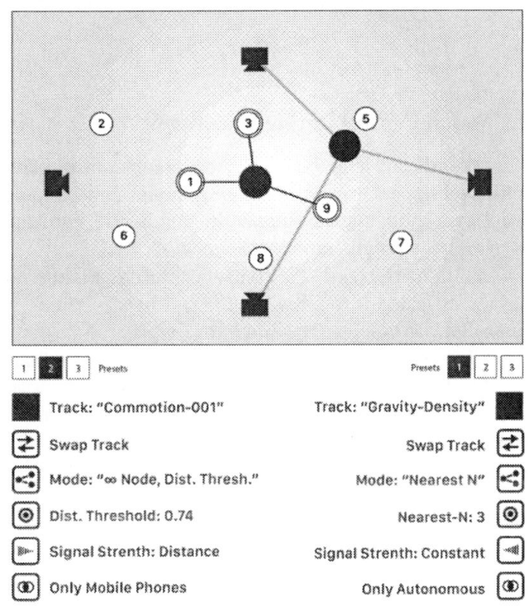

Figure 1. Controller interface during *Performance Phase*.

3.2.3 Performance Phase

The Performance Phase begins when the controller starts a new performance. All connected devices (mobile phones and autonomous hubs) have registered their positions and interfaces remind audience members to unmute and turn their volumes up.

All devices, mobile phones, and autonomous hubs, are considered 'nodes' in the 'performance space'. [3]

[1] https://www.collab-hub.io/

[2] https://p5.js

[3] Due to current web-based interaction and iOS/Android programming limitations, audiences must unmute their devices. One side effect to this for MoNoDeC is notifications, alerts, and reminders from such devices may potentially sound during performances. At the time of this writing, the authors have no programming solution, but a workaround is to ask the audience to unmute and turn off all notifications while in performance.

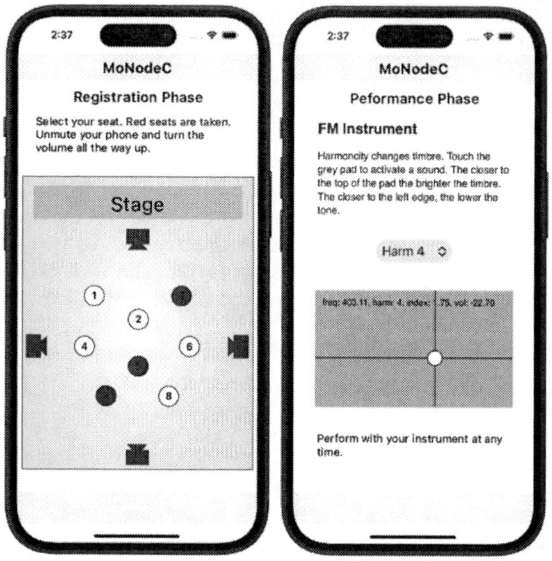

Figure 2. Audience Mobile Interfaces. Left: Registration. Right: A Performance Interface

3.3 Sound Control During Performance

The controller is able to select and change control parameters during performance, including main audio material, nearest neighbor distance threshold, number of nearest neighbors, signal strength, devices to include.

Main Audio Material - the controller can choose one sound file for diffusion throughout the performance space. The controller can change the sound file anytime.

Number of Nearest Neighbors - A nearest neighbor algorithm is employed to identify the closest node(s) (Mobile phone or autonomous hubs). The number of nearest neighbors is the maximum number of the possible neighbor nodes. This parameter is used in conjunction with the Nearest Neighbor Max Distance.

Nearest Neighbor Max Distance - This distance is the maximum distance to calculate nearest neighbors from the current touch location in the layout. The algorithm sorts nodes by shortest distance first then number of neighbors.

Signal Strength - This setting can be either ‘Distance’ or ‘Constant’ and refers to the amplitude value sent to nodes based on their Nearest Neighbor evaluation. If the parameter is ‘Distance’, a node within the Nearest Neighbor grouping will receive a ratio of their distance from the controller’s touch divided by the Nearest Neighbor Max Distance. Any excluded node would receive a signal strength value of zero. Signal Strength value will not exceed 1. Signal Strength value is the Node Distance divided by the Nearest Neighbor Max Distance. If the parameter is set to ‘Constant’, all included Nearest Neighbor Nodes will receive a value of 1.

MoNoDeC’s approach to diffusion is different than techniques practiced with conventional loudspeaker orchestras [11]: Rather than using multiple channels of audio routed to specific speakers, MoNoDeC uses two audio files routed to all phones with amplitude touch gestures creating the sense that the sound is following that touch path.

4. USE OF DIGITAL INSTRUMENTS

MoNoDeC makes use of digital instruments as one part of its audio synthesis with mobile phones and autonomous hubs. Prior versions used the WebAudio API for audio synthesis on mobile phones with Tone.JS. [4] The current versions on the mobile and autonomous hubs use different exports of RNBO patches. RNBO is an extension of the Max patching environment designed to export software creations to other frameworks. [5] RNBO patch export destinations include Web, C++, and others. These digital instruments exported from RNBO have differing designs because of their expected level of interaction: the hardware instruments will be discussed in the next section. The mobile phone instruments which are controlled by the audience members have simplified controls such as the frequency and modulation index of an Frequency Modulation instrument are mapped to an XY-pad touch area. A single finger’s touch and gesture would initiate the onset of sound and continuous control while that finger is down. Part of the digital instrument that the controller commands is obscured from the audience member. This part of the instrument has sound file playback controls and simple oscillators. The controller can select a sound file that will play on the mobile phones. The amplitude of the sound file is controlled by touch gesture through a mouse or finger touch mentioned in *Sound Control During Performance*. These instruments do not stream nor receive streaming audio data. Pre-selected audio files are uploaded on the server prior to the performance, and the digital instruments load those files when performance begins.

During a performance, the controller commands the sound on mobile phones including sound file playback, oscillators and their envelopment, and the amplitude of all sound from MoNoDeC.

The controller changes the interface on the participating mobile phones including instrument controllers or choice-based options.

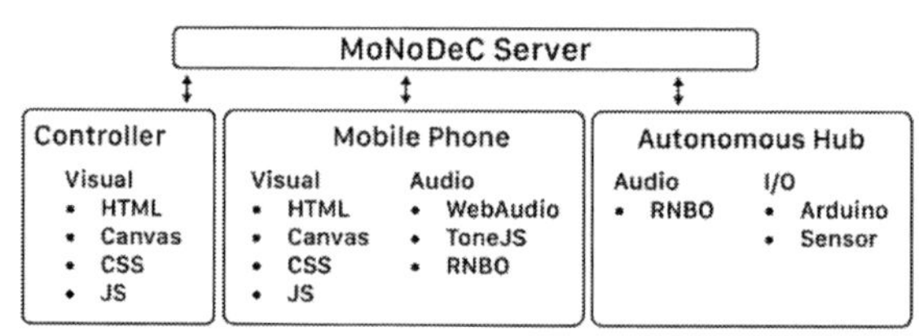

Figure 3. Server-Client Model for MoNoDec

5. HARDWARE

Extending the distributed/networked musical performance device set beyond mobile devices and laptops, MoNoDeC users can incorporate our autonomous hub devices into their network topology. Autonomous hubs are capable of playing simultaneous roles in a MoNoDeC project: each device can serve as a point source in the wireless speaker array, a self-performing and remote-controllable computer music

[4] `https://tonejs.github.io/`

[5] `https://cycling74.com/products/rnbo`

instrument, and a sensor-laden interface for communicating with other MoNoDeC clients. The current version of our autonomous hubs are built using a Raspberry Pi Zero W2, a stereo DAC shield with onboard amplifiers, and two 3-watt speakers. This setup can be expanded to incorporate additional shields that add connections for analog and digital sensors or add multichannel audio IO. A custom server runs in tandem with the RNBO runner or web browser on each hub and handles OSC message transmission between the audio engine, sensors, and the main MoNoDeC server.

With the ability to host either a webpage or an instance of a RNBO virtual instrument, autonomous hubs provide MoNoDeC users with a wide variety of options for featuring IoT hardware alongside mobile devices in their creative works. The same audio engine running on participants' phones can be run on each hub, allowing a one-to-one comparison between the sonic contributions of both devices. With the addition of proximity or motion sensors, physical interaction with each hub can allow audience participants to generate control data along the network. The physical computing Hub hardware is compact and lightweight, making it easy to hide or enclose inside fabricated housings, podiums, sculptures, and more. The flexible form factor of the autonomous hubs coupled with their connectivity and audio processing ability provide an alternative to the ubiquitous shape and user experience of consumer mobile electronics.

6. FUTURE WORK

Areas for future development include enhancements to MoNoDeC's software and rendering, digital instrument, and hardware capabilities. The authors plan to develop interfaces into native applications for tablets and mobile devices. MoNoDeC currently does not stream audio, and the authors intend to add that capability. To reduce possible network latency, the authors intend to release a version of the server software capable of running on a single-board computer. A variety of compositional examples, digital instruments, and more audience choices will expand the performance capabilities available to users.

7. CONCLUSIONS

MoNoDeC melds mobile music computing, networked music performance, sound spatialization techniques, and the development of software and hardware systems. By integrating audience mobile phones and IoT-driven speakers into immersive audio experiences, MoNoDeC combines notions of electronic music performers and audience, creating a dynamic and interactive soundscape that extends beyond traditional performance paradigms.

8. REFERENCES

[1] J. Harrison, "Sound, space, sculpture: some thoughts on the 'what', 'how' and 'why' of sound diffusion," *Organised Sound*, vol. 3, no. 2, pp. 117–127, Aug. 1998.

[2] B. Taylor, "A History of the Audience as a Speaker Array," in *Proceedings of the International Conference on New Interfaces for Musical Expression*. Copenhagen, Denmark: Aalborg University Copenhagen, 2017, pp. 481–486. [Online]. Available: http://www.nime.org/proceedings/2017/nime2017_paper0091.pdf

[3] A. Tanaka, "Mobile Music Making," in *Proceedings of the International Conference on New Interfaces for Musical Expression*, Hamamatsu, Japan, 2004, pp. 154–156. [Online]. Available: http://www.nime.org/proceedings/2004/nime2004_154.pdf

[4] O. Hödl, C. Bartmann, F. Kayali, C. Löw, and P. Purgathofer, "Large-scale audience participation in live music using smartphones," *J. New Music Res.*, vol. 49, no. 2, pp. 192–207, feb 2020.

[5] S. Robaszkiewicz and N. Schnell, "Soundworks - A Playground for Artists and Developers to Create Collaborative Mobile Web Performances," in *Proceedings of the International Web Audio Conference*, ser. WAC '15, S. Goldszmidt, N. Schnell, V. Saiz, and B. Matuszewski, Eds. Paris, France: IRCAM, January 2015.

[6] B. Matuszewski, "Soundworks - A Framework for Networked Music Systems on the Web - State of Affairs and New Developments," in *Proceedings of the International Web Audio Conference*, ser. WAC '19, A. Xambó, S. R. Martín, and G. Roma, Eds. Trondheim, Norway: NTNU, December 2019, pp. 65–70.

[7] A. T. Marasco and J. Allison, "SoundSling: A Framework for Using Creative Motion Data to Pan Audio Across a Mobile Device Speaker Array," in *Proceedings of the International Web Audio Conference*, ser. WAC '18, J. Monschke, C. Guttandin, N. Schnell, T. Jenkinson, and J. Schaedler, Eds. Berlin, Germany: TU Berlin, September 2018.

[8] D. Poirier-Quinot, B. Matuszewski, N. Schnell, and O. Warusfel, "Nü Soundworks: Using spectators smartphones as a distributed network of speakers and sensors during live performances." in *Proceedings of the International Web Audio Conference*, ser. WAC '17, F. Thalmann and S. Ewert, Eds. London, United Kingdom: Queen Mary University of London, August 2017.

[9] J. Allison and C. Dell, "AuRal: A Mobile Interactive System for Geo-Locative Audio Synthesis," in *Proceedings of the International Conference on New Interfaces for Musical Expression*. Ann Arbor, Michigan: University of Michigan, 2012. [Online]. Available: http://www.nime.org/proceedings/2012/nime2012_301.pdf

[10] N. Bryan-Kinns and P. G. Healey, "Daisyphone: Support for Remote Music Collaboration," in *Proceedings of the International Conference on New Interfaces for Musical Expression*, Hamamatsu, Japan, 2004, pp. 27–30. [Online]. Available: http://www.nime.org/proceedings/2004/nime2004_027.pdf

[11] L. Austin, "Sound diffusion in composition and performance: An interview with Denis Smalley," *Computer Music Journal*, vol. 24, no. 2, pp. 10–21, Jun. 2000.

Analog ring modulation: a DIY approach inspired by historical techniques

Tomás Koljatic S.
Music Institute
Pontificia Universidad Católica de Chile
takoljat@uc.cl

Michel Rozas
Department of Electrical Engineering
Pontificia Universidad Católica de Chile
mvrozas@uc.cl

Cristian Garcés
Department of Electrical Engineering
Pontificia Universidad Católica de Chile
cngarces@uc.cl

Juan Parra Cancino
Research Fellow
Orpheus Institute
Ghent
juan.parra@orpheusinstituut.be

Rodrigo F. Cádiz
Music Institute and
Department of Electrical Engineering
Pontificia Universidad Católica de Chile
rcadiz@uc.cl

ABSTRACT

In this paper, we present a device that implements a ring modulator intended to recreate historical analog audio. As simple as it sounds, the multiplication of two analog audio signals is not a straightforward task, mainly due to phenomena such as saturation or non-linearity. Drawing inspiration from historical realizations of ring modulation, we experimented with the most common methods described in the literature. Our device, which is comparatively inexpensive, improves upon the aforementioned alternatives from a DIY *perspective. It is predominantly analog, adhering to the practices of the first decades of electroacoustic music, with the notable exception of the digital control for the sinusoidal carrier. We aim to strike a balance between analog audio technology and modern components and techniques. Additionally, this paper includes audiovisual demonstrations that showcase the practical uses of our ring modulator. A comprehensive GitHub repository provides open access to all the resources required for* DIY *enthusiasts to replicate our implementation.*

1. INTRODUCTION

In the realm of electroacoustic music, the pursuit of historically informed performances has become a compelling discussion for practitioners and researchers [1]. An area of particular interest is how to recreate sonic effects originally produced with obsolete or obsolescent technology. Ring modulation, an important element in the sonic palette of historical electroacoustic compositions, especially in the 60s and 70s, is one such effect.

In this article, we introduce an electronic implementation of analog ring modulation, simple enough that it could be done as a DIY electronics project. Our proposed device relies on analog components to carry out the signal processing. The exception to this analog paradigm lies in the digital control for the sinusoidal carrier, offering a blend of analog audio, and digital precision in the control.

2. A BRIEF EARLY HISTORY OF RING MODULATION

Ring modulation is theoretically very simple: it consists of the multiplication of a signal (typically called a modulator) by another signal, usually a sinusoid (typically called a carrier). Historically, ring modulation was developed at Bell Labs in 1934 (by Frank A. Cowan), initially for telecommunications applications. Its musical potential was explored through early experiments in electronic music, for instance, those led by Louis and Bebe Barron, whose rudimentary circuits were featured in the iconic soundtrack for the film "Forbidden Planet" (1956). Harald Bode further explored the technology in 1961, and it became an integral element of modular synthesizers of the era, including those by Moog, Buchla (prominent in the work of pioneering experimental electroacoustic composers of the 60s and 70s, such as Pauline Oliveros and Suzanne Ciani [2]), and ARP. Éliane Radigue utilized the ARP 2515 containing the 1005 Modamp ring modulator module in her work *Ψ 847* (1973). [1]

Morton Subotnick used ring modulation extensively as well, exploring "ghost electronics" in his work *Until Spring* (1976) wherein "recorded control voltages are patched to synthesizer components – envelope and frequency followers, then ring modulators, frequency shifters, voltage controlled amplifiers (VCA's)–which use the information to process signals from oscillators, noise generators and so forth" [3]. Additionally, David Behrman demonstrated the use of the ring modulator as a musical instrument in *Players with Circuits* (1966) [4].

The most celebrated use of ring modulation in historical electroacoustic music may be found, perhaps, in the œuvre of Karlheinz Stockhausen, in works such as *Kontakte* (1958-1960), *Mixtur* (1964), *Telemusik* (1966), *Mantra* (1970), as well as other early and later pieces.

3. RING MODULATION IN THE PERFORMANCE TRADITION OF KARLHEINZ STOCKHAUSEN'S *MANTRA*

The rich performance tradition of *Mantra*, with at least eight commercial recordings since its premiere (the most

[1] https://amsynths.co.uk/home/my-synths/2500-rack/elaine-radique-arp-2515/

recent, released in 2021), has been widely documented and discussed in the literature. To the best of our knowledge, even though the high-level components and the interface of the MODUL 69 B (the device Stockhausen commissioned for the premiere of this work [5]) have been described in print [6] [7], the actual electronic circuitry has not been publicly documented to date. Similarly, very scant information about technical details can be inferred from the diagram of MODUL 69 A [8], another electronic device custom built for Stockhausen, which also did include a ring modulator.

The old MODUL 69 B devices being no longer serviceable, a wide spectrum of implementations, from fully digital ones to others that attempt to preserve the analog technology of the premiere, have been utilized in performance, and discussed in print. Moreover, the relative merits of different approaches, and their relationship to historical performance practice, have been addressed in the preface of the score, in dedicated academic articles, such as [9] and [7], as well as other outlets.

In 2008, Pestova, Marshall, and Sudol [9] examined the sustainability of the work, exploring several possibilities (from analog to digital), in terms of sonic quality, authenticity, sustainability, cost-effectiveness, ease of transportation and set-up, claiming that the portability of *Mantra* to the digital domain, "offers the best solution for preserving this important piece for future generations". Furthermore, the authors asserted that performing the ring modulation digitally offers "better sound quality" than an analog rendition of the effect.

Of course, all of this is open to debate. Admittedly, Stockhausen himself wavered between an adamant defense of using historical devices and the pragmatic solutions offered by updating audio technology (see, for example, the sources cited in [9]). However, Bryan Wolf, one of Stockhausen's assistants, stated in the 2012 edition of the score [5] that "the sound quality of the analog [ring] modulators is not easily dismissed. The very precise and somewhat frigid tone of digital modulation cannot be compared to the warm, organic, animated, and highly detailed tone produced by the analog ring-modulators." It is not likely that the digital/analog debate will be settled (or go away) any time soon.

Moreover, the digital solution proposed by Pestova et al., presupposes the existence of analog modulators with which performers can experiment, as they suggest "working with analog equipment that resembles the original as closely as possible and comparing the 'feel' and sound with the digital version". As for "the cost-effectiveness and ease of portability and set-up," the solution presented in this paper for carrying out ring modulation in the analog domain represents a first step towards building a DIY, cost-effective, stand-alone, portable analog modulator for the performance of *Mantra* (among other capabilities), offering an alternative to the common digitalization of historical pieces of electroacoustic music, and without the need for third-party equipment (as, for instance, the modular set-up proposed by Bryan Wolf in the preface to the score [5]).

4. COMMON TECHNICAL APPROACHES

Multiplying two signals in the analog domain is not as trivial as in the digital domain, and it can be achieved by various methods and approaches (the most common are based on transformers, op-amps, and transistors, along with diodes, and sometimes hyperbolic approximations). We will describe these methods and discuss their applicability to the ring modulation of analog audio signals. As we shall see, all of these common methods have evident drawbacks.

4.1 Transformers - diodes

One method of analog signal multiplication involves the use of transformers, which are passive devices that can be employed to modulate one signal by another. Passing one of the signals through a primary winding, and the other through a secondary winding, the interaction of magnetic fields induces a multiplication-like effect. The resulting signal carries the product of the two inputs. However, this method entails practical limitations (such as saturation effects and non-linearity in transformer cores). This approach is the one used in the lattice version of the Mumma-Tudor famous ring modulator [10, 261] and it is also the one described in [11].

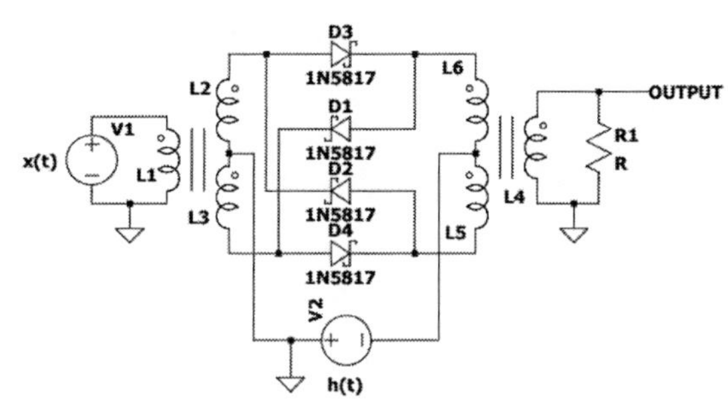

Figure 1. Typical design of a ring modulator using transformers and diodes.

In Figure 1, an example schematic diagram of a generic configuration of a ring modulator is depicted. A function $x(t)$ is applied at the input of the transformer, while a signal $h(t)$, of higher frequency and amplitude than $x(t)$, is applied at the intermediate terminals of each transformer. The secondary winding of each transformer is connected through diodes, which act as switches to allow current flow depending on the polarity of the voltages of the signals $x(t)$ and $h(t)$. The signal $x(t)$ can control the modulation amplitude. For instance, if, at a given instant, the amplitude of $x(t)$ is 0, regardless of whether $h(t)$ is positive or negative, two currents of equal magnitude will reach the secondary of the right transformer, resulting in zero magnetic flux. Therefore the output voltage of the modulator is 0. In the case where $x(t)$ is non-zero, the resulting polarity will be determined by the polarity of the signal $h(t)$, and in consequence, it will only be affected in terms of amplitude by $x(t)$.

From the schematic diagram presented in Figure 1, a basic simulation of this circuit was carried out using Analog

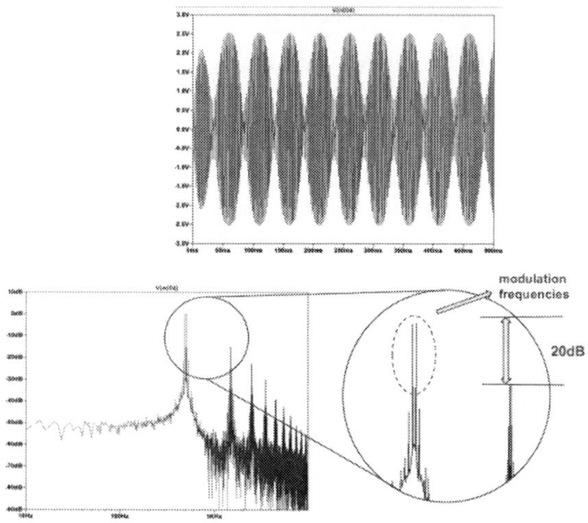

Figure 2. Time and frequency domain response using a circuit based on transformers and diodes.

Devices' LTspice software. The results are shown in Figure 2, which illustrate the outcome of applying a 10 Hz signal to the ring modulator along with a 500 Hz signal. The top of the graph displays the simulation results in the time domain for 500 ms. The lower image shows the FFT obtained using a rectangular window, revealing typical frequencies of ring modulation. However, the FFT exhibits distortion in the desired frequencies, accompanied by a series of harmonics. Given that the amplitude of these harmonics is significant and may be audible, as they are only 20 dB lower in magnitude, we discarded this solution, intending to enhance the gap between the signal's harmonics and the modulation frequencies.

4.2 Approximations using Op-amps - Diodes

Op-amps and diode-based circuits can also be employed for analog signal multiplication. Non-linear characteristics of diodes can be exploited to generate the product of two signals. For instance, a circuit using diodes in a ring modulator configuration can achieve signal multiplication. The diodes create non-linearities in the signal paths, allowing for the extraction of both sum and difference frequencies, with the latter being the desired product of the two input signals. However, careful circuit design is necessary to mitigate unwanted distortion and harmonics.

To simulate the signal operations performed by transformers, operational amplifiers can be used. Therefore, this version of the circuit replaces the transformers with the use of op-amps, while maintaining the diode arrangement of the previous circuit described in Figure 1.

Figure 3 shows an implementation of this circuit carried out in LTspice for testing and simulations, based on a proposal by Sebastian Azevedo. [2] He describes a circuit based on the use of operational amplifiers and the same arrangement of diodes as in the previous case.

According to Azevedo, the operation performed by the diodes precisely corresponds to squaring two inputs, V_1 and

[2] `https://www.edn.com/easy-four-quadrant-multiplier-using-a-quad-op-amp/`

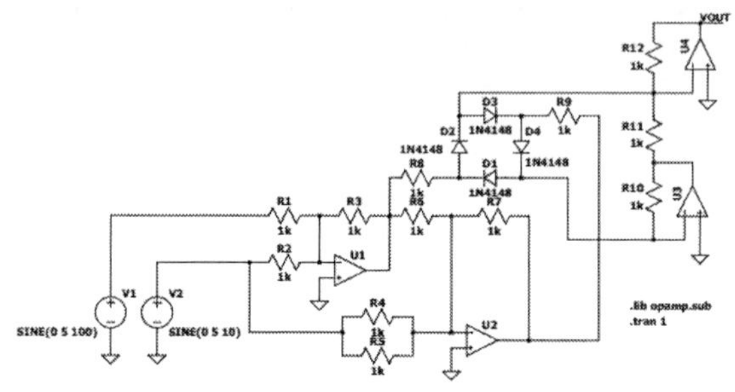

Figure 3. Four-quadrant multiplier simulated in LTspice with op-amps and diodes. Based on `https://www.edn.com/easy-four-quadrant-multiplier-using-a-quad-op-amp/`.

V_2. However, it is possible to achieve analog multiplication if both signals, V_1 and V_2, are combined into two signals $V_1 + V_2$ and $-V_1 + V_2$, respectively. These signals can be squared, generating a sum of squares, which ultimately results in $4V_1V_2$ at the output. Therefore, this circuit greatly simplifies the errors and problems that may arise from using transformers, since it only involves combining the signals V_1 and V_2, and the two signals explained above. This is easily achievable with the use of op-amps configured as inverting summing amplifiers.

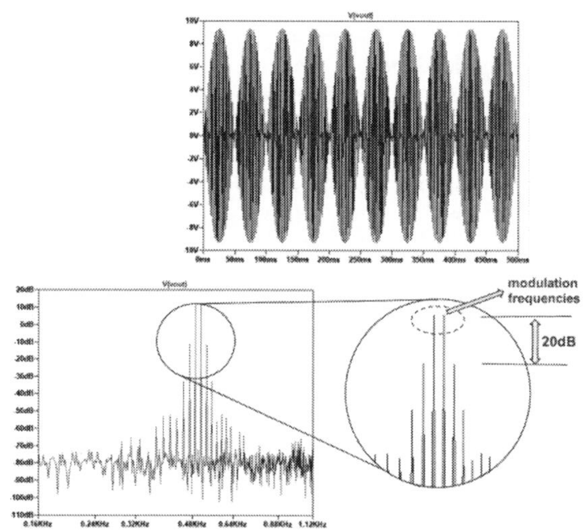

Figure 4. Time and frequency domain response for the circuit with diodes and op-amps.

In Figure 4, we can observe the result of running the simulation conducted in LTspice for the circuit in Figure 3. The top section of the image depicts the modulation result in the time domain for two sinusoids of 10 Hz and another of 500 Hz, respectively, throughout 500 ms. The lower section of the graph shows the FFT of this simulation, displaying the fundamental frequencies corresponding to the modulation. However, it is evident that many harmonics of these signals still exist, with a difference in amplitude of only 20 dB, as was the case with the transformer-based approach. This is still not sufficient to meet our desired expectations. However, one advantage of the diode-based circuit is that its implementation is straightforward and can

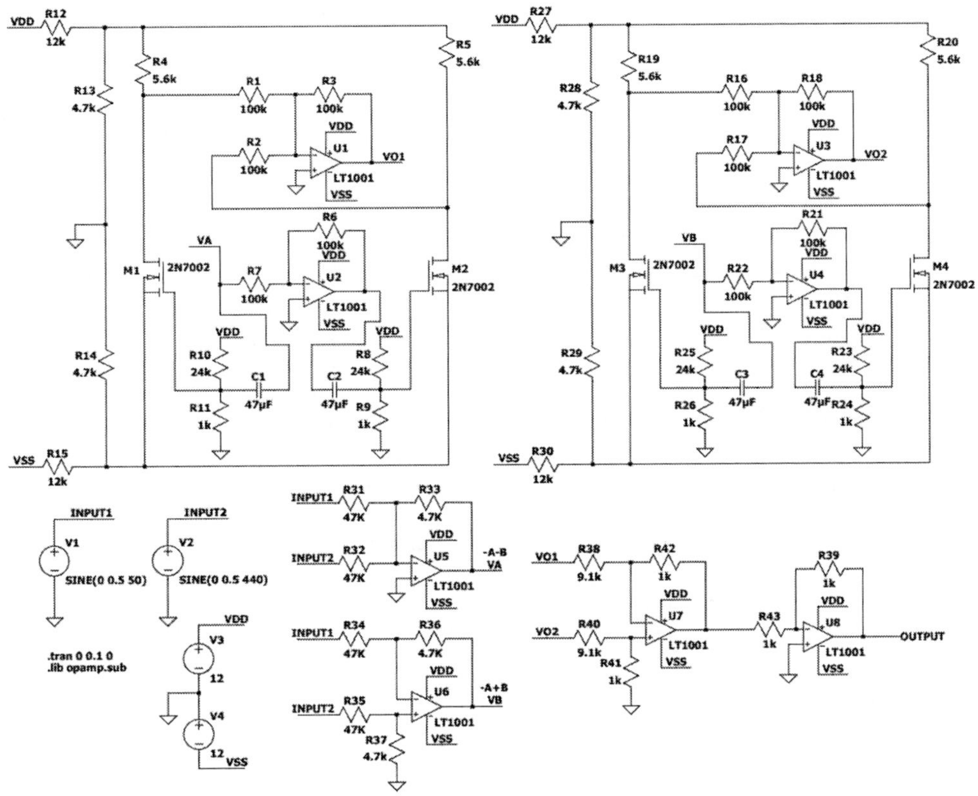

Figure 5. Schematics of the modulator using opamps and transistors simulated in LTspice with the corresponding adaptations. Based on [12].

be easily integrated into a PCB (printed circuit board), in comparison to the previously discussed transformers and diodes-based solution.

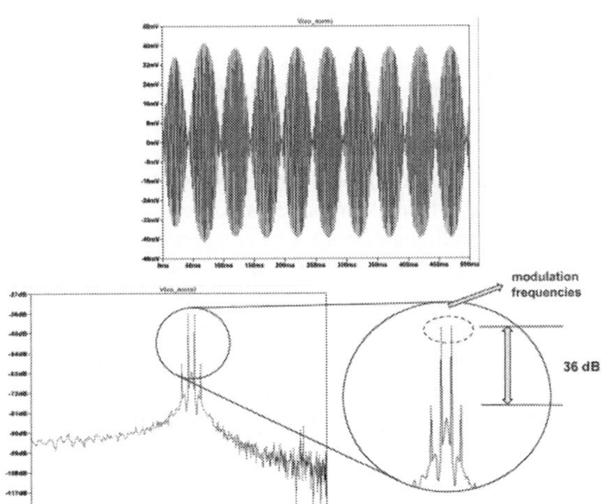

Figure 6. Time and frequency domain response for a circuit designed based on the use of MOSFET transistors.

4.3 Approximations using transistors

Mathematical approximations provide a foundation for analog multiplication. A circuit using NMOS or PMOS transistors [3] can be configured to approximate quadratic functions that can be used to create analog multipliers. For instance, a four-quadrant multiplier circuit can be implemented using differential pairs of transistors and op-amps to produce an output proportional to the product of the input signals. Fine-tuning is required to ensure accurate multiplication and to manage non-linearities inherent in the circuit.

Each of these methods has its advantages and challenges. The choice depends on factors such as the desired level of accuracy, the frequency range of the signals, and the available components. Additionally, the careful consideration of potential distortions and unwanted harmonics is crucial in designing effective analog signal multiplication circuits.

After studying several existing circuits that use the same principle of sum of squares, we studied a particular one designed by Abdul Kareem and Rusul Salah [12]. They implemented a design that first transforms the signals using the same arrangement of operational amplifiers to express them as sums of squares, and then, perform the mul-

[3] NMOS and PMOS transistors are types of field-effect transistors (FETs) where NMOS conducts when a positive voltage is applied to the gate, while PMOS conducts when a negative voltage is applied.

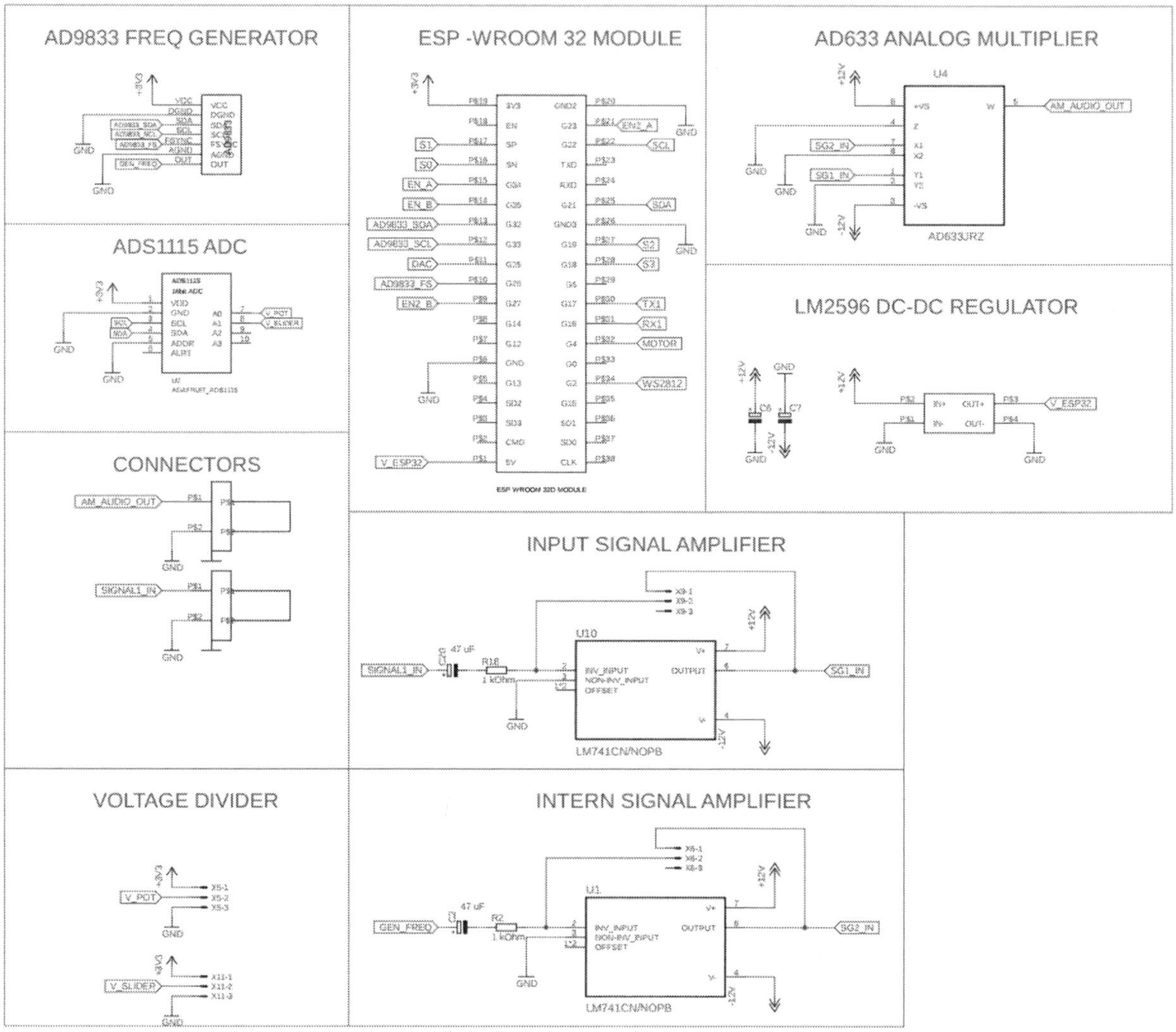

Figure 7. Schematics of our complete implementation made in Autodesk EAGLE, available at our GitHub repository: `https://github.com/rodrigocadiz/analog_ring_mod`

tiplication by activating MOSFETs.[4] The authors present a circuit using ideal transistors. However, in this case, modifications were made to the design to improve and consider the non-idealities of the transistor. For this purpose, a simulation was conducted in LTspice, as shown in Figure 5.

In this case, 2N7000 MOSFETs were used, and stages for coupling and decoupling DC voltages were added to provide the necessary threshold voltages to each of the transistors so that they operated in the active region. After implementing these improvements and changes to the circuit presented in [12], the results shown in Figure 6 were obtained.

It can be observed that when multiplying two sinusoidal signals using this approach, significant unwanted harmonic signals are produced, whose difference from the desired modulation frequencies reaches up to 36 dB. This provides an attenuation of approximately 100 times greater than the harmonics in comparison to the case of using diodes. However, one of the problems with this type of circuit is that it uses many electronic components, including high-precision resistors, making its manufacturing complex. Additionally, due to the high internal gain stages, this circuit type is very sensitive to external noise. Therefore, the optimal implementation solution for this type of circuit would be to design and build an integrated circuit (IC), as a PCB implementation would be complicated. This is, of course, expensive and requires advanced knowledge of electronic design, rendering it an impractical solution for DIY implementations.

5. OUR IMPLEMENTATION

For optimal audio quality, our goal was to attenuate any extra harmonics or noise at least 40 dB with respect to the de-

[4] MOSFETs (Metal-Oxide-Semiconductor Field-Effect Transistors) are semiconductor devices used for amplifying or switching electronic signals by controlling the flow of current between the source and drain terminals via a voltage applied to the gate terminal.

sired frequencies (to ensure that unwanted harmonics will not be perceptible). It became necessary, therefore, to use a circuit based on hyperbolic approximations. However, due to the complexity of developing an IC solely for a DIY prototype, a search was conducted for existing ICs that employed this type of approximation. We found that the chip AD633 IC from Analog Devices [5] fitted the bill.

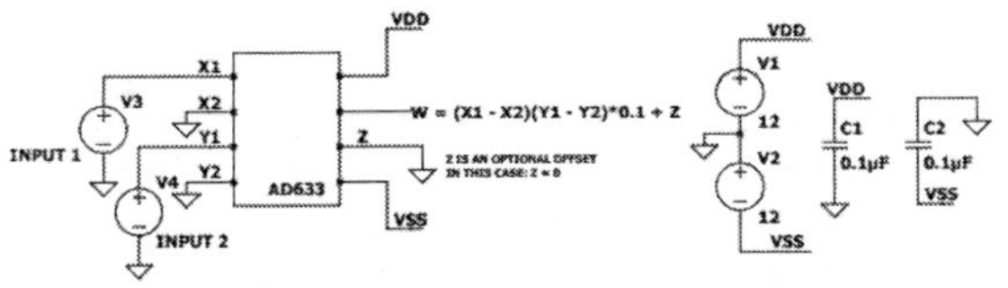

Figure 8. Schematics of our modulator using the AD633 analog multiplier simulated in LTspice, available at our GitHub repository: `https://github.com/rodrigocadiz/analog_ring_mod`

Based on the official model of the AD633 integrated circuit provided by Analog Devices for LTspice software, simulations were conducted for two sinusoidal inputs of 10 Hz and 500 Hz respectively. Figure 9 shows the modulation results using the AD633 integrated circuit. The response in the time domain for 500 ms is observed in the top image. In the bottom section of the figure, the FFT of this simulation is depicted. It clearly shows an attenuation of more than 40 dB between the modulation signals and any unwanted harmonics or noise. Therefore, we concluded that this circuit is more than suitable for the proposed design requirements.

After conducting the necessary research and simulations, the physical implementation of the ring modulator was carried out using the IC AD633, based on the schematics depicted in Figure 7 available at our GitHub repository. [6] For this purpose, a PCB was developed to pre-amplify an audio input signal before feeding it into the AD633. The other input signal is generated locally using an ESP32 microcontroller in conjunction with an AD9833 DAC. We chose the ESP32 for our solution because the project's requirements include handling data reading through an external ADC, a function generator, real-time data mapping, and a graphical interface. These needs are met by a microcontroller with an internal DAC, support for SPI and I2C protocols, a sufficient number of GPIOs for encoders and actuators, an internal voltage regulator, and enough processing power to manage all these tasks in real-time. The ESP32, with its 240MHz dual-core processor, integrated support for all necessary protocols, and cost-effectiveness, makes it the ideal choice for our project.

In Figure 7, a comprehensive block schematic of the implemented solution is depicted, also available at our repository. The usage of the ESP32 microcontroller, in conjunction with the DAC and frequency generator AD9833, act as the local signal generator. In the central section of the figure, there is an audio input that is conditioned before being fed into the AD633 multiplier. This signal corresponds to the sound before modulation. Finally, the modulated audio

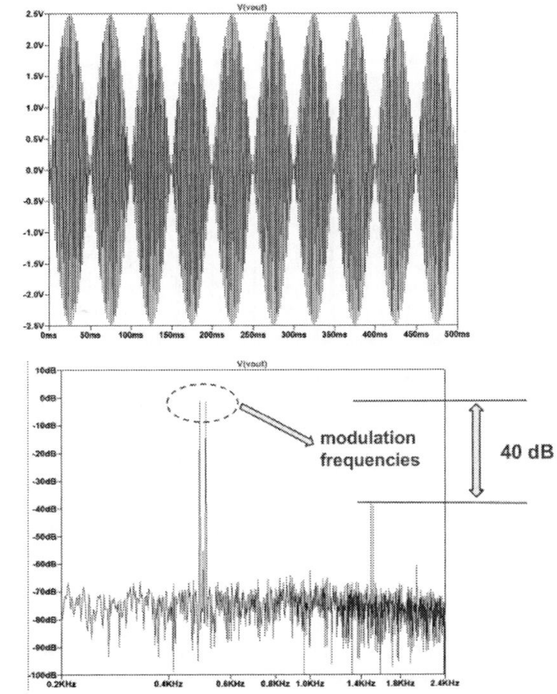

Figure 9. Time and frequency domain response using a circuit based on the AD633.

is conditioned and exits the circuit to be input into a mixer, and subsequently into an audio amplifier.

This implementation of the ring modulation produces a very clear output (as it eliminates unwanted hiss, parasite frequencies, and distortions), and approaches remarkably well the ideal mathematical operation, as it can be observed in a Tektronix TDS 1002B oscilloscope as displayed in Figure 10.

Arguably, the use of a higher precision IC, designed and first produced in the late 1980s (as opposed to lower-performance, earlier ICs), might be considered anachronistic if one wants to apply it to the realization of prior electroacoustic works. Indeed, a case could be put forward that by seeking to minimize to the utmost the imperfections present in the electronic components, part of the distinctive sound of the earlier decades is being removed. To use the colorful turn of phrase that Stockhausen himself used in a 1991 lecture on electroacoustic performance practice, the characteristic sound of the earlier devices, might "go to hell" [13] if they are replaced with later technology. On the other hand, the decision to handle the control of the carrier frequency digitally (in our case, by means of the ESP32 microcontroller), which affords incomparably greater precision and flexibility, is, to be sure, wholly uncontroversial even among analog hard-liners, as the carrier generator, and thus the whole signal processing chain, remains in the analog domain.

Of course, the application of this device (or any other technology, for that matter) in the context of recreating musical works with a historic approach poses many challenges that must be resolved on a case-by-case basis. This process often involves arriving at compromise solutions (sub-

[5] `https://www.analog.com/media/en/technical-documentation/data-sheets/AD633.pdf`

[6] `https://github.com/rodrigocadiz/analog_ring_mod`

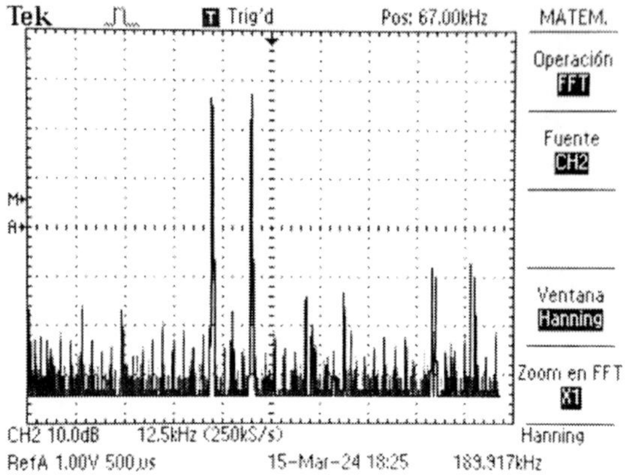

Figure 10. Frequency domain response of a PCB implementation of our solution based on the AD633 measured with a Tektronix TDS 1002B oscilloscope. Each box on the vertical axis represents a difference of 10 dB. On the horizontal axis, each box represents a difference of 12.5 kHz. The sampling frequency is 250 kS/s.

stituting modern equipment for defunct ones may be one such compromise), because in the context of historically informed performance, "there is a significant gap between the ideal and the possible; we must temper what may be historically desirable by what is practically and aesthetically reasonable" [14]. The dialectic between the ideal and the possible can be seen, for example, in Sean Williams' fascinating and detailed discussion about the recreation of Stockhausen's work, *Studie II* [1].

It is beyond the scope of this article to delve into the specifics of how a modulator (such as ours) should be tailored and refined for performance, let alone a historically informed performance, of *Mantra* (or any other specific electroacoustic work). Suffice it to say, that this particular implementation of ring modulation may be considered an alternative whenever the preservation of analog audio is required. The combination of analog equipment (including modern, accurate, and reliable electronic ICs), along with precise digital controllers, may offer a viable middle ground between the historicity of analog audio and the preference for high-quality audio and control.

6. SOUND AND VIDEO EXAMPLES

To demonstrate the actual status and capabilities of our approach to analog ring modulation based on the AD633 IC chip, we provide two video examples of its practical application, available as additional materials at our GitHub repository: `https://github.com/rodrigocadiz/analog_ring_mod`.

The contents of the videos are the following:

- Video 1: Extract of the beginning of *Mantra* (1970), by Karlheinz Stockhausen (piano I, bars 1 - 10). The modulating frequency is set to 220 Hz.

- Video 2: Short demonstration of a prototype analog ring modulator. The knob being manipulated is, in fact, connected to a digital control (ESP32 microcontroller) that sets the modulating carrier frequency. The incoming microphone signal modulator, the sinusoidal carrier generator, and the processing itself (the signal multiplication) are all conducted in the analog domain, recreating the audio technology used in premieres of historical works such as *Mantra*.

7. CONCLUSIONS

After examining several implementations of analog ring modulation (using transformers, op-amps, and diodes), we selected a circuit based on hyperbolic approximations utilizing the component chip AD633 from Analog Devices, to achieve our desired signal multiplication requirements with minimal distortion. Our physical implementation, integrating the AD633 with pre-amplification circuitry and digital signal generation, offers a practical solution for researchers, musicians, and technicians who wish to pursue DIY analog set-ups for the performance of historical electroacoustic works.

Acknowledgments

The authors would like to thank Stockahusen Stiftung für Musik for their support; María Julia Mancero for her participation as a piano performer in the videos; and the anonymous reviewers for their insightful comments and suggestions. This project was funded by the Office for the Arts and Culture of the Vice Presidency for Research, Pontificia Universidad Católica de Chile (ArTeCiH grant) and by ANID/Fondecyt 1230926 and ANID/Anillo ATE220041.

8. REFERENCES

[1] S. Williams, "Interpretation and performance practice in realising Stockhausen's Studie II," 2015. [Online]. Available: https://api.semanticscholar.org/CorpusID:84181511

[2] T. Pinch and F. Trocco, *Analog Days: The Invention and Impact of the Moog Synthesizer*. Harvard University Press, 2002.

[3] H. W. Whipple, "Beasts and Butterflies: Morton Subotnick's Ghost Scores," *The Musical Quarterly*, vol. 69, no. 3, pp. 425–441, 1983.

[4] A. Strange, "Electronic music: systems, techniques, and controls," J. Nolan, Ed. Responsive Ecologies Lab, 2022.

[5] K. Stockhausen, "MANTRA für 2 Pianisten, Werk Nr. 32 (score)," Kürten: Stockhausen-Verlag, 2012.

[6] H. P. Haller, *Das Experimentalstudio der Heinrich-Strobel-Stiftung des Südwestfunks Freiburg 1971-1989: die Erforschung der elektronischen Klangumformung und ihre Geschichte*. Nomos Verlagsgesellschaft, 1995, vol. 2.

[7] M.-L. Hundelshausen, "Mantra auf der Bühne: Zwei Aufführungsfassungen der Komposition Karlheinz Stockhausens im analytischen Vergleich," *Rundfunk und Geschichte*, vol. 46, pp. 76–84, 2020. [Online]. Available: http://dx.doi.org/10.25969/mediarep/18864

[8] K. Stockhausen, *Texte zur Musik 1970–1977*. Stockhausen Verlag, 1998.

[9] X. Pestova, M. T. Marshall, and J. Sudol, "Analogue to digital: Authenticiy vs. sustainability in Stockhausen's Mantra (1970)," *Proceedings of the 2008 International Computer Music Conference*, 2008.

[10] M. Johnsen and Y. Nakai, "The Mumma-Tudor ring modulator," in *Handmade Electronic Music*, N. Collins, Ed. Routledge, 2020, pp. 259–265.

[11] J. Parker, "A simple digital model of the diode-based ring-modulator," in *Proc. Int. Conf. Digital Audio Effects (DAFx-11), Paris, France*, vol. 14, 2011, pp. 163–166.

[12] R. S. Khadair *et al.*, "Design of a high linearity four-quadrant analog multiplier in wideband frequency range," *Journal of University of Babylon*, vol. 25, no. 2, 2017.

[13] K. Stockhausen and J. Kohl, "Electroacoustic performance practice," *Perspectives of New Music*, vol. 34, no. 1, pp. 74–105, 1996. [Online]. Available: http://www.jstor.org/stable/833486

[14] P. H. Lang, *Musicology and Performance*. Yale University Press, 1997.

MOBILE LOUDSPEAKERS AS AN ALTER EGO

Peter Faerber
ICST
peter.faerber@zhdk.ch

Junghae Lee
Homo Ludens / ICST
junghael@gmail.com

Giorgio Tedde
Homo Ludens / ICST
giorgio@tedde.net

ABSTRACT

In electronic music, sound, space, spatial sound, and sound movement are pivotal. Our research aims to enriche sound distribution by developing a system that generates sound movements through effective movement of the sound source. This required collaboration across technicians, mechanics, engineers, programmers, and composers. The outcome is a system allowing mobile loudspeakers during chamber music concerts, expanding sound into new acoustic realms and creating variable sound spaces. This greatly enhances the listening experience, freeing listeners from fixed positions. The interaction of the mobile speaker system with music creates a dynamic theatrical and choreographic interplay, with speakers acting as musical alter egos.

1. INTRODUCTION

1.1 Foreword

Artistic music research aims to enhance the auditory and performative aspect of the performer-audience relationship. One way to achieve this is by creating music where sound, typically from fixed sources with simulated movements, is perceived as physically moving due to real motion. Over the past decades, several sound systems have been devised to simulate sound movement virtually. Additionally, some systems have used moving sound sources, originally designed for non-musical artistic performances, to physically create sound motion (refer to Chapter 2: State of the Art).

1.2 Goals

Our main research goal is to create a sound system where speakers move as sound sources within chamber music, expanding music's interaction with the audience. This development, undertaken at the *Institute for Computer Music and Sound Technology* in Zurich (ZHdK) during 2021/22, has broad implications for multiple research areas. Key questions arising from this project include:

What's the link between real-space sound movements and the perception of motion from virtual sounds produced by stationary speakers? How do moving speakers interact with motionless acoustic instruments? What are the listener's responses to sounds moving in space compared to simulations from stationary sources? How does our perception of music change when familiar static sound sources begin moving?

1.3 Concrete object of the research

The mobile sound system's development was inspired by the *Heldendämmerung* concert project, featuring a piano trio, quadraphonic system, and three mobile speakers.

These speakers can move among the audience using radio-controlled vehicles and perform other *local* movements on the vehicle: rotation, combined two-axis polar motion, or elevation (refer to Figure 1). The team included two composers who contributed to the technology and engineering aspects of the research for musical applications.

1.4 Motivation and new domains

The technical advancements stemmed from the requirements of music production and were refined through multiple perceptual experiential workshops, uncovering both challenges and potentials. The impactful presence of mobile speakers not only expanded the auditory dimension but also introduced a concurrent theatrical and choreographic element. These mobile entities assumed a mediating role, akin to personalities, between musicians and the audience. The quest to enrich these novel dimensions of music reception spurred further technical innovations aimed at enhancing perceptual, musical, and theatrical values. The objective was to ensure that the technology seamlessly addressed these diverse aspects, guaranteeing reliable and silent vehicle movement while delivering high-quality, immersive sound to enhance the experience of sound source movement.

1.5 Why all this?

Composition: Develop a system for composers to enhance music and performance across mono, stereo, or quadra-surround (virtual) setups, integrating real acoustic instrument sounds with dynamic moving sound sources.

Perception: Deepen understanding of mobile sound source perception, enriching music recognition and experience in novel contexts while offering composers new creative avenues.

Education: Train a new generation of artists through study and research opportunities, including doctoral positions for composers, choreographers, and others.

Production and Research: Address critical issues in mobile sound source systems to support research and production centers in creating and advancing similar systems. Document the technology and its perceptual implications to encourage wider use and garner improvements from external users.

2. STATE OF THE ART

2.1 Moving speakers as effect devices (1940-1960)

Spatial sound and sound movements are crucial in acousmatic and electronic music creation and perception. In the 1950s, Pierre Schaeffer and Jacques Poullin introduced the *pupitre d'espace*, enabling sound distribution across four speakers via gestures during playback of recordings [1, 2].

Karlheinz Stockhausen introduced space as the fifth parameter (sound location) in music [3], allowing precise positioning and movement of sonic events in serial music. In the past, limited studio technology and lack of effect devices meant that rapid or fluid sound movements and the Doppler effect were achieved only by physically moving speakers. For instance, Stockhausen utilized three rotating tables in works like *Kontakte* (1959), *Hymnen* (1967), and *Sirius* (1975), exploring non-musical effects such as motor hum, brake squeaks, and wind noises [4].

2.2 Moving speakers as a design tool (from 1960)

Since the 1960s, speakers have been moved not just due to the absence of effect devices but driven by artistic considerations. This shift occurred because the artistic simulation of a moving sound source became possible and could not be adequately substituted. The moving speaker has become a fundamental element in both visual and musical design, transforming from an invisible playback device to the focal point of spatial sonic presentations, essentially becoming an instrument or sonic personality.

An early example of mobile speakers is found in David Tudor's *Bandoneon! (a combine)* (1966), where his *Instrumental Loudspeakers* [5] move on five remote-controlled platforms [6, 7, 8]. Christian Clozier and Jean-Claude le Duc developed *Les Antonymes* from 1974 onwards, mobile sound and image structures acting as a counterpoint to the fixed speakers of the *Gmebaphone* [9]. Alvin Lucier, in *Words on windy corner* (1980), shifts speakers on carts, altering the spatial relationship between microphones and speakers [10].

Echo Moiré (2011) by Matteo Marangoni resembles our project [11]: Two wheeled horn speakers enact a *robotic opera-ballet*. The space functions as a musical instrument, with bursts and clicks emanating from the speakers, revealing and amplifying the acoustic properties of the surroundings.

3. OUR MOBILE SPEAKERS

Three mobile speakers are utilized in the *Heldendämmerung* concert. They comprise a **mobile platform** with an attached **loudspeaker**. The platform, serving as a subwoofer, remains consistent across all three models, whereas the speakers vary in their movement capabilities.

3.1 Mobile platforms - spatial movement

The carriage is powered by two unsteered stepper motors, with the third wheel being an omnidirectional wheel that stabilizes the vehicle. Small rollers on the running surface enable movement in all directions by turning at right angles. Differential speeds of the two drive wheels dictate the direction of travel. Control is achieved via a steering wheel and two pedals for forward and backward motion. These vehicles are utilized to position and maneuver the speakers within the space.

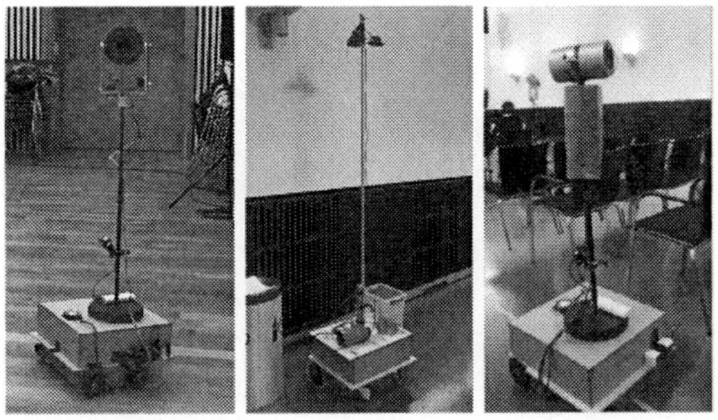

Figure 1. The names of the speakers are derived from its movement. Left: *Angela* from tilt and pan (aggregat). Center: *Eliane* from elevation movement. Right: *Roger* from rotation.

3.2 Loudspeaker - local movement

To direct sound precisely, the speakers on the platforms are movable, known as *local movement*. The first platform features a rotating directional loudspeaker that emits sound in a specific direction, offering infinite rotation in both directions or precise alignment (refer to Figure 1: *Roger*). The second platform includes a speaker that swivels and tilts horizontally and vertically by 340 degrees using two servomotors (refer to Figure 1: *Angela*). The third platform has a bar with three small speakers that can be raised and lowered (refer to Figure 1: *Eliane*).

3.3 Control and audio transmission

The vehicles are remotely controlled via WLAN, with a designated driver for each vehicle managing *spatial movement*. In contrast, *local movements* of the speakers are controlled by live electronics patches. This approach ensures precise synchronization with the musical content, which is crucial and cannot be achieved manually.

Audio transmission occurs through radio links, with mid and high frequencies emitted via the moving speaker. Low frequencies are directly transmitted to the vehicle's housing, designed as a subwoofer, through a built-in transducer.

3.4 Path finder

The drivers navigate the platforms along predefined routes marked with adhesive tape on the venue floor (refer to Figure 2a). A camera on the speaker pole allows the driver to maintain control of the vehicle and its path, even if direct visibility is lost (refer to Figure 2b). This camera wirelessly transmits a live view of the vehicle and the immediate area in front of it to the driver, enabling them to follow the adhesive strips accurately.

4. OUTCOME (RESULTS)

An important result was the enhancement of physiological values of sound perception and thus induced musical values. This fact also makes these values accessible to a larger spectrum of users (independent of cultural background).

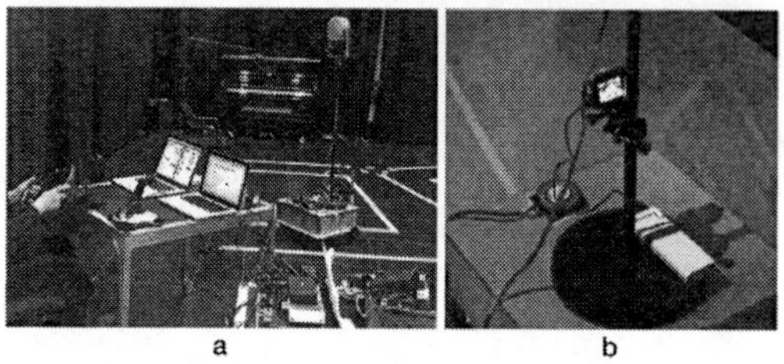

Figure 2. a) Driving lanes are indicated in white. b) Camera.

The results of the project are then shown below sorted into the different sectors involved.

4.1 Sound system with mobile sound sources

An audio diffusion system was developed for a chamber music ensemble with live electronics, optimizing interaction across three acoustic propagation levels: musicians with acoustic instruments (Absolut Trio: violin, Bettina Boller; cello, Judith Gerster; piano, Stefka Perifanova); amplified audio and live electronics on a quadraphonic system; and amplified audio and live electronics on a mobile speaker system (three radio-controlled vehicles capable of local sound source movement).

The *Heldendämmerung* project, featuring compositions tailored for this system, has been performed four times. A key musical objective is crafting vibrant sound spaces and corresponding virtual scenarios, resulting in dynamic and ever-changing soundscapes. These endeavors occasionally transform temporal and spatial perception into an ethereal, timeless ambience, achieved through the floating recognition and localization of individual sound elements (e.g., slow motion and spatial ambiguity).

Monitoring audience perceptions has provided valuable insights into perceptual values. This expanded understanding of the physiological aspects of music perception offers composers fresh avenues and enhanced interactions with audiences when conceptualizing and composing music.

4.2 Hall setting up

To enhance the expressive capabilities and functionality of the mobile speaker system, a hall setup model was devised to delineate movements within the space: audience islands, vehicle pathways between islands, and crossing points (see Figure 3a).

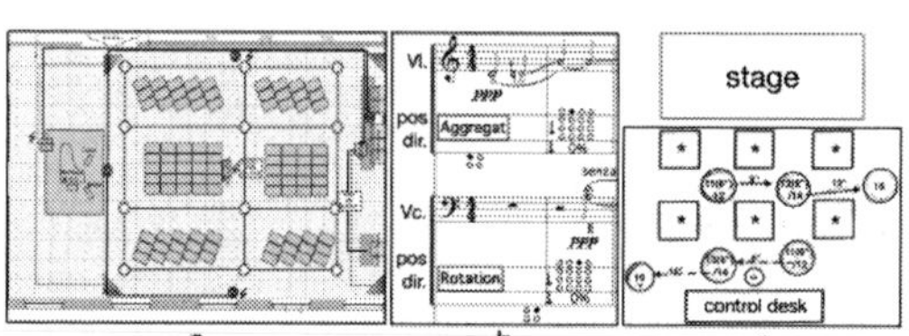

Figure 3. a) Setting concert hall. b) score instruments. c) vehicle movements. (* = audience island)

4.3 Notation

The movement of the vehicles were notated in the score as well as in a diagram (see Figure 3b) or also as verbal description. For both case there was a seperate driving score specifically detailing vehicle movements, aimed at drivers (see Figure 3c).

Additionally, we integrated instructions for local movements executed through live electronic commands (Max) transmitted via WLAN.

4.4 System constraints and possible solutions

From concerts and workshops, we learned about constraints and potential solutions for system improvement:

The system faced physical limitations such as speed, stability, noise, accuracy, and safety concerns in moving within the audience. The solution involved enhancing mechatronic engineering, motion control, and programming systems.

Each audience position required a tailored listening experience. This was addressed by ensuring a uniform distribution of spatial motion effects in composition.

Managing spatial movements in the hall necessitated multiple vehicle drivers, each responsible for a specific area. This challenge was tackled by implementing automatic lane following, executing driving commands, avoiding collisions through autonomous systems (AI), and using RFID chip bands on lanes for position detection.

5. VISITOR SURVEY

Among the 114 concert visitors during four concerts, 61 completed and returned the questionnaire.

5.1 Variable sound spaces

Loudspeakers combine to form a sound space over an area. With moving sound sources, this space can vary as speakers on vehicles shift in the hall, altering the space between them. Three speakers can ideally create a triangle, but when integrated with the quadraphonic system's fixed speakers, the possibilities multiply. The variable sound space is no longer confined to the three mobile speakers' area; it expands through different fixed and mobile speaker combinations.

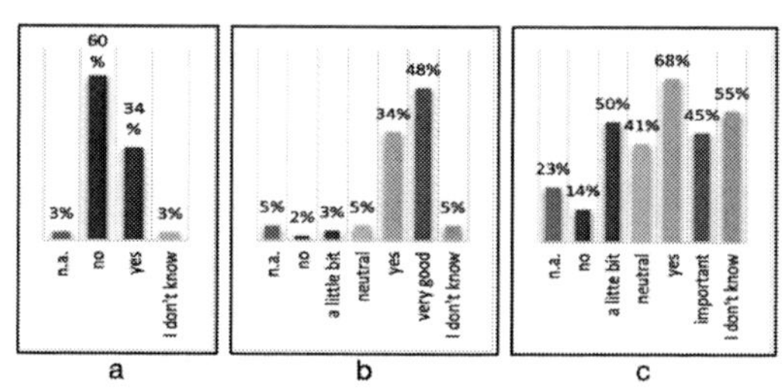

Figure 4. Survey results.

In the survey, 59% of participants responded negatively to the question *Have you ever encountered the term 'variable sound spaces'?* (Figure 4a). However, 82% acknowledged familiarity with the term *variable sound spaces* when asked *Have you perceived 'variable sound spaces'?* (Figure 4b). Just 2% claimed they had not perceived *variable sound spaces*.

It's unclear if respondents understood *variable sound spaces* as defined in the project or if they interpreted other perceived situations as such, potentially explaining the high agreement rate.

5.2 Dependence on the seat

Mobile speakers offer the advantage of localized sound, irrespective of seating position, eliminating the need for a traditional sweet spot. How does this impact the overall listening experience?

On the one hand, the perception of the sound field depends on individual listening habits. People who frequently attend concerts may look for a central location in order to enjoy the best possible sound. However, if the mobile speakers are used and their location changes, this can lead to confusion and give the impression that they are not always in the best position.

Individual's perception of the sound field is influenced by their listening habits. Concertgoers often seek a central spot for optimal sound. Yet, with mobile speakers altering positions, this can cause confusion and the feeling that the speakers aren't always optimally placed.

The responses to the question *Did it matter where you sat?* regarding the perception of mobile speakers fall out accordingly (see Figure 4c).

6. CONCLUSIONS

Overall, the use of mobile speakers presents both pros and cons. Considering individual listening habits and speaker visibility is crucial for an optimal experience. While the mobility of speakers offers a fresh way to perceive sound, it necessitates adjustments to seating choices and can pose challenges for visual immersion.

Unexpectedly prominent in the project was the theatrical and choreographic influence of the mobile speakers. In concerts, they became a visual alter ego of musicians, amplifying or distorting acoustic features akin to a magnifying lens, adding a unique dimension to the performance.

6.1 Insights

This project uncovered numerous new phenomena, particularly intriguing is the mechanics of perception within this audio system, offering composers fresh insights and compositional avenues. It's clear that further exploration is warranted across various domains. Below are the guiding research questions:

What happens when moving speakers become visible during music listening? Can changes in brain activity be detected in the relevant areas? Is there a neurophysiological impact of moving speakers on listening? Are there physiological indicators of acceptance or rejection of moving speakers (akin to food preferences or aversions)? Can we infer ways to design movements that enhance acceptance in cases of rejection? Alternatively, should efforts concentrate on reinforcing existing acceptance? Do cultural influences shape how moving speakers are perceived, directed, or understood? What specific cultural imprints might play a role?

6.2 Impressions

Three composers in this project have stated as below what was very different for them to compose for different kind of *time-space relations* than usual; here the perception is diverse; necessity of sound dramaturgical concept.

6.3 Outlooks

Improving vehicles with mobile speakers involves quieter movement and enhanced sound quality. Extensive studies are needed to understand the perceptual effects of moving sound sources, involving experts from diverse fields. This includes refining existing speakers and incorporating technical advancements such as artificial intelligence for motion control and more mobile speakers for better sound coverage. Additionally, exploring new topics in music perception through psychoacoustic and neuroacoustic research is essential.

7. REFERENCES

[1] P. Schaeffer, *Sept Ans de Musique Concrete, 1948-1955*, Centre d' études radiophoniques, Ed. Paris: Université Paris VII, 1955.

[2] B. Merlier, "Vocabulaire de La Perception de l'espace Dans Les Musiques Électroacoustiques Composées Ou Spatialisées En Pentaphonie," in *L'espace Du Son III*, A. V. Gorne, Ed. Ohain: Lien, 2011, pp. 9–20.

[3] K. Stockhausen, "Musik Im Raum (1958)," in *Texte Zur Elektronischen Und Instrumentalen Musik. Aufsätze 1952-1962 Zur Theorie Des Komponierens*, D. Schnebel and K. Stockhausen, Eds. Köln: DuMond, 1963, vol. 5, pp. 152–175.

[4] C. von Blumenröder, "Zur Bedeutung der Elektronik in Karlheinz Stockhausens Œuvre," *Archiv für Musikwissenschaft*, vol. 75, no. 3, pp. 166–178, 2018.

[5] J. H. Appleton, *The Development and Practice of Electronic Music*. Englewood Cliff: Prentice-Hall, 1975. [Online]. Available: http://archive.org/details/developmentpract0000appl

[6] Y. Nakai, *Reminded by the Instruments: David Tudor's Music*. New York: Oxford University Press, 2021.

[7] J. Driscoll and M. Rogalsky, "David Tudor's "Rainforest": An Evolving Exploration of Resonance," *Leonardo Music Journal*, vol. 14, no. 980039, pp. 25–30, 2004.

[8] J. Martin, Ed., *David Tudor Bandoneon! (A Combine)*, ser. 9 Evenings: Theatre & Engineering. E.A.T and ARTPIX, 2009, vol. 3.

[9] C. Clozier, *Les Antonymes 1974/1995, Robots Audio et Vidéo, Mobiles Téléguidés*, 1995.

[10] A. Lucier, *Reflections : Interviews, Scores, Writings = Reflexionen : Interviews, Notationen, Texte*, ser. Edition MusikTexte 3. Köln: MusikTexte, 1995.

[11] M. Marangoni, "Echo-Moire-page," 2011. [Online]. Available: https://matteomarangoni.com/Echo-Moire-page

Levels of Spectral Diffusion

Julián Ávila
Royal Conservatory of Music of Madrid
julian.avilasausor@rcsmm.es

ABSTRACT

Spectral Diffusion techniques in the context of electroacoustic composition and computer-aided composition explained in this text, can bring a new dimension to the spatial compositional techniques available for immersive musical contexts and spaces surrounded by speakers.

The author proposes a systematisation of Spectral Diffusion methodologies organised into three different levels of complexity, which represent the depth of these techniques and the new compositional concepts and vocabulary emerging from them. This organized system not only enhances our understanding of Spectral Diffusion but also opens new avenues for musical expression in the field of electroacoustic and computer-aided composition.

THE CONCEPT OF SPECTRAL DIFFUSION

Spectral Diffusion (hereinafter SD) is a sound processing technique in which two sub-processes are involved. Firstly, the frequency domain is decomposed into frequency bands. Secondly, these frequency bands are spatialised or located in the performance space. The term *Diffusion* refers to the spatial aspect of this technique. *Spectral* references the fact that the spatialisation is related and linked to the frequency content of a sound.

Spatialisation of sound has been well studied[1]. A considerable number of tools are available to spatialise sound in many different ways using different systems. Similarly, filtering by frequency analysis is a common technique in electroacoustic composition. Although there exists compositional research focusing on the two key individual elements (spatialisation or spectral content), there is less research and compositional outcome focused on how to successfully embrace both.

1.1 Examples of SD in other fields

Although SD might be seen as very specific to sound process, it is present in a number of other fields.

In radio frequency band organisation, country legislation often dictates which bands of radio frequency (in the telecommunications spectra) should be used in media broadcast. Similarly, digital TV channels have a fixed band width and have frequency constraints. Comparably, emergency service telecommunications, Wi-Fi or free spectral bands for wireless audio communications are defined and organised across the radio-frequency spectra.

In nature, as described by Bernie Krause in the book *The Great Animal Orchestra* [1], Krause depicts audio using spectrograms of how natural ecosystems have a particular spectral footprint in which each animal species or living organisms occupy different spectral bands. In this case, a concrete spectral division, as well as a spatial distribution of them, depends on the observed ecosystem. Krause uses this phenomenon to demonstrate how different environments have been damaged over decades, losing their spectral richness.

In the field of biophysics, *Spectral Diffusion* is the term that describes a process for analysing liquids [2] or proteins [3] using Fast Fourier Transform (hereinafter FFT) techniques similar to those used in sound analysis.

Figure 1 shows band divisions and subdivisions in the electromagnetic field (as used in biophysics and radio frequency communication) and sound spectra division created by different instruments.

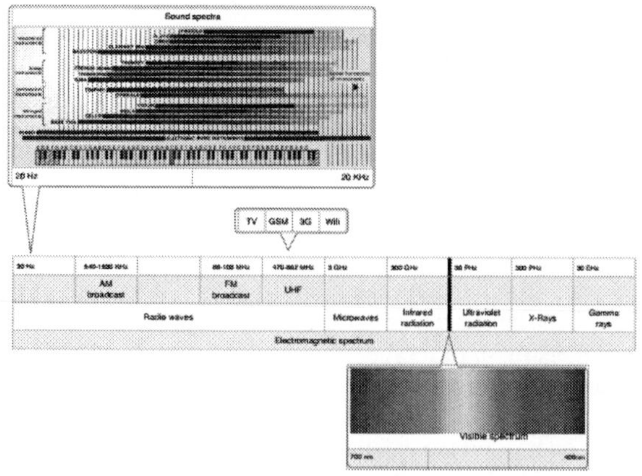

[1] See **Three-level system** (3rd level of SD) in section 3.

Figure 1. Band frequency table in electromagnetic spectrum and sound spectra.

This paper does not directly transfer these examples into the compositional field, however, it is informed by them. In the same manner, related techniques mould the emerging vocabulary from SD.

1.2 Implementations of SD in composition

Digital Signal Processing and FFT analysis as a creative process are found in many electroacoustic music compositions which make use of signal analysis and processing for the transformation of sonic materials. These include convolution, cross-synthesis, vocoders and spectral gates, to mention but a few. They use FFT analysis and resynthesis as a way to transform sound in the frequency domain.

Another example of FFT application in composition is spectralism[2]: frequency analysis and resynthesis via instrumental forces. This school of thought uses FFT sound analysis as a way to identify sonic features to be used as ground material for instrumental resynthesis. These include partial tracking, virtual fundamental, interpolations, modulations, frequency shift, etc.[3]

Although SD is not based on spectralist compositional techniques it does share some of the concepts and methods of spectral analysis and band division. However, it takes it further by linking them to sonic diffusion and spatialisation techniques. It does so by providing each individual band with its own spectral energy, different from the original sound source. As a result, the spectral energy will always be a consequence of band division and will be dependent upon the spectral content of the former sound.

SPECTRAL DIFFUSION UP-TO-DATE

SD techniques are often found as signal audio processes in which FFT analysis and resynthesis are used as the main tool for connecting sound spatialisation and frequency. Since the 1990s, when FFT sound processes became a standard for spectral analysis (and resynthesis), SD has received different names (as listed below), although they describe similar processes. Although there is plenty of musical research and composition based on the use of FFT, as part of the compositional methodology, there is much less investigation which focuses on the connections between sound spectra and spatial diffusion, which go beyond creating an '*interesting musical effect*' [4].

In this section, different points of view related to signal audio processing are outlined, where frequency is linked to spatialisation over the last 30 years.

In 1994 the idea of creating spatialisation linked to frequency arose: *'Frequency Dependent Spatialisation'* [5]. This sound process highlights the possibilities of IRCAM's *Signal Processing Workstation* and the Max programming language. This is in addition to other FFT techniques such as convolution, cross-synthesis or spectral gates. The main idea behind this paper on *'Frequency Dependent Spatialisation'* is that it is possible to change the energy of each bin[4] or FFT band to create a panning image of the sound and to allocate each bin into different positions between two loudspeakers.

A follow up paper explained how to implement this technique in stereo or quadraphonic systems. In this article the idea of spatialising sound linked to frequency is named *'Spectral Spatialisation Technique'* [6]. This explored the possibility of making divisions of 64, 128 or more bands (powers of 2 that matches half of the FFT window size), and their spatialisation in stereo or quadraphonic systems. In addition, a process module is implemented in order to achieve circular distribution of binaries in a quadraphonic system.

In 2004, Keyes explains how to root a stereo signal in a system of 8 loudspeakers using a SD technique called *'Spectral Spatialiser'* and defined as *'frequency-domain filtering to spatialize (one could also use the term 'animate') stereo sources over an even number of playback channels'* [7]. This sound processing proposal could be seen as an extension of the previous proposal but using stereo sound as input source.

The papers reviewed so far handle spatiality between pairs of loudspeakers from the point of view of ILD[5] (Interaural Level Difference). It seems logical that ITD[6] (Interaural Time Difference) could also be used as a system for virtualising sound sources. Nevertheless, the problem with this idea is that the minimum delay of a FFT process is determined by window size. Using the minimum window size obtains a minimum delay of 11 milliseconds approximately, while ITD delays around 0 to 0.6 milliseconds. Kim-Boyle designed a method to work around the problem. His *'Spectral Delay'* is able to create, in the author's own words, *'interesting musical effects'* [4].

Kim-Boyle proposes another implementation for spectral spatialisation based on the spatial principles described by Torchia & Lippe in 2004 [6]. In this case a *boids*[7] algorithm controls the location of the different bands of frequencies. The big difference with this implementation, as well as the previous ones, is that band

[2] Spectralism is a tendency in contemporary art music that takes the material attributes of sound as the point of departure for composition. Originating in France and Romania in the 1970s, partly in reaction to the perceived hegemony of serialism and other high modernist styles, since the 1980s the influence of spectral ideas and techniques has spread across Europe, Asia, and North and South America. Its most prominent representatives are Gérard Grisey (1946–98), Tristan Murail (1947--), and Horatiu Radulescu (1942–2008) [31].

[3] To mention a few spectral techniques [32].

[4] A bin is each FFT band defined by $\text{Number of bands} = \frac{\text{FFT window}_{size}}{2}$; Eg. if 512 samples are defined as a FFT window size, there will be 256 FFT bands or bins.

[5] ILD, interaural level differences that our ears receive when listening a sound and our brain uses for locating a source in space. ILD is recreated in panning systems for sound virtualisation, for example mixers, plugins, etc.

[6] ITD, interaural time difference that our ears receive when listening to a sound and our brain uses for locating a source in space. ITD could be implemented for virtualising sounds in space by delaying one channel between 0 and 0.6 milliseconds.

[7] *Boids* algorithm implements the movements of flocks of birds in Max.

division is dissociated from spatialisation; on the one hand, the FFT processes band division, and on the other hand, the *boids* algorithm processes the spatialisation. Spatialisation, however, is still implemented as a quadraphonic system [8]. In addition, Kim-Boyle wrote a paper, *'Spectral Spatialization – An Overview'* in which all the techniques explained are reviewed, adding the possibility of controlling spectral spatialisation by stochastic means [9].

The solution that is closest to SD is described by Normadeau as *'Timbre Spatialisation'*:

> 'What is unique in electroacoustic music is the possibility to fragment sound spectra amongst a network of speakers. [...] This is what I call timbre spatialisation: the entire spectrum of a sound is recombined only virtually in the space of the concert hall' [10].

This concept is implemented in works by Normandeau (for example in *Clair de terre* 1999-09, *StrinGDberg* 2001-03, *Éden* 2003 *and Palindrome* 2005-07) using 4 band-pass filters for splitting a source sound and routing each filter output to one loudspeaker. When one or more parameters of the band-pass filters change in time domain, the concept of a *'Dynamic Filter'* emerges.

Two more concepts that resemble SD are *'Spatial Decorrelation'* and *'Spectral Splitting'*. The first one is related to the paper *'The Decorrelation of Audio Signals and Its Impact on Spatial Imagery'* [11] and implies different audio processing techniques for decorrelating[8] a sound source and routing each output to one loudspeaker. The second term is very close to SD nevertheless its focus is on the sound quality difference of loudspeaker systems:

> 'This notion perhaps has it origins in non-homogenous loudspeaker systems intended for diffusion, in which, due to the varying frequency responses of different loudspeakers, their relative proximity and orientation, the onset times of different sounds or components, and a number of psychoacoustic considerations, sounds seem to separate out spatially to different parts of the array'[12].

There is a follow-up paper entitled *'Considerations on the Handling of Space in Multichannel Electroacoustic Works'* [13], in which the term *Spectral Diffusion* is included and attributed to Keyes [7], notwithstanding, this term does not appear in Keyes's text. For this reason, the term *Spectral Diffusion* can be attributed to Barreiro. In Barreiro's 2010 article, there is an implementation of an SD system for Max in which FFT bins are grouped to create bands. That means that the bandwidth is not determined by FFT window size but by the length of each band, and each frequency band is integrated by one or more FFT bins.

Lynch and Sazdov in 2017 introduce another term and technique, *'Dynamic Spectral Subband Decorrelation'* [14]. This research emerges from a previous paper in which this technique is included as a *'future work'* [15] and later in Lynch's thesis [16]. *'Dynamic Spectral Subband Decorrelation'* consists of applying the same technique as in Normandeau's *'Timbre Spatialisation'* and decorrelating the output of each band-pass filter by adding different delay times to each loudspeaker. This technique could be seen as a sort of spectral diffusion delay.

The above studies have focused on SD techniques in a direct or indirect way. Nevertheless, SD form could be used to reference any sound process or compositional process in which frequency is linked to spatialisation. Similarly, most of the articles that have been referenced in this section have two things in common: 1) band division is obtained through FFT and 2) spatialisation is driven by changes of intensity in the FFT bins. As a result, a simple panning is used to spatialise sound.

Nonetheless there are other filtering techniques that could be applied to SD to obtain band division; for example, traditional filters, bandpass filters with more or less overlapping, etc. There are also a number of spatialising procedures (Vbap, Spat, Ambisonics, etc.) which are not discussed in these papers.

In the section *'New methods of spatialisation based on sound analysis'* and referring to Torchia & Lippe (2004), Curtis Roads says:

> "These are all experimental methods. Analysis-based spatialisation methods face both technical and aesthetic challenges in terms of choosing appropriate sounds for applying them, as well as issues of interactive control. Effective use of these techniques will likely require a great deal of testing and tuning." [17]

LEVELS OF SPECTRAL DIFFUSION

1.3 The systematisation of the compositional process

In order to systematise and catalogue the use of SD and to analyse all the combinatorial possibilities of the technique, three levels of SD have been established. This classification is based on compositional parameters that are controlled by SD. As a result, there are pieces in which only one level of SD has been used and there are other works in which any combination of levels of SD simultaneously are possible. This means that the simultaneous use of different levels of SD is not incompatible as each level controls different musical parameters.

1.4 One-level system (1st level of SD)

At this level, concepts and techniques of spectral diffusion are applied to instrumental composition. Consequently, harmonic material is divided into bands, and those bands have characteristic processes of band frequency transformation (for example, elastic

[8] Sound decorrelation 'refers to a process whereby an audio source signal is transformed into multiple output signals with waveforms that appear different from each other, but which sound the same as the source" [33]. These multiple outputs can be obtained via reverb, chorus, delay and filters, to mention a few.

deformations, divisions into glassy systems[9] or disordered systems, etc.). This is the same idea that Grisey applies in *Partiels* [18], but with a new technique. In *Partiels,* the concept of additive synthesis is applied to harmony and orchestration, transforming an electroacoustic technique (additive synthesis) into a technique for orchestration. In this case, the parallelism is the same since the techniques of SD in the electroacoustic field are applied to instrumental works.

Of the three levels this level represents the most open framework, due to the fact that the application of band division could be handled in many different ways and applied either to vertical or temporal organisation. Similarly, this level is largely metaphorical in terms of the spatial element as instrumental forces have spatial limitations compared to electroacoustic media.[10]

The main aspects dealt with at this level include examples of successful applications as well as a glossary of terms that have developed into a specialist vocabulary (listed in section 4).

1.4.1 Work examples of 1st level of SD

Crescencia [19] is a piece for symphonic orchestra that applies the concept of first level of SD in its harmonisation. As well as in loudspeaker systems, in which each part of the array reproduces one portion of frequencies, each instrument in this piece has its own pitch (with the physical limitations of the orchestra). Harmonic material for this work derives from the computer-assisted analysis of different recorded sounds played at different dynamics, which provide a root chord with more or less extended partials.

Kantaber [20] is a work for tuba with amplification in which a `first-level system`[11] of SD is applied to the instrumental writing as well as to instrumental techniques, by preparing a valve slide. Having said this, the piece could be considered a work between `first` and `second-level` when the instrument is amplified. *`Spectral position, spectral jumps, blinking,`* and *`sound wandering`* are the SD concepts investigated in this score.

1.5 Two-level System (2nd level of SD)

At this level, SD techniques are applied to electroacoustic forces. There are two principal variables; the first one is the loudspeaker band division, and the second one is the features of the sound that are introduced in the system. These two variables can be dynamic or static. A static surrounding matrix is a glassy system in which all the band ranges are fixed and, therefore, no changes can be applied. In contrast, a dynamic system is a surrounding matrix with elastic deformations in the time-domain. In these systems, the features of the sound introduced in the surrounding matrix represent another variable that interacts with the final diffusion of the sound through the system. If the sound is static (with no changes over time), it will spread into space according to band division and distribution, although it will not change in time, therefore it will be a topographic filter.[12] If the sound has variations, the content of each band will change and the diffusion of sound will vary.

In this level, as well as in the third, there are several techniques that could be used to divide spectral content into bands. For instance, traditional filters, biquads, FFT process, etc. The use of one or other of these techniques does not change the essential two variables in the level (band division and loudspeaker routing). As a consequence, these are technical elements that do not affect the level definition.

Most of the readymade tools available to perform SD are suitable to implement this level of SD (Eg. BeastTools[13] or plugins such as MSpectralPan[14]). Nevertheless, there is room for new implementations and specific developments applied to particular compositions inside the second level of SD.

1.5.1 Work examples of 2nd level of SD

Worstward [21] is a piece for bass clarinet and live electronics in which the `1st` and `2nd level` of SD with *`spectral jumps, elastic deformations`* are controlled by hyperbolic paraboloids[15] as well as *`elastic deformations`* applied to instrumental writing. The electroacoustic part allows the performance in stereo, quadraphonic and octophonic arrays implementing a system of *`spectral jumps`* in the *`surrounding matrix`* with *`system impurities.`*

Time Folds II [22] implements Helmholtz resonators in toms using surface-loudspeakers, and investigates *`1st`* and *`2nd level`* of SD techniques in a *`glassy system`* with *`transitions`* between *`neighbour bands,`* enhancing 4 marimba notes as *`burning frequencies.`*

1.6 Three-level system (3rd level of SD)

A three-level system consists of adding the last possible variable to the previous level. This new variable is applied to the position of the bands in the concert space. At this level, the different audio signals of each band are not routed to a single loudspeaker. Rather, each audio signal is one audio source that is moved inside the performance

---

9 Glassy systems and other novel SD terminology are explained in section 4.

10 The spatial element in the 1st level of SD resonates with Smalley's *Spectral Space* that is also a metaphor of spectral content. Similarly, the spatial element in the 1st level can be seen as a metaphor of harmonic formalisation (as happens for example in *Crescencia*).

11 Special typography has been used for new vocabulary developed for SD. These terms are explained in point 4.

12 A topographic filter is a sequence of band-pass filters each one allocated in a different position inside the concert space.

13 Beast Tools are multichannel sound tools programmed for developing sound material. https://www.birmingham.ac.uk/facilities/ea-studios/research/beasttools.aspx

14 MSpectralPan is a plugin that allows panoramas at each individual frequency. https://www.meldaproduction.com/MSpectralPan

15 Hyperbolic paraboloids are curves created by superposing lines. These structures were used in the Philips Pavilion as a main architectural structure.

space using any of the spatialisation tools available, for example Vbap [23], Spat [24], Ambisonics [25], etc.[16]
In this level, the variable of sound spatialisation is added to the variables of the previous level. Whilst in the second level, the spectral bands are directly routed to a loudspeaker, in the third level each spectral band is treated as a sound object that will be spatialised with 2D or 3D virtual sound systems.
Figure 2 depicts the three levels of SD as well as the combinatorial possibilities:

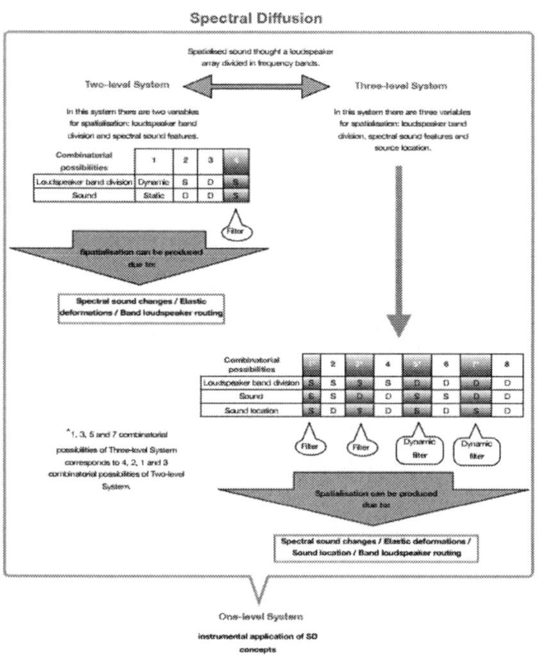

Figure 2. Conceptual synthesis of SD levels.

Figure 3 shows a block diagram of the step processes of the 2nd and the 3rd level of SD enhancing the similarities and differences between both levels.

1.6.1 Work examples of 3rd level of SD

Unfold [26] is a work for alto flute and electronics in which the third-level system of SD is applied to the spatial implementation of the electronic part, whilst the instrumental writing uses techniques related to *spectral jumps*. *Unfold* is a work that is informed by the construction of a *Dragon Curve,* using similar methods as seen in *Time Folds II.* In *Unfold*, these fractal shapes have been used to determine the trajectories of the fixed media sound materials that are distributed across space in a surrounding ring of 8 loudspeakers.

Garabatos [27] is a piece for clarinet, cello, percussion and electronics works on the 1st, 2nd and 3rd levels of SD using *burning frequencies* as an implementation of formant filters in an *asymmetric* and *disordered* SD system with frequency *holes*.

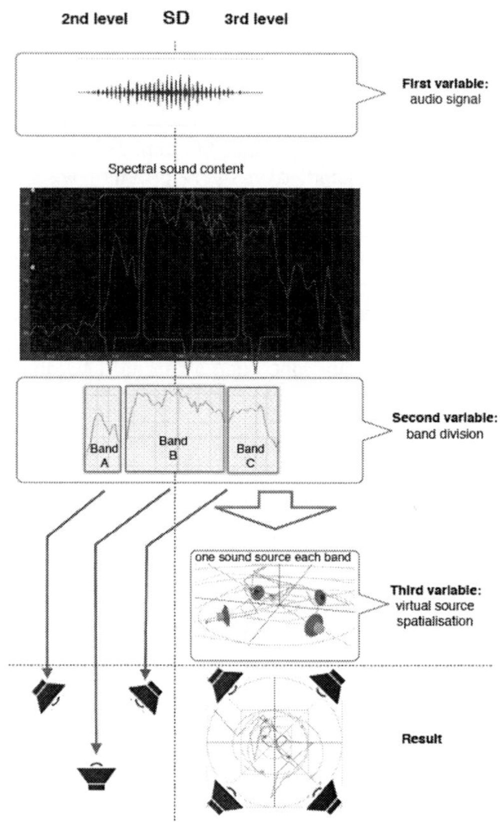

Figure 3. Differences and similarities between 2nd and 3rd level of SD.

NEW CONCEPTS AND VOCABULARY DEVELOPED FOR SD LEVELS

The rationale for developing tailored vocabulary and grammar surrounding the implementation of SD techniques in composition stems from the fact that existing literature often focuses on typologies of sound spectra or spatial spaces and forms. However, in the context of this article, which mainly covers the application of electronics to instrumental forces, not enough vocabulary exists to describe the merging of timbre and space.

To develop an adequate vocabulary, this paper focuses on the relationship between the terminology found in Spectral Diffusion in biophysics[17] (to determine the vocabulary of 'Levels') and Spectral Diffusion in the context of electroacoustic and computer-aided composition. It also includes reference to existing terminology found in Space and Spatial Audio.

[16] [34], [35], [36], [37] have guidance on the use of the different spatialisation techniques available in terms of source location accuracy in each piece included in this research.

[17] According to Miller-Keane Encyclopedia and Dictionary of Medicine, biophysics is 'the science dealing with the application of physical methods and theories to biological problems.

However, this does not mean that SD composition has been driven by biophysics processes, even if the terminology used in SD in biophysics has inspired new terminology applied to SD musical composition. For example, papers such as *Spectral diffusion and the energy landscape of a protein* [3], *Spectral diffusion in liquids* [2], *Vibrational line shapes and spectral diffusion in fluids* [28], or *Spectral Diffusion and Electron-Phonon Coupling of the B800 BChl a Molecules in LH2 Complexes from Three Different Species of Purple Bacteria* [29], have simply informed and influenced terminology decisions, which the author has found more suitable for SD composition, in preference to other sources of spectral and spatial vocabulary.

Table 1 presents new terminology applied to SD in musical composition, its compositional concept and Smalley's closest Space-form [30] definition.

Term	Compositional concept	Smalley's closest definition
One-level system (1st level of SD)	SD techniques applied to instrumental music.	
Two-level system (2nd level of SD)	System with two variables: band division and spectral sound variations.	
Three-level system (3rd level of SD)	System with three variables: band division, spectral sound variations and band location.	
Band	Portion of frequency domain.	
Neighbour band	Contiguous bands.	
Transition	Overlapping frequencies between bands.	
Spectral jumps	Neighbour bands without transitions.	
Surrounding matrix	One particular distribution of bands in the space.	(1)
Spectral position	Place in the space of a determinate frequency or band of frequencies.	
Elastic deformations	Band limits changes in time domain.	(2)
System impurities	Duplication of frequencies in 2 o more different bands.	
Holes	Loss of some frequencies or bands.	
Burning frequencies	Enhancement of frequencies or bands of frequencies.	
Blinking	Sound that is situated in the boundary of a band and changes between bands due to sound changes or elastic deformations.	
(Ground) states	How a concrete sound is divided into the system or surrounding matrix.	(3)
Glassy systems	Band limits that do not change its range.	(4)
Disordered systems	Random distribution of bands.	
Asymmetric system	Non-integer relationship between band distribution.	
Jump rate	When all bands are equally distributed, there is a jump each X Hz or Y musical interval.	(5)
Wander / Sound wandering	Fast change of sound location between bands because of the nature of sound or huge elastic deformations.	
Surrounding matrix	Each speaker that configures the system.	

	Smalley's definition and explanations or comments
(1)	***Circumspectral space:*** *The spatial distribution or splitting up of the spectral space of what is perceived as a coherent or unified spectromorphology.* Only the first part of the definition applies. The aim is not to present a unified spectromorphology sound but to explore timbral-spatial characteristics of a sound.
(2)	***Diagonal Forces & Planes:*** *The motion of spectral energy towards or away from a spectral region which acts as a plane. Planes can be expressed or implied.* Also could be seen as a change of spectral energies of bands.
(3)	***Spectral Space:*** *The impression of space and spaciousness produced by occupancy of, and motion within, the range of audible frequencies.* Combination of Ground State and Surrounding Matrix.
(4)	***Scale:*** *Relative Scale across spectromorpholgies.*
(5)	***Tonal Pitch Space:*** *The subdivision of spectral space into incremental steps that are deployed in intervallic combinations, a sub-category of spectral space.* Not necessary intervallic combinations.

Table 1. SD terminology applied to composition related with Space-form.

CONCLUSION

A well-defined methodology for the construction and implementation of a Spectral Diffusion system in the compositional process is proposed, starting with the definition of the three levels of Spectral Diffusion techniques and a suitable vocabulary (informed by biophysics and spatial audio and form terminology). These levels of SD were applied across a diverse range of compositions and musical genres, not only to evaluate the potential and limitations of the techniques but also to demonstrate the potential for musical expression, from which others can benefit.

A difficult aspect of the SD techniques was to find a suitable vocabulary across spectral analysis and sound diffusion in spatial audio and form. Therefore, the author had to amalgamate new terminology which involves existing vocabulary in spectral taxonomy and spatial form with non-musical vocabulary (e.g. in spectral diffusion biophysics) for the purpose of navigating the methodologies and musical thinking behind SD works.

The first level of SD is probably the most open-ended and conceptual level out of the three, as it is often applied as a different metaphor in instrumental music contexts.[18] This may also apply to any other type of external structure mapped on to musical parameters though. For example, there is an infinite number of ways of implementing the same fractal structure to a piece. However, it is key for the composer to identify which options work better for each need.

The second level of SD is far more concrete than the others, as each spectral band is always routed to a spatial source (e.g. a loudspeaker). As a consequence, composing with this level implies an extensive use of *elastic deformations* and, in general, the use of techniques that allow spectral changes on each spectral band, as a way to avoid a static sound image in the *surrounding matrix*. This

[18] As can be seen in *Crescencia*.

level has a good balance between the use of computational resources used and the efficient diffusion of the sound image.

Finally, the third level of SD is, technically speaking, the level with more variables available for implementation and mapping. This level is a clear extension of the second one because it adds sound virtualisation and it widens its range for potential implementation, since this process could be applied to a variety of different technologies. It is particularly suitable for the formalisation of musical trajectories, as this is one of the main features that distinguish it from the others.

Beyond the scope of this paper but certainly a future implementation of SD, which the composition community could benefit from, would be to programme a general tool for applying first and second levels of SD to a sound input. A type of plugin or standalone program could be developed to share with other composers for alternative applications in the creation of new pieces, formalising new structures or transforming sound.

REFERENCES

[1] B. L. Krause, *The great animal orchestra : finding the origins of music in the world's wild places*. Profile, 2013.

[2] A. D. Stein and M. D. Fayer, "Spectral diffusion in liquids," *J Chem Phys*, vol. 97, no. 5, p. 2948, 1992, doi: 10.1063/1.463036.

[3] K. Fritsch, J. Friedrich, F. Parak, and J. L. Skinner, "Spectral diffusion and the energy landscape of a protein.," *Proc Natl Acad Sci U S A*, vol. 93, no. 26, pp. 15141–15145, 1996, doi: 10.1073/pnas.93.26.15141.

[4] D. Kim-Boyle, "Spectral Delays with Frequency Domain Processing," *Proc. of the 7th Int. Conference on Digital Audio Effects*, pp. 42–44, 2004.

[5] Z. Settel and C. Lippe, "Real-Time Timbral Transformation: FFT-based Resynthesis," *Contemporary Music Review*, vol. 10, no. 2, pp. 171–179, 1994, doi: 10.1080/07494469400640401.

[6] R. H. Torchia and C. Lippe, "Techniques for Multi-Channel Real-Time Spatial Distribution Using Frequency-Domain Processing," *Proceedings of the 2004 Conference on New Interfaces for Musical Expression (NIME04), Hamamatsu, Japan*, pp. 116–119, 2004.

[7] C. J. Keyes, "Three Approaches to the Dynamic Multi-channel Spatialization of Stereo Signals," 2004.

[8] D. Kim-Boyle, "Spectral and Granular Spatialization with Boids," *Proceedings of the 2006 International Computer Music Conference*, no. Reynolds 1987, pp. 139–142, 2006.

[9] D. Kim-Boyle, "Spectral Spatialization - An Overview," *Proceedings of the 2008 International Computer Music Conference*, 2008.

[10] R. Normandeau, "Timbre spatialisation: The medium is the space," *Organised Sound*, vol. 14, no. 3, pp. 277–285, 2009, doi: 10.1017/S1355771809990094.

[11] G. S. Kendall, "The Decorrelation of Audio Signals and Its Impact on Spatial Imagery," *Computer Music Journal*, vol. 19, no. 4, p. 71, 1995, doi: 10.2307/3680992.

[12] S. Wilson and J. Harrison, "Rethinking the BEAST: Recent developments in multichannel composition at Birmingham ElectroAcoustic Sound Theatre," *Organised Sound*, vol. 15, no. 3, pp. 239–250, 2010, doi: 10.1017/S1355771810000312.

[13] D. L. Barreiro, "Considerations on the Handling of Space in Multichannel Electroacoustic Works," *Organised Sound*, vol. 15, no. 03, pp. 290–296, Oct. 2010, doi: 10.1017/S1355771810000294.

[14] H. Lynch and R. Sazdov, "A Perceptual Investigation into Spatialization Techniques Used in Multichannel Electroacoustic Music for Envelopment and Engulfment," *Computer Music journal*, vol. 41, no. 1, pp. 13–33, 2017, doi: 10.1162/COMJ.

[15] H. Lynch and R. Sazdov, "An Investigation Into Compositional Techniques Utilized For The Three- Dimensional Spatialization Of Electroacoustic Music," *EMS : Electroacoustic Music Studies Network*, no. June, pp. 1–9, 2011.

[16] H. A. Lynch, "Space in Multi-channel Electroacoustic Music : Developing Sound Spatialisation Techniques for Composing Multi-channel Electroacoustic Music with Emphasis on Spatial Attribute Perception," Univesity of Limerick, 2014.

[17] C. Roads, *Composing Electroacoustic Music*. New York: Oxford University Press, 2015.

[18] G. Grisey, "Partiels : pour 18 musiciens." Milano : Ricordi, Milano , 1978.

[19] J. Ávila Sausor, *Crescencia*, 2024th ed. Paris: Babelscores, 2014.

[20] J. Ávila Sausor, *Kantaber*, 2024th ed. Paris: Babelscores, 2015. [Online]. Available: www.babelscores.com

[21] J. Ávila Sausor, *Worstward*, 2024th ed. Paris: Babelscores, 2016.

[22] J. Ávila Sausor, *Time Folds II*, 2024th ed. Paris: Babelscores, 2016. [Online]. Available: www.babelscores.com

[23] V. Pulkki, "Virtual Sound Source Positioning Using Vector Base Amplitude Panning," vol. 144, no. 5, pp. 357–360, 1997.

[24] T. Carpentier, M. Noisternig, and O. Warusfel, "Twenty years of Ircam Spat: looking back, looking forward," *International Computer Music Conference Proceedings*, pp. 270–277, 2015.

[25] D. G. Malham and A. Myatt, "3-D Sound Spatialization using Ambisonic Techniques," *Computer Music Journal*, vol. 19, no. 4, p. 58, 1995, doi: 10.2307/3680991.

[26] J. Ávila Sausor, *Unfold*, 2024th ed. Paris: Babelscores, 2016. [Online]. Available: www.babelscores.com

[27] J. Ávila Sausor, *Garabatos*, 2023rd ed. Paris: Babelscores, 2016.
[28] J. L. Skinner, "Vibrational line shapes and spectral diffusion in fluids," *Mol Phys*, vol. 106, no. 16–18, pp. 2245–2253, 2007, doi: 10.1080/00268970802454778.
[29] J. Baier *et al.*, "Spectral diffusion and electron-phonon coupling of the B800 BChl a molecules in LH2 complexes from three different species of purple bacteria," *Biophys J*, vol. 97, no. November, pp. 2604–2612, 2009, doi: 10.1016/j.bpj.2009.07.052.
[30] D. Smalley, "Space-form and the acousmatic image," *Organised Sound*, vol. 12, no. 01, p. 35, Apr. 2007, doi: 10.1017/S1355771807001665.
[31] E. Drott, "Spectralism." Taylor and Francis, Jul. 25, 2016. doi: 10.4324/9781135000356-REM1010-1.
[32] J. Fineberg, "Guide to the basic concepts and techniques of spectral music," *Contemporary Music Review*, vol. 19, no. 2. pp. 81–113, 2000. doi: 10.1080/07494460000640271.
[33] G. S. Kendall, "The Decorrelation of Audio Signals and Its Impact on Spatial Imagery," *Computer Music Journal*, vol. 19, no. 4, p. 71, 1995, doi: 10.2307/3680992.
[34] D. R. Begault, *3-D sound for virtual reality and multimedia*, Nachdr. Boston: AP Professional, 1995. [Online]. Available: http://www.gbv.de/dms/bowker/toc/9780120847358.pdf
[35] M. a.J. Baalman, "Spatial Composition Techniques and Sound Spatialisation Technologies," *Organised Sound*, vol. 15, no. 03, pp. 209–218, Oct. 2010, doi: 10.1017/S1355771810000245.
[36] E. Bates, G. Kearney, and D. Furlong, "Localization accuracy of advanced spatialisation techniques in small concert halls," *Journal of the Acoustical Society of America*, vol. 121, no. 5, pp. 3069–3070, 2007, [Online]. Available: http://www.mee.tcd.ie/~gkearney/ResearchPapers/Bates, Kearney, Boland, Furlong ASA07.pdf
[37] E. Bates, "The Composition and Performance of Spatial Music," Trinity Collage Dublin, 2009.

Spatialization Revisited: Preserving Perceived Sound Source Angle Projected in Distance

John M. Chowning
Center for Computer Research in Music and Acoustics, (CCRMA), Stanford University
jc@ccrma.stanford.edu

ABSTRACT

The presentation of distance percept is often ignored in contemporary multi-channel spatialization, even though it is a richly extensible localization cue when a sound is projected in an illusory space, the others being angle and elevation. Multi-channel projections, both planar and hemispherical, brilliantly effect angular information but rarely that of distance. In closed spaces, the distance cue requires a reverberant signal, which gives the listener information as to the loudness of a sound source at a distant position when compared to the loudness of the direct signal. This is equivalent to perspective in vision. But reverberation masks the angular position of the direct signal at great distances. Reducing the reverberant signal is not desirable as it changes the character of the space. In this paper, we present an alternative that preserves both the character of the reverberation and the angle of the direct signal.

1. INTRODUCTION

Auditory localization functions with or without light, a 360-degree scanner, and it is rooted in our shared human experience of at least 250Ka. Over this period, our species lived half of every day in darkness on average. So, our auditory system was highly tuned to "hearing our way." In prehistoric times, humans depended upon hand lamps, candles, and torches, followed by lanterns, and gas lights to find our way.

The perception of angle and distance is associated with the amygdala in all mammals, the flee, freeze, or fight response; is the auditory signal of the predator's presence loud but far, or soft and close, right, left, or behind? However, living today in a world of widespread electrification, we sapiens rely minimally on auditory information to guide us in complicated spaces, but the capacity has not been lost, simply rarely used and therefore out-of-mind. A recent comprehensive paper about distance research notes that "auditory distance perception has received comparatively little scientific attention relative to other aspects of spatial hearing [1].

In the following sections, we define the localization cues and their simulation. Finally, we present a method that overcomes the masking effect of reverberation on the perceived angle of a source when the source is projected in distance.

2. LOCALIZATION CUES

To locate any real sound source in an enclosed space the listener requires three kinds of information relative to the location of the listener: angular location, distance, and elevation.

The cues for the angular location are:

(1) the different arrival time or delay of the signal at the two ears when the source is not centered before or behind the listener, and

(2) the pressure-level differences of high frequency energy at the two ears resulting from the shadow effect of the head when the source is not centered [2].

The cues to the distance of a source are:

(1) the ratio of the direct energy to the indirect or reverberant energy [3] where the intensity of the direct sound reaching the listener falls sharply with distance than does the reverberation, and,

(2) the loss of low-intensity frequency components of a sound with increasing distance from the listener.

1.1 Simulation of Cues

In the following, we define the configuration of loudspeakers and listeners and how the angular location and the distance cues may be simulated.[1] In this system, two groups of 8 loudspeakers are placed at the outer perimeter of the desired listener space, one at a high enough level such that there is a line-of-sight path to every member of the audience as shown in Figure 1.

[1] 4-channel (quad) has become the minimal standard in most studios and 8-channel is now common.

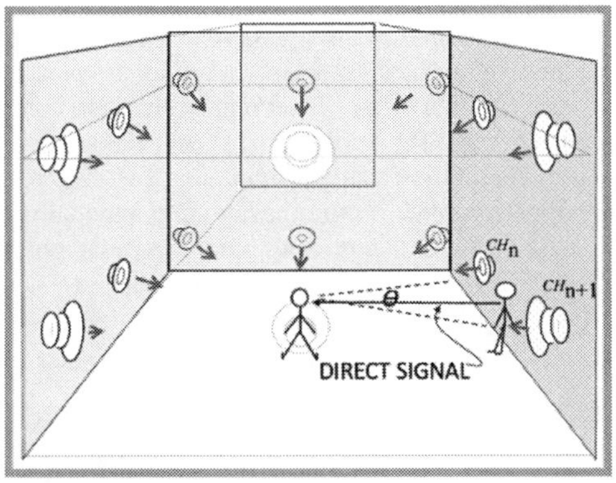

Figure 1. The vectors (arrows) represent the relative amplitudes of the signals from each loudspeaker. In this diagram, the source is at the innermost boundary and the amplitude of the direct signal is sufficiently great not to be masked by the reverberation.

The second group of eight can be placed at a higher level according to the presentation room. The listener is located inside of this boundary as close to the center as possible. Because the localization cues are computed for the listener who is an equal distance from the 16 loudspeakers, there will be a geometric distortion of the spatial image for any other listener depending on his distance from the center, but the distortion is constant for all angular and distance projections. Experience shows that artificial reverb masks the natural reverb of the room if the latter is not too great. Large and dead is best, of course.

Since the precise position of the listener is not known, any cues to the location of a source that are dependent upon delay, phase, and orientation of the listener's head are not appropriate. The cue to angular location, then, must be introduced by the energy ratio of the direct signal applied to pairs of loudspeakers in the eight-speaker array. As shown in Figure 1, the 360-degree space is divided into pairs of loudspeakers at angles of 33° relative to the listener. The means of changing the ratio of the direct signal to the sound source is to make the energy applied to loudspeaker pairs proportional to the angle of the source displacement [4]. Thus,

$$\%SignalCH_n = 1 - \theta/\theta_{max}$$

and where

$$\%SignalCH_{n+1} = \theta/\theta_{max} \quad (1$$

where

$$\theta_{max} = 33°$$

1.1.1 Distance Cues

To simulate the distance cue, we control the reverberant signal as well as the direct signal, such that the intensity of the direct signal decreases with distance while the reverberant signal is constant [2]. The direct signal's amplitude is proportional to $1/D$ where D equals the distance from the listener to the source.

1.1.2 Velocity Cues

In the presence of a moving sound source, a listener receives velocity information from the rate of the angular shift in energy (angular velocity), the rate of the radial shift in energy, and frequency shift due to the Doppler effect (radial velocity). The simulation of the Doppler effect is achieved, simply, by sampling the trajectory, scaling the unit distance D to some distance in meters, and making changes in frequency proportional to dD/dt, as seen in Figure 2 [4].

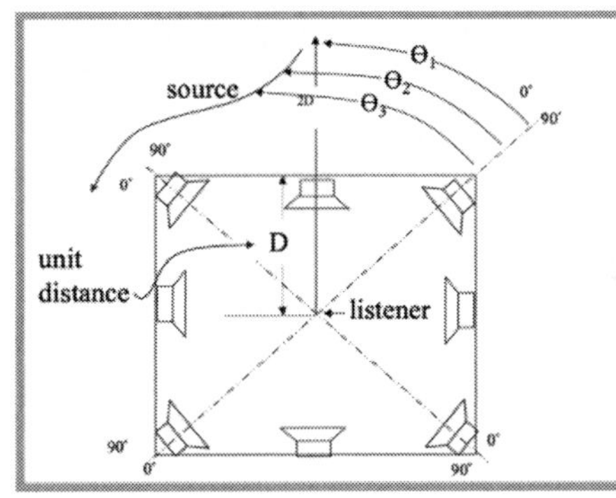

Figure 2. The unit distance is the physical distance between the listener and the closest loudspeaker in meters. The moving source can, of course, move to any distance beyond the trajectory shown here.

1.2 Reverberation

As was noted above, reverberation is an essential part of the distance cue. Reverberation also supplies the room information, giving general cues as to size, shape, and material construction. In simulating a sound source in an enclosed space, then, it is desirable for the reverberation to surround the listener and to be spatially diffuse.

To achieve the surround effect and the diffuse quality each output channel has uncorrelated phase outputs [5]. In the simplest case, some percent of the direct signal is scaled according to and passed to the reverberators equally. The percent governs the overall reverberation time within the characteristics of the reverberators.

It should be noted, however, that if the reverberant signal were to be distributed equally to all channels for all apparent distances of the direct signal, at distances beyond the *critical distance*, that point between the source and the listener where the SPL of the direct sound is equal to the reverberant sound (first referred to as *echo radius* in 1961 by Wendt[2]), the reverberation would tend to mask the direct signal and eliminate the cue for angular location. In the following section, we propose a means to overcome this limitation, which leads to the main contribution of this paper.

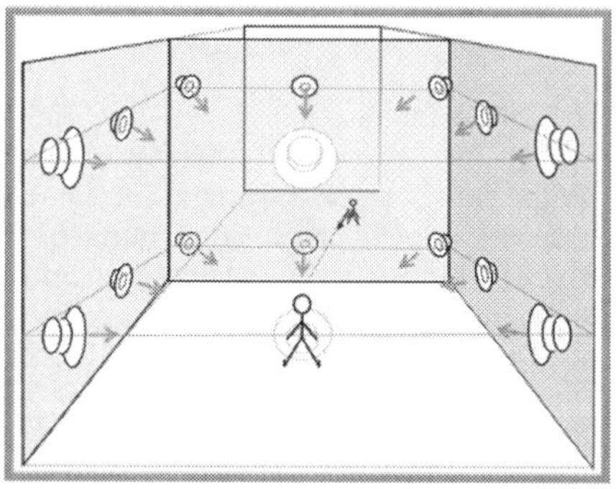

Figure 3. The vectors (arrows) represent the relative sound pressure of the signals from each loudspeaker. In this diagram, the direct signal of the source, shown at a great distance, is masked by the reverberation.

3. TWO PART REVERBERATION

1.1. Local and Global Reverberation

As noted above, reverberation begins to mask the direct signal, and therefore its angular information when the direct signal is projected at distances beyond the *critical distance*, as shown in Figure 3. To overcome this perceptual limitation, the reverberant energy is controlled in the following two ways:

(1) Global reverberation is that part of the overall reverberant signal that emanates equally from all channels and is proportional to 1/D and,

(2) Local reverberation is that part which is distributed between adjoining speakers and is proportional to 1-1/D.

Thus, with increasing distance of the virtual source, the reverberation becomes increasingly localized, compensating for the loss of direct signal energy, as seen in Figure 4. This may be a fair approximation of a real acoustical situation, for as the distance of a sound source increases, the distance to a reflecting surface decreases thereby giving the reverberation some directional emphasis. As the distance of the source increases toward infinity, the angular information of the reverberation and the direct signal become the same.

In their 2002 article [7], Moore et al. refine the conception of a room within a room, however, they do not account for the loss of sound source angle as its distance increases beyond the *critical distance*.

4.0 CONCLUSION

By controlling the output of the reverberation through all of the loudspeakers, such that the more distant the direct signal, the more localized the reverberation toward the angle of the direct signal, the angular information is preserved. We have presented a method for implementation that will be demonstrated in an in-place graphics sound-synchronous presentation.

Les Stuck, a programmer and application contributor for MaxMSP, implemented an elegant real-time implementation of this processing [6]. MaxMSP is a popular graphic programming language that is widely used in popular and academic computer music. Les Stuck is also a mentor of this author.

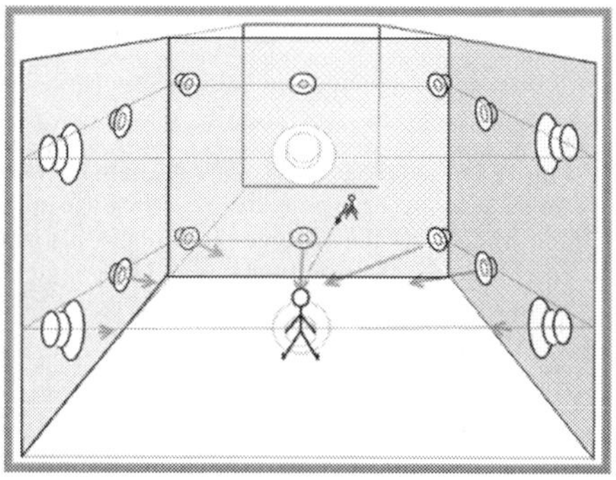

Figure 4. Reverberant signals from the loudspeakers are weighted toward the angular position just right of the center to compensate for the loss of angular information from the distant source, which would be completely masked otherwise.

5.0 REFERENCES

[1] P. Zahorik, B. Brungart, A. Bronkhorst. "Auditory Distance Perception in Humans: A Summary of Past and Present Research," *ACTA Acustica united with Acustica, vol.* 91, no. 3, pp. 409-420, 2005.

[2] M. Gardner, "Binaural Detection of Single-frequency Signals in Presence of Noise," *J. Acoustical Society of America*, no. 34, pp.1824-2830, 1962.

[3] K. Wendt. "The Transmission of Room Information," J. Audio Engineering Society," 9, 1961.

[4] J. Chowning. The simulation of moving sound sources," vol. 19, no. 1, pp. 2-6, 1971.

[5] M. Schroeder. "Natural Sounding Artificial Reverberation," J. Audio Eng. Soc. 10, 219, 1962.

[6] L. Stuck, MaxMSP(v.8.1.6)/Applications/ Max.app/Contents/Resources/Examples/ spatialization/quad-spatiaizer-folder/quad-spatializer.maxpat, 2022.

[7] S. Yadegari, F. Moore, H. Castle. A. Burr, T. Apel. Real-Time Implementation of a General Model for Spatial Processing of Sounds," ICMC, 2002.

This page intentionally left blank.

Cincinnati Center for Computer Music 2024

Kieran McAuliffe
University of Cincinnati
bkieranmcauliffe@gmail.com

Felipe Tovar-Henao
University of Cincinnati
tovarhfe@ucmail.uc.edu

Mara Helmuth
University of Cincinnati
mara.helmuth@uc.edu

Yunze Mu
Xavier University
muy@xavier.edu

Carl Jacobson
University of Cincinnati
jacobcf@mail.uc.edu

Hefang Ma
University of Cincinnati
mahf@mail.uc.edu

ABSTRACT

An update on the post-pandemic situation at the Center for Computer Music, College-Conservatory of Music, University of Cincinnati details recent music, research and activities of faculty and students. Research areas include several sonification projects, one using pulsar data, and another contributing sound signifying substances in a game application. Granular synthesis techniques were extended further by Kieran McAuliffe in the Rtcmix language, and MaxMSP externals. Creative activity was high with inventive performance strategies, an installation event and concerts at CCM, at the Cincinnati Art Music, in Seoul, S. Korea, Morelia Mexico, New York City, and many other locations.

1. INTRODUCTION

Following the pandemic studio situation described in the 2022 studio report [1], the Center for Computer Music at the College-Conservatory of Music (CCM), University of Cincinnati has resumed an intense level of in-person activity. Areas of research include projects in sonification, granular synthesis techniques, RTcmix programming and tuning systems. Music by Professor Mara Helmuth, the director of the studios, and student composers was presented at CCM and at many national and international events. Turner Post-Doctoral Fellow Felipe Tovar-Henao contributed new courses and exciting musical perspectives to concerts. At this writing Soundmesh for Internet2 Performance has been updated by alumnus Yunze Mu to be used for group improvisational composition, Endangered Sound 2, which is in rehearsal.

2. RESEARCH

2.1 Granular Synthesis

Kieran McAuliffe and Mara Helmuth have updated Helmuth's `RTcmix` granular synthesis instruments, allowing real time control and multichannel panning among other features. This also involved creating new `sgran~` and `stgran~` externals for MaxMSP [2]. McAuliffe has additionally created a `luagran~` MaxMSP external, allowing the use of Lua scripts for crafting complex grain parametrization routines.

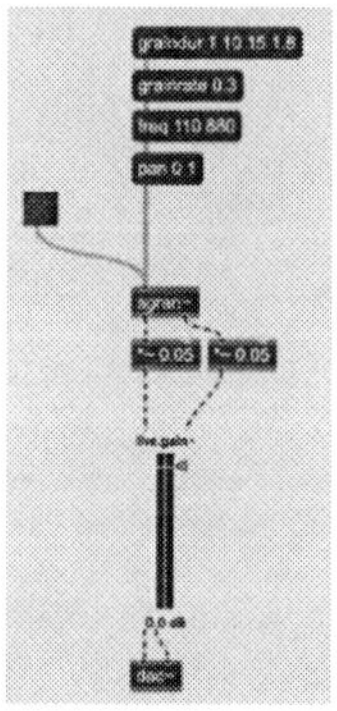

Figure 1: Basic usage of the new `sgran~` external for `Max`.

2.2 Pulsar Sonification

Mara Helmuth sonified astronomical data of pulsars using the new RTcmix granular synthesis instrument `SGRAN2`, creating *From Orion to Cassiopeia*, a fixed media work for stereo audio, and a multimedia version with video by astrophotographer and musician Bill Gwynne. A forthcoming article in the Journal of the Audio Engineering Society describes this project.

2.3 Swarmix

`swarmix`[1] (Swiss-army knife for cmix) is a third-party library for the `RTcmix` scripting language, developed by Felipe Tovar-Henao. The library includes a wide variety of new functions for data processing, unit conversion, mathematical operations, and more. To our knowledge, this is the first third-party library to be developed and released for `RTcmix`.

2.4 SoundMesh 3

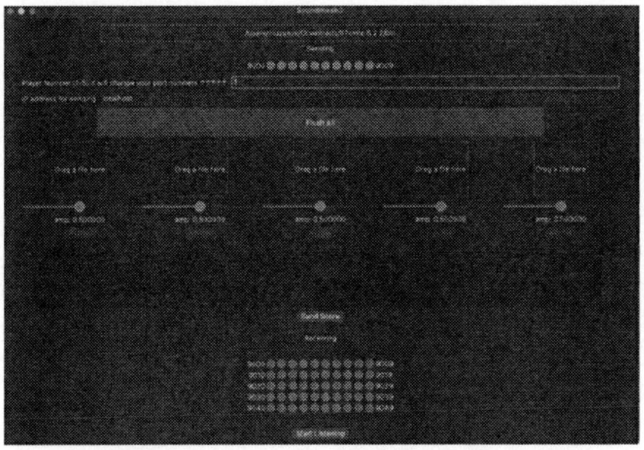

Figure 2: `SoundMesh` 2.1.4 User Interface

Yunze Mu and Mara Helmuth reinvented `SoundMesh`, an application for sending uncompressed audio over an internet connection. It is based on the RTcmix music programming language, configured with the netplay option. It has been used in a number of improvisatory performances or demonstrations at CCM, at the *2002 Internet 2 Conference*, the *2002 Society of Electroacoustic Music in the U.S. Conference*, the *2010 International Computer Music Conference at SUNY Stony Brook*, and in collaboration with musicians at Columbia University, Yale University, University of Montana and others.

The original version was built by Mara Helmuth [4]. Ivica Ico Bukvic made a Linux implementation. Zhixin Xu updated version 2 in 2016, and Yunze Mu has programmed the 2024 version 3, and a webaudio version as well.

2.5 Sonic Environment Generator

Kieran McAuliffe and Mara Helmuth received a Faculty-Student Collaboration grant during the summer of 2023 to prototype a device for generating background audio for public spaces. It produces three different sonic environments: *Piano and Strings*, *Granular Winds* and *From Australia*. They used a Raspberry Pi with a touchscreen, with `Pure Data` for as an audio engine and `Electron.js` for a user interface.

[1] https://github.com/felipetovarhenao/swarmix

2.6 Interactive Musical Software

Many students have explored the interaction between interactive video games and musical sound.

2.6.1 The Powder Toy

`The Powder Toy` is a free, open source "falling sand" game. This genre involves players freely experimenting with powdered substances in a rich simulated environment. Kieran McAuliffe developed an audio engine for `The Powder Toy` which maps analysis of the simulation to clouds of frequency modulated sound grains.

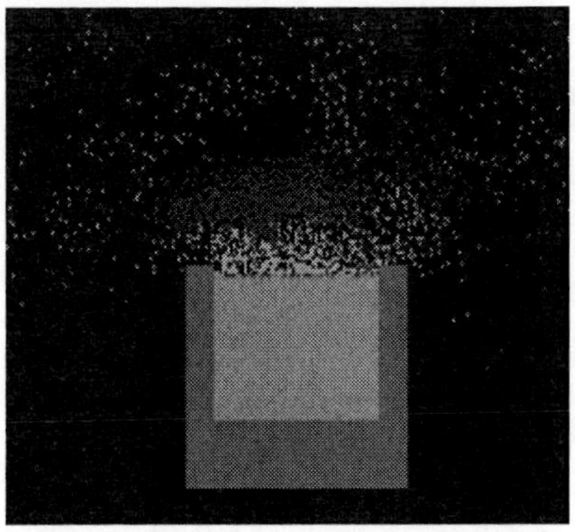

Figure 3: The Powder Toy

2.6.2 Sound City

Andrew McFarlane created *Sound City*, an open world interactive musical environment. It uses `Unity` for gameplay and `urtcmix` for embedded generative audio (https://youtube.com/embed/bi00tPlPq8E?start=90&end=120).

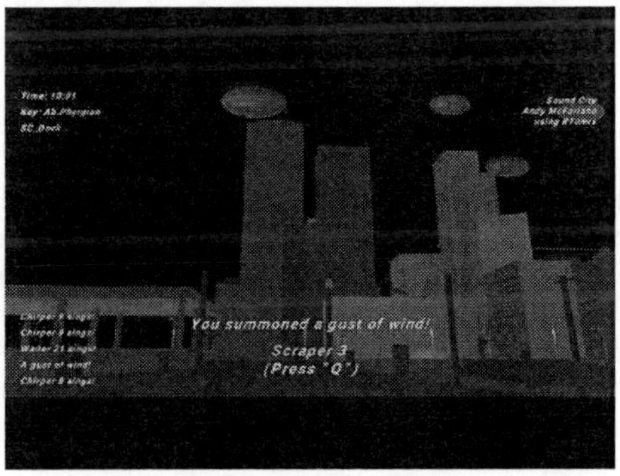

Figure 4: *Sound City*

2.6.3 Luminous

Carl Jacobson's *Luminous* presents players with a pattern-based composition environment, in which rows of pitch, duration, and timbre are realized by several algorithms. The musical parameters are stylized as crystals, runes, and glyphs within a dark cave. It is built in `Unity` and the embedded `Chuck` engine, `Chunity`.

2.7 Analysis

Alumna Margaret Schedel and Mara Helmuth published an article with analyses of compositions by Bob Sturm, George Lewis, Annea Lockwood and Carla Scaletti, exploring links between generative music and sonification [3].

3. PROGRAM/COURSES

3.1 New Tuning Theory Course

As part of his residency at CCM, Felipe Tovar-Henao offered a new course titled *Topics in Composition: Alternate Tuning Systems*. This course resulted in the development of `jinx`[2], a suite of interactive pedagogical tools for tuning theory and composition. This project, built in `Max`, consists of a variety of educational and interactive tools for teaching and learning about just intonation, xenharmonic music, and tuning theory more broadly. The primary goal of this project is to provide users with accessible and explorative tools, such that they can learn through play, and further solidify their musical intuition in tuning theory by connecting it to practice. Additionally, the long-term plan for this `jinx` is to eventually become a `Max` package, such that it's widely and easily available to the `Max` community at large.

3.2 Live Electronic Music Course

Mara Helmuth offered the Live Electronic Music course, which was documented in the CCM Digital Recording featuring music by Grace Choi, Carl Jacobson, Kieran McAuliffe and the class improvising together (https://youtu.be/U9e2diDqXNo).

4. CONCERT AND PERFORMANCES

4.1 Sonic Explorations

Every fall and spring semester, the *Sonic Explorations Concert* features electronic works by students, faculty, alumni and guests. Multichannel works and pieces for performers and electronics are often presented. A highlight was Mutien Lai's *Farewell* for piano and live electronics, involving live granulation of her virtuosic playing (https://youtube.com/embed/aqrK_FL_N_E?start=90&end=120).

Undergraduate Ian Marr created *IMANOK*, for game controller and `MaxMSP` visuals, an homage to early text-based video games. The music was created using a chiptune sequencer.

4.2 New Event: Sonic Installations

The new *Sonic Installations* involved students, faculty, and guests to present gallery style installations centered around sound. Using the two floors of Cohen Family Theater, participants throughout the day were free to wander around watching and interacting with the various installations. Former faculty Brad Garton's *My Places* Carl Jacobson's algorithmic *Luminous*, Andy McFarlane's *Sound City*, and Kieran McAuliffe's *Altar* were presented.

4.3 Recordings

The CCM Digital department produced a high quality video recordings for the computer music studio in addition to the course video above. A large team of students focussed on digital media produced a recording of the spring 2023 *Sonic Explorations* concert.

Helmuth's *Heart Sutra* for choir and electronics, conducted by Brett Scott, was released on Ablaze Records in 2023 (https://www.ablazerecords.net/new-choral-series/new-choral-voices-vol-6).

4.4 Recitals and Other Works

Mara Helmuth's faculty recital in September, 2023 included a new work for 4 trombones and electronics, *Astral Reflections*, *Expanding Space* (tuba and electronics), and two collaborative works composed with Esther Lamneck playing Tarogato: the 8-channel *Sound Dunes*, and multimedia *Burren Wind* (Alfonso Belfiore, video).

Kieran McAuliffe's *A History Told in Grains* for three laptop performers, live electronics was performed on his recital, in February, 2024 (https://youtube.com/embed/cdYdlf3YOuE?start=60&end=90). Another multimedia work entitled *Sunshower* was created by euphonium DMA student Nicolas McDermott (https://youtube.com/embed/IGj22WzUhm4?start=270&end=300).

Wenbin Lyu created *Duke's Fantasy* for open instrumentation and electronics (https://vimeo.com/845551435).

4.5 Endangered Sound

The Cincinnati Composers Laptop Orchestra Project (CiCLOP) composed a new piece *Endangered Sound* in which they all brought in sounds that they viewed as "endangered" to serve as materials for a group improvisation. This involved the cries of endangered animals, the sounds of outdated technology, recordings of forgotten music, and more. This piece was performed on Sonic Explorations at CCM, at the *2024 WebAudio Conference* at Purdue University and on a special concert at the Cincinnati Art Museum, April 20, 2024.

[2] https://github.com/felipetovarhenao/jinx

5. BEYOND CCM

Kieran McAuliffe was commissioned to write a composition for the *Holding Space SEAMUS Concert* held at NYU Bobst Library in May, 2024.

Mara Helmuth was in residency with Esther Lamneck in Morelia, Mexico at *Centro Mexicano para la Música y las Artes Sonoras* (CMMAS) and *Universidad Nacional Autónoma de México* (UNAM), Morelia, Mexico, with a concert of several performances, and a lecture. Helmuth was a Resident Fellow at The Virginia Center for the Creative Arts, Mt. St. Angelo, Virginia in May, 2022. She also presented several performances and an invited workshop with Esther Lamneck on Tarogato and Computer Music: *Hungarian Tarogato in Collaborative Composition* at *Platform-L*, at the *Seoul International Computer Music Festival*, the *Korea Electroacoustic Music Festival* and the *Seoul National University of Education* in 2022.

5.1 SNUE-CCM Conference

CCM Alumnus Professor Sangbong Nam at the Seoul National University of Education organized the *Creative Space* concert of music from composers currently or previously affiliated with UC-CCM, including Helmuth, Nam, Grace Choi, Carl Jacobson, Michael Lukaszuk, Kieran McAuliffe, Andy McFarlane and Yunze Mu.

6. CONCLUSIONS

The notable activities of people at the Center include numerous performances at CCM and at conferences and festivals. Ongoing research projects in granular synthesis and internet performance were expanded, and a focus on sonification strategies resulted in several new composition. Other projects explored interactive music, sonification, computer music programming, interactivity and virtual reality. Mara Helmuth was recognized with the George S. Rieveschl Faculty Award for Creative and Scholarly Works at the University of Cincinnati in 2023.

7. REFERENCES

[1] M. Helmuth, Y. Mu, K. McAuliffe, G. Choi, C. Jacobson, A. McFarlane and W. Lyu, "Cincinnati Computer Music 2022," *Proceedings of the 2022 International Computer Music Conference,* Limerick, Ireland. 2022, pp. 145–148. https://hdl.handle.net/2027/fulcrum.nk322

[2] K. McAuliffe, and M. Helmuth "StochGran: Expanded Granular Synthesis Tools," *Proceedings of the International Computer Music Conference*, Shenzhen, China, 2023, pp. 96–101.

[3] M. Helmuth and M. Schedel, "Links between sonification and generative music," *Interdisciplinary Science Reviews*, vol. 47, no. 2, pp. 215–242, 2022, doi: 10.1080/03080188.2022.2035106.

[4] M. Helmuth, "Virtual musical performance and improvisation on Internet2," Organised Sound, vol. 10, no. 3, pp. 201-107, 2005, doi: 10.1017/S1355771805000944.

Studio Report: Purdue University Music Department

Clay Williams
Dept. of Music
LAMP
will2400@purdue.edu

Monte Taylor
Dept. of Music
LAMP
mhtaylor@purdue.edu

Tim Nadolsky
Dept. of Computer Science
LAMP
tnadolsk@purdue.edu

Mark French
Purdue Polytechnic Institute
LAMP
guitar@purdue.edu

Kristen Yeon-Ji Yun
Dept. of Music
LAMP
yun98@purdue.edu

Tae Hong Park
Dept. of Music
LAMP
thp@purdue.edu

ABSTRACT

This studio report introduces the recently launched Department of Music at Purdue University and its new Music Technology Program. We provide an overview of initiatives, research, and growth in the music technology area, including the establishment of the Laboratory for Acoustics and Music at Purdue (LAMP) in fall 2023. Additionally, a summary of various academic curriculums, facilities, resources, faculty, and event programming is provided.

1. INTRODUCTION

The Department of Music at Purdue University is part of the Rueff School of Design, Art, and Performance under the College of Liberal Arts on Purdue University's main campus in West Lafayette, Indiana, USA. The Bachelor of Arts (BA) in Music is built around a 42-46 credit coursework structure, with concentrations in Music Technology and General Music Studies. In Fall 2024, we will offer concentrations in Composition and Jazz. Additionally, the Department offers a 21-credit certificate in Music Technology and a 15-credit minor in Music History and Theory. A wide range of courses is open to all Purdue students, including classes such as music theory, composition, music history, sound and AI, rock music, jazz, and world music. In fall 2024, we will introduce additional concentrations in Jazz as well as Music Theory/Composition.

Currently, there are approximately 130 majors, minors, and Music Technology Certificate students enrolled in the Department of Music. The Music Technology program comprises the majority of our current music students. Many of our music students participate in Purdue's signature Degree+ program, which provides opportunities for students to combine a STEM and music degree, resulting in two degrees within the traditional four-year timeframe.

2. CURRICULUM

2.1 Courses

The Department of Music formally offers a total of 23 courses. Within the Music Technology program, students are required to take classes covering topics including DAWs, sound synthesis and sampling, recording, mixing, mastering, electronic music history, and composition. Additionally, courses covering interactive audio, digital signal processing, and music-centric AI are currently offered as special seminars, with the intent to make them permanent course offerings within the program. These include courses such as *Music, Sound, and Computing* and *Sound and AI*. Furthermore, students also have opportunities to enroll in courses outside of the department, including those offered by the Theater Department and the Purdue Polytechnic Institute. These courses include *Introduction to Sound Studios*, *Electronic Systems*, *Data Acquisition And Systems Control*, *Introduction to Digital Systems*, and *Stringed Instrument Design And Manufacture*.

2.2 Faculty

Faculty at the Department of Music specialize in music technology (Tae Hong Park and Monte Taylor), composition (Harry Bulow, Allen McCullough, Bradley Bodine, Park, and Taylor), musicology (Lynn Hooker and Nolan Warden), music education (Christopher Cayari and Nadya Dubikovsky), jazz (Jarrard Harris and Drew Cox), and performance (Alfred Abel, Renee Anderson, Ellen Bulow, Nadya Dubikovsky, Danny Weiss, and Kristen Yeon-Ji Yun). The Department and the Music Technology program also benefit from the richness of Purdue's robust community in Theater with its Sound Design program, STEM-focused departments, research centers, and other sound and audio-centric programs, including the Audio Engineering Technology program and Guitar Lab at the Purdue Polytechnic Institute, the Center for Global Soundscapes, and the Ray W. Herrick Laboratories which focuses on acoustics and noise research.

3. FACILITIES AND RESOURCES

The Department of Music is housed in Pao Hall and the Elliott Hall of Music on the Purdue University West Lafayette campus. Pao Hall is a US$47 million , 176 thousand square-foot facility that houses classrooms, practice rooms, the Hansen and Mallet Theaters, galleries, acting and dance studios, labs, a recording studio, and faculty offices.

3.1 Concert Spaces

The Nancy T. Hansen Theater and the Carole and Gordon Mallet Theater serve as the primary performance venues at Pao Hall. The Hansen Theater is a 300-seat proscenium theater equipped with a 14-audio channel sound system and a Yamaha CL5 console, while the Mallet Theater is a configurable black box theater capable of seating up to 150 people, featuring the same console and a sound reinforcement system similar to that of the Hansen Theater. Both spaces are utilized year-round, hosting a variety of events not only from the Theater and Music Departments but also accommodating gatherings such as professional meetings and high school events, including the 34th annual Purdue Jazz Festival held this past January 2024, which featured jazz bands from middle schools and high schools across the Midwest.

Figure 1. Hansen Theater.

Figure 2. Mallet Theater.

In addition to the aforementioned ongoing updates, the school is currently renovating spaces at the Elliott Hall of Music, Purdue University's primary concert hall and performance venue. Elliott Hall has been a cornerstone of campus culture since its dedication in 1940. With seating for over 6,000, it hosts a diverse range of ceremonies, lectures, and performances from around the world, including a recent concert by the Kronos Quartet. Formerly the home of Purdue Bands and Orchestras, its main rehearsal space, seating approximately 80-100, is being repurposed as a hybrid classroom and multimedia performance space. This area is currently undergoing updates to include a dedicated multichannel sound system, projection capabilities, and configurable lighting.

Figure 3. Elliott 15.

3.2 Recording Studio

The recording studio is located in Pao Hall's basement and is used for recording, research, and instruction. The current control room contains a DynAudio 7.1-channel surround sound system, two Genelec near-field monitors controlled by a Yamaha DM2000 mixing console that connects to the live room, Hansen and Mallet theaters, and Music Computing Lab (MCL) via Dante. Additionally, the control room houses a Kurzweil master keyboard, a large screen display for course instruction, and a Mac Pro computer equipped with Logic Pro, Pro Tools, Digital Performer, Native Instruments Komplete, Waves Plugins, and various other software. The live room features an isolation chamber, Aviom Dante headphone mixers, a Yamaha baby grand piano, and a microphone closet with over 30 dynamic, condenser, and ribbon microphones. A large screen display and a set of studio monitors are installed in the live room to allow it to be flexibly converted to a supplementary instructional space. Alongside the control and live rooms, there is a storage and mixing room containing an iMac and several vintage analog synthesizers. Currently undergoing a major upgrade, the recording studio will soon boast a state-of-the-art Mac Studio workstation, a Yamaha DM7EX digital console, an Arturia Keylab 88 keyboard MIDI controller, the latest Aviom headphone mixers, and updated speakers, among other enhancements.

3.3 Laboratory Spaces

The Music Computing Lab (MCL) presently functions as an instructional space and computer lab primarily dedicated to teaching courses in music technology. It includes 16 individual student workstations, each equipped with sound monitoring and Yamaha piano MIDI controllers. The instructor's station mirrors the setup of the student workstations. We are currently updating the MCL by converting the space into an open, re-configurable instructional area for teaching, experimentation, and research, which can also serve as a recital space when needed. As part

Figure 4. Pao Hall Recording Studio.

of these ongoing updates, the MCL will undergo remodeling to feature a smaller number of state-of-the-art Mac Studio workstations and a 12-channel DynAudio immersive reconfigurable sound projection system. This transformation will enable the MCL to serve as an instructional space, recital venue, "hacking space," and adapt to the diverse needs of students and faculty.

Figure 5. Music Computing Lab.

The Laboratory for Acoustics and Music at Purdue (LAMP) operates as a research and collaboration hub, fostering connections among faculty, staff, and students with a central emphasis on advancing research in diverse areas of music technology, composition, and performance. Ongoing research initiatives at LAMP encompass projects such as citygram (real-time sound sensor network and soundmapping) [1, 2], electro-acoustic music mine (EAMM archiving and exploration) [3], soundscaper (soundscape resynthesis engine) [4], MatFly (on-the-fly music/sound coding in MATLAB), and various other endeavors involving faculty from other departments, including Aviation Technology and Theater.

Along with these venues, the Department of Music regularly utilizes the Rueff Galleries in Pao Hall and the Hiler Theater in the Wilmeth Active Learning Center as performance spaces. Additionally, the department collaborates with the Fusion Studio for Entertainment and Engineering, which is currently under construction at Stewart Center, the center of the Purdue campus. Operating under the Department of Theatre, the Fusion Studio focuses on innovations in theater technology, themed entertainment, and technology-centered interdisciplinary work.

4. RESEARCH

With the launch of the Department of Music in fall 2022, significant emphasis has been placed on supporting research projects and initiatives. This includes the hiring of faculty in the areas of music technology, composition, and performance, including Park, Yun, and Taylor.

Park is the most recent addition to the Department, joining after an 11-year tenure at New York University. He joined Purdue in fall 2023, assuming the role of Chair of the Department of Music. He continues his work in music composition, research, and the application of machine learning to music informatics, soundscape studies, and "cyber-physical computing," and sound sensor networks. Works by the faculty have received funding from organizations such as Google, IBM, NSF, and other grant agencies, leading to the establishment of startups such as GetNoisy LLC, which focuses on creating a smart airplane noise tracking system.

Park's most recent NSF-funded project focuses on developing novel digital voice biomarker software for clinical insights from short voice clips during phone calls, resulting in the establishment of the startup VitalAudio, Inc.

Yun is the PI of a research project on artificial intelligence for musicians called AIM. AIM recently received an NSF grant titled "Artificial Intelligence Technology for Future Music Performers". The project focuses on making reactive, human-like, and multi-modal music applications for string musicians. The topics include Evaluator, which evaluates musicians' posture, intonation, and rhythmic accuracy during performance, suggests musical improvements, and improves musicians' practice habits; Companion, which plays along with a human player during a chamber music piece, and actively responds to voice commands like a real human; and Mus2Vid, which uses diffusion models to generate video depictions in response to music in real-time and improves audience experience.

Taylor's research has focused on in electro-acoustic music composition with particular emphasis on interactions between performers, and live-generated sound and digital signal processing. Some of Taylor's most recent work explores the use of open-source machine learning platforms as a means of facilitating accessible approaches to creating intuitive and interactive systems for electro-acoustic music performance and improvisation. The most current iteration of this work will be showcased as part of a collaborative performance at College of Wooster in April 2024.

4.1 Collaborators

While the department is still in its infancy, we have already embarked on numerous cross-campus collaborations, including partnerships with the Aviation Technology Department, ECE, and Purdue Polytechnic. Currently, we are actively exploring avenues for collaboration with the Guitar Lab, overseen by Mark French, who has worked with the guitar industry for about 30 years, developing relationships with major companies like Fender, Taylor, and Gibson. [5] Established in 2006, the Purdue Guitar Lab is a dedicated facility supporting teaching, research, and industrial engagement. Housed in a purpose-built room within a newly constructed building at the Polytechnic Institute, its most notable activity is the unique class titled "Stringed Instrument Design and Manufacture" (MET 349). In this course, student teams design guitars and manufacture one for each team member over a semester. Through this hands-on experience, students learn principles of product design and series production while managing schedules, budgets, and their supplier base. The Guitar Lab serves as a platform for students to acquire essential skills applicable across various industries, with guitars serving as the medium for learning. Notably, at least three graduates currently work as engineers in the guitar industry, with more expected to follow suit.

Figure 6. Purdue Guitar Lab.

5. CONCERTS, EVENTS, AND ENSEMBLES

5.1 Concerts and Events

The department produces concerts and events throughout the year and one formal concert series per semester dedicated to compositions and performances of all styles by students, faculty, and guests. Most recently, Austin, Texas-based percussionist Jordan Walsh visited Purdue to perform a concert of electro-acoustic percussion music, including the premiere of a new piece by Taylor.

From March 15th to 18th, 2024, the Purdue Department of Music hosted the annual Web Audio Conference (WAC), an international event focusing on web audio research and the innovative use of web technologies for musical expression. The conference featured workshops, paper presentations, demos, and installations during the day, followed by evening concerts. Notably, a keynote speech by Hongchan Choi from Google enriched the program by providing insight on the future of Web Audio and the WebAudioAPI. Additionally, a special concert showcasing the Purdue Orchestra (directed by Adam Bodony) happened in the Niswonger Hall of Aviation Technology at the Purdue Airport. Drawing on Park's extensive experience in chairing events such as the 2013 International Conference on Auditory Display (ICAD), 2014 Sound, Image, and Data (SID), 2015 Noisegate Festival, and ICMCs in New Orleans (2006), South Korea (2018), and NYC (2019), the Purdue Department of Music aims to continue actively producing events. These endeavors not only foster collaboration and knowledge exchange but also attract members of the international music community to the region, further enhancing its cultural and academic landscape.

5.2 Ensembles

Though the Department of Music has only begun offering a Bachelor of Arts in Music as of Fall 2022, Purdue Bands and Orchestras, as well as Purdue Music Organizations, have been managing the various student ensembles at Purdue for over 130 years. Purdue Bands and Orchestras oversee the major marching bands, concert bands, jazz bands, orchestras, and student chamber ensembles, while Purdue Music Organizations primarily manage the many choirs, a cappella groups, and small student vocal ensembles. Additionally, Purdue's Black Cultural Center hosts the Black Voices of Inspiration, a choir dedicated to the performance of spirituals, gospel music, and songs of inspiration by African American composers.

6. FUTURE PLANS

The establishment and rapid expansion of the Department of Music has initiated a strategic endeavor aimed at systematically fostering innovative avenues for student engagement in research, creative pursuits, and collaboration with experts in the fields of music technology, especially computer music. A forthcoming objective for the Music Technology program involves the development of a specialized graduate program in music technology. Both our undergraduate programs and the new graduate initiative will prioritize a comprehensive exploration of research topics across a diverse spectrum of technical, artistic, and performance-oriented domains. These include areas such as physical AI, DSP, NIME, HCI, cyber-physical systems, sound sensor networks, sound mapping, acoustic ecology, composition, performance, and the practical application of music, engineering, and scientific principles.

7. REFERENCES

[1] T. H. Park, "Mapping urban soundscapes via citygram," *Seeing Cities Through Big Data: Research, Methods and Applications in Urban Informatics*, pp. 491–513, 2017.

[2] T. H. Park, B. Miller, A. Shrestha, S. Lee, J. Turner, and A. Marse, "Citygram One: Visualizing Urban Acoustic Ecology." in *DH*, 2012, pp. 313–317.

[3] T. H. Park, "The Electro-Acoustic Music Mine Project (EAMM): Collecting, Archiving, Sharing, and Exploring," *array.*, pp. 21–30, 2020.

[4] T. H. Park and S. Murakami, "The Soundscaper: A Tool for Soundscape Re-Synthesis," in *2021 International Computer Music Conference, ICMC 2021*. International Computer Music Association, 2021, pp. 356–360.

[5] R. M. French, *Engineering the guitar: theory and practice*. Springer, 2009.

From Composing History to Composing with History

Saadi Daftari
University of Montreal
saadi.daftari@umontreal.ca

ABSTRACT

The sound installation described herein combines the sounding-listening synergy of oral history with ideas from acoustemology and theory of emergence. It employs a network of microphones and loudspeakers that is algorithmically controlled to capture and replay some of the sonic events of their environment. This allows for fragments of the environmental sonic events to persist beyond their acoustic limit and echo a version of the aural history of the place. Passers-by are enticed to weave together the sonic traces left in an environment, including their own, with their electronically treated echoes, displaced and distorted, and in the process of doing so, become aware of the history of a given location and the memories it hosts.

1. INTRODUCTION

Microphones and loudspeakers have long been used not only for reproducing and supporting conventional musical instruments but also as standalone sound generating instruments. Typically, this has been accomplished either through creating a feedback loop between the microphone and the loudspeaker or through creating a line of amplification such that the material and/or spatial qualities of the network of microphones, loudspeakers and the environment is amplified [1]. Microphones and loudspeakers are also the defacto instruments in oral history [2], creating both a line of amplification, that of the past voices and personal recollections, and a feedback loop, albeit metaphorically and over a much-stretched time scale, that of "supra time scale" [3].

The work described herein attempts to integrate and explore the sounding-listening synergy of oral history in the context of a sound installation. It follows ideas from anthropology of sound [4] and the formal practices of oral history [5] to bridge the two worlds and to evoke a situational and relational environmental listening that emphasises on sound acting as a perceptual agent of knowledge pertaining to its environment and the memories it hosts.

2. ORAL HISTORY

"Oral history involves telling stories about stories people tell about themselves" [5, p. 89]. Much like an electroacoustic piece composed from a myriad of sound fragments and snippets, in oral history a larger history is pieced together from the assemblage of personal recollections [5, p. 93]. Also, much like an electroacoustic musician that uses microphones to collect raw material to compose with, oral historians use microphones to collect stories of bygone times to compose history with. Finally, much like a musical endeavor, the process of composing the past has as much to do with the historians' mode of composition as it has to do with what is contained perceptually within the raw material. In other words, in oral history, in addition to stories, sound itself is the medium that deals with how things are said and not only the facts it might convey through semantics [5, p. 92]. It is therefore tempting to consider oral history as a model to investigate history in sound art.

3. LISTENING AND SOUNDING AGENTS

Figure 1 depicts a typical microphone and loudspeaker configuration where the network of loudspeakers, microphones and electronics forms a line of amplification that shapes the piece through interaction with its environment. It is through this configuration that this work establishes the sounding-listening synergy that we seek with location being the focal point of interaction where history, in its most basic sense, is unfolding.

Similar configurations can be found in Agostino Di Scipio's *Audible Ecosystemic n.3a (Background Noise Study)* (2003) where the properties of the performance space, including the room characteristics and the sound of the audience are integrated into the piece and in fact are the only sound sources for the piece [1, p. 139].

Another seminal work exploring the network of microphones and loudspeaker in a place, along with a cycle of recording and playback, is *I Am Sitting in a Room* by Alvin Lucier [6]. Here, place is treated as a unique point of interaction and transformation where sound in its natural acoustic form is constantly subject to spacetime evolution to a point where only traces of the original phrase remain discernible [7, p. 312]. In the context of current discussion, this latter affect can also be interpreted as the capacity of a place to hold on to its memories before they diffuse into the spacetime continuum.

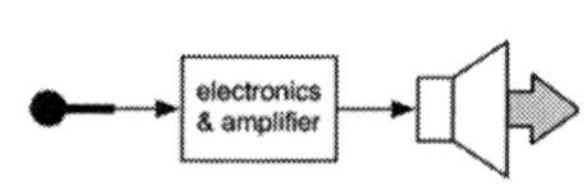

Figure 1. A line of amplification. [1, p. 103]

But how is sound treated in such a setup? How can one make the link between sound with its inherent perceptual qualities to the environment that hosts it? The answer to these questions holds the key to enabling the network of microphones and loudspeakers interact with their environment in such way that the temporal evolution of the environment, hence its history, becomes the subject of audition.

4. SOUND, KNOWLEDGE AND ENVIRONMENT

Acoustic ecology and soundscape composition, pioneered by Murray R. Schafer [8], are obvious candidates to provide the theoretical framework that focuses on the relationship between the composer, the listener, and the sound environment [9]. However, despite the relevance of the mode of listening and the compositional technics that they fostered, they fall short of the sort of the relationship between sound and environment that is sought for in this work. Notions such as hi-fi vs lo-fi soundscapes [8] pertaining to how and environment *ought* to sound like and how composing with referential forms of sound are privileged over the more abstract ways of treating sound [9] are some of the examples of the sort of the inherent ideological and aesthetic tensions that these approaches impose upon a sound environment that would ironically distort the actual context and the relationships it hosts.

Proposing a more inclusive, more heuristic, and less vertical framework that is more aligned with the theoretical processes of oral history, with no good or bad soundings, acoustemology, conjoining "acoustic" and "epistemology", is the theoretical framework that gives sound the status it needs to lead to knowledge. Coined by Steven Feld, in acoustemology sound is treated as a way of knowing that is concerned with "what is knowable and how it becomes known, through sounding and listening" [10, p. 12]. To the ears of acoustemology, sound and sounding is always situational, relational, ecological, dialogical, subjective and emergent [10, p. 13].

In reference to the sounding-listening synergy that we seek, the following is particularly relevant:

> *"[...] acoustemology favours inquiry that centralizes situated listening in engagements with place and space-time. Acoustemology prioritizes histories of listening and attunement through the relational practices of listening and sounding and their reflexive productions of feedback."* [10, p. 15]

Space and place become distinct keywords in this framework with place being the parameter of interest hosting "human engagement with the world" as opposed to the "abstract conceptions of space, time and spacetime" [11, p. 198]. This latter definition of place highlights the ecological approach to environment as a space of relations [11, p. 197], an idea central to this work.

The liberating aspect of this approach allows for all sorts of sound, be it referential or abstract, to become the building blocks of any sound environment and the composition that arises from it. But more importantly, acoustemology puts sound, sounding and listening in relation to one another and to their environment in such way that knowledge can emerge directly from the environment. A compositional approach informed by these ideas leads to the kind of listening that would enhance the awareness of the environment and the relationships it might hold.

5. PROTOTYPE DESCRIPTION

5.1 Physical Setup

Figure 2 depicts the diagram of the physical setup of the installation for a four-channel configuration. *Agents* are identified as the microphone-loudspeaker pairing each capable of listening and sounding through their own recorded buffers. Sounds of the environment are recorded by one agent at a time while all other agents play the algorithmically treated version of some of their buffer's content, hence creating a circulating sounding-listening synergy. Although each agent uniquely plays back its own buffer content, they are often part of a global musical gesture or phrase with a timbral and spatial movements due to the varying buffer contents and the unique location of the agents. For example, a phrase starting with a crescendo in agent 1 would finish with a decrescendo in agent 2 thus allowing for some form of spatial movement while maintaining perceptual continuity between the two agents.

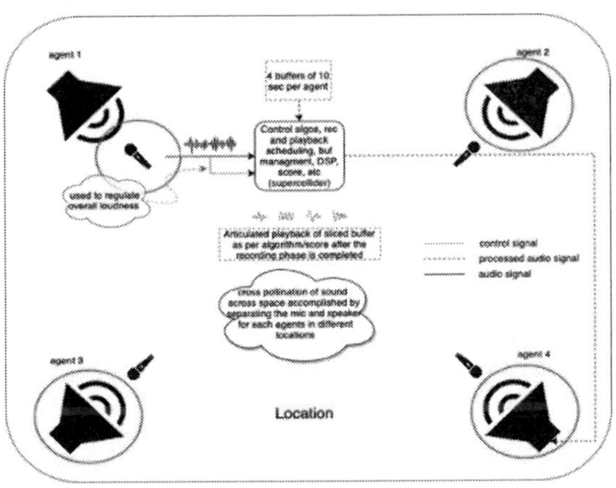

Figure 2. Diagram of a four-agent setup with the recording and sounding agents identified with red circles.

Central to the work is the treatment of space and place. Recalling the distinction made earlier between space and place, in this setup sound is continuously subject to spatial and environmental evolution. Sound events played back by one agent travel through space, pick up "the current state of the physical space" [9] and the environment before being picked up by the recording agent's microphone. The space related effects include the processing associated with the room, i.e., reverberation, spectral coloring, etc.

and are linked to the relative positioning of the loudspeaker-microphone pairs and their absolute position within the room. These effects can be enhanced by splitting the microphone-loudspeaker pair associated with a given agent across the room such that a sound picked up in one location is played back elsewhere and so on (Figure 2). This leads to a spatial fluidity of a sort where displacement renders location a rather fragile notion. Place related effects are simply the fragments of the environmental sounds that are picked up by a playback gesture before it is recorded again by another agent, much a snowball picking up more snow as it rolls down its path.

Equally important to this work is the temporal treatment of sound and place. Through this setup, sonic events persist through spacetime beyond their acoustic limit, reminiscent to *I am Sitting in a Room*. Since there is always one agent that listens this persistence in time is beyond the total time of the buffers, i.e. 40 seconds, and is achieved through the cycling of information between the agents through the medium of space. Past sonic events often re-emerge in another form from another agent in a location different from where the original event took place thus carrying the history of the location they traveled through. A clean discernible gesture will become only the silhouette of its original self but now carries information pertaining to the history of the location. Here the ecological definition of location as the space of relations, stretched beyond the here-and-now, becomes the subject of a relational and situational listening. Therefore, becoming aware of the history of the place emerges as one of many products that this mode of listening could lead to.

5.2 Algorithm and Software

The characteristics of the physical setup described in the previous section are exploited through careful deployment of algorithms. Implemented in SuperCollider, the code architecture can roughly be divided into three interlinked modules: *agent management, sound analysis, and playback*.

Agent management is mainly concerned with allocation and rotation of the recording agents as described above and depicted in Figure 2. Spatialization is also implemented here via a sequential or random allocation of the agents.

Sound analysis is concerned with the analysis of sound buffers before a new recording/playback cycle is initiated. Here, information pertaining to the location of significant sound events within the buffers and their mean loudness is extracted. This information is used by the playback module to trigger significant sound events and not a silent section within the buffer. The loudness detection is also used by the system to interact with its environment and adjust its behaviour accordingly. This is the characteristics of systems capable of *auto-organization* which is another idea borrowed from Agostino Di Scipio's *Audible Ecosystemic n.3a (Background Noise Study)* (2003), albeit in a much looser manner [12]. Noting that loudness is a property of the environment and not the system alone, here, higher overall loudness is countered by lower tempos to reduce the number of events produced by the device. This approach is more aligned with the acoustic ecology view on natural soundscapes where there is less overlap in sounds [9] and also contributes to the overall stability of the algorithm.

Finally, the playback module uses the information provided to it by the analysis module, for event onsets, and by the agent management module, for spatialization, to trigger sound events throughout space as per a quasi-algorithmically composition. Upon reaching the end of the sequence specified by the score, another cycle of recording, analysis and playback is initiated.

6. HOW TO COMPOSE

At this point, notions such as space, place, environment, presence of sound in its acoustic form, temporal persistence of sonic events, and the ecological sounding-listening synergy of oral history have all become active contributors to the overall experience of the work.

Going forward, it is the challenge of the composition to exploit and unify all these elements such that sound becomes an agent of knowledge with respect to its environment and the history it hosts. In fact, these elements only create the favourable condition for a situational and relational listening to take place and unveil the larger sound ecology of the place. Evoking this mode of listening is therefore the main goal of a composition for this setup. In doing so, the temporal and spatial evolution of the place becomes the subject of listening.

In our case, little to no information is available on the environmental context and the nature of the possible sound environment to compose with. What we do know however is the *relations* within that environment as discussed in the previous section. Thus, a fitting compositional approach for this work is that employed in *Audible Ecosystemic n.3a (Background Noise Study)* (2003) by Di Scipio. Based on the theory of *emergence*, in such as approach higher-level properties of a system arise from the lower-level processes [12]. That is, in a musical context, instead of creating wanted sounds via interactions, one focuses on "creating wanted interactions having audible traces" [12]. This shifts the focus for composition from sound to relations, and in our case, the *place* as the space of relations.

One relational element that stands out in our setup is *echo*. Sonic elements are born form the physical environment and echo through it via the network of microphones, loudspeakers and electronics. This dichotomy between the sounds coming out of the loudspeaker and the sounds of the environment is the source of the temporal fluidity that emerges from such a set up since a constant dialogue is established between the "now" and the "then" of the environment, a sort of a temporal ecosystem, further enhancing the interaction of the auditor with the environment and its temporal evolution. In an ideal situation the auditor is as much involved in reconstructing and composing history as is the algorithm.

Extending its meaning beyond the acoustic realm, echo in this work is omnipresent and could even be considered as the *material* to compose with. In fact, the notion of echo as being "nothing if not historical" and the acoustic world in which echoes are generated being a historical world, might be the key to this entire discussion [13, p. 55]

Composing for this setup should, therefore, encourage listening to the environment as much as to its echoes emitted from the loudspeakers. The challenge is to keep the two worlds distinguishable yet uniform. The generated sounds are singularities that should act as sonic events that articulate the environment and divert the attention to the broader environment in and through which both the subject and the sonic objects interact. In other words, the environment is the medium!

7. SAMPLE COMPOSITION

Although void of any spatial plays and interactions, and removed from the sonic environment it is injected into, an extract of the stereo reduction of the recording of loudspeakers' output is available for listening [14]. Informed by the discussion presented in the previous section, the composition used to run the demo consists of two main categories of sounds. One aimed at *diverting the attention to music by articulating the environment*. This mainly consists of a sequence of discrete familiar musical gestures of non-referential sound events. The other aimed at *making the relationship with the environment* consisting of a sequence of discrete referential events superimposed on a quasi-referential, slow transforming layer. In doing so, hearing and listening are evoked continuously, i.e. one listens to something that was just heard!

Distant events become naturally more distant due to reverberation they accumulate upon each traveling through space. Timbral evolution is also a function of space and room coloration. This generally trends towards an increasingly diffused sound shaped by the room acoustics. Gestures on the other hand tend to remain more recognizable over time. In short, shape persists while material morphs.

8. CONCLUSION

Making the bridge between oral history and a sound installation inspired by it requires a careful examination of the significance of sound in the process of history recollection and composition. The key to this transition is the treatment of sound as a way of knowing that is both situational and relational. In light of such understanding of sound, notions such as listening and place take on a new significance leading to a deeper engagement with place and space-time. This proved to be crucial for this sound installation that aspires to integrate and investigate oral history and its mode of knowledge pertaining to location and time. The physical/algorithmic configuration and the compositional strategies that were utilized for this work were the direct result of such understandings.

Notions such as space, place, environment, presence of sound in its acoustic form, temporal persistence of sonic events and the ecological sounding-listening synergy of oral history were all integrated into this work and actively contribute to a relational and situational listening that leads to awareness about space, time and history.

Acknowledgments

The author is grateful to Dr. Nicolas Bernier for his invaluable feedback and support and to the secteur multimedia (SMM) of the faculty of music of university of Montreal for providing the much-needed equipment.

9. REFERENCES

[1] C. van Eck, *Between air and electricity : microphones and loudspeakers as musical instruments*. New York: Bloomsbury Academic, an imprint of Bloomsbury publishing, Inc, 2017.

[2] D. A. Ritchie, *Doing oral history : a practical guide*, 2nd ed., 1 online resource (318 pages) vols. Oxford: Oxford University Press, 2003.

[3] C. Roads, "Microsound," Cambridge, Mass.: Cambridge, Mass. : MIT Press, 2001.

[4] D. Novak and M. Sakakeeny, *Keywords in sound*. Durham ; Duke university press, 2015.

[5] R. Rosaldo, "Doing Oral History," *Soc. Anal. Int. J. Soc. Cult. Pract.*, no. 4, pp. 89–99, 1980.

[6] A. Lucier, *I Am Sitting In a Room*. 1969. [Online streaming]. Available: https://www.ubu.com/media/sound/source/Lucier-Alvin_Sitting.mp3

[7] A. Lucier, G. Gronemeyer, R. Oehlschlägel, and A. Lucier, *Reflections: interviews, scores, writings, 1965-1994 = Reflexionen : Interviews, Notationen, Texte, 1965-1994*, Zweite erweiterte und überarbeitete Auflage. in Edition MusikTexte, no. 003. Köln: MusikTexte, 2005.

[8] R. M. Schafer, *The soundscape: our sonic environment and the tuning of the world*. Rochester, Verm. ; Destiny Books, 1994.

[9] A. McCartney, "Soundscape Composition and the Subversion of Electroacoustic Norms," *eContact!*, vol. 5, no. 1, 2002.

[10] S. Feld, "acoustemology," in *Keywords in Sound*, D. Novak and M. Sakakeeny, Eds., Duke University Press, 2015, pp. 12–21.

[11] A. J. Eisenberg, "space," in *Keywords in Sound*, D. Novak and M. Sakakeeny, Eds., Duke University Press, 2015, pp. 193–207.

[12] A. Di Scipio, "'Sound is the interface': from interactive to ecosystemic signal processing," *Organised Sound*, vol. 8, no. 3, pp. 269–277, 2003.

[13] M. M. Smith, "echo," in *Keywords in Sound*, D. Novak and M. Sakakeeny, Eds., Duke University Press, 2015, pp. 55–64.

[14] Daftari, Saadi, *Here-Now-Then*. Montreal, 2021. [Online]. Available: https://on.soundcloud.com/quAmu

Problems in Accessing Music for Piano and Electronics in Japan

Hyunmook Lim
Tokyo University of the Arts
s2323914@ms.geidai.ac.jp

ABSTRACT

This paper will describe the problems in accessing music for Piano and electronics in Japan. Although more than 100 composers have composed a considerable amount of music for Piano and electronics since 1958, most remain unpublished or unarchived and have not been performed again after their premiere. The performers are still having difficulties obtaining the score and electronic materials in Japan. Upon recognizing the situation, we will discuss the current archiving issue in Japan while comparing several cases inside and outside Japan, and future possible practices to improve the current situation. Although this paper is limited to the case of Piano repertoires in Japan, the author expects the cases of other instruments and countries could be expanded by subsequent researchers in the future based on this research.

1. INTRODUCTION

After Toshiro Mayuzumi (黛敏郎, 1929-1997) composed the first Japanese concrete music (musique concrète), "X, Y, Z" in 1953, numerous composers in Japan have challenged to compose electronic music up to the present. Most of the compositions were recorded on magnetic tape and mainly played through the speaker. As time passed, the Japanese composers have also challenged to compose electroacoustic music integrating electronic sounds and conventional musical instruments. The first composition for Piano and electronics was "Concertant 4 Movements with Piano and Electronic Sound (ピアノと電子音響による協奏的四章)" in 1958, composed by Hideko Ohki (大木英子, 1919-2008). However, the tape has been unfortunately lost. Although the manuscript score currently has been preserved, obtaining a copy outside Tokyo is difficult because of its strict legal issues which we will discuss in the next chapter. After Ohki, many compositions for Piano and electronics have been currently composed. However, the situation of other compositions is not significantly different from Ohki's composition in 1958. Most compositions are not archived well, and the performers are still having difficulties accessing the score, the electronic material, or both. Many early compositions have been especially lost or damaged. In the next chapter, we will discuss situations inside and outside Japan in more detail, and suggestable practices to improve the situation.

2. CASE STUDIES

2.1 Cases outside Japan (Europe-America)

We must acknowledge that not all the cases in Europe-America on archiving electronic music were successful. For example, an estimated 7,000 electronic compositions presented at ICMC have already been lost or inaccessible since the mid-1970s (Park, 2020). Recognizing this situation, the author will introduce certain remarkable and sustaining cases of Europe and America in this chapter, to compare the situation of Japan and overseas.

there has been an organized publication system in the European-American electronic music scene since more than half a century ago. For example, analog reel tape or digital audio tape was provided with the printed score when the performer ordered the early publication of Luigi Nono (1924-1990)'s "...sofferte onde serene..." (1976) by its publisher, Casa Ricordi. This tape is currently digitalized to a compact disc and can be obtained as an attached form with the score.

Figure 1 Digitalized compact disc for performance attached to the back cover of the score of "...sofferte onde serene..." by Luigi Nono (published by Casa Ricordi). Owned and photographed by the author.

It is currently common to provide electronic materials in the form of compact discs with scores. Moreover, there are even cases using contemporary technologies. For example, the early electronic materials of Andrzej Dobrowo olski (1921-1990)'s "Music for Magnetic Tape and Piano Solo" (1972) used to be provided as a vinyl record with a printed score. However, this can be obtained as a digitalized audio file through its current distributor, Hal Leonard, with an internet website link and download code printed on the score so that the performer can download it online after entering the code. Several prominent music publishers including Boosey and Hawkes, Donemus, Faber Music, Schott Music, et cetera are also providing electronic materials after purchasing the score online through their official website or email transfer. After 2010, More publishers were established whose electroacoustic music catalogs and their performance materials are fundamentally available online such as Babelscores, Maison ONA, Note en Bulle Editions, Tetractys Publishing, et cetera. Despite the lack of published research on this practice, we can observe that this tendency is becoming increasingly common at present.

Figure 2 downloadable webpage from the publisher Maison ONA. The user can download the purchased score and electronic materials online. screenshot captured by the author.

There is another remarkable case in France. Institut de Recherche et Coordination Acoustique/Musique [IRCAM] has its archive website "Sidney[1]". This website archives almost every work composed in IRCAM. The performer can obtain information about electronic materials, required equipment, setup instructions, et cetera for the actual performance.

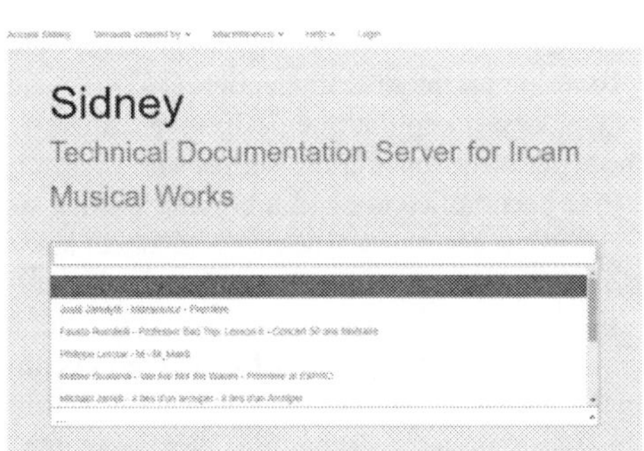

Figure 3 main page of Sidney. The visitor of this website can choose the composition they are looking for from the dropdown menu and can access the detailed documentation, including required equipment, setup instructions, et cetera. (electronic materials are also downloadable as digital files, but contacting the webmaster is necessary for the outside member of IRCAM). Screenshot captured by the author.

[1] https://brahms.ircam.fr/sidney.

2.2 Cases inside Japan

Meanwhile, the situation in Japan is relatively more vulnerable than overseas. As mentioned in the Introduction, most electroacoustic music compositions in Japan remain unpublished. In this case, the performer must contact the composer privately. However, receiving the performance materials or even a response is not always guaranteed. Furthermore, it is difficult to contact if the composers do not have their public contact address or website.

The situation would be more intricate if the composer was already deceased. For instance, Ohki's score of "Concertant 4 Movements with Piano and Electronic Sound" is currently preserved in The Archives of Modern Japanese Music (日本近代音楽館), Tokyo. However, to obtain the score, individuals are required to get permission from both the composer's heirs and the Japanese Society for Rights of Authors, Composers and Publishers [JASRAC] (日本音楽著作権協会). The situation will be more complicated to obtain a copy of the recording. In this case, additional permissions from each heir of the pianist, tape part composer, and recording engineer are required. Unless the composer's heirs' addresses are known, there is no way to obtain the score or other materials.

Not only for Ohki's case, but this also corresponds to electroacoustic compositions by other deceased composers preserved in The Archives of Modern Japanese Music or other Japanese libraries. Since these archives are normally not provided online, it is more difficult to access the necessary performance materials without directly visiting the location. Although we admit this copyright regulation is for protecting the rights of the composers, it is also considerable that more flexibility is needed for research and performance purposes.

It does not mean there have been no cases of electronic music publishing in Japan. For example, Japanese publisher, "Casa de la Guitarra (ギタルラ社)" has published Kenjiro Ezaki (江崎健次郎, 1926-2017)'s "Music for Guitar and Electronic Sound (ギターと電子音のための音楽)" (1967). In this case, no electronic materials were attached. Instead, the tape could have been obtained by asking the publisher directly. However, since this score is already out of print and the publisher does not currently have the tape, there is no way to obtain the score or electronic material officially at present.

We can also remark on the case of a publisher "Mother Earth (マザーアース)", which mainly publishes Japanese contemporary composer's works, including the composition for instruments and electronic sounds. In this case, a compact disc containing an audio file is attached t o the score. However, we should remember that this is a r ather exceptional case from the publisher's catalog and is also not common in Japan. Major publishers in Japan – such as ZEN-ON (全音楽譜出版社) or Schott Japan, et cetera – are still publishing minimal amounts of electroacoustic music. Nevertheless, most are publishing and selling only printed scores, but not with any attached electronic materials.

It contrasts that Japan has almost no electroacoustic publications with provided electronic materials, while Japanese major publishers already have been publishing numerous scores for student choirs, lesson books, or other popular works (Chopin or Schubert for instance), which have the attachments of demo recordings for practice as a compact disc, printed website link, et cetera. Since it is obvious they have enough environment to publish the scores in the form of books and attachments, we can assume one of the reasons is a problem between publishing cost and lack of demand, or it is only because the electronic materials of past compositions – especially composed before 2000 – are not properly digitalized or preserved (which we will discuss in the next chapter).

There are also several websites of Japanese contemporary music databases in Japan. The most representative case would be "Japanese composers and their works（日本の作曲家とその作品）[2]" by the Japanese Society for Contemporary Music [JSCM]（日本現代音楽協会）. This website introduces its members' compositions, as well as Sidney. However, electronic materials cannot be obtained since this is not an archival website but only for databases. Furthermore, it still lacks sufficient information as a database. It doesn't have any information on the electronic parts, such as the required equipment list, technical setup guide, et cetera. Although they are providing some of the composer's official website links, it does not mean all the provided links are accessible since they are not updated and managed in real-time. Certain websites are not updated anymore or are even not accessible. Occasionally, there are also cases in which email addresses or contact forms written on their website are unavailable (as of May 2024).

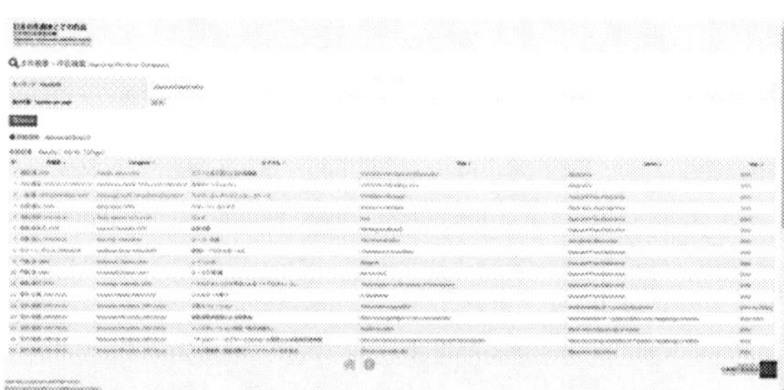

Figure 4 screenshot of the website "Japanese composers and their works" from the JSCM website. Screenshot captured by the author.

The case of the Japanese Society of Electronic Music [JSEM] (日本電子音楽協会) will be collatable. Mikako Mizuno (水野みか子, 1958–) has established with her colleagues a project for archiving JSEM members' past works (Mizuno et al. 2020). Yoshihisa Suzuki (鈴木悦久, 1975–) also has recently proceeded with a research project since 2022 (Suzuki & Watanabe, 2023), which is about researching methodology for reperforming Japanese electroacoustic music based on the cases of the association's past concerts. Although JSEM currently does not have an official database or archive online, we could expect these projects to improve the situation in the future.

There are also several websites produced by individual musicians using their networks of colleagues. For example, Ryuta Nishikawa（西川竜太, 1972–）published a website "Composer Database（作曲家データベース）[3]", which can access the entire work lists, official websites, and email addresses of several Japanese composers. There are also similar database websites by different authors such as "Oto wo Asobu: Japanese Composers（音ヲ遊ブ）[4]" or "Japanese Contemporary Composers Library（日本現代作曲家ライブラリー）[5]". However, all of them are currently updating only one or two composers. These websites also still have the same difficulties searching for desired results since they are focusing on a limited number of composers and have inconsistent, obscure information on instrumentation, electronic materials, or technical guides (see Figure 4 for instance). The author speculates that there is an obvious limitation that the individual cannot update all the recent compositions from every composer, since most of the websites are managed personally by each individual.

3. FUTURE WORKS

3.1 Organizing a Database of Japanese Compositions

The Author speculates that the main reason for the low accessibility of Japanese electroacoustic music is that they are not maintained due to the low occasions of reperformance after their premiere, and the reason for scarce performance is that there is a lack of information that the performers barely realize, which is about what compositions exist in Japan. Although several examples of databases on Japanese compositions are discussed in the previous chapter, most of them still have difficulty searching for desired information.

Practically, it is obvious that organizing a new database solely focusing on the instrumentation for Piano and electronics is necessary so that the performers can search and find the repertoires much more simply and precisely. The author has been collecting and archiving the list of compositions[6] in the form of a Google spreadsheet since 2022, which is accessible through the author's website[7]. This spreadsheet contains the composer's name and the work's title (both in Japanese and English), detailed instrumentation including required devices, publication information, contact information to access the electronic materials, listenable recording link online, and the technical notes on electronic material written by the author which will be discussed in the next chapter. The visitors can contact the author directly through the email address written in the list for additional inquiries.

[2] https://www.jscm-db.net/db/search/.

[3] https://contemporary-composer.jp/.

[4] https://japanesecomposers.info/jc/.

[5] https://composerworklist.wixsite.com/composerworklist.

[6] http://tinyurl.com/33tck5h2.

[7] https://www.hmlim.com/works.

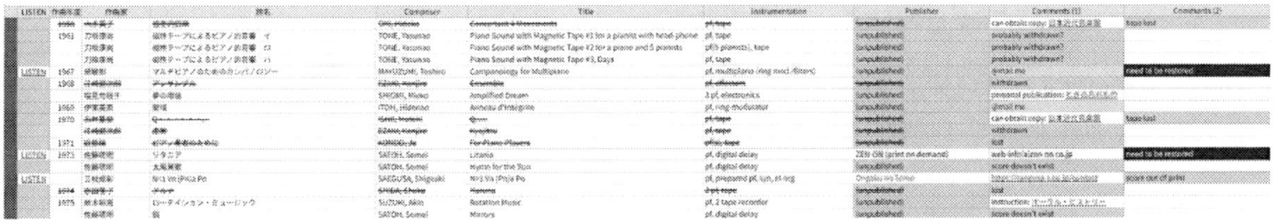

Figure 5 "List of Electroacoustic Works for Piano and Electronics by Japanese Composers [LOPEJ]" Written and screenshot captured by the author. Text with strikethrough refers to the lost or withdrawn compositions. The colored text in red indicates the score is currently out of print

There is still a limitation that the author – as an individual researcher – cannot update every new composition in real-time. To overcome this situation, the author made the database editable. So that every visitor can add the compositions they know or their own. The vandalization could be prevented since the Google spreadsheet can revert to the previous version.

3.2 Restoring Japanese Compositions

There are also several electroacoustic music compositions, which were composed with specific electronic technologies or devices at that time, which are currently not available. Occasionally certain compositions cannot even be reperformed since the composer cannot remember how they have operated the program although it still exists. As an example of possible practice for archiving, the author has also been working on restoring those compositions that are currently not performable.

In the database, the author has recorded 159 compositions for Piano and electronics in total (as of May 2024) and regards that at least 40 works from 142 (excluding certainly lost, withdrawn works) cannot be reperformed with their original technology and need an improvement or restoration.

The author is conscious that all compositions cannot be restored since not every composition has sufficient information to understand. Instead, the author has set certain standards and has been restoring regarded as representative compositions from each standard: 1) A composition with a currently unavailable device (technology). 2) An available composition but regarded as improvable with the current technology. 3) A composition that has never been realized.

For instance, we can regard restoring the works of Somei Satoh (佐藤聰明, 1947-) as an example of standard 1. He has composed several compositions for Piano and digital delay using a Three-head tape recorder from the 1970s, which could monitor the recorded sound while recording simultaneously. For instance, in his work in 1978, "Incarnation II (化身 II)", an instruction on how to operate the recorder and set the delay timing is written on the score. Although this recorder is currently not available, we can consider performing this work by simply using a physical delay effect or making a program with Max or Pure Data, et cetera.

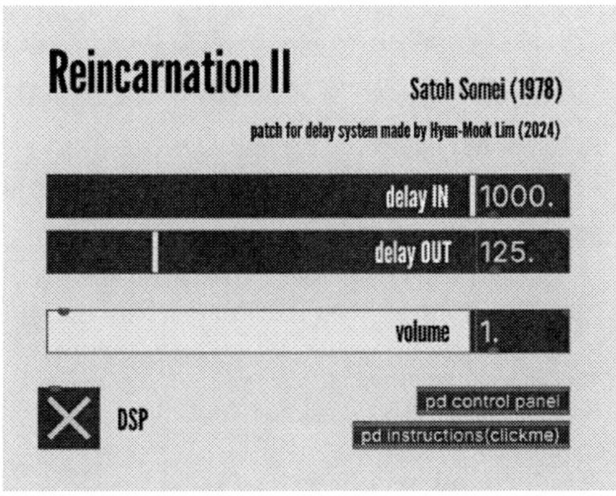

Figure 6 Program patch for performing Satoh Somei's "Reincarnation II". Patch made and screenshot captured by the author.

The author is writing every technical note on restoration and will make it public in the case where current technology might be unavailable in the future. The author expects this set of notes and database will make the performer, engineer, or researcher understand certain representative cases in Japanese electronic music history, and also how the electronic materials have been operated in detail, without contacting the author or the composer.

4. CONCLUSIONS

In this paper, we have discussed the current situation of accessing electroacoustic works in Japan while comparing the situation inside and outside Japan. Although many composers in Japan are currently privately publishing and distributing their works mainly through their websites or email contacts, there is still a need for a more organized publication and archive management system in the Japanese electronic music field.

The author is still working on restoring past Japanese works with outdated technologies. Although the author admits the limitation that this is only admitted to the limited number of works that the author understands, the author expects that this research could lay the groundwork for subsequent research. We will discuss the further results in the following research in the future.

5. REFERENCES

[1] A. Dobrowolski, *Music for Magnetic Tape and Piano Solo*, Polskie Wydawnictwo Muzyczne, 1973.

[2] A. Dobrowolski, *Music for Magnetic Tape and Piano Solo*, Rob. Forberg Musikverlag, 2007.

[3] K. Ezaki (江崎健次郎), *Music for Guitar and Electronic Sound (ギターと電子音のための音楽)*, Casa de la Guitarra (ギタルラ社), 1968.

[4] L. Nono, *...sofferte onde serene...*, Casa Ricordi, 1977.

[5] S. Satoh (佐藤聰明), *Incarnation II (化身 II)*, EXPERIM ENTAL HOUSE (EX ハウス), 1978.

[6] K. Kawasaki (川崎弘二), *Japanese Electronic Music seco nd edition (日本の電子音楽　増補改訂版)*. Aiikusha (愛育社), 2009.

[7] M. Mizuno (水野みか子) et al. "Journal of Sonic Arts (先端芸術音楽創作学会 会報) Vol.12, No.3" *Archiving of Japanese Electroacoustic Music - preliminary report of the JSEM archive project (日本の電子音響音楽アーカイヴについて ―日本電子音楽協会アーカイヴ・プロジェクトの経過報告―)*, Tokyo, 2020, pp. 12-16.

[8] T. H. Park. "array2020" *The Electro-Acoustic Music Mine Project (EAMM) Collecting, Archiving, Sharing, and Exploring*, California, 2020, p.21-30.

[9] Y. Suzuki, and A. Watanabe. "Journal of Sonic Arts (先端芸術音楽創作学会 会報) Vol.14, No.1" *Report of Symposium "Methodology of Archiving Electroacoustic Music – From a Practical Perspective in Concert Archiving (シンポジウム「電子音楽におけるアーカイブの方法論―コンサートアーカイブにおける実践的視点から―」開催報告)*", Tokyo, 2023, pp. 6-9.

[10] H. Lim (임현묵), *List of Electroacoustic Works for Piano and Electronics by Japanese Composers [LOPEJ]*. http://tinyurl.com/33tck5h2.

[11] R. Nishikawa (西川竜太), *Composer Database (作曲家データベース)*, https://composerworklist.wixsite.com/composerworklist.

[12] H. Yamamoto (山本裕之), *Oto wo Asobu: Japanese Composers (音ヲ遊ブ)*, https://japanesecomposers.info/jc/.

[13] Ensemble Free WEST (アンサンブル・フリー WEST) and Ensemble Free EAST (アンサンブル・フリー EAST), *Japanese Contemporary Composers Library (日本現代作曲家ライブラリー)*, https://contemporary-composer.jp/.

[14] Institut de Recherche et Coordination Acoustique/Musique, *Sidney: Technical Documentation Server for Ircam Musical Works*, https://brahms.ircam.fr/sidney.

[15] Japanese Society for Contemporary Music（日本現代音楽協会）, *Japanese composers and their works (日本の作曲家とその作品)*, https://www.jscm-db.net/db/search/.

This page intentionally left blank.

Technical Implementation and Artistic Expression Characteristics of Multimedia Electronic Music Creation in China

DAI Shan Shan
Communication University of China
ss_cuc@163.com

GUI Ren
City University of Hong Kong
GUI.Ren@my.cityu.edu.hk

ABSTRACT

Based on the past competitions, performances and exhibited works of the Beijing International Electronic Music Festival, this paper analyzes and interprets the Chinese multimedia electronic music works from technology and art. It categorizes these works into three types based on their creative technical methods means: unidirectional audio-visual creation, bidirectional audio-visual creation, and immersive audio-visual creation. We analyze the artistic characteristics of these works from the perspectives of media symbols and audio-visual symbols. With the development of 5G and artificial intelligence technologies, Chinese electronic music continuously extends to other art forms for cross-disciplinary integration. In retracing traditional arts, it constantly derives new, subversive forms of musical artistic expression.

Keywords: Electronic Music; Multimedia Music; Visual Images; Music Creation

1. INTRODUCTION

Electronic music entered China in the 1980s, with a "serious lag" of about 40 years compared to developed countries in the West. However, in the forty years since the early 1980s, Chinese electronic music has developed rapidly, not only in the fields of audio-visual electronic music, hybrid electronic music, multimedia electronic music, and interactive electronic music, but also in the fields of electronic music combined academic and applied music. Under the influence of immersive, interactive, and multimedia technologies, electronic music has presented a multi-media integration art form. In this integration, electronic music evolves from auditory to audio-visual and even multisensory trends. Technology and art intertwine throughout the ontological creation of electronic music, leading it to a multimedia era that combines with other art genres and media across disciplines.

The primary form of expression is now digital images and audio media, representing the sound materials, rhythms, and themes of electronic music through concrete or abstract visual content. In the trend of new technologies, the creation methods of electronic music works presented with digital images and audio media have also changed. Creators can not only create visual images closely related to musical ideas but also use real-time interactive technologies to simultaneously carry out music creativity and visual creation. For example, through computer programming, the pitch, amplitude and other attributes of music can control the changes in visual graphics, colors, and speeds in real time.

From the viewpoint of domestic and international electronic music forums and competitions, as well as the electronic music professional activities of domestic music colleges, and the emergence of forms of audiovisual works created with electronic music as the leading force, there are many different differences. In terms of numerous ways of audiovisual realization, different technologies have endowed electronic music methods combined with visual arts with distinct characteristics, giving works unique features in audio-visual language.

This paper breaks away from previous classification methods and explores the relationship between audio-visual symbols and production techniques in audio-visual electronic music. Multimedia electronic music is categorized into unidirectional, bidirectional, and immersive creation modes based on technical means, with artistic expression manifested in both audio-visual form and audio-visual connotation layers.

2. INTEGRATION OF TECHNICAL IMPLEMENTATION AND ARTISTIC EXPRESSION

Professor Zhang Xiaofu once said that audio-visual electronic music is not a simple superposition of visual images and music, but a "1+1>2" creative achievement, which is a poetic and pictorial expression of sound imagery and visual imagery abstracted again. The artistic language of contemporary electronic music has transformed from purely artistic attributes to highly technological cultural symbols in an environment of multimedia integration and various technology integration. Choosing any medium and using any technology must endow it with cultural significance, and the expression of musical connotation cannot be separated from the symbolization of the medium. In multimedia electronic music works, not only can computers be used to distribute and process digital information such as sound, light, and images, but technology and art together constitute each cultural symbol in the artistic image, which can be homogeneously placed. In the multimedia environment communicated in digital language, the heterogeneous combination of different sensory media is "connected" together in a special "interactive" relationship. Based on this, the author proposes a five-dimensional analysis method for multimedia electronic music, including:

Immersion level. The immersion level of visuals and music determines the immersion level of multimedia electronic music in the listener's experience, divided into: unidirectional (audio or video projected from a single side), multidirectional (multiple screens or multichannels), immersive.

Degree of freedom. The degree of freedom of visuals and music depends on the level of interaction with performers or audiences, divided into: fixed media (FixMedia, partial interaction, free interaction.

Visual source. The source of visuals, from the degree of interaction of visual sources, is divided into: pre-produced video materials, live real-time capture video, live real-time generated video.

Visual imagery. The directness of the source of visual imagery elements, from direct to indirect, is: music ontology (e.g., musical pitch, rhythm, timbre, etc.), external sources (e.g., the body movements of performers or audiences), abstract sources (some abstract interpretations, such as text, language, brain waves).

Visual connotation. Whether the visual and musical aspects of the work are culturally representational, in descending order: no cultural representation, musical symbols (e.g., using elements of Chinese calligraphy, opera, etc.), musical language (constructing a unique musical language).

In this paper, we selected five representative Chinese multimedia electronic music works, covering three generations of Chinese electronic music composers as well as different creative eras, to illustrate the above five-dimensions in detail. The first work, Professor Zhang Xiaofu's multimedia version of "Norilang" premiered in Beijing in 2004. The music part uses Tibetan female voices and sampled chanting voices from Tibetan Buddhism as the main sound materials, transforming and developing them through audio technology and electronic production techniques.It combines the concept of the cycle of life in Tibetan culture with the cyclical sound motives (Loop) in electronic music composition, expressing the cultural creativity of "circle" and "cycle" from small cycles to large cycles. This is connected and matched with the spiral development of the overall music structure, forming a unified and complete musical logic. The visual image part uses photos and images taken in Tibet, using image production techniques corresponding to electronic technology, such as reverse playback, constructing the composer's unique audio-visual language. Although there were already interactive means of expression during this period (as discussed in the following example), composers still finished music and visual creation on separate production platforms, composed the music first, and then used the visual material to interpret it in one direction. Although music and visuals cannot interact, this way of composing allows for a more tangible representation of cultural connotations to a certain extent. The following is a five-dimensional analysis diagram of the work:

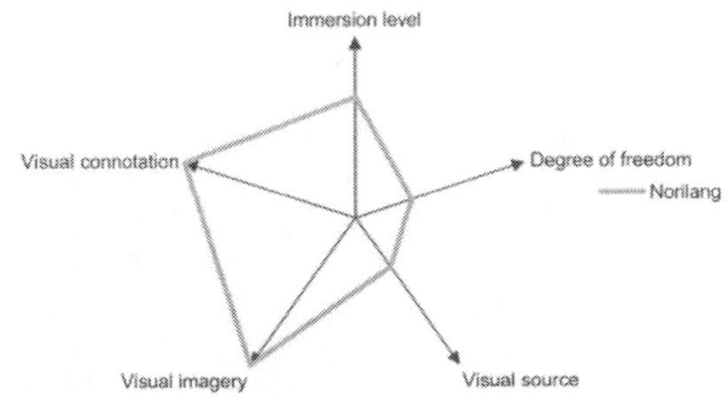

Figure 1. Five-dimensional analysis diagram of "Norilang" .

Figure 2. The performance of"Nuorilang" .

"Music in Calligraphy" by Cheng Yibing, created in 2004, which is a partially interactive musical work, the work captures the writing actions of a calligrapher, converting the actions into a part of the music during the performance. During the performance, the calligrapher's hand is tied with 6 sensors, with 5 bending sensors tied to the 5 fingers and 1 balance sensor tied to one side of the wrist. Thus, the calligrapher's writing actions in terms of force, displacement, bending, etc., are converted into MIDI signals in real time, forming the main body of the music, with two other elements: pure electronic improvisation on the "guqin"(Chinese instrument) and traditional ancient words sung through electronic processing (Vocoder). The following is a five-dimensional analysis diagram of the work:

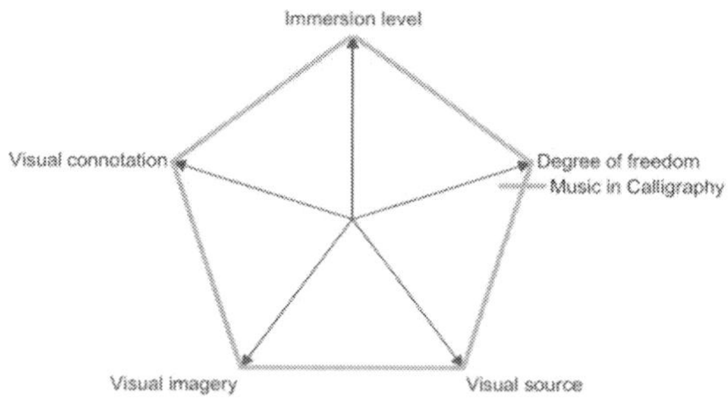

Figure 3. Five-dimensional analysis diagram of "Music in Calligraphy".

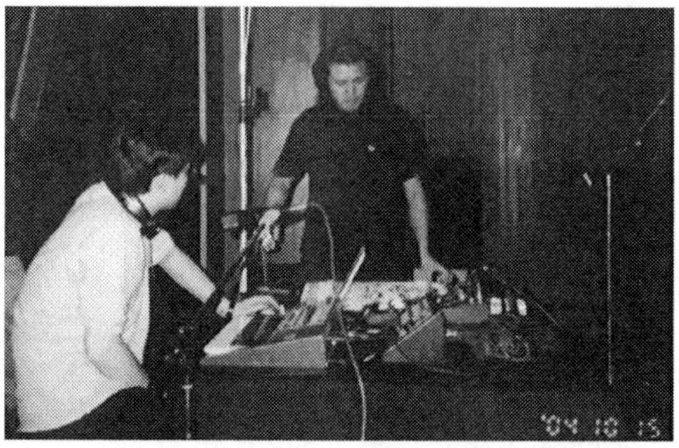

Figure 4. The performance of "Music in Calligraphy" in 2004 Beijing International Electronic Music Festival Opening Ceremony Concert .

The work "Boundless" is a live real-time generated piece, where the spatial movement of music performance is related to visual modeling, allowing the visual content to complete the same spatial movement trajectory in the image space as the sound's phase parameters. This work is highly abstract from sound to vision, and in the process of real-time generation, sound as the dominant feature, translating timbre, dynamic expression, and spatial movement into a data-driven process that generates the modeling elements, colors, and spatial lighting effects, etc, of the image. The work is led by sound, designing the visual material's modeling elements, colors, and spatial lighting effects according to the characteristics of sound material's timbre, dynamic expression, and spatial movement; defining different image components according to the time structure of the music work, adjusting the image's expression effects at any time according to the time of the music work; and flexibly adjusting the output image's size and shape according to the live performance environment, allowing the visual content to complete the same spatial movement trajectory in the image space as the sound's phase parameters. The following is a five-dimensional analysis diagram of the work:

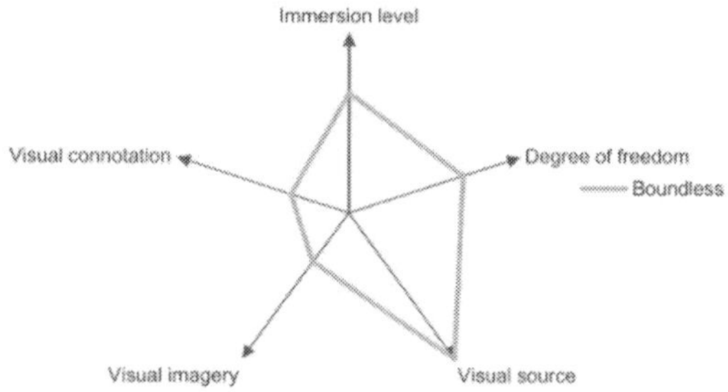

Figure 5. Five-dimensional analysis diagram of "Boundless" .

Figure 6. The performance of "Boundless" in 2017 Beijing International Electronic Music Festival .

The work "Whispering Water" has similarities in visual imagery with the previous work, which is mainly based on abstract point, line, and surface modeling elements, but there are obviously differences in the creative techniques. This work is a pre-produced video electronic music piece, focusing on "water" as the narrative object, using metallic sound materials and some instrumental performance sounds as the creative materials for electronic music. The work attempts to express the forms and characteristics of water through completely abstract sounds. Based on the main body and sound style of the work, the work uses abstract color language and graphic image language to map multiple musical elements in the music, such as sound segments, sound forms, dynamics, spatial forms, etc.The following is a five-dimensional analysis diagram of the work:

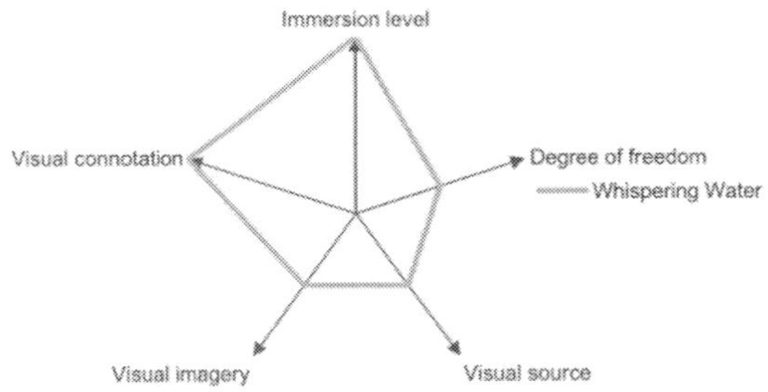

Figure 7. Five-dimensional analysis diagram of "Whispering Water".

Figure 8. The performance of "Whispering Water" in ICMC.

Living Room Drama uses artificial intelligence technology, which is one of the latest creative approaches in the trend of multimedia electronic music in China. During the performance, music and visuals can interact completely, freely and in real-time. The work sets up a "virtual theater", using artificial intelligence algorithms combined with video technology, using AI cameras to recognize objects, movements and scene locations, and realizing real-time interaction between the body and objects in the scene. In this kind of work, the visual material consists of the performer's body movements, without specific cultural connotations, but rather a kind of referential or "command" symbols. The following is a five-dimensional analysis diagram of the work:

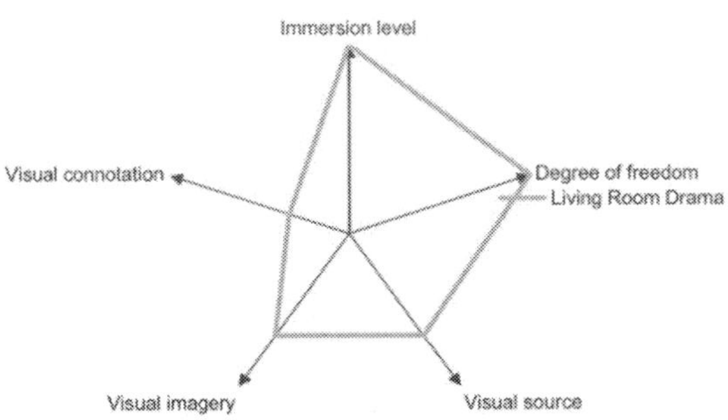

Figure 9. Five-dimensional analysis diagram of "Living Room Drama".

Figure 10. The performance of "Living Room Drama" in 2023 Hangzhou International Electronic Music Festival .

3. CONCLUSIONS

From the above, it seems that the complexity of musical composition determines how visual are presented. The more complex the musical texture or the higher the cultural expressiveness of the visual connotation in the work, the less freedom between auditory and visual; the visual sources generated in real time are associated with abstract visual imagery, in which the visual is the referential "symbol" of the music, and changes in the techniques and elements of the musical composition can be visually presented to the listener in real-time. All in all, Electronic music, from the concrete music period, tape music period, and electronic acoustics stage focusing on creating and exploring "new sounds" as purely auditory forms of music. To the computer music period, not only continues the pursuit of "new sounds", but also, in recent years, as everyday life becomes networked and interactive, technology as an accelerator between different media has fostered cross-boundary cooperation among various art forms. The public's requirements for the appearance or form of art have changed to some extent, and multimedia technology is continuously used in the artistic creation of electronic music. The essence of electronic music is the art of sound, but in the new era, new environment, and under the influence of new technology, its expression as an integrated art form becomes increasingly strong. With the development new technology, our music creation ways will become increasingly affluent, and future electronic music creation and stage art will continue to extend to other art forms for cross-disciplinary integration, in retracing traditional arts, it will continuously derive new, subversive forms of musical artistic expression.

Acknowledgments

Thanks to the National Social Science Foundation of China for the support of the Art Project "Chinese Contemporary Electronic Music Works and Composers".

4. REFERENCES

[1] Zhang Xiaofu, "Review and evaluation of the development of electronic music in China," *J. Art Review*, no. 04, pp. 27-40, 2012.

[2] Zhang Xiaofu, Zhang Zhaoxia, Liu Yantao, "Three important categories in Chinese new media art research " *J. Journal of Renmin University of China*, vol. 27, no. 01, pp. 44-51, 2013.

[3] Wang Xuan, Dai Shanshan, "Presentation of Chinese electronic music audio-visual art under the fusion of immersive multiple media," *J. People's Music*, no. 10, pp. 32-34, 2019.

[4] Guan Peng, "Sound objects and sound symbols - On the rational perception and perceptual perception of the sound of "Acousmatic music," *J.Huang Zhong (Journal of Wuhan Conservatory of Music, China)*, no. 02, pp. 17-26, 2010.

[5] Zhao Xiaoyu, "Energy aggregation and radiation—the development of Chinese electronic music creation styles from the Beijing International Electronic Music Festival," *J.Chinese Music,*no. 04, pp. 186-192, 2020.

[6] LU Agile,JIANG Xiaoli, "A preliminary exploration of new samples of new media music in China,"J. *Contemporary Literature Forum*, no. 02, pp. 149-153, 2017.

[7] Chen Yun. "Visual representation of visual music," *J.Cultural Studies*,, no. 02, pp. 170-186, 2016.

[8] Wang Xuan. *Interactive Music*. Chongqing University Press, 2010.

This page intentionally left blank.

Changing terms – naming categories. A systematic approach to performance information

Miriam Akkermann
FU Berlin
miriam.akkermann@fu-berlin.de

ABSTRACT

Performance details contain many information that go beyond pure concert details, providing both insights in artistic work processes and hints to inherent performance traditions. This accounts also for musical works that are genuinely linked to technology. Both insightful with regard to the role of the embedded technology and challenging for analytical approaches is hereby the variety of terms and categories for describing music technologies, which is, amongst others, mirrored in program lists and concert notes. This paper presents the collection and systematization of performance information on mixed music compositions which have been created and performed at IRCAM in the 1980s and 2000s, and discusses how performance details can serve as a starting point for examining performance practices with regard to the use of music technologies from a musicological point of view.

1. INTRODUCTION

Musical works that employ technology as a significant element for carrying out the artistic ideas, such as, e.g., computer music and mixed music [1] are strongly influenced by the technology in use, as well as by technological changes. This becomes especially evident when looking at musical works developed in the 1980s and 2000s: while it can be assumed that there exists a strong mutual relationship between the musical idea and the embedded technologies, which influences the genesis of a piece and is mirrored in its appearance and performances, many of the initial technologies are no longer functional in the 21st century due to rapid technological developments. In order to be able to perform those pieces, technologies in use have to be regularly updated or replaced – a process which is also observable in the compositions' documentations, as well as programs and concert notes which often contain a heterogeneous field of varying terms to describe the embedded technology of one and the same piece. This fuses with two further challenges: There is no standard for describing music technologies, and the definition and use of some terms have changed over time [2]. At the same time, the discrepancies in the descriptions also hint at larger developments: selective information or the detail level chosen to describe technology can depend on a documentalist's interest but also hint at a 'common sense' among documentalists and the documented artists and technicians. When examining the descriptions of the embedded technology, the terminology in use, can serve as a starting point to explore a composition's creational background and underlying artistic and sonic ideas, and to reveal insights in ongoing performance practices. Performance details may hence offer both, information on how musical pieces were seen at the time of description and hints to inherent musical performance traditions related to music technology.

In the following, this is investigated using an exemplary dataset of mixed music compositions which have been created and performed at the Institute de Recherche et Coordination Acoustique/Musique IRCAM in the 1980s and 2000s. The main data set has been established in June-August 2015 in context of the presented research project. The exemplary section was chosen as IRCAM's archive provides comprehensive sources on annuals concerts and performances and has been operating continuously since the examined decade. This allows to contextualize observations deriving from the systematic observations also from historic perspective and create synergy effects with regard to the interpretation of the findings [3].

The leading questions for observing of the collected dataset were: Which terms are used to describe technology in musical works, and how do they change? How can the occurring terms be categorized? And what can we learn from the observable (in-)consistencies regarding inherent musical performance practices?

Underlying hypotheses are that firstly, characteristics of musical performance practices manifest themselves in performance data, and, secondly, that these characteristics are structurally similar for different performance practices, which allows to compare developments of possibly different branches of performance practice.

The focus of this paper is to outline the assembly of the retrievable performance information as well as the process and challenges concerning systematizing the terms and categories which are used to describe the (music) technologies, and to show how observing shifts in the use of terms and their definitions may help to learn about inherent performance practices.

The aim of this paper is to present a systematic approach to performance details and show the necessary interplay between an analytical and historical viewpoint for establishing a dataset from performance details. The resulting dataset is part of an ongoing research project.

2. CHALLENGES OF SYSTEMATIZING PERFORMANCES DETAILS

When establishing a dataset from source content, two aspects have to be considered: what can be examined in a dataset also depends on how this dataset is structured, and how a dataset is structured depends on the way in which the content is systematized and hence transferred into information units. This requires a content-related (historical) knowledge in order to ensure the correct implementation of the content, as well as an evaluation-related (statistical) perspective in order to create suitable categories which re meaningful for the content's context. However, a dataset cannot provide both the greatest possible level of detail and the creation of superordinate categories that summarize the individual pieces of information obtained from the content.

In the context of mixed music, one major challenge is the lack of a uniform classification of the technologies involved. Instead of categories for technical settings and technology-based instruments, terms such as 'electroacoustic music,' 'computer music,' and 'mixed music' can be found, serving as both classes of compositions with seemingly comparable technical structures, vague technical indications, as well as a genre-like group assignments independent from the actual embedded technology [3]. This lack of a uniform classification is also a challenge to areas such as, e.g., archiving and content management in meta-databases, where these inconsistencies are faced with various strategies.

The IRCAM database *Sidney,* for example, integrates a data model developed by Serge Lemouton and Samuel Goldszmidt that specifically takes care of systematizing performance relevant technical information. Dedicated to storing, archiving and providing access to the documentation of performances developed and carried out in context of IRCAM, the database's structure relys on a data model designed to archive information with regard to different versions of a composition's performance, including different types of descriptions (such as technical plans, set-up descriptions, program codes), and technologies. Lemouton and Goldszmidt hereby subdivide the information into two major categories: group (work, event, natural person, person function, user) and content (WorkSidney, WorkFile, VersionFile, Version, VersionNaturalPerson, VersionEquipment), and relate them to each other [4]. *Sidney* provides no overall classification of the compositions or basic systematization of the involved technology; the search interface is structured by person, composition title, and performance date, whereas a search for specific instrumentation or technical settings is not provided.

The meta-database *Identifiants et Référentiels pour l'enseignement supérieur et la recherche IdRef* published by the Agence bibliographique de l'enseignement supérieur (ABES), in contrast, integrates findable information from several different sources, indicating basic content and the source providing the information. While *IdRef*'s search interface is also primarily oriented towards searching for names/persons and works/objects, the field "Tous le index" seems to implicitly offer a glimpse on categorization approaches: the search engine contains a vast collection of keywords based on the implemented databases' indexing. This includes categories such as 'Musique électroacoustique mixte,' 'Musique mixte,' 'Musique mixte acoustique et électronique,' 'Musique élektroacoustique,' 'Computer Music,' and 'Electronic Music.' However, searching these kinds of terms only offers the results that are individually connected to this specific search term; it will not be shown if a category doesn't exist in an implemented source [5].

Having started based on three main sources (works developed and performed in context of the Electronic Studio of TU Berlin, the Institute of Sonology, and the Festival Interventionen, Berlin), *EMDoku* is a (to date) privately maintained database specialized on providing details on compositions and performances of electroacoustic music. It integrates information from several international festivals, amongst others the ICMC concerts. Hereby, *EMDoku* combines several approaches, containing on the one hand an (access-restricted) database with performance information and recordings from TU Berlin, and serving on the other hand as a complex meta-database. Besides the search for basic information such as composer/name, composition/titles, and date of composition, *EMDoku* also offers the search for a specific instrumentation as well as a selection of "genres," which, however, include different levels of classification, ranging from media type (e.g., "Dia," "Film") to type of work (e.g., "Installation") and individual classifications of technology (e.g. "live elec") [6]. Assumably, these "genres" have been largely taken over from (self-)announcements deriving from the related sources such as program notes, concert programs, and composers' descriptions.

While *Sidney* and *IdRef* avoid the challenge of the prevalent inconsistent use of terms by neither offering nor creating their own (search) categories, the very same challenge of not having an overarching terminology for groups of technology and unified genre classification already in the sources is illustrated by "genre" integrated in *EMDoku* – the latter a situation that applies to most concert information when transcribed directly from these sources.

3. THE DATA SET

In this project, a dataset was established containing performance details on mixed music compositions developed and/or performed at IRCAM in the time span of 1979–1990 and 1999–2010. The focus is set on compositions embedding technology in real-time in the broadest sense, ranging from tape to (digital) synthesizer and (digital) real-time sound processing – compositions, whose technical outline is assumingly traceable influenced by the technical developments. The time periods under examination were chosen with regard to the technological developments in the decade in between: in the 1990s, rapid developments in music technology took place. Amongst others, real-time music programming languages became processable on PCs, becoming not only accessible to a broader public but also quite flexible to cover different needs. At the same time, IRCAM offers a well-documented and clear working structure as well as continuous reporting on concerts and performances available in the institution's Mediatheque. This provides an excellent basis for gathering performance details for the envisioned time periods from seasonal and festival programs, booklets for special (additional) concert series, program notes for individual concerts, and mentions of guest performances and tours in the season program or in IRCAM's annual report. The gathered information was cross-checked with the IRCAM data bases *Brahms* and *Sidney* in case of doubt or missing information. The data collection took place from June to August 2015 at IRCAM Mediatheque in Paris, accompanied by online research throughout 2019-2022.

In a first step, the relevant performance details were extracted from the sources, roughly split up in individual information, and transferred into an excel-sheet. In a second step, the content was 'cleaned up' which included correcting typos, removing extra blanks, checking special characters, making sure that first and last name of the composer are in the intended order, as well as removing doubletted entries. It results a first basic systematization of the content presented in an excel-sheet in which each line represents a performed piece of music which is described by the related details structured in columns. Besides basic categories such as composer/name, title/piece, year of composition, performance date, year of premiere, involved soloists, RIMs, conductors if applicable, and sometimes re-performance dates, also information such as self-description of genre and the instrumentation structured as a collection of instruments and (if mentioned) technologies were added.

As expected, the categorization of the instruments and technologies came along with several challenges, notably three major ones:

a) Terms to describe the technology-based instrument are not always coherent with the description of the technology. In Marc-André Dalbavie's composition *Diadèmes* (1986), e.g., the instrumentation includes a "célesta (also 2 claviers électroniques/MIDI/synthétiseurs [Yamaha DX7])," while the following description points out that is consisted of an "électronique composé de deux synthétiseurs Yamaha DX7," but the documentation of the premiere points out that a Yamaha TX816 was used. [7, see also 8].

b) Terms refer to superior categories which do (usually) not describe the technology-based instruments in use, e.g., in Thomas Kessler's piece *Flute Control* (1984), the description "électronique" signifies the use of a Fairlight synthesizer [9, see also 10].

c) Terms appear in different languages (majorly French, English, German) or different terms describe the same technology. Even though some terms and definitions may be linked to a respective language and terminological changes over time are no longer easy to observe, the terms have been standardized in one language. Though, these changes have to be kept in mind and taken into account in the interpretation of the dataset. In addition, descriptions such as 'lecteur CD' and 'CD' have been merged into one category. In the same procedure, instruments such as electric piano (if no synthesizer), electric guitar, Onde Martenot, and 'orgue' (if identifiable as an organ) have been excluded from the group of technology-based instrument and appear in line with the acoustic instruments instead.

In order to enable statistical examinations of the dataset, missing information – blank cells within the excel sheet – were filled with "0." In case of an unclear entries, the information on these performances was (as far as possible) cross-checked.

The resulting dataset comprises of 929 identifiable performances with 160 distinguished attributes [3].

4. SOME OBSERVATIONS

The collected performances derive from 559 identifiable compositions composed by 340 namable composers and assigned 14 groups (e.g., the 'Cursus' classes); for 33 performances, no name of an individual or group is listed. In addition, 62 performances do no show a work's title [3].

When looking at the number of performances per composer in both decades of focus, most performances took place of compositions by Pierre Boulez (61 performances), followed by Karlheinz Stockhausen (37 performances), Johnathan Harvey (33 performances), Phillippe Manoury (23 performances), and Kaija Saariaho as well as Georges Aphergis (both 20 performances) [3].

The two compositions listing by far the highest number of performances are Boulez' compositions *Dialogue de l'hombre double* (31 performances) and *Anthème 2* (19 performances). *Dialogue de l'ombre double* is hereby special in several respects: The piece is not only the most performed piece in the 2000s in context of IRCAM – 30 times between 1999 and 2001 including in the original version for clarinet, as well as arranged for other solo instruments such as saxophone, bassoon, and oboe –, it is also the most frequently performed work composed in the 1980s, although it was only performed once in the decade of its composition. This low re-performance rate in the 1980s is quite coherent with the overall impression: less than 20% of the compositions that have been premiered in the 1980s have been reperformed in this decade; in the 2000s, the re-performance rate is slightly higher [3].

When looking at the assigned instrumentation and the self-assigned categories it shows up that 26 different technology-based instruments details can be identified, which are mentioned a total of 377 times. 267 performances are listed without information on the instrumentation, and 412 performances name one (plus technology not listed in the instrumentation) or two instruments (with or without technology) in their details. The highest number of mentions accounts to the instrument "bande" ('tape') with 205 mentions. Hereby, the term appears under ten different self-classifications, most often assigned to "sons fixés sur support" (also in some cases with the addition of "temps reel") and a few times as "dispositive électronique/électroacoustique," "musique acousmatique," "musique concrete" or as "électronique" [3]. As the overall tendency goes rather towards self-assigning broader, unspecific categories, the classification "4X" for the two performances of *Epigénèse* (1986) by Jean-Baptoste Barrière appears as an outliner. Here, the instrumentation includes both "bande et ordinateur 4X" [11], being embedded in parallel in the performance of the piece, and the self-classification relates to the real-time digital sound synthesis, not to the tape. The details concerning the technologies mentioned reveal that the description of the embedded technology is not coherent – neither throughout various performances of one nor across different compositions. It is not possible to link the self-classifications to either the technology assigned within a composition's description or the technology in use at a specific performance.

What can be concluded is that most of the performances cover compositions in chamber music size: ~73% of the performances list to employ one or two instruments, another 55 performances list three instruments. This goes well along with the observation that 744 out of the 929 performances (~80%) do not list a conductor; for the remaining 185 performances mentioning a conductor, 58 male and four female conductors can be identified. Hereby, Péter Eötvös stands out with conducting 33 performances, followed by Denis Cohen (nine performances), Jean Deroyer, Jonathan Nott and Pierre Boulez (eight performances each), and Susanna Mälkki (six performances) [3].

These basic observations illustrate vividly the challenges that are already apparent in the preparation of the dataset. At the same time, it is interesting to note that most of the systematic incoherencies can be framed or contextualized when going back to the sources. The challenge of categorizing the information as visible e.g. in the instrumentation accumulates on top of two parallel and interlinked challenges: on the one hand, the sources appear inconsistent and incomplete which may derive from the fact that they have been created by various persons with potentially differing interests and needs; on the other hand, the vague indications may also derive from quite practical reasons due to the nature of the source, e.g., that concert announcements can be requested before a commissioned composition is completed, or that the intended set-up was not yet decided when the concert was announced, or changed, adjusted or updated due to practical restrictions. In some cases, using vague terminology also seems be a strategy to provide a seemingly comprehensible description.

5. CONCLUSION

The process of systematizing performance details shows that the way of categorizing source-based information has a strong and direct impact on the possible results subsequent analyses of the resulting dataset can provide. In parallel, this very same process already requires to reflect on existing definitions and inherent assumptions in order to be able to establish suitable categories: the whole process hence bases on an interplay and negotiation process between a historic and a systematic viewpoint.

While some of the systematic observations depict what can be also assumed from a historical perspective – that the musical performances in the1980s and the 2000s are strongly influenced by Boulez's works, also rather little noticed aspects come to light, e.g., that compositions by Stockhausen were the third most frequently played pieces in the observed decades, foremost the 1980s. While it may not surprise that, given the examined periods, 'tape' is the technology listed in most performances, it is interesting to see that the description 'tape' stays within the instrumentation details of a piece despite the fact that obviously other (digital) technologies were used in the announced performances of this very same piece. Hence, it can be argued that the examination of the terminology in use mirrors both, individual (institutional) trends in musical performance practice and an understanding of how to express certain phenomena and name objects.

The observation that there exists a largely varying accuracy of information within a set of sources that have been created for communicating and promoting musical performances, suggests that there exists a strong uncommunicated self-conception shared between the creators of the sources and their addressed recipients. This can be interpreted as an indication for a common-sense knowledge with regard to the music performed as well as the technology in use, especially as some terminological definitions are bound to short time periods.

For this exemplary dataset, a future examination can thus ask for correlations between the terms used in the compositions' descriptions, especially the naming and framing of the embedded technology, and the various descriptions' purposes and authors. The observation of performance details of mixed music presented at IRCAM in the 1980s and 2000s can hence be used as a starting point to foster further discussions concerning ongoing performance practices and inherent common (musical) knowledge.

Working on the categorization of the terms describing technologies shows, however, that not all content can be summarized in overarching categories. In some cases, details must be retained visible in order to enable a historically meaningful data representation, and translation challenges, cultural biases, and individual perspectives of composers and electronic musicians have to be acknowledged more in dept – a framing that depends on both the scope and type of available data as well as the intended research question.

6. REFERENCES

[1] V. Tiffon, *Recherches Sur Les Musiques Mixtes*. Université d'Aix-Marseille I, 1994.

[2] M. Akkermann. "Vocabulary ruts in Mixed Music – multifarious terms with many ascriptions," in: *Proceedings of the ICMC 2021*, Santiago de Chile. 10.5281/zenodo.4161673.

[3] M. Akkermann, "Performance details dataset IRCAM music performances including technologies; 1990s and 2000s"; in idem. *Neue Praxis vergangener Ideale*, Universität Bayreuth 2023.

[4] S. Lemouton and S. Goldszmidt, "La préservation des œuvres du répertoire IRCAM: Présentation du modèle Sidney et analyse des dispositifs temps réel," *Journées d'Informatique musicale*, 2016, hal-01944619.

[5] Agence bibliographique de l'enseignement supérieur ABES (ed.), *Identifiants et Référentiels pour l'enseignement supérieur et la recherche IdRef*, www.idref.fr/ (Jan 28, 2024).

[6] F. Hein, EMDoku, https://emdoku.de/de (Jan 28, 2024).

[7] IRCAM (Ed.), "Marc-André Dalbavie (1961). Diadèmes (1986)," *Brahms*, https://brahms.ircam.fr/works/work/7549/ (Feb 4, 2022).

[8] M. Akkermann, "This hardware is now obsolete" *Proceedings of the ICMC 2017*, Shanghai, https://hdl.handle.net/2027/spo.bbp2372.2017.021

[9] IRCAM (Ed.), "Thomas Kessler (1937). Flute Control (1984)," *Brahms*, https://brahms.ircam.fr/works/work/9671/ (Feb 8, 2022).

[10] L. Koblyakov. "Thomas Kesslers 'Control-'Stücke." *Dissonances* 2010.

[11] IRCAM (Ed.). "Jean-Baptiste Barrière (1958) Epigénèse (1986)," *Brahms*, https://brahms.ircam.fr/fr/works/work/6633/ (Feb 4, 2022).

OMM: an OpenMusic library for Mathematical Morphology

Carlos Agon
Sorbonne Université,
CNRS, IRCAM, STMS,
Paris, France
agonc@ircam.fr

Gonzalo Romero-García
Sorbonne Université,
CNRS, IRCAM, STMS,
Paris, France
romero@ircam.fr

Isabelle Bloch
Sorbonne Université,
CNRS, LIP6,
Paris, France
isabelle.bloch@sorbonne-universite.fr

ABSTRACT

This article introduces OMM, a new OpenMusic library based on Mathematical Morphology. After conducting several years of research on the potential usages of Mathematical Morphology operators in composition, musical analysis, and music education, we are convinced that it is now opportune to develop computer tools for music creation, analysis, and education based on Mathematical Morphology concepts. Our primary objective is to demonstrate the relevance of these techniques in the musical domain. In pursuit of this goal, we present one illustrative example based on rhythmical transformations. OMM represents an initiative aimed at bridging the gap between theoretical ideas and practical applications in the musical domain. This contribution reflects our commitment to democratizing access to advanced musical tools, thereby promoting a more inclusive musical landscape.

1. INTRODUCTION

This article introduces OMM, an OpenMusic [1] library which applies Mathematical Morphology to music. Mathematical Morphology (MM) is a domain at the intersection of mathematics and computer science. It was originally formulated in the mid-1960s in [2] and [3].

MM has been highly successful in the field of image processing. We argue that MM can also be relevant in the musical domain, without the need to represent music as an image. The paper [4] suggested for the first time a possible strategy to approach musical information research by combining tools and ideas belonging to MM. More recently, two doctoral theses [5] and [6] have improved this research domain proposing relevant representations both in the symbolic and signal processing domains.

We argue that the application of MM to the musical domain is advantageous, mainly because its algebraic characteristics. The fundamental idea is to define abstract operators for the generation and analysis of musical materials in general. Once these operators are defined, it is crucial to find suitable representations where these tools can be applied in a musically relevant manner. OMM provides a graphical interface for connecting various mathematical morphology operators to musical objects. We present in this paper one specific application case concerning rhythms. Furthermore, OMM establishes the necessary conditions to apply mathematical morphology operators to new musical materials, thereby offering users the opportunity to pursue new musical research.

This article is organized as follows: in Section 2, we define the basics of MM [1], specifically its two fundamental operators: dilation and erosion. Then we show how these operators combine to define two other fundamental ones: opening and closing. These four operators, which may seem abstract initially, will gain meaning through their applications in the following sections. In Section 3, we introduce a first application domain: rhythmic canons. In this section, we employ what is known as binary morphology. Section 4 is dedicated to outlining the protocol necessary for extending applications to other types of representations, provided that they adhere to the conditions imposed by MM. We quickly showcase in this section an application concerning melodies by using what is known as grayscale morphology. The last section allow us to draw conclusions and envision other potential scenarios for future research.

2. MATHEMATICAL MORPHOLOGY

Lattice structures are at the basis of MM. We start by giving the definition of complete lattices (see [8] to know more about lattice theory).

[Poset : partially ordered set] A poset is a pair $\langle P, \leq \rangle$ where P is a set equipped with a binary relation $\leq$, called the order of P, with $\leq$ being reflexive, antisymmetric and transitive.

We focus on a particular class of posets, namely lattices.

[Lattice] A poset $\langle L, \leq \rangle$ is a lattice if every pair of elements $x, y \in L$ has both a least upper bound and a greatest lower bound.

[Upper and lower bounds] Let $\langle L, \leq \rangle$ be an ordered set and $S \subseteq L$. Then

- $x \in L$ is a *lower bound* of S if $\forall y \in S, x \leq y$,
- $x \in L$ is the *greatest lower bound* of S if $\forall y \in S^\ell, x \geq y$.

when S^ℓ denotes the set of all the lower bounds of S.

This research is supported by European Research Council ERC-ADG-883313 REACH, and Agence Nationale de la Recherche ANR-19-CE33-0010 MERCI.

[1] For a real introduction to MM, we recommend [7].

The *(least) upper bound* and the set of all upper bounds S^u are defined dually by reversing the order (using $\geq$ instead of $\leq$).

[Complete lattice] A lattice $\langle L, \leq \rangle$ is complete if every subset of $S \subseteq L$ has both a least upper bound and a greatest lower bound, called supremum and infimum. A complete lattice is always bounded: there is a greatest element $\top \in L$ such that $\forall x \in L.x \leq \top$ and a least element $\bot \in L$ such that $\forall x \in L.\bot \leq x$.

A lattice is an algebraic structure $\langle L, \sqcup, \sqcap \rangle$ where the binary operation $\sqcup$ is called the join and $\sqcap$ the meet. The join $x \sqcup y$ is the least upper bound of the set $\{x, y\}$ and the meet $x \sqcap y$ is its greatest lower bound. We use the notation $\bigsqcup S$ (resp. $\bigsqcap S$) to compute the least upper bound (resp. greatest lower bound) of the set S.

Let $(L, \leq)$ and $(L', \leq')$ be any two arbitrary lattices, the two basic operations of MM, erosion and dilation, are defined as follows:

[Dilation] $\delta : L \to L'$ is a dilation if $\forall x_i \in L$, $\delta(\bigsqcup x_i) = \bigsqcup' \delta(x_i)$.

[Erosion] $\varepsilon : L \to L'$ is a erosion if $\forall x_i \in L$, $\varepsilon(\bigsqcap x_i) = \bigsqcap' \varepsilon(x_i)$.

In other words, an operator δ (resp. ε) is a dilation (resp. erosion) if it commutes with the supremum (resp. the infimum).

In this paper, we will define these two operators in a simplified framework called deterministic MM with structuring element. The main idea is to transform an element $A \in L$ using another element $B \in L$ called the structuring element. It is to note that in our case, the domain and codomain of erosion and dilation are the same lattice, i.e. $L = L'$.

We define algorithms for dilation and erosion using structuring element as follows:

-For dilation, we take the origin of the structuring element B, and translate it to occupy successively all positions within the space A. For each position, if B intersects A then this position is part of the dilation. We will note the dilation of A by B as $A \oplus B$.

-For erosion, we take the origin of the structuring element B, and translate it to occupy successively all positions within the space A. For each position, if B is completely included within A then this position is part of the erosion. We will note the erosion of A by B as $A \ominus B$.

The problem with these algorithms is that the notions of translation, intersection, inclusion and the origin of the structuring element depend entirely on the lattice that we use. In the following section, we will provide a specific example using what is called binary morphology.

Before concluding this section, we define two new operators based on erosion and dilation: opening and closing.

[Opening] $A \circ B = (A \ominus B) \oplus B$.

[Closing] $A \bullet B = (A \oplus B) \ominus B$.

In image processing it is said that opening removes narrow parts of the object and deforms convex corners of the object while closing fills narrow parts of the background and deforms concave corners of the object [7]. If we want to apply MM to music, it is necessary that we can make similar assertions about the application of these operators to musical structures.

The next section will provide specific examples of these four operators applied to rhythmical structures.

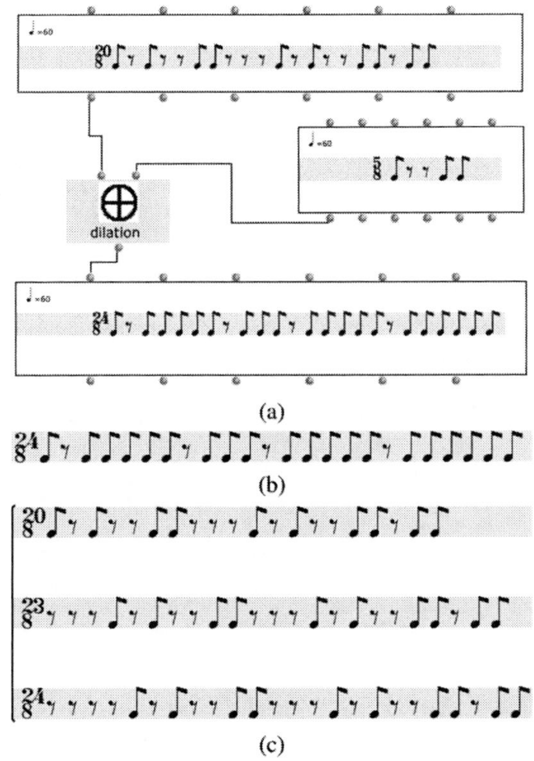

Figure 1. Dilation of one rhythm by another one.

3. RHYTHM

In this section, we work on what is called binary morphology. Binary morphology is often referred too as morphology on sets because it uses the lattice $(\mathcal{P}(E), \subseteq)$ with E a set and $\mathcal{P}(E)$ the power set of E.

The lattice that we will use here is defined by $(\mathcal{P}(\mathbb{Z}), \subseteq)$. Intuitively, we interpret a set X as a rhythmic pattern. For instance, {0,2,4,5} corresponds to the following rhythm . In this example, we have taken the quarter note as the beat. There is a quarter note at position e for each element e in our set, and a rest otherwise.

In this context, we define the dilation of a rhythm A by a structuring rhythm B by the equation:

$A \oplus B = \{a + b \mid a \in A, b \in B\}$ with the usual addition in $\mathbb{Z}$.

Figure 1 (a) illustrates a program that performs the dilation computation of a rhythm $R_1 = \{0, 2, 5, 6, 10, 12, 15, 16, 18, 19\}$ by a structuring rhythm $R_2 = \{0, 3, 4\}$.

Analyzing the result in Figure 1 (b), we observe that it arises from the flattening of a rhythmic canon with internal rhythm R_1 and external rhythm R_2. This canon is shown in Figure 1 (c). Dilation proves to be a straightforward method for constructing rhythmic canons, as defined in [9]. This observation is not surprising, given that we have defined binary dilation using the Minkowski addition in $\mathbb{Z}$. Rhythmic canons have been widely employed as techniques in various compositions, see [10].

Let us now see if we can attribute a rhythmic meaning to erosion. We define the erosion of a rhythm A by a structuring rhythm B by the equation:

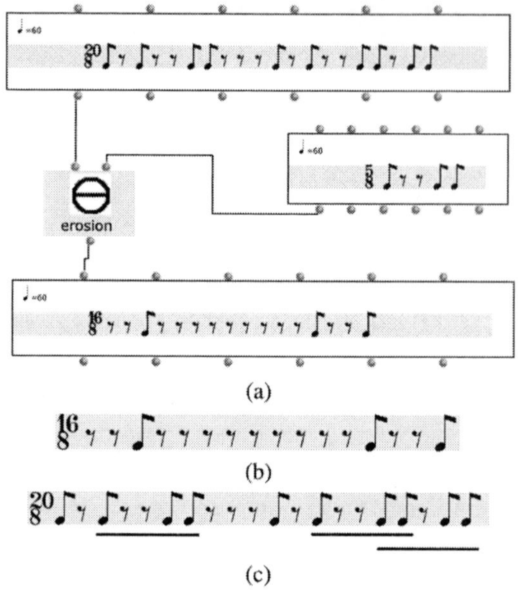

Figure 2. Erosion of one rhythm by another one.

$A \ominus B = \{p \in A \mid B_p \subseteq X\}$, where $B_p = \{x + p \mid x \in X\}$.

Figure 2 (a) shows a program that calculates the erosion of the rhythm R_1 by the structuring rhythm R_2.

Erosion computes a new rhythm, displayed in Figure 2 (b), wherein the attack points align with the starting moments in R_1 where one can find the rhythmic motif R_2. From a musical analysis standpoint, this is comparable to seeking occurrences of R_2 within R_1, similarly to searching for a word in a text (see Figure 2 (c)).

Let us now examine the rhythmic opening and closing operations. Figure 3 (a) illustrates a program that calculates the opening of R_1 by R_2.

The result, depicted in Figure 3 (b), is equivalent to the flattening of the rhythmic canon in Figure 3 (c). This canon is obtained by taking as internal rhythm R_2. The external rhythm is determined by the positions of R_2 within R_1, that is, $R_1 \ominus R_2$.

The opening removes the attacks from the original rhythm that do not belong to any instantiation of the structuring rhythm. These can be thought of as a kind of rhythmic noise.

Figure 4 (a) illustrates a program that calculates the closing of R_1 by R_2. Unlike opening, closing adds new attacks to the original rhythm (see Figure 4 (b)). This is due to the fact that the rhythmic space is first saturated by the construction of the rhythmic canon $R_1 \oplus R_2$ (Figure 4 (c)).

Experimentally, OMM incorporates additional operators specific to MM (e.g., hit-and-miss, area opening, area closing, see [7]). However, since their musical relevance is not evident, we have chosen not to present them in this article.

4. WORKING WITH OTHER LATTICES

OpenMusic is written in Common Lisp. For a user eager to extend OMM to other musical domains, the procedure consists in defining methods for the following generic functions:

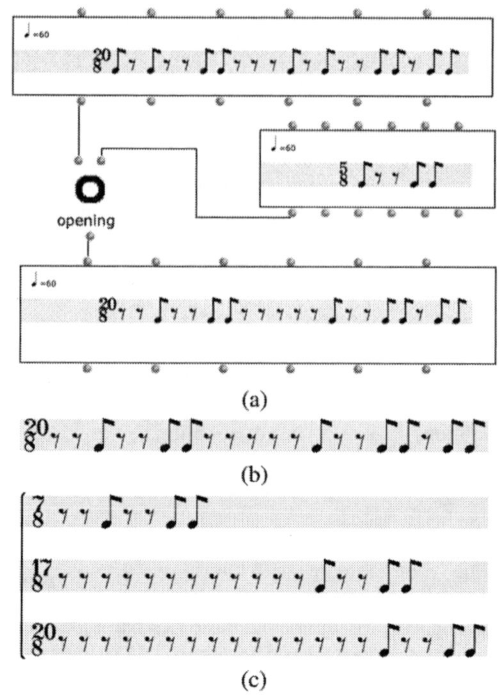

Figure 3. Opening of one rhythm by another one.

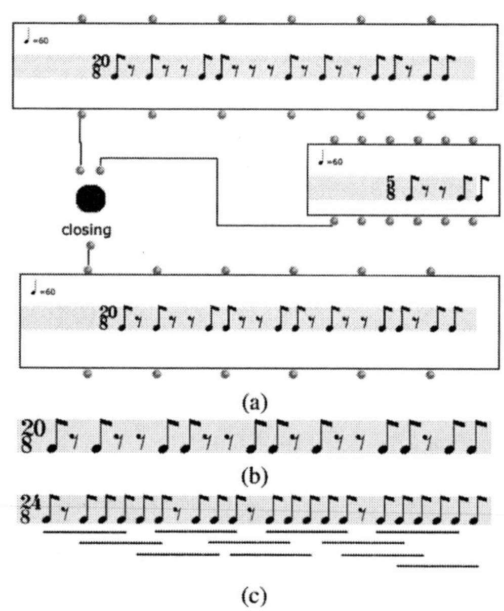

Figure 4. Closing of one rhythm by another one.

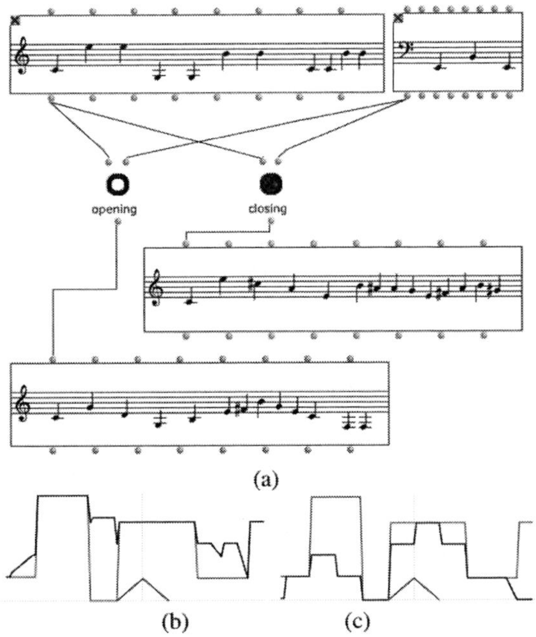

Figure 5. Opening and closing of melodies.

```
(defgeneric supremum ((obj1 t) (obj2 t)))
(defgeneric infimum ((obj1 t) (obj2 t)))
(defgeneric minus ((obj t)))
(defgeneric translate ((obj t) (x t)))
```

For instance, the binary morphology used for rhythms in Section 3 was defined by the following code:

```
(defmethod supremum ((obj1 list) (obj2 list))
  (union obj1 obj2))
(defmethod infimum ((obj1 list) (obj2 list))
 (intersect obj1 obj2 ))
(defmethod minus ((obj list))
  (loop for item in obj collect (* item -1)))
(defmethod translate ((obj list) (x integer))
  (loop for item in obj collect (+ item x)))
```

OMM also implements the protocol for working in grayscale morphology, that is, morphology where the lattice used is made of functions. Musically, this allows us to work with melodies if we model them as functions from time to pitches. For instance, in Figure 5 (a), we see a program that performs the opening and the closing of one melody by another one. We observe that the results produce new melodies where the range of the melodic contour has been modified depending on the structuring melody, a fifth in this example. To better understand these new melodies, let us note that in the case of the opening (Figure 5 (b)), the narrow peaks of the melodic contour were removed and the slope of jumps at the top reduced. In turn, the closing operation (Figure 5 (c)) eliminated narrow valleys and reduced the slope of jumps at the bottom. The generation of new melodies using MM operators remains highly experimental and heavily depends on the structuring melody. We have noticed a loss of control when the number of notes increases (i.e., from 4 notes onwards).

5. CONCLUSIONS

We have provided an overview of a new OpenMusic library called OMM and argued for the utility of mathematical morphology in the analysis and generation of musical structures. In this article, we have primarily highlighted the relevance of MM operators for the analysis and generation of rhythmic structures. Integrating these techniques into the OpenMusic computer-assisted composition language allows for testing the theoretical results stemming from this algebraic formalization while also providing composers or analysts with the opportunity to interact at various levels of the calculation process.

The quest for a unified method to create and transform any musical material represents, in our point of view, one of the most stimulating challenges of this musical formalization. In addition to rhythmic canons and melodies, OMM defines methods for working with lattices of rhythmic trees [11]. Details on implementations and experiments will be the subject of future work.

6. REFERENCES

[1] C. Agón, "OpenMusic : un langage visuel pour la composition musicale assistée par ordinateur," PhD., Paris 6, 1998.

[2] G. Matheron, *Eléments pour une théorie des milieux poreux*. Masson et Cie, 1967.

[3] J. Serra, *Image Analysis and Mathematical Morphology*. Academic Press, 1982.

[4] C. Agón, M. Andreatta, J. Atif, I. Bloch, and P. Mascarade, "Musical Descriptions Based on Formal Concept Analysis and Mathematical Morphology," in *23rd International Conference on Conceptual Structures*. Springer, 2018, pp. 105–119.

[5] G. Romero Garcia, "Mathematical Morphology for the Analysis and Generation of Time-Frequency Representations of Music," PhD, Sorbonne University, 2023.

[6] P. Lascabettes, "Mathematical Models for the Discovery of Musical Patterns, Structures and for Performances Analysis," PhD, Sorbonne University, 2023.

[7] I. Bloch, H. Heijmans, and C. Ronse, "Mathematical Morphology," in *Handbook of Spatial Logics*. Dordrecht, The Netherlands: Springer, 2007, pp. 857–944.

[8] B. A. Davey and H. A. Priestley, *Introduction to lattices and order*. Cambridge: Cambridge University Press, 1990.

[9] D. T. Vuza, "Supplementary Sets and Regular Complementary Unending Canons," *Perspectives of New Music*, vol. 29, 30, 31, 1991-1992.

[10] D. Andreatta, "Constructing and Formalizing Tiling Rhythmic Canons : A Historical Survey of a 'Mathemusical' Problem," *Perspectives of New Music*, vol. 1-2, n° 49, 2011.

[11] C. Agon, K. Haddad, and G. Assayag, "Representation and rendering of rhythm structures," in *WEDELMUSIC 2002. Proceedings.*, 2002, pp. 109–113.

An Extension of the Note-Based Tonnetz to 31-Tone Equal Temperament

Jason Hoopes
Northeastern University
hoopes.j@northeastern.edu

ABSTRACT

When musicians approach composing in the visual domain, they are usually working with the traditional notation of markings on staff paper. While other visual representations do exist, like those that leverage the geometric relationships of notes, these models are usually created, and used in the context of musical analysis. However, the visual properties of these geometric representations can be also utilized in the process of musical creation, which is particularly useful when composing in unfamiliar conditions, like microtonal tuning systems. In this paper, I propose the use of the Tonnetz as a compositional tool in 12-tone ET, and its extension to 31-tone ET.

1. INTRODUCTION

In *A Geometry of Music*, Dimitri Tymoczko defines a series of chord-based graphs. These basic versions represent a geometric model of *n*-dimensional voice leading, where the *n* refers both to the spatial dimension of the structure, as well as the amount of notes in each chord. In both of these examples, the notes that make up the chords are undordered, and agnostic of register, and thus they can be wrapped into a repeating structure, like a mobius strip in the 2-dimensional case.

While the movement of individual notes can be inferred from these chords, it is difficult to conceptualize. To model the intervalic relationships of the individual notes themselves, we can create a similar structure, where a node represents a single note, and an edge represents the interval between two notes. In its generalized form, this is called a *Tone Network*, or in the more common German translation, a *Tonnetz*.

2. THE TONNETZ

2.1 Basic Structure

The basic foundations of the *Tonnetz* rely on 3 intervals, the major third, the minor third, and the perfect fifth[1]. As seen in figure 1, moving to the right in the horizontal direction ascends by a *perfect fifth*, moving up at a 60° angle ascends by a *major third*, and moving downwards, at a 300° angle, descends by a *minor third*. It is clear from this diagram that these three notes form a tradic chord, specifically a C major triad. The utility of this structure is that

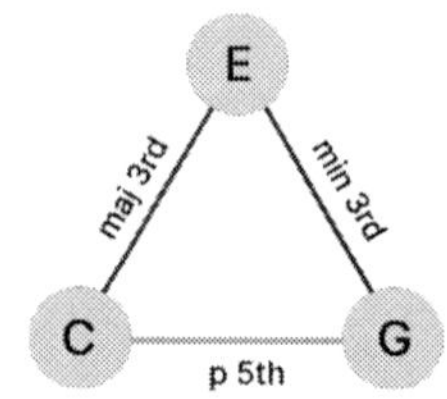

Figure 1. The basic structural building block

it allows us to model *Neo-Riemannian* transformations, by inverting these notes over one of its 3 edges.

Neo-Riemannian Theory refers to a set of writings and ideas proposed by Hugo Riemann, and extended by modern theorists like David Lewin, and Richard Cohn [2]. The work is based on a series of basic transformations that describe the overlap between triads, regardless of their diatonic relationship. These transformations, *Parallel*, *Leading-Tone*, and *Relative*, describe two chords that share a perfect fifth, minor third, and a major third, respectively [2]. Since these shared intervals, all represent an edge on our triangle, we can map this relationship onto our structure. In the case of the *Parallel* transformation, we can add the note Eb to our structure, such that there is an edge connecting C-Eb that is parallel to the E-G edge, and that there is an edge connecting G-Eb that is parallel to the C-E edge. Figure 2, shows that the resulting structure, looks like the mirror image of our original triangle. In fact, this intuition reveals another useful property, that each of these transformations over an edge, can also be modeled as an OPTIC inversion, as defined by Tymoczko [3]. Specifically, the axis of inversion is the axis that evenly subdivides the two notes in the transformation's shared edge. In this case, this axis is I_E^{Eb} (located at the midpoint between E and Eb), which cuts the perfect fifth interval of C-G in half.

If we recursively repeat these transformations, for each edge of the triangle, we can create the full, infinite *Tonnetz*, that models each of the 3 transformations, for every possible basic triad. Because there only 24 possible basic triads in 12-ET (major/minor for each of the 12 tones), this structure tends to repeat relatively quickly. If we start at C major, it will only require 8 transformations leftward, to arrive back at C major. Because of this infinitely repeating property, The *Tonnetz* can be folded, so that the bolded lines touch, creating a toroidal structure [1].

This note-based structure can even be abstracted another level, to represent the chords themselves. This is referred to as the "chicken-wire" *Tonnetz*, initially proposed by Jack Douthett and Peter Steinbach [4]. To create the chord-based abstraction, a new node can be placed in the center

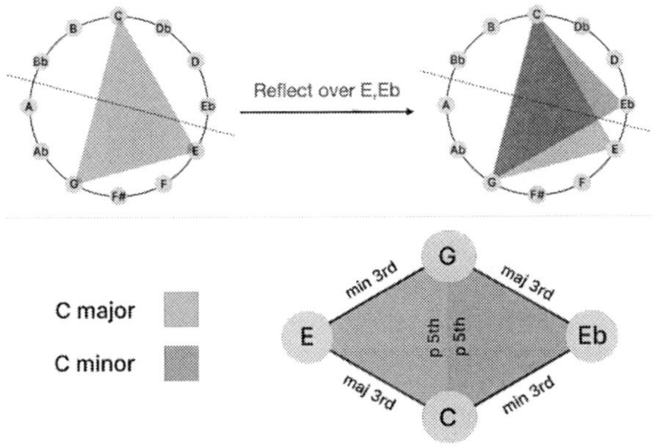

Figure 2. A Neo-Riemannian Parallel transformation, and its Tonnetz analog

of each triangle, and then connected to the other 3 chords in which it shares a transformation with. This process is visualized in Figure 3. Now, the nodes represent chords, and the edges represent the transformations. Like its note-based cousin, this structure is also repeatable, and can again be folded over the Torus.

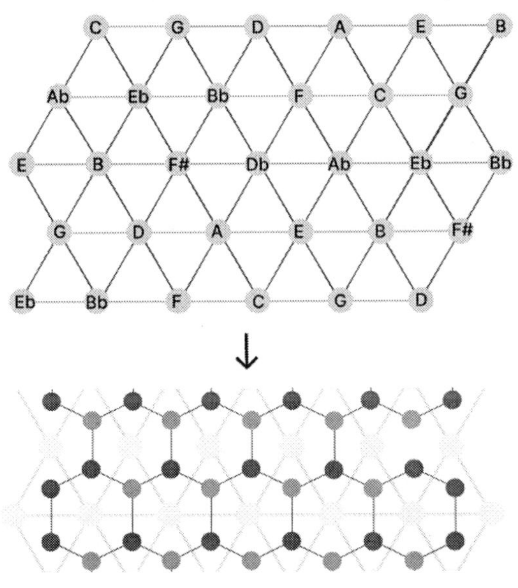

Figure 3. Construction of the chord-based dual graph

2.2 Compositional Use

As the *Tonnetz* provides a visual framework for the harmonic overlap between chords, it can be used as a compositional roadmap, that can help a composer create harmonic support for a melody, transition to a target chord, or simply break natural composition tendencies that they may have when compositing strictly in notation. For example, if a composer wanted to migrate tonal centers from Cmajor to Bmajor, they might be tempted to simply transpose down by a semitone. However, by using the *Tonnetz* as a framework, they can reach the same destination as transposition, instead by chaining together inversions, perhaps leading to a more harmonically rich, and interesting transition.

3. EXTENSION TO 31-TONE EQUAL TEMPERAMENT

The visually-based compositional capabilities of this structure lend itself well to unfamiliar conditions, which for myself, and likely many western composers, describes microtonal composition well. Because the *Tonnetz* structure requires consistent intervals in a given direction, it would not apply well to any non-equal temperament scale, as there would be significant pitch drift every time we completed one repetition of single Tonnetz tile. However, this makes the Tonnetz a perfect candidate for any equal temperament scale, regardless of how many notes it has. In this case, I chose to study the 31-note ET scale as there is not much current literature that describes its relationship to these geometric tools.

The 31-tone ET system is composed of single octave that is equally divided by 31 tones. In this tuning, the frequency ratio between consecutive tones is $2^{\frac{1}{31}}$, or 38.71 cents[5].

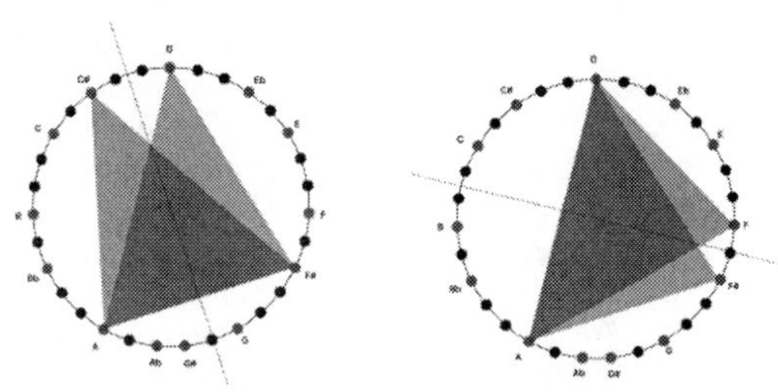

Figure 4. Inversions in 31-ET space

Since we have consistent intervals, the inversions outlined above in section 3.1, also hold true for 31-ET, as seen in 4. This means that the basic *Neo-Riemannian* transformations will also hold true. Thus, the Tonnetz can be generated using the same interval structure as 12-tone, except now a perfect fifth is 18 steps, a minor third is 8 steps, and a major third is 10 steps. The only difference from 12-tone, as seen in Figure 5 is that our repeating tile will be much bigger, since now there are many more possible chords - 62 to be exact.

While the size of the tile is not in itself a limiting factor, the types of chord qualities that can be modeled is somewhat limiting to our use-case. In 12-Tone, there are only 2 basic triads, so our Neo-Riemmannian Tonnetz is fairly comprehensive of many possible harmonic sequences. However, in 31-tone, there are 3 additional basic triad qualities. These triads are downminor (tone steps 0-7-18), mid (0-9-18), and upmajor (0-11-18)[5]. Thus, in order to fully leverage the benefits of 31-tone harmony, the Tonnetz structure needs the ability to frequently lower, or raise a note by a single tone. In our current basic Tonnetz structure, this is not possible, as this is not accounted for by the traditional 12-tone Neo-Riemannian theory. Any of these three triads, cannot be created, without breaking the structure of our

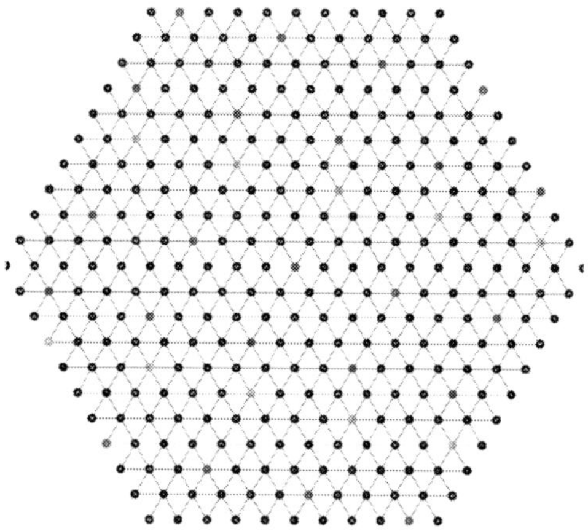

Figure 5. The 31-ET Tonnetz

Tonnetz. To solve this, I propose the modification of this 2d structure, to include a z (depth) dimension. At each step in the z direction, A new Tonnetz would be placed, where every note in the network is transposed by a single step, such that shifting a single node backwards in the Z direction would transpose it down by a step, and shifting it forwards in the Z direction would transpose it up by a step. A slice of this structure is shown in Figure 6, where the notation "vC" means "down C", representing a downward step wise transposition. The bolded lines represent the Tonnetz edges, while the thin lines are just spatial markers to model depth. It is implied that an additional layer, instead starting from "⋀C" or "up C", would be placed *in front* of the original, orange layer, in the opposite direction. These layers would extend, like the *Tonnetz*, into infinity, requiring 31 steps in z direction, to return the original. Figure 7 models a slice of this multi layer stacking.

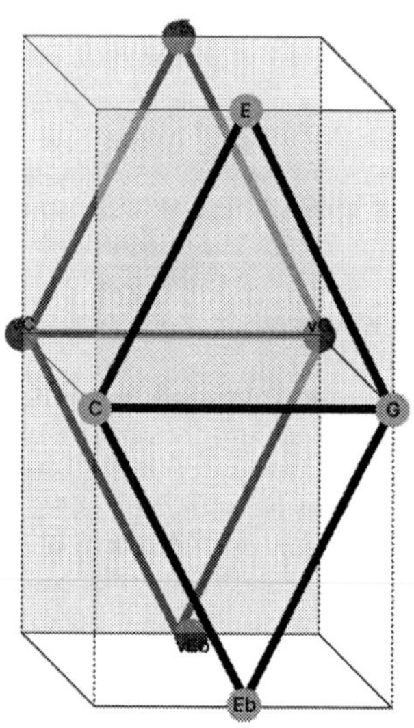

Figure 6. A single chordal slice of the proposed 31-Tone Tonnetz

With this structure, it is now possible to efficiently and visually create harmonic, inversion-centric sequences in the Tonnetz structure, whilst also leveraging all five of the basic triads in 31-tone equal temperament. Shown in Figure 8 is a basic example of a chord progression, created with this new extended structure. From right to left, the chords are C major, C mid (or C neutral), Down C major, and Down C Up Major (or Super Major).

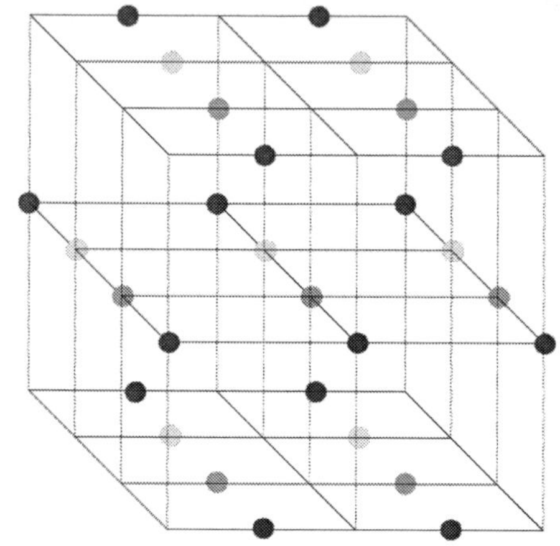

Figure 7. Slice of the multi-layer Tonnetz

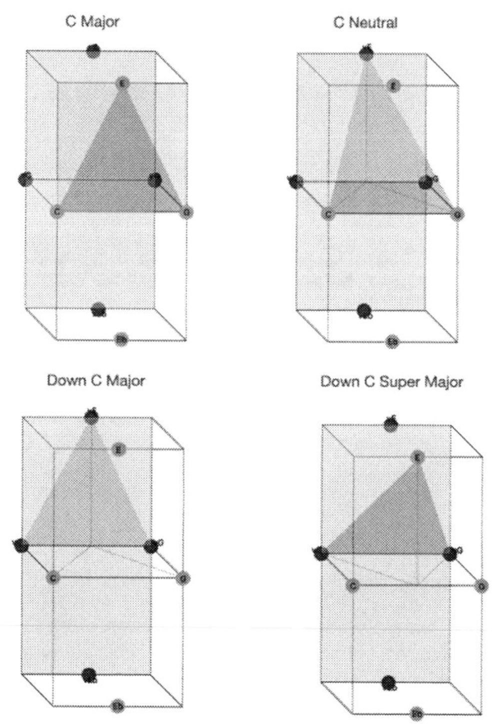

Figure 8. An example chord progression in 31-ET

4. CONCLUSION AND FUTURE WORK

While this new Tonnetz is useful, there are a few limitations. Mainly, it has not yet become clear that there is a way to tile this structure, like the torus, without a need for a fourth dimension. Currently, in my definition of the structure, an infinite plane, extending in all directions must be assumed to conceptualize its use. However, in the context of a virtual 3D software space, like a VR/AR environment, this is not much of an issue. In fact, this context could bolster the compositional benefits that this tool provides, and is likely where a model like this will thrive the most. Future work includes the development of a tonnetz-to-MIDI/CV software environment for the mapping of arbitrary data sources to 3-Dimensional Tonnetz position, aiding in the creation of generative micro-tonal music.

5. REFERENCES

[1] D. Tymoczko, "The Generalized Tonnetz," p. 1–52, Apr. 2012. [Online]. Available: http://dx.doi.org/10.1215/00222909-1546958

[2] R. Cohn, "Neo-Riemannian Operations, Parsimonious Trichords, and Their "Tonnetz" Representations," *Journal of Music Theory*, vol. 41, no. 1, pp. 1–66, 1997. [Online]. Available: http://www.jstor.org/stable/843761

[3] D. Tymoczko, *Geometry of Music Harmony and counterpoint in the extended common practice*. Oxford University Press, USA, 2014.

[4] J. Douthett and P. Steinbach, "Parsimonious Graphs: A Study in Parsimony, Contextual Transformations, and Modes of Limited Transposition," *Journal of Music Theory*, vol. 42, no. 2, pp. 241–263, 1998. [Online]. Available: http://www.jstor.org/stable/843877

[5] "31edo - Xenharmonic Wiki." [Online]. Available: https://en.xen.wiki/w/31edo

A Networked Musico-Spatial Virtual Environment

Jeremy J Ham
Musico-Spatial Researcher
jeremy@surfcoastarchitecture.com.au

Uwe Woessner
HRS Stuttgart
woessner@hlrs.de

ABSTRACT

This paper describes a Networked Musico-Spatial Virtual Environment (NMSVE) as a virtual reality (VR) based spatialisation of music and sound in motion. Using MIDI instruments, live and recorded sound and controllers and consumer-level VR gaming technologies, the NMSVE provides a potential platform for new forms of musico-spatial performance (combining the musical and spatial arts) and expression for geographically- distant performers. We describe the new affordances of the NMSVE as 'Synaespatia'- the spatial experience of music and sound in VR, and propose potential new areas of research for the computer music community.

1. INTRODUCTION

The Networked Musico-Spatial Virtual Environment (NMSVE) operates from the technological confluence of musical instrument inputs (as both MIDI data and line-in sound), live or recorded sound inputs outputs and virtual reality-based spatialisation[1]. For this paper, we describe spatialisation as the transformation of music and sound into 3D spatial forms in VR. Together, these create a performance environment that combines synthesisers, digital drum kits and pads, virtual instruments, acoustic instruments, digital theremin and dynamic and spectacular real-time output in VR. The NMSVE is designed principally as a research vehicle to explore new modes of 3D spatial notation and musico-spatial performance.
The NMSVE setup utilises the following basic equipment (refer Figure 1):

- The CAVE (Cave Automatic Virtual Environment) at the HLRS Stuttgart and/ or HTC Vive virtual reality gaming setup;
- Microphone inputs used as a sound source;
- 8 channel mixing desk: this allows multiple inputs, including instrument sound inputs (eg drums, keyboards and guitar), input from a digital audio workstation and live inputs;
- Laptop for Studio One or Reaper DAW;
- VR-ready laptop;
- Digital interface;
- Moog Theremini digital theremin (or other MIDI instruments)
- DJ controller configured to manipulate VR objects.

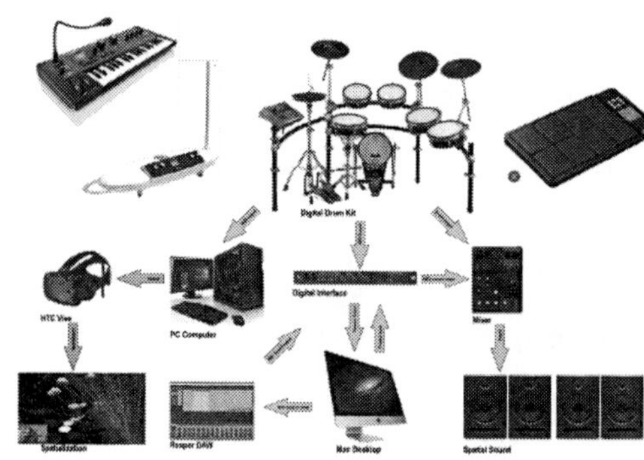

Figure 1. NMSVE equipment and workflows.

1.1 Spatialisation of Music and Sound in VR

The NMSVE operates from the OpenCOVER VR rendering system within the COVISE software framework[2], developed at the HLRS Stuttgart. COVISE is a parallel distributed rendering system which supports rendering for high end VR environments such as CAVEs but also scales down to consumer-level gaming hardware such as the HTC Vive. OpenCOVER is primarily used for the visualisation of complex data such as simulating heat flows in cooling towers, however the capacity for processing real-time data has proven quite useful for the spatialisation of sonic and musical data.
The VR spatialisation is first person user-centric and based on projections around eye level in the HMD and CAVE, with X-Y planes as setout for 3D VR notes which project forward from the HMD in the Z plane. From this position, 3D VR notes can be configured to appear around the user and project forward into 3D virtual space forward of the user. The note size, note path and velocity of each 3D VR note projection is set as a function of the velocity of each MIDI note.

[1] See https://www.jjham.com/one for NMSVE Demo.

[2] See https://www.hlrs.de/solutions/types-of-computing/visualization/covise

In addition to MIDI data, live sound is spatialised as a 'sound tunnel', with the top arc projecting (in real time) real-time sound wave forms and the bottom arc projecting fast Fourier transform of frequency banding from 100 to 20,000Hz. These live data can be spatialised in the VR as data points, vertices or rendered as coloured gradient surfaces (see Figure 2). Parameters such as projection speed, note path, note size, 'Sound Tunnel' shape and sound spatialisation attributes can be configured to be controlled by the TableUI or MIDI-enabled controller surfaces such as DJ controllers or keyboard knobs and sliders. Thus, all parameters of the NMSVE are parametrically flexible and user-controllable to suit specific performance and research purposes.

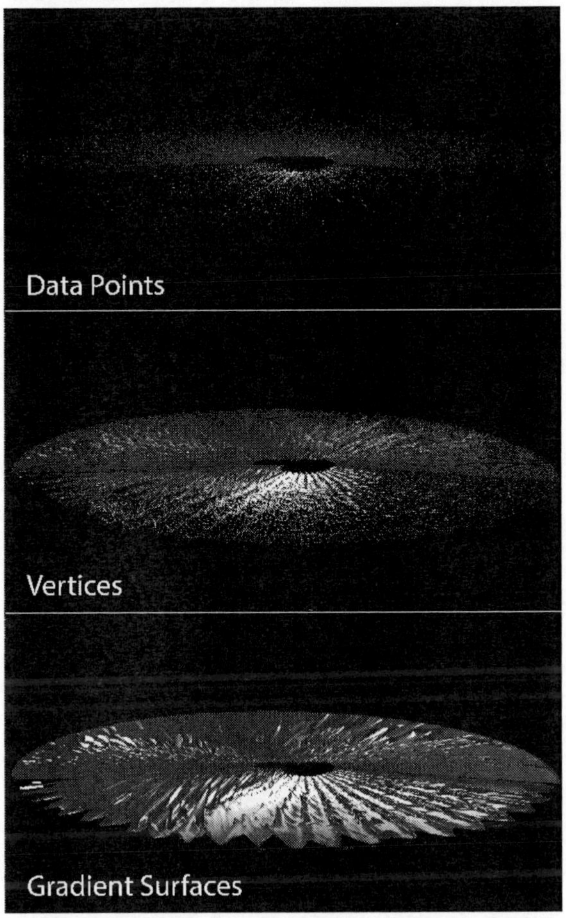

Figure 2. NMSVE Sound Tunnel rendered as data points, vertices and gradient surfaces.

1.2 MIDI musical instrument input

The C++ COVISE OpenCOVER configuration file manages the VR spatialisation parameters and provides individual configurations for multiple MIDI-enabled instruments such as the Moog Theremini, Roland TD50 digital drum kit, Roland SPD30 pads, MiniNova synth.

The config file assigns 3D VR notation to the MIDI notes used by each instrument. By default, coloured spheres are used, however new forms of musical notation are enabled by the use of parametric 3D CAD software (eg Rhino3D Grasshopper and 3D Studio Max) to build dynamic new forms of dynamic 3D spatial notation in .obj, .wrl and other formats.

As an example, config file below assigns to MIDI note 12 a modelled object named oval3.obj at a scale of 1.0 with an RGB colour of 250/110/10. This is visualised in figure 3, below.

<Key name="12" r="250" g="110" b="10" modelName = "/data/NOTES/oval3.obj" modelScale = "1.0"/>

Note objects can animated using GLSL shaders. Where MIDI information such as frequency, velocity, pitch and others can be routed to the shader programs in form of Uniforms, thus any type of visual effect can be achieved for each of the notes.

Figure 3. 3D VR drum notes (oval forms) projected on screen as viewed through the HMD.

2. NETWORKED VR

OpenCOVER can be networked to provide a collaborative virtual environment between multiple remote VR installations or co-located HMDs (or both). Application state is shared through a central Virtual Reality Broker (VRB). State can be stored on a VRB which provides persistence between sessions while also providing support for late joining participants. Application state in this application is for example the selected rendering mode as seen in Figure 4, below.

Realtime data such as audio or MIDI streams can also be routed through the VRB. This data is transmitted as UDP streams while the state information is sent through reliable TCP connections. This ensures reliable application state while allowing for low latency transmission of real time data. Network configuration is flexible enough to support NAT and only requires limited firewall configuration. While the HLRS provides a VRB service, one can run a VRB on any system which is accessible by all participants through a single TCP connection. One VRB can serve many parallel collaborative sessions.

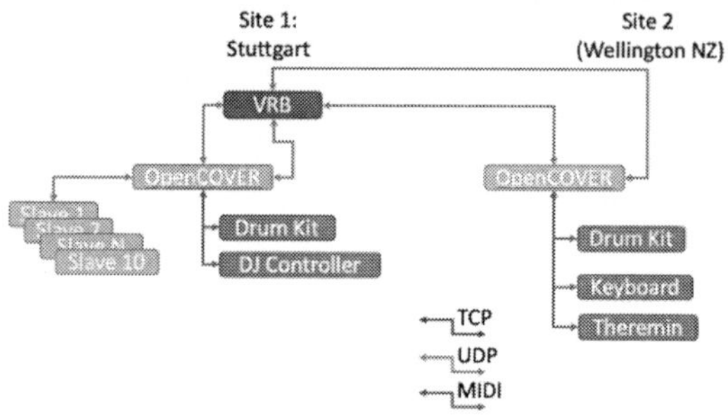

Figure 4: NMSVE networking schematic.

The NMSVE has not been used in a formal performance, however has been tested at an installation at the 2022 Ars Electronica Aoteoroa Garden[3] (see Figure 5, below). In this iteration, drummers in New Zealand and Stuttgart staged a 'drum battle' using Skype to transmit sound and the NMSVE to transmit 3D spatial notation and data to the Sound Tunnel. We experienced similar issues of latency and buffering as reported in Rottondi et. al., 2016, with the principal issue being the quality of sound transmission via Skype. In this regard, the technologies inform the performance potential. The NMSVE environment does not intend to replicate the quasi-realistic virtual environments of many developments in Patch XR (see Loveridge, 2020) however provides a virtual environment for musico-spatial improvisation. With this evolving modality, improvisation is based on both musical and spatial cues- and, by combining these; musico-spatial cues.

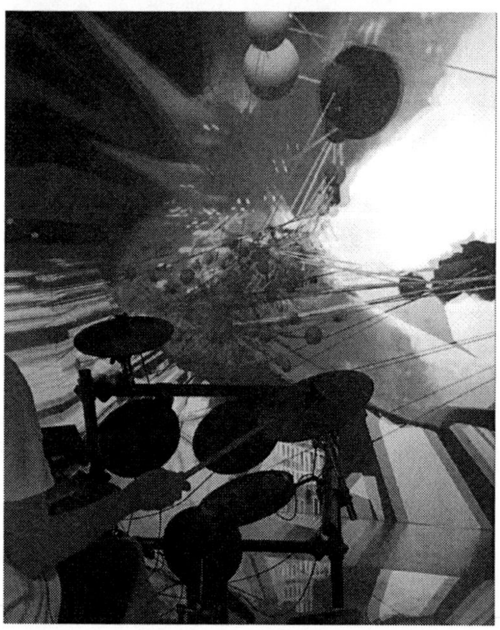

Figure 5. Networked performance at Ars Electronica. View inside the CAVE in Stuttgart of notes sent from Wellington NZ.

[3] See https://www.hlrs.de/news/detail/virtual-reality-brings-musicians-together-for-long-distance-jamming

3. SYNAESPATIA

The concept of *affordance* has its origins in the field of evolutionary psychology and was related to an animal's relationship with the environment (Gibson, 1979). Donald Norman in *The Design of Everyday Things* introduces the idea of affordance relating Gibson's ideas to the field of design. In this domain, an 'affordance is what one system (say, an artefact) provides to another system (say, a user).

We propose that the bridging of the nexus between the musical domain and the spatial domain provides affordances to music that are otherwise unavailable. These affordances relate to the combined spatialisation of the parameters of sound and the dynamic, real time generation of 3D VR musical notation within a 'Sound Tunnel' virtual environment. These affordances are enhanced by the navigability and interrogation of sonic and musical VR artefacts in real time, enabling cognitive associations between music, sound and notation.

We introduce the concept of Synaespatia. This concept borrows from the condition of synaesthesia as the involuntary stimulation of a secondary cognitive pathway (the sensation of colour) in conjunction with the stimulation of a primary cognitive pathway (hearing sound)[4]. Synaespatia is experienced through the interface of the HMD in the HTC Vive or through 3D glasses inside the CAVE. The networking capacity of the NMSVE allows synaespatia to be experienced, interactively, from geographically-distant users.

Synaespatia is enhanced by the following aspects of the NMSVE:

- Spatialisation in real time in VR;
- The representation of musical performance as *both* 3D VR notes and through the Sound Tunnel;
- The ability to navigate through VR space to interrogate interesting aspects of sound and music spatialisations;
- The ability for users to change parametric settings on the NMSVE to enhance and tailor the experience to individual needs;
- The CAVE allows ten or more people to share their experience without the limitations of the HMD;

Between the experience of sound and music through the sense of hearing, the spatial perception of the sound waves, frequency and multiple types of 3D spatial notational translation and the ability of participants to freely navigate within the virtual environment and control the size, speed, rotation and other parameters of the projection; synaespatia is a wholistic construct.

4. RESEARCH POTENTIAL OF NMSVE

The NMSVE provides significant potential to advance research at the intersection of computers, music and spatial design. The first area is graphic, animated and 3D musical notation (see for example Hope and Vickery, 2015; Bell and Carey, 2019). We currently have the capacity to freeze

[4] See https://en.wikipedia.org/wiki/Synesthesia

and capture musical phrases to generate virtual galleries of 3D VR notation, which can be exported as .obj 3D CAD files to be 3D printed. The NMSVE can also import VRML, .obj and other 3D CAD models to provide for a full VR-based notation system. Using parametric modelling software such as Grasshopper provides significant further capabilities for the generation of complex musical scores based on algorithmic or parametric design.

The NMSVE has the potential to contribute to the study of the acoustic properties of music, as well as the architectural acoustics places and spaces. The wide range of technologies employed across these fields each have intrinsic limitation- brought about by issues such as their hardware and software, static representation of dynamic events and environments and limitations of the interface (Vorländer et. al., 2015). The NMSVE, as a VR-based, parametrically flexible platform that provides full navigation in 3D space, offers a complimentary set of affordances to existing sound research technologies that could contribute to the body of knowledge of acoustics and other fields.

Perhaps the most interesting and novel potential of the NMSVE relates to the cross-domain representation of music and sound in the spatial domain for deaf or hearing impaired people. Given that deaf individuals do not participate to the degree that hearing individuals do in most common ritual uses of music (Darrow, 1993), music researchers could find new ways to engage the wider community with music and sound. The dynamic 3D VR notation accompanied by spectacular spatialisation of sound in the Sound Tunnel potentially allows deaf people to experience the joys of music as synaespatia. Future research would involve working with the hearing impaired community to design synaespatial experiences in settings such as live music performance- as a spatial accompaniment, or 'music for the eyes'.

Taking this a step further, the NMSVE has the current capacity as a vehicle to facilitate musical (or musico-spatial) interaction and 'jamming' between musicians and deaf persons. In this scenario, both parties (playing MIDI instruments) could use the 'call and response' modality of jazz and blues music to improvise and jam. The call of musicians playing music could be met with the response of deaf people playing with VR notation using musical instruments. Using the networking capability of the NMSVE, this interaction could occur across international waters, thus creating more potential for cultural interaction. With consultation with the deaf community, the NMSVE could provide an important platform for shared musico-spatial experiences.

5. CONCLUSIONS

The NMSVE utilises the OpenCOVER visualisation platform to facilitate the cross-domain representation of music- from the musical domain to the spatial domain. We have developed sets of 3D VR notation for MIDI instruments, including keyboards, drum pads, digital drum kit and theremin. Work is ongoing to spatialise stringed instruments. Working in synergy with notation, we have developed a parametrically flexible spatialisation of sound in VR. The VR environment if fully navigable, allowing users to interrogate interesting aspects of sound and music by moving through virtual space, picking up 3D objects and moving and rotating them.

Together, these spatialisations provide affordances for the experience of sound and music for both hearing abled and hearing impaired persons as 'synaespatia'. Whilst the focus has been on technological development for installations we propose that the NMSVE has significant potential as a research vehicle for 3D notation, networked performance, acoustics studies and new forms of musical interaction for the wider community.

Acknowledgments

This research is supported by the High Performance Computing Lab at the University of Stuttgart.

6. REFERENCES

[1] Bell, J. and Carey, B. 2019. "Animated Notation, Score Distribution and AR-VR Environments for Spectral Mimetic Transfer in Music Composition" in Proceedings of the International Conference on Technologies for Music Notation and Representation – TENOR'19, Melbourne, Australia, pp 7–14.A.

[2] Darrow, A. A. (1993). The role of music in deaf culture: Implications for music educators. *Journal of Research in Music Education*, *41*(2), 93-110.

[3] Gibson, J. (1979). The Theory of Affordances in the Ecological Approach to Visual Perceptual, Houghton Mifflin. Boston, USA.

[4] Ham, Jeremy (2018) Improvising Polyrhythmic Space: Exploring a Continuum of Musico-Spatial Creative Practice, RMIT University

[5] Ham, Jeremy, (2017) An Architectural Approach to 3D Spatial Drum Notation, TENOR International Conference 2017, University de Coruna, a Coruna Spain.

[6] Hope, C. & Vickery, L. (2015). Decibel ScorePlayer - A digital tool for reading graphic notation. Proceedings of TENOR 2015 (The first International Conference on Technologies for Music Notation and Representation), IRCAM, Paris, France

[7] Loveridge, Ben. "Networked Music Performance in Virtual Reality: Current Perspectives." *Journal of Network Music and Arts* 2, 1 (2020)

[8] Norman, D. (2002). The Design of Everyday Things. Basic Books. New York, USA

[9] Rottondi, C., Chafe, C., Allocchio, C., & Sarti, A. (2016). An overview on networked music performance technologies. *IEEE Access*, *4*, 8823-8843.

[10] Vorländer, M., Schröder, D., Pelzer, S., & Wefers, F. (2015). Virtual reality for architectural acoustics. *Journal of Building Performance Simulation*, *8*(1), 15-25.

'Distant Concerto', a Genre of Network Computer Music: Realisation and Possibilities

Gabin Kim
Department of Music
University of Birmingham
gxk233@student.bham.ac.uk

ABSTRACT

The main focus of this paper is the realisation of 'Distant Concerto' (telematic performance) and its potential extension of networked performance possibilities. This experiment implemented during the pandemic to discover a way of performing music together in an isolated environment. The paper examines the limitations encountered in this networked music, such as audio latency, and proposes practical approaches based on experiments carried out during rehearsals and concerts from 2021 to 2023, primarily from the performer's perspective. These approaches are divided into two aspects: the technical side and the performance practice side. Specifically, the discussion investigates how Max/MSP/Jitter is utilised in 'Distant Concerto' to simultaneously process live electronics music and real-time video by integrating inputs from performers at various locations.

1. INTRODUCTION

The history of network music traces back to John Cage, particularly with his piece *'Imaginary Landscape No. IV for twelve radios'* in 1952 [1], and additional figures such as David Tudor, Gordon Mumma, Pauline Oliveros, Max Neuhaus. Numerous articles reference them to provide a historical context. [2, 3] Starting from them, Renwick's thesis classifies the diverse forms of network music, such as laptop ensembles with networked live coding performances, telematic performances, distributed performances, game music-derived approaches to network music, and some other extended forms. [4] In addition, Akkermann's research referred more kinds of network music with examples. [3] Among the rich history of network music, this paper focuses on telematic performance.

Lemmon's article, along with Cook's and Renwick's theses, all mention two early figures in this genre. [4,5,6] Firstly, Roy Scott's journal article (1990) defined the term 'telematic' (*télématique*) as a combination of telecommunication and computer science (*informatique*), a concept originating from Nora and Minc's published report in 1978, France. [7] Subsequently, Pauline Oliveros exemplifies how technological evolution has impacted her performances, from a six-city connected improvisation using telephone lines and still images in 1991, to a concert with internet, sound painting, and forty-four improvisers in 2007. [8] Scott and Oliveros both emphasised the significance of sharing creativity interchangeably between multiple locations, surpassing the mere transmission of information.

Based on those backgrounds, the main concept of 'Distant Concerto' is a telematic performance which performs concerto between the instruments and live electronics using network. The composer Yong-Gyu Gregory Kim, who also experimented the remote performances amid the pandemic, called his telematic pieces as 'distant concerto' and explained it as 'connecting performers in various regions with network and using their sound as sources of a computer concerto to process real-time music and video, creating a real-time multimedia work'. The terms 'distant concerto', 'distant performance', and 'remote performance' share the same meaning with 'telematic performance' in this discussion.

This paper centres on the realisation of remote performance using Max/MSP/Jitter and its potential extension of networked performance possibilities. The discussion is grounded in the author's practical experiments conducted during rehearsals and performances with the composer and performers from 2021 to 2023, documented for scholarly analysis mainly from the performer's perspective.

2. REALISATION OF 'DISTANT CONCERTO'

My initial attempt on remote performance were when performing Yong-Gyu Gregory Kim's pieces at his composition recital titled *'Distant Concerto Concert'* in April-May 2021.[1] The composer has been experimenting with various ensemble formations, from duo piece to piece for five ensemble players, facilitating remote performances during the Covid-19 pandemic. It originated from the idea of finding a way to perform together in separate spaces. For example, the duo piece performed in 2021 was *'Multimedia Concerto for Violin, Cello and Computer 'ARIA''* which the violinist performed in York, UK, the cellist Jiwon Huh performed in Munich, Germany and the computer (electronics) performed in Daegu, South Korea. The ensemble piece *'Multimedia Concerto 'Andromeda' for Ensemble and Computer'* was more

[1] Youtube link of Yong-Gyu Gregory Kim's 'Distant Concerto Concert' in 2021. https://youtu.be/jOY_9SlkhUw?si=Qb52SjPD4-MK0bcw

intricated as flute performed in Seoul, South Korea; first violin, second cello and computer were in Daegu, South Korea; second violin in York, UK; lastly the first cello performed in Munich, Germany (refer the Figure 1). Five performers and computer in four different cities performed together and I would like to say the performances were successful for these reasons. As a performer, I was able to compare rehearsals to live concerts and observed significant improvements as we gained experience. Also, the video recordings can serve as another objective criteria. For instance, we achieved a better musical flow in the concerts than in rehearsals, and we learned how to handle with telematic performance through encountering diverse situations caused by audio latency.

Figure 1. Five performers and computer in four different cities performing *Multimedia Concerto 'Andromeda' for Ensemble and Computer* at Yong-Gyu Gregory Kim's *Distant Concerto Concert* in May 2021.

This remote performance has two essential aspects: technical requisites as a fundamental element and, thereafter, the intuitive and pragmatic practice of performers. The most important thing to consider in performing this was dealing with the audio latency between performers. The first idea was using Zoom, but this software was not appropriate to play music together as there were high audio latency and compression of sound. The solution was using a SYNCROOM, which is an online ensemble performing software produced by Yamaha in June 2020. According to the Yamaha, they were developing on this software and the technology called 'NETDUETTO (R)' even ten years before the pandemic has started. [9] From my experience, this software has proven to be efficient tool offering relatively low audio latency, typically ranging from 5 to 20 milliseconds. This low latency facilitates interaction and synchronisation between performers. However, as it only provides to transmit audio capabilities, additional video call application such as Zoom is still necessary for observing each other's gestures during the rehearsal or performance.

Lastly, the pieces performed in the remote performances discussed in this paper are all real-time live electronics music using Max/MSP/Jitter with real-time videos (refer the Figure 2). However, this is not limited solely to live electronics or specific software; rather, I believe it could be extended to any other genre of music or software that can potentially bring about this capability, opening up further research on this.

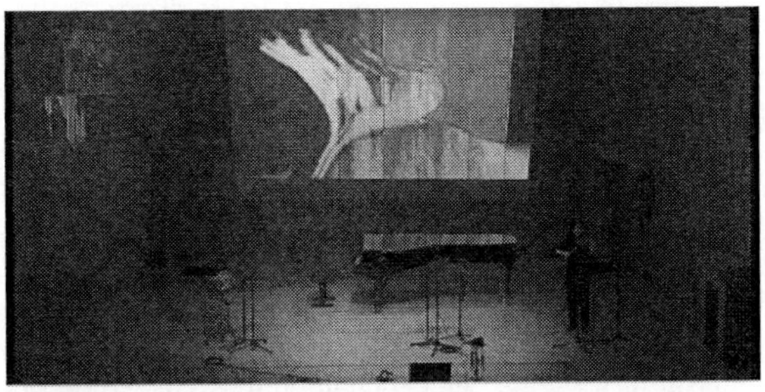

Figure 2. A remote performance at DICMF (Daegu International Computer Music Festival, South Korea) in 2022.[2] The left side of the wall is showing the display of a violinist performing in the concert hall in Daegu, South Korea, and a cellist performing remotely from Munich, Germany. The central display is a real-time generated video interacting with the sounds produced by the instruments and electronics.

3. TECHNICAL REQUISITES

To realise the 'distant concerto', these are main technical issues to be solved: need of stable network environment to minimise the audio latency, equipment that best keeps the audio quality, using Max/MSP to realise this live-electronics performance.

Firstly, the essential requirement for the performance is transmitting the audio with minimised latency. Using SYNCROOM could be one of the ways to achieve this and it needs a LAN cable with a stable and high-speed internet environment. Although Akkermann showed the example of 'Chloé' case using Wi-Fi on the network performance which gave audience an opportunity to take part in the performance, mentioning still some limitations were existed. [3] Eventually, Wi-Fi is not suitable for this remote performance, as stability and internet speed significantly impact the performance. In my experience, internet speed determined the audio latency and the quality of the transmitted sound. We were able to gauge the latency or loss rate of each location through the SYNCROOM display. Also, in the simplified version of display, a smiling emoticon indicated a good connection with high internet speed, whereas a frowning emoticon signified a relatively slow speed with extended latency. If a performer is in a location with relatively low-speed internet, it can directly result in unwanted noise and low-quality sound. This also affects the latency rate and synchronicity of the music. Therefore, Yamaha indicated on their website that 'to achieve optimal outcomes, it is advisable to use optical fibre or an alternative broadband connection, along with an audio interface that is compatible with ASIO[3]'. [9]

[2] Youtube link of Distant Concerto performance at DICMF (Daegu International Computer Music Festival, South Korea) in 2022. https://youtu.be/s2k5bK8PF6c?si=H8cxxVvCv1dDqClj&t=1431

[3] ASIO (Audio Stream Input Output) is a protocol software developed by Steinberg which enables the Window computer to communicate directly with external hardware device like audio interface.

Secondly, the next requirement is preserving the audio quality using the audio interface, as the soundcard equipped in the computer is usually insufficient for transmitting high-quality sound. And the microphones for the better-quality input of the instrument sound is another required equipment which connected to audio interface. This set must be setup with every performer. The sound-check process is crucial due to the diverse spatial and technical environments in which participants are engaged in this performance. Variations include individuals situated in dry studios with soundproofed walls, while others may find themselves in concert halls with nice resonances. Additionally, each participant utilises different input and output settings on their audio interfaces. Consequently, it becomes imperative for individuals to adjust their volumes appropriately while listening to others during sound testing. This adjustment can be manually done by manipulating the controls on the audio interface device itself, software (i.e. RME TotalMix FX), or SYNCROOM. The volume level setting is also particularly important in the concert venue with an audience. The sounds should be balanced between remote performers, performers in the concert venue, and the computer sound. Also, it is important to ensure that every cable is connected tightly; loose connections can lead to additional noises. Additionally, to avoid excessive instrument feedback, I strongly recommend using headphones or earphones for the performers who are performing away from the concert hall. One of the realistic limitations that hindering the generalisation of this performance is that there is possibility that not every performer may be equipped with the required technical equipment.

Lastly, to use the sound and visual source from the remote performers as a material and to generate real-time music and video, the composer used the Max/MSP/Jitter. It needs high performance computer to process sound and video simultaneously in real time. As you can see the Figure 3, the violinist in the concert venue and the cellist in remote place both send the sound input by SYNCROOM and video input by Zoom to the computer in the concert venue. Then the computer receives the inputs from the performers, process the data, and generate the sounds to the four channel speakers and video outputs into two displays in the concert hall. The main video output displays real-time video that interacts with sounds processed through Max/MSP. It uses inputs from both Zoom and the webcam in front of the violinist as sources for the video processing. The second video output displaying the performers on Zoom allows them to see each other's gestures during the performance, and it also gives the audience a sense of the existence of distant performers by showing them on the screen.

Audio Modeling Srl (2024) Available at: https://kb.audiomodeling.com/en/c/grow-your-knowledge/d/what-is-core-audio-what-is-asio/

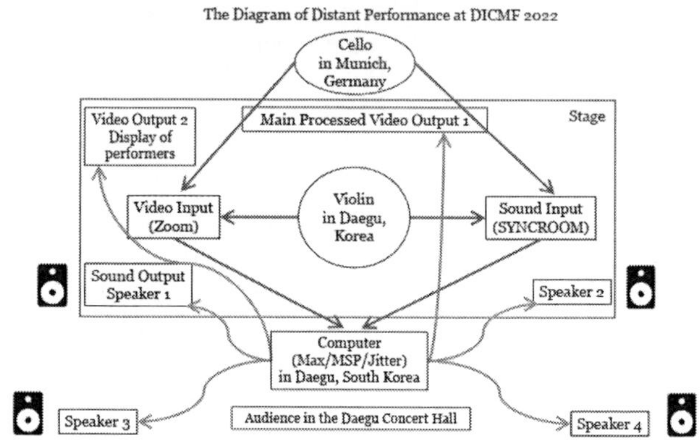

Figure 3. Diagram of a distant performance at DICMF (Daegu International Computer Music Festival, South Korea) in 2022.

4. PRAGMATIC APPROCHES FOR THE PERFORMERS

The telematic performance has been performed a diverse kind of music, from free improvisation to scored pieces. The approaches discussed in this paper are specifically based on the scored pieces. Once the technical groundwork is settled, performers need to shift their focus to how they will interact with each other. To achieve this, we must first recognise that performers are divided into two situations in this performance. The first involves playing in a concert venue with computer sound and an audience, while the second entails playing in a different location away from the concert venue. In this scenario, the timing benchmark will be the performer in the concert venue with the audience, largely leading the music.

Drawing from my experience playing in both situations, I found it easier to perform in the former situation. The primary reason is that this condition is the most familiar or similar form to a 'normal' performance. In this setting, the performer is less likely to be confused by occasional feedback sounds, and the computer sound can be heard directly on the stage. In this situation, concentrating on and following the distant performers is key to achieving better interaction. This interaction could be realised, for example, by setting additional cues throughout the piece to confirm whether all performers are at the same point and context.

Performers in the latter condition will encounter some challenges. Despite efforts to minimise feedback sound using headphones, it may still occur. This can be confusing and disruptive, akin to an unskilled performer suddenly breaking into the stage, interfering with the entire performance by playing out of context. In such a situation, it becomes difficult for anyone to ignore the intruder and continue playing. The beat of the feedback sound is entirely out of synchronicity, greatly disrupting our ability to count the music.

Although there is no solid solution for this issue yet, I would like to suggest two options based on the cases performing ensemble pieces by Yong-Gyu Gregory Kim. I have encountered some passages where I need to be in exact time and provide others with regular and stable beats but having difficulty with counting myself due to the mixed sound feedback of my own latency feedback sound and other players sound. This usually happened when more than three players were engaged. In this case, I tried reducing the volume of my headphones even if this makes it is hard to listen to others. However, this approach is not universally applicable, as it is only possible when there is sufficient time to play the instrument and control the volume simultaneously. If this method cannot be applied, the only alternative is repeated training to ignore the feedback sound during rehearsals.

During the rehearsal with the cellist in Germany, we encountered difficulty in connecting the melodies properly due to sound delays in the passages where the violin and cello intertwine. To address this challenge, we experimented with various approaches and discovered the most effective solution: determining the extent of the delay in the sound from Germany. For instance, if we assume the sound from Germany is approximately a crotchet later than the benchmark place, the cellist compensates by playing a crotchet earlier. We applied this method to every part where we felt uncomfortable due to audio latency, and it proved to be the most efficient approach. As a result, the audience perceived the performance as if we were playing in the same place without any musical awkwardness. This approach shares the same context with Cáceres and Renaud's paper which suggested to compromise the latency as a musical technique which could be used as a theoretical framework for the future research. [10]

Due to limitations and a lack of generalisation, finding pieces for remote performance, aside from those I had performed previously, was challenging. Considering the mentioned limitations, the composers should be aware of the audio latency issues. For instance, it is advisable to avoid overly complex interactive pieces, such as those with intricate interweaving factors for an acoustic string quartet. Allowing enough spaces for the instruments to synchronise would be ideal. Finally, another approach to expand the repertoire of remote performance pieces is to explore ways of adapting existing compositions for remote settings.

5. CONCLUSION

Based on the cases of performing several concerts during 2021 to 2023, I discussed the practical solutions for dealing with the network performance with two aspects: technical and practical requisites. Given that remote performance contains limitation with these inherent traits, the main objective of this is not only connects the network but also preserve the musical quality. Though it is still impossible to play without any latency, performers supplement the deficiency of technology by their trained ability of ensemble and using their intuitive sense of performing music. At this point of the end of the pandemic, it is less likely to utilise this kind of performance in a reality, however, I suggest this 'distant concerto' as a way of performing computer music using media and network, advocating for the further research which has potential possibility of network music. Drawing on Dresser, the telematic performance enables the possibility of performative expansion rather than solely replacing live performance. [8] The ongoing development of technology prompts anticipation for the resolution of the limitations discussed in this paper. I look forward to observing how future advancements will improve the current constraints.

Acknowledgments

All concerts mentioned in this paper (2021-2023) were funded by the Daegu Foundation for Culture & Arts, and a telematic performance in my recital (2023) was funded by Arts Council Korea. I would like to acknowledge the composer and director of DICMF, Yong-Gyu Gregory Kim, as well as the talented Korean performers with whom I had the privilege to work: violinist Hyeryeong Kim, cellists Jiwon Huh and Un Lee, and flutist Grace Eunhae Oh. Additionally, I extend my gratitude to my supervisors, Prof. Scott Wilson and Prof. Andrew Kirkman, for their supportive guidance throughout my first year of PhD.

6. REFERENCES

[1] F. Turner, *The Democratic Surround: Multimedia and American Liberalism from World War II to the Psychedelic Sixties*. The University of Chicago Press, 2013, pp.143-148.

[2] S. Gresham-Lancaster, "The Aesthetics and History of the Hub: The Effects of Changing Technology on Network Computer Music," *Leonardo Music Journal*, vol. 8, pp. 39–44, 1998.

[3] M. Akkermann, "Performing Computer Network Music. Well-known challenges and new possibilities," *Proceedings of the International Computer Music Conference*, Utrecht, Netherlands, 2016, pp. 394-400.

[4] R. Renwick, "Topologies for network music," Ph.D. thesis, Queen's University Belfast, UK, 2017. [Online]. Available: https://pure.qub.ac.uk/en/studentTheses/topologies-for-network-music

[5] E. C. Lemmon, "Telematic Music vs. Networked Music: Distinguishing Between Cybernetic Aspirations and Technological Music-Making," *Journal of Network Music and Arts*, vol 1, no. 1, Art. no. 2, 2019. Available: https://commons.library.stonybrook.edu/jonma/vol1/iss1/2

[6] M. Cook, "Telematic Music: History and Development of the Medium and Current Technologies Related to Performance," DMA thesis, Bowling Green State University, USA, 2015. [Online]. Available: https://etd.ohiolink.edu/acprod/odb_etd/etd/r/1501/10?clear=10&p10_accession_num=bgsu1447261468

[7] R. Ascott, "Is There Love in the Telematic Embrace?," *Art Journal*, vol. 49, no. 3, pp. 241-247, 1990. doi: https://doi.org/10.2307/777114.

[8] P. Oliveros *et al.*, "Telematic Music: Six Perspectives," *Leonardo Music Journal*, vol.19, 2009.

[9] SYNCROOM. (2020). Yamaha. Accessed: 9 Feb 2024. [Online] Available: https://syncroom.yamaha.com/global/about/

[10] J.-P Cáceres, and A. Renaud, "Playing the network: the use of time delays as musical devices," *Proceedings of International Computer Music Conference*, Belfast, UK, 2008, pp. 244-250.

DAFNE+: A blockchain platform for preservation and valorisation of experimental music and sound production

Hugues Vinet
IRCAM Centre-Pompidou
Hugues.Vinet@ircam.fr

Greg Beller
IRCAM Centre-Pompidou
Greg.Beller@ircam.fr

Miller S. Puckette
IRCAM Centre-Pompidou
Miller.Puckette@ircam.fr

Guillaume Piccarreta
IRCAM Centre-Pompidou
Guillaume.Piccarreta@ircam.fr

ABSTRACT

A new international research and innovation project supported by the European Union, the DAFNE+ project for fair creative content distribution aims to empower creators and communities though new digital distribution models based on digital tokens. The purpose of DAFNE+ is to design a blockchain and NFT based platform providing digital content creators with new forms of creation, registration, distribution and monetization of their works of art. DAFNE+ addresses several creative communities and the purpose of this article is to focus on those of its features intended to the experimental sound and music community. Halfway between IRCAM's Forum and archives of interactive music/sound repertoire, and based on an autonomous organization and distributed infrastructure, the platform will enable artists, researchers and engineers to share and monetize pieces of technology for producing music and performing works - libraries, patches, documentations. This paper presents the general objectives of the project, its foundations, the specification process it followed, the target features that resulted from it and its current state of development.

1. INTRODUCTION

A new international research and innovation project supported by the European Union, the DAFNE+ project[1] for fair creative content distribution aims to empower creators and communities though new digital distribution models based on digital tokens. The purpose of DAFNE+ is to design a blockchain and NFT (non fungible token) based platform providing digital content creators with new forms of creation, registration, distribution and monetization of their works of art. In an intuitive and simple way, without the need for technical knowledge in blockchains/NFTs, creative communities are invited to join a decentralized autonomous organization (DAO) offering new services and tools that allow the creation and co-creation of content in a blockchain. DAFNE+' research focuses also on the definition of new business models through the distribution of content, allowing creators and users to monetize multimedia creations. The project was started in July 2022 for 36 months and gathers an international consortium of 10 European partners including universities and public research centres, companies specialized in digital infrastructures and organizations federating creative communities. It is structured in 3 use-cases addressing the following communities:

1. User generated content at large for heritage (prosumers and multimedia students)
2. Experimental sound and music production (composers, computer music designers, sound designers and sound engineers)
3. Novel forms of artistic content exploitation (makers, designers)

This paper focuses on the second use-case led by IRCAM.

2. BACKGROUND

2.1 IRCAM

The Institute for Acoustic/Music Research and Coordination IRCAM is one of the largest public research centres in the world articulating musical creation and scientific research. IRCAM's original framework as an organization has been since its inception in 1977, as a component of the Centre Pompidou's project in Paris, to gather researchers, engineers and artists in the same place and organize productive interactions between them. Its research lab entitled STMS (Science and Technology of Music and Sound) gathers 120 researchers, faculty and engineers specialized in all scientific fields related to music and sound. The artistic and production departments commission and host some of the greatest composers and performers for producing 30 new artworks every year, mostly live performance pieces based on IRCAM's latest technology. Beyond the presence of artists, a specificity of the lab in the academic world is that most research teams include engineers who develop and maintain over years dozens of technical environments and modules (mostly software but also hardware) that integrate new research results and make them available to artists for their own production.

[1] https://dafneplus.eu

2.2 The IRCAM Forum

The IRCAM Forum was founded in 1994 to make the IRCAM non-commercial technologies available to external users, mostly artists - composers, performers, sound designers, sound engineers, but also researchers and teachers, engineers, etc. 30 years after, the IRCAM Forum gathers a community of 50,000 users following a yearly growth of 25% in the last years. The main vectors for this interaction between IRCAM research teams as technology producers and these users are the forum.ircam.fr web platform and the organisation of the IRCAM Forum Workshops gathering part of the community every year at IRCAM and in various countries in collaboration with partner institutions. From a platform of distribution of IRCAM technology, the IRCAM Forum website[2] turned from 2019 to a community platform, enabling members to publish their own content (software distributions, articles, events), exchange in specialised discussion groups and collaborate on code through an internal git-based repository system. An important component of the IRCAM Forum is also to manage the documentation and promotion of the technology through the editorial production of related tutorials, teasers, user documentations in various forms (text documents, sound examples, videos, etc.). Technology distribution in the Forum platform is done through the Project model that can include any set of digital elements including code and data, examples, tutorials, etc. in dedicated archives. Projects can be created directly in the platform CMS, as well as mirrors from external open-source repositories such as GitHub.

2.3 The IRCAM Sidney patches archive

In addition to the IRCAM Forum, which hosts sound and music production tools, the Sidney private platform [1] includes versions of the technical repositories for pieces produced at IRCAM. This database contains archives of all the digital elements required to produce interactive works (patches, sounds, documentation, etc.).

2.4 Collaborative archiving and creative preservation: the Antony project

Storing, documenting and sharing contemporary music materials is a problem faced by many organizations. Beyond the usual difficulty to find financial resources to work on databases before they can even exist and the challenge to specify and implement a data model that ideally fits for everyone, the specificity of such data is both related to the extreme heterogeneity of the file repositories and their evolution in time.

Starting from the base of the Sidney application and methodologies, a workgroup has been created inside the French computer music association with several actors of the ecosystem in order to study and propose some common methodologies that would provide better approaches to manage musical data in the long term, especially for generative and interactive pieces [2]. Several guidelines that resulted from this 2-year study including the following ones:

1. The workflow rules should engage external contributions to maintain the playability of a piece although the technical execution environment varies [3].
2. The granularity of the repositories needs to be exposed for pedagogical and dissemination reasons.
3. The versions of an artistic work should reference the original one [4].

To meet these objectives, a git-based code management was proposed. Not only it provides a continuity and historicity of the contributions, but it also ensures that the versions of the code can be differentiated and identified uniquely as commits or tags. Practically, it also gives the possibility to create branches to develop, test and prototype new future versions. Of course, this is a very common workflow in engineering and code development but not as usual in the musical use cases.

3. FEATURES FOR EXPERIMENTAL SOUND AND MUSIC IN DAFNE+

3.1 Initial assumptions

Given the initial purpose of DAFNE+ as a blockchain/NFT platform aimed at empowering artists for publishing and monetizing their works, and building on the experience of IRCAM Forum, Sidney and Antony, the initial assumptions of targeted features for experimental music production were the following:

- Experiment new possibilities of registration and distribution of creative technologies (applications, libraries) using the blockchain. Provide access to existing tools, support their extensions and the development of new ones;
- Extend managed assets to artistic productions. More precisely, the objective was not to pretend replacing existing circuits of music right collection and management, for music composition, audio recordings or performance; in the continuity of Sidney and Antony, the focus was put on a category of productions mostly unaddressed by right collecting societies but central for experimental music: the technical elements needed to produce the work.
- Manage explicitly successive versions of a work and the rights granting process for enabling the production of new versions.
- Manage, through NFTs and associated smart contracts, access rights to these assets including through cryptocurrency-based monetization processes.
- Implement a decentralized content management architecture ensuring the best conditions for long-term sustainability.
- Unlike IRCAM-centered Forum and Sidney, organize the community in the form of a DAO (Distributed Autonomous Organization) in which members would be part of the organization and decide on the asset management and monetization rules.

[2] https://forum.ircam.fr

3.2 Specification process

These assumptions were integrated in a process of specification that gathered the project DAFNE+ partners and involved representatives of the targeted communities. It started with several internal project workshops to exchange on the different use-cases through a common analysis grid based on *storylines* identifying managed assets, user types and roles and their potential interests for each storyline. This process enabled to identify aspects specific or common to several use-cases. Although very different on the addressed communities and types of digital contents managed, a lot a similarity emerged on the main categories of assets to be managed and user roles in relation to these categories. A common vocabulary was adopted and converged on the concepts of *Components* and *Repositories*. *Components* are technical modules (code scripts, libraries, executables, databases…) that intervene in digital creative tools, whereas *Repositories* gather technical elements needed for a creative process, mostly creative application documents and data. The distinction between them lies less on their technical form than on their purpose: *Components* are produced by technical experts and perform a generic technical process independently of a specific artistic project, whereas *Repositories* are the support of a creative process, in particular for the production or reproduction of the artifact. Another important dimension resulting from theses exchanges was the collective dimension of the involved creative processes with possibly different roles assigned to various categories of users.

In parallel, DAFNE+ technical, business and legal partners elaborated a set of general questions that cut across the various use cases.

This stage of elaboration by the DAFNE+ consortium was then confronted to a user feedback process. An online survey was publicly announced through various communication channels. Following its launch of the survey, use case managers organised live exchanges with representatives of their communities through a set of workshops and interviews. The qualitative feedback they obtained helped interpret the survey responses to feed into the platform specification. Another outcome of this feedback was to feed an update of the use case specifications from the initial assumptions. What emerged then was the necessity of structuring each use-case in several scenarios, involving different assets and/or user communities and roles. The answers to the survey enabled to prioritize the features to be developed and were then translated to functional and technical specifications, that fed the platform development during the second semester of 2023.

3.3 Features for experimental sound and music production

Some platform features are common to all DAFNE+ use-cases and communities, such as:

- the use of a distributed content management system,
- the possibility of declaring ownership on uploaded contents, possibly between several users with defined shares, and/or on the organizations to which they are affiliated,
- then to mint them as NFTs, and publish them in the platform's marketplace and possibly to external marketplaces,
- the availability of a set of creative tools resulting from research carried out as part of the project, including on AI-based image processing and 3D modeling,
- the setup of a DAO for managing the exchanges within the community.

The platform features more specifically intended for experimental sound and music production are summarized in the following scenarios and tool sets.

3.3.1 Scenario 1: Software components

This scenario concerns the distribution and use of software components for audio/music creative processes (libraries, applications, datasets, etc.). Novel possibilities enabled by the blockchain include its use for declaring software anteriority, NFTs supporting crowdfunded code development in the spirit of Patreon, and its complementarity to open-source software distribution for protecting non-public domain components, such as datasets resulting from artistic processes (performance recordings) that can be stored in the platform and made available conditionally to the acquisition of an NFT associated to a license in the form of a smart contract.

3.3.2 Scenario 2: Work repositories

This scenario is central to the project and aims to support the technical and legal foundations of an open database of sound/music work repositories: in the international computer music community, and despite various expressed marks of interest and local approaches there has been up to now no large-scale infrastructure developed for that purpose. The setting of such an open work repertoire gathers converging interests of composers, computer music designers, performers, performance venues and musicologists, and even possibly collectors who would like to acquire rights on the technical form of major works that are expected to be milestones in the history of sound and music aesthetics. The initial focus was on computer music, but positive feedback from artists and sound designers has led us to extend the scope to the latter: in commercial sound design or urban installations, declaring the work in the blockchain before submitting it for tender can provide a kind of security against copying. The possible formats are very open and can include the algorithms used to compose the piece, the patches to perform it, but also multichannel recordings, that are currently not supported by most NFT marketplaces. A major problem identified in many cases is that work repositories can include copyrighted content, such as scores or recordings. The approach being pursued, which is the subject of legal studies currently underway at international level, is to store such content privately and only allow access to it subject to the acquisition of an NFT associated with a smart contract license that will specify the conditions of use acceptable to the holders of these neighbouring rights. In addition, the platform specification foresees the management of work versions, i.e. several blockchain assets pointing to the same piece, with the choice given to the initial owner either to allow anyone to produce a new version, or to prevent it by default and be able to select users of his/her choice who will be trusted for respecting the original artistic intention and make relevant choices therefore.

3.3.3 Scenario 3: Private spaces

This last use-case was not initially foreseen and emerged from exchanges with composers in workshops and interviews. The idea is to transpose crowdfunding processes to contemporary music creation using NFTs: fans and collectors will be invited to contribute to the funding of an ongoing creation process against counterparts ("private spaces") to be defined by the artists and their commissioners in smart contracts, including VIP access to the work premiere, invitation to follow the production process, exchange sessions with the artists, mention of their names as part work sponsors, etc.

3.3.4 Creative tools

The IRCAM Forum already proposes many creative tools and an API has been developed to enable the access to its projects metadata from the DAFNE+ platform's tools catalogue. DAFNE+ also supports the development of existing or new creative tools. This support has been dedicated up to now to the following advances:

- The development of version 2 of RAVE[3][5], a real-time audio processing technology based on a variational autoencoder featuring timbre transfer and generativity.
- A contribution to the development of WebPd[4], a web interface that enables to play Pure Data patches in a browser, with all patch parameters specified in the URL. WebPd may be used for instance as a preview interface for some Pure Data work repositories.
- The development by Miller Puckette and test in a large scale production project by Philippe Manoury of Reality Check [6], a system dedicated to assessing the conformance of a new version of a Pure Data patch by comparing its audio outputs with those of a reference patch, using the same set of recorded inputs. In DAFNE+, it is intended to support the development of new versions of a patch.

4. CURRENT STATUS AND NEXT STEPS

As of January 2024, a first version of the platform[5] is publicly open and manages user registration, upload of content, declaration of ownership rights, publication of uploaded assets on the platform's marketplace etc. The used blockchain is Polygon and the platform release runs on testnet, i.e. with bitcoins with no exchange value –here MATICs of Polygon's Mumbai testnet. Moreover, the starting licensing conditions are restricted to the Creative Commons license, so to public-domain work repositories contents. Planned updates foresee the possibility of more restrictive access and licensing conditions, the management of work versions, and the setup of the DAO. Beyond the technical and legal validation of its concepts during the project's timeframe, the sustainability of the developed platform will be only possible if a sufficiently large community is involved so that recurrent means can be found for its operation.

Acknowledgments

This work is supported by the DAFNE+ project under Horizon Europe Grant Agreement number 101061548. We also would like to thank all the persons who devoted time to give us feedback on the project's proposals and fed its specification.

5. REFERENCES

[1] Lemouton, S. and Goldszmidt, S. "La préservation des œuvres du répertoire IRCAM: Présentation du modèle Sidney et analyse des dispositifs temps réel". *Actes des Journées d'Informatique musicale*, Albi, GMEA, 2016.

[2] Wetzel, D. B., "A model for the conservation of interactive electroacoustic repertoire: analysis, reconstruction, and performance in the face of technological obsolescence". *Org. Sound* 11(3), 2006, pp273-284.

[3] Zattra, L., "Collaborating on composition: The role of the musical assistant at IRCAM, CCRMA and CSC", *Live-Electronic Music. Composition, Performance and Study*, Friedemann Sallis, Valentina Bertolani, Jan Burle, Laura Zattra eds., Routledge, 2018, pp. 59-80.

[4] Lemouton, S., Bonardi, A., Pottier, L., & Warnier, J., "On the Documentation of Electronic Music". *Computer Music Journal* 42(4), MIT Press, 2019. https://doi.org/10.1162/comj_a_00486

[5] Caillon A., Esling P., "RAVE: A variational autoencoder for fast and high-quality neural audio synthesis", *International Conference In Machine Learning*, 2021. arXiv:2111.05011

[6] Puckette M., "Reality Check - a framework for preserving real-time electronic music realizations", ICMC, Seoul, Korea, 2024.

[3] https://forum.ircam.fr/projects/detail/rave/

[4] https://forum.ircam.fr/projects/detail/webpd/

[5] https://dafneplus.eng.it/

The Future is Here, Opportunities and Challenges of Avatar Technology for Music Performance

Wanjun YANG
Sichuan Conservatory of Music, CHINA
yangwanjun@163.com

Haokun YANG
Sichuan Conservatory of Music, CHINA
1663590016@qq.com

Mingliu YANGXU
Sichuan Conservatory of Music, CHINA
1458303409@qq.com

ABSTRACT

With the advent of the post-epidemic era, changes in human lifestyles and technological transformations have made it necessary for humans to accept and embrace new technologies and futures. The ever-evolving technology of virtual digital people will become the basic trend of future performances. This paper takes ABBA Reunion and Alter Ego of Fox News as entry points, and combines them with other cases of virtual digital person application in music performance to explore the opportunities and challenges brought by virtual digital person for music performance.

1. INTRODUCTION

From a technical point of view, an Avatar can be understood as an interactive virtual image created through computer graphics, graphic rendering, motion capture, deep learning, speech synthesis and other technological means, and having the appearance, behavior and even thoughts of a human being.

In this paper, we take ABBA's comeback of the young image of actors reconstructed with virtual technology, the concert guaranteed by new media technology, the launch of the world's first avatar singing competition Alter Ego with the Fox News, and other avatars as examples, to illustrate the changes that the avatar technology has brought about to music performances in this era. As well as the impact of online concerts and performances with virtual digital people in the post epidemic era, providing new ways of performing.

2. ABBA REUNION

2021, ABBA, one of pop music's most prestigious evergreens with 400 million albums sold and 17 number one singles, announced that they are returning for the first time after four decades, holding a grand virtual concert in 2022. It was conducted in the form of an online concert, taking virtual technology to sample the band's performers and then reconstructing the young appearance of them.

2.1 Who is ABBA

ABBA is a famous Swedish pop band, the name of the band comes from the initials of the four members' names, the band was active in the 1970s and 1980s, with a variety of styles of music covering pop, rock, disco and folk, and with fans all over the world.

2.2 Technical analysis of ABBA's reunion

This concert blurs the boundaries of reality through the latest motion capture technology, recreating the image of the band members in their youth, and the audience saw the same virtual image as the image of the band members in 1979. The technology in the human motion capture, through the human body key parts set up tracker, after computer processing to get the three-dimensional spatial coordinates of the data, so as to build the virtual image of the trajectory of the virtual image, this technology will make the virtual image more humane.

The virtual quartet performed at a bespoke venue called the ABBA Arena at the Queen Elizabeth Olympic Park in London on 27 May 2022. *The ABBA Voyage* offers many unique ways for audiences to enjoy the show, including the ability to see everything that can be viewed from their seats in the auditorium via the internet, as well as dancing to the music and more, as if they were there!

3. FOX NEWS ALTER EGO SINGING COMPETITION

3.1 What is Alter Ego?

Alter Ego is the world's first avatar singing competition on American Fox News. The term "Alter Ego" comes from the Latin word meaning "other self", and is often considered to be a sharp departure from a person's normal or original personality. The show premiered on the 22nd and 23rd of September, 2021. The show is judged by Grammy-winning singers and hosted by Rocsi Diaz. The contestants of this show all stayed backstage and compete by manipulating their virtual digital characters to perform on stage. The avatars in the show have different skin color options, and are free to choose their body type and gender. Contestants can choose the image that they think best represents their inner self, or best catches the attention of the audience. The winner of the first season of Alter Ego receives a cash prize of $100,000 and has the opportunity to be mentored by a panel of judges. The contestants are given the opportunity to bring these avatars into real life, and that they are able to perform on stage and take part in interviews.

3.2 The impact of Alter Ego

For Grimes, shows like this give an opportunity to many people who are behind the scenes but also like to perform. This is definitely a good thing for people who have stage fright; it fulfils the need to show off their ego, but also does a good job of avoiding the trepidation of facing an audience head on.

Grimes, who created and released her own 3D character, War Nymph, said in an interview with magazine *The Face* that with War Nymph, she was able to perform on stage even during her pregnancy and had more time to spend with her new baby. It's hard for her to do photo shoots or wear the clothes she wears for those shoots. But War Nymph can promote her album here. The avatar is a solution to the problem of women being afraid to have children in the workplace because of their jobs, a benefit Grimes describes as "e-feminism".

4. VIRTUAL DIGITAL PERSONS FOR OTHER MUSICAL PERFORMANCES

4.1 Luo Tianyi and her activities

The development of virtual technology is not limited to television programs or concert performances, for example, the Chinese virtual singer Luo Tianyi, who was the first virtual singer to make a profit in China. In September 2021, Luo Tianyi was involved in the Winter Olympics and Paralympics, performing the musical composition '*Time to Shine*' on stage.

4.2 Microsoft Xiaobing

Xiaobing, a teenage girl, is a poet, singer, presenter, painter and designer. Unlike other AIs, Xiaobing focuses on the development of AI in the dimension of anthropomorphic human emotional intelligence, emphasises AI emotional intelligence rather than task completion, and continuously learns from the abilities of excellent human creators to create works of the same quality level as the corresponding human creators.

4.3 A-SOUL

A-SOUL is a virtual idol girl group created by Lehua Entertainment, consisting of Ava, Bella, Carol, Diana, and Eileen, who debuted in November 2020 as "Lehua Entertainment's first virtual idol group". On 2 December 2020, the group's first single "Quiet" was released, and on 11 December, the group's first online live broadcast took place.

5. CREATION AND USE OF VIRTUAL DIGITAL PEOPLE

5.1 What is a virtual digital person

From the perspective of future media forms and service modes, computer graphics, voice synthesis technology, deep learning, brain-like science, biotechnology, computational science and other converging technologies will bring about a new space for semantic communication and barrier-free communication, and the resulting avatar (Metahuman) will be widely used in the metaverse in the new ecosystem with the role of a new medium, assuming the core hub function of information manufacturing, content delivery, human-computer interaction and interpersonal communication.

5.2 Identity Creation of Virtual Digital Person in Music Performance

The identity creation of virtual digital people has a high degree of freedom, and the identity information can be created according to the creator's needs.

The identity of all virtual digital people in musical performances is the digital content created by the creators. And the digital content created by the creators through digital creation, after determined through the property rights attribute, is the digital asset, which can lay the foundation for the next digital transaction.

Virtual human technology also plays an important role in the metaverse, one of the components of which is "identity", in which users can obtain one or more new identities that have nothing to do with the real world. The identity system of the metaverse is an independent and unique digital human identity, which has the characteristics of a personality and has the right to freely participate in activities in the metaverse and enjoy a common identity with others. The identity of the meta-universe refers to decentralised digital identity (DID), which is supported by underlying technologies such as blockchain and distributed originals. In the metaverse environment, the DID identity is completely detached from the real world, through which people reconstruct themselves in the virtual world. The identity of an avatar in real life is also the same as in the metaverse, forming an identity that needs to assume corresponding rights and obligations, but this identity can sometimes not be regarded as independent of the real world, but rather as a digital alter ego of the real world identity.

5.3 Purposes of use of virtual digital people in music performance

The contestants in ABBA and Alter Ego are all trying to make their images in front of the audience and perform more in line with their own expectations, so they have retained their own characteristics when using their virtual digital persona, so as to better expand their acting career. Virtual idols such as A-soul and Luo Tianyi, on the other hand, are entirely products that bring profits to the acting companies behind them.

As can be seen, the purposes for which virtual digital people are used in musical performances are diverse. Firstly, they ultimately aim to create a better performance effect and bring a better aesthetic experience to the audience. However, it is worth noting that the virtual digital person characters created by the contestants in ABBA and Alter Ego are based on their own characteristics and carry their own social nature, and the purpose of creating virtual digital people is also to facilitate their use and shape their own social influence. The virtual idols, however, go on to create the social influence of the virtual digital person characters themselves.

6. APPLICATION OF VIRTUAL DIGITAL MAN TECHNOLOGY IN THE MUSIC PERFORMANCE MARKET

6.1 Background of the application of virtual digital person technology in the music performance market

Since the Coronavirus Pandemic, human beings have to accept the changes brought about by segregation, so this makes people more nostalgic for the warmth and revelry of live music performance and appreciation in the past. The transformation of live performances into online virtual performances through network technology and virtual technology can maximize the closeness to live performance. For years, for example, opera as an art form has been in a phase of transition: audiences are declining, and streaming services raise hopes of gaining new and younger audience segments, such as the European Opera Streaming Initiative Opera Visions. In Ann-Kristin Zoike's study, seven in-depth interviews with Opera Vision recipients from Germany, the UK, Ireland and the US were conducted and their experiences with streaming opera were analyzed using qualitative content analysis. The results show that for the interviewees, streaming opera is often a complement to, rather than a replacement for, existing live opera. Respondents perceived certain benefits of streaming opera over attending live opera, particularly in terms of more time flexibility and a wider range of program choices. And virtual digitizer technology, in this zeitgeist, has more performance opportunities and usage scenarios.

In terms of technological development, metaverse related technologies, such as artificial intelligence, AR/VR and so on, have been applied by all walks of life in the past few years. The emergence of the metaverse, with higher requirements for new technologies, can prompt related technology companies that want to reap the dividends of the metaverse to invest more in order to upgrade their technologies. For example, Apple's Vision Pro released in 2024 implements a combination of XR, artificial intelligence and other technologies to shape a new generation of spatial image processing devices. It makes a newer and better platform for the use of virtual human technology and the way to experience it.

6.2 Changes brought by virtual digital man technology to the music performance market

Before the use of virtual digital person technology, the idol of the music performance market is mainly discovered and cultivated by star scouts or acting companies, or by individuals to participate in talent shows and other ways to create an idol. However, after the virtual digital person technology gradually matured and was used in the performing arts market, the idol can not only be a natural person, but also a virtual digital person. The virtual digital person can be generated in full accordance with the requirements of the technology media performing arts company. In this way, not only reduces the difficulty of talent excavation, management costs, and in the image of the artiste works to create performances and other aspects of the company has a higher degree of control of copyright, the formation of a new product operation, capital operation mode. For musicians, the competition with virtual digital persons also needs to be considered.

7. OPPORTUNITIES BROUGHT BY THE VIRTUAL DIGITAL PERSON TECHNOLOGY IN MUSIC PERFORMANCE

Through the comeback of ABBA can be seen, any age group of appreciators have their specific popular music and memories, in the music industry has more ability to consume and the potential to tap into the music consumption needs of this type of crowd, can be presented again through the virtual digital person technology, and as a basis for the development of new works. This will be a huge business opportunity for music consumption and a new direction that the music performance market should think about.

From the musician's point of view, virtual digital person technology, brings many new possibilities to our music performance. The application of virtual digital person technology gives ordinary people an alternative when they need an image but don't want to use their own appearance image. Such an application is not only found in live music performances but also in other forms of online performances such as webcasting. The performance mode of using virtual characters for online performance is conducive to expanding the source of performers in the music performance industry, so that some music performers or ordinary people who are not satisfied enough with their own appearance or stage performance can make up for their own shortcomings through the virtual digital person technology, and thus bring better performance to the audience.

Avatar performers such as Microsoft Xiaobing and Luo Tianyi are different from natural human performers, since their own identities are created, the creators can customize the generation of identity information according to market demand. This allows performing arts companies to quickly have avatar performers with an image that meets market demand through co-operation with technology companies. And such performers can still have the same social influence as natural performers, while the company can reduce the worry about the performer's management, copyright, profit sharing and other issues, such a new business model so that the distribution of benefits between the performer and the performing arts company appeared to change the pattern. The business model of virtual digital performances, in terms of human resources, requires traditional performance-related performers, publicity and other positions, but also requires the participation of more virtual technology-related practitioners, thus creating more jobs for these related technology practitioners. Moreover, under the mode of avatar performance, virtual human characters can be used to perform online in the virtual world, as well as offline performances in the real world, and even perform on the same stage with other natural human performers. Such performance activities break through the time and space limitations, the same time cycle, the virtual performer can get more performances, thus bringing more profits for the company.

In short, the use of virtual digital person technology for music performances has brought new technical points of view, giving the performer's image, identity optimization and creation of more possibilities, bringing more new market development direction, conducive to digging more practitioners involved in the music performance industry, but also the formation of a new business operating model, creating more jobs.

8. CHALLENGES OF THE APPLICATION OF AVATAR TECHNOLOGY

Whether or not the performance technology standards and regulations related to the application of virtual digital person technology in music performances are sufficiently complete remains a concern. At present, the general standard of virtual digital person for performance has not yet appeared, but the virtual digital person industry has formed two ITU-T international standards: "digital person application system basic framework and evaluation index" and "non-interactive 2D real human image class digital person application system index requirements and evaluation methods ", from the product definition, technology, services and other dimensions of the indicator requirements and assessment methods, is an important practice of industry generalization exploration. The rapid development of the virtual anthropomorphic digital human industry cannot be separated from the personalization, intelligence and interoperability of products, and there is an urgent need to form an industry consensus and standards for technical standards, platform interoperability interfaces, compliance and ethical guidelines. And with musical performances as a major scenario for the use of avatar beings, a common standard can only make it easier and more efficient for avatar beings between different technology companies to perform at the same time as well as to cooperate with natural persons in their performances.

The operation of virtual digital persons is still faced with the dilemmas of high technical threshold, high cost, unpopularity of operation tools, and insufficient professional operation organizations and operation talents. At the same time, virtual digital person operation is a set of technology, design, content production, marketing planning and other elements of the "cross-professional", professional institutions, the lack of operating personnel, making the operating costs remain high. In addition to the regular development and operation of virtual digital persons, it also involves the innovation of the performance method and the operation of the performance business, in which the operation cost and what innovation of the operation method is needed have also become a matter of concern. However, even with huge investment, combined with the current technical means, virtual idols are also difficult not to bug in front of the fans. In the live broadcast of the members of the A-SOUL, through the mould, lagging, facial capture crash, audio and video out of sync and other phenomena also occur from time to time, the picture quality of the rendering and the live broadcast of the push stream problems occur frequently.

Although there have been many real-life cases of avatar music performances, the degree of public acceptance of this model and the upper limit of the market size are still unclear. Even if the artistic creation and product development model behind virtual digital person music performance are not yet mature, the impact of the new business model brought by virtual digital person technology on the music market can no longer be ignored. It remains to be seen what changes the technological innovation of avatar has brought to the music performance business.

9. CONCLUSIONS

The development and application of virtual digital person technology and the advent of the post epidemic era have made changes in human lifestyles inevitable. Accepting and embracing new technologies and lifestyles is the proper mindset for humans to continue to thrive and prosper. The innovative application and development of avatar technology will also be the basic trend of future artistic creation and performance. New media technology and virtual technology have become the hotspot and focus of music performance research. And the application of these new technologies also has many impacts on our society and culture, bringing about many changes.

10. REFERENCES

[1] Rao Qiong, Li Xiang. New Ideas for the Development of Chinese Art Market in the Post-Epidemic Era - Thinking triggered by the Cohen Lecture and the New Crown Epidemic[J]. Beauty and Age (Next),2021(03):44-46.

[2] Steffen Lepa, Ruth Müller-Lindenberg, Hauke Egermann. Classical Music and Opera During and After the COVID-19 Pandemic - Empirical Research on the Digital Transformation of Socio-cultural Institutions and Aesthetic Forms[M],2023:95

[3] Xu Miao. A book to read and understand the meta-universe [M]. Beijing: China Federation of Industry and Commerce Press, 2022:189

[4] State Key Laboratory of Media Convergence and Communication, Communication University of China. 2022 Report on the Influence Index of China's Virtual Digital People [R].2023:1-14

The Interpretive-Generative Spectrum and Its Role in the Form of Live-Performed Electroacoustic Music

Victor Zheng
North Central College
vzheng2696@noctrl.edu

ABSTRACT

Live-performed electroacoustic music refers to music that incorporates both an acoustic and electronic component in its composition. The integration of acoustic and electronic composition represents a bridge between traditional and modern musical techniques, making works incorporating this integration receptive to formal approaches taking inspiration from, but not wholly rooted in, traditional descriptors of form. In its own right, this integration constitutes a fast-evolving field of electroacoustic music as technology continues to innovate on methods to consolidate the human performer and their interaction with the electronics in a manner conducive to real-time music performance.

I describe three general technical categories that define integrated live and electroacoustic performance, those being fixed media, live electronics, and augmented performer. I then propose the concept of the interpretative-generative spectrum to describe the relationship between the performer and electronic components: the generative end of the spectrum represents an electronic component producing material independently of musical material within the acoustic, while the interpretive end of the spectrum involves the electronics directly processing or developing a performer's gestures. This framework provides a means to describe the balance between the acoustic and electronic components in terms of its place on the interpretive-generative spectrum, and opens possibilities of using that spectrum to describe the formal and structural connotations said interaction.

1. INTRODUCTION

Live-performed electroacoustic music refers to music involving any degree of integration between any number of live performers, or acoustic elements, and electronic elements. Compositionally, the synthesis and sampling possibilities of electronics allow for near complete freedom in the sonic realm, while live performers must contend with performance practices and acoustic limitations of their instruments or voice. The crucial question that arises in the presence of live performers is the relationship between the electronics and the sounds produced by the performers and how a composer bridges the seeming gulf in the natures of these two categories.

2. TECHNICAL CATEGORIES

In defining the genre of live-performed electroacoustic music, I first propose three categories of acoustic-electronic integration as determined by the technological setup of the electronics and its behavior in interacting with the acoustic.

2.1 Fixed Media and Performer

Fixed media and performer uses preprepared sound, whether recorded or synthesized, as a monolithic companion to one or more live performers. This is certainly the most easily implemented form of integration between live and electronic performance, requiring only a means of playback and no responsivity to input, and as such was the means by which the earliest attempts at such integration were made.

Fixed media is uniquely inflexible, subordinating performers to the electronic sounds exactly as recorded or rendered with the only control available being stopping and starting the media. In any ensemble, even one with a clear leader-follower hierarchy, the human interaction between the leader and follower uses input from both sides to facilitate communication. Hence, the introduction of fixed media to the musical ensemble places a rigid, unchanging musical framework around the human ebb and flow of the performer(s). The composer must therefore decide on a means of composing around the one-sided nature of the human-electronic interactions, leading this logistical concern to have compositional ramifications.

Using fixed media does not necessarily demand mathematical precision from the performer(s) in every musical gesture. Composers have the choice to counter the rigidity of the electronic component by loosening the requirements of the human performers, designing aleatoric segments of electronic gesture around which a performer can exercise some freedom.

2.2 Live Electronics

Live electronics introduces the possibility of electronic interaction between the performer(s) and the electronics. Electronic interaction involves taking the sound produced by a performer as an input signal and using the computer to interpret the signal in some way. The means of interaction between the performer and the electronics can range from a simple effect applied to the performer's part, such as adding a reverberation, to programming the electronics to recognize different gestures and respond accordingly in complex ways.

Philippe Manoury describes temporal control as a crucial difference between live electronics and fixed media. Electronics can exist in "real time" (temps réel) or "non-real time" (temps différé). Fixed media is designed asynchronously, being composed before any performer can interact with it; once it plays, it is unable to adapt in the moment to the performer. Fixed media and a live performer, according to Manoury, therefore operate in non-real time, being completely independent of each other conceptually and only coexisting in a moment rather than occupying a common temporal progression. With live electronics, even if the sounds themselves are precomposed and immutable, they could respond to the performer's gestures, allowing the performer to influence the timings. With this tenet of interactivity, the performer and electronics now progress in response to each other and occupy the same temporal dimension, in real time.

2.3 Augmented Performer

Augmented performer features electronically enhancing the controls of an instrument or performer themself beyond producing their own sound, allowing their performative gestures to include additional control over different sound parameters or technical functions in the software. For example, modifying the instrument to magnify its sounds could create more possibilities out of normally quiet techniques, such as keyclicks on a flute. In addition, by augmenting the body of a performer with devices such as motion sensors, non-sound based performative gestures such as body movement or miming could play a role in controlling electronics.

There is necessarily a great deal of similarity between the category of augmented performer and the previous category of live electronics; for example, one could expand a flute's sound possibilities with attached microphones and also process its sound, straddling both categories. Augmented performer makes one important distinction between itself and live electronics in its use of microphones: in the augmented performer category, the integration of the microphones into the instrument and/or body of the performer is done where their placement is integral to the physical body of the instrument or performer as well as the content they are meant to capture. A microphone placed in the general vicinity of a flute would fall under live electronics, but a microphone fixed to the keys of a flute specifically to capture keyclicks would be augmented performer. Such incorporation of the physicality of the instrument and performer sets it apart from live electronics.

3. THE INTERPRETIVE-GENERATIVE FRAMEWORK

I propose two general categories that define a musical idea's relationship between the electronic and acoustic components on a formal level. There is a crucial distinction between analyzing a gesture in the moment versus analyzing it on a formal level, i.e. in the context of its large-scale surroundings. Comparing the electronic and acoustic elements has no formal implications unless taking into account the temporal dimension, i.e., the gesture's development over time. To that end, the two categories I propose relate to how a material unfolds over time, not just its presentation.

3.1 Interpretive Gestures

An interpretative gesture features the electronics subordinated to the acoustic, by following a developmental trajectory directly related to that produced by the live performer, thus interpreting the performer's gesture. This category often takes the form of live effects applied to an acoustic line and played back in real time, such as an instrument being harmonized live during performance. A similar effect can be achieved with fixed media, where there is no live processing being applied but the precomposed materials in the acoustic and electronic components still follow deliberately corresponding trajectories, such as a performer playing a motive simultaneously with a recording of that same motive with effects applied. The previously mentioned technical categories are independent of this categorization, as an interpretive gesture can be realized in any technical category: whether using live effects or precomposing the corresponding segments with fixed media is only a distinction in methodology.

Interpretative gestures need not be simultaneous nor tightly corresponding to their acoustic stimulus, only following in some way. For example, recording a live-performed sample and replaying it later in the work would be interpretive, as would be fragmenting, time-stretching, reversing, scrambling, or otherwise twisting it beyond recognition, even after the listener has long since lost any semblance of association between the materials.

3.2 Generative Gestures

A generative gesture involves the electronic component producing or developing material independently of the acoustic, regardless of whether the starting material itself is related or not. This does not disqualify motivic connection between the two components; if an electronic component shares a common motive with the acoustic but develops it in its own trajectory free from acoustic influence, then the process would fall under a generative role. By extension, a generative gesture could involve the electronic component developing a material completely unrelated to what occurs in the acoustic. The crucial element is the electronics generating their own developmental trajectory rather than being anchored to the acoustic.

Whether a gesture in the electronics follows the acoustic, as with an interpretive gesture, or vice versa, as with a generative gesture, is an important distinction, as the compositional role of the electronics is fundamentally different between these two cases. Mere similarity between the two does not automatically result in an interpretive gesture. For example, a scratch tone in a violin echoing bursts of noise in the electronics with the electronics growing louder while the violin follows suit is composed so that the violin reacts to the electronic gestures. In such cases where the acoustic follows the lead of the electronic, I categorize this as a generative gesture in the electronics, despite the similarities in the material, as it is not dependent on the trajectory of an acoustic gesture, but the other way around. An interpretative gesture refers strictly to an electronic process designed to follow the gestures of a performer, and when reversed, the electronics take on a generative function.

4. BRUNO MADERNA'S *MUSICA SU DUE DIMENSIONI* (1952): APPLYING THE FRAMEWORK

There are two works by Bruno Maderna titled *Musica su due dimensioni* (*Music in two dimensions*), one written in 1952 and the other in 1958. *Musica* '52 is written for flute, cymbal, and tape, though the cymbal is limited to a single appearance near the end of the work and is performable by the flutist, making the work largely for flute and tape, usually played by one performer. *Musica* '58 is entirely for flute and tape. The two works are otherwise unrelated. This analysis covers specifically *Musica* '52.

4.1 Form and Structure

Musica '52 is in a tripartite form, divided into clear zones of precedence between the live performer and the tape. Section A is entirely tape, followed by Section B which is entirely a flute solo. Section C returns to entirely tape apart from a single cymbal strike near the end.

Section A immediately demonstrates Maderna's combination of set-based and serial techniques, by playing entirely within 12-tone equal temperament and producing trichordal sets that develop into a complete row at the end of the section, bridging into Section B and its extended flute solo. Maderna's choice to restrict Section A's electronics entirely to 12-TET is noteworthy in the face of the synthesis and sampling possibilities that were readily available in 1952; this choice is a clear tying of the electronics to the pitch-based realm of the flute.

Section B then takes the row presented in Section A and develops it via the iteration method described by Christoph Niedhöfer, in which the intervals between successive notes of the row are rotated to produce new iterations of the row.

Section C reintroduces the electronics, but this time presenting largely in percussive noise. This again connects back to the instrumental dimension at the end, in which the percussive-reminiscent electronics are answered with a single cymbal crash. Finally, the work closes out with a final iteration of the row originally generated in Section A and developed in Section B, thus tying the work together with their shared developmental trajectory in the tone row.

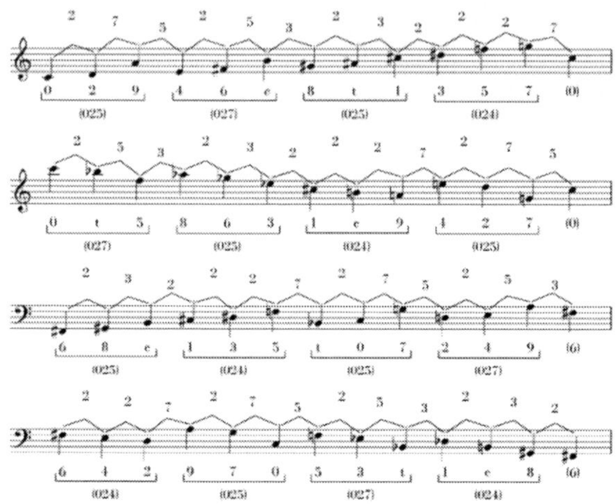

Figure 1. The four rotations of the row, first introduced at the end of Section A (electronics) and developed through Sections B (flute) and C (electronics). Note the rotating intervals (in semitones) between the row members.

4.2 Developing Along the Interpretive-Generative Spectrum

The connecting of the electronic and flute gestures via iterations of the same row as well as the affinity between the percussive noise in the electronics and the cymbal crash raise the fundamental question regarding the relation between the gestures – are the electronics performing an interpretive or generative function against the flute and cymbal? The ambiguities that this work presents blur the boundaries of the two categories, and demonstrate that they constitute not a dichotomy but opposite ends of a continuous spectrum.

The first, most obvious characterization to Section A is that the electronics gestures are generative. Regardless of any affinity they may share with the flute material, the electronics develop first without any input from the flute. Independently of any live element, the electronics slowly coalesce into complete twelve-tone rows that act as the culminating objective of the first section's development and provide the springboard from which the flute takes over proceedings, permuting and developing the rows. With such a direct, unambiguous presentation of the flute following the development of the electronics, there seems no question that the electronics are generative.

But alternatively, one could interpret 12-TET as inherently belonging to the realm of acoustic music, represented by the flute. Even if the electronics occur temporally before the flute, the rows presented in the flute can be interpreted as the source material for the electronics in the first section. This can also be supported by examining the material shared across the flute and electronics: the row fragments presented in Section A hint at the trichordal construction that eventually form the complete rows that bridge the two sections; the complete row is the basis from which the fragments were derived. Could then the electronics of Section A be seen as a development of the figures presented in the flute, thus being interpretive in nature?

The electronics return in Section C with a percussive, noisy sound profile and are the clearest example of generative electronics in this work, as Maderna presents this section as a showcase of the timbres with no direct analogue in the flute, thus having no inherently pitch-based material that could be construed as a developmental basis. The cymbal crash arriving near the end of the work is the culmination of this section, arriving after several repetitions of a rhythmic ostinato in different timbres in the electronics; the single crash carries little indication of ambiguity in developmental direction compared to the debatable functions of the dodecaphonic pitch structures between Section A and the flute: the electronics are developing and arriving at the cymbal, not the other way around.

The closing gestures of C, a final presentation of two rows in the electronics, is in turn the most unambiguous instance of an interpretive gesture as it presents a permutation of the row arrived on in Section A and developed in Section B, a clear interpretation of the developmental trajectory that was previously presented in the flute. It is crucial that the electronics are continuing the permutation operations that led to the flute's introduction in Section B, as these operations were absent in Section A and therefore is a direct connection to the flute's development and not the previous pitch-based electronic material. It is equally crucial that the end of Section C connects to the flute's method of development, the permutation operation, and not the material itself. Referencing the actual developmental technique is the critical element identifying these final rows as an interpretive gesture.

Musica '52 thus presents two developmental trajectories with regards to the interaction between the electronics and the acoustic. Firstly, either the tone rows forming in the electronics of A are answered by the flute's development of the rows in B, or the electronic trichords in A are a fragmentation of a preconceived set of rows that is only revealed by the flute in B; regardless, these are answered by a single interpretive gesture at the end of Section C in the form of the unbroken row at its closing, continuing the development of the work's row structure. Secondly, the electronics develop their percussive possibilities throughout Section C in a generative gesture that culminates in a single cymbal crash. Despite the continued affinity between the electronic and the acoustic components, the developmental direction is clearly starting from the electronics' generated material and answered by the acoustic, in the cymbal.

The ambiguity seen in Section A between the interpretive or generative nature of the electronics blurs the boundaries between the two categories, demonstrating not a dichotomous categorization but a flexible spectrum on which a gesture can be found. Such a spectrum opens a new dimension for analysis of development and form: in *Musica* '52, we can observe the trajectory of the electronics begin in ambiguity before developing into its role and definitively stating both ends of the interpretive-generative spectrum.

5. CONCLUSIONS

The interpretive-generative spectrum is a flexible, succinct framework for characterizing the relationship between the electronic and acoustic elements of a live-performed electroacoustic work, and a work's place on the spectrum is a characteristic that a composer can control and thus develop. More broadly, a gesture's place on the spectrum reflects the hierarchy between the human performer and electronics, a question that has challenged composers of the genre since its inception. How does a performer truly interact with electronics, which cannot interpret their gestures or communicate like a fellow human could?

The technical categorizations of live-performed electroacoustic music provide configurations that have implications toward the hierarchy of the entities, but ultimately give no guarantees to the nature of the relationship between them. The technical configuration of *Musica* '52, of fixed media and performer, necessarily subordinates the performer to the electronics, which cannot respond to the performer in any way whatsoever. But this is in fact no hindrance to the distribution of its gestures along the interpretive-generative spectrum – the design of the electronic gestures in fact shows a dynamically evolving relationship in affinity and hierarchy between the performer and electronics in their gestural content.

The inherently contrasting approaches between electronic and acoustic are not only a logistical concern but integral enough to the genre of live-performed electroacoustic music that the relationship between the two components becomes a compositional parameter and a structural consideration. The interpretive-generative spectrum is a framework to evaluate the degree of affinity between the electronic and acoustic components of a live-performed electroacoustic work. This categorization is meant to be applicable regardless of a work's technical characteristics and facilitate an approach to form that centers around the composer's approach to consolidating the electronic-acoustic divide. By introducing this dimension of form, analyses can better consolidate formal, technical, and thematic implications into a unified interpretation of the music and open new directions for composers operating in the medium.

6. REFERENCES

[1] P. Manoury, *La musique du temps reél*, Paris, France: Éditions MF, 2012.

[2] B. Maderna, *Musica su due dimensioni per flauto e nastro magnetico*, Nicola Scaldaferri, Mario Baroni, and Rossana Dalmonte, Eds., Milan, Italy: Edizioni Suvini Zerboni, 2001.

[3] C. Niedhöfer, "Bruno Maderna's Serial Arrays," *Music Theory Online*, vol. 13, no. 1, 2007. [Online]. Available: https://mtosmt.org/issues/mto.07.13.1/mto.07.13.1.neidhofer.html

Queer Soundscapes: Deconstructing Gender Identifiers in Vocal and Bodily Sounds through a Technologically-Aided Music Composition

Fotis Rovolis (φø)
NKUA
faux.tease@gmail.com

Thanos Polymeneas-Liontiris
NKUA
athpoli@gmail.com

ABSTRACT

This paper presentation is based on the exploration of technological processes applied on bodily sounds, both as a means for research on music making, as much as for the personal review and observation of one's gender identity and fluidity. The research is founded upon an intellectual dialogue between queer theory and contemporary music practices. The results of this discourse support theoretically a technologically aided music practice, the subject matter of which is the gender identity of bodily and vocal sounds. The investigation follows an autoethnographic method on a creative-critical practice. It explores the capacity of music to highlight gender aspects of voice, it looks into processes that remove such gender identifiers, aiming towards the making of queer soundscapes. This paper is aiming to present the theoretical background of the research, alongside the creative processes and methods employed to develop a queer soundscape.

1. INTRODUCTION

Focusing on the body, and more specifically its sonic essence, the processes presented in this paper investigate a potential redefinition of gender, within a creative sonic project. Sound, listening and technology might aid a better understanding of one's gender experience. They also challenge the assumption that bodies, as much as voices, are taken for granted as binary gender identity carriers. This research project puts into question such assumptions through a creative critical practice. The work we will present is called *Cyborgutt*, and was made by sound artist φø (pronounced Faux, aka Fotis Rovolis). This paper originates from the conception of "non-existence", a recurring experience for many LGBTQIA+ individuals, which can be understood as the lack of understanding of their non-binary identity in the social sphere. The paper initially examines the existence of gender and its boundaries. Subsequently, it observes the voice and the way it's perceived as a gender identifier. It presents music compositions examples where the voice is deconstructed, rendering any gender identifiers more fluid, or other music practices that call for a redefinition of listening, pointing out how such aural gender assumption may get deconstructed by the listeners themselves.s The paper concludes with the assimilation of these processes in the making of a queer soundscape.

2. GENDER CONSTRUCTS

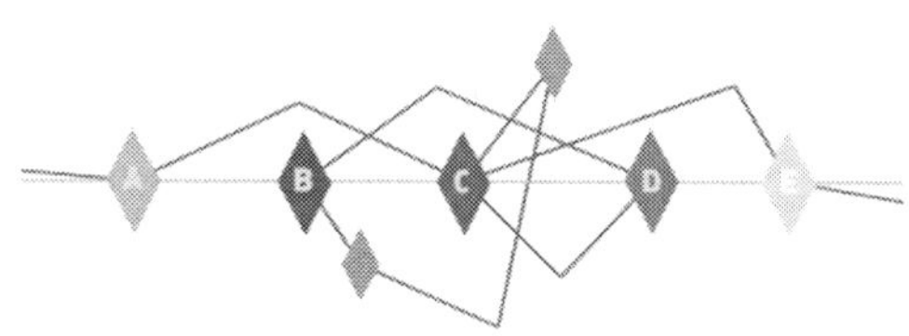

Figure 1. Queer temporalities graphic structure

To begin with, it is important to understand or approach the term queer as a fluid concept. It is rather an action, a verb, that indicates the departure from predetermined conventions and filtered recruitments of the environment, such as bodies, genders, sounds and in general relationships, avoiding to put everything into boxes. Judith Butler posits gender as a social construct, shaped by individual performances influenced by societal norms. Gender roles aligned with binary biological categories can constrain identity and render certain ones invisible. For Butler, gender emerges through repeated bodily gestures, and is not predetermined at birth but constituted over time, through repetitions, which eventually create the illusion of a fixed gendered self. However, societal prejudice towards binary gender norms marginalizes queer identities, leading to temporal displacement and the formation of alternative queer temporalities, as described by Jack Halberstam. As heteronormative culture, translates age, into stages of maturityqueer people might not have the linear heteronormative coming of age milestones in their lives (figure 1), nor might they conquer adulthood within a linear timeline. The concept of queer temporalities, could hence be transcribed into soundspaces, and is a concept that responds to heteronormative standards. Similarly, the concept of queer proposes constant fluidity, redefinition of boundaries and recognition of how queer bodies explore new relationships with time. Such disruptions of the heteronormative linearity, consequently lie in the very act of repetition, as Butler proposes. No gesture repetition can be identical to another, therefore such discrepancy causes variations, and the uniqueness of each person's identity. Gender identification is not static, it is a dynamic process, a process of constant configuration. Within each repetition lies the potential of re-proposing the essence of what is being repeated, hence the redefinition of one's own identity.

3. VOICE AND LISTENING

The voice is considered to be one of the main gender stereotypical identifiers. It is one of the first characteristics that may pin down the body as male or female in a binary gender system. Labels are automatically placed through stereotypical assumptions. Voice mimicking is one of the very first means used to mock and insult any person whose gender identity does not fit within the binary split, a common transphobic practice. Alexa Woloshyn [4] points out that the body is marked by the voice. When the physical body is not visible, the voice carries all its characteristics, delineates it and regurgitates it on a symbolic level. Stephen Conor [5] proposes the term "vocalic body" to describe the ability of the voice to suggest and "produce" a body. Just as every sound is connected to its source object, the voice is associated with a body. This leads to the assumption that any voice, coming from a non-visible body, will produce its own symbolic body. Similarly to a certain extent, Mladen Dolar [5] suggests that the voice is the surplus of the body, a description that captures the non-materialistic aspect of its nature.

For Joke Dame, the voice on its own does not possess a gendered imprint. Rather the act of listening is the process that assigns gender to each voice. This means that our reception operates on predetermined conventions. She suggests that listening must be reinvented every time it encounters a new voice.

Such a process of constant reinvention cannot be undisrupted or linear, since the imaginary production of a body through the sound of a voice may not always be accurate. When we hear a voice and associate it with a certain body of an imaginary shape, the chances that our imagination matches reality are not always high. That depends on many factors, starting from the very ambiguity of each voice regarding to how its characteristics fit into the spectrum of stereotypical frequency values or timbre [6].

Gender is produced and gets embodied only through its iterative actions and imperfect repetitions of its performativity [1]. The very process of performing and its precarious stamp of an impossible absolute reproduction that constantly creates the space of new forms and, therefore, of new identities. For Jarman Ivens [5], the voice needs two bodies to be "heard". The receiver and the transmitter, "the voicer and the listener": the voice thus functions as a tool for connecting two or multiple bodies together (figure 2). Thus, she proposes a "third space" between the body and the voice (transmitter and receiver): the moment where sound waves are emitted by the body and before they are received by the ears of another. In this third space, the voice contains its infinite manifestations simultaneously [7]. This way, she describes listening as the process of filtering out the multiplicity of possibilities and assigning gender to any voice. The third space therefore, if explored appropriately and in depth, is capable of giving birth to new possibilities, by highlighting queer qualities.

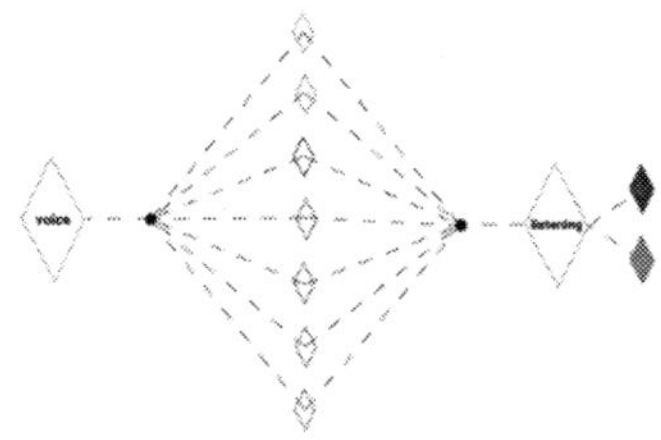

Figure 2. Queer temporalities graphic

As Woloshyn mentions, queer as a verb denotes a practice of unbiased perception, which in the case of gender binary breaks down the fixed dichotomy through which bodies, sounds and voices are filtered [4, p.69]. Truax's composition "Song of Songs" - based on the romantic dialogue between Solomon and Salomoth - exemplifies this, distorting voices to erase gender markers. Through granular synthesis, Truax fragments and blends voices with ambient sounds, blurring distinctions between human and nature. This challenges heteronormativity in auditory reception, creating aural events detached from physical origins. Truax's approach represents a queer practice, redefining conventional romantic contexts by removing gender identifiers, thus dissolving the ties between sound object and source. In this way, the composition suggests a redirection from binary constraints, offering insights beyond gender, towards a broader disconnection from fixed forms.Another approach is that of Pauline Oliveros, who in her *Deep Listening* (2005) workshops attempts to introduce a deeper conception of the listening process. According to Oliveros [9], Deep Listening involves listening in a non-judgmental and open way, without preconceptions or need to categorise and classify sounds and to associate them to identifiers. This means embracing all sounds, including those considered noise or non-musical, and incorporating them into the listening experience. Listening in the process of Deep Listening is not only about hearing sounds, but about being fully present in the moment and experiencing the environment in a new, non-judgmental and ephemeral way. One of the key aspects of deep listening is incorporating the body into the listening experience: Oliveros encourages listeners to actively engage their bodies in the listening process, through movement, breathing and other physical activities. This helps to create a deeper connection with the sounds and the environment, as well as to develop a closer relationship between the listener and the sounds [9].

4. *CYBORGUTT* THE COMPOSITION

The theoretical analysis of this research led to the development of an acousmatic composition,

Cyborgutt, a fixed media work, composed in 2022 by sound artist φø (pronounced Faux, aka Fotis Rovolis), based on recorded sound material produced by their own body. The reasons for this creative-critical work were composite: on the one hand, φø was interested in applying the theoretical framework of their previous research onto their own sound art practice. Therefore the composition in itself is one of the outcomes of a larger scale research. On the other hand, the composer wanted to make a work produced through an autoethnographical process. Inevitably, the work itself had a very personal charge, as it led the composer towards a deeper and more sincere understanding of themselves and their own body. Hence, the composition ended up becoming one possible "vehicle", a means of communication of such a relationship with oneself and the general audience, a way to transmit their research output in a non verbal manner.

The first stage of the practical process consisted in the exploration of all possible bodily sounds. φø made numerous recordings, building up an audio library. These sounds were divided into 3 categories: the external sounds (all sounds except vocal sounds); the intermediate sounds (voice and sounds produced inside the oral cavity); and lastly the internal ones (sounds from the internal organs: stomach sounds, heart beats, breathing etc.). For the external sounds, the recordings were made using directional condenser microphones. The intermediate sounds were recorded by both binaural microphones and directional condenser microphones. Binaural microphones were explored in order to capture the personal perspective and the spatial aspects related to these sounds. Lastly, the internal sounds were recorded by electronic stethoscopes. Before recording the external sounds, the composer started by compiling a list of sounds that can be produced on the surface of a body (externally), such as body parts moving (rubbing) or hitting (clicking, clapping, etc), air, liquid or gas production, and then they proceeded to their recording. A similar process was followed for the intermediate sounds, the sounds produced in the mouth, in the overall oral cavity including for example breathing through the nostrils. A sort of ingenuity, playfulness and improvisation employed during this process offered the possibility to cover the widest range of sounds that can be produced by the combination of the tongue, lips and teeth. At first the artist recorded all well known and widely used consonants and vowels, to engage into a "play" with their combination, leading into the production of sound coincidences and rare vocal sound events. Regarding the voice, the composer's intention was to register their entire frequency range and capture as many qualities as possible. The artist's aim was to find the limits of their voice range, therefore they explored the full range of it, recording it in different ways and qualities. In addition, they explored the possibilities of multiphonics, the continuous jumps and fluctuations between their highest and lowest notes, and attempted layering that to throat sounds, whispers and other vocal sounds in different intensities, and qualities. The internal body sounds including heartbeats, abdominal sounds, stomach sounds and other bowel movements, were discovered impromptu and recorded ad hoc using the electronic stethoscope through a process of body cartography. This stage of bodily sounds research was a proprioceptive challenge, as most of the internal sounds are produced during unconscious movements of the integral organs. The use of the stethoscope links the process of listening with the edges of the hand, while it allows to delve into sounds produced by one's own body that are normally unheard, therefore provoking the recorder/listener cognitively and proprioceptively. Exploring and recognising the sounds produced by different parts of the body was a physically active and engaging bodily process requiring a lot of concentration, yet it was equally inspiring, creative and experimental.

After exploring the internal sounds' potential, The main reason and aim for it was to focus on keeping the body calm. The artist laid down and the recordings were made while moving the stethoscope from point to point on their body. By augmenting the sense of hearing through a device, and by enhancing the perception of the inner body through meditation, a feedback system between listening and awareness emerged as the process progressed. This stage was a key for the overall research journey. During this the composer came into full contact with the sounds produced by their bodily processes and gained a deeper understanding of its rhythms and qualities. For example, The heart makes two basic tones, a pulse, The rhythmicality of in the overall aural experience a sense of vitality and a feeling of connection to the body's core. Listening to the changes of the sounds and their subtle fluctuations, activity, rendered each recording an exploration of an internal soundwalk,Sounds in the region of the abdominal cavity, corresponding to the stomach and gastrointestinal system, compose a soundscape So the randomness of the sound environment of the abdomen can be characterised as "directed" by the food that has entered the body and the time distance from each meal. For the acoustic study of this area, long-term recording sessions were scheduled. This internal process is characterised by a sort of randomness, which gives the feeling of loss of control and lack of agency by the composer. Listening to a soundscape produced by one's own body makes one become aware of their bodily functions and accentuates their proprioception. As mentioned previously all the internal recordings were done in a meditative state, and ended up being a deep auditory observation underlined by a sense of intriguing curiosity. After the recording phase was over, It was only then that the second stage of the compositional process could start with the editing, processing and mixing of these sounds into the final soundscape.

The sounds were divided into small fragments (mostly the external sounds), or mid to long durational sections (the inner sounds). The sounds were further processed, gaining new qualities and thus distancing themselves from any cognitive association to their sources of origin, through frequency modulation and granular synthesis. Such processes were meant as allegories, referencing the conceptual part of the research and the erasing of gender identifiers from the sound material. The structure of the work was based on the periodic cycles of the breath, the heart and the stomach. Three parallel layers of sound events were built (heartbeat, breath and stomach), while the external sounds were used to enhance the transitions between the layers and to accentuate the rhythms generated by these three layers.

Cyborgutt begins with rhythms made by the heartbeat and the breath and then the element of digestion is added to the mix. It evolves and escalates, with sounds deriving mainly from internal sounds and variations in the rhythmicality of two initial layerst. The composition leads to a section in which all the different sound elements get synchronised and it concludes with a process of deconstruction of the different sound qualities. After that, there is a movement in the work with many successive silences, until the final return of the original sounds unprocessed. Throughout the work, the layers of breath and heartbeat alternate between each other allowing silences, restoring therefore the sense of rhythm and repeatability, while functioning as transitions between the different sections of the overall work.

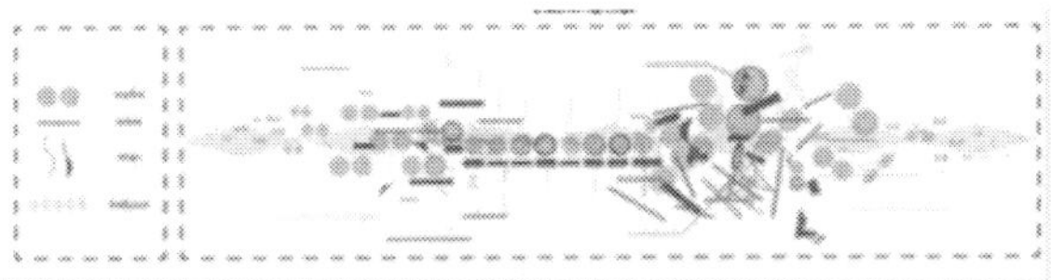

Figure 3. “Cyborgutt” script

5. CONCLUSIONS

A collection of vocal and bodily sounds, used in their original form or processed through technological methods may give way to soundscapes distanced from heteronormative frameworks, thus acquiring a queer character. On a practical level, various methods of gender deconstruction have been applied by artists who have dealt with voice, gender and sexuality, in the field of sound. By observing their practices and exploring new methods that increase the possibility of redefining gender, sound artist φø devised a creative-critical audio work that encompasses such compositional and technological processes. Using bodily sounds unbound by gender identifiers, processing the frequency of the voice, using filters, altering basic characteristics of timbre and intensity by using granular synthesis, stretching or reverb, the artist manages to conceal the vocal bodies from the ones they originate from, removing therefore any of their gender traces. Particularly the use of sounds that are intrinsically shared by any organism, regardless its gender, but somehow belong to the realm of the unheard, such as stomach sounds or heart sounds, weave the aural narration on a non binary canvas, which prevents the listener from predetermined gender assignment predispositions.

At a first level, Cybergutt can be defined as queer, due to the fluid dynamics that define the condition of the whole piece [11]. In a second and more essential level, the soundscape is a queer entity, due to the content of the sounds it consists of, either processed or not [12]. Recorded sounds that are not deemed acceptable either in a musical or in social context (stomach sounds, sounds of bodily pleasure, etc.), as well as sounds from non-included bodies, such as non-binary bodies, when mixed together, result in a composition that by definition can only be understood as queer. Queer qualities in an organism can eventually be observed, when they are not included in certain socially acceptable structures and offer ways to deconstruct the boundaries of the sonic organism itself.

Thus, the possible developments of Cybergutt (in its current form) are varied and could be explored in greater depth and in numerous courses. Issues of perception and gender assignment are open to formation and further development, as they reinforce the overall nature of the project as an organism in constant fluidity that adapts, redefines and reveals new patterns. Another possible area of development is the extension of the element of randomness and the inclusion of the element of non-linearity, through the performance of the piece in a live setting.

Acknowledgments

We would like to thank Thanos Vovolis for providing references and valuable information and M. Eugenia Demeglio for her help and overall support.

6. REFERENCES

1. J. Butler, *Bodies that matter*. New York: Routledge, 1993
2. J. Butler, Gender Trouble: Feminism and the Subversion of Identity. New York: Routledge, 1990
3. J. Halberstam, “What’s that smell?,” *International Journal of Cultural Studies*, vol. 6, no. 3, pp. 313–333, Sep. 2003. doi:10.1177/13678779030063005
4. A. Woloshyn, “Electroacoustic Voices: Sounds queer, and why it matters,” *Tempo*, vol. 71, no. 280, pp. 68–79, Mar. 2017. doi:10.1017/s0040298217000092
5. F. Jarman-Ivens, Queer Voices Technologies, Vocalities, and the Musical Flaw. New York: Palgrave Macmillan, 2011
6. S. Guarracino, “An effortless voice: Queer Vocality and Transgender Identity in Kim Fu’s for today I am A boy,” *Queering Masculinities in Language and Culture*, pp. 127–147, Dec. 2017. doi:10.1057/978-1-349-95327-1_7
7. C. A. Marchiselli, “Queer sonorities: Sound as persuasion in Gertrude Stein’s*tender buttons*,” *Women’s Studies in Communication*, vol. 39, no. 1, pp. 69–85, Jan. 2016. doi:10.1080/07491409.2015.1127302
8. D. Sofer, “The macropolitics of microsound: Gender and sexual identities in Barry Truax’s*song of songs*,” *Organised Sound*, vol. 23, no. 1, pp. 80–90, Dec. 2017. doi:10.1017/s1355771817000309
9. P. Oliveros, Deep Listening: A Composer’s Sound Practice. New York, NY: iUniverse, 2005
10. D. Sofer, Sex Sounds: Vectors of Difference in Electronic Music. Cambridge, MA: MIT Press, 2022
11. “Queer Abstraction (or how to be a pervert with no body). some notes toward a probability,” Mousse Magazine and Publishing, https://www.moussemagazine.it/magazine/queer-abstraction-travis-jeppesen-2019/ (accessed Feb. 13, 2024).

Rap is Art: Creating Spaces for the Interpretation of Misunderstood Voices

TeAiris Majors
Georgia Institute of Technology
tmajors6@gatech.edu

ABSTRACT

This paper explores the integration of rap music, an auditory art form conveying powerful sociopolitical commentary, into visual arts spaces to create immersive multimedia experiences. A virtual museum was developed in Unity, spatializing music from prominent rap artists to amplify their messages. Interactions allow users to visualize lyrics and access sources linked to deeper analysis. Parallels are drawn to soundscape composition techniques and the World Soundscape Project's exploration of acoustic ecology. Goals include highlighting lyrical depth in rap by extracting and projecting vocal and song lyrics, uniting visual and auditory arts through an inclusive museum space, and providing an innovative template for future virtual experiences. This paper argues that rap music deserves recognition as impactful artistic expression, not just mere entertainment, containing deeper meaning beyond its aural perspective. It concludes that embracing rap music in cultural institutions and virtual interactive experiences can increase accessibility and awareness, foster dialogue about social justice, identity, and empowerment, and resonate with more diverse audiences.

1. INTRODUCTION

Paintings and music both serve as channels for artistic expression [1], evoking emotions and opportunities for personal perceptions to emerge. One being a visual medium and the other an auditory, each having its own unique way of engaging and impacting our surroundings. Museums are great spaces for centralizing art, as they capture the history, diverse cultures, and stories of a particular time or space. Traditionally known for showcasing visual art, museums have also explored embracing the history and significance of music genres such as hip-hop culture and rap music by means of photos, visuals, relevant artifacts, and auditory experiences [2]

Rap music has embraced various forms of storytelling and narrative techniques, allowing artists to provide a voice for marginalized communities and shed light on their experiences [3]. Unfortunately, stereotypical narratives and misconceptions about rap music focus solely on explicit language, violence, and misogyny, failing to recognize the deeper messages and social commentary embedded within the lyrics [4, 5]

Fortunately, artists within the genre continue to push boundaries and challenge these stereotypes, using their platform to address important social issues such as systemic racism, poverty, police brutality, and inequality [6]. Artists, such as Kanye West, have used their platform to challenge societal norms and initiate meaningful discussions [7]. Kendrick Lamar's album "To Pimp a Butterfly" is a powerful example of the social and political commentary that rap music can provide, addressing issues of racial inequality, self-love, and the Black experience in America. Undoubtedly, the impact of rap music in society goes beyond mere entertainment.

The discourse of rap music cannot all be fully understood without contextualizing it within the environment in which it emerges. Some may turn to the news to stay informed about current events. However, this is usually derived from an outside perspective, often influenced by dominant narratives and biased interpretations. While this can provide some level of awareness, rap music offers a unique and unfiltered perspective within communities.

Similarly, soundwalks and soundscape compositions provide a different way of experiencing and understanding our environment [8]. By incorporating the sounds of everyday life, these audio experiences allow us to listen to our surroundings with intention and curiosity. The composers of this genre target the nuances of the sounds around us, highlighting the intersection between sound, space, and emotion.

With the advances of technology, now it is even easier to deliver art and entertainment to a wider audience through the use of virtual experiences [9]. Creators have access to tools, such as game engines accompanied with spatial audio features, to design the virtual spaces of our imagination, inviting remote elements that may have not co-existed or shared similar physical and/or aural environments.

This project aims to explore this concept of coexistence and augment the perspective in which we experience art and music. By localizing the music, lyrics, and internal voices of prominent rap artists in a virtual space, I aim to amplify these narratives and foster dialogue about social justice, identity, and empowerment.

2. RELATED WORK

Composers such as Hildegard Westerkamp have really pushed to expose the deeper embedded meanings of sounds in our environment and the roles they have in society [10]. Part of this force is to deliver an experience of a space that we may have not traveled to. Another part, being the soundwalk, is to provide a different perspective in real time. This project, while not an exact mirror of their philosophies, aims to explore innovative ways to experience sound in an environment beyond static recordings. By making a system that is somewhat varying, this soundwalk experience invites multiple perspectives within space.

Soundscape composers traditionally captured sounds in a space as they present themselves in nature, later reproducing the sound as a form of art. Some composers in this genre even use special techniques to process the source, yet still resemble its native origin. With advances in technology, such as 3d renders, we have access to defining these virtual spaces. In this project, I make use of a virtual museum. While a museum does not have a distinct sound itself, the augmentation of its use echoes these concepts.

Observing the work of Annea Lockwood, mother nature has voice that can speak for itself. Still, we may stumble upon more of her universal beauty if we search deeper. Advances in audio recording technology have given us innovative ways to capture and reproduce the sounds we hear in our daily and remote physical environments. For example, a listening session and talk with artists, such as Listening to Rivers - with Leah Barclay and Annea Lockwood include examples of hydrophones (waterproof omnidirectional microphones) used to capture the auditory scene beneath earth's oceans and rivers [11] Likewise, in this project, I aim to expose a messages that were always present, but submerged beneath instrumental beats. I also strive to express the many ways in which sound can be experienced and appreciated in different environments.

Stepping back to its roots, the World Soundscape Project (WSP) was founded by R. Murray Schafer at Simon Fraser University in the early to study acoustic environments [12]. In relation, soundscape composition composers, such as Hildegard Westerkamp aimed to emphasize and explore the interrelationship between sound, nature and society (Acoustic ecology) [10]. In her article "Linking soundscape composition and acoustic ecology ", Westerkamp discusses the composer's affordances to convey a point of view through soundscape pieces and their impact [10]. While flexible in terms of definition, soundscape compositions are not all mere reproductions of a recorded environment. In Westerkamp's Beneath the Forest Floor, she explores transformations of sounds within an environment to metaphorically represent sounds akin to a typical rainforest [13]. She also uses unconventional ways to capture sound in the environment in addition to stationary field recordings. Barry Truax's analysis of this practice adequately justifies the flexibility within the soundscape genre [14]. This practice can synonymous to the art of sampling in hip-hop music. While a sample may undergo many chops, manipulations, and processing, it can always be traced back to its origin.

3. GOALS

One focal goal of this project is to bring attention to the powerful messages and social commentary embedded within rap music. Although we normally listen to songs as they are produced and delivered, I believe that by extracting vocal stems, the interpretation of lyrics can be amplified. I also aim to unite the visual and aural art-forms by creating a space that welcomes them equally. Another goal of this project is to explore the use of spatial audio to realize creative interactions with sound that do not exist in the physical world. Additionally, this project serves as a resource and template for creating virtual soundscapes, and other multimedia interactive experiences.

4. IMPLEMENTATION

4.1 Development Environment

Unity Game Engine was used as the main development platform for this project. With features such as sound spatialization, 3d model importing, and video playback, it was an ideal choice. Another advantage of using Unity is its well supported developer community and the Unity Asset Store. This allows for easy integration of extended features and assistive editor add-ons. Furthermore, the access to visual scripting tools, such as Flow Canvas[15] [1] empower artists, even with little programming knowledge, to implement innovative interactions and behaviors and allowing for more experimentation and creativity in the development process.

4.2 Visual Design

To emphasize music as an art form, the virtual space was designed to resemble a small museum. Rap music can sometimes be regarded to as just entertainment or "noise", even if regarded in a metaphorical sense, rather than a true form of art [16] . The walls are decorated with styled paintings of rap artists to emphasize their status as worthy works of art themselves. In addition, a few of the paintings display famous rap lyrics of songs that have had a significant impact in the rap genre. The canvases were intentionally designed to be very reflective. Since the lighting was baked (rendered) in advance, the artwork is still reflected even when changing textures for *Mode 2* discussed later in this paper. The walls themselves were programmed to be forever changing. This is implemented to resemble the evolution and growth that rap music and hip-hop culture has seen over the past 50 years since its birth in 1973. It is also meant to serve as a symbol of inclusiveness and welcome diversity within this artistic space. The color of the walls is determined by the hue value of its inherited material; see Figure 2. Over a period of 30 seconds, the hue is increased from 0 to 360 to complete the color wheel. This method is triggered by a custom Update function, which has an interval of 30 seconds also. Sharing space with the canvases, styled text accompanies the walls. The Kayne.rest API is used to retrieve quotes made by the rapper Kayne West, in real-time; see Figure 1. This is included to further support the project's goals and amplify voices that are often suppressed and/or silenced.

4.3 Song Selection

The selection of songs for this project were made with careful consideration to represent a diverse range of rap artists and themes. The songs included are as follows:

"Neighbors" by J. Cole: portrays his personal experiences with racial profiling and the assumptions made about

[1] Flow Canvas "a powerful and feature-rich Visual Scripting Solution for Unity, empowers others to create and manipulate virtually any aspect of game-play elements for your games in a very similar fashion to Unreal Blueprints, but with far less programming knowledge required all around".

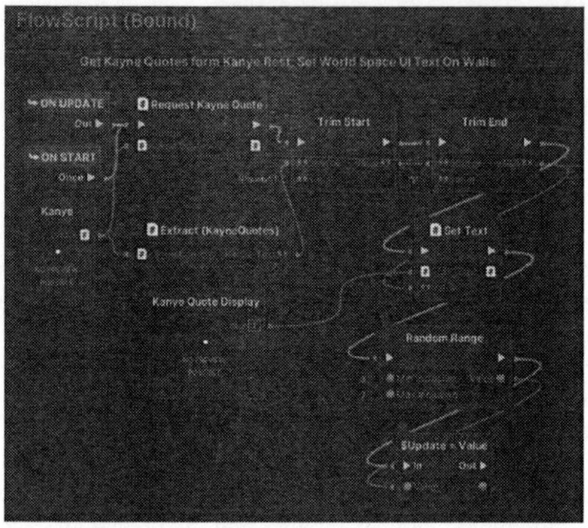

Figure 1. This Flow Script Graph contains nodes to request and display quotes created by Kayne West, delivered from https://api.kanye.rest.

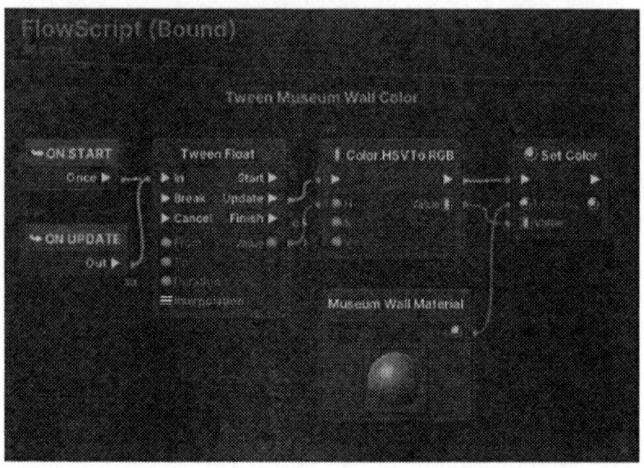

Figure 2. This image displays logic created using Flow Canvas, a third-party visual scripting solution for Unity Game Engine. This Flow Script Graph contains nodes to implement changing the hue of walls of the environment at a defined interval of 30 seconds, in an infinite loop.

him as a successful African American man living in an affluent neighborhood.

"Apparently" by J. Cole: reflects on his life and his relationships, particularly with his mother. This song carries themes of repentance, forgiveness, and understanding the significance of loved ones.

"Alright" by Kendrick Lamar: viewed as an anthem for hope and resilience. It delves into the struggles faced by the African American community and emphasizes a message of determination and confidence that things will get better.

"DNA" by Kendrick Lamar: showcases Kendrick Lamar's complex lyrical ability and strong pride in his African American heritage. This song explores his personal and cultural identity and the qualities that define him.

"All Falls Down" by Kanye West: critiques consumerism, self-consciousness, and the search for self-worth in material possessions. It also discusses the challenges faced by African American communities and the pressure to conform to societal expectations.

"U.N.I.T.Y." by Queen Latifah: a powerful feminist anthem that confronts issues of sexism, misogyny, and disrespect towards women. This song advocates for female

Figure 3. This image displays a wall decorated with text delivered from https://api.kanye.rest.

empowerment and respect for women from all walks of life.

Individual audio files were essential for the purpose of this project in order to facilitate analysis and exploration of the lyrics, stem separation, and other exploratory audio processing. Each song used in this project was purchased from Apple's iTunes Store. A digital copy was then downloaded locally. These files are used specifically for research and educational purposes and within the boundaries of fair use. To comply with copyright laws, the audio files will not be shared or distributed with future template versions of this project.

4.4 Interaction and Sound Design

4.4.1 Mode 1

The interaction and sound design for this project were crucial in creating an immersive and engaging experience [9]. To organize the experience, two modes were implemented. In *Mode 1*, I included a human character for realism, which a user can navigate through the virtual museum. Virtual pillars are placed in the space containing videos of hip-hop pioneers such as Afrika Bambaataa and Grandmaster Flash, symbolizing the foundation of the rap genre. As a user approaches each pillar, the video's sound is spatialized, accompanied by a visual display of the song's lyrics projected into the virtual environment. As the user gets closer, the acapella version of the song is tweened in.

To achieve lyrical text projection, the third-party asset "sound text transcriber asset" was used. This asset uses OpenAI's automatic speech recognition system "Whisper" to transcribe audio, then divides the text into synced phrases [17]. Next, the synced text events are passed into a text mesh pro component. Lastly, another third-party asset, "3d text asset," was used to instantiate and animate 3d text objects into the environment, while fading after a specified duration. This integration aims to provide a multi-sensory experience [18], allowing the users to engage with both the auditory and visual elements. Beyond the pillars, users can enjoy viewing the art work just as you would in a museum.

4.4.2 Mode 2

In *Mode 2*, I aimed to emphasize the goal of highlighting lyrical depth and intricacy in rap music. The character is now modeled as a robot. This interacts with ideas presented in Hildegard Westerkamp's article "Linking Soundscape Composition and Acoustic Ecology". She proposed

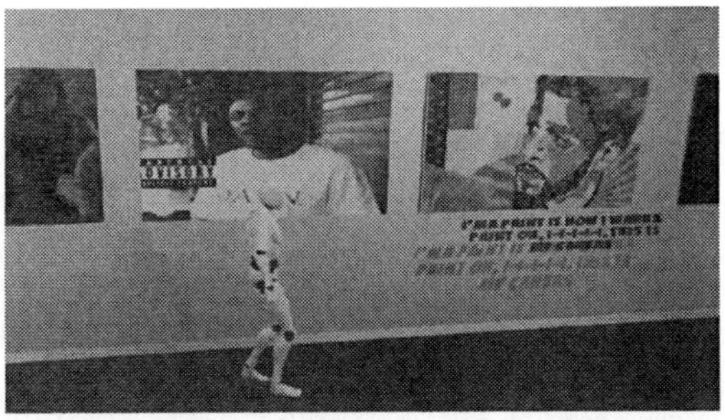

Figure 4. This image displays the canvases on the wall of the museum. It also includes the 3d world space text used to display lyric visuals with spatialized audio.

Figure 5. This image displays the area created as a tribute to Soundscape Composition composer Hildegard Westerkamp.

that the human ear has the ability to focus in and out, but the microphone's way of hearing is non-selective[10]. The robot character here serves as a neutral observer, encouraging the listener to listen from a similar perspective.

Triggered using the bottom face button of a controller, or the space bar, most of the art work in the virtual museum transforms into live music videos of the selected rap songs by J. Cole, Kanye West, Kendrick Lamar, and Queen Latifah projected from each canvas; see Figure 4 All videos references were stored in a list, then randomly distributed among the canvases, ensuring that each experience is unique. The Fisher-Yates shuffle algorithm was used in a C# script to achieve this function. The playback start times of each video are randomized also. To achieve this, the Get Frame Count method is used on each Video Component. Next, a random range function is called using 0 as the minimum, and the total frame count for the video clip as the maximum. To set the playback, the Set Fame method is called using the randomly generated number as an argument.

Again, the sound of each video is spatialized to enable a controlled listening environment. Although the videos are positioned closely for an intimate feel, the music occupies its own local space. The maximum distance variable for the audio source spatialization was purposely set to slightly overlap with adjacent videos. This decision was made to explore the artists as two unique voices sharing the same resonate space to convey similar messages from different perspectives. Using a similar function in Mode 1's pillars, a box trigger was used to detect the presence of the user near a video, calling the Acapella function which tweens the transition from the full audio track to the isolated vocal stem.

4.5 Soundscape Composition Tribute

While conceptualizing and fulfilling the creation of this experience, I was greatly inspired by the history, purpose, and practice of soundscape composition and composers of the genre. To express my gratitude and appreciation for their efforts, a portion of the space was dedicated one particular composer, Hildegard Westerkamp, to display one of her aural artworks "Beneath the Rain Forest" [13]; see Figure 7. A pillar, accompanied by a video recorded in a rain forest, is also placed near the entrance of this area to situate users before entering. While placing Westerkamp's voice among the other rap artists was considered, I chose to separate the two to clearly express the intended gesture.

4.6 Song Comparison

As an extension of the first two modes, I have added a few prototype examples to further enrich this virtual experience. To start, I created a matrix in Word to cross-reference each song once. After creating this generic layout, I proceeded to form comparisons for each song, highlighting similarities and differences in themes, lyrics, storytelling, delivery, and production. Next, I created a Unity script containing a dictionary for each song pair, parallel to its comparison text. Lastly, I created a function that would accept two different songs as arguments, returning the comparison text from the dictionary. The song titles were stored in an Enum for easy selection using UI Dropdown menus. Due to the process of hard coding each comparison, extending this functionality for more songs can be a very time-consuming task. In future iterations, I plan to use OpenAI 's API request to retrieve comparison texts automatically, reducing the manual effort involved in creating comparisons for multiple songs. While I have tested this alternate approach with accurate results, I would also include options for entry of human curated comparisons which would take precedence.

4.7 Lyric Extraction

Additionally, this project includes a lyric extraction feature. This feature gives users the option to query lyrics with keywords to find direct similarities in words and optional synonyms. After supplying text into the input field, users are instantly supplied with buttons displaying the lyric line for each match found. Each button, when clicked, plays the corresponding matched lyric line. To summarize how this feature was implemented, most of this was made possible by using LRC (lyrics synchronization) files. I created a custom parser for Unity to extract the time stamps for each line. Next, I used the current timestamp and following timestamp of each line to calculate the duration of each line. This duration is then used to determine when to play and stop the audio clip of the corresponding lyrics, accommodated by an variable offset time to implement an audio fade. Each song was then parsed into a Scriptable Object containing data for each line. The previously mentioned keyword functionality was then expanded to utilize a collection of parsed songs to query all songs at once. For lyric audio playback, I also included a toggle to isolate the vocals. Overall, I believe that this is a great tool for self-discovery, complimenting the song comparisons matrix.

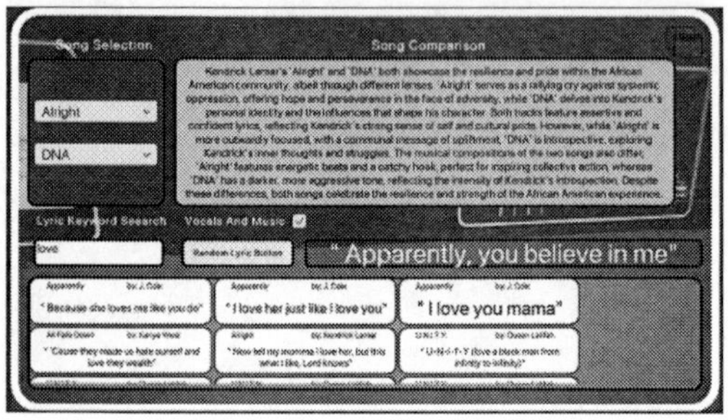

Figure 6. This image displays the song comparison and lyric extraction features.

4.8 Node Based Interaction

As a final extension, I added a node-based interactions system, allowing users to visually create their own song mixes. This concept was inspired partly by the use visual scripting, which has made much of the data to UI connections in this project possible in the limited amount of time to develop. The main node block allows users to select a song from the 6 select songs used in this project. The interface affords users with options to playback and even access to stems of the selected song, such as vocals, bass, drums, and others. While stemming of the tracks could have been done using API web request, I opted to do this offline to avoid cost while testing. Other nodes were supplied for environmental sounds. This interacts with the practice of soundscape composition artists who repurposed snippets of sounds with small edits. A last node was created to display lyrics of a connected node. Overall, this node system is meant to be used as a playground to explore new ideas and make connections with elements that may not have been connected in everyday settings.

5. CONCLUSIONS AND FUTURE WORK

With the support of innovative tools and the inspiring force of creativity, this project unites the worlds of visual arts and rap music into a unique interactive experience. Using sound spatialization techniques, users are immersed in a controlled auditory setting that allows for multiple voices to coexist, respectful to each other's contribution to the virtual environment. Appreciation is expressed for the pioneers of hip-hop culture who have constructed spaces for rap music and its artists, which has greatly expanded and continues to do so today.

For future iterations of this project, my goal is to extend this template to provide a platform for other movements, cultures, groups, messages, and voices to be elevated and promoted. There is more room to explore the delivery of symbolic references of rap music. In particular, more in-depth analysis of lyrical and metaphorical word play comparisons amongst artists will provide insights of their personal and shared creative techniques. Multi-user capabilities will provide opportunities for joint and shared experiences. Voice and text chat rooms can also invite interesting discourse around the art and music pieces, changing the dynamics of how we typically experience museums. By providing custom editors with ready-made tools and functions, the barrier of entry can be lowered to give visual and music artists additional unique ways to present their artwork.

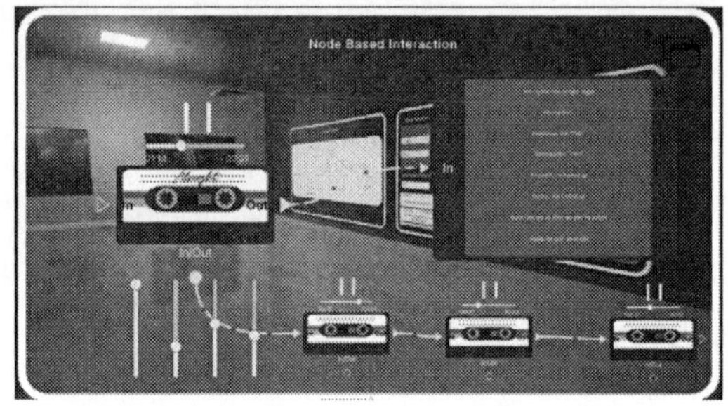

Figure 7. This image displays the node-based interaction remix features.

In conclusion, the integration of rap music in museums, soundwalks, and soundscape compositions presents an exciting opportunity to explore new dimensions of artistic expression and storytelling. By embracing rap music, these cultural spaces can foster inclusivity, amplify marginalized voices, and create dynamic experiences that resonate with diverse audiences.

Acknowledgments

I would like to thank my family for their continued support throughout my academic journey. I would also like to thank the Georgia Institute of Technology, School of Music faculty, and the I.M.P.A.C.T. Lab (Interactive Music, Performance, Audio, and Creative Technologies) for guidance and supporting this project.

6. REFERENCES

[1] B. Yucel, "The Interaction of Painting and Music," Nov. 2012. [Online]. Available: https://www.sciencedirect.com/science/article/pii/S1877042812032831

[2] "The Hip Hop Museum - The Home of Hip Hop History." [Online]. Available: https://uhhm.org/homepage/

[3] A. d. Paor-Evans, "The Intertextuality and Translations of Fine Art and Class in Hip-Hop Culture," *Multidisciplinary Digital Publishing Institute*, vol. 7, no. 4, pp. 80–80, Nov. 2018. [Online]. Available: https://doi.org/10.3390/arts7040080

[4] J. W. Richardson and K. Scott, "Rap Music and Its Violent Progeny: America's Culture of Violence in Context," *Howard University*, vol. 71, no. 3, pp. 175–175, Jan. 2002. [Online]. Available: https://www.jstor.org/stable/3211235?origin=crossref

[5] C. T. Powell, "Rap Music: An Education with a Beat from the Street," *Howard University*, vol. 60, no. 3, pp. 245–245, Jan. 1991. [Online]. Available: https://doi.org/10.2307/2295480

[6] A. Leach, ""One Day It'll All Make Sense": Hip-Hop and Rap Resources for Music Librarians," Sep.

2008. [Online]. Available: https://doi.org/10.1353/not.0.0039

[7] J. Bailey, "The Cultural Impact of Kanye West," Jan. 2014. [Online]. Available: https://doi.org/10.1057/9781137395825

[8] D. W. Paquette, "Soundwalking and the Bodily Exploration of Places," *Jilin Academy of Agricultural Sciences*, vol. 37, no. 1, pp. 135–145, Apr. 2012.

[9] C. Summers and M. K. Jesse, "Creating immersive and aesthetic auditory spaces in virtual reality," Mar. 2017. [Online]. Available: https://ieeexplore.ieee.org/document/7938144/

[10] H. Westerkamp, "Linking soundscape composition and acoustic ecology," *Cambridge University Press*, vol. 7, no. 1, pp. 51–56, Apr. 2002. [Online]. Available: https://www.cambridge.org/core/journals/organised-sound/article/abs/linking-soundscape-composition-and-acoustic-ecology/FBE211836B584EB92E960B10392E5A5B

[11] PRAKSIS Oslo, "Listening to Rivers - with Leah Barclay and Annea Lockwood," Oct. 2020. [Online]. Available: https://www.youtube.com/watch?v=dGAcUChycp4

[12] "Soundscape Composition." [Online]. Available: https://www.sfu.ca/~truax/scomp.html

[13] musicaincidental1984, "Beneath The Forest Floor -Hildegard Westerkamp," Jan. 2020. [Online]. Available: https://www.youtube.com/watch?v=n-U8iTyqKRA

[14] B. Truax, "Genres and techniques of soundscape composition as developed at Simon Fraser University," *Organised Sound*, vol. 7, no. 1, pp. 5–14, Apr. 2002.

[15] "FlowCanvas | Modern Visual Scripting for Unity." [Online]. Available: https://flowcanvas.paradoxnotion.com/

[16] T. Swiss, "Black Noise: Rap Music and Black Culture in Contemporary America. By Tricia Rose. Hanover & London. Wesleyan University Press, 1994. xvi + 241 pp." *Cambridge University Press*, vol. 14, no. 1, pp. 135–136, Jan. 1995.

[17] A. Radford, J. W. Kim, T. Xu, G. Brockman, C. McLeavey, and I. Sutskever, "Robust speech recognition via large-scale weak supervision," in *Proceedings of the 40th International Conference on Machine Learning*, ser. ICML'23, vol. 202. JMLR.org, Jul. 2023, pp. 28 492–28 518.

[18] M. Obrist, G. Boyle, M. v. Brakel, and F. Duerinck, "Multisensory Experiences & Spaces," Oct. 2017. [Online]. Available: https://dl.acm.org/doi/10.1145/3132272.3135086

Phil Winsor: An Exemplar of the Artist Technologist

Ken Paoli, DMA
College of DuPage
Glen Ellyn, IL
paolik@cod.edu

ABSTRACT

American composer and visual artist Phil Winsor (1938-2012) lived through a time of exciting and accelerating change in technology. His long academic career in America and Asia displayed consistent excellence and the determined integration of the technological resources at his disposal. His journey in academia and art can serve as a model and perhaps, an inspiration for emerging artists who are only beginning their artistic journey. This paper examines his career in four stages; from his post baccalaureate studies until his retirement.

1. INTRODUCTION

Phil Winsor was born in Morris, Illinois in 1938 the same year that magnetic tape was invented, a year before frequency modulation was discovered and three years before the Z3 computer was developed. When he began his undergraduate studies in composition, two decades later, with Wilbur Ogden, at Illinois State University in 1958, several important developments in technology and music occurred: the BBC had established its Radiophonic Workshop, the first integrated circuit was invented by Texas Instruments and Edgard Varese composed *Poème Électronique*.

It is axiomatic that one can only make use of the technological tools that exist during one's lifetime and so it was for Winsor. In those twenty years technological developments were put into motion that would influence and shape Winsor's direction as a creative artist. His artistic journey was a rich one and while his voice has been stilled for twelve years, his artistic life can serve as an example of an artist pursuing his goals while embracing and mastering emergent technologies.

2. EARLY CAREER

Upon completion of his undergraduate work Winsor migrated to the San Francisco area and was involved with the San Francisco Conservatory of Music. Winsor was studying composition with Robert Erickson and received a performance award from the Conservatory's Composer Workshop for his *Song Cycle* on poems of William Blake. While Winsor was supporting himself as a trumpet performer in a wide variety of genres, he was also involved with the emerging San Francisco Tape Music Center. This provided Winsor with exposure to the cutting-edge techniques of the West Coast avant-garde [1]. Besides his work with reel-to-reel tape decks and early signal processors, his involvement with improvisation, minimalism and multimedia made an indelible impression that influenced his artistic palette throughout his life. It was through the San Francisco Tape Music Center that Winsor became aware of Don Buchla's synthesizer, the Buchla Box, one of the earliest modular synthesizers. While embryonic, he embraced analog synthesis which became an integral part of electronic studios he established and directed. Winsor's' *Sound Study One* was performed at the Sonics I concert in 1961. He shared the program with Terry Riley, Ramon Sender and Pauline Oliveros [2].

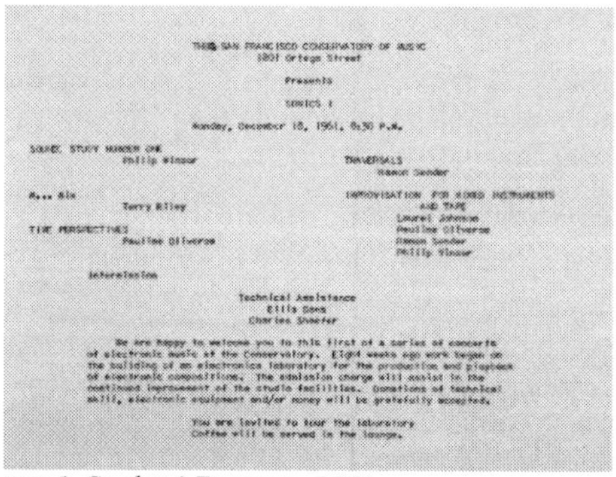
Presents
Sonics I
Philip Winsor
Terry Riley
Pauline Oliveros
Ramon Sender
Technical Assistance

Figure 1. Sonics 1 Program, 1961

During his involvement with the San Francisco Tape Music Center, Winsor met Milton Cohen, a professor from the University of Michigan who was an Artist-in-Residence at the Firehouse Theater in San Francisco. Cohen constructed a large scrim-covered icosahedron (a twenty-sided figure in an abandoned firehouse. This seated ten people who watched projections on the inner surface. The center of the viewing area had a round platform fitted with small turntables that were used as projection stations for the experimental slides. The audience viewed the projections while a group of musicians around the outside of the icosahedron improvised music [6]. Influenced by these techniques Winsor began experimenting with 2"x 2" hand-built slides to create abstract images that he intended for use during multimedia concerts. Winsor details his process:

"I experimented with many different materials commonly found in the kitchen, including corn syrup, baking soda, salt, colored sugars, cotton fibers, pieces of colored plastic, and so on. I used plastic cement...to form a boundary on the edges of the glass. Transparent colored inks, dyes, and viscous fluids were applied by eye dropper or cotton swab, and I observed the motion of the materials as the various colors flowed and interacted [5]."

Another technique Winsor became acquainted with was a process referred to as "Light Painting." To produce light paintings the camera lens is placed on a long exposure setting and the artist uses a light source to "paint." These photographic techniques were used by Winsor to generate images for his intermedia works until the ability to work with videos via computer became available. See Figures 2 and 3.

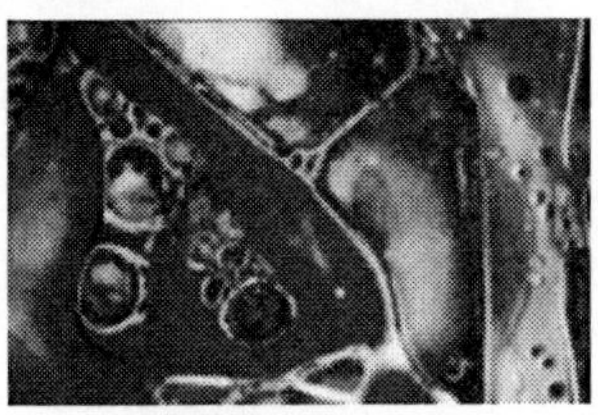

Figure 2. Glass plate example.

Figure 3. "Light Painting" example.

After receiving his MA in composition from San Francisco State University, in 1964, Winsor was awarded a Fulbright Fellowship for compositional studies in Milan with Luigi Nono. This was an opportunity to work in an important studio in the growing area of electronic music. The RAI (Radiotelevisione italiana) Musical Phonology Studio had eight sine and square wave oscillators, pulse and white noise generators patched manually through a bank of processors. Processors included frequency shifters, filters and various types of echo and reverberation units [3]. According to Winsor the studio also had the capability to make tape loops of large lengths that allowed for multiple loops that would synchronize at varying time intervals.

The studio also had a "Tempophon" a tape device with rotating heads that varied the duration of the playback of a previously recorded sound while maintaining the original pitch. In the illustration that follows, the rotating head in the middle can be variably adjusted by both speed and direction. The belt speed can also be manipulated. The Tempophon (Figure 4.) was an early time stretching device in the analog domain [4]. The audio output at the RAI studios was monitored on a system of five speakers and recorded to a four-track tape recorder.

Figure 4. The Tempophon.

Winsor returned to the San Francisco area and taught theory at the San Francisco Music and Arts Institute. In 1965 Winsor began to pursue a Doctorate degree at the University of Illinois studying with Salvatore Matirano. Matirano is now remembered for the SAL-MAR Construction, which was a hybrid system using TTL logical circuits to drive analog modules, such as voltage-controlled oscillators, amplifiers and filters. It allows the operator to interactively produce real-time composition with twenty-four spatialized channels. The SalMar Construction cannibalized parts from the aging Illiac II Supercomputer and was widely considered to be the world's first composing machine [5]. It was a hybrid analog-digital system that primarily used random number generators to produce musical sequences. Winsor's studies with Matirano exposed him to the early computer music developments that had put the University of Illinois at the forefront in computer music research. Phil had great respect for Matirano and always remembered him fondly.

In September, 1966, Winsor was the recipient of the Prix di Rome which awarded study at the American Academy in Rome and his orchestra piece *Conflations* was premiered by the Rome Radio Orchestra. *Conflations* is a serial work in the style of Webern making use of the pointillistic technique, Klangfarbenmelodie. Financial considerations caused him to leave his studies in Rome early to accept a position as an Assistant Professor at Moorhead State University, in the fall of 1967. Though he was there for only a short time he established an electronic music studio, a contemporary music series and a New Music publication program. Winsor felt that the University was reneging on promises for the electronic music program and the following year Winsor was appointed Chairman of Theory-Composition at DePaul University in Chicago.

3. DEPAUL UNIVERSITY 1968-1982

Chicago, like San Francisco, had numerous academic institutions but also a vibrant arts environment which suited Winsor well. Winsor served as the Director of DePaul's Contemporary Music Ensemble and the Electronic Music Studio. This studio featured a monophonic Moog installation with 4-channel capability. The audio output was recorded on four Viking tape decks that were modified to record in synchronization. This resembled the studio in Milan but was centered around analog synthesis. Winsor was also involved in artistic endeavors outside the academic institution. He served as Musical Director and Resident Composer for the Chicago Contemporary Dance Theatre and was a Co-director with the Chicago Interarts Ministry remaining involved in intermedia and improvisatory endeavors [8].

This was also a fertile time for Winsor the composer. Several pieces were published by Carl Fisher for various performance types. He composed chamber works for acoustic instruments, tape pieces, works that combined acoustic instruments with pre-recorded tape and intermedia pieces. He often made use of extended performance techniques and graphic notation as can be seen in *Gorge,* written for Bertram Turetzky, and *Asleep in the Deep,* for tuba and tape. Winsor also made use of tape "loop" techniques applied to acoustic instrument performance as demonstrated in *Coronation* (Figure 7), a work for four trumpets. Winsor's work for two pianos, *Melted Ears,* was a quotation piece of famous Classic-Romantic "piano licks" that earned him a measure of notoriety.

Figure 7. Opening page of Coronation, 1966

Winsor won the Oregon College of Education Summer Arts Festival Award for *Missa Brevis*, an intermedia work in 1970. In 1979 he received a Shell Foundation Development Award to compose *Rondulet Concertante* for orchestra and was the Grand Prize Winner of the Amherst College New Music Contest for *Kyrie Eleison* a work for double choir and tape.

Winsor was also the recipient of several fellowships while at DePaul. In 1969 he received a composition fellowship from the Bennington Composer's Conference. In 1973 he received a Ford Foundation Fellowship in Electronic Music. In 1977 and 1979 Winsor received fellowships from the National Endowment for the Arts. In 1980 and 1981 he received composition fellowships from the Illinois Arts Council.

4. NORTH TEXAS AT DENTON 1982-2005

In the 1982-1983 academic year Winsor accepted a position as an Associate Professor of Composition at the University of North Texas at Denton. He was also appointed as Co-director of the Center for Experimental Music and Intermedia joining Larry Austin. The studio at North Texas had analog systems, digital systems and eventually, a computer-music facility equipped with computer-controlled video production studios. This was a fortuitous mid-career opportunity for Winsor who would have access to far greater facilities and equipment than at DePaul University. It would prove to be the impetus for an important period in his career as composer and author.

1987 saw the release of Winsor's first book on computer music composition, *Computer-Assisted Music Composition: A Primer in Basic.* Three additional texts followed: *The Computer Music Composer's Toolbox, Computer Music in C: Compositional Algorithms* and *Automated Computer Music Composition.* These texts were well received and documented Winsor's deep interest in Algorithmic Composition. Winsor viewed the computer as the logical replacement for the piano for the contemporary composer. The ability of MIDI to translate musical gestures into data and the speed of the computer to manipulate that data became an important aspect of Winsor's compositional technique [7].

In 1988 Winsor was promoted to the rank of Professor and also began his long relationship with National Chiao Tung University as a visiting professor. He was tasked with establishing computer music at NCTU based on the developments at UNT, Denton. Still actively composing, Winsor won first prize at the Festival of Contemporary Choral Music in America at Bowdoin College. In 1989 he received a Republic of China National Science Council Computer Music Research Grant.

Winsor created several pieces of software that came as a result of his research into algorithmic composition. *Music Sculptor*, which ran on early PCs (Windows 3.1 and DOS 5.0) reflected the ideas put forth in *Automated Computer Music Composition* which allowed for compositional data manipulation via MIDI with audio output using firmware soundcards. Designed as a compositional tool, Music Sculptor far surpassed typical MIDI sequencers in its ability to manipulate data. Another software program was *CWest* which algorithmically generated country music incorporating the sieve theories of Xenakis. Any mention of this software would elicit a wry smile from Winsor. It was a demonstration of how easily popular genres could be generated algorithmically.

Winsor also mounted several photographic exhibits. He had showings at Ball State University, the Sun-Gallery and the Kaoshung Gallery in Taiwan [8]. He also presented master classes on intermedia art in China and Korea, reflecting the importance of intermedia approaches in his art.

Winsor was now splitting his academic duties between North Texas and NCTU. He received additional research grants in Taiwan and also received a Rockefeller Foundation Composition Fellowship in 1996.

5. NCTU 2004-2010

In 2004 Winsor took a Faculty Development leave from UNT to conduct compositional research at NCTU. Winsor would retire from UNT the following year and devoted the remainder of his career to the development and nurturing of computer music in Taiwan. Winsor established the Master's degree program in Computer Music in the Music Institute at NCTU. Due to the governmental imposition of quotas, the growth of the program was slow, although interest exceeded the available positions. Winsor established the Center for Audio and Video Experiment (C.A.V.E.) at NCTU which was an eight-channel studio/classroom with video capabilities.

In 2007, in an attempt to increase the enrollment of the program, the computer-music program moved to the College of Engineering and was renamed Sound and Music Innovative Technologies (SMIT). Again, the demand exceeded the available student chairs and in the first year fifteen students were enrolled.

With the advent of hard-drive recording Winsor involved himself with works that made used of sample manipulation. His software of choice was Adobe Audition 3.0 and he made great use of time and pitch stretching and convolution synthesis. His method for sample manipulation began with simple samples undergoing multiple transformations. His file naming conventions would often include descriptions of the processes applied. Most interesting are sample manipulations that he deemed worthy to earn the "MUSIC" descriptor in the file name.

A notable synth build was called Myst, which was realized in MAX/MSP (Figure 9). Myst was used later to generate the sound track for a music video with the same title. The Myst instrument was designed for use in a therapeutic project involving schizophrenia. This was a joint research project with the University of Pisa, North Texas and NCTU. Unfortunately, the research did not progress beyond the embryonic stage but it is an example of the wide range of research topics that Winsor wished to initiate at NCTU [11]. His original proposal for the program included: music technology, multimedia technology, artificial intelligence, neural networks, cognition, psychoperceptual phenomena, brain research, data mining, data expert systems and acoustics [10].

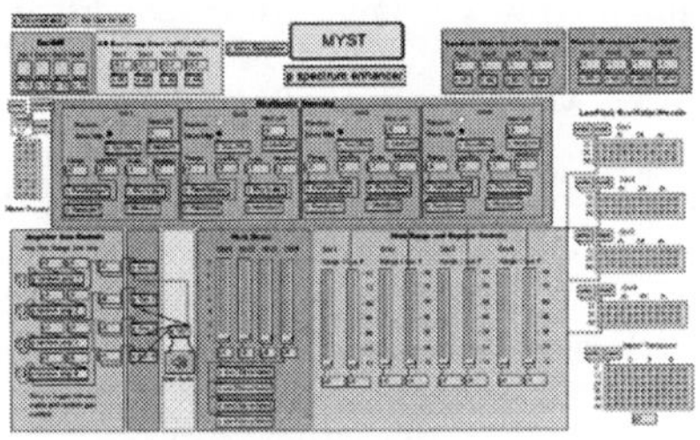

Figure 9. The Myst Control Panel.

This final period of Winsor's creative output was devoted to the creation of Computer Music Videos. Winsor used Chaos Pro, a program that generated fractal pictures that were animated and rendered into films in Adobe Premiere. He would compose original soundtracks for many of these videos, but several videos used previously composed music for the soundtrack. From 2001 to 2008 thirty-six computer music videos were produced comprising the final works of Winsor's output.

The computer music video seemed to satisfy Winsor's desire for abstract intermedia works; the computer music video appears to be the vehicle that fulfilled his artistic vision.

In 2010 Winsor returned to America to retire and there was a marked decrease in his creative activities. He succumbed to cancer in 2012.

6. CONCLUSIONS

One studies with a composer to gain knowledge in the musical sphere to advance ones art. But there are lessons to be learned beyond the musical dimension. A composer's artistic perspective, their creative life and career path can provide inspiration, and a model for young composers to aspire to as they develop their own artistic voice. Phil Winsor's life demonstrates the journey of an artist who worked in instrumental genres, wrote award winning choral pieces and intermedia works and achieved success as an experimental photographer. He became an expert in compositional research and computer music. In all of his endeavors he embraced not only emerging musical techniques but also the technical advancements of the day. He worked with tape decks and musique concrete, extended performance techniques for acoustic instruments, samplers and sample manipulation, micro-computers, MIDI and computer programming. His compulsion to create art caused him to continually forge forward. Whatever the technique being used, Winsor displayed an ability to sculpt sound commensurate with composers of the highest order. Phil Winsor made full use of multiple technologies in an untiring fashion to fully realize his artistic conceptions.

7. REFERENCES

[1] Reyes, Jordan. *The San Francisco Tape Center was an Early Home to the Avant-Garde.* 18 September 2018. Web Page. 20 November 2023.

[2] Bernstein, David (ed.). *The San Francisco Tape Music Center: 1960s Counterculture and the Avant-Garde* . Oakland: University of California Press, 2008. Print.

[3] Crab, Simon. *Milan Electronic Music Studio or RAI Studio of Phonology*. n.d. Web Source. 20 November 2023.

[4] *Spring Tempophon.* 1 January 2010. Web Page. 24 January 2024.

[5] Illinois Distributed Museum. *Sal-Mar Construction.* n.d. Web Page. 21 November 2023.

[6] Winsor, Phil. "Hybrid Photographic Processes in Experimental Media Art." 2006. Document.

[7] —. *Automated Music Composition.* Denton: University of North Texas Press, 1989. Book.

[8] —. *Curriculum Vita.* 2008. Word Document.

[9] —. "Resume." Denton, 1988. Document.

[10] —. "CAVE Research Proposals and Projects" 20 October 2005. Word Document.

[11] Paoli, Ken. "Phil Winsor's Myst: Research and Art: A Technical and Aesthetic Consideration." Daegu, 2018. Proceedings of the 2018 International Computer Music Conference. Conference Paper.

Towards Sustainable Sonic Arts Practices: Less Glitz, More Grit

PerMagnus Lindborg
School of Creative Media, City University of Hong Kong
pm.lindborg@cityu.edu.hk

ABSTRACT

In the context of the climate crisis, what makes for a sustainable practice for contemporary sound artists? It is clear that musicians, producers, composers, and sound designers can no longer blindly pursue the creation of beauty - emotional melodies, exciting rhythms, lush timbres - simply to lure listeners on a leisurely, alas temporary, escape into Scharaffenland. Art is more than entertainment. This paper argues that it is incumbent upon sound artists to dedicate their skill, time, and efforts towards the greater good of climate change mitigation. While many sound artists, including me, are closely connected to academic institutions that provide material resources and ample time for reflection, we must recognise that positions of privilege come with great responsibility. In fact, we cannot be content with raising awareness but must strive to stimulate action. I will review initiatives towards sustainable practices amongst pop musicians, working in industry, and sound artists, working in niche or academic contexts. From there, I discuss four matters of concern for sound artists working in academia. Firstly, a rethinking of the aesthetics, purposes, sonic materials, and methods that composers and sound artists use, if their output is to generate meaning-filled experiences that reach beyond the serotonin rush of instant gratification and instead influence listeners to reflect and react to the crisis. Secondly, finding ways to calculate CO2 footprint for the production, presentation, and distribution of sonic artwork, while carefully weighing reasonable costs against potential (if not measurable) impact on audiences, in terms of positive behavioural change. Thirdly, stimulating students and other stakeholders by reviewing curricula and teaching practices in educational institutions. Fourthly, strengthening the network of initiatives geared towards sustainable practices among professionals in the field of sound art.

1. INTRODUCTION

As a composer & sound artist working in academia, I believe it is incumbent upon me to dedicate whatever skills and experience I might have in support of sustainable art practices, through teaching and research. Sound art is in many ways a niche practice within the larger umbrella of "music" or 'music business'. It is closely linked to academic institutions [1] and enjoys privileges in terms of access to equipment, facilities, and other resources that are largely supported by the taxpayer.

Beethoven might be the first artist in history to be free from, in a paradigmatically different way, overbearing and external economic pressure. He famously yelled "Cattle!" at an audience and was largely able to pursue his work regardless of what the audiences might think of his musical compositions. Therefore he has been referred to as a "proto-Modernist", the very first to create 'art for art's sake'. As a supporter of absolute music, Igor Stravinsky stated emphatically (first published in 1942), that "music means nothing outside itself" [2]. One of his most astute followers, Frank Zappa claimed that 'art is entertainment' (perhaps echoing Nietzsche, who claimed that "every kind of reading belongs among my recreations"). Much as I appreciate Zappa's musical instincts (especially when connecting 'high' and 'low' art, as the Yellow Shark album), I've never believed this dictum to be true. And today, music and sound art have come a long way from Beethoven's disdainful attitude.

As Kurt Langer says, decadence is synonymous with the music industry: it is a "fantasy that we created for our audience" [3]. Analysing the historical context of art and entertainment, Andy Hamilton [4] argued that the distinction between them is artificial and relatively recent. 'Fine arts' is "a modern concept, and... entertainment contrasts with any serious activity—science, politics, religion". He continues to define the aims of entertainment as "giving pleasure or delight by amusing, exciting or otherwise diverting the audience, in a way that calls on them to make little concentrated effort". In contrast, art has a "conscious aesthetic end that richly rewards aesthetic attention... [within a more] complex relation to an audience".

COP27 [27th Conference of the Parties, 2022] [5] and even more so the following COP28 were heavily criticised by commentators unwilling to consider its message (or eager for some Egypt-bashing). These events appeared to be largely ignored in Hong Kong (people don't talk about it, and e.g. the South China Morning Post carried very minimal reporting, mainly based on the occasional 'reader opinion letter'). But make no mistake: there is no contemporary matter more critical than the climate crisis. So what can musicians and sound artists do in this situation?

It might be true that much of current sound art and music takes the listeners mind off serious concerns. Shusterman [6] ventures a "hypothesis concerning the cognitive contribution of entertainment: its relaxing function not only provides relief or diversion that can restore concentration but it can also sharpen sensitivity of perception by lowering the sensory interference caused by surplus tensions of muscular contraction resulting from excessive effort or straining". This leads us to ask whether the value of such artwork lies partly in escapism. Hamilton seems to reduce the role of sound art and music to consolation, a practice meant to comfort those in pain in face of inevitable death and destruction. Art, he therefore claims, might offer a temporary escape from immediate reality, yet it "is not escapism. Art may console, where consolation means helping through bad times, while recognising that times are bad. Escapism means forgetting; consolation does not—a vital contrast between art and entertainment" [4].

1.1 Pop music: post-Covid, but mid-Crisis

The three years of Covid-19 panic have presented extreme difficulties for professional musicians hitherto relying on live performance and paying audiences to make a living. Now that social restrictions are easing (at least in the West), many see this as an inflection point, suggesting that this presents an opportunity for music business, if the recovery from Covid-19 can be green. Those who adopt leaner practices may enjoy a competitive advantage. But how can it be done?

It might be true that when counting CO2, sound artists and their output make a minuscule dent in the 'hockey stick' curve (based on climate analysis by Michael Mann and collaborators in 1999). But let us start by considering the trade value of the 'music industry' as a whole: it is not small. Goldman Sachs estimates that by 2030 the total "global music streaming revenues (on a retail/gross basis) will hit $89.3 billion", mostly from emerging platforms [7]. In the big picture, this might still seem like not a whole lot. However, and importantly, music culture has always played a key role to inspire and fuel social movements. "Music, musicians and music businesses, through their unique cultural and economic power, can lead the way in demanding the systemic changes required to secure all life on earth." A survey by researchers at the University of Glasgow found that 82% of music fans were concerned about climate change compared to 72% of non-music fans. Fans are "both more concerned about climate change in general and expect the music industry to do extra on the issue". Furthermore, they are "prepared to change their consumption habits to support more sustainable products and practices" [8].

So what can be done? Langer [3] claims that right now, at the tail end of Covid-19, there is an opportunity to "create an industry like few others: leading by example, powered by creativity, and working to make a better world for the next generation... to leverage this power of influence to course-correct on climate, while still growing our bottom line. If our own sense of self-preservation doesn't ask this of us, then we need only look to the audiences and artists who are calling for it" (op.cit.).

1.2 Case study: DJs CO2 footprint

The most important way for anyone living in affluent countries and contexts to reduce their personal climate crisis impact is by avoiding flying. The total contribution of aviation to climate change is about 3.5% [9]. For musicians, the practice of "relentless touring – driven by low income from streams and physical format sales – is precarious and environmentally unsustainable" [10]. As a case in point, consider DJs, the high-flying masters of ceremony at large-crowd music events. The top 1000 DJs touring in 2019 used 51,000 flights, with a CO2 footprint equivalent to "20,000 households' electricity for one year, powering 8000 festivals for three days, or pressing 25 million records" [11]. The average touring DJ emits "35 tonnes of CO2 annually, which is over 17 times more than the sustainable carbon budget... of approximately 2 tonnes of CO2 per individual" [12]. Elidh McLaughlin proposes six actions to mitigate DJs negative impact on the environment: a focus on Future Equity; Accountability; Celebrate Local; Rethinking Exclusivity; Efficient Tour Routing; and Collaboration. These concepts are developed in their report [11].

As Parncutt writes: "Until a few years ago, academics thought nothing of flying from anywhere in the world to a single location and enjoying a few days of intense communication. We returned home with new ideas, plans, and sense of purpose. In 2021, after a year of virtual communication triggered by the COVID- 19 epidemic, many are longing to go 'back to normal'. That is hardly likely, given the worsening global climate situation. Whereas COVID-19 happened more suddenly, climate change is more important in the long term" [13]. In addition, musicians in industry can switch to energy-efficient lighting and sound equipment, and prioritise venues that rely on renewable energy [12], and if they output records on a physical, vinyl-like medium, the material itself can be recyclable [14].

1.3 Climate Action

But music industry has to show that their engagement is more than just a fashion statement: "eco-enthusiasm has to come with concrete, identifiable actions" [3]. "After pledging to reduce emissions, record labels, musicians and other stakeholders have to put their money where their mouths are" [15]. Individual actions do matter: "When we come together and collectivise those actions, we can rewire the system to favour justice, equity and equality. That's the power of community." [16]. These sentiments are shared by musician action groups, such as DJs for Climate Action. See [17] for an analysis (from 2010?) of the carbon footprint of music festivals in the USA. These associations are taking on the ideas of 'green jobs' [18] and 'just transition', with links to the global trade union movement to prioritise workers' rights and reduce inequalities (e.g. the Climate Justice Alliance).

2. TOWARDS SUSTAINABLE SOUND ART PRACTICES

Having reviewed the current situation in the profit-oriented music industry, I discuss matters of concern for sound artists working in academia, and give examples from what we are currently doing at SoundLab at the School of Creative Media, City University of Hong Kong. In SoundLab's approach to working with sound art at a higher education institution, we are adopting a four-pronged strategy that involves 1) rethinking the aesthetics; 2) calculating CO2 footprint; 3) reviewing curricula, and: 4) strengthening the networks. In what follows I will briefly discuss them and give examples from our practice.

2.1 Rethinking the aesthetics

Sound artists are practice-based: we tend to work with the materials and contexts that are immediately available to us. I suspect that the highly technical nature of the work and comparatively introverted mentality of many sound artists, when compared to for example visual artists or film makers, makes it harder for them to take in concerns that still seem to be far away, both in the future and geographically. But they are not.

I argue that we need to re-focus contents and materials, compositional purposes, sonic materials, and methods that we use, if our output is to generate meaning-filled experiences that reach beyond the serotonin rush of instant gratification and instead influence listeners to reflect and react to the crisis. As Richard Parncutt points out, "Visible green behaviour can help reduce the value-action gap... people need to be shown what to do, and how... Another approach is climate change communication that anthropomorphizes nature... explaining that the atmosphere "doesn't negotiate" and "doesn't care where the emissions come from." [13].

At SoundLab, we setting up All Ears All Eyes, a project to chart environmental data sonification and visualisation with recent analyses of the Data Sonification Archive [19, 20].

2.2 Calculating CO2 footprint

With his 'categorical imperative, Emmanuel Kant affirmed that the best fundamental for ethical decisions was to "act only according to that maxim whereby you can, at the same time, will that it should become a universal law". Meanwhile, Ayn Rand heavily criticised Kant, and emphasised the individual's personal responsibility for making moral decisions based on a rational understanding of existence.

What does this mean for academics and ethical action in the face of a climate crisis that truly *exists*? For starters, we have to establish ways to calculate CO2 footprint for the production, presentation, and distribution of sonic artwork, while carefully weighing reasonable costs against potential (if not measurable) impact on audiences, in terms of positive behavioural change. It can easily be shown that a long-haul return flight in economy class corresponds to roughly a tonne of burned fossil carbon (creating 3.7 tonnes CO2). That figure, which does not consider other greenhouse gases (atmosfair.de), is comparable with driving a car for a year (consuming 30 l of gasoline per week) or eating beef for three years (500 g per week, at 50 kg CO2 per kg beef)" [13]. In this perspective, the single most effective action an individual can do is to reduce taking flights, preferably to none at all. "For many academics, the carbon emissions associated with air travel dominate personal carbon budgets, dwarfing other contributions such as from driving or eating a meat-based diet" [21]. It follows that considerations of research ethics, as commonly discussed by ethics committees, might usefully include questions about conference organisation [22, 23], and hence the need to implement new conferencing formats that produce much less CO2 than what we have become used to previously. The proposed model also holds great promise to promote diversity, equity, and inclusion, which was the topic of a recent special issue in Array, the journal of the International Computer Music Association (Akkermann, Lindborg et al. 2021).

2.3 Reviewing curricula

We must stimulate students and other stakeholders by reviewing curricula and teaching practices in educational institutions. As a case study, we are reviewing the undergraduate courses at the School of Creative Media. There are currently 123 courses in the catalogue). Scanning these, we found only three (3) with a description that contains either 'sustain /able /ability' or 'climate change /action /crisis /mitigation'. One of them is dedicated to the issues we are here discussing, even though it is not centred on music or sound art, and the description will be cited in full: *"The course introduces students to sustainable values in art and product development by highlighting the responsibility of the artist/designer towards the ecological, economical and social influence of his/her creation. Ecological sustainability in art and design includes a holistic understanding of production and transportation methodologies and their application in a digital environment. It also includes notions energy efficiency and the use of eco-friendly materials in products and art pieces. Social sustainability in art and design encompasses clear and honest communication of a product, information or art piece and its positive influence on the society."* (SM3726 Sustainable Art and Design). The two other courses mention, respectively, *"questions of resource-use (for instance energy consumption, carbon emission, or impact on climate)"* and *"environmental narrative design"*.

We will have to do more work to chart the terrain of curricula: within our own institution and in comparison with sister institutions. The important goal should be to identify best practices.

The course descriptions together with content (teaching and learning activities) will need to respond to the current climate crisis, to the demands of students, and reflect deep insights into what the most productive and reflected action are in the present situation. The first part of this paper outlined the pressure from multiple international organisations within the field of music (some of which are part of the coordination spearheaded by the COP27), and as the Glasgow survey showed [8], music fans are more sensitive than the average population towards adapting their habits and practices for climate change mitigation.

At SoundLab, we are creating workshops to generate and collate materials for sound artists to work with. The point is to stimulate approaches to climate data sonification and music-making that have a clear connection to the issues brought about by the climate crisis. In the DACA Workshop in September 2022, students worked with meteorological data from Hong Kong Observatory. Materials, blog, and examples output are available at the website. Another example of how to stimulate students and young people to join their passion for creative sound art and engagement with climate action is the 'sample pack' by DJs for Climate Action.

2.4 Strengthening the networks

The final argument I want to make is that we need to strengthen the network of initiatives geared towards sustainable practices among professionals in the field of sound art. This is about creating platforms for awareness and sharing of climate-aware practices.

One example is the 2022 Conference on Data Art for Climate Action, which was organised by the author in collaboration with nine organisations in Hong Kong and EU, together with colleagues and contributors. *"DACA is about sonification and visualisation of climate data with a purpose of exploration, awareness, education, and action… a focal point for researchers, artists, activists, and students, to meet, discuss, and learn from each other. DACA will support a wide, open source dissemination of knowledge. The organisers actively work towards diversity… participants are researchers, academics, and graduate students in arts, computer science, media, journalism, and environmental studies, as well as laymen and interested parties in the general population. … We reach out to climate scientists who are interested in sonification for dealing with their own data. The overarching goal of DACA is to support scientists and artists who seek to work more closely together and create perceptualizations of climate data that excite and surprise people"*. The conference proceedings are available here, and selected articles are published in an associated Research Topic [24].

In his keynote address, Moritz Stefaner stated that "We don't have an awareness problem. We have an action problem." Analysing historical, recent, and own work, he showed that now is the time for artists and designers to make a mental shift away from 'creating awareness' to 'generating action'. While Stefaner focuses on visual design, the same case can be made for sound art and sound design.

3. CONCLUSION

There is such a thing as 'sound art for climate action'. In this paper, I have outlined a background to the current state of affairs by considering the philosophy of aesthetics, the recently awakened climate awareness in the music industry, and the thinly spread and mostly disjoint field of sound art (at least, the part that connects with academia). I argue that we, as students and professionals in the field, have a responsibility to turn our attention, skills, and aesthetics towards answering the inescapable demands put up by the climate crisis. This firstly concerns conference travel, but also and at a deeper level, the kinds of musical work that we produce. At present, it is hard to find evidence that this attitude is stimulated in higher education, exactly where it is needed and in fact quite likely to be well received. Many conferences in the fields relevant to sound art have a genuine concern for climate action, including ICAD, ICMC, NIME, and UbiMus, but our actions are heterogeneous and not well connected. Much work remains to be done.

Acknowledgments

The author thanks Gui 'Gooey' Ren for assistance in the review of SCM course descriptions and final reading of the manuscript. The author declares having no economic interests in any part of materials presented in this paper.

4. REFERENCES

[1] R. Ikeshiro, D. Charrieras, and P. Lindborg, "Charting the scene (s) of sonic arts in Hong Kong: An overview based on 23 interviews with local practitioners and organisers," *Organised Sound*, 2022.

[2] I. Stravinsky, *Poetics of Music in the Form of Six Lessons*. Harvard University Press, 1970-02-26, google-Books-ID: UwrtfNYIylQC.

[3] K. Langer and J. Aswad, "Here's How the Music Industry Can Help Fight Climate Change," *Vanity*, 2022. [Online]. Available: https://variety.com/2022/music/news/music-industry-fight-climate-change-1235313805/

[4] A. Hamilton, "Against Modernism and Postmodernism on Art and Entertainment: A Kristeller Thesis of Entertainment," *The British Journal of Aesthetics*, 2022.

[5] UnitedNations. (2022) Climate Change Conference [COP27]. [Online]. Available: https://www.unep.org/events/conference/un-climate-change-conference-unfccc-cop-27

[6] R. Shusterman, "Entertainment: A question for aesthetics," *The British Journal of Aesthetics*, vol. 43, no. 3, pp. 289–307, 2003.

[7] T. Ingham, "Goldman Sachs: The global music industry is going to be worth even MORE than we thought," *Music Business Worldwide*, 2022-06-13. [Online]. Available: https://bit.ly/3RrgeTB

[8] D. Shaw, M. Brennan, D. McKeever, and M. Wong, "'Turn Up the Volume'Survey: Music Fan Attitudes towards Climate Change and Music Sustainability-Initial Report," 2022. [Online]. Available: https://eprints.gla.ac.uk/270449/

[9] D. S. Lee, D. W. Fahey, A. Skowron, M. R. Allen, U. Burkhardt, Q. Chen, S. J. Doherty, S. Freeman, P. M. Forster, and J. Fuglestvedt, "The contribution of global aviation to anthropogenic climate forcing for 2000 to 2018," *Atmospheric Environment*, vol. 244, p. 117834, 2021.

[10] A. Corner, "Time to shake things up: music industry confronts climate crisis as gigs resume," *The Guardian*, 2021-04-27. [Online]. Available: https://www.theguardian.com/music/2021/apr/27/music-industry-confronts-climate-crisis-gigs-resume

[11] E. McLaughlin, E. Fineberg, and F. MacWilliams, "Last Night a DJ toook a Flight: Exploring the carbon footprint of touring DJs and looking towards alternative futures within the dance music industry." 2021-03. [Online]. Available: https://cleanscene.club/

[12] V. Tachev, "How to Reduce the Music Industry's Climate Impact," *Energy Tracker Asia*, 2022-07-12. [Online]. Available: https://energytracker.asia/how-to-reduce-the-music-industry-climate-impact/

[13] R. Parncutt, P. Lindborg, N. Meyer-Kahlen, and R. Timmers, "The multi-hub academic conference: global, inclusive, culturally diverse, creative, sustainable," *Frontiers in Research Metrics and Analytics*, p. 53, 2021.

[14] J. Wickes, "Vinyl records are bad for the environment – it's time for that to change," *The Face*, 2021-08-12. [Online]. Available: https://bit.ly/3V1WXZx

[15] R. Trapunski, "The music industry changes its tune on climate change," *Corporate Knights*, 2022-10-24. [Online]. Available: https://www.corporateknights.com/category-culture/the-music-industry-changes-its-tune-on-climate-change/

[16] K. Langer. (2022) Climate Control Projects. [Online]. Available: https://www.linkedin.com/company/climatecontrolprojects/

[17] D. Singleton, "Carrying the Tune of Sustainability Addressing Climate Change in Creative Ways," 2010. [Online]. Available: https://www.oxy.edu/sites/default/files/assets/UEP/Comps/2010/Singleton_Carrying%2520the%2520Tune%2520of%2520Sustainability.pdf

[18] E. Johnson. (2022-08-22) What are Green Jobs? [Online]. Available: https://cpdonline.co.uk/knowledge-base/business/green-jobs/

[19] P. Lindborg, S. Lenzi, and M. Chen, "Climate data sonification and visualization: An analysis of topics, aesthetics, and characteristics in 32 recent projects," *Frontiers in Psychology*, vol. 13, 2023-01-25.

[20] P. Lindborg, V. Caiola, M. Chen, P. Ciuccarelli, and S. Lenzi, "Re(de)fining Sonification: Project Classification Strategies in the Data Sonification Archive," *Journal of the Audio Engineering Society*.

[21] J. N. Quinton, "Cutting the carbon cost of academic travel," *Nature Reviews Earth & Environment*, vol. 1, no. 1, pp. 13–13, 2020.

[22] R. Parncutt and A. Seither-Preisler, "Live streaming at international academic conferences: Ethical considerations," *Elementa: Science of the Anthropocene*, vol. 7, 2019.

[23] ——, "Live streaming at international academic conferences: Doing rather than talking," *Elementa: Sci. Anthropocene*, vol. 9, no. 1, p. 00435, 2021.

[24] P. Lindborg, K. Groß-Vogt, and S. S. Chopra, "Data perceptualization for climate science communication [Research Topic]," *Frontiers in psychology*, vol. 14, 2023. [Online]. Available: https://www.frontiersin.org/research-topics/20827/data-perceptualization-for-climate-science-communication

This page intentionally left blank.

Nightports at Hull Minster: Transporting a Site-Specific Musical Work Across Physical and Virtual Spaces

Matthew Barnard
Music, School of The Arts
University of Hull
Hull, United Kingdom
m.barnard@hull.ac.uk

Adam Martin
Music, School of Arts & Humanities
University of Huddersfield
Huddersfield, United Kingdom
a.martin2@hud.ac.uk

Mark Slater
Music, School of The Arts
University of Hull
Hull, United Kingdom
m.slater@hull.ac.uk

ABSTRACT

'Nightports at Hull Minster' is a musical project that harnesses spatialisation techniques to present music composed of the sounds of Hull Minster, UK, in both the location itself and alternative performance spaces, whilst still expressing the spatiality of the location. The root of the project is a live electronic music performance by Nightports (The Leaf Label), using only sounds recorded in the Minster itself, spatialised in real-time by another performer across a 25-loudspeaker array in situ. Three variant performance approaches are detailed that allow this original principle of spatialisation to endure in contrasting locations: a physical acousmonium in-situ; a hybrid acousmonium and virtualmonium; and headphone-targeted virtualisations for radio. The compositional and performance processes, influenced by architectural and acoustic considerations, necessitated the development of a scalable and adaptable spatialisation system by the Hull Electroacoustic Research Organisation (HEARO). Alongside the technical implementations, this paper details performance observations including the interplay between spatial dynamics, audience interaction, and sonic immersion, while also offering insights into potential refinements and advancements in the spatialisation methods.

1. INTRODUCTION

The initial concept and primary execution of this musical project involved a live electronic music performance within Hull Minster. The music was derived from sounds recorded in the bell tower, which were then diffused through a 'loudspeaker orchestra' array, utilising amplitude-panning to exploit the distinct acoustic characteristics of the space, following the fundamental traditions of the acousmonium: the intention of 'diffusing' signals across loudspeakers distributed in a performance space [1]. The resulting musical work is intimately entwined with the location: parts of the Minster date back to circa 1285 [2] and it features a rich, pronounced acoustic as to be expected of a large, stone church. The performance of the work requires three people – two triggering and manipulating sounds (referred to as Nightports or performer 1 or 2), and one gathering the various categories of sound feeds and spatialising them in real-time (referred to as the diffusion performer). Subsequent, unanticipated iterations of the project (for example, a live performance broadcast for BBC Radio 3) have required reactive adaptations of the spatial presentation and virtualisation of the acoustic properties of the Minster and the loudspeaker array that was implemented in the Minster in August 2022 [3].

2. ORIGINS

The origin of *Nightports at Hull Minster* was one of opportunity. Hull Minster is a welcoming public space at the heart of the city, but access to its bell tower is typically restricted. However, Nightports were granted rare access to the upper floors of the bell tower, where a complex arrangement of ropes and intersecting wooden beams converge to form the time-keeping apparatus of the structure. For centuries, the building has marked time for the population of Hull, with its bells reverberating across the city and out across the river Humber. This iconic building presents a fascinating challenge for the creation of new music because of its symbolic status, rich history and acoustic properties.

3. MATERIALS

In September 2021, a stereo and ambisonic recording rig was taken to the uppermost reaches of the bell tower, some 45 meters above ground level, up a narrow spiral staircase. The day was dedicated to capturing five categories of sounds: 1) individual bell tolls; 2) peals occurring at quarter-hourly intervals; 3) clock mechanisms; 4) mechanical noises of ropes in movement during peals alongside sundry metallic objects forming the fabric of the apparatus; and 5) a sample set of the 25-bell/2-octave carillon. This extensive palette of audio then formed the basis of an 8-month creative process which gave rise to a 30-minute ambient electronic composition designed for live performance, involving a mixture of pre-composed and improvised elements, distributed across 7 stereo busses for discrete spatialisation via acousmonium-style diffusion.

4. COMPOSITION

First, the building as an architectural space carries with it its original intended function as a place of worship for the people of Hull (a factor that could be deemed a 'cultural' or 'dramaturgic' influence [4]). Since a significant refurbishment project that was completed in 2017, the use of the building has expanded to embrace non-religious segments of the population in a kind of ethos of celebratory welcoming. This wider use was reflected in the selection and organisation of musical materials: the preservation of the time-keeping function of the bells recalls the building's long-standing function, while invocations of the synths and beats of Berlin industrial music or ambient soundscapes work to 'break expectations' [5] of what the place might mean. Second, the acoustic properties (or 'physical' influence [4]) of the building were always intended to be woven into the fabric of the music and its performance. The music is thoroughly in and of that place, with sounds recorded at an earlier point in the building's history intermingled with those of the immediate, performed present to effect 'a kind of doubling or layering or space' [6].

There are two key compositional concerns here. First, a space is not simply a container for the intended future musical performance, it is a dynamic and integrated aspect of the compositional process that forms the materials in a teleological play of what may come to pass. The performers will not just play in the acoustic, they play with it. In this instance, as Elblaus and Eckel would suggest, 'without a site, there is no piece' [7]. Second, this sense that the acoustic would be an integral aspect of the music in performance exerted a natural limit on the possible density and intensity of any one moment. This impacted compositional decisions particularly with regards to percussion onsets and how sound could become obscured by pronounced acoustic responses. Though this was often unrewarding during the creative process, this sense of incompleteness was, in retrospect, some indication that this dialogue with space was necessary and inherent.

5. SPATIALISATION SYSTEM

The Hull Electroacoustic Research Organisation (HEARO) is a collective focusing on the creation and spatialisation of musical works based at the University of Hull, often utilising a loudspeaker orchestra. A bespoke spatialisation system, built within a modular software environment, has been designed to support traditional and diffusion techniques [8] and contemporary spatialisation approaches, akin to the 'BEASTMulch' software system [9]. This system encompasses functions such as loudspeaker array definition, input routing, virtual channel propagation, and mapping of physical controllers to virtual channel amplitudes. Adaptations were made for the Nightports at Hull Minster project to accommodate multiple stereo feeds for spatialisation: the system processes 14 audio inputs from Nightports, arranged into 7 stereo pairs, each transmitting discrete components of the musical arrangement to afford both musical flexibility and sympathy in the spatialisation approach (see Table 1). These inputs are propagated to 80 virtual channels, facilitating precise spatialisation across the loudspeaker array, with amplitudes controlled via diffusion performance interfaces.

Arrangement Component(s)	Spatialisation Affordances
Bass & Rumbles	Fixed
Drums	Anchored with widening dynamic across front of 'main ring'
Percussion FX	Dynamic across full array
Bells & Swells	Dynamic across full array
Synths & Pads	Dynamic across full array
Performer 1 Return	Fixed in 'diffuse ring'
Performer 2 Return	Dynamic across 'main ring' and 'diffuse ring'

Table 1. Arrangement components created by Nightports and the respective spatialisation affordances.

5.1 The Primary Array

In August 2022, a loudspeaker array based on the acousmonium principle was installed in Hull Minster (see Figure 1). It comprised 25 loudspeaker channels positioned to provide both envelopment and extension along the building's length, covering a 70-meter span. This primary array served as the basis for subsequent iterations, featuring eight large loudspeakers forming a main ring, six small, rear-facing loudspeakers for a diffuse ring, and eight small loudspeakers arranged in pairs for distant projection as a column. Three subwoofers provided low-frequency coverage, with additional ones used for extension. Time-alignment was implemented only within the nave due to significant delay compensations being required for the most distant portions of the array (~130ms).

5.2 Spatial Room Impulse Response Capture

An audio-visual format was adopted for online dissemination for the initial presentation of the project (as part of Freedom Festival 2022 in Hull, UK). A recorded live performance by Nightports was used, with virtual spatialisation applied in post-production. To achieve this, Spatial room impulse responses (SRIRs) were captured for each loudspeaker component in the Primary Array, excluding

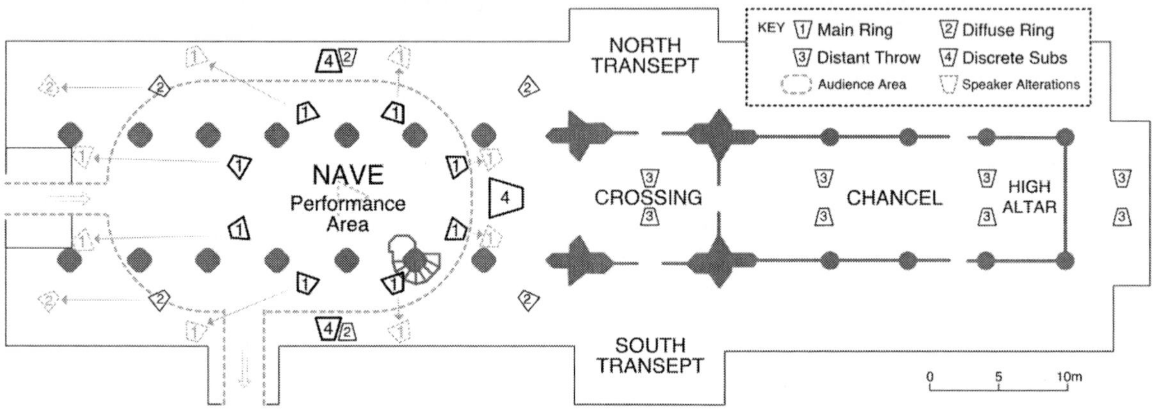

Figure 1. The primary array as realised in Hull Minster in August 2022 for a filmed performance, with alterations required for a realisation in March 2023, accommodating a public audience. [23]

subwoofers, using a 1st-order ambisonic microphone and the sine-sweep method [10]. These SRIRs facilitated ambisonic virtualisation through multiple convolution processes, utilising efficient non-equal partitioned convolution for near-zero latency processing [11].

6. PERFORMANCE INTERFACES AND AFFORDANCES

As the performance of the work would become unmanageable without a pragmatic approach to control design due to the number of sonic elements, the array of interfaces was selected to balance ergonomic efficiency with a degree of flexibility needed to maintain an improvisatory ethos. Performer 1 triggers the bulk of the pre-prepared sounds (which are organised into six blocks – roughly equating to six 5-minute segments) along with some software and outboard signal processor sends to be applied in the moment; performer 2 has responsibility for live synthesisers and the application of a range of signal processors to the sounds triggered by performer 1 to create another layer of processing. Outboard signal processors include reverbs and granulations, delays, noise and saturation. The performance is structured around the strict time-keeping function of the bell tower, beginning precisely on the hour, reaching the half-way point at exactly 15-minutes in, and culminating at half past. Within these main structural pillars (not unlike the columns, capitals and buttresses of the church itself) there are in-built places for improvised freedoms, which include addition and subtraction of audio elements within a texture, the intensity of send-return signals, and the combination of signal processing via pre- and post-fader configurations to further blur the source sounds.

The spatialisation of live materials in all settings was accomplished by the diffusion performer using a 32-fader OSC device and a MIDI device with XY controllers. These controllers manage virtual channel amplitudes, offering varying spatial control resolutions based on the intended spatial dynamics. Illustratively, the 'Bass & Rumbles' component is controlled by a single fader for overall dynamic amplitude, without spatial movement. The 'Drums' component employs two faders for amplitude control in a fixed position and optional broadening of the image across the 'main ring'. Meanwhile, the 'Synths & Pads' component utilises eight faders for front/back dynamic control and an XY controller for movement between the 'main ring' and 'diffuse ring', along with another XY controller for amplitude jitter control. This arrangement component model is consistently applied with slight variations across other components, enabling nuanced spatial control conducive to musical expression and performance variations. This spatial curation encompasses anchored/vectorial space, anchored/dynamic diffuseness, proximate/distal space, prospective/lateral space, and more [12]. The performance control resolution allows for a 'polyphonic', discrete diffusion of arrangement elements. A method was developed that allowed the diffusion performer to recall a snapshot of motorised fader positions that were devised for opportune moments between movements of the work. When recalled, an interpolation from the current fader position to the one predetermined is performed at a customisable rate. Any faders with active finger/thumb contact are excluded from the recall which enables dynamic spatialisation to continue simultaneously.

Adding this functionality created opportunity to choreograph some spatial movements that were unfeasible to realise with only performer input. An example of this is the staging of the clock mechanisms at precisely the quarter-past the hour point, featuring extreme close-perspective capture of the clockwork mechanism (accentuated with pronounced saturation and dynamics compression processing) set against a framing soundscape capture from the bell tower that brought external sounds of the city (vans reversing complete with warning beeps, traffic rushing, distant human laughter) inside the space. These specific moments were structural markers, partly due to the sonic material, but also due to the spatial staging. These junctures emerged during rehearsals in the space and across the repeated performances as intuitively affective moments that were then recalled using the snapshot method explained above. Importantly, these moments were afforded by the musical materials in a dynamic and immediate relationship with the space – the structural scheme of the musical work was an emergent property in tandem with the architectural and acoustic resonance of the place. Finally, the recall method created an ecologically unlawful moment in the design of the sound because such sudden non-linear changes (beyond the capabilities of a single human performer due to the physical realities of the body in relation to the sprawling bed of faders laid before them) created a perceptual 'jump cut' that was disorientating and self-signalling. These are ideal perceptual artefacts for important structural markers that the creators of the work want an audience to understand.

7. SPATIALISATION METHODS

The project has been realised (as both performances and recordings) in a variety of forms, which wasn't initially anticipated. The following is a summary of the key forms of realisation. In each case, the arrangement components have been performed by Nightports and spatialised by the diffusion performer in the manner outlined, which has supported a coherence across the different performance contexts. Three approaches are detailed: a physical acousmonium in-situ (A); a hybrid acousmonium and ambisonic virtualmonium [13] [14] (B); headphone-targeted ambisonic virtualisations (C1 and C2).

7.1 A: Acousmonium in-situ

A public performance at the Awakening arts festival in Hull, UK, in March 2023 represented the primary-intended context of the work. This implementation employed a conventional amplitude-panning approach for spatialisation. The spatial dynamics relied on the physical loudspeaker positioning within the Minster and real-time routing of arrangement components. Notably, adjustments were made to the loudspeaker array to accommodate the movement of a substantial public audience around the performance area (see Figure 1), leading to alterations in the response of the 'main ring' to be less direct and an increased reliance on elevated sound pressure levels.

7.2 B: Hybrid acousmonium and ambisonic virtualmonium

The HEARO loudspeaker orchestra was implemented in Middleton Hall, a concert venue situated on campus at the University of Hull, UK, as a 56-loudspeaker array utilising the acousmonium approach and higher-order ambisonic decoding via a 31-channel irregular array portion. This afforded a hybrid presentation of the project, which amalgamated amplitude-panning with real-time convolution of the Primary Array SRIRs. The performance by Nightports as recorded in August 2022 was used as source for a concert of real-time spatialisation in November 2022. The performance embraced an 'electroacoustic coupling' of the existing hall acoustic and a rendered simulation of the Minster's acoustic, akin to the 'active acoustic' method [15][16]. Notably, SRIR rotations were made to superpose with the equivalent loudspeaker positions in Middleton Hall where they existed, compensating for any discrepancies in array layout, supporting the 'electroacoustic coupling'. The resulting system provided precise control over both the direct and reverberant characteristics of each loudspeaker. For those loudspeaker sources intended to convey the spatial depth of the virtualised Primary Array, the decoded SRIR convolution feeds were used exclusively, ensuring accurate reproduction of distance-related auditory cues that were otherwise prevented by the contrasting shape of the concert hall. This methodology amalgamates techniques from both a conventional loudspeaker orchestra acousmonium and an adaptation of Barrett's virtualmonium, a loudspeaker ensemble rendered in ambisonics, crafting an 'augmented' auditory experience [17].

7.3 C: Headphone-targeted virtualisations

Two iterations of the project have exploited ambisonic virtualisation of the primary array for binaural stereo: a fixed-media audio-visual presentation of the work for Freedom Festival 2022 and a live performance for broadcast on BBC Radio 3.

7.3.1 C1: Fixed Media

The Freedom Festival 2022 film showcased a rendition of the project which harnessed 3rd-order ambisonics [18]. Recorded from a live performance by Nightports, post-recording spatialisation was applied via a native ambisonic method, emulating the primary loudspeaker array, akin to a virtualmonium. Signals intended for physical loudspeakers were redirected instead to two processing destinations: SRIR convolution for the reverberant response and a room encoder for a direct response emulation. These encoded signals were time-aligned and processed in a binaural decoder. The approach aimed to recreate the perceptual experience of the performance in the Minster more accurately than using SRIRs alone, which sounded too indirect. Spatialisation was performed in real-time by the diffusion performer, using familiar interfaces, with control data recorded for automation. However, the method's latency, stemming from utilising both modular and Digital Audio

Workstation (DAW) environments, rendered live performance an impossibility.

7.3.2 C2: Live Performance for Radio

A live performance of the work was recorded at the Trades Club in Hebden Bridge, UK, for BBC Radio 3's 'Northern Drift' broadcast. This performance, recorded in November 2022 and broadcasted in January 2023, featured live sources from Nightports and real-time spatialisation by the diffusion performer. To optimise responsiveness, the density of SRIRs and room-encoded loudspeaker positions was reduced, from 8 to 4 for the 'main ring' and from 6 to 4 for the 'diffuse ring'. This reduction in coverage resulted in a more efficient channel count and improved latency, critical for the live performance. The ambisonic signals were decoded to binaural stereo and aligned with selected non-ambisonic components (Bass & Rumbles, Drums). Performers monitored via headphones and utilised familiar performance interfaces, with the diffusion performer having the ability to dynamically rotate the ambisonic image across the azimuth.

8. PERFORMANCE OBSERVATIONS

There are six inter-related dynamics at play in the real-time exploration of the space during a performance: distance/proximity, diffusion/localisation, stasis/movement, clarity/noise, purity/distortion, focus/blur. These dynamics are the site of in-the-moment decision making, which elevates the performance from simple play-back of prefabricated sounds to a responsive, unique performance moment. They also relate to all modes of performance whether live multi-speaker spatialisation or stereo radio broadcast recording.

As part of the Awakening arts festival in Hull in March 2023, four consecutive performances were given starting at 6, 7, 8 and 9pm. A defining characteristic of the performance (which aligns with the ethos of the festival) was to permit maximum autonomy to the audience to move freely around the space. The nave of the church was clear of pews and other furniture, leaving a wide-open space from which audience members could pick a perspective or move between any part of the church. This free flow of people was made possible by utilising different entry and exit points to the venue. Over the course of the evening of performances, 3,800 people experienced the work. There was a sense of accumulating willingness for risk across this evening of performances as increased familiarity with the material and the space gave rise to an increased desire to explore how far (quite literally in the space) the performance could be taken, and how much noise the venue could withstand. The use of sends to pedals to distort and glitch sounds further became much more liberal in application and the whole effect was a form of sonic envelopment of and with the performance space. In short, the spatialisation became more dynamic as did the degree of intervention and treatment of the source audio.

In comparison to this, a performance for BBC Radio 3's 'Northern Drift' program (made in front of a live audience at a former working men's club in Hebden Bridge, UK) adopted a headphone-centric approach that was a markedly different experience in a way that was unexpected, and which challenged the location-specific purity of the original concept. The headphone version felt sonically 'pure' whereas the acoustics of the in-situ live performance, in comparison, had a quality of 'interference'. Additionally, when the work is taken outside of the Minster itself, the opportunity to manage the direct and reverberant portion of the loudspeaker array responses (in this case by simply balancing the SRIR-convolved and non-convolved signals) was considered creatively essential, if not aesthetically 'pure' in terms of the original concept. Each iteration outside of the Minster is a departure from the source situation and becomes an inflection of the work with qualitative contrasts because of the 'folding or doubling' of different spaces, but also provides novel opportunities for spatialisation.

The choreography of the spatialisations across iterations shared similarities, partly due to predetermined compositional cues and consistent means of control. While primarily lateral in nature due to practicalities and available resources, some loudspeaker angling and reverberation in the Minster extended spatial dynamics upwards. Middleton Hall's layout variation (spatialisation method B) introduced height dynamics, showcasing site-specific aspects and the project's adaptability across contexts while maintaining coherence through emulated acoustic properties and consistent means of spatialisation.

Ambisonic virtualisation offered certain benefits, including isotropic flexibility allowing rotation of array portions during spatialisation. This enhanced the sense of spatial movement across the 'main ring' in method C2 compared to C1, which lacked rotational affordance. However, transitioning to a virtualised and non-navigable perspective restricted the ability to explore the sonic environment through head movements, affecting localisation. While this may benefit performers' spatial experience, as it offers a firm grip on the presentation, it limits audience engagement spatially.

Monitoring the performance on headphones during method C2 also meant a sense of being removed from the social setting and entering an individual performance space. From the moment of putting headphones on at the beginning of a piece, the performers experienced the sudden attenuation of room and audience noise due to the closed-back and sonically isolating headphones being used. Sonic isolation was akin to social isolation. There was no longer a shared soundscape between performer and audience. This resulted in the monitoring being detailed and highly accurate (revealing aspects of sound that had not been perceptible within the Minster performance (method A) due to the size of the building and location of, in particular, the very furthest speakers) but situationally abstracted. In the Minster, sounds were frequently moving around within the space and the performers could not fully be sure of the relative loudness of the parts they were playing as they could be positioned near or far away. As a result, the process became about intuition and returned the electronics performance imperative to one perhaps more like the proprioceptively-connected relationship between body and instrument. On headphones, where all performers and audience had the same mix, this seemed to create a more cautious approach to the balancing of each musician's parts as no one wanted to stand out or above the others.

9. TECHNICAL OBSERVATIONS & DEVELOPMENTS

While the SRIRs were limited to 1st-order due to inventory constraints, upmixed versions were generated [19]. However, employing a HOA microphone capture could potentially improve localisation and spatialisation methods, especially considering the density of loudspeakers in the array. The spatial impulse response rendering (SIRR) method [20] offers an alternative approach, exclusively utilising convolution for spatialisation and potentially enhancing localisation without the ambisonic decoding layer. It should be noted that the SIRR method, in the context of this project, would necessitate a considerable number of convolutions to be processed. For future headphone contexts, decoding/transcoding SRIRs or SIRR-processed SRIRs to emulated binaural room impulse responses (BRIRs) before convolution could reduce the number of convolutions and improve latency. This 'virtual ambisonic' approach [21] could also incorporate ambisonic interaural level difference optimisation (AIO) [22] for further perceptual benefit. While latency wasn't a significant issue in current iterations, it could become problematic for future musical variations that necessitate more responsive systems. Additionally, head-tracked implementations and user-navigable dissemination methods offer further potential for developing the spatial experience in viable contexts.

10. CONCLUSIONS

Given the initial aim of presenting a site-specific performance through an acousmonium in the Minster itself, the emergent opportunities of dissemination and performance required the creators to adjust the approaches to spatialised performance in a reactive manner, harnessing combined methods and techniques. This situation has raised inquiries about the significance of the acoustic origins of the work, the viability of transferring a live, large-scale, site-specific piece, and how these factors have influenced the execution of the performances. Additionally, the process of SRIR capture became essential to providing a viable method of transportation and is considered a critical component of the technical approach of the project. Although there is scope for refinements and extensions within each iterative version of Nightports at Hull Minster, the project highlights the potential for adapting and transporting a site-specific work that is otherwise entwined with a location's acoustic and architecture.

Acknowledgments

Funded by the PRS Foundation's Open Fund for Music Creators.

11. REFERENCES

[1] F. Bayle, 'Space, and more', *Organised Sound*, vol. 12, no. 3, 2007, doi: 10.1017/S1355771807001872.

[2] National Churches Trust, 'Hull Minster'. Accessed: May 16, 2023. [Online]. Available: https://www.nationalchurchestrust.org/church/hull-minster-hull

[3] M. Barnard, A. Martin, and M. Slater, 'Nightports at Hull Minster: Physical, Hybrid and Virtualized Live Loudspeaker Array Spatialization of Electronic Music Performance', in *2023 Immersive and 3D Audio: from Architecture to Automotive (I3DA)*, IEEE, Sep. 2023, pp. 1–7. doi: 10.1109/I3DA57090.2023.10289518.

[4] A. Knight-Hill, 'Theatres of sounds: The role of context in the presentation of electroacoustic music', *Scene*, vol. 6, no. 2, pp. 165–175, Dec. 2018, doi: 10.1386/scene_00016_1.

[5] F. Macedo, 'Investigating Sound in Space: Five meanings of space in music and sound art', *Organised Sound*, vol. 20, no. 2, pp. 241–248, Aug. 2015, doi: 10.1017/S1355771815000126.

[6] M. Gallagher, 'Field recording and the sounding of spaces', *Environ Plan D*, vol. 33, no. 3, pp. 560–576, Jun. 2015, doi: 10.1177/0263775815594310.

[7] L. Elblaus and G. Eckel, 'Acoustic modelling as a strategy for composing site-specific music', in *ACM International Conference Proceeding Series*, 2020. doi: 10.1145/3411109.3411141.

[8] J. Harrison, 'Sound, space, sculpture: some thoughts on the "what", "how" and "why" of sound diffusion', *Organised Sound*, vol. 3, no. 2, 1998, doi: 10.1017/s1355771898002040.

[9] S. Wilson and J. Harrison, 'Rethinking the BEAST: Recent developments in multichannel composition at

Birmingham ElectroAcoustic Sound Theatre', *Organised Sound*, vol. 15, no. 3, 2010, doi: 10.1017/S1355771810000312.

[10] A. Farina, 'Advancements in impulse response measurements by sine sweeps', in *Audio Engineering Society - 122nd Audio Engineering Society Convention 2007*, 2007.

[11] L. Battisti, A. Farina, A. Bevilacqua, and L. Tronchin, 'Implementation of non-equal partitioned multi-channel convolver', in *Internoise 2022 - 51st International Congress and Exposition on Noise Control Engineering*, 2022. doi: 10.3397/in_2022_0220.

[12] D. Smalley, 'Space-form and the acousmatic image', *Organised Sound*, vol. 12, no. 1, pp. 35–58, Apr. 2007, doi: 10.1017/S1355771807001665.

[13] N. Barrett, 'A Musical Journey towards Permanent High-Density Loudspeaker Arrays', *Computer Music Journal*, vol. 40, no. 4, 2016, doi: 10.1162/COMJ_a_00381.

[14] N. Barrett, 'A 3D future for loudspeaker orchestras emulated in higher-order Ambisonics', in *ICMC 2016 - 42nd International Computer Music Conference, Proceedings*, 2016.

[15] W. Woszczyk, 'Active acoustics in concert halls - A new approach', *Archives of Acoustics*, vol. 36, no. 2, 2011, doi: 10.2478/v10168-011-0028-6.

[16] W. Woszczyk and D. H. Benson, 'Experiencing room acoustics through a library of multichannel high-resolution room impulse responses', in *Proceedings of the International Congress on Acoustics*, 2019. doi: 10.18154/RWTH-CONV-239920.

[17] J. Blauert and R. Rabenstein, 'Providing surround sound with loudspeakers: A synopsis of current methods', *Archives of Acoustics*, vol. 37, no. 1, 2012, doi: 10.2478/v10168-012-0002-y.

[18] Freedom Festival Arts Trust, 'Nightports at Hull Minster'. Accessed: Jun. 14, 2023. [Online]. Available: https://www.freedomfestival.co.uk/what-we-do/freedom-online/night-ports/

[19] S. Berge and N. Barrett, 'High Angular Resolution Planewave Expansion', in *Proc. of the Second of International Symposium on Ambisonics and Spherical Acoustics*, 2010.

[20] L. McCormack, V. Pulkki, A. Politis, O. Scheuregger, and M. Marschall, 'Higher-Order Spatial Impulse Response Rendering: Investigating the Perceived Effects of Spherical Order, Dedicated Diffuse Rendering, and Frequency Resolution', *Journal of the Audio Engineering Society*, vol. 68, no. 5, pp. 338–354, Jun. 2020, doi: 10.17743/jaes.2020.0026.

[21] M. Noisternig, T. Musil, A. Sontacchi, and R. Holdrich, '3D binaural sound reproduction using a virtual ambisonic approach', in *IEEE International Symposium on Virtual Environments, Human-Computer Interfaces and Measurement Systems, 2003. VECIMS '03. 2003*, IEEE, 2003, pp. 174–178. doi: 10.1109/VECIMS.2003.1227050.

[22] T. McKenzie, D. Murphy, and G. Kearney, 'Interaural Level Difference Optimization of Binaural Ambisonic Rendering', *Applied Sciences*, vol. 9, no. 6, p. 1226, Mar. 2019, doi: 10.3390/app9061226.

[23] M. Barnard, M. Slater, and A. Martin, 'Adapting live loudspeaker array spatialisation methods for a site-specific live electronic music performance in physical, virtual and hybrid contexts', in *Audio Engineering Society Conference: AES 2023 International Conference on Spatial and Immersive Audio*, Aug. 2023.

This page intentionally left blank.

Enough: a Radically Vulnerable Composition Approach for Gesturally Mediated Human Voice

Sophie Rose
University of Melbourne &
Australian Institute of Music
sophie.rose@aim.edu.au

ABSTRACT

Enough is a composition for voice, live electronics, and projections that employs radical vulnerability as a foundational concept, pushing boundaries in the artistic expression of trauma and recovery. The piece utilises the MiMU dataglove system to transmit movement data, transforming it into musical and visual elements through Max and Ableton Live. Routing draws from conducting movement practices to support the vocal line thematically. This interdisciplinary work explores the intersection of trauma, feminist praxis, and technology in music composition, using gestural interfaces and datagloves to express deeply personal experiences of sexual trauma. The piece draws from a trauma-informed approach to consider aspects of trauma's psychological aftereffects in sonic and lyrical content, challenging conventional narratives and offering an alternative portrayal of survivors' complex emotional landscapes. The paper discusses the use of trauma-informed practices, the concept of radical vulnerability, and the implications of music and technology as tools for personal expression and societal commentary.

Keywords: *sonification; trauma; gestural music; interaction design; radical vulnerability; voice.*

1. INTRODUCTION

Enough is a composition for voice, live electronics, and projections. The performer wears datagloves (electronically augmented gloves), which capture their positional movement (yaw, pitch, and roll), emblematic hand gestures (such as a fist, open palm, OK sign, et cetera), accelerometer strikes, and button presses. Thematically, the piece outlines the ongoing burden of advocating for fundamental rights as women, as society says one thing (sure, you can be equal) and performs the other (but we will continue to exploit and diminish you). It is about surviving and persisting through repeated sexual crimes and the fatigue of remaining resilient in the face of the overwhelming statistical probabilities. This piece draws from radical vulnerability [1], a feminist praxis, to externalise the aftermath of sexual trauma. The performer's movements frame the content and sonify psychological states that arise in the resulting aftershock. It is part of a more extensive doctoral folio of creative works investigating a trauma-informed approach to gesturally mediated vocal composition. Please see either link or an audiovisual recording of this work:

- www.youtube.com/watch?v=euagyRJJpTg
- DOI: 10.5281/zenodo.8197969

By embodying trauma through gestural mediation and vocal expression, *Enough* challenges conventional narratives and offers an alternative, more nuanced portrayal of the complex emotional landscapes of survivors [2]. This interdisciplinary study has implications for music composition, performance, and fields like psychology and feminist studies. It also demonstrates the potential of music and technology for personal expression and societal commentary. This paper explores the intersection of trauma, feminist praxis, and technology in music composition. Its relevance lies in the innovative use of gestural interfaces and datagloves to articulate profoundly personal and often stigmatised experiences [2]. The rationale and importance of this work (and others like it) is to give voice to experiences that are frequently marginalised or misrepresented in mainstream discourse, particularly in the context of women's narratives of systemic trauma.

2. BACKGROUND

Here, I briefly outline trauma's mechanisms, trauma-informed practices, the approach used in this research, and radical vulnerability.

2.1. Trauma and Trauma-Informed Practices

Traumatic events can cause the function of parts of the brain to diminish and cause behaviour pattern reinforcements in individuals [3], [4]. Unresolved trauma can create cycles of abuse because traumatised individuals may have been unable to execute fight or flight responses, instead reacting with freeze or fawn[1] behaviour patterns [5], [6]. Individuals may be pre-disposed to be victims again because they may not know the process of "fighting back" or be unable to identify warning signs where the behaviour patterns have been normalised [4], [7]. The events are not the individual's fault but become their undeserved responsibility. These obligations have emotional repercussions, especially when not effectively treated [8].

Trauma-informed therapies seek to navigate this process and facilitate our innate ability to heal the body and

[1] Where the person seeks to appease the perpetrator in order to avoid additional harm [5].

brain. They originated from feminist movements in the 1970s and 1980s. They were merged into medical care structures in the 1990s [9]. The approach shifts focus from determining what is "wrong" with the individual or their experiences to the need to understand how it impacts their life. While the outward-facing profile of these therapies differs, the core tenets aim to consider the individual's traumatic experience(s) and environment in relation to each other [9]. *Enough* uses a trauma-informed approach through radical vulnerability in considering aspects of trauma's aftereffects in the sonic and lyrical content.

2.2. Radical Vulnerability

Vulnerability is a universal, inevitable, and constant of the human condition [10]. Radical vulnerability encourages openly and daringly exposing one's thoughts, emotions, and experiences, even when doing so may result in judgment or potential hurt [10], [11]. It is considered "radical" because it goes against the common practice of shielding one's vulnerabilities against discomforts or threats.

Despite notable advancements in women's rights within social and political realms, prevalent depictions in art and society often adhere to reductive stereotypes [12], [13]. Furthermore, publicly discussing sexual trauma (which also remains widespread) remains a societal taboo [14]. Radical vulnerability challenges the dominant narrative by offering an alternative perspective on personal growth and empowerment, fostering a broader, more inclusive understanding of resilience, resistance, and recovery. It embodies a unique form of emancipation, wherein one confronts their history and refuses to conform to established and contradictory narratives that circumscribe personal experience [1]. Furthermore, these expressions of "weakness" can extend a lifeline to fellow survivors, allowing them to feel acknowledged and less isolated [10], [14], [15]. The larger doctoral research project investigates various facets of trauma, offering a perspective on singular and collective phenomena by showcasing reactions to themes in different contexts, combinations, and self-attitudes – *Enough* centres on reconciliation and reclamation.

3. RELATED WORKS

This project builds on the concepts and ideas of interdisciplinary artworks of different art forms. This section outlines the most relevant works by Pamela Z, Imogen Heap, and Terry Pratchett.

Pamela Z uses speech, sampling, extended vocal techniques, and Bel Canto[2] singing techniques. Her 2010 installation *Baggage Allowance* [16] symbolises personal and historical relationship trauma through the concept of travelling with heavy luggage. The work uses sound, music, and sculpture to reframe the emotional and physical luggage we bring from location to location and each relationship. It acknowledges the excess weight we drag throughout our lives and its impact on individuals and groups.

The vulnerability and sense of space within Imogen Heap's body of work and the incorporation of frailer vocal textures have influenced my practice for many years[3]. However, her MiMU-specific work has not influenced this piece as extensively. These singing elements are most noticeable in *Bad Body Double* [17], where she humorously critiques her body from a negative and externalised locus that invades her private spaces during inopportune moments. Heap's song is a miniature of relatable lyrics based on society's expectations for women and an element of radical vulnerability in popular music – with no gestural mediation used in this work. *Enough* also has similarities to Imogen Heap's song *Hide and Seek* [18], which uses a vocoder to synthesise her voice to create a choir accompaniment. The effect of Heap's synthesized voice is "eerie and haunting"; the unseen choir produces a "disembodied, mechanical, somewhat supernatural presence – one that bears little resemblance to the acoustic world" [19, p. 91].

Shaking Hands with Death [20] is a lecture and short book by Terry Pratchett in which he talks about his progressing Alzheimer's disease and support of euthanasia as the execution of mercy, compassion, and ultimate granting of free will – the freedom to decide when it is time to die. The book discusses grief, fear, and resignation at the prospect of one's mortality and the complications with which it comes. Death appears as a kindly (and anthropomorphised) character in many of Pratchett's Discworld novels which demonstrates his more neutral attitude to the spiritual mystery of what comes next.

These creative works have a tongue-in-cheek approach to the subject matter while remaining earnest. They explore societal issues through vulnerability as evident in their words, timbre, and the surrounding contextualisation. Additionally, these artworks share a courageous approach to confronting and communicating personal and universal vulnerabilities through their respective artistic practices, connecting with the broader discourse on portraying difficult human experiences and the empowerment that can arise from such candid expression.

4. METHODOLOGY

This piece was composed through practice-based, performative autoethnography [21], [22]. Trauma often eludes linguistic expression, hindering the expression of events, feelings, and emotions. Yet, the human voice holds a distinct power to reveal and mitigate trauma's effects. Vocalising one's experiences allows for reassembling past fragments, weaving them into the fabric of one's personal story. Autoethnography acts as a channel to elevate individual voices, addressing and denouncing violence, and navigating personal or traumatic experiences within a broader framework [21], [22]. Additionally, I wrote this piece to fuse my newer experimental composi-

[2] A style of Western classical singing.

[3] Additionally, I had recently conducted a short analysis on women performer-composers in Popular music from the last 20 years for another piece – of which Imogen Heap's work was a part. This analysis is beyond the scope of this paper.

tion style with my past contemporary practice and (self-perceived) melodic, lyrical, and vocal performance strengths.

4.1 Composition Process

I began by improvising over a C Lydian scale at the piano while contemplating the mini-analysis (summarised in my doctoral thesis) of women singer-songwriter's presentations of interpersonal trauma in popular music over the last 20 years, a fresh instance of sexual harassment, and Terry Pratchett's *Shaking Hands with Death* [20]. I captured the MIDI information from this improvisation and layered six vocal lines over it. Then, I transformed those vocal lines into additional MIDI information and refined the harmony and note density from the overall mass. Lastly, I composed the lead line by singing lyrics and melody line by line over the backing without consideration of the mode. This line-by-line construction results in each lyric fitting instinctively to the rich harmony and through-composed structure. The vocal textures then deepen the meaning of the chosen words and subject matter to depict facets of traumatic experience. Instead of hinging on repeated chord patterns, this format cycles through extreme timbre and pitch waves.

The vocal techniques selected draw from contemporary music usage and general speech affectations, and, as such, the vocal range required is relatively large, spanning from C3 to B5. The piece is highly melodic, with lush chords and harmonic movement generated from the performer's motion and conducting gestures. This piece has no improvisation except for vocal embellishments and freedom with the tempo and timings. A score can be found here: 10.5281/zenodo.8197969

4.2 Technology

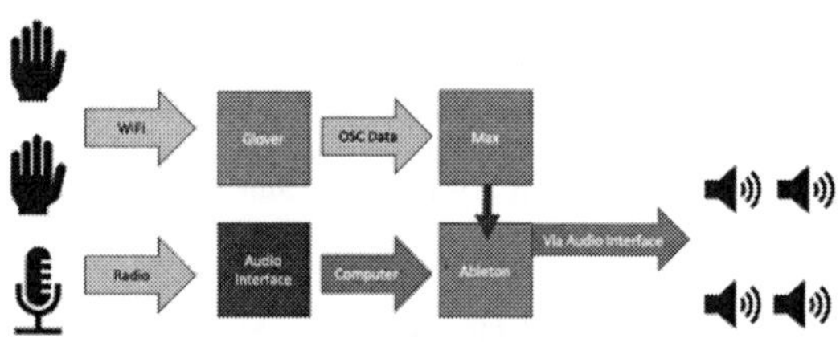

Figure 1. Signal and data information flow for all triptych pieces.

Data is captured by MiMU datagloves [23] and transmitted over Wi-Fi as OSC (Open Sound Control) information to MiMU's proprietary software, Glover [24]. It is then sent to Max [25] and translated into musical information. This information is sent to Ableton Live [26], where it is combined with the vocalist's live output and spatialised in a four to eight-channel surround environment. See Figure 1 for a diagram of the signal and information flow. The projections are generated through the digital transformation of video footage where ink is poured into milk, edited in Final Cut Pro [27]. The lyrics are superimposed and particle-displaced on this video in Max and the effects and text is controlled by the gesture. See Figure 2 and Figure 3 for a screenshot of the general Max-patch and excerpt of the video projections.

Figure 2. The performance view in Max shows the chord number in the sequence, accompanying lyrics, audio monitoring (controlling visual effects), and absolute difference video processing.

Figure 3. Screenshot of the projections without `[jit.sprinkle]` effect applied (for legibility).

4.3 Final Gesture Mapping and Conducting

Table 1. Mapping gesture (left column) to effect/audio consequence (right column).

Gesture	Routing
L Fist + Button	Start/Record Start max patch video
R Fist + Button	Recording Start/Stop Stop max patch video
L & R OK	Set Forwards
R 1FP + Flick	Mute Vocal Synths
R Open + Wrist Flick	Advance Chord (vibrate)
R Fist + Wrist Flick	Retreat Chord
R Open + Pitch	Velocity/Synth Volumes To Max: X-range displacement for projections
L Puppet + Pitch	Backing focus
L Puppet + Yaw	Backing rotation To Max: Y-range displacement
L Puppet + Roll	Backing centre
L 2FP + Roll	Live delay (decay time)
L Open + Palm Up + Yaw	Reverb (dry/wet)
In Max:	Probability % for `[jit.sprinkle]` object

Gestural routings were adapted from choir conducting movements for this work. These were used to nod to the unseen chorus of other survivors. Conducting gestures are part of the cultural zeitgeist thanks to film, television, concert hall music, and theatrical works. I also reference Elena Jessop's work with Virtual Augmentation and Manipulation Prosthesis (VAMP) [28] in this routing strategy. Jessop's controller enables a singer to capture and manipulate single notes using a movement vocabulary drawn from choral conducting.

In *Enough*, this choir sound and conducting movement style thematically infers the presence of a group, choir, band, orchestra, et cetera. This represents the isolating but all too familiar narrative of sexual trauma. Often, through societal taboos, institutional investigation structures, and victim-blaming, survivors are made to feel isolated and alone, which causes significant psychological harm in the process. The performer, thus, stands alone on the stage. The choir then represents the multitude of other survivors' narratives, which echo the individual experience.

Table 1 contains the movement to audio mapping for this piece. The right-hand advances the choir harmony through accelerometer strikes with an open hand, which confirms its recognition through a haptic feedback vibration. The chords are contained in Max as MIDI numbers. A closed fist with a wrist flick goes back one step in the progression. This contingency-routing counters double strikes registered by the accelerometer that may act prematurely on the score. The left controls the choir's position, spatialisation, and amplitude while the performer holds a "puppet hand". See Figure 4 for photographs of each emblematic hand gesture used in this work. Not pictured are the mute audio and position zeroing controls (one-finger point and okay hand symbols). A two-finger point and an open hand with the palm facing up add delay and reverb, respectively. Performer movements also control the probability and displacement of particles on the `[jit.sprinkle]` object in Max, which adjusts the visual intelligibility of the lyrics in the projections. The chords are numbered in sequence in Max, as shown in Figure 2.

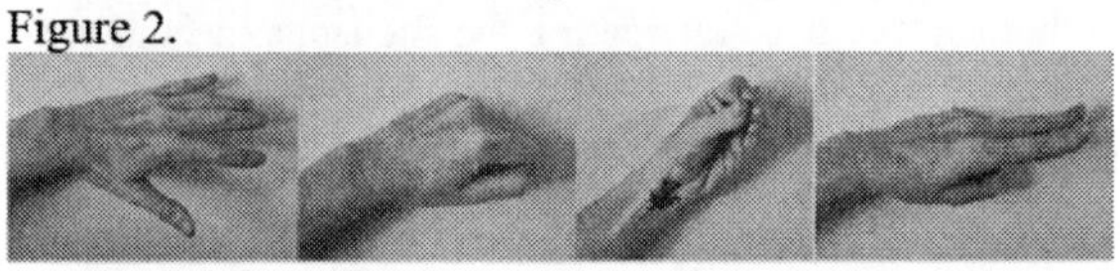

Figure 4. The gestures used in *Enough* are (left to right) open hand, fist, puppet hand, and two-finger point.

The simple nature of the controls returns the gestural language to that commonly used on stage as performative intensifiers. The hands are raised in supplication, exasperation, and desperation. They form a part of the whole through facial expressions, musical cues (voice pitch, texture, and context within the chord and phrase interpretation), staging, projections, and physicality. Additionally, this reduced the complexity of the choreography required, making a virtuosic vocal performance more achievable for the singer and readable by an audience. From discussions with non-technology-based performers and laypeople at performances and conferences, I have found that a general understanding of sound-action relationships is impenetrable without a substantial music-technology background. Even with simple routings, an audience is not guaranteed to correctly interpret the controls. Thus, the theatricality and overall artistic output are the principal concerns of this piece.

5. DISCUSSION

In this section, I discuss the implications of the musical content and the importance of radical vulnerability. Section 5.1 discusses the intersection of music and lyric cues and timbre choices. 5.2 outlines the broader social context for embodiment, gestural performance, and tool use as *agency*, *play*, and empowerment. Finally, 5.3 discusses rejected routings and the transformation of gesture use over time in this work.

5.1 Music and Lyrics

The lyrics describe sorrow and pressures of resilience, which are expected of survivors in order to engage with general society [2], [29]. The text refuses to express positive sentiments towards becoming better or stronger due to mistreatment, subverting a resilience narrative by turning towards despair and vulnerability [29]. This can be seen in lines such as "Fear of death is passée" and "sleepily conforming". The text is laden with first-person language, reflecting the themes of the #metoo era of fourth-wave feminism through the lyrics – for example, "I have had enough" and "I will speak out". At several points, the psychological state pivots through different societal, self-attitude states, and just reactions to mistreatment, for example: "I just can't go on… being fragile, being scared by, being fractured, being scarred by… men like you". In this line, the voice goes from soft and slightly breathy, gradually crescendoing through timbre and volume to belt voice to communicate anger, frustration, and desperation on "being scarred by" and back to a soft, light texture for "men like you". This transition moves through emotional waves quickly to represent those that can arise through these experiences and the turbulence of one's internal experience in the aftermath of trauma.

As mentioned in the Section 3, this vocoder choir has similarities to Imogen Heap. She uses a vocoder that sands off the voice's imperfections, while I chose a plugin that introduces artefacts. Given the similarity in timbre and harmonic use, I believe the effect of the disembodied choir is similar between the two works because the burbling and glitching sound produced by the VocalSynth 2 plugin [30] highlights the unreality of the mechanical choir without disrupting the presence of the invisible ensemble. These imperfections increase as the pitches become progressively lower and descend far below my range.

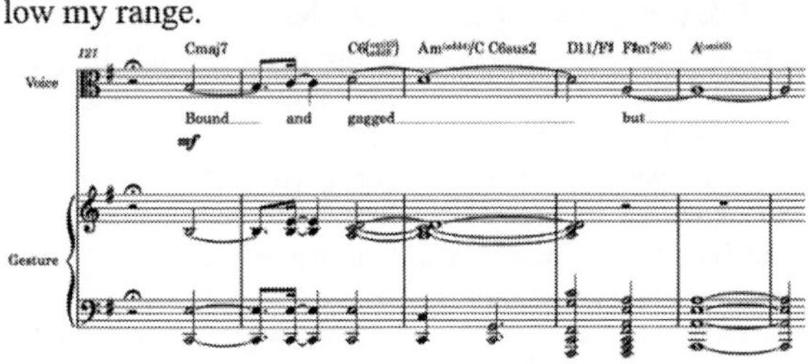

Figure 5. Excerpt of *Enough* score showing accompaniment and melody pitches.

The sung voice often follows the choir into the depths of these lower notes (see Figure 5). The female voice becomes softer and breathier on the low end of one's vocal range, where physiology increases projection difficulty. This huskiness melds with the burbling artefacts to enhance the voice's lowness and bolsters its strength in the song's final moment. This provides supplementary strength to the last statement of resolution while underscoring the tentativeness due to the tenuous vocal timbre.

This piece presents vocal performance challenges; thus, the gesture routing was simplified to facilitate execution (discussed further in 5.3). Using familiar movements as a mapping strategy facilitates embodiment (and therefore facilitates artistic performance) of a work by lowering the cognitive load. This enables me to do the expressive heavy lifting with the instrument most fit for purpose and support the performance through the movements. The refined controls heighten the expression of instrumental proficiency rather than being a potential distraction. The work's position in the folio is the final development and voicing of the ideas. Theatrically and musically, this song is positioned as a swansong. However, instead of being the final lament before fading away (to death or obscurity), it concludes unresolved, ending Dm7/F to an E with thirds omitted and neutralising the F# of the key signature.

5.2 Radical Vulnerability

This work practices radical vulnerability by allowing people into the uncomfortable space and the uncertainty, grief, fear, and despair. It opens space for individuals to feel seen and reflected on a stage within the context of their general world and the magnified artistic experience, less anomalous than one might think from similar events. The harmony, voice, and interpretation operate as one to encapsulate the emotional progression, openly acknowledged painful experiences. In addressing the cyclical nature of gendered violence, the long-term and progressive (through repeated instances) damage, and resulting body dysmorphia candidly, the narrative fails to overcome where the voice soars [29], see Figure 6. The vocal timbre moves from raw, belt-edged qualities through head voice into a thin vocal fold closure throughout my high register, drawing from emotional expression as found in ordinary voice use [31], [32]. The rawer, louder timbres draw on confidence, desperation, and anger. Pure, flute-tinged head voice pulls an ethereal quality through its power (volume), which contrasts with the lyrics. Thin-fold closure on the B5 reinforces the lyric "[demise of…] confidence" as (texturally) weak, shaky, and small. Using timbre this way may catapult the pain beyond the individual by employing empathy pathways for emotional contagion [33], [34].

Embodied knowledge emerges from extensive practical expertise in liminal performance spaces, where one can feel fully present and empowered. During performance, whether in front of an audience or not, one can experience the feeling of being fully present in one's body and the moment. Embodiment in performance translates to *agency* and empowerment. Performing, where the artist is free to make choices and can fully embody the piece, is *play*. As forms of active participation, *play* and *agency* inherently facilitate embodied knowledge in an individual [35], [36]. Using datagloves to disrupt the mundane paradigms of my voice and transcend ordinary engagement made me feel intensely connected to every layer of my being. However, this sudden bodily awareness can be jarring as it throws the hollowness of one's conscious engagement with the world into sharp relief.

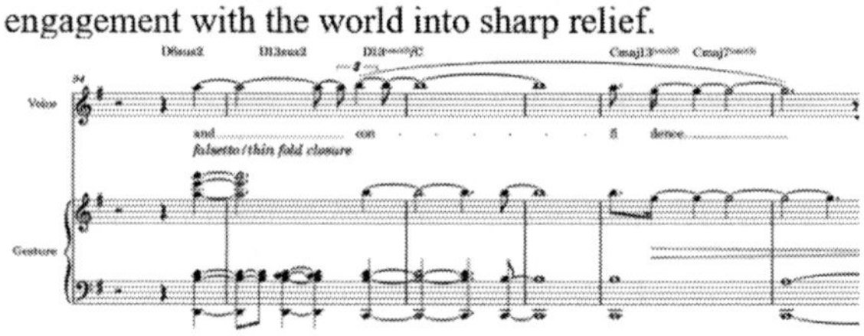

Figure 6. Excerpt of *Enough* score showing the vocal line and technique at the highest pitch in the piece.

Agency and empowerment play a significant role in recovery, which makes them a critical thematic stratagem for works about trauma. Gestural interaction aided in directing my focus on routing sound as play, which mitigated some risks associated with performing this type of content. The effectiveness of these technological interactions may fluctuate, particularly as routine experiences dampen the initial thrill or unique incidents, and technical difficulties hinder engagement. Nonetheless, they remain potent catalysts. This could signify a substantial area for further exploration in fields such as complementary activities for therapies, embodiment, human-computer interaction, and musical interface design.

Vulnerability and sensitivity are often stigmatised. In these works, I embrace them as a source of empowerment, reasserting control of personal agency from past abuse. Such an approach offers visibility and solidarity to other survivors, counteracting the societal expectation for marginalised individuals[4] to demonstrate resilience merely to participate in social norms [2], [14].

5.3 Rejected Routing Methods

Initially, more complicated frameworks centred around sequenced bilateral movements (akin to semaphore) and Australian sign language were trialed initially. These rejected methods were chosen due to my desire to push boundaries of capabilities and competencies in performance. Thematically, they are visual signals for communication which can be understood without vocally uttered words. Both were ultimately rejected in favor of simpler conducting movements, primarily due to their excessive cognitive load. Data drift caused by my MiMU systems' magnetometers added to performance problems, and though disabling them remedied aspects of the difficulty, it was insufficient for the performance rationale.

This singing in this piece is technically challenging due to the extremes in range and timbre and the large interval leaps which mark section changes. The added cognitive load in complex choreography rendered the work cumbersome. Additionally, it reduced embodiment of voice cues which are necessary to elicit an audience response. This work draws on musical and emotional elements typical of arias and power ballads, such as high ranges, loud singing, slow tempos, and rubato passages.

[4] Particularly women, gender diverse, or non-white people.

Any tech-based interference that disrupts performativity in turn disrupts established performers and audience expectations alike. Furthermore, reviewing footage of the tests confirmed that the semaphore-style and sign language choreography did not aesthetically complement the work. Their use amounted to unnecessary virtuosity that detracted from the music and performance. The complicated choreography only served to cloud the text, rather than underscoring it.

While both semaphore-style choreography and Australian sign language have merit and could be considered for future projects, there are more elegant and impactful ways to integrate them. For instance, semaphore could control industrial sounds, such as pitch-shifting the noise of airplane engines to reflect calls to close the Ukrainian airspace. Sign language could be used to make music for (and with) hearing impaired and deaf people that is catered to the technological and musical requirements of hearing aids.

6. CONCLUSIONS

The narrative of this work is, unfortunately, not unusual. Traumatic experiences are not merely internal or interpersonal; they engage the whole body and mind, directly impacting the amygdala and, thus, are challenging to express in words. The voice, an instrument of body and mind [32], offers timbres that provide context for semantic language concepts and knowledge. This piece encapsulates the gamut of psychological states which can arise from traumatic experiences. The use of and flexibility of the gesture controls pulls in the audience through familiarity with the conducting motions and the open-armed body posturing. The lyrics cover the before, during, and aftermath of traumatic experiences and the emotions that are proper and logical consequences of said incidents. As a piece of performative autoethnography and radical vulnerability[5], this is my life turned back onto and through the world as a mirror of society and an example of all too typical life narratives among (particularly and statistically) women. The lush chords and emotive performative content tap into the general audience connections through the music's songwriting style, presentation, and balladlike style.

7. FUTURE WORK

This work is part of a more extensive folio of doctoral works submitted in 2024. It spurred the development of a piece premiered in February 2024 in Melbourne for soprano and wearable electronics called *To Echoes and Lines* [37]. In this new work, I investigate simplicity as a mapping tenet to enable novice gestural performers to learn and gain confidence in electro-acoustic music and technology-based performance. This work addresses women's experience of aging in society, particularly that of queer people. The music is framed as a conversation between the electronics, a joyful rebellion of expectations, and the shedding of limitations. Furthermore, I am developing an algorithmic chordal piece for throat-singing techniques and wearable gesture interfaces.

[5] The practitioner reflects the world, political climate, personal values, and practice.

8. REFERENCES

[1] R. Nagar and R. Shirazi, "Radical Vulnerability," in *Keywords in Radical Geography: Antipode at 50*, First., USA: John Wiley & Sons, Ltd, 2019, pp. 236–242. doi: 10.1002/9781119558071.ch44.

[2] D. Lyon, S. Owen, M. Osborne, K. Blake, and B. Andrades, "Left / Write // Hook: A mixed method study of a writing and boxing workshop for survivors of childhood sexual abuse and trauma," *Int. J. Wellbeing*, vol. 10, no. 5, Art. no. 5, Dec. 2020, doi: doi.org/10.5502/ijw.v10i5.1505.

[3] S. W. Porges, "The polyvagal theory: New insights into adaptive reactions of the autonomic nervous system," *Cleve. Clin. J. Med.*, vol. 76, no. Suppl 2, pp. S86–S90, Apr. 2009, doi: 10.3949/ccjm.76.s2.17.

[4] B. van der Kolk, *The Body Keeps the Score: Mind, Brain and Body in the Transformation of Trauma*. UK: Penguin UK, 2014.

[5] A. Marschall, "The Four Fear Responses: Fight, Flight, Freeze, and Fawn," Verywell Mind. Accessed: Jul. 11, 2023. [Online]. Available: https://www.verywellmind.com/the-four-fear-responses-fight-flight-freeze-and-fawn-5205083

[6] R. Paredes, "Understanding Trauma: The 6 Types of Trauma Responses," Mindbetter. Accessed: Jul. 19, 2023. [Online]. Available: https://mindbetter.com/trauma-response-types/

[7] K. A. Gleiser, "Psychoanalytic Perspectives on Traumatic Repetition," *J. Trauma Dissociation*, vol. 4, no. 2, pp. 27–47, Mar. 2003, doi: 10.1300/J229v04n02_03.

[8] E. Levy-Gigi and G. Richter-Levin, "The hidden price of repeated traumatic exposure," *Stress*, vol. 17, no. 4, pp. 343–351, Jul. 2014, doi: 10.3109/10253890.2014.923397.

[9] C. Wilson, D. M. Pence, and L. Conradi, "Trauma-Informed Care," *Encyclopedia of Social Work*. National Association of Social Workers Press & Oxford University Press, UK, p. 1, Nov. 04, 2013. doi: 10.1093/acrefore/9780199975839.013.1063.

[10] J. Butler, "Rethinking Vulnerability and Resistance," in *Vulnerability in Resistance*, USA: Duke University Press, 2016, p. 348. Accessed: Apr. 27, 2023. [Online]. Available: https://doi.org/10.1215/9780822373490

[11] J. Butler, "Giving an Account of Oneself," *Diacritics*, vol. 31, no. 4, pp. 22–40, 2001.

[12] Geena Davis Institute, "The Geena Benchmark Report," Geena Davis Institute, USA, Gender in Media, Feb. 2019. Accessed: Aug. 14, 2023. [Online]. Available: https://seejane.org/wp-content/uploads/geena-benchmark-report-2007-2017-2-12-19.pdf

[13] R. Kahalon, O. Bareket, A. C. Vial, N. Sassenhagen, J. C. Becker, and N. Shnabel, "The Madonna-Whore Dichotomy Is Associated With Patriarchy Endorsement: Evidence From Israel, the United

States, and Germany," *Psychol. Women Q.*, vol. 43, no. 3, pp. 348–367, Sep. 2019, doi: 10.1177/0361684319843298.

[14] D. Lyon, C. Gaskin, and G. Everall, "writing + boxing = Left / Write // Hook," *TEXT J.*, vol. 26, no. Special 67, pp. 1–18, Aug. 2022, doi: 10.52086/001c.37824.

[15] S. Banet-Weiser, "Radical vulnerability: Feminism, victimhood and agency," in *Re-writing Women as Victims: From Theory to Practice*, First Edition., London, UK: Routledge, 2019, pp. 167–180. Accessed: Apr. 24, 2023. [Online]. Available: doi.org/10.4324/9781351043601

[16] P. Z, *Baggage Allowance*. 2010. Accessed: Nov. 13, 2023. [Installation: found objects with embedded sound and video]. Available: https://pamelaz.com/work/baggage-allowance-installation/

[17] I. Heap, *Bad Body Double*. in Ellipse. UK: Megaphonic, RCA Victor, 2009. Accessed: Oct. 11, 2018. [CD]. Available: https://open.spotify.com/track/2rkQtnknRZivK7saBryrjm

[18] I. Heap, *Hide and Seek*. in Speak for Yourself. UK: Megaphonic, RCA Victor, 2005. Accessed: Aug. 01, 2023. [CD]. Available: https://www.youtube.com/watch?v=UYIAfiVGluk

[19] M. Young, *Singing the Body Electric: The Human Voice and Sound Technology*. Routledge, 2016.

[20] T. Pratchett, *Shaking Hands with Death*. UK: Random House, 2015. [Online]. Available: https://www.terrypratchettbooks.com/books/shaking-hands-with-death/

[21] T. Spry, *Body, Paper, Stage: Writing and Performing Autoethnography*. California; USA: Routledge, 2011. Accessed: Apr. 07, 2020. [Online]. Available: http://ebookcentral.proquest.com/lib/unimelb/detail.action?docID=843865

[22] D. E. Reed-Danahay, Ed., *Auto/Ethnography: Rewriting the Self and the Social*. in Explorations in Anthropology. New York; USA: Oxford, 1997. Accessed: Sep. 13, 2019. [Online]. Available: https://content.ub.hu-berlin.de/monographs/toc/ethnologie/BV025182531.pdf

[23] MiMU Gloves LTD, "MiMU," Gestural Interface: Datagloves, 2010. Accessed: Oct. 18, 2021. [Online]. Available: https://mimugloves.com/

[24] MiMU Gloves LTD, "Glover." MI.MU Gloves Ltd, UK, 2022.

[25] Cycling '74, "Max." Cycling '74, USA, 2018. [macOS]. Available: https://cycling74.com/

[26] Ableton, "Ableton Live." Ableton, Germany, 2021.

[27] Apple INC., "Final Cut Pro." Apple Inc., California; USA, 2023. Accessed: Sep. 03, 2023. [macOS]. Available: https://www.apple.com/au/final-cut-pro/

[28] E. Jessop, "The Vocal Augmentation and Manipulation Prosthesis (VAMP): A Conducting-Based Gestural Controller for Vocal Performance," in *Proceedings of the international conference on new interfaces for musical expression*, Pittsburgh, PA, United States: NIME, 2009, pp. 256–259. [Online]. Available: http://www.nime.org/archives/

[29] R. James, *Resilience & Melancholy: Pop Music, Feminism, Neoliberalism*. USA: Zero Books, 2015. [Online]. Available: https://archive.org/details/resiliencemelanc0000jame_x6n7

[30] S. Nercessian and iZotope Inc, "VocalSynth 2." iZotope, Inc, Massachusetts, United States, 2018. [VST]. Available: https://www.izotope.com/vocalsynth

[31] T. Wishart, *On Sonic Art*, New and rev. Ed., vol. 12. in Contemporary music studies, vol. 12. Amsterdam: Harwood Academic Publishers, 1996.

[32] A. Cavarero, *For More Than One Voice: Toward a Philosophy of Vocal Expression*. USA: Stanford University Press, 2005.

[33] E. Hatfield, R. L. Rapson, and Y.-C. L. Le, "Emotional contagion and empathy," in *The social neuroscience of empathy*, in Social neuroscience. , Cambridge, MA, US: Boston Review, 2009, pp. 19–30. doi: 10.7551/mitpress/9780262012973.003.0003.

[34] S. Davies, "Music to Listener Emotional Contagion," in *The emotional power of music: Multidisciplinary perspectives on musical arousal, expression, and social control*, T. Cochrane, B. Fantini, and K. R. Scherer, Eds., in Series in affective science. , UK: Oxford University Press, 2013, p. 12. [Online]. Available: https://doi.org/10.1093/acprof:oso/9780199654888.003.0013

[35] J. H. Kim and U. Seifert, "Embodiment: The body in algorithmic sound generation," *Contemp. Music Rev.*, vol. 25, no. 1–2, pp. 139–149, Feb. 2006, doi: 10.1080/07494460600647592.

[36] J. J. Sykes, "Tools and peripersonal space: an enactive account of bodily space," *Phenomenol. Cogn. Sci.*, vol. 23, no. 1, p. 21, Mar. 2023, doi: 10.1007/s11097-023-09903-4.

[37] S. Rose, *To Echoes and Lines*. 2024.

This page intentionally left blank.

Multiplayer Performance Scores for VR

David Kim-Boyle
The University of Sydney
david.kim-boyle@sydney.edu.au

ABSTRACT

The mid-twentieth century witnessed radical experiments with musical notation aimed at exploring open musical forms that granted performers greater agency and interpretive freedom. In this paper, the author discusses the creative and technical process behind the development of a multiplayer, virtual reality adaptation of a work from this period, Earle Brown's 4 Systems (1952-53). The expressive affordances of VR are explored and solutions to various technical challenges including those presented by multiplayer networked performance in VR space are described. The paper concludes with a brief overview of other VR adaptations currently in development.

1. INTRODUCTION

The radical experiments with musical notation explored in the mid-twentieth century by composers such as Cage, Brown, Cardew and others were fundamentally predicated on the desire to explore the musical possibilities of open, fluid musical forms which afforded greater musical agency and interpretive freedom to performers. [1] The abstract notational language often employed in works of the period invited performers to engage with the visual elements of the score in highly personalized ways predicated on a heightened visual sensibility and awareness of how the spatial presentation of symbols, typography, and graphic structures might be sounded and correlated to musical gestures. In many ways, therefore, the notational presentation of such works went well beyond the traditional prescriptive function of traditional music notation.

Moreover, the medium itself upon which such scores were inscribed often became an element intrinsically connected to the aesthetic and compositional questions being explored. In the scores for Cage's *Fontana Mix* (1958) and Takemitsu's *Corona for Pianist(s)* (1962) for example, the use of printed transparencies afforded correlations between inscribed notational depth and musical structure, [2] while the use of mobile elements within the score of Stockhausen's *Refrain* (1959), for example, connected physical manipulations of the score itself to musical form. The musical possibilities of reactive scores responsive to performance and even audience agency has continued to be a topic of creative exploration until today. [3]

While the aesthetic questions that drove much of the experiments with musical notation in the 1950s have remained and have become increasingly active areas of investigation, [4, 5] the rapid evolution and accessibility of mixed reality technologies, immersive visualizations, and reactive multiplayer networked environments have opened exciting new ways in which composers can revisit some of these themes. This paper delves into some of these possibilities through a detailed examination of an adaptation of Earle Brown's *4 Systems* (1952-53) for pianist and virtual reality participants. The project is part of a broader series of XR adaptations of classic open form works currently in development including Brown's *December 1952*, Cage's *Fontana Mix*, and Wolff's *Jasper* (1991) where the scores are presented as interactive virtual reality instruments.

2. VR ADAPTATION

2.1 4 Systems

Earle Brown's *4 Systems* (1952-53) was written for pianist David Tudor and is part of a larger series of works named *FOLIO* which feature graphic scores the most well known of which is undoubtedly *December 1952* (1952). The score of *4 Systems* presents the pianist with a single page of four systems upon which black, rectangular blocks are inscribed, see Figure 1. The pianist is afforded considerable interpretive freedom although Brown does provide the following helpfulnote - "May be played in any sequence, either side up, at any tempo. The continuous lines from far left to far right define the outer limits of the keyboard. Thickness may indicate dynamics of clusters." [6]

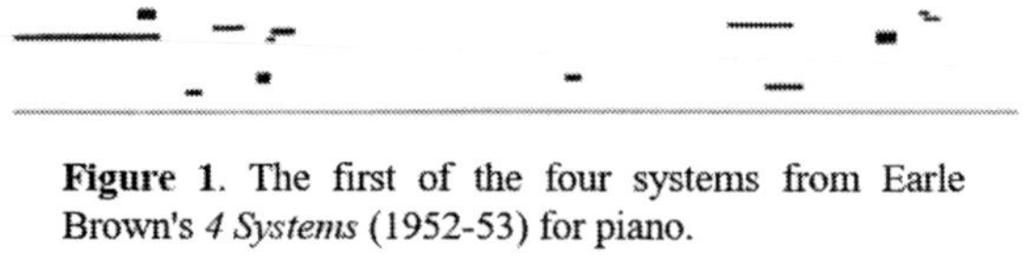

Figure 1. The first of the four systems from Earle Brown's *4 Systems* (1952-53) for piano.

The transformation of *4 Systems* into a multiplayer, interactive VR performance significantly broadens the interpretive scope of the work and was motivated by Brown's prefatory notes to *FOLIO* where he identifies two approaches for how notation might help support open musical forms predicated on performer agency. While the notes are fragmentary, Brown writes of - "...a mobile score subject to physical manipulation of its components, resulting in an unknown number of different, integral, and "valid" realizations." and later of "a *conceptually* "mobile" approach to basically fixed graphic elements; subject to an infinite number of performance realizations through the involvement of the performer's immediate responses to the intentionally ambiguous graphic stimuli relative to the conditions of performance involvement." (italics in original) [7]

The musical possibilities for how such a VR adaptation might be realized are enormous and present a range of unique technical challenges. The author's adaptation extends his previous research in immersive, [8] reactive scores [3] and is built on the following performance framework. A 3-dimensional score is situated within a VR space and interpreted by a pianist wearing an Oculus Quest 3.

Multiple users (clients) connect from anywhere around the world to the VR space in which the score is presented and manipulate via hand tracking the rectangular blocks that comprise it, see Figure 2. These manipulations include spatial relocation via grabbing, and transformation of object sizes via scaling of the distance between thumb and index finger. The size of the objects is correlated to musical pitches - larger objects correspond to lower pitches while smaller objects correspond to higher pitches. These pitches are reproduced using pre-recorded piano samples, which are activated when objects collide or when a user "pinches" them within the VR space.

Figure 2. Manipulations of the score in virtual space. The red lines represent raycasts attached to the hands of a user.

For the pianist, the score is presented in what is known as "pass-through mode" which allows the real-world to be seen underneath the virtual, refer to Figure 3, thus allowing the pianist to maintain sightlines with the keyboard.[1] The ability to include video imagery from the Quest's built-in camera was only recently made available via a significant upgrade to the Meta Oculus SDK.

Figure 3. The VR score of the first of the *4 Systems* (1952-53) for piano presented from the perspective of the pianist with the Quest 3 in pass-through mode.

The objects comprising the score are subject to physics in the virtual world in which they are presented such that they spin and move subject to gravity and inertia settings. The sounds triggered by the virtual participants are broadcast back to the performance space and the interpretation of the pianist is streamed to all clients within the room. While the musical performance foregrounds the live interpretation of the pianist, the manipulation of the score and its sounded results is itself another mode of performance. A full schematic of the performance framework is presented in Figure 4.

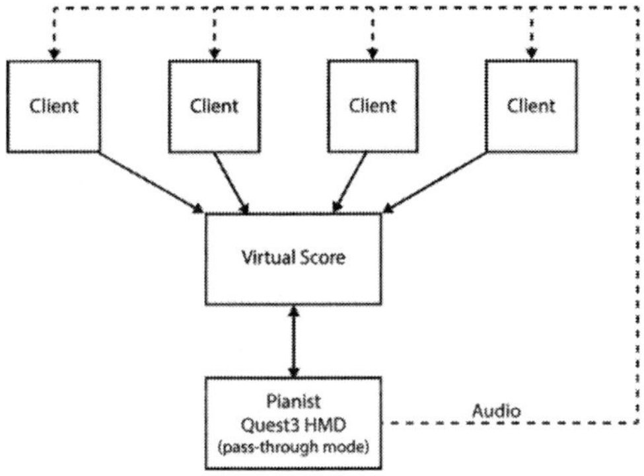

Figure 4. Performance framework for the VR adaptation of *4 Systems* (1952-53).

To the extent that such an adaptation is still able to be identified as the work *4 Systems* is an ontological question that this paper will not pursue. Nevertheless, the author has strived to ensure thematic, aesthetic, and musical continuity with Brown's original conception of the work even though the various expressive affordances of multiplauyer VR have expanded their scope significantly.

2.2 Development Framework and Hardware

The technical capabilities of VR head-mounted devices (HMDs) have accelerated markedly over the past few years and their affordability has made them increasingly

[1] Prior to the release of the Oculus Quest 3, pass-through mode on the Quest HMDs was greyscale and exceptionally low resolution (800x600), effectively making it unsuitable for musical applications such as this.

available to a growing community of users. The development of *4 Systems* was specifically designed to leverage the technical affordances of one the most popular series of HMDs, the Oculus Quest, with the Unity3D platform used for application development. A variety of SDKs were installed within the Unity environment to enable Oculus integration (Meta XR Core) [9] and multiplayer functionality (Photon Fusion and Photon Voice). [10]

2.3 Hand Tracking

A striking feature of the Quest HMD, considerably improved with a late-2023 update to the Meta Interaction SDK, is the capacity to track hand movements and the spatial positions of individual joints and digits. This facilitates a more natural form of interaction with objects presented in virtual space than the device's hardware controllers.

In *4* Systems, participants are able to "grab" and reposition score objects. Much as in the real world, however, virtual hands cannot in themselves interact with objects at a distance. For the *4 Systems* adaptation, two different approaches were developed to address this problem. In the first, raycasts were attached to the hands which are used to target distant objects. In the second, the boundaries established when launching the application are changed to "Roomscale" so that users can physically wander over the distant objects and manipulate them directly. Such wandering is by default not available when an application is launched for obvious safety reasons.

A fundamental technical constraint of hand-tracking lies in its capability to precisely measure rapid gestures. [11] In the context of *4 Systems* this was not a significant issue as the manipulation of score objects was a task deliberately designed to require slow, continuous movements. A secondary consideration, however, proved to be more critical. Hand-tracking on the Quest, and hand-tracking in general, requires adequate lighting conditions for optimal performance. While most domestic lighting environments in which the research was tested proved adequate, darker settings more typical of dedicated performance spaces presented some challenges. Finally, the correlation of hand gestures, namely the pinching of thumb and index finger, to the triggering of audio cues and resizing of score objects naturally required that wrists and digits be visible to the front-facing camera of the Quest.

2.4 Multiplayer Networking

An essential feature of the VR adaptation of *4 Systems* is its multiplayer functionality which enables clients to connect from any location in the world and manipulate score objects. To achieve this, the project utilized the *Photon Fusion 2* SDK. *Photon Fusion 2* supports various network topologies with the "Shared" model the optimal choice for *4 Systems*, see Figure 6. In this topology, the room in which the virtual score is presented retains state authority over objects, each of which have a unique Network ID when instantiated. State authority is transferred to clients if they are manipulating an object which allows all connected clients to view transformations as they occur. The room is hosted on a Photon server which has a fixed region to enable multiplayer interaction.

Remote procedure calls are sent to the server when an action by a client needs to be distributed to all connected clients. In *4 Systems*, such RPCs are made when score objects collide or are "pinched" in both cases of which, audio cues need to be played on all connected HMDs. The inherent latency of such calls is affected by geographical distance from the server. For the testing of *4 Systems*, the application was hosted on a server based in Singapore with connected clients in Sydney (2 clients) and Marseille (1 client).[2] As of writing Photon Fusion applications can be hosted on servers in fifteen regions around the world with a maximum number of clients able to simultaneously connect to a room in the hundreds.[3] During testing, network performance was measured, using Photon network statistical tools. The consumed bandwidth per client, averaging around 710 bytes per second, and average number of packets in and out (ca. 30 and ca. 65 per second) were low enough to minimize the impact of packet loss on performance and usability.

The issue of latency has historically been the core technical challenge of network-based musical performances, [12] and various artists have delved into its artistic potential, exploring how the inherent delays and temporal dynamics of network communication can help shape the overall aesthetic of musical works. [13] For any musical performances that hinge on the precise synchronization of event, latency indeed poses a formidable challenge with the slightest delay disrupting the rhythmic integrity of a piece whereas in projects like *4 Systems* the need for strict synchronization of musical events is notably absent. Instead, these works embrace a more fluid approach to performance, where the timing and sequencing of musical elements is open to interpretation, mitigating the impact of network latency and allowing for greater spontaneity in artistic expression.

2.5 Audio Streaming

In *4 Systems* the performance of the live pianist is captured in real time and streamed to all connected clients through the *Photon Voice* SDK. While this SDK was originally designed to facilitate live voice chat between players within a multiplayer gaming environment it can nevertheless support chat at 48kHz with a bitrate up to 512kbps. To ensure an optimal audio capture of the live pianist, the instrument is miked with a single, high-quality condenser microphone connected to an external audio interface. This interface was in turn connected to a laptop running a PC build of the *4 Systems* application with audio settings of 48kHz and 512kbps. Anecdotal evaluations of the audio performance, as heard through the internal loudspeakers of the Quest

[2] As of writing, Photon Fusion applications can be hosted on servers in fifteen regions around the world.

[3] This is a theoretical upper limit with most multiplayer applications typically numbering between two and sixteen clients.

HMD reported the quality as satisfactory although this this is somewhat contingent on the frequency response of the internal Quest 2 loudspeakers with a significant roll off below 150Hz and above 5kHz. [14] External headphones are one straightforward way in which the audio quality can be improved.

FUTURE DEVELOPMENT

Various technical enhancements to the *4 Systems* adaptation are currently underway. One significant improvement involves the inclusion of avatars for each participant in the virtual room. This feature allows for easy identification of the number of partcipants present, and for coordination to be more strategically planned. In its current implementation, it is possible for participants to unintentionally manipulate the same score object simultaneously which is problematic.

As previously noted, the VR adaptation of *4 Systems* is one of a series of multiplayer VR adaptations of classic open-form works from the 1950s that the author is developing. These include the aforementioned *December 1952*, which features a score similar in design to *4 Systems*, Cage's *Fontana Mix* (1958), Wolff's *Jasper* (1991), and excerpts from Cardew's *Treatise* (1963-67). This work is motivated by a fascination with the musical and aesthetic concepts explored in these historically important works and a desire to consider how these themes might be expanded through the expressive affordances of multiplayer VR.

CONCLUSIONS

This paper has explored the creative possibilities and technical challenges involved in translating Earle Brown's experimental graphic scores into an interactive VR experience, showcasing the potential of immersive technologies to reimagine traditional musical forms and performance practices. The project was motivated by a fascination with the aesthetic themes embodied within seminal open-form works of the 1950s which challenge traditional concepts of musical composition and performance.

The VR adaptation of *4 Systems* builds upon this legacy, offering performers and participants unprecedented levels of agency and engagement. Through hand tracking, spatial manipulation, and multiplayer networking, users are invited to actively shape the sonic and visual landscape of the performance, blurring the boundaries between composer, performer, and audience. Through leveraging the expressive and technical affordances of VR, the project endeavors to explore how the aesthetic themes of these works can be recast and extemded within a contemporary context. The technical framework outlined in this paper provides valuable insights into the challenges and opportunities inherent in such adaptations, each aspect of which required careful consideration and innovation.

Multiplayer VR introduces exciting new possibilities for collective improvisation and spontaneous creativity and offers new modes of musical performance. The fluidity and interactivity afforded by the technology offers a fertile ground for experimentation, enabling new modes of artistic expression and collaboration to emerge. In doing so, the project not only honors the legacy of these groundbreaking works but also charts new pathways for creative expression.

Acknowledgments

Many thanks to Dr. Jonathan Bell (PRISM Lab, Marseille) for his helpful suggestions and testing of the work, and Sébastien Poivre from the Photon development team for his technical advice and expertise in helping implement the multiplayer functionality of the work.

REFERENCES

[1] D. Behrman, "What Indeterminate Notation Determines," *Perspectives of New Music*, vol. 3, no. 2, 1965, pp. 58-72. https://doi.org/10.2307/832504

[2] D. Kim-Boyle. The 3D Score. In Proceedings of the 2017 International Conference on Technologies for Music Notation and Representation (TENOR 2017) (A Coruña, Spain May 24-26).

[3] D. Kim-Boyle. Reactive Scores. In Proceedings of the 2023 International Conference on Technologies for Music Notation and Representation (TENOR 2023) (Boston, U.S.A. May 15-17).

[4] https://network.tenor-conference.org/

[5] C. Vear, *The Digital* Score - *Musicianship, Creativity and Innovation*. Routledge, 2019.

[6] E. Brown, *4 Systems*, AMP/G. Schirmer, 1952.

[7] E. Brown, "Prefatory Note," Available at https://earle-brown.org/wp-content/uploads/Folio-and-Four-Systems-Prefatory-Note.pdf

[8] D. Kim-Boyle. Immersive Musical Notations in AR/VR. In Proceedings of the 2023 International Computer Music Conference (Shenzhen, China October 15-20).

[9] https://developer.oculus.com/documentation/unity/unity-package-manager/

[10] https://www.photonengine.com/fusion

[11] M. Oudah, A. Al-Naji, and J. Chahl, "Hand Gesture Recognition Based on Computer Vision: A Review of Techniques," *Journal of Imaging*, vol. 6, no. 8, 2020. https://doi.org/10.3390/jimaging6080073

[12] C. Bartlette and M. F. Bocko, "Effect of Network Latency on Interactive Musical Performance," *Music Perception*, vol. 24, no. 1, pp. 49-62, September 2006. https://doi.org/10.1525/mp.2006.24.1.49

[13] A. Tanaka and K. T. Toeplitz, "Global String," *Leonardo*, vol. 35, no. 5, p. 536, October 2002.

[14] J. Nichter, "Oculus Quest 2 Speaker Impulse Responses." http://jeffnichter.weebly.com/ (Accessed Jan. 18, 2024).

The Robo-Cajon: An Example of Live Performance with Musical Robotics

Austin Franklin
Mälardalen University
austin.franklin@mdu.se

ABSTRACT

The Robo-Cajon is a robotic musical performer capable of real-time improvisation and live performance with a human performer. It is a wooden cajon, or box-shaped percussion instrument played with the hands, mounted with two push/pull solenoids that receives input from a separate cajon mounted with piezo contact microphones performed by a human. Rhythmic data from the human performer is first classified using a Multi-Layer Perceptron (MLP) and a Hidden Markov Model (HMM) is used for prediction and generating rhythmic patterns based on this prior classification. The Robo-Cajon demonstrates a novel and lightweight approach to human-computer interaction and real-time applications for various machine learning algorithms. The Robo-Cajon was realized using Max and Arduino.

1. INTRODUCTION

Musical robotics is a field which explores the intersection and relationship between creativity and robotics. The potential for machines to express creativity is important to the field of robotics and AI, but it is especially relevant for machines that replicate human activities that are generally described as creative, such as music making [1]. Humans are especially good at predicting, synchronizing, and harmonizing amongst rapidly changing environments in real-time, while the challenges faced by current robotics architecture to detect, interpret, and respond quickly make these tasks difficult. Music making is a well-structured setting for determining a robots ability to perform these tasks, and the implications of high performance are applicable throughout the field of robotics [2].

The author presents *The Robo-Cajon*, a robotic musical performer capable of real-time improvisation and live performance with a human performer. [1] Capable of detecting and interpreting rhythms from a human performer on a separate cajon using a Multi-Layer Perceptron as described by J. Bullock and A. Momeni [3], *The Robo-Cajon* generates new rhythmic sequences in real-time using a Hidden Markov Model at a fixed tempo predetermined by the human performer in the Global Transport in Max. A Bluetooth enabled foot pedal is introduced that allows the human performer additional agency over robotic performer and can be used to retrain the MLP and HMM at any time.

[1] Demo video available at https://www.youtube.com/watch?v=mJ5rTQk3Uct=115s

2. RELATED WORK

Several basic types of "beater" or "mallet" based robotic instruments were explored and used as the mechanical basis for *The Robo-Cajon*, such as **Dartron** [4] and the **MahaDeviBot** [5] seen in Figure 1. As a proof of concept, the *The Robo-Cajon* was designed without the use of mallet based rotational motion in favor of the linear motion provided by the solenoid plunger itself.

Figure 1. *MahaDeviBot*

In 1999 Trimpin created an installation entitled **Conloninpurple**, which is "a 7-octave instrument with wooden bars and metal resonators" [6]. Each bar is excited using a push/pull solenoid which strikes the bar when a specific MIDI message is received (Figure 2). It is this simple mechanical framework that allows for easy experimentation and portability with *The Robo-Cajon*. Routing MIDI messages to trigger a hardware controller is also inherently slower than feeding analog signals to solenoids via Arduino.

A number of systems included in the category of interactive music have been developed to enable human-machine improvisation. Examples utilizing software to interpret the gestures of human performers and produce synthesized sounds include **Cypher** [7], **Voyager** [8], and **The Continuator** [9]. Other systems interpret the gestures of human performers and produce sound using physical electro-mechanical instruments. These include **Haile** and **Shimon** [10] seen in Figure 3, both of which exhibit musical expression through the embodiment of musical actions [11]. *The Robo-Cajon* implements a software and hardware component and is positioned somewhere in between these two categories.

Figure 2. *Conloninpurple*

Figure 3. *Shimon*

3. INTERACTIVE DESIGN

The design for *The Robo-Cajon* is intentionally minimal (Figure 4) as a prototype design that is cost effective, using only two cajons and a Bluetooth enabled foot pedal. [2] The human performer first sets the tempo in Max using the Global Transport, performs on their cajon in that tempo, and uses the foot pedal to initialize training on the second cajon of all rhythmic material performed since the last foot pedal trigger. The addition of the footpedal originally made developing and testing *The Robo-Cajon* easier, and was decidedly kept due to its ease of use. The robotic performer begins improvising on this material instantly and can be retrained at any time by the human performer. This gives the human performer some degree of control over the robotic performer, allowing them to shape the overall phrasing and musical structure.

Both cajons are identical in size with the robotic performer being custom built using the dimensions from the human performer (12x12x17.25 inches). [3] The solenoids on the robotic performer are secured with a brace that is set approximately 1/2 inch from the front face. One solenoid is positioned at the center of the brace to produce a lower sounding pitch mimicking the bass sound of the human performer while the other is positioned near the edge to mimic the snare sound (Figure 4). This brace holds the

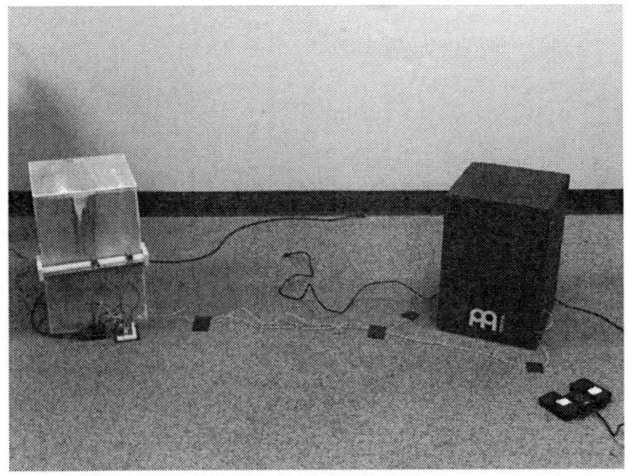

Figure 4. *The Robo-Cajon*

solenoids in this position and at this distance to insure that each strike from the plunger results in an optimal and consistent sound.

4. TECHNICAL DETAILS

The software component for *The Robo-Cajon* utilizes Arduino to read from analog pins and write to digital pins, and Max to interpret this data in a way that can be classified and used to generate new sequences. Each of these components are described in more detail below.

4.1 Arduino

The Robo-Cajon uses an Adafruit METRO 328 Arduino-Compatible board [4] to act as a bridge between both cajons and Max (Figure 5). It takes the analog pin values from two piezo contact microphones and sends them to Max using the 'serial' object. Concurrently, Arduino receives values back from Max and uses them to determine which digital pin to set as high or low. The state of these digital pins control the state of two 12V push/pull solenoids, where high equals extended and low equals retracted. The most efficient way to control the state of two digital pins simultaneously in Arduino is with a switch case:

```
switch(pinValue) {
    case 0;
        digitalWrite(solenoid1, LOW);
        break;
    case 1:
        digitalWrite(solenoid1, HIGH);
        break;
    case 2:
        digitalWrite(solenoid2, LOW);
        break;
    case 3:
        digitalWrite(solenoid2, HIGH);
        break;
}
```

[2] https://www.sweetwater.com/store/detail/Duo200–airturn-duo-200-transmitter-with-2-pedals?utm$_{s}ource = googleutm_{m}edium = organicpla$

[3] https://www.amazon.com/Meinl-Percussion-Internal-Europe-Baltic-BC1NTWR/dp/B00LJP78Q4/ref=psdc$_1 1972491_t 2_B 0799BM6KN$

[4] https://www.adafruit.com/product/2488

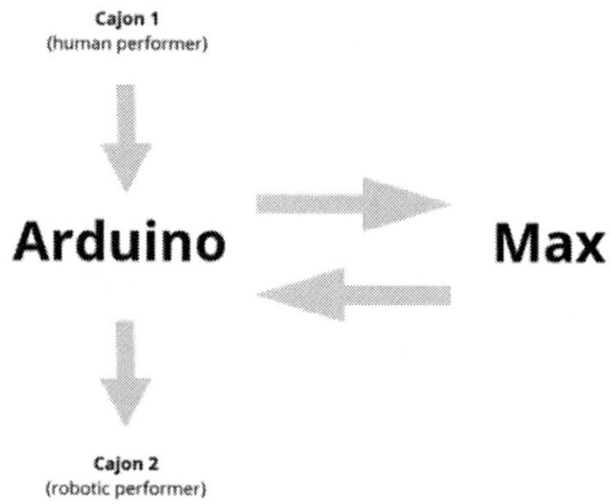

Figure 5. Diagram of *The Robo-Cajon*

4.2 In Max

The piezo values are sent to Max using the 'serial' object and are used to trigger a bang when a threshold has been met. The time (in ms) between bangs is then taken and scaled from an existing tempo first set in the Global Transport to a normalized range between 0-1 (Figure 6). The specific piezo contact microphone is also recorded to indicate whether a slap, tone, or both were played. This list of numbers containing the piezo contact microphone and normalized length of the note are then classified using a Multi-Layer Perceptron Neural Network developed by Ben Smith as part of the ml.star package [12].

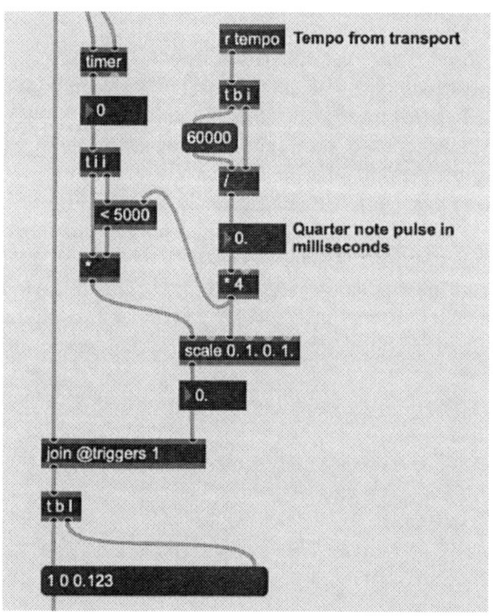

Figure 6. Scaling tempo from the Global Transport

Training data for the Multi-Layer Perceptron only includes note lengths shorter than a whole note and longer than a 1/16th note. The difference between the normalized note lengths shorter than this is so small that it often leads to incorrect classification if not performing perfectly in time (0.041667 of a bar for 1/16th note triplets and 0.03125 for 1/32nd notes) [13]. Two additional training sets are also used to classify and discard note lengths that are larger and smaller than whole notes and 1/16th notes. Once classifications are made, the floating point values are rounded, sorted by slap (1), tone (2), or both (3), and the correct classifications are selected using the 'select' object. All other classifications are discarded and return an error message to the console (Figure 7).

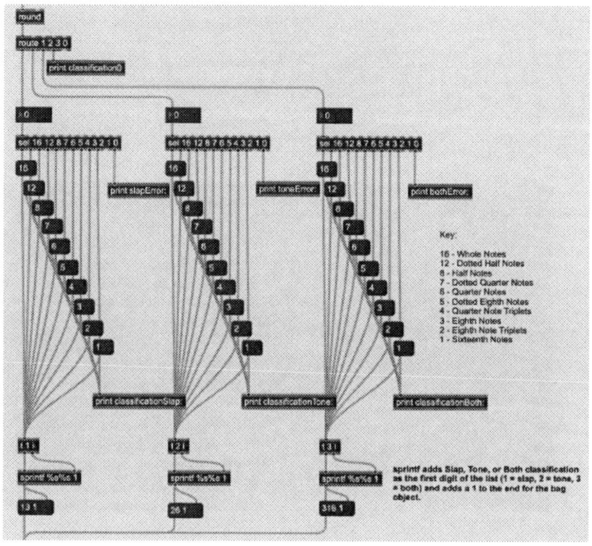

Figure 7. Rounding and Selecting Classifications in Max

All classifications are then stored in the 'bag' object. This object stores a collection of values and dumps them when triggered. Using the Bluetooth foot pedal, the human performer can trigger and dump the contents of the bag into a Hidden Markov Model from the ml.star package [12]. Once dumped, the Hidden Markov Model is immediately trained and begins generating new rhythmic sequences based on the data. These new sequences are then scaled back from normalized values to their corresponding lengths (in ms), originally determined by the Global Transport, before being sent back to 'serial' object to control the solenoids.

5. FUTURE WORK

While the interaction and improvisation between the robotic and human performer is straight-forward, it does require prior knowledge of how the 'bag' and foot pedal collectively stores, dumps, and trains models. Future work could include devising methods for training and interpreting data automatically, such as syncing dumping and training to a downbeat that occurs every N number of measures or beats. Future work could also include BPM estimation algorithms that could set the Global Transport tempo automatically, which would allow musically and non-musically trained users to simply play and allow the robotic performer to self-adjust to a wide variety of tempos and rhythms. The touch or fingers pressure (or amplitude) of the human performer could also be measured and used to control various parameters making the Robo-Cajon more expressive. The addition of instruments (hardware or software) could provide other interesting areas for experimentation, and other parameters could be classified and used to control audio synthesis or non-linear systems. For example, pitched instruments such as a disklavier could be used and MIDI data related to pitch and velocity could be used to train an MLP.

6. CONCLUSIONS

The Robo-Cajon is a robotic musical 'performer' capable of real-time improvisation and live performance with a human performer. It uses Arduino to receive piezo contact microphone analog values and control two push/pull solenoids and Max to detect and interpret rhythms and generate new rhythmic sequences using a Multi-Layer Perceptron and Hidden Markov Model. *The Robo-Cajon* demonstrates a novel and lightweight approach to human-computer interaction and real-time applications for various machine learning algorithms.

7. REFERENCES

[1] S. Kemper, "Locating Creativity in Differing Approaches to Musical Robotics," *Frontiers in Robotics and AI*, vol. 8, p. 52, 2021. [Online]. Available: https://www.frontiersin.org/article/10.3389/frobt.2021.647028

[2] C. Crick, M. Munz, and B. Scassellati, "Synchronization in social tasks: Robotic drumming," in *ROMAN 2006-The 15th IEEE international symposium on robot and human interactive communication*. IEEE, 2006, pp. 97–102.

[3] J. Bullock and A. Momeni, "Ml.Lib: Robust, Cross-Platform, Open-Source Machine Learning for Max and Pure Data," in *Proceedings of the International Conference on New Interfaces for Musical Expression*, ser. NIME 2015. Baton Rouge, Louisiana, USA: The School of Music and the Center for Computation and Technology (CCT), Louisiana State University, 2015, p. 265–270.

[4] A. Kapur and M. Darling, "A Pedagogical Paradigm for Musical Robotics." in *NIME*, 2010, pp. 162–165.

[5] A. Kapur, A. Eigenfeldt, C. Bahn, and W. Schloss, "Collaborative Composition For Musical Robots," *Journal of Science and Technology of the Arts*, vol. 1, 05 2009.

[6] A. Kapur, "A History of robotic Musical Instruments," in *ICMC*, 2005.

[7] R. Rowe, *Interactive music systems: machine listening and composing*. MIT press, 1992.

[8] G. E. Lewis, "Too many notes: Computers, complexity and culture in voyager," *Leonardo Music Journal*, vol. 10, pp. 33–39, 2000.

[9] F. Pachet, "The continuator: Musical interaction with style," *Journal of New Music Research*, vol. 32, no. 3, pp. 333–341, 2003.

[10] G. Weinberg and S. Driscoll, "The interactive robotic percussionist-new developments in form, mechanics, perception and interaction design," in *2007 2nd ACM/IEEE International Conference on Human-Robot Interaction (HRI)*. IEEE, 2007, pp. 97–104.

[11] S. Kemper and S. Barton, "Mechatronic Expression: Reconsidering Expressivity in Music for Robotic Instruments," 06 2018.

[12] B. D. Smith and G. E. Garnett, "Unsupervised Play: Machine Learning Toolkit for Max," in *NIME*, 2012.

[13] L. Noriega, "Multilayer perceptron tutorial," *School of Computing. Staffordshire University*, 2005.

Collaboration Between Robots, Interfaces and Humans: Practice-Based and Audience Perspectives

Anna Savery
University of Technology Sydney
anna.Savery@uts.edu.au

Richard Savery
Macquarie University
richard.savery@mq.edu.au

ABSTRACT

This paper provides an analysis of a mixed-media experimental musical work that explores the integration of human musical interaction with a newly developed interface for the violin, manipulated by an improvising violinist, interactive visuals, a robotic drummer and an improvised synthesised orchestra. We first present a detailed technical overview of the systems involved including the design and functionality of each component. We then conduct a practice-based review examining the creative processes and artistic decisions underpinning the work, focusing on the challenges and breakthroughs encountered during its development. Through this introspective analysis, we uncover insights into the collaborative dynamics between the human performer and technological agents, revealing the complexities of blending traditional musical expressiveness with artificial intelligence and robotics. To gauge public reception and interpretive perspectives, we conducted an online survey, sharing a video of the performance with a diverse audience. The feedback collected from this survey offers valuable viewpoints on the accessibility, emotional impact, and perceived artistic value of the work. Respondents' reactions underscore the transformative potential of integrating advanced technologies in musical performance, while also highlighting areas for further exploration and refinement.

1. INTRODUCTION

In music technology research, collaboration between independently developed new interfaces and robotic musicianship remains a relatively under-explored domain [1]. Despite the transformative potential, collaborations within these areas are infrequent, possibly due to the challenges inherent in merging disparate technological systems and the often limited resources allocated for such interdisciplinary endeavors. In work on new musical interfaces 78% of practitioners fulfil the role of designer, composer and performer [2].

However a key component of musical creation and appreciation lies within communal activity—ensemble performances, composer-performer collaborations, and the shared experiences between performers and their audiences [3]. This inherent collectivity in music poses unique challenges within the context of new music technologies, where the integration of diverse technologies is not always straightforward, and the development of music for new technological mediums can be particularly complex.

The introduction of novel interfaces and robotic musicians into traditional performance settings raises questions regarding their impact on both performers and audiences. How do performers adapt to and integrate their technologies into the practice of others, and how does the audience perceive and engage with these technologically augmented performances? This paper aims to develop new understanding into these questions by exploring a case study on integration of robotic musicianship and innovative interface design within a mixed-media experimental music framework.

This paper describes and analyzes a specific experimental musical performance that integrates a novel violin interface, human and AI improvisation, interactive visuals, and robotics (see Figure 1). This grouping offers a unique area to explore the tension between traditional and technological modalities in music. Our documentation and discussions aim to dissect these dynamics, shedding light on the challenges and inherent potential in integrating cutting-edge technology with human artistry in musical performance. Our analysis is grounded in the case study provided by the referenced performance, serving as a detailed example of the broader implications of technology in the arts.

We start with a technical description of each system, detailing the design and implementation of *Keirzo*, the robotic musician, followed by a breakdown of the violin interface and interactive visuals developed for this piece. In our description, we examine both, the hardware and software parameters of each technology, highlighting the intention behind their development and explaining their functionalities. We then present our views on what we consider to be significant discussion points associated with this practice-led research project. These points include our perspectives on embodiment and disembodiment of sound, human musician interaction with a robotic musician collaborator, staging and physicality of the referenced work and strategies for designing the visualisation.

The final section of this paper presents an analysis of our piece from an audience perspective, with data derived from an online study conducted using Prolific. Participants were asked to view a video of the performance with no prompt and then described their reactions. Audience perspectives from our survey predominantly echoed our own discussion points as well as providing fresh insight and view points which will likely influence and shape our future composi-

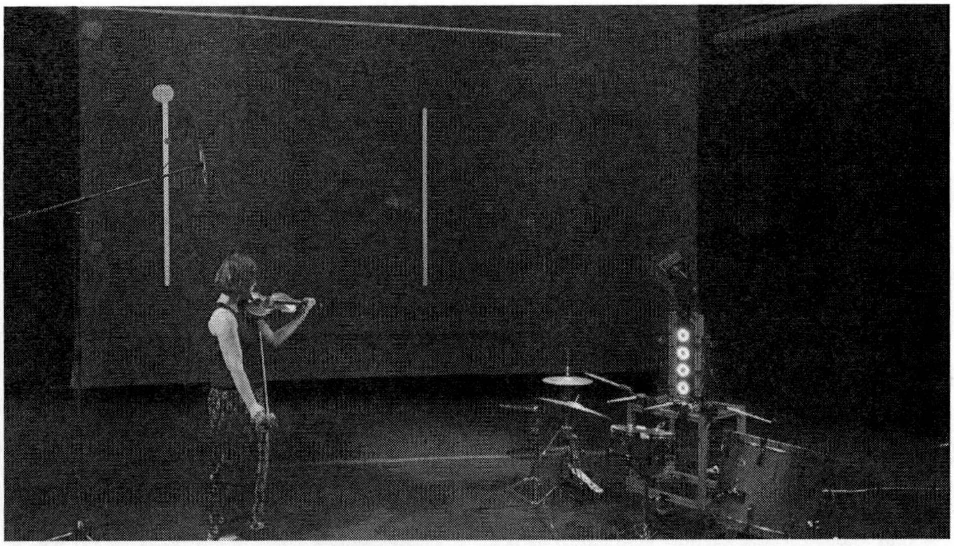

Figure 1. Performance of the combined work

tions. One of the key takeaways is the importance in audience accessibility and education when presenting new experimental works, specifically mixed-media pieces involving robotics and AI, where audience members may experience feelings of prejudice and hostility unless full transparency is displayed. After analysing the survey data, we have come to the conclusion that incorporating these strategies into future compositions will result in better ways of communicating artistic intentions and create a more inclusive space for audiences unfamiliar with new technologies.

A demonstration video can be seen online. [1]

2. RELATED WORK

2.1 Instrument Augmentation

Bowed string instruments have been extensively enhanced with a wide range of sensor-based technologies [4]. The *Hyperinstruments* research project, founded by Tod Machover 1981 [5] has produced a series of augmented instruments aimed at extending an existing skill set of an expert practitioner through sophisticated gesture analysis and bespoke software environments [6, 7]. Notable projects include the *Hypercello*, developed for Yo-Yo Ma's performance of Machover's *Begin Again Again...* [8], the *Hyperviolin*, originally developed for Ani Kavafian [4] followed by a more recent version, updated in association with Joshua Bell [9]. Both versions used iterations of Young's *Hyperbow* [10], with embedded sensors allowing real-time gesture and bow stroke analysis.

Kimura's *Augmented Violin Glove* [11] builds on the *Hyperinstruments* research by incorporating gesture analysis technology into a custom designed glove. Built in collaboration with IRCAM researchers, Kimura's *Augmented Violin Glove* allows an expert violinist to extend their creativity using a non-invasive approach [11]. Veering away from the *Hyperinstruments* project and natural gesture capture, Overholt's *Overtone Violin* [12] and Ko and Oehlberg's *TRAVIS II* [13] offer the violinist an opportunity to learn new extended techniques in order to master these augmented instruments. Both violins retain the essence of traditional acoustic instruments with the addition of real-time interaction tools in the form of attached sensors and other instrument modifications.

Other new musical interfaces that aim to extend an existing skill-set of an expert practitioner with sensor-based technologies include Impett's *Meta-Trumpet* [14] and more recently, Reid's *MIGSI* [15]. Although differential in methods and design, these sensor-enhanced musical interfaces offer expert practitioners opportunities to extend their performance practice through unique and creative approaches to technological applications.

2.2 Robotic Musicianship

Robotic musicianship is an interdisciplinary field combining music, computer science, performance studies, AI, and mechatronics (the physical creation of robotics) [16]. The field of robotic musicianship aims to develop robots with musical abilities, such as to listen and improvise with human performers [17]. Music styles explored in robotic musicianship, including jazz improvisation and free style hip hop interaction, offer communicative dialogue-based mediums that require extensive domain knowledge [18]. Robotic musicianship is often considered a separate field to musical mechatronics, which instead focuses on actuation or control of instruments, without necessarily developing agency or a robot persona [19]. Robotic musicians can be compared in different ways, for example, Kemper classifies robots into anthropomorphic representation of robots, their ability to produce nuanced sounds, the level of control over their musical expression, and their overall musical output [20].

3. VIOLIN INTERFACE

In this piece, the violinist's bow is augmented with a custom-designed musical interface that is used to interact with both,

[1] https://bit.ly/violinrobot

Figure 2. Violin bow interface used in this piece

Keirzo and the visuals. This interface has been in development since January 2021 [21] and is designed to be minimally invasive, with all the sensors attached to a stretchy cotton fabric that slides on and off the violin bow (Figure 2). This design approach prevents any permanent modifications to the existing bow. Data from the interface is sent wirelessly using the ZigBee protocol [2]. This is achieved by using an XBee radio module within the interface and an XBee receiver unit attached to a computer via USB. The interface is fitted with an accelerometer sensor that tracks the bow movements in real-time, an RGB NeoPixel, three push-buttons and a potentiometer slider. These sensors are wired into an Arduino Fio which is powered by a small lithium polymer 3V battery, allowing for freedom of right-hand movement without cables or heavy battery packs.

The virtual component of this interface uses Max/MSP and Processing software environments, to create an audio and visual output unique to each composition project. By utilising this interface, an expert violinist is able to interact with a custom-made system that integrates both, natural gesture tracking and extended techniques through finger manipulation of the various sensors.

4. VISUALS

The visuals for this work were developed using the Processing software environment, exploring three concepts:

- Real-time bow gesture tracking using particle systems
- Real-time visualisation of *Keirzo's* drum hits
- Simple collision behaviour between three ellipses and the lines representing *Keirzo's* drum hits

The particle system follows the violin bow using an algorithm that maps bow placement in relation to horizontal motion and positioning within each string using the accelerometer sensor x and y coordinates. This mapping approach is effective in visualising the horizontal and vertical motion of the violinist's bow in real-time. Further mappings utilised acceleration values to create a relationship between fast and slow bow strokes, incorporating a wind force to mimic the speeding up and slowing down of the system in relation to the music.

[2] ZigBee Wireless Mesh Networking

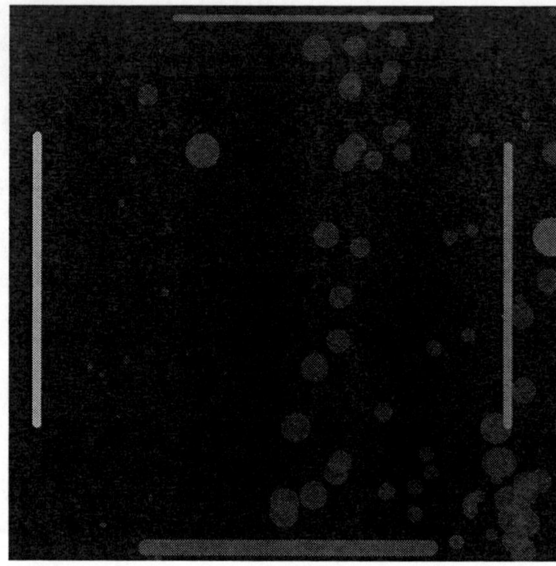

Figure 3. Interactive visuals capturing violinist's bow gestures and Keirzo's drum hits

Max/MSP is used to receive both, the interface data and midi values from Keirzo. Each time Keirzo's drum sticks come into contact with one of his four drums, a value is sent into the violinist's Max patch. These are numbered 1-4 and correspond to the four lines shown within the Processing canvas window. For every hit, the lines move forward and sideways using randomised but constrained values so that each line will not leave the dimensions of the window. Once a line travels to the end of the canvas window dimensions, it reverses its direction.

The lines are also interacting with the three larger ellipses using simple collision detection. The spheres bounce off the lines as well as each other. These collisions affect the changes in colour and size of each ellipse, creating a playful augmentation to the physical performance presence (Figure 3.

Figure 4. Keirzo the Robotic Musician in Performance

5. KEIRZO

In this work, we utilize Keirzo, a custom-built robot with capabilities in drumming and improvisation 4. Keirzo is specifically designed to engage with musicians and other humans. The system has been constructed to facilitate extensive live performances and emphasises human interaction. Keirzo is contains five interactive components, drumming arms, a rib cage, LED rings, head movement and an eye display.

The drumming uses four dynamixel XH430-W210-R servomotors, each manipulating a drumstick through. These arms are intentionally designed with an emphasis on visual transparency of their function, opting for exaggerated, large-scale movements. This design choice prioritizes the visibility of the robot's actions over mechanical efficiency, deliberately placing the arms in a position on the robot and away from drum set rather than integrated directly onto the drum set.

Encircling the central structure of Keirzo is what is referred to as the 'rib cage.' This element does not contribute directly to the musical output but is essential for the robot's visual expressiveness. It is designed to simulate the appearance of breathing and other human-like gestures, aiming to enhance the robot's ability to communicate movement and engage with onlookers and fellow performers. The LED rings are used to demonstrate pulse, and placed in custom enclosures for 4 Neopixel rings.

The robot's head is equipped with three degrees of freedom, enabling it to convey beats and musical patterns through motion. This movement serves as a non-verbal cueing system, allowing Keirzo to signal changes in the musical arrangement or to synchronize with other musicians. Finally, the 'eye display' of Keirzo responds in real-time to audio inputs. This display is powered by a custom-programmed interface developed in Max/MSP/Jitter, offering a highly flexible platform for visual feedback that can be adapted to various performance contexts.

For this robot performance Keirzo's drumming was integrated with a deep learning based, virtual synthesized orchestra. The rhythm of the orchestra was generated by a rule-based algorithms controlled by the violin. There were three modes of performance, in-tempo staccato backings, longer sustains, and short tremolo interjections. Each mode placed beats on a grid, with predefined probabilities for each grid space. The violinist was able to choose which mode with their interface, as well as the density of texture and the tempo of the grid (between 80 and 200 bpm). In addition to the backing their were generated melodies that were created using the set density and the z angle of the bow, with movements from the bow triggering melody notes.

To generate harmony from the rhythms we used a unidirectional auto-encoder, modeled on Piano Genie [22]. The generated rhythms were assigned a number between 0 and 7, which corresponded with low to high pitches. Melodies would always be in the range 4 to 7, with the accompanying parts 0-3. This allowed us to input any number of chord and melody notes, before the system return the pitches. The system is trained on data from International Piano-e-Competition, which includes a range of piano performances. Violin playback was done with and 8 Dio Orchestra Kontakt Library.

6. SYSTEM INTEGRATION

Two computers were used to perform this work, one dedicated to the violin bow interface (Laptop 1, Figure 5 and the other to the synthesized string orchestra and Keirzo (Laptop 2, Figure 5. Keirzo's drum hits were also sent to Laptop 1. Data from the interface was parsed into Max/MSP using the serial port object and was received directly from the Zigbee receiver module. Max then communicated necessary data to the Processing sketch using the Open Sound Control protocol. Processing was able to receive information from Max via the external OscP5 library [3]. Keirzo's drum hits were sent into the same Max patch as MIDI values using serial communication via Wifi, using a dedicated router.

Within this work, each sensor was specifically mapped to musical and visual parameters. The slider influenced the speed of Keirzo's drumming and synthesised strings. The buttons were mapped to change modes of performance and density of orchestral texture, controlling levels of intensity within each mode. These mappings gave the violinist a degree of interactive control and allowed them to structure the musical composition harmonically and according to timbral variance in real-time. The acceleromter provided values for both, the visuals and the synthesised orchestral strings, which were designed to be reactive but not controlled.

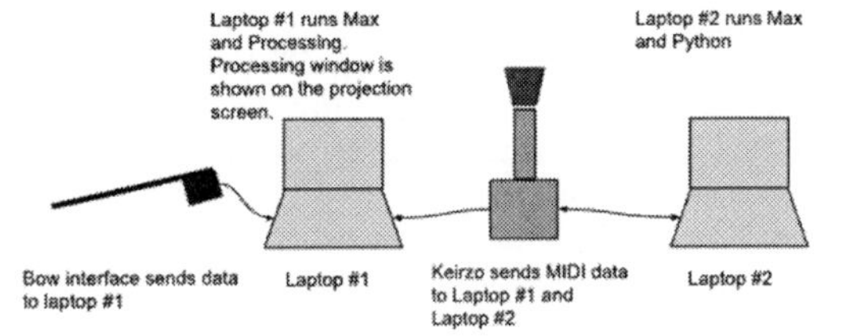

Figure 5. Communication Protocol

7. PRACTICE-LED PERSPECTIVE

Following the development we aimed to critically engage with the intricacies of designing, implementing, and interacting with new musical interfaces and robotic musicianship. This section aims to unpack issues and concepts that arose from our artistic intention, technical challenges, and aesthetic considerations that underpin the development and realization of the work.

7.1 Acoustic vs. Synthesized Sound: Embodiment and Disembodiment

A common consideration within robotic musicianship is the role of acoustic physical sound that is embodied and from the robot, compared to sounds emanating from a speaker and disembodied from any physical source [23]. This embodiment adds a tangible, visceral layer to the performance,

[3] OscP5 for Processing

as audiences can visually connect the sound source with its auditory output. In contrast, the synthesized string orchestra, while rich in tonal quality, lacks a physical form or visual counterpart.

This performance created a stark contrast between the embodied acoustic sounds of the drums and violin and the disembodied nature of the synthesized string orchestra. A continual concern of the creators was what agency would be perceived from the synthesized string orchestra, and whether it would be perceived as part of the robot or separately. For this reason the drumming was synchronized to the string sounds, through almost complete rhythmic unison.In the future, the contrast between embodied and disembodied sounds offers unique opportunities for creative expression, with opportunity to explore audience expectation, and variation in synchronization.

7.2 Playing with Artificial Agent

The process of developing this work came about in three stages - technical development (mapping interface sensor values, mapping Keirzo's MIDI values), rehearsing (learning how to use the mappings, getting used to playing with Keirzo) and finally, performing the piece. The initial phase opened up new creative possibilities to design approaches of interacting with an Artificial Agent as a playful performance partner. The second stage was the most challenging due to its high cognitive load on the violinist, as they learned to play the bow interface with its new mappings, develop the structure of the performance and choreograph interactions with a robotic musician in a meaningful way.

Playing with an Artificial Agent challenged the violinist both physically and creatively. The compositional requirement of controlling a performance partner through a musical interface required patience and practice. On the other hand, lacking control due to external parameters associated with the nature of this work also took some getting used to. For instance, not knowing the tonality of the string samples at the start of each performance iteration, or the novel sonic nature of controlling intensity and texture density rather than volume. Improvising alongside an Artificial Agent also meant developing a new listening approach, forcing the violinist to allow Keirzo's time to respond and contribute musically, whilst simultaneously driving the direction of the piece through interface manipulation and intuitive decisions. Throughout this process, the violinist had developed a creative relationship with Keirzo, which evolved into a new performance style and improvisation strategies, unique to this experience.

The opportunities that present themselves within an experimental work such as this, where the technologies are evolving alongside the composition are vast and exciting. A piece of music where learning to use the technology is part of the composition process pushes the human artist to explore new creative approaches, extending their existing skill-set and vastly expanding their creative scope.

This collaboration was a robust learning experience and future work with Keirzo will benefit from the groundwork laid down in this composition. Exploring more intricate control parameters within the mapping solutions could result in a more cohesive composition structure, where the synthesized strings are more sympathetic to the acoustic audio. Developing Keirzo's drumming vocabulary would also enhance the human/robotic musician interactions with a richer pallet of sonic and rhythmic variance.

7.3 Stage Layout

Based on the physicality of the performers and the visual component, our staging choices were somewhat limited. The projection screen inside our occupied space was positioned against the back wall, meaning the violinist and Keirzo needed to be either directly in front or beside it. The violinist chose to be positioned stage right, so that sound holes of the instrument would project towards the audience. Having Keirzo positioned stage left, allowed for the two collaborators to watch each other whilst also being able to see the screen. Although the space was large, the positioning of the video camera created a slightly minimised representation, especially of the projection screen, which had a much grander presence within a live setting.

The triangular set-up used for this performance had its benefits from a performer perspective, allowing good collaborative visibility. However, the violinist felt somewhat restrained and awkward in their positioning and gestural freedom. This was primarily due to the positioning of the projection screen, as well as the physical strain of manipulating the interface for musical and visual interactivity and compositional structure.

In future works, deeper consideration could be placed into staging lighting and wardrobe. A new experimental work that combines multiple elements that may be unfamiliar or uncomfortable for a general audience, could create a sense of ease through deliberate performer positioning as well as colour codes and projection surfaces. The human performer juxtaposed beside a robotic musician, taller and larger than them could appear as menacing or disconnected. This issue could be muted by experimentation in performer positioning as well as colour schemes in performer wardrobe against the robotic musician colour schemes. The sterile placement of the projection screen could also be improved by incorporating softer fabrics such as silk scrims or bleeding the projection onto adjacent surfaces. As the audience looks to decipher meaning within an unfamiliar setting, making conscious staging decisions could help communicate the intentions of the creative artists, building a more inclusive performance environment.

7.4 Visual Design Strategies

The visual element of this work was intended to be an augmentation of the physical performance acting as an extension of the performer's gestures whilst aiding in communicating the meaning behind the experiment. Each component of the visual design was tied in closely with the music, morphing with the violinist's gestures and changes in sonic modalities. As the violinist manipulated the interface, the data would simultaneously affect the synthesised sound and the projected visuals. A button pressed changed the colour of the particle system and differing slider values changed the wind force.

With a strong physical onstage presence from the violinist and Keirzo, designing visuals that would complement the performance was difficult, raising questions about how the visuals could be effectively incorporated into the piece as an integral element rather than a background distraction. One solution was to derive colours from Keirzo's design as well as visualising the drum hits as moving lines, which resemble drumsticks and spatially organised in correlation to their pitch, with hi-hat positioned top center, bass drum, bottom center and the ride and tom, vertically on either side. The violinist's bow gestures would then compliment Keirzo's drumming with a softer looking particle system that changed its appearance in response to bow strokes and bow speed. The three bouncing ellipses were the only independent element of the visual design, aimed to offset the direct drumming and bow gesture translation whilst creating a playfulness that the work inherently possesses.

Future works for Keirzo and augmented violin will benifit from exploring visuals that contribute to the narrative development of the work, using more sophisticated mapping solutions, such as machine learning and genetic algorithms. The visuals in this project were overly simplistic and could have been absent. If visuals are to be incorporated within this setting, they would need to be an equal contributor to the piece, acting as a third collaborator.

8. AUDIENCE-LED PERSPECTIVE

In the course of our research we conducted an exploratory online study aimed at gathering a broad spectrum of views on the performance. The primary objective was to ascertain the general audience's perceptions and to contrast these with our observations, particularly focusing on the variance in issues raised by both parties. We intentionally aimed to present the work without program notes or context, to attempt to contextualize broader opinions on the work without first directing attention or focus, or biasing the audience in anyway.

To facilitate this study, we recruited 50 participants through Prolific, a platform known for academic and market research recruitment. These participants were exposed to a four-minute condensed version of the performance, which was made accessible online. Following the viewing, participants were prompted to respond to two open-ended questions. The first question sought their initial perspective on the performance, while the second question, visible only after the first had been answered, aimed to understand the perceived role of technology in the project.

Compensation for participation was set at £2 per participant, with an incentive structure in place to encourage detailed and insightful responses. The top 25 responses, selected based on their attention to detail and the novelty of their perspectives, whether positive or negative, were awarded an additional £1.50. Furthermore, the top 5 responses received an increased bonus of £3.00. Of the 50 individuals recruited for the study, 6 were disqualified due to incomplete video viewing, submission of brief or irrelevant responses, or failure to engage with the content meaningfully. Consequently, the study's final participant count stood at 44 individuals. The demographic breakdown of these participants included 30 women, 13 men, and 1 non-binary individual. The statistical analysis of participant demographics revealed a median age of 32 years, with a standard deviation of 11.92 years and an age range spanning from 21 to 75 years.

8.1 Latent Dirichlet Allocation

Thematic analysis of viewer feedback on a robot-violinist collaboration video was conducted using Latent Dirichlet Allocation (LDA), a topic modeling approach that identifies topics within documents. The analysis utilized the `sklearn` library's functions for pre-processing and topic modeling [24]. Data was processed to remove common stopwords, facilitated by `CountVectorizer`. This step produced a document-term matrix representing term frequencies across responses. LDA was then applied to this matrix, configured to extract five topics, revealing the distribution of words significant to each theme.

The LDA model identified five key themes, with the topic names added by the authors:

1. **Musical Performance**: Discussions centered on the artistry and performance quality.
2. **Human-Robot Interaction**: Insights into the collaborative dynamics between the human and robot.
3. **Technological Enhancement**: The role of technology in augmenting the performance experience.
4. **Emotional Response**: Viewer emotional reactions to the performance.
5. **Technical Execution**: Comments on the technical aspects of the performance and robot's involvement.

8.2 Audience Themes

In addition to the algorithmic theme analysis we hand-coded the interviews and found multiple reoccurring themes. At times these themes matched our own concerns while also raising new issues.

8.2.1 New Technology and Musical Aesthetics

The integration of technology into musical performance often introduces audiences to an unprecedented artistic experiences. Viewers noted the uniqueness of witnessing technology play an instrument, marking a departure from traditional musical performances. Critiques of the musical output highlighted a divergence from conventional musical tastes, with some viewers finding the combination of drums and violin, mediated by technology, abstract and unfamiliar. One participant noted:"My initial thoughts are that I don't understand or appreciate the music that was performed. I like both classical music and pop music in general but that was just a bit too abstract." Many participants however said they enjoyed hearing a new approach to music and that it was an interesting role for the technology to help create new approaches to music.

We also believe the work may have benefited from a more gradual introduction to each piece of technology in the work. Multiple participants noted an initial confusion, such as "I watched the video trying to make sense of all the moving parts – the violinist, the drumming robot and the screen. I could not figure out how these were interrelating and influencing each other. It seems that the violinist was improvising off of the drums and the orchestral music, but not the screen. I couldn't figure out if the robot was making all of the non-violin music, or just the beats. In general, I liked the improvised music – reminded me of jazz.'

In future work gradual introduction and education about the roles of each technology could improve how audiences unfamiliar with the work understand the technology.

8.2.2 Anthropomorphize

The design of the robot elicited primarily positive reactions, however there were mixed reactions to the human-like elements. While some found the humanoid gestures of the robot endearing, others perceived it as deceptive, preferring a clear distinction between the robotic and human elements. One participant described "Had they not tried to anthropomorphize the robot, I would have enjoyed it more. It would have seemed somehow less deceptive to have it presented as a machine without any attempt to personify it." This dichotomy raises questions about the role of anthropomorphism in technology, particularly in artistic contexts, and its impact on audience reception.

8.2.3 Interaction

Viewer responses varied on the perceived interaction between the musician and the robot, with many praising the interaction, such as "I thought the video was very interesting because it was clear that the musician and robot were interacting" and "it felt like a performance given by a duo". Others felt the robot was too dominating and "not complementing the performer well", perhaps suggesting they believed the robot should play more of an accompanying role.

8.2.4 Robotic Soul

The essence of human creativity emerged as a central theme, with some viewers commenting on the robot's inability to replicate the soulfulness and emotional depth characteristic of human performances. Quotes included "It lacked the soul and flavor a human would produce when playing an instrument." and "It felt like it was lacking something, and that was probably some emotion.". Other participants noted that "A robot making music isn't as appealing as a person." and "In my view, humans are best at creating art". Nevertheless the vast majority of participants treated the robot as another collaborator on stage.

8.2.5 Ethical Concerns

Although not predominant, some comments touched on ethical considerations related to the use of musicians' data in training the robot, highlighting concerns over consent and compensation. One participant wrote "My first thought was to wonder if the actual musicians whose data had been used to train the robot had consented. I then wondered if they were at least compensated". This was not a key concern however, and almost all participants instead focused on the end product.

8.2.6 Robot Agency

Questions about the robot's autonomy and the extent of its pre-programmed versus live-responsive capabilities indicated a curiosity about the technology's sophistication. This interest in robot agency leads to a broader discussion on the evolving role of artificial intelligence in live performances, examining the balance between programmed routines and adaptive, interactive behaviors. Participants asked "was someone controlling the robot or did the robot control itself.", "It is hard to tell how much of the music playing was pre-programmed for the Robot or if it was able to sync up with the lady live on the stage." and "Was it randomly responding or doing something pre-programmed".

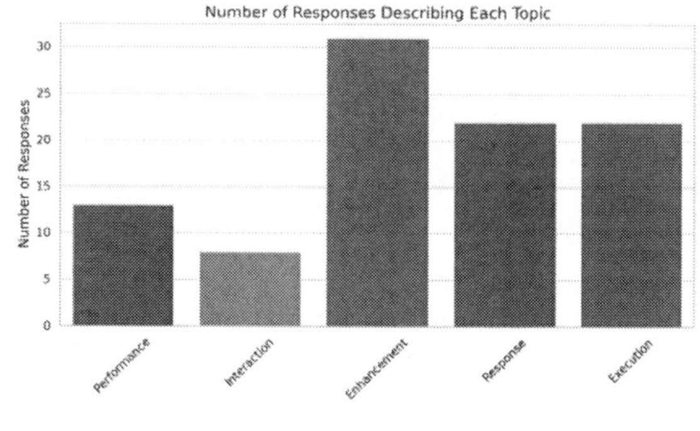

Figure 6. Distribution of viewer feedback across identified themes.

9. DISCUSSION, FUTURE WORK AND CONCLUSION

In this paper, we discussed the process of creating a mixed-media, experimental work for augmented violin, robotic musician and interactive visuals. We also presented discussion points around themes that we, as developers of this project were most concerned with. Our perspectives are grounded in our own personal relationships with the technologies used within this project as well as external constraints that shape the final outcome of the work. These include time, existing technology, available resources such as performance spaces and documentation tools and our own limitations as practice-based researchers and creative artists.

Although driven to create a musically and visually engaging work, our primary concerns are associated with the development processes of this and future works, shaped by ongoing personal and external evaluation. Having lived with this piece from its conception, it can be difficult to ascertain a removed, holistic view of the final product.

The audience perspectives as presented in the survey were derived from a point of unfamiliarity with the project and the music, arming them with a fresh perspective. Although using slightly different terminology, it is important to note, that much of the discussion points brought up by the participants aligned with our own concerns. For instance, *Musical Performance*, although broad, relates back to both, embodiment/disembodiment of sound and the human-computer interaction approaches as seen by the violinist. Concerns raised about anthropomorphism could also be linked to the strategies taken by the violinist in interacting with Keirzo and shaping the structure of the piece.

In future works, placing greater significance on audience accessibility through points of departure surrounding familiarity of style and introduction to the technologies being used will decrease audience confusion and feelings of alienation. Transparency in data being used for training models will also aid in softening feelings of hostility. Overall, we feel optimistic that as our technologies develop alongside our composition strategies, there is robust potential for engaging and novel works incorporating robotic, virtual and human collaborators.

10. REFERENCES

[1] J. Sullivan and M. Wanderley, "Stability, Reliability, Compatibility: Reviewing 40 Years of NIME Design," Ph.D. dissertation, McGill University/Université McGill, 2018.

[2] F. Morreale, A. McPherson, M. Wanderley *et al.*, "NIME Identity from the Performer's Perspective," 2018.

[3] C. Small, *Musicking: The meanings of performing and listening*. Wesleyan University Press, 1998.

[4] D. Overholt, "Advancements in violin-related human-computer interaction," *International Journal of Arts and Technology*, vol. 7, no. 2-3, 2014.

[5] B. C. Baroni, Nicola, "Sound Gesture and Rhetoric. Hyper-cello as an Algorithmic Composer Nicola Baroni Carlo Benzi," *Proceedings of the Electroacoustic Music Studies Network Conference*, 2014.

[6] F. Bevilacqua, N. H. Rasamimanana, E. Fléty, S. Lemouton, and F. Baschet, "The augmented violin project: research, composition and performance report," in *International Conference on New Interfaces for Musical Expression*, 2006.

[7] T. Machover, "Interactive instruments for experts and amateurs," *The Journal of the Acoustical Society of America*, vol. 95, no. 5, 1994.

[8] J. A. Paradiso and N. Gershenfeld, "Musical applications of electric field sensing," *Computer music journal*, vol. 21, no. 2, 1997.

[9] D. Young, "The Hyperbow Controller: Real-Time Dynamics Measurement of Violin Performance," *New Interfaces for Musical Expression*, 2002.

[10] N. Rasamimanana, "Gesture analysis of bow strokes using an augmented violin," *Memoire de stage de DEA ATIAM, Tech. Rep*, 2004.

[11] M. Kimura, N. Rasamimanana, F. Bevilacqua, B. Zamborlin, N. Schnell, and E. Fléty, "Extracting Human Expression For Interactive Composition with the Augmented Violin," *New Interfaces for Musical Expression*, 2012.

[12] D. Overholt, "The Overtone Violin," in *Proceedings of the New interfaces for musical expression*, 2005.

[13] C. Ko and L. Oehlberg, "Construction and Performance Applications of an Augmented Violin: TRAVIS II," *Computer Music Journal*, vol. 44, no. 2-3, 2020.

[14] J. Impett, "A Meta Trumpet (er)," in *Proceedings of the international computer music conference*, 1994.

[15] S. Reid, R. Gaston, C. Honigman, and A. Kapur, "Minimally Invasive Gesture Sensing Interface (MIGSI) for Trumpet." in *New interfaces for musical expression*, 2016.

[16] E. Frid, "Musical Robots: Overview and Methods for Evaluation," *Sound and Robotics*, pp. 243–284, 2023.

[17] R. Savery and G. Weinberg, "Robotics: Fast and Curious: A CNN for Ethical Deep Learning Musical Generation," in *Artificial Intelligence and Music Ecosystem*. Focal Press, 2022, pp. 52–67.

[18] R. Savery, L. Zahray, and G. Weinberg, "Shimon the rapper: A real-time system for human-robot interactive rap battles," *arXiv preprint arXiv:2009.09234*, 2020.

[19] N. Yang, R. Savery, R. Sankaranarayanan, L. Zahray, and G. Weinberg, "Mechatronics-driven musical expressivity for robotic percussionists," *arXiv preprint arXiv:2007.14850*, 2020.

[20] S. Kemper, "Locating Creativity in Differing Approaches to Musical Robotics," *Frontiers in Robotics and AI*, vol. 8, p. 647028, 2021.

[21] A. Savery, "Enhancing Violin Performance through Real-Time Interaction: Design and Evaluation of a Wireless Audio-Visual Interface," *Chroma: Journal of the Australasian Computer Music Association*, vol. 39, no. 2, 2023.

[22] C. Donahue, I. Simon, and S. Dieleman, "Piano genie," in *Proceedings of the 24th International Conference on Intelligent User Interfaces*, 2019, pp. 160–164.

[23] R. Savery, L. Zahray, and G. Weinberg, "Shimon sings-robotic musicianship finds its voice," *Handbook of Artificial Intelligence for Music: Foundations, Advanced Approaches, and Developments for Creativity*, pp. 823–847, 2021.

[24] F. Pedregosa, G. Varoquaux, A. Gramfort, V. Michel, B. Thirion, O. Grisel, M. Blondel, P. Prettenhofer, R. Weiss, V. Dubourg *et al.*, "Scikit-learn: Machine learning in Python," *the Journal of machine Learning research*, vol. 12, pp. 2825–2830, 2011.

Author Index

International Computer Music Association
1819 Polk Street #330
San Francisco, CA
94109

ISBN 979-8-3313-1131-5
9 798331 311315

CURRAN ASSOCIATES INC.
proceedings
.com

17th Russian Youth Conference on Physics of Semiconductors and Nanostructures, Opto- and Nanoelectronics (RYCPS 2015)

Journal of Physics: Conference Series Volume 690

St. Petersburg, Russia
23 – 27 November 2015

IOP
Institute of Physics